TOEFL iBT® 온라인 실전 테스트 사용법

설치

웹사이트 www.mhprofessional.com/toefl7e를 방문하면 책에 있는 접속 코드를 입력하라는 메시지가 뜹니다. 이 코드는 책 구매자에 한해 최대 2회까지 이용할 수 있습니다. 접속 코드를 입력하면 자동으로 다운로드가 시작됩니다.

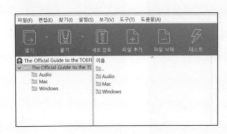

프로그램 실행

오디오 파일뿐만 아니라 PC와 Mac® 포맷의 실전 테스트 파일도 함께 다운로드 됩니다. 이 중 Windows PC를 사용하신다면 Windows 폴더를 클릭하여 TOEFL Official Guide Setup 파일을 실행하면 됩니다.

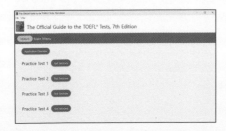

온라인 실전 테스트

프로그램을 실행하면 다음과 같은 화면이 나타납니다. Main Menu에서 Practice Test 1, 2, 3, 4 중 수행하고 싶은 테스트를 선택합니다. 그런 다음 읽기, 듣기, 말하기, 쓰기 등 수행하고 싶은 영역을 선택합니다. 각 영역은 한 번 이상 풀어 볼 수 있습니다.

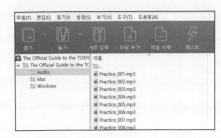

MP3 오디오 파일 활용

컴퓨터가 아니라 책에 인쇄된 실전 테스트로 공부할 때도 오디오 트랙을 들어야 합니다. 'Audio Files'라는 폴더를 컴퓨터에 복사하면, 교재에 표시된 오디오 트랙 번호와 일치하는 파일을 찾아 들을 수 있습니다.

Digital Access Code

The
Official
Guide to the
TOEFL iBT® Test

SEVENTH EDITION

The Official Guide to the TOEFL iBT Test, 7ᵗʰ Edition

1 2 3 4 5 6 7 8 9 10   YBM   20 24

Original: The Official Guide to the TOEFL iBT Test, 7ᵗʰ Edition © 2024
      By Educational Testing Service (ETS)
      ISBN 978-1-265-47731-8

TOEFL is a registered trademark of ETS, Princeton, New Jersey, U.S.A. and is used under license.

ETS, the ETS logo, TOEFL, and TOEFL iBT are registered trademarks of Educational Testing Service (ETS) in
the United States. TOEFL GOLEARN! and MyBest are trademarks of ETS in the United States and other countries.

This authorized Korean translation edition is jointly published by McGraw-Hill Education Korea, Ltd. and YBM.
This edition is authorized for sale in the Republic of Korea.

This book is exclusively distributed by YBM.

When ordering this title, please use ISBN 978-89-17-23985-0

Printed in Korea

The Official Guide to the TOEFL iBT® Test | Seventh Edition

발행인   허문호
발행처   YBM

저자   Educational Testing Service(ETS)
편집   정윤영, 이시현
마케팅   정연철, 박천산, 고영노, 김동진, 박찬경, 김윤하

초판인쇄   2024년 6월 14일
초판발행   2024년 6월 30일

신고일자   1964년 3월 28일
신고번호   제 1964-000003호
주소   서울시 종로구 종로 104
전화   (02) 2000-0515[구입문의] / (02) 2000-0328[내용문의]
팩스   (02) 2285-1523
홈페이지   www.ybmbooks.com

ISBN 978-89-17-23985-0

Preface

많은 이들의 관심 속에서 2006년 9월부터 우리나라에서도 TOEFL iBT® 시험이 시행되기 시작했습니다. PBT(Paper-Based Testing)에서 CBT(Computer-Based Testing), 그리고 iBT(Internet-Based Testing)에 이르기까지 TOEFL® 시험은 발전을 거듭해 왔으며 세계에서 가장 널리 채택되고 인정 받는 영어시험입니다.

이 시험은 영어권 대학 지원자들이 현지에서 공부하는 데 적합한 영어 실력을 갖추었는지 평가하는 시험으로 전 세계 200개 국 이상에서 실시되고 있습니다. TOEFL iBT® 시험은 수험자의 종합적인 영어 능력뿐만 아니라 실질적 의사소통 능력을 평가한다는 점에서 가장 효과적인 영어 능력 평가 시험이라고 할 수 있습니다.

TOEFL iBT® 시험은 최근 2023년 7월 이후 시험 시간과 문항 수 등에서 변화가 있었습니다. 전체 시험 시간이 기존 3시간에서 2시간 이내로 줄었고, 읽기 영역의 문항 수 감소 및 쓰기 영역의 일부 유형이 바뀐 것이 주요 변화입니다. 먼저 읽기 영역은 기존 3개에서 2개로 출제 지문 수가 줄어 지문당 10문항씩 총 20문항이 출제됩니다. 듣기 영역은 28문항이 출제되어 시험 시간이 36분으로 줄었습니다. 쓰기 영역의 경우, 독립형 문제가 학술적 토론에 관한 글쓰기로 변경되었습니다.

이 책은 TOEFL 시험 출제기관인 ETS와 독점 계약을 체결하고 TOEFL iBT® 시험을 처음 접하는 수험자들을 돕기 위해 만들었습니다. 특히, 2023년 7월 이후 바뀐 TOEFL iBT® 시험 형식이 반영된 최신 개정판입니다. 시험 출제기관이 직접 만든 가장 믿을 수 있는 안내서로서 수백여 개의 기출 문제, 명확한 해설, 점수 향상 전략, 평가 방식들을 수록했습니다. 이와 더불어 TOEFL iBT® 시험 환경을 체험할 수 있는 온라인 실전 테스트 4회분을 제공하여 교재에 수록된 실전 테스트를 온라인에서도 풀어볼 수 있습니다.

이 책을 활용한다면 최신 개정 시험에 전략적으로 대비하여 목표로 하는 토플 점수를 달성하는 데 도움이 될 것입니다.

2024년 6월

Contents

Chapter 1

About the TOEFL iBT® Test

About the TOEFL iBT® Test

이 장의 구성 • TOEFL iBT®의 주요 특징
　　　　　　　• 영역별 구성과 문제 유형

Getting Started

토플 시험은 무엇이며, 토플 시험은 왜 필요하며, 토플 성적은 어떻게 활용되는지 알아보자.

1. TOEFL: 상급학교 진학을 위한 시험

- 토플 시험은 전 세계 대학의 학부·대학원 과정 지원자의 영어 의사소통 능력을 증명한다.
- 토플 시험은 교수와 학생들이 강의, 실습, 스터디 그룹을 비롯한 일상적 대학 생활에서 실제로 사용하는 영어를 그대로 반영한다.
- 학술적 읽기 영역 지문은 학교 교재 및 기타 학술 논문에서 발췌한다.

2. 토플 성적의 활용

- 토플은 전 세계적으로 타당성과 신뢰도를 인정받는 시험이다.
- 공정하고 객관적인 채점으로 학생들의 실제적 영어 구사력을 측정해 해당 학생이 영어 환경에서 학업을 성공적으로 수행할 능력이 있음을 확인한다.
- 세계적인 공신력을 인정받아 전 세계 160개국의 만 천여 개 대학과 기관에서 토플 점수를 인정한다.
- 180개국 이상에서 보안이 철저한 수천 개의 ETS 공인 시험 센터가 운영되고 있으며 1964년 이래 3천 5백만 명 이상이 토플 시험에 응시했다.

3. 토플 시험은 누가 만드는가?

ETS(Educational Testing Service)는 토플 시험을 개발하고 운영하는 세계 최대 규모의 사설 교육 평가 및 측정 기관이다. ETS의 임무는 교육 분야에 있어 질과 공평성을 개선하는 것이다. 공정하고 유효하며 신뢰할 수 있는 평가를 제공하는 것이 핵심적인 ETS의 존재 이유이다.

4. 토플 시험 응시자는 누구인가?

영어로 강의를 하는 대학교의 대부분은 영어 능력 시험 성적을 요구한다. TOEFL iBT®는 세계적으로 가장 널리 인정받고 있는 시험으로 이러한 요구에 부응하는 최적의 선택이다. 지원하는 학교에서 요구하는 성적을 미리 확인하도록 한다.

5. 토플은 입학사정에 어떻게 활용되는가?

토플 성적은 학교에 제출하는 다른 자료와 함께 정규·응용과정에 입학할 수 있는 학문적·언어적 배경을 갖추었는지 판단하는 자료로 활용된다. 학문 분야와 학부·대학원 진학 희망 여부에 따라 필요한 토플 점수가 달라지는 경우가 많다.

6. TOEFL iBT®는 어떤 방식의 시험인가?

TOEFL iBT®는 보안이 철저한 시험 센터에서 전 세계적으로 시행되는 인터넷 기반 시험(iBT)이다. 컴퓨터 기반 시험(CBT)을 대체하는 시험이며, iBT 시행이 불가능한 지역에서는 여전히 지필고사(PBT)를 시행한다.

7. 최저 인정 점수가 있는가?

각 학교는 최저 인정 점수를 규정하고 있다. 이 점수는 지원자의 학문 분야, 학업 수준(학부·대학원), 조교 희망 여부, 해당 학교의 영어교육 지원 여부에 따라 학교별로 다르다.

All About the TOEFL iBT® Test

TOEFL iBT®는 읽기, 듣기, 말하기, 쓰기의 4개 영역으로 구성된다. 전체 시험은 약 2시간 소요되고, 모든 영역이 시험 당일에 순차적으로 시행된다.

1. TOEFL iBT®의 주요 특징

- TOEFL iBT®는 효과적인 의사소통에 필요한 네 가지 언어 능력(말하기, 듣기, 읽기, 쓰기)을 평가한다.
  TOEFL iBT®는 학습 환경에서 영어를 효과적으로 구사하는 능력을 평가한다.
- TOEFL iBT®는 언어의 실제 사용 방식을 반영하므로 다음과 같은 통합형 문제를 포함한다.

  - 읽고 들은 후 답변 말하기
  - 듣고 구두로 답변하기
  - 읽고 들은 후 답변 작성하기

2. TOEFL iBT®의 시행 방식

- TOEFL iBT®는 세계 곳곳에 위치한 시험 센터 및 집에서 안전하고 편리하게 응시할 수 있다.
- 각 영역마다 답변에 관한 지시 사항이 제시된다.
- TOEFL iBT®는 수험자의 읽기, 듣기, 말하기, 쓰기 능력을 평가한다.
- 수험자는 시험 내내 필기를 할 수 있다. 시험 종료 시 보안을 위해 모든 필기용지를 폐기한다.
- 듣기와 말하기 영역에서는 북미, 영국, 호주, 뉴질랜드 출신의 영어 원어민 액센트를 포함함으로써 수험자가 외국 유학 생활 중 들을 수 있는 다양한 액센트를 반영한다. 샘플을 들으려면, www.ets.org/toefl/ibt/about/content/를 방문하면 된다.
- 말하기 영역에서는 수험자가 소음 차단용 헤드폰을 착용하고 마이크에 말한다. 답변은 디지털 방식으로 녹음되어 ETS로 전송된다.
- 쓰기 영역에서는 수험자가 자신의 답변을 키보드로 입력해야 한다. 입력된 답변은 ETS로 전송된다.
- ETS 공인 채점자들과 인공지능을 사용해 말하기와 쓰기 답변을 채점하여 수험자들의 정확한 능력을 측정한다.
- 시험이 끝난 후, 수험자들은 읽기와 듣기 영역의 비공인 환산 점수를 볼 수 있다. 말하기와 쓰기 영역의 채점은 시험 시행 후에만 가능하므로 실시간으로 제공되지 않는다.
- 공인 점수는 인터넷과 우편으로 통보한다.

3. 영역별 문제 수와 소요 시간

다음 표는 영역별 문제 수와 시간을 나타낸다. 각 영역의 제한 시간은 문제 수에 따라 변동될 수 있다.

영역(Test Section)	문항 수(Number of Questions)	시간(Timing)
읽 기(Reading)	2개 지문, 각 10개 문제	35분
듣 기(Listening)	3개 강의, 각 6개 문제 2개 대화, 각 5개 문제	36분
말하기(Speaking)	4개 문제: 독립형 1개 + 통합형 3개	16분
쓰 기(Writing)	통합형 문제 1개 학술 토론에 관한 쓰기 1개	20분 10분

4. 화면 상단의 Tool Bar

화면상의 툴바를 클릭하면 손쉽게 시험 화면을 전환할 수 있다. 다음은 읽기와 듣기 영역의 툴바이며, 각 영역의 명칭은 화면의 좌측 상단에 항상 명시된다.

1) 읽기 영역

- 수험자는 전체 지문을 볼 수 있다.
- Review를 클릭하면 수험자가 선택한 답을 확인할 수 있다. Review에서는 어떤 문제든 되돌아가 답을 변경할 수 있고, 답을 선택하지 않고 지나간 문제도 확인할 수 있다.
- 읽기 영역에서는 언제든 Back을 클릭하고 이전 문제로 되돌아갈 수 있다.

2) 듣기 영역

- 수험자는 툴바에서 현재 진행중인 문제와 남은 답변 시간을 항상 확인할 수 있다. Hide Time을 클릭하면 시계를 감출 수 있다.
- Volume을 클릭해서 소리 크기를 조절할 수 있다.
- Help를 클릭하면 도움말 창이 열린다. Help 기능을 이용할 때도 시계는 멈추지 않는다.
- Next를 클릭하면 다음 문제로 넘어간다.
- Next를 클릭한 다음 OK를 클릭하면 답변이 확정된다. 듣기 영역에서는 한 번 OK를 클릭하면 해당 문제를 다시 볼 수 없다.

Reading Section

1. 읽기 영역의 구성

지문 분량	문항 수	시간
약 700단어	2개 지문 각 지문당 10개 문제	35분

2. 읽기 영역의 특징

TOEFL iBT®의 읽기 영역은 특정 전공이나 주제를 소개하는 대학 수준의 교재를 이용한다. 학생들의 실제 학술적 글 읽기 능력을 측정하기 위해 발췌문의 변경은 가능한 한 최소한으로 제한된다. 읽기 지문은 다양한 주제를 다룬다. 읽기 지문에는 정답 찾기에 필요한 모든 정보가 포함되어 있으므로, 수험자는 익숙하지 않은 주제에 관해 걱정할 필요가 없다. 읽기 지문에 어려운 단어나 구가 포함되어 있을 경우에는 밑줄 친 단어를 클릭하면 좌측 하단에 정의나 설명이 나타난다.

용어 사전

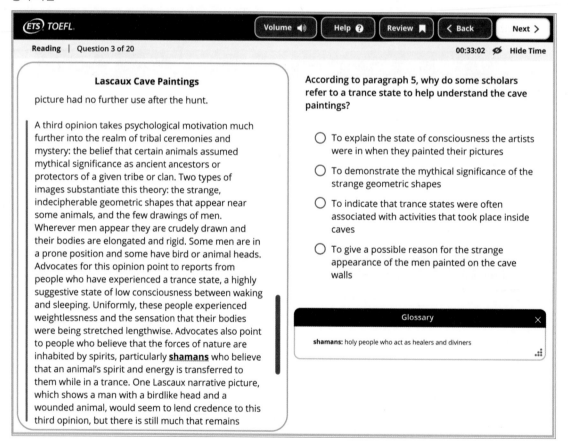

3. 읽기 영역의 문제 형식과 예시

- 일반 사지선다형 문제: 4개의 보기 중에서 1개 혹은 1개 이상의 정답을 선택한다.
- 문장 재구성 문제: 4개의 보기 중에서 해당 문장의 핵심 정보를 가장 잘 나타내는 문장을 선택한다.
- 문장 삽입 문제: 4개의 보기 중에서 해당 문장을 삽입하기에 가장 적절한 곳을 지문에서 선택한다.
- 지문 요약 문제: 6개의 문장 중에서 지문 요약에 필요한 3개의 문장을 찾아서 순서대로 배열한다.

지문 내용 종합하기 (Reading to Learn)

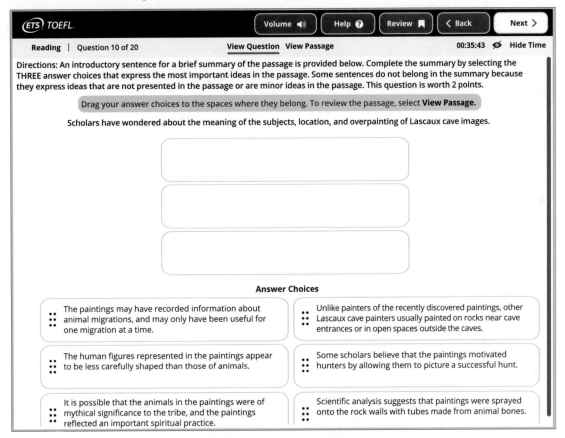

Listening Section

1. 듣기 영역의 구성

지문 분량	문항 수	시간
3개 강의, 강의당 4–5분 500–750단어	강의당 6개 문제	36분
2개 대화, 대화당 약 3분 약 12–25번의 대화가 오고 감	대화당 5개 문제	

2. 강의와 대화 비교

1) 강의

실제 강의에서 일어나는 상황을 반영한다. 교수가 강의를 진행하면서 학생들의 질문을 받기도 하고, 교수가 학생들에게 질문하거나 학생들의 토론에 참여하기도 한다. 컴퓨터 화면에 나오는 사진은 수험자가 화자들의 역할을 확인할 수 있도록 도와준다.

교수의 수업

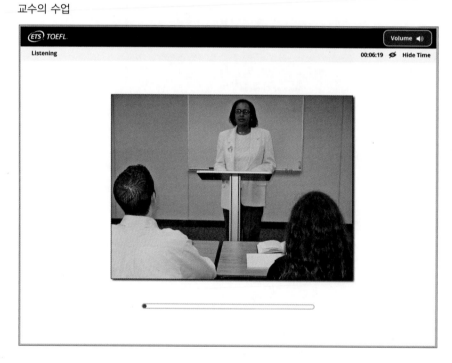

교수와 학생들의 소통

2) 대화

학생이 교수, 조교, 행정 직원, 기숙사 담당자, 도서관 사서, 혹은 다른 학생과 나누는 대화가 주를 이룬다. 컴퓨터 화면에 나오는 사진은 대화의 상황을 짐작하는 데 도움이 된다.

학생과 교수의 대화

3. 듣기 영역의 문제 형식과 예시

- 4개의 보기 중에서 1개의 정답 선택하기
- 4개 이상의 보기 중에서 1개 이상의 정답 선택하기
- 과정의 단계나 사건을 순서대로 나열하기
- 특정 대상이나 텍스트를 도표의 적절한 항목에 일치시키거나 표에 체크 표시하기

도표 문제

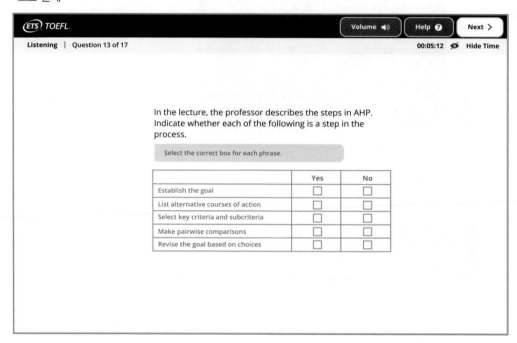

4. 듣기 영역의 특징

듣기 영역에서는 강의와 긴 대화를 들려준다. 시험 시간 동안 노트 필기를 할 수 있고, 필기 용지는 보안을 위해 수험자가 시험장을 나서기 전에 폐기한다. 듣기 영역의 예상 소요 시간은 대략 36분이지만 최대 41분이 주어진다. 말하는 이의 태도, 확신성, 목적에 대한 수험자의 이해도를 측정하는 문제도 있으므로 말하는 이의 어조, 감정을 비롯한 기타 단어를 귀담아 들어야 한다. 강의나 대화의 일부를 다시 들려주는 문제도 있으므로 반드시 기억에만 의존할 필요는 없다. 거의 모든 문제가 각각 1점에 해당하지만, 2점이 배당된 문제가 있다. 2점짜리 문제일 경우 지시문을 통해 미리 알려준다. 2점짜리 문제는 시험당 최대 1개이다.

다시 듣기 문제의 지시 사항

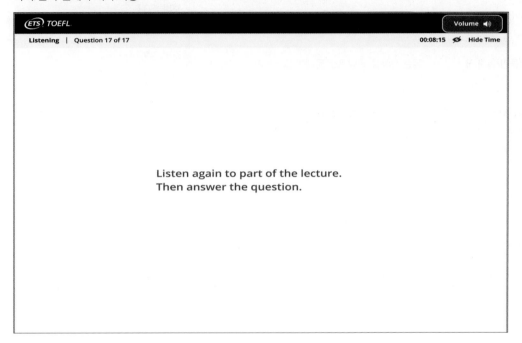

의도 파악 문제

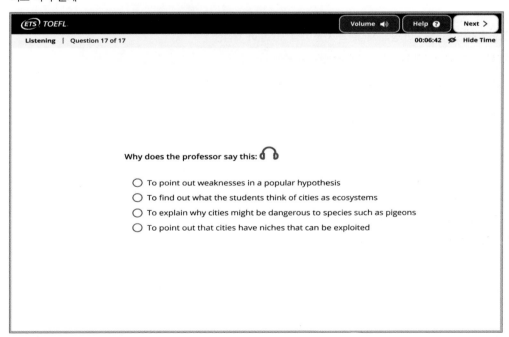

Speaking Section

1. 말하기 영역의 구성

과제 유형	특징	문항 수	시간
독립형	친숙한 주제에 관해 개인적 의견 말하기	1	준비: 15초 답변: 45초
통합형(읽기/듣기/말하기)	읽고 들은 내용을 바탕으로 문제에 답변하기	2	준비: 30초 답변: 60초
통합형(듣기/말하기)	들은 내용을 바탕으로 문제에 답변하기	1	준비: 20초 답변: 60초

2. 말하기 영역의 특징

말하기 영역은 4개의 문제로 구성되어 있으며, 1개의 독립형 과제와 3개의 통합형 과제로 구분된다. 시험에는 약 16분이 소요된다.

– 독립형 과제

처음에 나오는 독립형 1문제는 수험자에게 친숙한 주제에 관해 선택하도록 한다. 수험자는 자신의 생각, 의견, 경험을 토대로 답변을 뒷받침해야 한다.

– 통합형 과제

나머지 3개의 통합형 문제에서는 수험자가 두 가지 이상의 능력을 활용해 답변해야 한다. 읽고 들은 후 구두로 답변하는 문제가 두 개, 들은 후 구두로 답변하는 문제가 1개 출제된다. 수험자는 읽고 들은 내용을 필기할 수 있고, 이를 참고해 답변할 수 있다.

3. 말하기 영역의 시험 방식

TOEFL iBT®의 다른 영역과 마찬가지로 말하기 영역도 컴퓨터를 통해 전송된다. 시험이 진행되는 동안 수험자는 답변을 마이크로 전달한다. 답변은 ETS로 전송되어 공인 채점관과 자동 채점 시스템이 채점한다.

4. 말하기 영역의 과제 유형과 세부 특징

	과제 유형		특징	준비 시간	답변 시간
독 립 형		1. 선택	대조적인 두 가지 행동이나 생각, 행동방침 중에서 개인적으로 선호하는 것을 선택하고, 자신의 의견을 뒷받침할 근거를 제시해야 한다.	15초	45초
통 합 형	읽 기 / 듣 기 / 말 하 기	2. 지문을 읽고 대화를 들은 후 요약하기	• 대학 생활과 관련된 문제를 알리는 지문(90-115단어)을 읽는다. • 지문에 나온 문제에 대해 두 사람이 논하는 대화(60-80초)를 듣는다. • 읽은 내용을 참고해 들은 내용을 요약해 말한다.	30초	60초
		3. 지문을 읽고 강의를 들은 후 요약하기	• 학술적 주제의 지문(90-115 단어)을 읽는다. • 예시와 세부정보를 이용해 지문의 내용을 설명하는 강의 (60-90초)를 듣는다. • 읽고 들은 내용을 종합해 중요한 정보를 전달한다.	30초	60초
	듣 기 / 말 하 기	4. 강의 요약하기	• 구체적 예를 들어 용어나 개념을 설명하는 강의(90-120초)를 듣는다. • 강의를 요약하고 전체 주제와 예시의 관계를 설명한다.	20초	60초

Writing Section

1. 쓰기 영역의 구성

과제 유형	특징	문항 수	시간
통합형	읽고 들은 내용을 바탕으로 글쓰기	1	20분
학술 토론에 관한 쓰기	한 가지 학술 주제에 대한 두 학생의 상반된 주장 중 하나를 뒷받침하는 글쓰기	1	10분

2. 쓰기 영역의 특징

쓰기 영역은 통합형 1문제와 학술 토론에 관한 쓰기 1문제로 구성된다. 시험은 30분 동안 진행되고, 수험자가 컴퓨터에 입력한 2문제의 답변은 ETS에 전송되어 공인 채점자들과 자동 채점 시스템이 채점한다.

- 통합형 과제
  - 듣고 읽은 내용을 필기하고, 필기 내용을 토대로 내용을 정리한다.
  - 원문의 내용을 정확히 요약, 바꿔쓰기, 인용한다.
  - 강의 내용과 독해 내용이 어떤 관련이 있는지 설명한다.

- 학술 토론에 관한 쓰기
  - 토론의 질문과 두 학생의 관련 의견을 읽고 자신의 의견을 글로 쓴다.

- 글쓰기 전반에 관한 조언
  - 내용을 체계적이고 논리적이며 일관된 방식으로 표현한다.
  - 적절한 연결어를 사용하여 여러 아이디어를 연결하고 독자의 이해를 돕는다.
  - 문법과 어휘를 정확히 사용하고, 숙어 표현을 적절히 활용한다.
  - 올바른 맞춤법, 구두점 사용법, 양식을 준수한다.

3. 쓰기 영역의 과제 유형과 세부 특징

과제 유형	특징	시간
1. 통합형 과제 읽기/듣기/쓰기	• 학술 지문 읽기(250-300단어, 읽기 시간: 3분) • 수험자는 읽기 지문의 내용을 필기할 수 있다. • 화면에서 읽기 지문이 사라진 후 강의를 듣는다. 읽기 지문은 수험자가 답변을 작성할 때 참고할 수 있도록 화면에 다시 나타난다. • 강의에서는 교수가 동일한 주제를 다른 시각에서 논한다. (250-320단어, 듣기 시간: 약 2분) • 강의에서는 읽기 지문의 요점과 관련된 부가 정보를 제공한다. 수험자는 강의 내용을 필기할 수 있다. • 수험자는 강의 요점을 조리 있는 영어 산문체로 요약하고, 읽기 지문의 요점과 어떤 관련이 있는지 설명한다. 답변의 권장 분량은 150-225단어이지만, 주제를 벗어나지 않는 한 더 많은 분량의 답변을 작성하더라도 점수가 깎이지는 않는다.	20분
2. 학술 토론에 관한 쓰기 학술적 주제에 대한 주장을 뒷받침하는 글쓰기	• 수험자는 온라인 토론에 참여하는 글을 쓴다. 토론은 교수의 질문으로 시작되고, 두 명의 동급생이 이미 글로 의견을 제시한 상태다. 최소 100단어 이상으로 이루어진 답변이 유효하다. • 수험자는 교수의 질문에 대해 동급생의 글을 참고하여 글을 써도 되고, 완전히 새로운 의견을 개진해도 된다. 수험자의 글은 논의와 관련성이 있어야 하고, 자신만의 언어로 명확하게 토론에 기여해야 한다. • 전형적인 토론 주제는 학생들에게 어떤 입장 또는 주장에 대해 찬반을 묻고, 다양한 입장 또는 주장 중 하나를 선택하거나, 자신들만의 의견을 개진하고 설명하도록 요구한다.	10분

About Test Scores

◆ 점수 환산(Score Scales)

TOEFL iBT®는 다음과 같은 네 가지 능력의 점수를 제공한다.

읽기(Reading)	0-30
듣기(Listening)	0-30
말하기(Speaking)	0-30
쓰기(Writing)	0-30
총 점 (Total Score)	**0-120**

총점은 네 가지 영역별 능력 점수를 합산한다.

MyBest® Scores

MyBest® 점수는 지난 2년간 수험자가 섹션별로 받은 최고 점수를 합산한 것으로, 수험자가 획득한 최상의 성적을 나타낸다. 이를 통해 희망 학교에서 요구하는 점수를 획득하기까지 시험 응시 회수를 줄일 수 있고 더 빨리 목표를 이룰 수 있다.

◆ 성적표(Score Report)

TOEFL iBT® 성적표는 학생이 영어 구사 환경에서 학문 연구에 참여하여 성공적으로 학업을 이어갈 수 있는 준비가 되었는지에 관한 소중한 정보를 제공한다. 성적표에는 다음 사항이 포함된다.

- 총점
- 각 영역(읽기, 듣기, 말하기, 쓰기)의 점수
- 수험자의 각 영역별 수행능력 수준
- MyBest 점수

이에 더하여 각 수험자의 TOEFL iBT® 계정에서 더 자세한 성적 피드백과 수행 평가 분석 내용을 확인할 수 있으며, 여기엔 다음과 같은 사항도 포함된다.

- 읽기와 듣기 영역에서 고득점 수험자의 수행 능력과 일치하는 성과를 보여준 문제 유형과 아직 더 수행 능력을 보완해야 하는 문제 유형에 대한 피드백
- 언어 사용, 문법 및 구두점 등의 기술적인 측면에 대한 분석을 포함한 말하기 및 쓰기 수행 능력에 대한 심층적인 분석
- 연습 및 능력 향상을 위한 말하기와 쓰기 영역 문제의 고득점 답변 추가 샘플 및 해설 제공

◆ 말하기 및 쓰기의 답변 평가

1) 말하기(Speaking)

말하기 영역의 네 문제에 대한 답변은 디지털 방식으로 녹음되어 ETS로 전송된다. 각 수험자의 답변은 4명의 공인 채점자와 자동 채점 시스템이 채점한다. 각 문제의 답변을 115-116쪽에 수록된 채점 기준에 의거하여 0-4등급으로 채점하고, 네 문항의 점수 총합을 환산점수 0-30으로 변환한다.

채점자들은 수험자의 답변에서 다음 주안점을 유의해서 듣는다.

- 전달 능력: 얼마나 명확하게 말했는가? 우수 답변은 유창하고, 명확하며, 발음도 정확하고, 속도와 억양이 자연스러워야 한다.

- 언어 사용: 수험자가 문법과 어휘를 얼마나 효과적으로 활용하여 생각을 전달하는가? 채점자들은 수험자가 기본적 언어 구조와 복합적 언어 구조를 모두 구사하고, 적절한 어휘를 사용하는 능력을 평가한다.

- 주제 전개: 수험자가 질문에 얼마나 제대로 대답을 하며, 생각을 얼마나 조리 있게 표현하는가? 통합형 문제에서 수험자가 내용을 얼마나 잘 종합하여 요약하는가? 우수한 답변은 대게 할당된 시간의 전체나 대부분을 사용하고, 의견들 간의 관계와 한 의견에서 다른 의견으로의 진행이 명확하고 이해하기 쉽다.

채점자가 수험자에게 완벽한 답변을 기대하지 않는다는 사실에 유념해야 한다. 심지어 고득점 답변에도 위에서 설명한 세 가지 주안점 중 어느 것에라도 간혹 오류나 사소한 문제가 포함되어 있을 수 있다.

2) 쓰기(Writing)

모든 쓰기 문제의 답변은 ETS로 전송된다. 답안은 2명의 공인 채점자와 자동 채점 시스템이 130쪽과 138쪽에 수록된 채점 기준에 의거하여 0-5등급으로 평가하고, 쓰기 2문항의 평균등급을 환산점수 0-30으로 변환한다.

- 통합형 쓰기 문제의 답변은 글의 수준(구성, 문법과 어휘의 적합하고 정확한 사용)과 내용의 완성도 및 정확성을 기준으로 채점한다.

- 학술 토론에 관한 쓰기 에세이는 글의 전반적 수준(전개, 토론 내용 뒷받침, 문법과 어휘의 정확한 사용)을 기준으로 채점한다.

수험자의 글이 초고임을 채점자들이 알고 있다는 사실에 유념해야 한다. 채점자들은 수험자가 훌륭한 연구를 바탕으로 한 포괄적 에세이를 작성하기를 기대하지는 않는다. 그러므로 수험자는 다소 오류가 있는 답변이라도 높은 점수를 받을 수 있다.

Sample TOEFL iBT® Score Report

 **TOEFL iBT** Test Taker Score Report

Kumar, Kaira
Last (Family/Surname) Name, First (Given) Name Middle Name
Email: Kaira.Kumar@123gmail.com

Kaira Kumar
33, Pantheon Rd
Chennai, Tamil Nadu
600008 INDIA

SAMPLE

Institution Code	Department Code
ABCD	40
M987	41
P654	42
i321	43

Test Date: May 15, 2023
Appointment #: 1234 8052 1411 0011
Native Language: Tamil
Test Center Country: India
Test Center: STN20038A – ANCONS International

Gender: F
Date of Birth: October 14, 2004
Country of Birth: India

Test Date: May 15, 2023   **ETS® Security Guard**
                                                See back for details

Total Score	🖽 Reading	🎧 Listening	🗣 Speaking	✎ Writing
91 out of 120	**27** out of 30	**23** out of 30	**21** out of 30	**20** out of 30

***MyBest®* Scores** | Your highest section scores from all valid test dates, as of May 17, 2023.

Sum of Highest Section Scores **94** out of 120	Reading (0–30) **27** Test Date May 15, 2023	Listening (0–30) **24** Test Date Apr 15, 2023	Speaking (0–30) **21** Test Date May 15, 2023	Writing (0–30) **22** Test Date Apr 15, 2022

SECURITY IDENTIFICATION
ID Type: Passport
ID No: xxxxx...0372
Issuing Country: India

A total score is not reported when one or more sections have not been administered. Expired scores are not included in *MyBest*® calculations.

80-80

Page 1 of 2

Sample TOEFL iBT® Score Report

 TOEFL iBT.

Kumar, Kaira
Test Date: May 15, 2023
Appointment Number: 1234 8052 1411 0011

For additional TOEFL iBT® scoring details, score ranges, and how to improve your skills, visit www.ets.org/toefl/ibt/scores.

Score Ranges
Total Score Range: 0–120

Reading	**0–30**
Advanced	24–30
High–Intermediate	18–23
Low–Intermediate	4–17
Below Low–Intermediate	0–3

Listening	**0–30**
Advanced	22–30
High–Intermediate	17–21
Low–Intermediate	9–16
Below Low–Intermediate	0–8

Speaking	**0–30**
Advanced	25–30
High–Intermediate	20–24
Low–Intermediate	16–19
Basic	10–15
Below Basic	0–9

Writing	**0–30**
Advanced	24–30
High–Intermediate	17–23
Low–Intermediate	13–16
Basic	7–12
Below Basic	0–6

Institution Codes

Department	Where the Report Was Sent
00	Admissions office for undergraduate study
01, 04–41, 43–98	Admissions office for graduate study in a field other than management (business) or law according to the codes selected when you registered
02	Admissions office of a graduate school of management (business)
03	Admissions office of a graduate school of law
42	Admissions office of a school of medicine or nursing or licensing agency
99	Institution or agency that is not a college or university

IMPORTANT NOTE TO SCORE USERS: To verify the scores on this report, please contact the TOEFL® Score Verification Service at **+1-800-257-9547** or **+1-609-771-7100**. Scores more than two years old cannot be reported or validated.

ETS® Security Guard text is printed with a special heat-sensitive ink for security. To activate this security feature, apply heat to the text, either by rubbing it or blowing on it, and the ETS Security Guard text will disappear.

150256-149717 • S722E1200 • Printed in U.S.A.
831186

General Skill-Building Tips

TOEFL iBT®가 평가하는 영어 능력을 키우려는 영어 학습자에게 최선의 방법은 다음 사항에 대해 강의를 제공하는 영어 학습 프로그램을 수강하는 것이다.

- 읽기, 말하기, 듣기, 쓰기 학습. 특히 말하기에 중점을 두어야 함.
- 통합적 능력 접근법(예: 듣고 읽고 말하는 능력과 듣고 읽고 쓰는 능력을 키우는 강의)

1. 읽기 비결(Reading Tips)

영어 학습자가 읽기 능력을 향상시키려면 규칙적으로, 특히 다양한 주제 영역(예: 과학, 사회과학, 인문학, 경영학 등)에 걸쳐 학술적 문체로 작성된 대학 교재 등을 읽어야 한다. 정기간행물과 학술지는 물론 인터넷에서도 매우 다양한 학술문서를 찾아볼 수 있다.

1) 정보 찾기

- 지문을 죽 훑어보면서 핵심 사실(날짜, 숫자, 용어)과 정보를 찾는다.
- 더욱 빠르고 유창하게 읽기 위해 읽기 연습을 자주 한다.

2) 기본적 이해

- 주제의 대의를 파악하기 위해 속독을 연습한다.
- 지문 전체를 빨리 읽은 후 꼼꼼히 다시 읽고 주제, 주요 요점, 중요 사항을 기록 한다.
- 지문에서 익숙하지 않은 단어를 찾아 사전에서 의미를 확인한다.

3) 내용 종합하기

- 지문의 유형(예: 원인/결과, 비교/대조, 분류, 문제/해결, 설명, 내레이션 등)과 구성을 파악한다.
- 지문의 정보를 정리한다.
  · 중요 사항과 부수 사항을 구분하기 위해 지문의 개요를 작성한다.
  · 지문에서 정보가 분류되어 있으면, 차트를 만들어 각 정보를 해당 항목에 넣는다.

2. 듣기 비결

구어체 영어를 정기적으로 들으면서 듣기 능력을 향상시킬 수 있다. 영화나 TV 시청, 팟캐스트나 라디오 청취가 듣기 능력 향상을 위한 좋은 기회를 제공한다. 다양한 학술 자료를 듣는 것이 학술적 듣기 능력을 향상시키는 최선의 방법이다. 다양한 형태의 비디오나 오디오 자료도 도서관, 서점, 웹사이트에서 찾아볼 수 있다. 대본이 포함된 자료는 특히 유용하다. 인터넷에도 좋은 듣기 자료가 있다(예: npr.org, bbc.co.uk/sounds, bbc.co.uk/learningenglish, or learningenglish.voanews.com 등).

1) 기본적 이해

- 어휘력을 향상한다.
- 잘 모르는 어휘가 나올 경우, 그것이 쓰인 문맥을 바탕으로 그 의미를 추론해 본다.
- 발화의 내용과 흐름에 주의를 기울인다. 말하는 방식이나 말투에 주의가 흐트러지지 않도록 한다.
- 집중 유지를 위한 수단으로 다음에 무슨 말이 나올지 예측한다.
- 스스로에게 질문하면서 적극적 자세를 취한다. (예: 교수는 무슨 주제를 전달하는가?)
- 주제가 바뀌거나 딴 이야기로 흐르는 것을 나타내는 단어나 구를 듣는다.
- 강의나 담화의 일부를 듣고 중요한 사항으로 구성된 개요를 작성한다. 들은 단어 전부를 받아 적으려고 하기보다는 요점이나 중요 세부 사항을 기록한다. 끝나면 다시 들으면서 자신이 쓴 내용을 점검하고 수정 또는 추가한다. 강의나 담화의 양을 점차 늘려가고 개요를 작성한다.
- 전체 강의나 담화를 듣는다. 들은 내용 중 주제를 나타내는 문장을 적는다. 다시 한번 들으며 쓴 내용을 확인하고 주요 세부 사항들을 적는다.

2) 화용론적 이해

- 말하는 이의 의도를 짐작해 본다. 주장이나 질문의 목적이 무엇인가? 사과하는가, 불평하는가, 아니면 제안하는가?
- 말하는 이가 얼마나 확신하고 있는지에 유의한다. 화자는 정보에 대해 얼마나 확신하는가? 화자의 어조로 화자가 어느 정도 확신하는지 알 수 있는가?
- 여담에 귀를 기울인다.
- TV 프로그램이나 코미디 영화를 녹화해 시청한다. 의미를 전달하기 위해 강세나 억양을 활용하는 방법에 주의하며 듣는다.

3) 구성 파악과 정보 종합

- 듣고 있는 강의의 구성 방식을 생각해 본다. 도입부, 주요 단계나 개념, 예시, 결론이나 요약을 나타내는 신호어에 유의하며 듣는다.
- 여러 개념 사이의 관계를 파악한다. 여러 개념들은 원인/결과, 비교/대조의 관계이거나, 전개의 각 단계이다.
- 여러 개념 사이의 연결이나 관계를 나타내는 단어에 유의하며 듣는다.
- 녹음 자료를 들으면서 여러 지점에서 잠시 멈추고, 그 다음에 어떤 정보나 개념이 나올지 예측한다.
- 청취 도중이나 청취 후 논의된 정보의 개요를 작성한다.

3. 말하기 비결

최선의 말하기 연습 방법은 원어민과 대화를 나누는 것이다. 비영어권 국가에 살고 있다면 영어권 강사를 찾아서 되도록 함께 말해 보는 것이 매우 중요하다. 인터넷을 통해서도 영어권 강사에게 배우거나 함께 영어 말하기를 연습할 대화 상대를 찾을 수 있다. 영화, 음악, 여행에 관해 영어로 대화하는 회원들로 구성된 영어 회화 클럽에 가입하는 것도 한 가지 방법이다. 주변에 그런 클럽이 없으면 직접 만들고, 도와줄 원어민을 초대해 보자.

1) 독립형 말하기 과제(Independent Speaking Tasks)

- 익숙한 주제의 목록을 작성하고 그 주제에 관해 말하기 연습을 한다.
- 선호하는 것을 말하고 그것을 선호하는 이유를 설명한다.
- 견해를 명확히 말하고 그 의견에 대한 명확하고 상세한 이유를 제시한다.
- 특정 사항을 추천하고 그것이 최선의 진행 방법인 이유를 설명한다.
- 여러 주제에 관해 1분간 답변하기를 연습한다.

2) 통합형 말하기 과제(Integrated Speaking Tasks)

- 본문 내용과 관련된 문제가 수록된 교재를 구해서 질문에 구두로 답하는 연습을 한다.
- 짧은 지문(100~200단어)을 읽고, 그 지문의 주요 핵심만 포함하는 개요를 작성하고 이를 이용해 지문의 내용을 요약하여 말한다.
- 지문에서 다루는 주제와 동일한 주제에 관한 듣기 자료와 읽기 자료를 찾는다. 각 자료의 관점은 유사하거나 상이할 수 있다(인터넷이나 도서관은 정보 찾기에 적합한 곳이다). 듣기 자료와 읽기 자료에 관해 필기하거나 개요를 작성한다.
  - 듣기 자료와 읽기 자료의 내용을 요약해 말한다. 반드시 다른 단어와 문법 구조를 활용하여 다른 말로 바꾸어 말한다.
  - 독해 자료의 정보와 듣기 자료의 정보를 통합해 내용을 종합하고, 설명한다.
  - 독해 자료와 듣기 자료에 제시된 아이디어와 정보에 관해 의견을 진술하고, 서로 어떤 관련이 있는지 설명한다.

3) 전반적인 말하기 능력 향상 비결(All Speaking Tasks)

- 매일 새로운 하나의 어휘, 혹은 숙어를 사용하려고 노력한다.
- 영어 화자의 말을 1분 동안 녹음한다. (당신의 지인 혹은 인터넷, TV, 라디오 등으로부터의 녹음일 수 있다.) 녹음을 두 번 들어서 화자의 억양에 익숙해진다. 그런 다음 세 번째로 녹음을 틀고 화자를 따라 크게 말해 본다.
- 위에서 소개한 요령으로 TOEFL iBT®를 연습할 때, 말하기 전에 무엇을 말할지 15초 동안 생각한다. 몇몇 핵심어와 주제를 적어 두되, 말할 내용을 문자 그대로 적어 두려 해서는 안 된다(채점자들은 미리 써놓고 읽은 답변을 알아차리고 낮은 점수를 줄 것이다).
- 영어 구사자의 말을 들을 때, 화자의 생각을 연결하는 데 도움이 되는 단어와 표현을 식별하도록 노력한다. 그런 다음 이러한 표현을 사용해 새로운 정보를 제시하고, 생각을 연결하며, 중요한 단어나 생각을 나타내도록 노력한다. 이렇게 하면 듣는 사람이 더 쉽게 이해할 수 있다. (예: "on the one hand," "what that means is," "one reason is," "another difference might be")

4. 쓰기 비결

1) 통합형 쓰기 과제(Integrated Writing Tasks)

- 본문 내용과 관련된 문제가 수록된 교재를 구해서 질문에 대한 답변을 글로 쓰는 연습을 한다.
- 약 300~400단어 분량의 지문을 읽고, 주요 핵심과 지문의 중요한 세부 사항을 포함하는 개요를 작성한다. 개요를 활용하여 내용과 아이디어를 요약한다. 요약은 간략하고 명확히 주요 핵심과 중요한 세부 사항만 전달해야 한다. 반드시 다른 단어와 문법 구조를 이용해 다른 말로 바꾸어 써야 한다.
- 인터넷이나 도서관에서 한 가지 주제에 관한 듣기 자료와 읽기 자료를 찾는다. 각 자료의 관점은 유사하거나 상이할 수 있다. 독해 자료와 읽기 자료에 관해 필기하고 다음 사항을 이행한다.
  - 듣기 자료와 읽기 자료의 내용을 요약한다.
  - 내용을 종합하고, 독해 자료와 듣기 자료가 서로 어떤 관련이 있는지 논한다. 제시된 아이디어가 어떻게 유사한지, 어떻게 한 아이디어가 다른 아이디어로 확장되는지, 또는 여러 아이디어의 차이와 서로 어떻게 대립되는지 설명한다.

2) 고쳐 쓰기 능력 향상 비결(Paraphrasing)

'고쳐 쓰기(Paraphrasing)'란 해당 자료에 제시된 내용을 본인의 말로 재진술하는 것이다. TOEFL iBT®에서는 수험자가 지문의 내용을 그대로 옮겨 쓰기만 했다면 점수를 전혀 받지 못한다. 다음 비결을 자주 활용하여 단어, 구, 문장, 전체 단락을 고쳐 쓰는 연습을 한다.

- 동의어를 손쉽게 찾는 방법을 익힌다. 독해 지문에서 10~15개의 단어나 구를 선정하고, 일반 사전이나 동의어 사전을 찾아보지 않고 동의어를 재빨리 생각해 본다.
- 필기 내용만 활용하여 한 단락의 지문을 고쳐 쓴다. 필기를 하지 않았으면 원문을 참고하지 않고 고쳐 쓴다. 그 다음 고쳐 쓴 글과 원문을 비교해 정확한 사실을 언급했는지, 다양한 단어와 문법 구조를 활용했는지 확인한다.

3) 학술 토론에 관한 쓰기 과제(Academic Discussion Writing Tasks)

- 각 주제로 최소한 하나 이상의 의견 글을 작성해 본다. 10분 안에 글쓰기와 검토를 마치도록 한다. 가능하면 같은 주제로 여러 의견 글을 써본다.
- 글을 쓰기 전에 두 가지 정도 아이디어를 내보고 가장 좋은 글이 될 만한 것을 고른다.
- 글을 쓰는 데 너무 많은 시간을 할애하지 않는다. 대신 전체적으로 일관되고 자연스럽게 읽히도록 노력한다. 아이디어를 잘 연결하고 발전시켜서 독자가 글쓴이의 의견이 무엇인지 왜 그렇게 생각하는지 명확하게 이해할 수 있도록 한다. 글을 검토하고 오류를 고칠 약간의 시간을 남겨 두는 걸 잊지 않는다.
- 암기한 글, 공식 같은 글, 모호한 언어를 사용하지 않는다. 자신만의 목소리를 글에 투영하고, 자신만의 언어를 사용하여 자신의 생각을 표현한다.

Test Preparation Tips from ETS

다음은 ETS에서 권장하는 토플 수험 전략이다.

- **지시 사항**

  각 영역의 지시 사항(Direction)을 준수하여 시간 낭비를 방지한다.

- **도움말 활용**

  도움말을 볼 때도 화면 우측 상단의 시계가 멈추지 않으므로 **반드시 필요할 경우에만** 도움말 기능을 활용해야 한다.

- **당황하지 말 것**

  지금 풀고 있는 문제에만 집중하고 지나간 문제들을 어떻게 풀었는지는 생각하지 말아야 한다.

- **신속한 판단**

  어떤 문제든 한 문제에 너무 많은 시간을 소요하지 말아야 한다. 잠시 생각해도 정답을 알 수 없으면 가능한 한 많은 선택지를 제거하고 가장 적절하다고 판단되는 선택지를 선택해야 한다. 읽기 영역에서는 **Review**를 선택하면 답변 상황을 확인할 수 있다. 모든 문제의 답을 선택한 후 답변 상황을 확인해야 집중력을 유지하고 시간을 절약할 수 있다.

- **적절한 시간 분배**

  시간 분배를 잘 해야 모든 문제에 답하기에 충분한 시간을 확보할 수 있다. 각 영역과 문제의 시간 제한에 유의하고, 시간을 적절히 분배해야 막판에 서두르지 않게 된다. 원한다면 화면 우측 상단의 시계를 감출 수 있지만, 진행 상태를 확인하기 위해 주기적으로 시간을 확인하는 것이 바람직하다. 읽기, 듣기, 쓰기 영역에서는 시험 종료 5분 전에 시계가 이를 자동으로 알려줄 것이다. 말하기 영역에서는 시계와 막대 그래프를 통해 제한 시간과 남은 시간을 확인할 수 있다.

Questions Frequently Asked by Test Takers

■ TOEFL iBT®의 장점

Q 토플을 응시해야 하는 이유는?

TOEFL iBT®는 미국뿐만 아니라 캐나다, 영국, 호주, 뉴질랜드의 많은 학교와 기관에서 채택하고 있으므로, 수험자는 사실상 전 세계 어느 학교에라도 지원할 수 있는 자격을 갖추게 된다.

Q TOEFL iBT®가 다른 시험보다 더 우수한 이유는?

TOEFL iBT®는 전 세계의 다른 모든 시험에 비해 시험 장소, 일자, 횟수의 선택폭이 훨씬 넓고, 더욱 풍부한 학습자료와 피드백을 제공하므로 수험자가 유연하게 대처할 수 있다. TOEFL iBT®는 성공적인 학업 수행을 위해 수험자에게 반드시 필요한 통합적 영어 구사력을 측정한다. 특히 다른 시험보다 말하기 능력을 더욱 공정하게 평가한다. 답변은 최소 4명 이상의 각기 다른 공인된 채점자와 자동 채점 시스템에 의하여 채점되어, 지역 시험장에서 한 명의 면접관만 이용하는 다른 시험들보다 수험자의 말하기 기술에 대한 더 객관적이고 신뢰할 수 있는 정보를 제공한다.

Q TOEFL iBT®는 수험자 이외의 누구에게 도움이 되는가?

대학 입학 심사관과 여러 기관이 지원자의 영어 능력을 판단하는 데 필요한 더욱 정확하고 풍부한 정보를 제공한다.

■ TOEFL iBT® 등록 절차

Q 등록 일자와 방법은?

가장 쉬운 방법은 온라인 등록이다. 우편이나 전화 등록도 가능하다. **www.ets.org/toefl**에서 자세한 정보를 얻을 수 있다. 등록은 희망 응시 일자 기준으로 5-6개월 이전에 가능하다. 조기 마감되는 경우가 많으므로 되도록 일찍 신청해야 한다.

Q TOEFL iBT® 시험 일자와 장소는?

TOEFL iBT®는 전 세계 200여 개국 및 지역에서 시행된다. 세 가지 방식으로 응시가 가능하여 자신에게 제일 알맞은 방식을 고를 수 있다. 테스트 센터나 집에서 컴퓨터로, 또는 테스트 센터에서 필기로 시험을 볼 수 있다. **ets.org/toefl**에서 자신에게 제일 편리한 응시 방법을 선택하면 된다.

Q TOEFL iBT®의 수험료는?

수험료는 국가별로 다르다. **www.ets.org/toefl**에서 국가별 수험료를 확인할 수 있다.

■ 시험 준비

Q 샘플 문제를 활용할 수 있는가?

그렇다. TOEFL 웹사이트인 https://www.ets.org/toefl/test-takers/ibt/prepare에서 TOEFL iBT® Free Practice Test를 풀어볼 수 있는데, 읽기, 듣기, 말하기, 쓰기의 4가지 영역의 실제 시험 문제를 반복해서 풀어 보고 연습할 수 있는 기회를 제공한다. 말하기와 쓰기 문제는 채점자 코멘트가 포함된 샘플 응답도 볼 수 있다. 이 웹사이트에는 이전 시험의 무료 TOEFL iBT® 문제들도 제공하고 있어 각 영역을 연습할 수 있다.

Q 모의고사에 응시하고 점수를 받을 수 있는가?

그렇다. www.ets.org/toefl/shoptestprep에서 토플 모의고사에 응시할 수 있다. 이 사이트는 다른 곳에서는 찾아볼 수 없는 4대 영역(읽기, 듣기, 말하기, 쓰기)의 연습 문제와 ETS 공인 채점관의 채점을 제공한다.

■ 성적과 성적표

Q 점수는 어떻게 알 수 있는가?

성적은 ETS 계정에서 확인할 수 있다. 시험 응시 방식에 따라 성적 발표 시기가 다르다.

- 테스트 센터 응시: 응시일로부터 4-8일 후
- 집에서 응시: 응시일로부터 4-8일 후
- 필기 시험 응시: 응시일로부터 영업일 기준 11-13일 후

Q 성적표에는 무엇이 포함되는가?

모든 성적표에는 다음이 포함된다.

- 해당 응시일에 받은 총점과 영역별 점수
- MyBest 점수(지난 2년간 받은 영역별 최고 점수를 더한 점수)

자신의 ETS 계정에서 개인별 수행 능력 피드백과 성적 결과의 심층 분석 내용을 확인할 수 있다.

Q 추가 성적표 신청이 가능한가?

그렇다. 소정의 비용을 지불하면 수험자가 원하는 대로 다수의 기관에 성적표를 발송할 수 있다. www.ets.org/toefl에서 자세한 정보를 얻을 수 있다.

Q 점수의 유효기간은?

ETS는 응시일 이후 2년간 성적표를 제공한다.

Q 기관에서 이전 점수를 인정하는가?

각 기관별 기준이 있으므로 해당 기관에 문의해야 한다.

■ 시험 진행

Q TOEFL iBT®는 어떤 능력을 측정하는가?

시험은 영어로 진행되고, 4영역(읽기, 듣기, 말하기, 쓰기)에 약 2시간 이하의 시간이 소요된다.

영역	예상 시간	문제 수
읽 기(Reading)	35분	2개의 지문, 지문당 10문제
듣 기(Listening)	36분	3개의 강의, 강의당 6문제 2개의 대화문, 대화당 5문제
말하기(Speaking)	16분	4
쓰 기(Writing)	29분	2

Q 1개 영역만 응시할 수 있는가?

불가능하다. 모든 영역에 응시해야 점수를 받을 수 있다.

Q TOEFL iBT®에는 어떤 키보드가 사용되나?

일반적으로 가장 흔한 QWERTY 키보드를 사용한다. 수험자는 영어로 답변을 작성해야 하므로 시험 전에 영문 타자 연습을 충분히 해야 한다.

Chapter 2

Reading Section

Basic Comprehension Questions

Inferencing Questions

Reading-to-Learn Questions

Reading Practice Sets

Chapter 2

Reading Section

이 장의 구성_   TOEFL iBT® 읽기 문제 9가지 유형
유형별 문제 식별 방법
유형별 문제 풀이 요령
점수 향상 전략

TOEFL iBT® 읽기 영역에서는 약 700단어 분량의 지문이 2개 나오고, 각 지문마다 10개의 문제
가 출제된다. 읽기 영역에는 36분이 소요된다. 읽기 영역에서는 제한 시간 안에 문제를 모두 풀 수
만 있다면 중간에 문제를 건너뛰고 나중에 다시 돌아와 풀 수 있다.

읽기 영역에 대한 소개

TOEFL iBT® 읽기 지문은 개론서로 사용될 만한 교재와 논문에서 발췌한 것으로 학생들이 학문적인 글을 얼마나 잘 이해
할 수 있는지 평가하는 것이 목적이다. 다양한 주제가 등장하지만 문제를 푸는 데 필요한 모든 정보는 지문 안에 있으므로
익숙하지 않은 주제라 할지라도 걱정할 필요가 없다. 모든 TOEFL 지문은 글쓴이가 글을 쓴 목적에 따라 설명, 논증, 역사
적 사실 기술 등의 범주로 분류되며 지문 구조의 유형에 따라 분류·비교, 원인·결과, 문제·해결로 분류된다.

문제 유형

1. Basic Comprehension Questions_기본적인 정보 및 추론 문제

1. Factual Information Questions_세부 사항 찾기 문제 (2–5문제)

2. Negative Factual Information Questions_틀린 정보 찾기 문제 (0–2문제)

3. Vocabulary Questions_어휘 문제 (1– 2문제)

4. Reference Questions_지시 대상 찾기 문제 (0–2문제)

5. Sentence Simplification Questions_문장 재구성 문제 (0–1문제)

2. Inferencing Questions_지문 내용 추론하기 문제 (1 문제)

6. Inference Questions_내용 추론 문제 (1–2문제)

7. Rhetorical Purpose Questions_수사학적 의도 파악 문제 (1– 2문제)

8. Insert Text Questions_문장 삽입 문제 (1문제)

3. Reading-to-Learn Questions_지문 내용 종합하기 문제 (1문제)

9. Prose Summary_지문 요약하기

Basic Comprehension Questions_기본적인 이해 문제

| Type 1 | 세부 사항 찾기 문제 |

이 문제는 지문에 명시된 객관적 정보를 파악하는 것으로, 사실, 세부 사항, 정의, 정보 등을 묻는다. 대개 지문의 일부분에만 언급된 구체적 정보를 파악할 것을 요구하며, 지문 전체가 이야기하고 있는 일반적인 주제를 묻는 경우는 별로 없다.

1. 문제 식별 방법

세부 사항 찾기 문제는 다음 중 한 가지 형태로 질문하는 경우가 많다.

- According to paragraph X, which of the following is true about Y?
- According to paragraph X, which of the following is the main reason that Y declined?
- According to paragraph X, Y declined mainly because...
- In paragraph X, which of the following is identified as an advantage of having Y?
- In paragraph X, which of the following is presented as evidence supporting the conclusion that...
- According to paragraph X, Y differs from Z in which of the following ways?

2. 문제 풀이 요령

1) 문제에 언급된 대상에 대해 정확히 어떤 내용이 쓰여 있는지 판단하기 위해 독해 지문을 참고한다.
2) 대부분의 보기가 정확한 대답을 선택할 수 있도록 말을 바꾸어 정보를 표현하고 있음을 인식하도록 한다.
3) 보기의 내용이 지문에 나온다고 해서 무조건 정답으로 선택하지 말고, 해당 문제에 대한 답변이 되는 보기를 택해야 한다.

ex.

"...Sculptures must, for example, be stable, which requires an understanding of the properties of mass, weight distribution, and stress. Paintings must have rigid stretchers so that the canvas will be taut, and the paint must not deteriorate, crack, or discolor. These are problems that must be overcome by the artist because they tend to intrude upon their conception of the work. For example, in the early Italian Renaissance, bronze statues of horses with a raised foreleg usually had a cannonball under that hoof. This was done because the cannonball was needed to support the weight of the leg. In other words, the demands of the laws of physics, not the sculptor's aesthetic intentions, placed the ball there. That this device was a necessary structural compromise is clear from the fact that the cannonball quickly disappeared when sculptors learned how to strengthen the internal structure of a statue with iron braces (iron being much stronger than bronze)..."

According to paragraph 2, sculptors in the Italian Renaissance stopped using cannonballs in bronze statues of horses because

Ⓐ they began using a material that made the statues weigh less

Ⓑ they found a way to strengthen the statues internally

Ⓒ the aesthetic tastes of the public had changed over time

Ⓓ the cannonballs added too much weight to the statues

Type 2 틀린 정보 찾기 문제

이 문제는 지문에 명시된 내용을 근거로, 어떤 정보가 사실인지 아닌지 확인하는 것이다. 이런 유형의 문제를 풀기 위해서는 먼저 관련된 정보를 지문에서 찾아낸 뒤, 네 개의 보기 중에서 사실이 아닌 것을 찾으면 된다.

1. 문제 식별 방법

문제에 NOT이나 EXCEPT 등의 단어가 대문자로 나오면 틀린 정보를 찾는 문제다.

- According to the passage, which of the following is NOT true of X?
- In paragraph X, the author mentions all of the following characteristics of Y EXCEPT...

2. 문제 풀이 요령

1) 보통 틀린 정보 찾기 문제는 세부 사항 찾기 문제보다 독해 지문을 좀 더 자세히 살펴봐야 한다. 보기에서 정답을 골라내는 데 필요한 정보들이 보통 여러 문장들에 걸쳐 나오기 때문이다.

2) 틀린 정보 찾기 문제의 정답은 지문의 내용과 모순되거나 지문에서 언급되지 않은 내용이다.

3) 문제를 다 풀고 나면 문제의 의도를 정확히 이해했는지 확인하고 답을 검토해야 한다.

ex.

"The United States in the 1800s was full of practical, hardworking people who did not consider the arts—from theater to painting—useful. In addition, the public's attitude that European art was better than American art both discouraged and infuriated American artists. In the early 1900s there was a strong feeling among artists that the United States was long overdue in developing art that did not reproduce European traditions. Everybody agreed that the heart and soul of the new country should be reflected in its art. But opinions differed about what this art would be like and how it would develop."

According to paragraph 1, all of the following were true of American art in the late 1800s and early 1900s EXCEPT:

Ⓐ Most Americans thought art was unimportant.

Ⓑ American art generally copied European styles and traditions.

Ⓒ Most Americans considered American art inferior to European art.

Ⓓ American art was very popular with European audiences.

<table>
<tr><td>Type
3</td><td>어휘 문제</td></tr>
</table>

이 문제에서는 지문에 사용된 특정 단어나 어구의 의미를 묻는다. 따라서 다의어의 경우에는 독해 지문에서 쓰인 의미를 찾아야 한다. 어휘 문제에서는 한 단어나 어구를 골라 질문하는데, 다양한 학문에 걸쳐 해당 단어나 어구가 관련 교재의 내용을 이해하는 데 중요하기 때문이다. 즉, 어휘 문제에서 다루는 용어는 해당 학문 분야의 기술적이고 전문적인 용어가 아니다. 전문 용어나 구가 지문에 나올 경우 보통 괄호나 하이퍼링크를 통해 정의가 제시된다.

1. 문제 식별 방법

어휘 문제는 대체로 파악하기 쉽다. 지문에서 음영 처리된 단어나 구가 보이며, 다음과 같은 문제가 나온다.

- The word "X" in the passage is closest in meaning to...
- The phrase "X" in the passage is closest in meaning to...
- In stating X, the author means that...

2. 문제 풀이 요령

1) 어휘 문제는 단순히 단어의 의미를 묻는 것이 아니라 지문에서 어떤 의미로 사용되었는지 묻는다. 그러므로 그 단어의 여러 의미 중 하나가 보기에 나왔다고 해서 이를 택해서는 안 된다.

2) 자신이 택한 단어나 어구를 지문에 대입해서 읽어 보고, 그 문장이 지문 전체의 맥락에서 의미가 통하는지 확인한다.

ex1.

"In the animal world the task of moving about is fulfilled in many ways. For some animals locomotion is accomplished by changes in body shape..."

The word "locomotion" in the passage is closest in meaning to

Ⓐ evolution

Ⓑ movement

Ⓒ survival

Ⓓ escape

ex2.

"Some poisonous snake bites need to be treated immediately or the victim will suffer paralysis..."

In stating that the victim will "suffer paralysis" the author means that the victim will

Ⓐ lose the ability to move

Ⓑ become unconscious

Ⓒ undergo shock

Ⓓ feel great pain

Type 4   지시 대상 찾기 문제

이 문제는 지문에 나온 단어들 간의 상호 지시 관계를 묻는 것으로 단어나 어구와 그 선행사(가리키는 표현 또는 개념)의 관계를 묻는 경우가 많다. 다른 종류의 문법적 지시 관계를 묻는 경우도 있다.

1. 문제 식별 방법

어휘 문제와 비슷해 보이지만, 지시 대상 찾기 문제는 지문에서 하나의 단어나 어구가 음영 처리되어 있으며 대명사인 경우가 많다. 다음과 같은 유형의 문제가 나오며, 그에 따른 네 개의 보기는 모두 지문에 나온 단어나 어구로 구성된다.

• The word "X" in the passage refers to...

2. 문제 풀이 요령

1) 대명사의 지시 대상을 묻는 문제에서는 자신이 고른 답안이 대명사와 수가 일치하는지(단수 또는 복수)와 같은 품사(예를 들어 명사, 동사, 형용사 또는 부사)인지를 확인한다.

2) 문장에서 음영 처리된 단어나 어구에 자신이 택한 보기를 대입해 문법적으로 올바르고 의미가 통하는지 확인한다.

ex1.

"...The first weekly newspaper in the colonies was the *Boston Gazette*, established in 1719, the same year that marked the appearance of Philadelphia's first newspaper, the *American Mercury*, where the young Benjamin Franklin worked. By 1760 Boston had 4 newspapers and 5 other printing establishments; Philadelphia, two newspapers and three other presses; and New York, three newspapers. The distribution, if not the sale, of newspapers was assisted by the establishment of a postal service in 1710, which had a network of some 65 offices by 1770, serving all 13 colonies..."

The word "which" in the passage refers to

Ⓐ distribution

Ⓑ sale

Ⓒ newspaper

Ⓓ postal service

ex2.

"...Roots anchor the plant in one of two ways or sometimes by a combination of the two. The first is by occupying a large volume of shallow soil around the plant's base with a *fibrous root system*, one consisting of many thin, profusely branched roots. Since these kinds of roots grow relatively close to the soil surface, they effectively control soil erosion. Grass roots are especially well suited to this purpose. Fibrous roots capture water as it begins to percolate into the ground and so must draw their mineral supplies from the surface soil before the nutrients are leached to lower levels..."

The phrase "this purpose" in the passage refers to

Ⓐ combining two root systems

Ⓑ feeding the plant

Ⓒ preventing soil erosion

Ⓓ leaching nutrients

Type 5 문장 재구성 문제

지문의 특정 문장과 핵심 의미가 동일한 문장을 고르는 문제다. 정답은 질문에서 묻는 특정 문장을 재구성한 형태이지만, 특정 문장의 핵심 정보를 포함하며 요점을 정확하게 표현한다. 모든 독해 지문에 문장 재구성 문제가 출제되지는 않으며, 한 지문 당 한 문제를 초과하지 않는다.

1. 문제 식별 방법

문장 재구성 문제는 항상 음영 처리된 한 개의 문장이 지문에 표시되고, 다음과 같은 형태로 출제된다.

- Which of the following best expresses the essential information in the highlighted sentence? Incorrect answer choices change the meaning in important ways or leave out essential information.

2. 문제 풀이 요령

1) 보기가 오답이 되는 다음 두 가지 경우를 알아 둔다.
   - 문제로 제시된 문장에 잘못된 정보를 포함시키거나 의미를 왜곡한다.
   - 문제로 제시된 문장에서 핵심 내용이 누락되었다.
2) 정답으로 택한 보기가 그 문장이 포함된 단락의 핵심 내용이나 지문 전체와 상충되지 않는지 확인한다.

ex.

"...Although we now tend to refer to the various crafts according to the materials used to construct them—clay, glass, wood, fiber, and metal—it was once common to think of crafts in terms of function, which led to their being known as the "applied arts." Approaching crafts from the point of view of function, we can divide them into simple categories: containers, shelters, and supports. There is no way around the fact that containers, shelters, and supports must be functional. The applied arts are thus bound by the laws of physics, which pertain to both the materials used in their making and the substances and things to be contained, supported, and sheltered. These laws are universal in their application, regardless of cultural beliefs, geography, or climate. If a pot has no bottom or has large openings in its sides, it could hardly be considered a container in any traditional sense. Since the laws of physics, not some arbitrary decision, have determined the general form of applied-art objects, they follow basic patterns, so much so that functional forms can vary only within certain limits. Buildings without roofs, for example, are unusual because they depart from the norm. However, not all functional objects are exactly alike; that is why we recognize a Shang Dynasty vase as being different from an Inca vase. What varies is not the basic form but the incidental details that do not obstruct the object's primary function..."

Which of the following best expresses the essential information in the highlighted sentence in the passage? Incorrect answer choices change the meaning in important ways or leave out essential information.

Ⓐ Functional applied-art objects cannot vary much from the basic patterns determined by the laws of physics.

Ⓑ The function of applied-art objects is determined by basic patterns in the laws of physics.

Ⓒ Since functional applied-art objects vary only within certain limits, arbitrary decisions cannot have determined their general form.

Ⓓ The general form of applied-art objects is limited by some arbitrary decision that is not determined by the laws of physics.

Inferencing Questions_추론하기

Type 6	내용 추론 문제
	내용 추론 문제는 지문에서 암시하고 있는(구체적으로 명시되지 않은) 정보를 알아내는 능력을 측정하며, 독해력이 요구된다. 읽기 영역의 추론 문제는 수험자가 적절한 지문을 찾아 글로 명백하게 언급되지 않은 주제와 관련된 정보와 생각을 파악할 수 있는지 묻는다. 지문 하나당 최소 1개에서 많게는 2개의 추론 문제가 출제된다.

1. 문제 식별 방법

내용 추론 문제에는 대개 infer, suggest, imply 같은 단어들이 나온다.

- Paragraph 1 suggests which of the following about X?
- The author of the passage implies that X...
- Which of the following can be inferred from paragraph 1 about X?

2. 문제 풀이 요령

1) 지문의 핵심 주제와 모순되지 않는 것을 답으로 골라야 한다.

2) 중요하거나 사실처럼 보인다고 답으로 선택해서는 안 된다. 정답은 반드시 지문으로부터 추론이 가능해야 한다.

3) 정답의 근거가 지문에 명시되어 있으므로 이를 정확히 파악해야 한다.

ex1.

"...The nineteenth century brought with it a burst of new discoveries and inventions that revolutionized the candle industry and made lighting available to all. In the early-to-mid-nineteenth century, a process was developed to refine tallow (fat from animals) with alkali and sulfuric acid. The result was a product called stearin. Stearin is harder and burns longer than unrefined tallow. This breakthrough meant that it was possible to make tallow candles that would not produce the usual smoke and rancid odor. Stearins were also derived from palm oils, so vegetable waxes as well as animal fats could be used to make candles..."

Which of the following can be inferred from paragraph 1 about candles before the nineteenth century?

Ⓐ They did not smoke when they were burned.

Ⓑ They produced a pleasant odor as they burned.

Ⓒ They were not available to everyone.

Ⓓ They contained sulfuric acid.

Fossils—the mineralized remains of plants and animals—provide important clues to life in the past. The fossils collected by Mary Anning (1799–1847) along the southwest coast of England helped shape modern science. Some fossils found or excavated by Anning were truly spectacular. While still a girl, Anning recovered the body of a large, strange animal whose skull was discovered by her brother in 1810. Thought to be a crocodile when only its head had been found, the fossil set off years of debate, with the animal eventually identified as an Ichthyosaurus, a previously unknown reptile. In 1824, she discovered the first intact skeleton of Plesiosaurus, a four-limbed swimming creature with a small head, and in 1828, the remains of the first flying reptile located outside of Germany. Finds such as these were rare and dangerous to unearth. The cliffs rising above Lyme Regis beaches were unstable with frequent mudslides in winter and during storms, yet these were best times for collecting fossils—the crumbling and washing away of parts of the cliffs left fossils newly exposed. Unless such fossils were collected right away, they would be washed out to sea. Given these conditions, it is hardly surprising that Anning narrowly escaped severe injury several times.

Which of the following can be inferred about Mary Anning from her efforts to search for fossils on the cliffs of Lyme Regis?

(A) She was brave and was not easily discouraged.

(B) She stopped searching for fossils when conditions became stormy.

(C) She suffered serious injuries multiple times as a result of her searches.

(D) She sometimes waited for fossils to wash out to sea before collecting them.

Type 7 수사학적 의도 파악 문제

수사는 효과적으로 말하거나 글을 쓰는 기술이다. 세부 사항 찾기 문제에서는 글쓴이가 어떤 정보를 제시했는가를 묻는 반면 이 문제에서는 글쓴이가 왜 특정 정보를, 특정 부분에, 특정한 방법으로 제시했는가를 묻는다.

1. 문제 식별 방법

수사학적 의도 파악 문제는 보통 다음과 같은 형태로 출제된다.

- The author discusses X in paragraph 2 in order to...
- Why does the author mention X?
- Why does the author compare X to Y?

2. 문제 풀이 요령

1) 수사학적 의도 파악 문제에 자주 사용되는 단어나 어구에 대해 알아 두도록 하자.

예증하다(illustrate), 설명하다(explain), 대조하다(contrast), 반박하다(refute), 주목하다(note), 비판하다(criticize) 등등.

2) 수사학적 의도 파악 문제는 독해 지문의 전체 구조에 대해 묻는 경우는 별로 없다. 그 대신 문장과 단락들 간의 논리적 관계를 묻는 경우가 많다.

ex.

"...Sensitivity to physical laws is thus an important consideration for the maker of applied-art objects. It is often taken for granted that this is also true for the maker of fine-art objects. This assumption misses a significant difference between the two disciplines. Fine-art objects are not constrained by the laws of physics in the same way that applied-art objects are. Because their primary purpose is not functional, they are only limited in terms of the materials used to make them. Sculptures must, for example, be stable, which requires an understanding of the properties of mass, weight distribution, and stress. Paintings must have rigid stretchers so that the canvas will be taut, and the paint must not deteriorate, crack, or discolor. These are problems that must be overcome by the artist because they tend to intrude upon his or her conception of the work. For example, in the early Italian Renaissance, bronze statues of horses with a raised foreleg usually had a cannonball under that hoof. This was done because the cannonball was needed to support the weight of the leg..."

Why does the author discuss the "bronze statues of horses" created by artists in the early Italian Renaissance?

Ⓐ To provide an example of a problem related to the laws of physics that a fine artist must overcome

Ⓑ To argue that fine artists are unconcerned with the laws of physics

Ⓒ To contrast the relative sophistication of modern artists in solving problems related to the laws of physics

Ⓓ To note an exceptional piece of art constructed without the aid of technology

Type	문장 삽입 문제
8	새로 제시된 문장을 지문의 어느 곳에 넣어야 가장 적당한지 묻는 문제이므로 문장 간의 문법적 연결 관계(대명사의 지시 관계 등)뿐만 아니라 논리적 흐름을 이해해야 한다. 모든 독해 지문에 문장 삽입 문제가 출제되며, 한 지문당 한 문제를 초과하지 않는다.

1. 문제 식별 방법

지문에 네 개의 검은 사각형이 나오며, 이 사각형은 문장의 시작 부분이나 끝 부분에 표시된다. 네 개의 사각형이 모두 한 단락 안에 있거나 한 단락의 끝 부분과 다음 단락의 시작 부분에 걸쳐서 나올 때도 있다. 사각형 네 개 중 하나를 클릭하여 굵게 표시된 문장을 지문 안에 삽입하라는 문제가 나온다.

[TOEFL iBT® 시험의 문장 삽입 문제 예시]

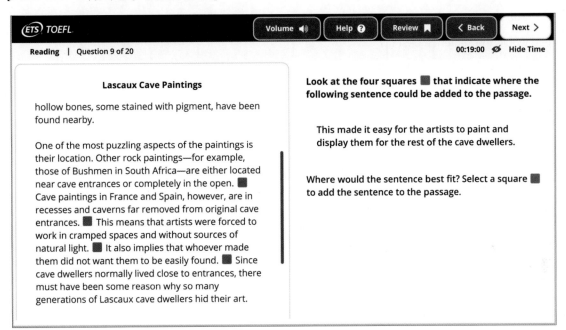

2. 문제 풀이 요령

1) 사각형으로 표시된 각 부분에 문장을 대입해 본다. 원하는 대로 얼마든지 문장을 넣어 볼 수 있다.

2) 삽입하고자 하는 문장의 구조와 논리를 모두 살펴본다. 논리적 연결어들은 문장이 어디에 들어가야 적당한지에 대한 중요한 단서가 될 수 있으므로 각별히 주의를 기울인다.

3) 자주 사용되는 연결어들은 다음과 같다.

On the other hand, For example, On the contrary, Similarly, In contrast, Further[Furthermore], Therefore, In other words, As a result, Finally

4) 삽입된 문장이 그 앞뒤 문장을 논리적으로 연결하는지 확인한다.

ex.

One of the most puzzling aspects of the paintings is their location. Other rock paintings—for example, those of Bushmen in South Africa—are either located near cave entrances or completely in the open. **(A)** Cave paintings in France and Spain, however, are in recesses and caverns far removed from original cave entrances. **(B)** This means that artists were forced to work in cramped spaces and without sources of natural light. **(C)** It also implies that whoever made them did not want them to be easily found. **(D)** Since cave dwellers normally lived close to entrances, there must have been some reason why so many generations of Lascaux cave dwellers hid their art.

Directions: Look at the part of the passage that is displayed above. The letters **(A)**, **(B)**, **(C)**, and **(D)** indicate where the following sentence could be added.

This made it easy for the artists to paint and display them for the rest of the cave dwellers.

Where would the sentence best fit?

Ⓐ Choice A   Ⓑ Choice B   Ⓒ Choice C   Ⓓ Choice D

Reading-to-Learn Questions_지문 내용 종합하기

Type 9 지문 요약하기

이 문제는 지문에 제시된 논지와 정보들의 상대적 중요성을 이해하고 파악하는 능력을 평가한다. 이 유형의 문제를 풀려면, 중요한 개념이나 정보를 체계화하고 기억하기 위한 생각의 틀을 만들 수 있어야 한다.

문제 풀이 요령

지문 요약하기 문제에서는 여섯 개의 보기 중에서 지문에 나온 가장 중요한 개념을 나타내는 보기 세 개를 택해야 한다. 정답을 선택하는 순서는 점수와 무관하지만, 정답의 개수에 따라 다음과 같이 점수가 달라진다.

1) 정답 수 0~1개

   0점 처리된다.

2) 정답 수 2개 이상

   2개면 1점, 3개면 2점을 받는다.

ex.

Applied Arts and Fine Arts

Although we now tend to refer to the various crafts according to the materials used to construct them—clay, glass, wood, fiber, and metal—it was once common to think of crafts in terms of function, which led to their being known as the "applied arts." Approaching crafts from the point of view of function, we can divide them into simple categories: containers, shelters, and supports. There is no way around the fact that containers, shelters, and supports must be functional. The applied arts are thus bound by the laws of physics, which pertain to both the materials used in their making and the substances and things to be contained, supported, and sheltered. These laws are universal in their application, regardless of cultural beliefs, geography, or climate. If a pot has no bottom or has large openings in its sides, it could hardly be considered a container in any traditional sense. Since the laws of physics, not some arbitrary decision, have determined the general form of applied-art objects, they follow basic patterns, so much so that functional forms can vary only within certain limits. Buildings without roofs, for example, are unusual because they depart from the norm. However, not all functional objects are exactly alike; that is why we recognize a Shang Dynasty vase as being different from an Inca vase. What varies is not the basic form but the incidental details that do not obstruct the object's primary function.

Sensitivity to physical laws is thus an important consideration for the maker of applied-art objects. It is often taken for granted that this is also true for the maker of fine-art objects. This assumption misses a significant difference between the two disciplines. Fine-art objects are not constrained by the laws of physics in the same way that applied-art objects are. Because their primary purpose is not functional, they are only limited in terms of the materials used to make them. Sculptures must, for example, be stable, which requires an understanding of the properties of mass, weight distribution, and stress. Paintings must have rigid stretchers so that the canvas will be taut, and the paint must not deteriorate, crack, or discolor. These are problems that must be overcome by the artist because they tend to intrude upon their conception of the work. For example, in the early Italian Renaissance, bronze statues of horses with a raised foreleg usually had a cannonball under that hoof. This was done because the cannonball was needed to support the weight of the leg. In other words, the demands of the laws of physics, not the sculptor's aesthetic intentions, placed the ball there. That this device was a necessary structural compromise is clear from the fact that the cannonball quickly disappeared when sculptors learned how to strengthen the internal structure of a statue with iron braces (iron being much stronger than bronze).

Even though the fine arts in the twentieth century often treat materials in new ways, the basic difference in attitude of artists in relation to their materials in the fine arts and the applied arts remains relatively constant. It would therefore not be too great an exaggeration to say that practitioners of the fine arts work to overcome the limitations of their materials, whereas those engaged in the applied arts work in concert with their materials.

Directions: An introductory sentence for a brief summary of the passage is provided below. Complete the summary by selecting the THREE answer choices that express the most important ideas in the passage. Some sentences do not belong in the summary because they express ideas that are not presented in the passage or are minor ideas in the passage. **This question is worth 2 points.**

This passage discusses fundamental differences between applied-art objects and fine-art objects.

- ◆
- ◆
- ◆

Answer Choices

A   Applied-art objects fulfill functions, such as containing or sheltering, and objects with the same function have similar characteristics because they are constrained by their purpose.

B   It is easy to recognize that Shang Dynasty vases are different from Inca vases.

C   Fine-art objects are not functional, so they are limited only by the properties of the materials used.

D   Renaissance sculptors learned to use iron braces to strengthen the internal structures of bronze statues.

E   In the twentieth century, fine artists and applied artists became more similar to one another in their attitudes toward their materials.

F   In all periods, fine artists tend to challenge the physical limitations of their materials while applied artists tend to cooperate with the physical properties of their materials.

Reading Practice Sets

PRACTICE SET 1

IMPACT OF RAILROAD TRANSPORTATION IN THE UNITED STATES

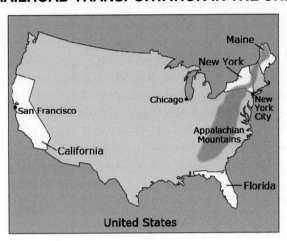

Both the steamboat and the railroad system with its steam-powered trains revolutionized transport in the United States in the nineteenth century. Entire regions that would hardly have been touched, especially in the West, were opened up to settlement and exploitation. In a geographic sense, the impact of the steamboat and railroad was simply immense. Some historians have argued further that they were the key to the rapid economic growth experienced by the United States in the middle decades of the century. The railroad, especially, not only lowered transport costs but caused a surge in the output of the iron, coal, and engineering sectors. It thus was a driving force in economic development.

In recent decades economic historians have attempted to quantify the economic impact of railroads. Both Robert Fogel and Albert Fishlow found that, with appropriate investments in canals and roads, the total of railroad services for a typical year in the late nineteenth century could have been provided by other means, at a cost of just a couple years' worth of economic growth. Moreover, the effect of railroads on the iron and coal industries had been greatly exaggerated.

Still, Fogel recognized that he could not measure the *dynamic* effects that railroads might have had. By tying markets together, they allowed firms to operate at a much larger scale than previously. By facilitating personal travel, they increased the flow of ideas and likely had a significant impact on the rate of innovation, because technological innovation generally involves the synthesis of diverse ideas. The fact that firms were exposed to a wider range of raw materials and new marketing opportunities must also have spurred innovative activity.

The railroad also speeded up the decline in travel times that had been underway for decades with improved roads, stagecoaches[1], canals, and steamboats. In 1790, it took one week to reach Maine from New York City and two weeks to reach Florida, and no stagecoaches crossed the Appalachian Mountains (courageous travelers would spend at least five weeks reaching the present site of Chicago). **(A)** By 1860, a New Yorker could reach Maine in a day, and Florida in three; most dramatic was the fact that by rail Chicago was now only two days away. **(B)** Soon, rail travel between East Coast and West Coast cities would occur at speeds that would have amazed earlier generations. **(C)** Although automobiles and airplanes would further reduce travel times in the next century, the impact of the railroad was arguably more profound. **(D)** Many regions that had previously been isolated were now enveloped in the national economy.

The social effects went beyond the strictly economic. Travel for pleasure became a possibility for many, given the high speed and low cost of railroad travel. With the freedom to travel came a greater sense of national identity and a reduction in regional cultural diversity. Farm children could more easily acquaint themselves with the big city, and easterners could readily visit the West. It is hard to imagine a United States of continental proportions without the railroad. Arguably, because of its speed, the railroad also changed the way that people from the United States viewed nature: as a distant and passing scene, rather than as an immediate experience.

The impact on local economies could be huge. Many towns began as division points where trains changed their crews and steam locomotives were resupplied with water. Others became industrial centers because the railroad linked them to materials and markets. On the other hand, those towns and regions without access by rail to coal suffered competitively in the age of steam. Farmers who would otherwise have been limited to a local market were able to specialize in crops best suited to their soil and climate. Local manufacturers based on local resources were affected in the same way.

Finally, the railroad had major impacts on how goods were distributed: first wholesalers, in the 1850s, and then department stores, chain stores, and mail-order companies from the 1870s created large national markets for goods. As happened with changes in distribution ushered in by improvements to roads in the eighteenth century, these developments changed the way that producers operated. In the final decades of the nineteenth century, some major companies created large hierarchical organizations to manage both large-scale production and national marketing of their goods.

---

1. **Stagecoaches:** passenger carriages pulled by horses for long-distance transportation

1. The word "immense" in the passage is closest in meaning to
   - Ⓐ unmatched
   - Ⓑ hard to believe
   - Ⓒ hard to understand
   - Ⓓ enormous

2. Which of the sentences below best expresses the essential information in the highlighted sentence in the passage? Incorrect choices change the meaning in important ways or leave out essential information.
   - Ⓐ Like most technological innovations, the means to facilitate personal travel came about as a result of the synthesis of diverse ideas.
   - Ⓑ Railroads probably increased the rate of technological innovation by making it easier for people in different places to meet and share ideas.
   - Ⓒ The flow of ideas that resulted from technological innovation led to an increased interest in personal travel by railroad.
   - Ⓓ Technological innovation generally involves the combination of diverse ideas and thus increases as the flow of information increases.

3. The word "courageous" in the passage is closest in meaning to

Ⓐ patient

Ⓑ brave

Ⓒ inexperienced

Ⓓ prepared

4. According to paragraph 4, why did railroads arguably have a bigger impact on the United States than automobiles or airplanes did?

Ⓐ Rail travel was less expensive than automobile or plane travel.

Ⓑ Railroads connected communities in a countrywide economic system.

Ⓒ Railroads made up a bigger proportion of the national economy.

Ⓓ The transition to rail travel happened more quickly.

5. According to paragraph 5, which of the following was NOT one of the social effects of railroads?

Ⓐ Widely separated areas of the country became more culturally similar.

Ⓑ Traveling for fun became much more common.

Ⓒ Many people began to worry about changes in the natural world.

Ⓓ People began to identify more strongly as citizens of the United States.

6. Which of the following is mentioned in paragraph 6 as one of the effects that railroads had on local economies?

Ⓐ Railroads divided many towns in half with the industrial center on one side and a residential area on the other.

Ⓑ Manufacturers that used local resources went out of business because they could not compete in larger markets.

Ⓒ New towns were created in places where fresh crews boarded trains and locomotives were readied for activity.

Ⓓ Towns and regions without access to railroads developed alternative ways to use steam power.

7. Paragraph 6 suggests that before the introduction of railroads some farmers did not grow the crops best suited to the local soil and climate because

Ⓐ they lacked knowledge about the most productive farming methods

Ⓑ they did not have access to the necessary tools and supplies

Ⓒ they had a limited supply of workers

Ⓓ they could sell their crops only to local markets

8. In paragraph 7, why does the author mention the large hierarchical organizations created by some major companies?

Ⓐ To argue that these types of organizations were based on the business model used in railroad companies

Ⓑ To provide examples of changes during this time period that were not related to the railroads

Ⓒ To identify a specific way that some producers changed in response to the effect of railroads on the distribution of goods

Ⓓ To explain why department stores, chain stores, and mail-order companies were able to expand in the 1870s

9. **Directions:** Look at the part of the passage that is displayed above. The letters **(A)**, **(B)**, **(C)**, and **(D)** indicate where the following sentence could be added.

On June 4, 1876, a train arrived in San Francisco, California, only 83 hours and 39 minutes after leaving New York City.

Where would the sentence best fit?

Ⓐ Choice A

Ⓑ Choice B

Ⓒ Choice C

Ⓓ Choice D

10. Directions: An introductory sentence for a brief summary of the passage is provided below. Complete the summary by selecting the THREE answer choices that express the most important ideas in the passage. Some sentences do not belong in the summary because they express ideas that are not presented in the passage or are minor ideas in the passage. **This question is worth 2 points.**

The development of the railroad transportation system in the nineteenth century greatly changed life in the United States.

- ◆
- ◆
- ◆

Answer Choices

A By making it possible for industries to reach needed resources and new markets, railroads significantly increased the country's economic growth.

B New studies by researchers like Fogel and Fishlow reveal the large impact that railroads had in tying together the markets for industrial goods like iron and coal.

C The fast and inexpensive personal travel provided by the railroad system allowed people to explore different parts of the country, leading to social change.

D Although railroads eventually connected the far West to the rest of the country, travel for personal enjoyment occurred mainly in the eastern part of the country.

E Because railroads connected local producers to distant markets, it made sense for many of them to specialize in what they grew or manufactured, and large-scale production companies appeared.

F In the late nineteenth century, the influence of the railroads declined with the rise of large hierarchical companies that engaged both in production and distribution.

DESERT FORMATION

The deserts, which already occupy approximately a fourth of the Earth's land surface, have in recent decades been increasing at an alarming pace. The expansion of desertlike conditions into areas where they did not previously exist is called **desertification**. It has been estimated that an additional one-fourth of the Earth's land surface is threatened by this process.

Desertification is accomplished primarily through the loss of stabilizing natural vegetation and the subsequent accelerated erosion of the soil by wind and water. In some cases the loose soil is blown completely away, leaving a stony surface. In other cases, the finer particles may be removed, while the sand-sized particles are accumulated to form mobile hills or ridges of sand.

Even in the areas that retain a soil cover, the reduction of vegetation typically results in the loss of the soil's ability to absorb substantial quantities of water. The impact of raindrops on the loose soil tends to transfer fine clay particles into the tiniest soil spaces, sealing them and producing a surface that allows very little water penetration. Water absorption is greatly reduced, consequently runoff is increased, resulting in accelerated erosion rates. The gradual drying of the soil caused by its diminished ability to absorb water results in the further loss of vegetation, so that a cycle of progressive surface deterioration is established.

In some regions, the increase in desert areas is occurring largely as the result of a trend toward drier climatic conditions. Continued gradual global warming has produced an increase in aridity for some areas over the past few thousand years. The process may be accelerated in subsequent decades if global warming resulting from air pollution seriously increases.

There is little doubt, however, that desertification in most areas results primarily from human activities rather than natural processes. The semiarid lands bordering the deserts exist in a delicate ecological balance and are limited in their potential to adjust to increased environmental pressures. Expanding populations are subjecting the land to increasing pressures to provide them with food and fuel. In wet periods, the land may be able to respond to these stresses. During the dry periods that are common phenomena along the desert margins, though, the pressure on the land is often far in excess of its diminished capacity, and desertification results.

Four specific activities have been identified as major contributors to the desertification processes: overcultivation, overgrazing, firewood gathering, and overirrigation. The cultivation of crops has expanded into progressively drier regions as population densities have grown. These regions are especially likely to have periods of severe dryness, so that crop failures are common. Since the raising of most crops necessitates the prior removal of the natural vegetation, crop failures leave extensive tracts of land devoid of a plant cover and susceptible to wind and water erosion.

(A) The raising of livestock is a major economic activity in semiarid lands, where grasses are generally the dominant type of natural vegetation. **(B)** The consequences of an excessive number of livestock grazing in an area are the reduction of the vegetation cover and the trampling and pulverization of the soil. **(C)** This is usually followed by the drying of the soil and accelerated erosion. **(D)**

Firewood is the chief fuel used for cooking and heating in many countries. The increased pressures of expanding populations have led to the removal of woody plants so that many cities and towns are surrounded by large areas completely lacking in trees and shrubs. The increasing use of dried animal waste as a substitute fuel has also hurt the soil because this valuable soil conditioner and source of plant nutrients is no longer being returned to the land.

The final major human cause of desertification is soil salinization resulting from overirrigation. Excess water from irrigation sinks down into the water table. If no drainage system exists, the water table rises, bringing dissolved salts to the surface. The water evaporates and the salts are left behind, creating a white crustal layer that prevents air and water from reaching the underlying soil.

The extreme seriousness of desertification results from the vast areas of land and the tremendous numbers of people affected, as well as from the great difficulty of reversing or even slowing the process. Once the soil has been removed by erosion, only the passage of centuries or millennia will enable new soil to form. In areas where considerable soil still remains, though, a rigorously enforced program of land protection and cover-crop planting may make it possible to reverse the present deterioration of the surface.

1. The word "threatened" in the passage is closest in meaning to
   - (A) restricted
   - (B) endangered
   - (C) prevented
   - (D) rejected

2. According to paragraph 3, the loss of natural vegetation has which of the following consequences for soil?
   - (A) Increased stony content
   - (B) Reduced water absorption
   - (C) Increased numbers of spaces in the soil
   - (D) Reduced water runoff

3. The word "delicate" in the passage is closest in meaning to
   - (A) fragile
   - (B) predictable
   - (C) complex
   - (D) valuable

4. According to paragraph 5, in dry periods, border areas have difficulty
   - (A) adjusting to stresses created by settlement
   - (B) retaining their fertility after desertification
   - (C) providing water for irrigating crops
   - (D) attracting populations in search of food and fuel

5. The word "progressively" in the passage is closest in meaning to
   - (A) openly
   - (B) impressively
   - (C) objectively
   - (D) increasingly

6. According to paragraph 6, which of the following is often associated with raising crops?
   - (A) Lack of proper irrigation techniques
   - (B) Failure to plant crops suited to the particular area
   - (C) Removal of the original vegetation
   - (D) Excessive use of dried animal waste

7. According to paragraph 9, the ground's absorption of excess water is a factor in desertification because it can
   - (A) interfere with the irrigation of land
   - (B) limit the evaporation of water
   - (C) require more absorption of air by the soil
   - (D) bring salts to the surface

8. Which of the sentences below best expresses the essential information in the highlighted sentence in the passage? Incorrect choices change the meaning in important ways or leave out essential information.

   Ⓐ Desertification is a significant problem because it is so hard to reverse and affects large areas of land and great numbers of people.

   Ⓑ Slowing down the process of desertification is difficult because of population growth that has spread over large areas of land.

   Ⓒ The spread of deserts is considered a very serious problem that can be solved only if large numbers of people in various countries are involved in the effort.

   Ⓓ Desertification is extremely hard to reverse unless the population is reduced in the vast areas affected.

9. **Directions:** Look at the part of the passage that is displayed above. The letters **(A)**, **(B)**, **(C)**, and **(D)** indicate where the following sentence could be added.

This economic reliance on livestock in certain regions makes large tracts of land susceptible to overgrazing.

Where would the sentence best fit?

   Ⓐ Choice A

   Ⓑ Choice B

   Ⓒ Choice C

   Ⓓ Choice D

10. **Directions:** An introductory sentence for a brief summary of the passage is provided below. Complete the summary by selecting the THREE answer choices that express the most important ideas in the passage. Some sentences do not belong in the summary because they express ideas that are not presented in the passage or are minor ideas in the passage. **This question is worth 2 points.**

Many factors have contributed to the great increase in desertification in recent decades.

- ◆
- ◆
- ◆

Answer Choices

A Growing human populations and the agricul- tural demands that come with such growth have upset the ecological balance in some areas and led to the spread of deserts.

B As periods of severe dryness have become more common, failures of a number of different crops have increased.

C Excessive numbers of cattle and the need for firewood for fuel have reduced grasses and trees, leaving the land unprotected and vulnerable.

D Extensive irrigation with poor drainage brings salt to the surface of the soil, a process that reduces water and air absorption.

E Animal dung enriches the soil by providing nutrients for plant growth.

F Grasses are generally the dominant type of natural vegetation in semiarid lands.

PRACTICE SET 3

EARLY CINEMA

The cinema did not emerge as a form of mass consumption until its technology evolved from the initial "peepshow" format to the point where images were projected on a screen in a darkened theater. In the peepshow format, a film was viewed through a small opening in a machine that was created for that purpose. Thomas Edison's peepshow device, the Kinetoscope, was introduced to the public in 1894. It was designed for use in Kinetoscope parlors, or arcades, which contained only a few individual machines and permitted only one customer to view a short, 50-foot film at any one time. The first Kinetoscope parlors contained five machines. For the price of 25 cents (or 5 cents per machine), customers moved from machine to machine to watch five different films (or, in the case of famous prizefights, successive rounds of a single fight).

These Kinetoscope arcades were modeled on phonograph parlors, which had proven successful for Edison several years earlier. In the phonograph parlors, customers listened to recordings through individual ear tubes, moving from one machine to the next to hear different recorded speeches or pieces of music. The Kinetoscope parlors functioned in a similar way. Edison was more interested in the sale of Kinetoscopes (for roughly $1,000 apiece) to these parlors than in the films that would be run in them (which cost approximately $10 to $15 each). He refused to develop projection technology, reasoning that if he made and sold projectors, then exhibitors would purchase only one machine—a projector—from him instead of several.

(A) Exhibitors, however, wanted to maximize their profits, which they could do more readily by projecting a handful of films to hundreds of customers at a time (rather than one at a time) and by charging 25 to 50 cents admission. **(B)** About a year after the opening of the first Kinetoscope parlor in 1894, showmen such as Louis and Auguste Lumière, Thomas Armat and Charles Francis Jenkins, and Orville and Woodville Latham (with the assistance of Edison's former assistant, William Dickson) perfected projection devices. **(C)** These early projection devices were used in vaudeville theaters, legitimate theaters, local town halls, makeshift storefront theaters, fairgrounds, and amusement parks to show films to a mass audience. **(D)**

With the advent of projection in 1895-1896, motion pictures became the ultimate form of mass consumption. Previously, large audiences had viewed spectacles at the theater, where vaudeville, popular dramas, musical shows, classical plays, lectures, and slide-and-lantern shows had been presented to several hundred spectators at a time. But the movies differed significantly from these other forms of entertainment, which depended on either live performance or (in the case of the slide-and-lantern shows) the active involvement of a master of ceremonies who assembled the final program.

Although early exhibitors regularly accompanied movies with live acts, the substance of the movies themselves is mass-produced, prerecorded material that can easily be reproduced by theaters with little or no active participation by the exhibitor. Even though early exhibitors shaped their film programs by mixing films and other entertainments together in whichever way they thought would be most attractive to audiences or by accompanying them with lectures, their creative control remained limited. What audiences came to see was the technological marvel of the movies; the lifelike reproduction of the commonplace motion of trains, of waves striking the shore, and of people walking in the street; and the magic made possible by trick photography and the manipulation of the camera.

With the advent of projection, the viewer's relationship with the image was no longer private, as it had been with earlier peepshow devices such as the Kinetoscope and the Mutoscope, which was a similar machine that reproduced motion by means of successive images on individual photographic cards instead of on strips of celluloid. It suddenly became public—an experience that the viewer shared with dozens, scores, and even hundreds of others. At the same time, the image that the spectator looked at expanded from the minuscule peepshow dimensions of 1 or 2 inches (in height) to the life-size proportions of 6 or 9 feet.

1. According to paragraph 1, all of the following were true of viewing films in Kinetoscope parlors EXCEPT:

   Ⓐ One individual at a time viewed a film.

   Ⓑ Customers could view one film after another.

   Ⓒ Prizefights were the most popular subjects for films.

   Ⓓ Each film was short.

2. The author discusses phonograph parlors in paragraph 2 in order to

   Ⓐ explain Edison's financial success

   Ⓑ describe the model used to design Kinetoscope parlors

   Ⓒ contrast their popularity to that of Kinetoscope parlors

   Ⓓ illustrate how much more technologically advanced Kinetoscope parlors were

3. Which of the sentences below best expresses the essential information in the highlighted sentence in the passage? Incorrect answer choices change the meaning in important ways or leave out essential information.

   Ⓐ Edison was more interested in developing a variety of machines than in developing a technology based on only one.

   Ⓑ Edison refused to work on projection technology because he did not think exhibitors would replace their projectors with newer machines.

   Ⓒ Edison did not want to develop projection technology because it limited the number of machines he could sell.

   Ⓓ Edison would not develop projection technology unless exhibitors agreed to purchase more than one projector from him.

4. The word "readily" in the passage is closest in meaning to

   Ⓐ frequently

   Ⓑ easily

   Ⓒ intelligently

   Ⓓ obviously

5. According to paragraph 4, how did the early movies differ from previous spectacles that were presented to large audiences?

   Ⓐ They were a more expensive form of entertainment.

   Ⓑ They were viewed by larger audiences.

   Ⓒ They were more educational.

   Ⓓ They did not require live entertainers.

6. According to paragraph 5, what role did early exhibitors play in the presentation of movies in theaters?

   Ⓐ They decided how to combine various components of the film program.

   Ⓑ They advised filmmakers on appropriate movie content.

   Ⓒ They often took part in the live-action performances.

   Ⓓ They produced and prerecorded the material that was shown in the theaters.

7. The word "It" in the passage refers to

   Ⓐ the advent of projection

   Ⓑ the viewer's relationship with the image

   Ⓒ a similar machine

   Ⓓ celluloid

8. According to paragraph 6, the images seen by viewers in the earlier peepshows, compared with the images projected on the screen, were relatively

   Ⓐ small in size

   Ⓑ inexpensive to create

   Ⓒ unfocused

   Ⓓ limited in subject matter

9. **Directions:** Look at the part of the passage that is displayed above. The letters **(A)**, **(B)**, **(C)**, and **(D)** indicate where the following sentence could be added.

When this widespread use of projection technology began to hurt his Kinetoscope business, Edison acquired a projector developed by Armat and introduced it as "Edison's latest marvel, the Vitascope."

Where would the sentence best fit?

   Ⓐ Choice A

   Ⓑ Choice B

   Ⓒ Choice C

   Ⓓ Choice D

10. **Directions:** An introductory sentence for a brief summary of the passage is provided below. Complete the summary by selecting the THREE answer choices that express the most important ideas in the passage. Some sentences do not belong in the summary because they express ideas that are not presented in the passage or are minor ideas in the passage. **This question is worth 2 points.**

The technology for modern cinema evolved at the end of the nineteenth century.

◆

◆

◆

Answer Choices

Ⓐ Kinetoscope parlors for viewing films were modeled on phonograph parlors.

Ⓑ Thomas Edison's design of the Kinetoscope inspired the development of large-screen projection.

Ⓒ Early cinema allowed individuals to use special machines to view films privately.

Ⓓ Slide-and-lantern shows had been presented to audiences of hundreds of spectators.

Ⓔ The development of projection technology made it possible to project images on a large screen.

Ⓕ Once film images could be projected, the cinema became a form of mass consumption.

PRACTICE SET 4

WATER AND OCEAN LIFE

The physical and chemical properties of water, unsurprisingly, determine much about life in the ocean. Water is dense (high mass per unit of volume), about 840 times as dense as air—roughly as dense as most life forms, as they are primarily made of water. This means that marine organisms fight no battle with gravity and possess none of the structures that we need on land to combat it. In the ocean, there are no tree trunks. The closest analogy would be the stipes (stalks) of the large seaweeds known as kelp, allowing kelp to form "forests." But these stipes do not hold the kelp up—they just hold it in place. At low tide the kelp collapses. Likewise, marine animals can have flexible skeletons or no skeleton at all. This makes it much easier to become large. The major problem with the density of the ocean comes in the depths, where the weight of all that seawater bears down, creating enormous pressures.

Related to density is viscosity—or, basically, thickness due to internal friction. It is about sixty times easier to move through air than water. The importance of this friction depends on how big one is and how fast one is moving. It is much more significant for the little creatures. As a result, while a killer whale can cruise at about ten kilometers per hour, krill, weighing about 0.2 grams, can achieve only about 0.2 kilometers per hour. So, in the viscous ocean the little animals move slowly, giving the big ones a significant advantage. There are no darting ocean insects. Some medium-sized animals, like flying fish and leaping dolphins, leave the water when they want to move really fast.

Water dissolves other substances better than any other common liquid. This allows it to function as the medium for chemical communication using hormones within animal bodies. Seawater includes all kinds of dissolved substances, including, of course, salt. Many of these substances are important for marine life, but none has the significance of oxygen, which all animals need to power their bodies. Seawater is about 0.5–0.9 percent oxygen at the surface. Most marine animals use gills to get oxygen from seawater into their bodies. A few, including the marine mammals, come to the surface and breathe the air. Coming to the surface may have costs in time, energy, or vulnerability to predators, but it has benefits, too, primarily that air is 21 percent oxygen.

Few animals just sit, or move aimlessly along, waiting for good things, like food or mates, or dangerous things, like predators, to come their way. They sense their environment and change their physiology or behavior, and they communicate with each other. One can sense and communicate through a variety of channels, primarily what we call the five senses: touch, taste, smell, hearing, and sight. Moving from the air to water changes the relative benefit of each of the senses. Chemical signals are not dispersed as widely or as predictably under water as in air, so taste and smell have less value for marine animals. Some penguins seem to be able to smell areas with high concentrations of organisms and swim toward them over large ranges, but, tellingly, they do so by smelling the air that they breathe, not by tasting the water that they swim through, even though the organisms they are aiming for are in the water. Sight is also degraded in the ocean because light is absorbed by water. At depths of a few hundred meters there is virtually no light, even in the middle of the day, and even just beneath the surface one can rarely see more than about twenty meters, less than the length of a blue whale.

(A) One sense that does do better underwater is sound. **(B)** Sound travels about four times faster than in air. **(C)** More important, and in contrast to light, sound is less weakened by water than air. **(D)** While there are a few sounds of terrestrial mammals that travel over kilometers—the roars of lions, the rumbles of elephants, and the howls of wolves—most sounds of most terrestrial mammals are lost at much shorter ranges. Many underwater sounds of marine mammals, on the other hand, can be heard in quiet conditions at a kilometer and some travel very much farther.

1. In paragraph 1, why does the author mention that kelp collapses at low tide?

    Ⓐ To illustrate the idea that organisms in the sea lack structures that overcome gravity

    Ⓑ To provide evidence that kelp is primarily made of water

    Ⓒ To explain why kelp needs stipes to hold it in place

    Ⓓ To demonstrate how the enormous pressures in the deep ocean are a major problem

2. According to paragraph 1, which of the following is a reason that ocean animals can grow very large?

    Ⓐ The number of life-forms in the ocean creates enormous pressure for animals to grow larger.

    Ⓑ Large ocean animals do not need rigid skeletons.

    Ⓒ Kelp forests provide a flexible habitat for large animals.

    Ⓓ There is a lot of room in the deep ocean for large animals.

3. In paragraph 2, why does the author compare the swimming speeds of killer whales and krill?

    Ⓐ To provide support for the idea that moving through air is much faster than moving through water

    Ⓑ To explain why krill are a common food for whales

    Ⓒ To support the claim that water's viscosity affects small animals more than large ones

    Ⓓ To provide evidence that a small size is a big advantage in the ocean

4. According to paragraph 3, which TWO of the following statements about seawater are true? To receive credit, you must select TWO answer choices.

    Ⓐ The salt it contains helps it to dissolve more oxygen than it otherwise would.

    Ⓑ It limits animals' ability to communicate by interfering with their hormones.

    Ⓒ It includes many substances that animals need.

    Ⓓ Its oxygen is taken in by the gills of many sea animals.

5. The word "primarily" in the passage is closest in meaning to
   Ⓐ normally
   Ⓑ commonly
   Ⓒ particularly
   Ⓓ mainly

6. Which of the sentences below best expresses the essential information in the highlighted sentence in the passage? Incorrect choices change the meaning in important ways or leave out essential information.
   Ⓐ Penguins that seem to be able to sense high concentrations of organisms over large ranges do so by smelling the air rather than tasting the water.
   Ⓑ Some penguins can sense areas of high concentrations of organisms and swim toward them over large ranges.
   Ⓒ Some penguins sense organisms by smelling the air they breathe, while others do so by tasting the water they swim through.
   Ⓓ Some penguins seem to be able to sense areas with high concentrations of organisms, but only when both the penguins and the organisms are in the water.

7. The phrase "in contrast to" in the passage is closest in meaning to
   Ⓐ more than
   Ⓑ apart from
   Ⓒ along with
   Ⓓ unlike with

8. Which of the following can be inferred from the passage about "the roars of lions, the rumbles of elephants, and the howls of wolves"?
   Ⓐ They can sometimes be heard by marine mammals.
   Ⓑ They are some of the farthest-traveling sounds made by land animals.
   Ⓒ They travel about four times faster than most sounds made by most marine animals.
   Ⓓ They can be heard over a much greater range than sounds made by marine animals.

9. **Directions:** Look at the part of the passage that is displayed above. The letters **(A)**, **(B)**, **(C)**, and **(D)** indicate where the following sentence could be added.

   There are a couple of reasons for this.

   Where would the sentence best fit?
   Ⓐ Choice A
   Ⓑ Choice B
   Ⓒ Choice C
   Ⓓ Choice D

10. **Directions:** An introductory sentence for a brief summary of the passage is provided below. Complete the summary by selecting the THREE answer choices that express the most important ideas in the passage. Some sentences do not belong in the summary because they express ideas that are not presented in the passage or are minor ideas in the passage. **This question is worth 2 points.**

The properties of water determine the properties of life-forms that live in the ocean.

◆

◆

◆

Answer Choices

A Because of the density of water, marine organisms do not need to overcome gravity, but the water's density causes extreme pressures in the deep ocean that can be a problem for life.

B Marine animals must deal with salt, hormones from other animals, and other harmful substances dissolved in seawater, and they require oxygen to power this process.

C Although its concentration in seawater is low, oxygen is the most important dissolved substance for marine life, and most marine animals collect it using gills.

D Oxygen in the ocean is much more concentrated near the surface, so many creatures rise toward the surface when they need the energy to move more quickly.

E One sense that marine animals have available that terrestrial animals lack is chemical signaling, since chemicals easily dissolve in water and can be distributed over large areas.

F The relative importance of the senses is different underwater, with sight, smell, and taste being less useful than they are on land, and hearing being much more effective.

FREDERICK TAYLOR AND UNITED STATES INDUSTRY

By the twentieth century, making workers more "cost-efficient" had become the single most important management goal in large-scale industries. Everywhere in industrial America managers were drafting work rules and designing tasks with an eye to increasing worker output.

The leading supporter of productivity was Frederick Winslow Taylor, whose time-and-motion studies revolutionized the industrial workplace and whose writings, especially *The Principles of Scientific Management*, had unquestionable authority among industrial engineers and factory managers. Taylor was obsessed with order and efficiency. Taylor also grew up at a time when the processes of motion were fascinating to many Americans. Artists such as Thomas Eakins were painting the human form in ways that showed its dexterity. **(A)** In the 1870s, in California, the English-born photographer Eadweard Muybridge was developing a multiple-camera technique to record an animal in motion. **(B)** Muybridge's experiments, which laid the groundwork for motion pictures, started out to settle a bet whether all four of a racehorse's hooves simultaneously left the ground at some point during its stride (he showed that they did), but they attracted national attention for demonstrating that machines could measure movement. **(C)** Picture frame by picture frame, Muybridge revealed what the naked eye could not see, and by breaking down complex movement his cameras made it understandable and potentially subject to control. **(D)**

In the iron and steel factories that Taylor visited during the 1870s and 1880s, he saw only disorder and inefficiency on shop floors where skilled workers controlled the rhythms and division of labor. Taylor believed that scientific study could break down the industrial process into its simplest parts, which, once understood, would allow managers to increase production and lower costs by reducing unnecessary motion and workers. Stopwatch in hand, he recorded the time workers spent on each particular task and then suggested changes in the jobs to improve efficiency. In his most famous demonstration, at the Bethlehem Steel Company in 1898, Taylor designed fifteen kinds of ore shovels, each for a specific task and each to be used in a specific way. He was able to show that 140 men could do the work of 600. The company thereupon fired the "excess" shovelers, cutting its ore-shoveling costs by half. It also gave the remaining shovelers a raise in salary.

The other side of Taylor's plan was to provide motivations for workers to exceed production goals by rewarding them with extra pay when they did so. Under Taylor's proposal, however, workers lost. Jobs became more tedious and monotonous, and the character and speed of work were defined by management rather than the workers themselves. Skill and tradition yielded to "scientifically" ordained rules from which workers could not deviate. Managers, the "white shirts" in workers' parlance, were not able to be on the floor all the time observing work, so they measured output instead. They weighed the tonnage of coal, for example, in determining the "efficiency" of miners, rather than going into the mines themselves. By evaluating workers mainly by looking at their output, managers lost effective contact with the work culture and failed to grasp and respect the difficulties or skills involved in producing. Managers also adopted Taylor's ideas piecemeal, preferring the emphasis on worker productivity while ignoring his calls for higher wages. Indeed, most managers looked for ways to cut wages for poor work rather than raising them for better work.

"Taylorism," as Taylor's ideas came to be known, did not take hold everywhere. His program called for redesigning the physical layout and work patterns of the whole factory and for precise record keeping and cost accounting to watch over every aspect of the flow of goods and work. Few manufacturers could bear the costs of complete retooling and reorganization of heavy industries, and workers fought against management's efforts to reduce them to robots. Also, the mechanization of industry itself was an uneven process. Such basic industries as logging, for example, continued to rely on manual labor and horse-drawn transportation into the early twentieth century. The widespread adoption of Taylorism waited until the twentieth century, especially the 1920s, when a "cult of productivity" and the widespread replacement of steam power with electricity encouraged fuller mechanization of both capital and finished goods industries.

1. According to paragraph 1, by the twentieth century the main aim of managers in large-scale industries had become to
   Ⓐ establish better work rules
   Ⓑ redesign tasks
   Ⓒ increase worker productivity
   Ⓓ revise management goals

2. According to paragraph 2, Eadweard Muybridge's experiments established each of the following EXCEPT:
   Ⓐ All four of a racehorse's hooves simultaneously leave the ground at some point during its stride.
   Ⓑ Movement can be measured by machines.
   Ⓒ Cameras can reveal aspects of complex movements that cannot be seen with the naked eye.
   Ⓓ Complex movements could be observed but not controlled.

3. According to paragraph 3, what was Taylor's impression of the iron and steel factories of the 1870s and 1880s?
   Ⓐ Their shop floors were not well organized or efficient.
   Ⓑ There was no control over the rhythms and division of labor.
   Ⓒ They had given too much power to industrial managers.
   Ⓓ They did not have enough skilled workers on their shop floors.

4. According to paragraph 3, what made it possible for 140 men to do the work of 600?
   Ⓐ Working half the time over more days
   Ⓑ Receiving more money for their work
   Ⓒ Being timed by Taylor with a stopwatch
   Ⓓ Using different shovels designed for different tasks

5. The phrase "contact with" in the passage is closest in meaning to
   Ⓐ connection with
   Ⓑ patience with
   Ⓒ control of
   Ⓓ faith in

6. According to paragraph 4, under Taylor's proposal, working conditions became worse in each of the following ways EXCEPT:

Ⓐ Work became less varied.

Ⓑ There was less respect for the skills involved in production.

Ⓒ Management looked for ways to cut wages for poor work.

Ⓓ Managers were constantly watching workers as they worked.

7. According to paragraph 4, what was an effect of managers' relying on output as the measure of worker efficiency?

Ⓐ Managers no longer understood what was really involved in doing the work.

Ⓑ Managers had to spend more time on the floor observing production.

Ⓒ Managers began justifying the enforcement of work rules by emphasizing that they were traditional.

Ⓓ Managers had to offer higher pay to get workers to exceed production goals.

8. In paragraph 5, why does the author provide information about the way the logging industry operated?

Ⓐ To help explain why the widespread adoption of Taylorism did not occur until the twentieth century

Ⓑ To argue that logging was an example of an industry that became more productive after it adopted Taylorism

Ⓒ To make the point that the logging industry lacked a tradition of precise record keeping and cost accounting

Ⓓ To help support the idea that full mechanization depended on the replacement of steam power with electricity

9. **Directions:** Look at the part of the passage that is displayed above. The letters **(A)**, **(B)**, **(C)**, and **(D)** indicate where the following sentence could be added.

Taylor was determined to apply this new understanding of motion to the improvement of industrial processes.

Where would the sentence best fit?

Ⓐ Choice A

Ⓑ Choice B

Ⓒ Choice C

Ⓓ Choice D

10. **Directions:** An introductory sentence for a brief summary of the passage is provided below. Complete the summary by selecting the THREE answer choices that express the most important ideas in the passage. Some sentences do not belong in the summary because they express ideas that are not presented in the passage or are minor ideas in the passage. **This question is worth 2 points.**

Frederick Taylor's program to increase productivity through time-and-motion studies revolutionized the industrial workplace.

- ◆
- ◆
- ◆

Answer Choices

A Taylor held that breaking down the industrial process into its simplest parts could identify and cut down on unnecessary motions, thus cutting costs by decreasing the number of workers needed.

B Taylor worked with the photographer Eadweard Muybridge to develop a technique for using machines to measure motion more precisely than could be done with the naked eye.

C Taylor's idea of paying workers more for exceeding production goals was not adopted by managers, and his scientifically defined work process was too expensive for most large industries to adopt right away.

D Taylor believed that the only way to increase worker productivity was to increase workers' pay before asking them to use more advanced tools.

E Since, under Taylor's proposal, managers would spend more time on record keeping and cost accounting and less time supervising the shop floor, workers would need to be more highly skilled.

F Taylorism became fully adopted in most industries only in the 1920s, when a "cult of productivity" and the replacement of steam power with electricity encouraged greater mechanization of production.

PRACTICE SET 6
THE DISTRIBUTION OF PLANTS AND ANIMALS

There is a much greater similarity between the flowering plant floras of different continents—South America, Africa, Asia, and Australia—than between the mammalian faunas (animals) of these regions. Only in the case of the African/Asian comparison are the plant and animal figures at a similar level. Three factors seem to have caused these differences.

First, the families of flowering plants evolved and dispersed earlier than the families of mammals. Recent palaeobotanical techniques have made it possible to retrieve and identify complete and partial flowers from sediments from the middle Cretaceous (144 to 65 million years ago). These demonstrate that several currently existing families had appeared by the middle Cretaceous, about 120 million years ago, and at least a dozen by 95 to 5 million years ago. Therefore, the angiosperms (flowering plants) commenced their dispersal across the world much earlier than the mammals, and thus had a much greater chance of reaching the different continents before they drifted far apart. In contrast, the diversification and dispersal of modern mammals only began in the earliest Cenozoic, 66 to 65 million years ago, by which time the continents had drifted farther apart and were more difficult to reach. However, those mammals that did succeed as colonists were able, in the isolation of each continent, to diverge into a number of unique, native groups that show little similarity to those in other continents, for example New World monkeys in South America, elephants and aardvarks in Africa, and marsupials like the kangaroo in Australia.

Secondly, there has been more extinction and replacement during the history of mammals than during that of flowering plants. For example, in addition to the approximately 100 living families of mammals, over 300 other families evolved and became extinct during the Cenozoic—some 70 percent of the families of mammals died out completely. Some of these were previously widespread families, which were replaced in the now-separate continents by new families found only in those particular regions. In other cases, the family became extinct only in some areas, so that it now had a disjunct distribution, with widely separated subgroups, as in the camel-llama group. Another example of the influence of extinction is seen if one compares the similarities between the mammal faunas of North and South America before and after a wave of extinctions in the Pleistocene (1.8 million to 10,000 years ago). **(A)** All these phenomena reduced the levels of similarity between the faunal regions. **(B)** In the flowering plants, in contrast, there has been much less extinction. **(C)** Furthermore, groups of plants are much longer-lived than are those of mammals. **(D)** For example, the distribution of the southern beech tree, *Nothofagus*, shows that it evolved in the Late Cretaceous, at least 70 million years ago, while the average longevity of mammalian groups is only eight million years.

Finally, of course, not all floral similarities were merely the result of early dispersal across insignificant barriers rather than a later colonization across wider gaps. The extent of the spread of flowering plants across the Pacific (over 200 different immigrant flowering plants have reached the most isolated island group, Hawaii) shows clearly that they can cross even quite wide stretches of ocean, especially where intermediate island stepping-stones were available.

For all these reasons, it is not surprising that the flora of the different continents shows more similarities to one another than do their mammalian faunas. However, there is one exception: the almost identical levels of similarity for the two groups when the African and Asian regions are compared. The floral similarity here is not surprising, for it is at the same general level as the similarities between the other tropical regions. It is therefore the faunal similarity between the African and Asian regions that is unexpectedly high. This is probably because of the faunal exchange that took place between Africa and Eurasia after the two continents became connected in the Miocene era (28.3 to 5.3 million years ago) and before deserts spread through the Middle East.

1. The word "demonstrate" in the passage is closest in meaning to

   Ⓐ argue

   Ⓑ show

   Ⓒ emphasize

   Ⓓ conclude

2. According to paragraph 2, how do we know that flowering plants had appeared before the continents drifted far apart?

   Ⓐ From the large number of living flowering plants that can be traced back to the Cenozoic

   Ⓑ From flowers found in sediments dating to the middle Cretaceous

   Ⓒ From the fact that the earliest flowering plants were not very successful at colonizing across oceans

   Ⓓ From the fact that flowering plants reached all the continents before mammals did

3. The author mentions "New World monkeys in South America" in order to

   Ⓐ give an example of the range of mammals that are now found only in isolated regions within continents

   Ⓑ support the point that mammals generally dispersed later than flowering plants did

   Ⓒ explain how groups of mammals were able to succeed as colonists on different continents as a result of diversification

   Ⓓ give an example of a group of mammals that developed in isolation and are now very different from their closest relatives on other continents

4. The word "Furthermore" in the passage is closest in meaning to

   Ⓐ However

   Ⓑ Therefore

   Ⓒ In addition

   Ⓓ In effect

5. According to paragraph 3, which of the following is true of mammals?

   Ⓐ All of the currently living families had evolved by the beginning of the Cenozoic.

   Ⓑ The families that still exist consist of widely separated subgroups.

   Ⓒ The majority of families became extinct during the Cenozoic.

   Ⓓ The families that became extinct during the Cenozoic were more widespread than those that survived.

6. According to paragraph 3, the similarity between the mammals of North America and those of South America was significantly reduced by

   Ⓐ the large number of mammal families that went extinct in the Pleistocene

   Ⓑ the spread of certain families of mammals at the expense of others

   Ⓒ differences in how rapidly different families of mammals dispersed through the continents

   Ⓓ differences in the number of subgroups that developed on each continent

7. The discussion of "Hawaii" supports the idea that families of plants would probably be more widespread than families of mammals even if

  Ⓐ there had not been significant barriers to the dispersal of mammals

  Ⓑ many families of plants had gone extinct in some areas but not in others

  Ⓒ plants had not dispersed before the continents drifted apart

  Ⓓ there had been more extinction among plants than among mammals

8. According to paragraph 5, what probably explains the high animal similarity between the African and Asian regions?

  Ⓐ The animal exchange between the two regions occurred earlier than exchanges between other regions.

  Ⓑ For a period after Africa and Eurasia connected, animals could cross from one region to the other relatively easily.

  Ⓒ The flora of the two regions were highly similar before the continents became connected.

  Ⓓ Mammals were able to adapt to the deserts that eventually spread throughout most of the Middle East.

9. **Directions:** Look at the part of the passage that is displayed above. The letters **(A)**, **(B)**, **(C)**, and **(D)** indicate where the following sentence could be added.

In fact, there is no record yet of the extinction of a major group of flowering plants.

Where would the sentence best fit?

  Ⓐ Choice A

  Ⓑ Choice B

  Ⓒ Choice C

  Ⓓ Choice D

10. **Directions:** An introductory sentence for a brief summary of the passage is provided below. Complete the summary by selecting the THREE answer choices that express the most important ideas in the passage. Some sentences do not belong in the summary because they express ideas that are not presented in the passage or are minor ideas in the passage. **This question is worth 2 points.**

Mammals on different continents are more different from each other than are flowering plants on the same continents.

- ◆
- ◆
- ◆

Answer Choices

A Unlike mammals, flowering plants appeared and spread before the continents drifted apart, which helps explain the greater similarity of flora than of fauna between continents.

B By reconstructing complete flowers from flower parts found in ancient sediments, scientists have shown that most currently existing families had not yet appeared by the middle Cretaceous.

C Research on the separation of continents and dispersal of species has shown that the oldest living groups of plants were first found in South America.

D Unlike plants, many families of mammals died out and were replaced by families unique to certain regions, or else evolved very differently on different continents.

E The floral similarity between isolated islands such as Hawaii and other tropical regions is not as great as that between continents that were connected when flowering plants first appeared.

F Plants can spread across wide stretches of ocean, but mammals generally can spread only when there is a land connection—such as that which appeared between Africa and Eurasia in the Miocene.

읽기 영역 점수 향상 전략

읽기 실력을 키우는 가장 좋은 방법은 다양한 주제(과학, 사회과학, 인문학, 경영 등)의 글을 자주 읽는 것이다. 인터넷이 가장 유용하지만 도서, 잡지, 정기간행물도 큰 도움이 된다. 대학 강의에서 사용하는 학문적 유형의 글을 정기적으로 읽어야 한다. TOEFL iBT® 읽기 영역에 대한 조언은 다음과 같다.

■ 정보를 찾기 위한 읽기(Reading to find information)
   1) 지문을 속독하면서 주요 사실(날짜, 숫자, 용어)을 찾아 강조 표시를 한다.
   2) 읽기 속도와 이해도의 향상을 위해 이를 자주 연습한다.

■ 기본적 이해를 위한 읽기(Reading for basic comprehension)
   1) 어휘력을 키운다.
   2) 각 단어와 문장을 꼼꼼히 읽기보다는 주제를 파악하기 위해 속독한다.
   3) 글을 속독한 후 면밀히 한 번 더 읽고 주제, 요점, 중요 사실을 필기한다.
   4) 지문에서 익숙치 않은 단어를 찾아 문맥적 의미를 추측해 본다.
   5) 지문에서 모든 대명사(he, him, they, them 등)의 지시 대상을 파악한다.
   6) 지문에서 전체적으로 암시하는 내용을 바탕으로 추론하고 결론을 내리는 연습을 한다.

■ 학습을 위한 읽기(Reading to learn)
   1) 지문 유형(분류, 원인/결과, 비교/대조, 문제/해결, 묘사, 서사 등)을 파악한다.
   2) 다음과 같은 방법으로 지문의 정보를 조직화한다.
      – 개요를 작성해 중요한 사항과 그렇지 않은 사항을 구분한다.
      – 지문에 정보가 분류되어 있으면 표를 만들어 항목별로 정보를 분류한다. (TOEFL iBT®에서 표를 작성할 필요는 없다. 대신 표의 각 항목에 적합한 선택지를 찾아 넣으면 된다.)
      – 지문에서 과정의 여러 단계를 설명한다면 각 단계의 순서대로 개요를 작성한다.
   3) 표와 개요를 이용해 지문의 요약문을 작성한다.
   4) 지문의 문장 바꿔쓰기는 물론 더 나아가 문단 전체를 바꿔쓰는 연습을 한다. TOEFL iBT® 읽기 영역은 바꿔쓰기에 대한 인식 능력을 측정한다는 것을 유념해야 한다. 바꿔쓰기 능력은 말하기 영역과 쓰기 영역에서도 중요하다.

Chapter 3

Listening Section

Listening Section

이 장의 구성_ TOEFL iBT® 듣기 문제 8가지 유형
유형별 문제 식별 방법
유형별 문제 풀이 요령
점수 향상 전략

TOEFL iBT® 듣기 영역에서는 3개의 강의와 2개의 대화를 듣게 되며, 강의 하나 당 6개의 문제, 대화 하나 당 5개의 문제가 출제된다. 모든 문제를 푸는 데 배정되는 시간은 41분이다.

듣기 영역에 대한 소개

TOEFL iBT®의 듣기 지문은 강의와 대화로 구성된다. 강의당 4~5분, 대화당 2~3분 분량이고 가능한 한 실제 상황처럼 전개된다. 예를 들면, 말 실수를 하고 스스로 고치거나 같은 말을 반복하기도 하고, 내용을 해치지 않는 범위 내에서 잠깐 멈추거나 머뭇거리는 등의 언어 습관이 자연스럽게 나타난다.

문제 유형

1. Basic Comprehension Questions_기본적인 이해 문제

1. Gist-Content_내용의 요점을 묻는 문제
2. Gist-Purpose_내용의 목적을 묻는 문제
3. Detail_세부 정보 찾기 문제

2. Pragmatic Understanding Questions_화용론적 이해 문제

5. Function_의도 파악 문제
6. Attitude_태도 파악 문제

3. Connecting Information Questions_정보 연결 문제

7. Organization_구성 파악 문제
8. Connecting Content_내용 연결 문제
9. Inference_추론 문제

듣기 지문의 종류

1. 대화

TOEFL에는 두 가지 유형의 대화가 있다. 이는 영어가 주로 사용되는 대학에서 볼 수 있는 전형적인 대화 유형들이다.

1) 연구실에서의 대화

연구실에서의 대화는 교수의 연구실에서 벌어지는 대화로 수업 내용 또는 과제와 관련된 내용일 수 있다. 예를 들면, 연구실에서 학생이 교수에게 보고서 마감일을 늦춰 달라고 요청하거나 특정 강의 내용을 자세하게 설명해 달라고 부탁할 수도 있다.

2) 서비스와 관련된 대화

서비스와 관련된 대화는 대학 캠퍼스에서 일어나는 상황으로 기숙사비 납부, 수강 신청에 관한 대화 등이 주를 이룬다. 각 대화당 5문제가 출제된다.

2. 강의

강의는 교수가 실제 강의하는 것처럼 구성된다. 따라서 발췌 내용은 교수가 설명하거나, 학생이 교수에게 질문하거나 교수가 학생들에게 질문을 던지고 한 학생에게 답을 말해 보라고 하는 것일 수 있다. 각 강의의 길이는 약 5분이며 강의 당 6문제가 출제된다.

강의는 개론 수준의 학문적인 내용들로 구성되며, 광범위한 분야의 과목들을 다룬다. 그러나 문제에 답하기 위해 필요한 모든 정보가 청취 지문에 나와 있으므로 강의 내용에 대한 사전 지식은 필요하지 않다. 아래 목록은 듣기 영역에 나오는 일반적인 주제들이다.

1) 인문학

건축 / 산업 디자인 / 도시 계획 / 공예: 천 짜기, 뜨개질, 섬유, 가구, 조각, 모자이크, 도자기 등 민속 미술 및 부족 미술 / 동굴 벽화·암면 미술 / 음악과 음악의 역사 / 사진술 / 문학과 작가 / 책, 신문, 잡지, 저널 / 화가와 그림

2) 생명과학

동식물 멸종 또는 보존 활동 / 어류 및 기타 수생 생물 / 박테리아 및 기타 단세포 생물 / 바이러스 / 의료 기술 / 공중 보건 / 감각 기관의 생리학 / 생화학 / 동물 행동학: 이동, 먹이 사냥, 방어 행동 / 동물들의 서식지와 서식지 적응 / 영양과 영양이 신체에 미치는 영향 / 동물의 의사소통

3) 자연과학

기상과 대기 / 해양학 / 빙하, 빙하 지형, 빙하기 / 사막과 기타 극한 환경 / 오염, 대체 에너지, 환경 정책 / 다른 행성의 대기 / 천문학과 우주론 / 빛의 성질, 광학 / 소리의 성질 / 전자기복사 / TV, 라디오, 레이더 기술 / 수학 / 무기 화학 / 지진학(판 구조, 지진, 구조학 또는 지질학, 대륙 이동, 화산의 구조)

4) 사회과학

비 산업화 문명의 인류학 / 문명 발달기의 표기 체계 / 역사 언어학 / 비즈니스, 경영 / 집단의 사회적 행동, 공동체 역학, 집단행동 / 아동 발달 / 교육 / 현대사(도시화 및 산업화의 역사, 도시화 및 산업화의 경제·사회적 효과) / 매스컴으로서의 미디어 방송과 디지털 미디어

Basic Comprehension Questions_기본적인 이해 문제

Type 1　내용의 요점을 묻는 문제

강의나 대화의 요점을 이해한다는 것은 전체적 주제나 논지를 이해한다는 것이다. 강의나 대화의 요점은 명시적이거나 암시적으로 표현될 수 있다. 요점을 이해했는지 평가하는 문제에서는 듣기 내용을 일반화하거나 종합해야 한다.

1. 문제 식별 방법

내용의 요점을 묻는 문제는 보통 다음과 같은 형태로 출제된다.

· What problem does the man have?
· What are the speakers mainly discussing?
· What is the main topic of the lecture?
· What is the lecture mainly about?
· What aspect of X does the professor mainly discuss?

2. 문제 풀이 요령

1) 내용의 요점을 묻는 문제는 청취 영역 내용 전반에 관한 것이므로 청취 지문의 지엽적인 사항에 대해서만 언급하는 보기는 제거한다.
2) 정답을 고르기 전에 강의나 대화의 주제를 한 구절이나 문장으로 요약해 보는 것이 도움이 된다.

Professor

...So the Earth's surface is made up of these huge segments, these tectonic plates. And these plates move, right? But how can, uh, motion of plates, do you think, influence climate on the Earth? Again, all of you probably read this section in the book, I hope, but, uh, uh, how—how can just motion of the plates impact the climate?

...when a plate moves, if there's landmass on the plate, then the landmass moves too, okay? That's why continents shift their positions, because the plates they're on move. So as a landmass moves away from the equator, its climate would get colder. So, right now we have a continent—the landmass Antarctica—that's on a pole.

So that's dramatically influencing the climate in Antarctica. Um, there was a time when most of the landmasses were closer to a pole; they weren't so close to the equator. Uh, maybe 200 million years ago Antarctica was attached to the South American continent; oh, and Africa was attached too, and the three of them began moving away from the equator together.

...in the Himalayas. That was where two continental plates collided. Two continents on separate plates. Um, when this, uh, Indian, uh, uh, plate collided with the Asian plate, it wasn't until then that we created the Himalayas. When we did that, then we started creating the type of cold climate that we see there now. Wasn't there until this area was uplifted.

So again, that's something else that plate tectonics plays a critical role in. Now, these processes are relatively slow; the, uh, Himalayas are still rising, but on the order of millimeters per year. So they're not dramatically influencing climate on your—the time scale of your lifetime. But over the last few thousands of —tens of thousands of years, uh—hundreds of thousands of years—yes, they've dramatically influenced it.

Uh, another important thing—number three—on how plate tectonics have influenced climate is how they've influenced—we talked about how changing landmasses can affect atmospheric circulation patterns, but if you alter where the landmasses are connected, it can impact oceanic, uh, uh, uh, circulation patterns.

...Um, so, uh, these other processes, if, if we were to disconnect North and South America right through the middle—say, through Panama—that would dramatically influence climate in North and South America— probably the whole globe. So suddenly now as the two continents gradually move apart, you can have different circulation patterns in the ocean between the two. So, uh, that might cause a dramatic change in climate if that were to happen, just as we've had happen here in Antarctica to separate, uh, from South America.

What is the main topic of the lecture?

Ⓐ The differences in climate that occur in different countries

Ⓑ How movement of the Earth's plates can affect climate

Ⓒ Why the ocean has less effect on climate than previously thought

Ⓓ The history of the climate of the region where the university is located

What is the main topic of the lecture?

Ⓐ A climate experiment and its lecture

Ⓑ A geologic process and its effect

Ⓒ How a theory was disproved

Ⓓ How land movement is measured

1. 문제 식별 방법

내용의 목적을 묻는 문제는 보통 다음과 같은 형태로 출제된다.

· Why does the student visit the professor?
· Why does the student visit the registrar's office?
· Why did the professor ask to see the student?
· Why does the professor explain X?

2. 문제 풀이 요령

1) 대화의 단일 주제가 무엇인지 잘 들어본다. 예를 들면, 한 학생이 교수에게 찾아와 빙하에 관한 보고서 작성에 도움을 요청한다. 두 사람의 대화에는 빙하에 대한 여러 사실이 포함되지만 대화의 주제는 학생이 보고서를 쓰는 데 도움을 필요로 한다는 것이다. 이 대화에서 두 화자가 논의하는 것은 빙하에 대한 내용이 아니다.

2) 서비스와 관련된 대화에서 학생은 어떤 문제를 해결하려고 하는 경우가 많다. 학생의 문제가 무엇이고, 그것을 어떻게 해결할 것인가를 이해하면 내용의 목적을 묻는 문제를 풀 수 있다.

ex.

N Narrator P Professor S Student

N Listen to a conversation between a professor and a student.

S I was hoping you could look over my note for my presentation... just to see what you think of it.

P Okay, so refresh my memory: what's your presentation about?

S Two models of decision making...

P Oh, yes—the classical and the administrative model.

S Yeah, that's it.

P And what's the point of your talk?

S I'm gonna talk about the advantages and disadvantages of both models.

P But what's the point of your talk? Are you going to say that one's better than the other?

S Well, I think the administrative model's definitely more realistic. But I don't think it's complete. It's kind of a tool... a tool to see what can go wrong.

P Okay, so what's the point of your talk? What are you trying to convince me to believe?

S Well, uh, the classical model—you shouldn't use it by itself. A lot of companies just try to follow the classical model, but they should really use both models together.

P Okay, good. So let me take a look at your notes here... Wow, you've got a lot packed in here. Are you sure you're going to be able to follow this during your talk?

S I was hoping to get some advice about that.

Why does the student visit the professor?

Ⓐ To get help understanding the difference between two decision-making models

Ⓑ To show her some examples of common errors in research

Ⓒ To review the notes for his presentation with her

Ⓓ To ask for help in finding a topic for his presentation

Type 3	세부 정보 찾기 문제

세부 정보 찾기 문제는 강의나 대화에 명시된 세부 정보나 사실들을 이해하고 기억해야 풀 수 있는 문제다. 세부 정보는 상세한 설명, 구체적인 사례, 기타 다른 방법을 통해 제시된다.

1. 문제 식별 방법

세부 정보 찾기 문제는 보통 다음과 같은 형태로 출제된다.

· According to the professor, what is one way that X can affect Y?

· What is X?

· What resulted from the invention of the X?

· According to the professor, what is the main problem with the X theory?

2. 문제 풀이 요령

1) 대화나 강의의 요점과 관련 없는 질문은 나오지 않는다. 그러므로 필기 내용에 대화나 강의의 중요한 세부 정보가 포함되어 있어야 한다.

2) 대화나 강의에서 사용된 단어가 보기에 있다고 해서 이를 선택하면 안 된다. 오답에는 주로 듣기 지문에 나온 단어가 포함되어 있다.

3) 정답이라는 확신이 없을 때는 대화나 강의의 주제와 가장 일치하는 보기를 택한다.

ex.

Professor

Uh, other things that glaciers can do is, uh, as they retreat, instead of depositing some till, uh, scraped-up soil, in the area, they might leave a big ice block, and it breaks off, and as the ice block melts, it leaves a depression, which can become a lake. These are called kettle lakes. These are very critical ecosystems in this region, um, because, uh, uh, they support some unique biological diversity, these kettle lakes do.

The Great Lakes are kettle lakes; they were left over from the Pleist—from the Pleistocene glaciers. Uh, now, as the glaciers were retreating, the Great Lakes underwent a change. Once the weight of the glacier ice decreased, and the pressure decreased, the land at the bottom of the lakes rose. In some places it rose by as much as one hundred feet.

So I just wanted to tell you a little bit more about glaciers...

What are kettle lakes?

Ⓐ Lakes that form in the center of a volcano

Ⓑ Lakes that have been damaged by the greenhouse effect

Ⓒ Lakes formed by unusually large amounts of precipitation

Ⓓ Lakes that form when pieces of glaciers melt

What happened to the Great Lakes when the glaciers retreated?

Ⓐ The lakes became less deep.

Ⓑ The lakes became larger.

Ⓒ The biodiversity of the lakes increased.

Ⓓ The amount of soil in the lakes increased.

Pragmatic Understanding Questions_화용론적 이해 문제

Type 4	의도 파악 문제
	화용론적 이해 문제의 첫 번째 유형은 진술의 의도를 이해했는지 묻는 문제다. 이 유형은 대개 듣기 지문의 일부를 다시 들려준다.

1. 문제 식별 방법

의도 파악 문제는 보통 다음과 같은 형태로 출제된다.

· What does the professor imply when he says this? *(replay)*

· Why does the student say this? *(replay)*

· What does the professor mean when she says this? *(replay)*

2. 문제 풀이 요령

의도 파악 문제는 화자가 직접적으로 말하는 것과 일치하지 않을 수도 있다. 다음 예제에서 여직원은 학생에게 기숙사 사무실이 어디 있는지 아느냐고 묻는다. 그러나 기숙사 사무실의 위치에 대한 정보를 얻기 위해 이런 질문을 하는 것은 아니다.

남학생과 여직원의 대화 내용으로, 두 사람은 남학생의 기숙사 비용에 대해 이야기하고 있다. **ex.**

N Narrator   S Student   A Administrative Assistant

N   Listen again to a part of the conversation. Then answer the question.

S   Okay. I'll just pay with a credit card. *[pause]* And where do I do that at?

A   At, um, the housing office.

S   Housing office, all right.

A   Do you know where they are?

What is the woman trying to find out from the man?

Ⓐ Where the housing office is

Ⓑ Approximately how far away the housing office is

Ⓒ Whether she needs to tell him where the housing office is

Ⓓ Whether he has been to the housing office already

Type 5 태도 파악 문제

화용론적 이해 문제의 두 번째 유형으로 화자의 태도나 의견을 이해하는지 묻는 문제다. 화자의 느낌, 좋아하거나 싫어하는 것, 걱정하거나 즐거워하는 이유 등에 대한 문제가 출제된다. 이 유형에는 화자가 어디선가 입수한 정보를 언급하는지, 아니면 개인적인 의견을 피력하는지, 또는 제시한 정보들이 일반적으로 인정되는 것인지 아니면 논쟁의 여지가 있는지를 묻는 문제도 출제된다.

1. 문제 식별 방법

태도 파악 문제는 보통 다음과 같은 형태로 출제된다.

· What can be inferred about the student?
· What is the professor's attitude toward X?
· What is the professor's opinion of X?
· What can be inferred about the student when she says this? *(replay)*
· What does the woman mean when she says this? *(replay)*

2. 문제 풀이 요령

이 유형의 문제를 풀 때는 화자의 어조를 주의 깊게 들을 필요가 있다. 화자가 미안해 하는지, 혼란스러운지 혹은 열광적인지 등을 파악하는 것이 도움이 된다.

남학생과 상담자의 대화 내용으로 남학생의 일에 대해 얘기하고 있다.   ex.

A **Advisor** S **Student**

A Well, good. So, bookstore isn't working out?

S Oh, bookstore's working out fine. I just, I—this pays almost double what the bookstore does.

A Oh, wow!

S Yeah. Plus credit.

A Plus credit.

S And it's more hours, which... The bookstore's—I mean it's a decent job 'n' all. Everybody I work with... that part's great; it's just... I mean I'm shelving books and kind of hanging out and not doing much else... if it weren't for the people, it'd be totally boring.

What is the student's attitude toward the people he currently works with?

Ⓐ He finds them boring.
Ⓑ He likes them.
Ⓒ He is annoyed by them.
Ⓓ He does not have much in common with them.

Connecting Information Questions_정보 연결 문제

<table>
<tr><td rowspan="2">Type
6</td><td>구성 파악 문제</td></tr>
<tr><td>구성 파악 문제에서는 듣기 지문의 전반적인 구성이나 듣기 지문 사이의 관계에 대한 질문이 나올 수 있다.

전체적인 구성을 묻는 것으로, 듣기 지문 전체의 연결 관계를 이해했는지 묻는다.

How does the professor organize the information that she presents to the class?
○ In the order in which the events occurred

지문의 일부 내용에 대해 묻는 것으로, 두 개의 서로 다른 개념들 간의 관계를 이해했는지 묻는다.

How does the professor clarify the points he makes about Mexico?
○ By comparing Mexico to a neighboring country

구성 파악 문제 중에는 특정 문장이 주변 내용과 연계해서 어떤 기능을 하는지 파악하라는 것이 있다. 주제의 전환 나타내기, 주제와 부제 연결하기, 서론이나 결론 제시하기, 예 제시하기, 주제에서 벗어나기, 또는 농담하기 등이 포함된다.</td></tr>
</table>

1. 문제 식별 방법

구성 파악 문제는 보통 다음과 같은 형태로 출제된다.

· How does the professor organize the information about X?

· How is the discussion organized?

· Why does the professor discuss X?

· Why does the professor mention X?

2. 문제 풀이 요령

1) 지문의 전체적인 구성을 묻는 문제는 대화 지문보다는 강의 지문에 나올 가능성이 많다. 교수가 강의 내용을 전개할 때 어떤 방식을 사용하는지 주의를 기울인다. 예를 들면, 시간의 순서대로 했는지 아니면 단순한 것에서 점차 복잡한 순서대로 했는지, 또는 기타 다른 방식으로 했는지 등인데 처음부터 명확하지 않을 수도 있으므로 노트 필기를 활용하자.

2) 교수가 주제에서 벗어난 내용을 언급한다면 무엇을 말하고자 하는지 생각해 보도록 한다.

ex1.

N Narrator P Professor

N Listen again to a statement made by the professor. Then answer the question.

P There's this committee I'm on... Th-the name of the thing, and it's probably, well, you don't have to take notes about this, um, the name of the thing is academic standards.

Why does the professor tell the students that they do not have to take notes?

Ⓐ The information is in their books.

Ⓑ The information may not be accurate.

Ⓒ She is going to tell a personal story.

Ⓓ They already know what she is going to talk about.

다음 예제에서 교수는 식물의 구조에 대해 논하면서, 신축 건물의 강철과 철근을 예로 들었다.

Professor

So, we have reproductive parts—the seeds, the fruit walls—we have leaf parts, but the great majority of plant fibers come from vasculature within the stem... fibers that occur in stem material. And what we do is consider these fibers *[false start]*—basically they're what are called *bast* fibers. Bast fibers. Now, basically bast fibers are parts of the plant that the plant uses to maintain vertical structure.

Think about it this way: what's the first thing you see when you see a building being built... uh, what's the first thing they put up? Besides the foundation, of course? The metalwork, right? They put all those steel girders up there, the framework. OK, well, think of *[false start]*—bast fibers basically constitute the structural framework to support the stem of the plant. OK? So as the plant grows, it basically builds a girder system within that plant, like steel, so to speak.

So suppose you cut across the stem of one of these plants... take a look at how the bast fibers are arranged, so you're looking at a cross section... you'll see that the fibers run vertically side by side. Up and down next to each other, forming a kind of tube, which is significant...'cause, which is physically stronger: a solid rod or a tube? The tube—physics tells you that. What's essentially happening—well, the plant is forming a structural ring of these bast fibers all around the stem, and that shape allows for structural rigidity, but also allows for bending and motion.

Why does the professor talk about steel?

Ⓐ To identify the substance that has replaced fiber products.

Ⓑ To explain a method for separating fibers from a plant.

Ⓒ To compare the chemical structure of fibers to metals.

Ⓓ To illustrate the function of fibers in a plant's stem.

Why does the professor mention a tube?

Ⓐ To explain how some fibers are arranged in a plant.

Ⓑ To show how plants carry water to growing fibers.

Ⓒ To describe an experiment involving plant fibers.

Ⓓ To explain why some plant stems cannot bend.

Type 7	내용 연결 문제

내용 연결 문제는 지문에 나오는 개념들 간의 관계를 이해하는지 묻는 문제다. 이러한 관계들은 명확히 드러나는 경우도 있지만 추론해야 하는 경우도 있다. 비교, 인과관계 등을 파악하거나 특정 항목들을 적당한 범주로 분류하는 문제, 또는 사건의 순서나 과정을 파악하는 문제가 나올 수도 있다.

1. 문제 식별 방법

내용 연결 문제는 보통 다음과 같은 형태로 출제된다.

· What is the likely outcome of doing procedure X before procedure Y?

· What can be inferred about X?

· What does the professor imply about X?

2. 문제 풀이 요령

도표를 채우거나, 사건을 순서대로 배열하는 문제가 이 유형에 속한다. 단계별 과정뿐만 아니라 용어와 그 정의를 명확하게 파악하면 이 유형의 문제를 푸는 데 도움이 된다.

ex.

Professor

OK, Neptune and its moons. Neptune has several moons, but there's only... we'll probably only worry about two of them, the two fairly interesting ones. The first one's Triton. So you have this little struggle with the word *Titan* which is the big moon of Saturn and the name *Triton*, which is the big moon of *Neptune*. Triton: it's, it's the only *large moon* in the solar system to go backwards, to go around its—what we call its parent planet—in this case Neptune, the wrong way. OK? Every other large moon orbits the *parent planet* in the same counterclockwise direction... same as most of the other bodies in the solar system. But this moon... the reverse direction, which is perfectly OK as far as the laws of gravity are concerned. But it indicates some sort of peculiar event in the early solar system that gave this moon a motion in contrast to the general spin of the raw material that it was formed from.

The other moon orbiting Neptune that I want to talk about is Nereid. Nereid is, Nereid has the most eccentric orbit, the most lopsided, elliptical-type orbit for a large moon in the solar system. The others tend more like circular orbits.

...Does it mean that Pluto and Neptune might have been related somehow in the past and then drifted slowly into their present orbits? If Pluto... did Pluto ever belong to the Neptune system? Do Neptune's moons represent Pluto-type bodies that have been captured by Neptune? Was some sort of... was Pluto the object that disrupted the Neptune system at some point in the past?

It's really hard to prove any of those things. But now we're starting to appreciate that there's quite a few junior Plutos out there: not big enough to really call a planet, but large enough that they're significant in history of the early solar system. So we'll come back to those when we talk about comets and other small bodies in the fringes of the outer solar system.

What does the professor imply about the orbits of Triton and Nereid?

Ⓐ They used to be closer together.

Ⓑ They might provide evidence of an undiscovered planet.

Ⓒ They might reverse directions in the future.

Ⓓ They might have been changed by some unusual event.

<table>
<tr><td>Type
8</td><td>추론 문제
정보 연결 문제의 마지막 유형은 추론 문제다. 이 문제 유형에서는 듣기 지문에 나온 사실들에 근거하여 결론을
도출해야 한다.</td></tr>
</table>

1. 문제 식별 방법

추론 문제는 보통 다음과 같은 형태로 출제된다.

· What does the professor imply about X?

· What will the student probably do next?

· What can be inferred about X?

· What does the professor imply when he says this? *(replay)*

2. 문제 풀이 요령

이 유형은 지문에 나오는 세부 사실들을 종합해 결론을 도출하는 문제다. 특정 사실을 직접적으로 말하지 않고 암시하는 경우가 많다. 대부분의 경우 정답에는 청취 지문에 없는 단어가 사용된다.

ex.

Professor

Dada is often considered under the broader category of Fantasy. It's one of the early directions in the Fantasy style. The term "Dada" itself is a nonsense word—it has no meaning... and where the word originated isn't known. The "philosophy" behind the "Dada" movement was to create works that conveyed the concept of *absurdity*—the artwork was meant to shock the public by presenting the ridiculous, absurd concepts. Dada artists rejected reason—or rational thought. They did not believe that rational thought would help solve social problems...

...When he turned to Dada, he quit painting and devoted himself to making a type of sculpture he referred to as a "ready-made"... probably because they were constructed of readily available objects... At the time, many people reacted to Dadaism by saying that the works were not art at all... and in fact, that's exactly how Duchamp and others conceived of it—as a form of "non-art"... or anti-art.

Duchamp also took a reproduction of da Vinci's famous painting, the *Mona Lisa*, and he drew a mustache and goatee on the subject's face. Treating this masterpiece with such disrespect was another way Duchamp was challenging the established cultural standards of his day.

What does the professor imply about the philosophy of the Dada movement?

Ⓐ It was not taken seriously by most artists.

Ⓑ It varied from one country to another.

Ⓒ It challenged people's concept of what art is.

Ⓓ It was based on a realistic style of art.

Listening Practice Sets

PRACTICE SET 1

Now listen to Track 1.

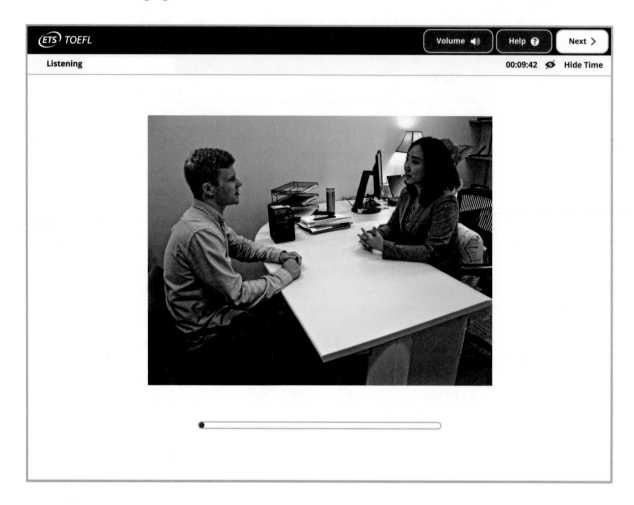

1. Why does the man go to see his professor?

   Ⓐ To borrow some charts and graphs from her

   Ⓑ To ask her to explain some statistical procedures

   Ⓒ To talk about a report he is writing

   Ⓓ To discuss a grade he got on a paper

2. What information will the man include in his report?
For each phrase below, place a check mark in the "Include" column or the "Not Include" column.

	Include in Report	Not Include in Report
Climate charts		
Interviews with meteorologists		
Journal notes		
Statistical tests		

3. Why does the professor tell the man about the appointment at the doctor's office?

   Ⓐ To demonstrate a way of remembering things

   Ⓑ To explain why she needs to leave soon

   Ⓒ To illustrate a point that appears in his report

   Ⓓ To emphasize the importance of good health

4. What does the professor offer to do for the man?

   Ⓐ Help him collect more data in other areas of the state

   Ⓑ Submit his research findings for publication

   Ⓒ Give him the doctor's telephone number

   Ⓓ Review the first version of his report

5. *Listen again to part of the conversation by playing Track 2. Then answer the question.*

Why does the professor say this?

   Ⓐ To question the length of the paper

   Ⓑ To offer encouragement

   Ⓒ To dispute the data sources

   Ⓓ To explain a theory

PRACTICE SET 2

Now listen to Track 3.

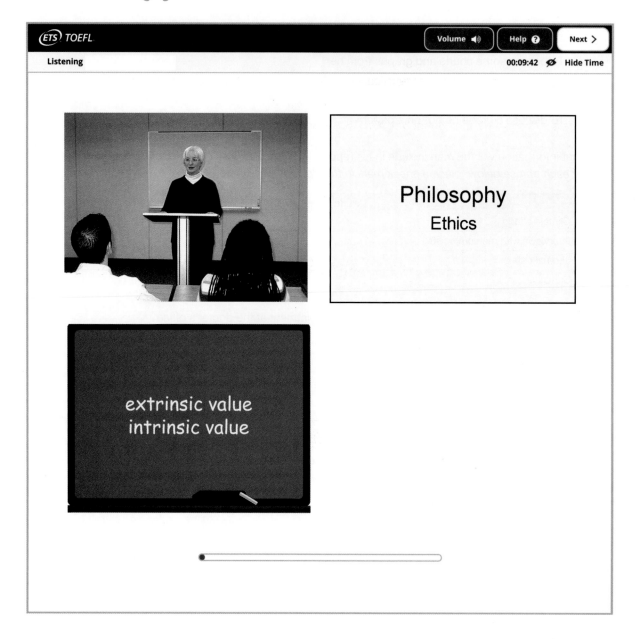

1. What is the main purpose of the lecture?

   Ⓐ To illustrate the importance of extrinsic values

   Ⓑ To explain Aristotle's views about the importance of teaching

   Ⓒ To explain why people change what they value

   Ⓓ To discuss Aristotle's views about human happiness

2. The professor gives examples of things that have value for her. Indicate for each example what type of value it has for her.

   Place a check mark in the correct box. **This question is worth 2 points.**

	Only Extrinsic Value	Only Intrinsic Value	Both Extrinsic and Intrinsic Value
Teaching			
Exercise			
Health			
Playing a musical instrument			

3. Why is happiness central to Aristotle's theory?

   Ⓐ Because it is so difficult for people to attain

   Ⓑ Because it is valued for its own sake by all people

   Ⓒ Because it is a means to a productive life

   Ⓓ Because most people agree about what happiness is

4. According to the professor, why does Aristotle think that fame cannot provide true happiness?

   Ⓐ Fame cannot be obtained without help from other people.

   Ⓑ Fame cannot be obtained by all people.

   Ⓒ Fame does not last forever.

   Ⓓ People cannot share their fame with other people.

5. *Listen again to part of the lecture by playing Track 4.*
   Then answer the question.

   What does the professor mean when she says this?

   Ⓐ Teaching is not a highly valued profession in society.

   Ⓑ She may change professions in order to earn more money.

   Ⓒ The reason she is a teacher has little to do with her salary.

   Ⓓ More people would become teachers if the salary were higher.

PRACTICE SET 3

Now listen to Track 5.

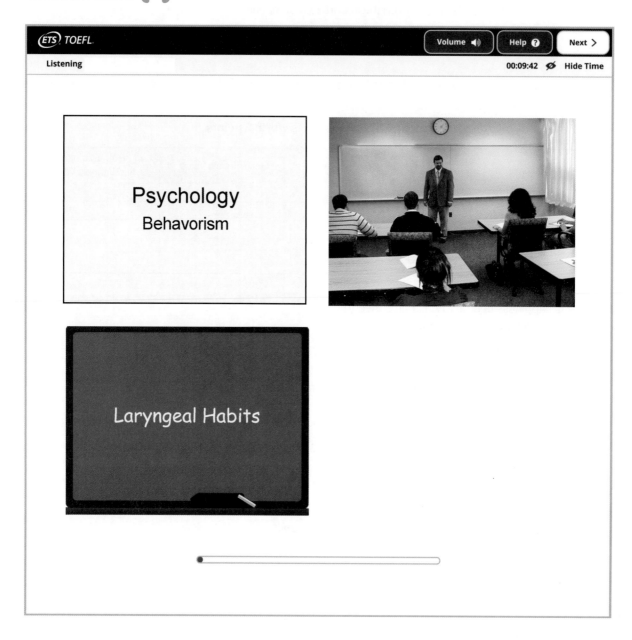

1. What is the professor mainly discussing?

   Ⓐ The development of motor skills in children
   Ⓑ How psychologists measure muscle activity in the throat
   Ⓒ A theory about the relationship between muscle activity and thinking
   Ⓓ A study on the problem-solving techniques of people who are deaf

2. What does the professor say about people who use sign language?

   Ⓐ It is not possible to study their thinking habits.
   Ⓑ They exhibit laryngeal habits.
   Ⓒ The muscles in their hands move when they solve problems.
   Ⓓ They do not exhibit ideomotor action.

3. What point does the professor make when he refers to the university library?

   Ⓐ A study on problem solving took place there.
   Ⓑ Students should go there to read more about behaviorism.
   Ⓒ Students' eyes will turn toward it if they think about it.
   Ⓓ He learned about William James's concept of thinking there.

4. The professor describes a magic trick to the class. What does the magic trick demonstrate?

   Ⓐ An action people make that they are not aware of
   Ⓑ That behaviorists are not really scientists
   Ⓒ How psychologists study children
   Ⓓ A method for remembering locations

5. What is the professor's opinion of the motor theory of thinking?

   Ⓐ Most of the evidence he has collected contradicts it.
   Ⓑ It explains adult behavior better than it explains child behavior.
   Ⓒ It is the most valid theory of thinking at the present time.
   Ⓓ It cannot be completely proved or disproved.

6. Listen again to part of the lecture by playing Track 6.
   Then answer the question.

   Why does the professor say this?

   Ⓐ To give an example of a laryngeal habit
   Ⓑ To explain the meaning of a term
   Ⓒ To explain why he is discussing laryngeal habits
   Ⓓ To remind students of a point he had discussed previously

PRACTICE SET 4

Now listen to Track 7.

1. What is Bode's Law?

   Ⓐ A law of gravitation
   Ⓑ An estimate of the distance between Mars and Jupiter
   Ⓒ A prediction of how many asteroids there are
   Ⓓ A pattern in the spacing of planets

2. Why does the professor explain Bode's Law to the class?

   Ⓐ To describe the size of the asteroids
   Ⓑ To explain how the asteroid belt was discovered
   Ⓒ To explain how gravitational forces influence the planets
   Ⓓ To describe the impact of telescopes on astronomy

3. How does the professor introduce Bode's Law?

   Ⓐ By demonstrating how it is derived mathematically
   Ⓑ By describing the discovery of Uranus
   Ⓒ By drawing attention to the inaccuracy of a certain pattern
   Ⓓ By telling the names of several of the asteroids

4. According to the professor, what two factors contributed to the discovery of the asteroid Ceres?
   Select 2 answers.

   Ⓐ Improved telescopes
   Ⓑ Advances in mathematics
   Ⓒ The discovery of a new star
   Ⓓ The position of Uranus in a pattern

5. What does the professor imply about the asteroid belt?

   Ⓐ It is farther from the Sun than Uranus.
   Ⓑ Bode believed it was made up of small stars.
   Ⓒ It is located where people expected to find a planet.
   Ⓓ Ceres is the only one of the asteroids that can be seen without a telescope.

6. *Listen again to part of the lecture by playing Track 8.*
   Then answer the question.

   Why does the professor say this?

   Ⓐ To introduce an alternative application of Bode's Law
   Ⓑ To give an example of what Bode's Law cannot explain
   Ⓒ To describe the limitations of gravitational theory
   Ⓓ To contrast Bode's Law with a real scientific law

PRACTICE SET 5

Now listen to Track 9.

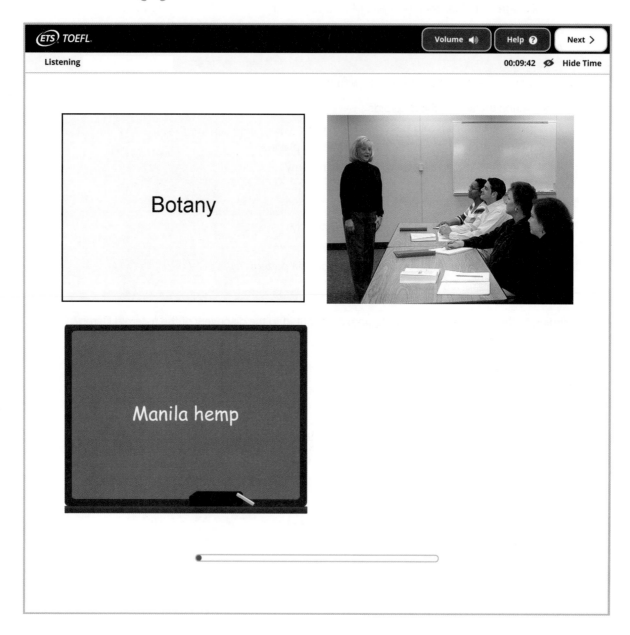

1. What aspect of Manila hemp fibers does the professor mainly describe in the lecture?

    Ⓐ Similarities between cotton fibers and Manila hemp fibers

    Ⓑ Various types of Manila hemp fibers

    Ⓒ The economic importance of Manila hemp fibers

    Ⓓ A use of Manila hemp fibers

2. What does the professor imply about the name "Manila hemp"?

    Ⓐ It is a commercial brand name.

    Ⓑ Part of the name is inappropriate.

    Ⓒ The name has recently changed.

    Ⓓ The name was first used in the 1940s.

3. Why does the professor mention the Golden Gate Bridge?

    Ⓐ To demonstrate a disadvantage of steel cables

    Ⓑ To give an example of the creative use of color

    Ⓒ To show that steel cables are able to resist salt water

    Ⓓ To give an example of a use of Manila hemp

4. According to the professor, what was the main reason that many ships used Manila hemp ropes instead of steel cables?

    Ⓐ Manila hemp was cheaper.

    Ⓑ Manila hemp was easier to produce.

    Ⓒ Manila hemp is more resistant to salt water.

    Ⓓ Manila hemp is lighter in weight.

5. According to the lecture, what are two ways to increase the strength of rope made from Manila hemp fibers?

    Select 2 answers.

    Ⓐ Coat the fibers with zinc-based paint

    Ⓑ Combine the fibers into bundles

    Ⓒ Soak bundles of fibers in salt water

    Ⓓ Twist bundles of fibers

6. *Listen again to part of the lecture by playing track 10.*
Then answer the question.

    Why does the professor mention going away for the weekend?

    Ⓐ To tell the class a joke

    Ⓑ To apologize for not completing some work

    Ⓒ To introduce the topic of the lecture

    Ⓓ To encourage students to ask about her trip

듣기 영역 점수 향상 전략

듣기 실력을 키우는 가장 좋은 방법은 과학, 사회과학, 인문학, 경영 등 여러 분야에 걸친 다양한 종류의 듣기 자료들을 자주 접하는 것이다. 영화나 TV를 보고, 라디오를 듣는 것도 좋은 방법이다. 오디오북과 기타 기록 자료들이 특히 도움이 될 수 있으며, 인터넷에서 유용한 오디오 및 비디오 자료들을 많이 찾을 수 있다. TOEFL iBT® 듣기 영역의 세 가지 유형에 따른 전략을 소개한다.

■ 기본적 이해 문제

1) 어휘 실력을 늘려야 한다.
2) 듣기 내용과 흐름에 집중한다. 화자의 말하는 스타일이나 말투에 구애되지 않도록 한다.
3) 화자가 다음에 어떤 말을 할지 예측하면서 들으면 집중도를 높일 수 있다.
4) 스스로 질문하면서 능동적으로 듣는다(예: 교수가 전달하려는 핵심 주제는 무엇인가?).
5) "핵심 주제", "핵심 요지", "중요한 세부 사실"이라고 항목을 만들고 주의 깊게 들으면서 각각에 해당하는 사항들을 적는다.
6) 강의나 대화의 일부를 듣고, 핵심 내용을 요약하여 적어 본다.

■ 화용론적 이해 문제

1) 강의나 대화의 목적이 무엇인지 생각해 본다. 화자는 사과하고 있는가, 불평하고 있는가, 아니면 제안을 하고 있는가?
2) 화자가 말하는 방식에 유의한다. 사용하는 언어의 수준이 형식적인가, 일상적인가? 화자는 어느 정도의 확신을 가지고 말하고 있는가? 화자의 목소리는 차분한가, 감정적인가? 화자의 어조로부터 무엇을 알 수 있는가?
3) 화자가 확신하는 정도에 주목한다. 화자는 정보에 대해 얼마나 확신하고 있는가? 화자의 어조를 통해 그가 어느 정도 확신하는지 알 수 있는가?
4) TV나 코미디 영화를 보면서 의미 전달에 사용되는 강세나 억양의 패턴에 주의를 기울인다.
5) TV나 코미디 영화를 보면서 다른 사람의 감정을 상하게 하지 않으려고 간접적으로 반대 의견을 표현하거나 제안하는 방식에 주의를 기울인다.

■ 정보 연결 문제

1) 강의가 어떻게 구성되어 있는지에 대해 생각해 본다. 서론, 본론, 결론, 예시 또는 요약의 의미를 나타내는 단어들을 잘 들어 본다.
2) 인과관계, 비교 · 대조 등 논의되고 있는 내용들 간의 관계를 파악한다.
3) 연결 및 관계를 나타내는 단어들을 잘 들어 본다.
4) 녹음된 자료를 들을 때, 중간에 멈춘 다음 그 다음에 이어질 내용을 예측해 본다.
5) 듣는 도중이나 다 듣고 난 후, 논의된 정보의 개요를 작성한다.
6) 주제의 전환이나 또는 화자가 잠시 주제에서 벗어났다가 돌아오는 여담에 유의해서 듣는다.

Chapter 4

Speaking Section

Speaking Section

이 장의 구성_	TOEFL iBT® 말하기 문제 4가지
	유형별 예제 답안과 답변 요령
	유형별 채점 기준표
	점수 향상 전략

TOEFL iBT® 말하기 영역에서는 개인적 경험, 캠퍼스에서 일어날 수 있는 상황, 다양한 학문적 주제에 관해 4문제가 출제된다. 각 문제당 준비 시간은 15~30초, 답변 시간은 45~60초이며 시험 종료까지 약 16분이 소요된다.

말하기 영역에 대한 소개

TOEFL iBT® 말하기 영역은 영어권 국가에서 학습할 때 필수적인 말하기 능력을 평가하며, 독립형 과제와 통합형 과제로 분류된다. 주요 내용은 교실 안에서의 수업 참여와 교실 밖에서의 일상적인 대화로 모두 대학 생활과 관계가 있다.

문제 유형

1. The Independent Speaking Task_독립형 과제

독립형 과제는 응시자의 생각, 의견, 경험으로부터 답변을 이끌어내야 하는 것이 특징이다.
– 질문에 제시된 두 가지 행동, 상황 또는 의견 중 하나를 선택하고, 선호하는 이유를 밝히는 과제 (1문제)

2. The Integrated Speaking Task_통합형 과제

통합형 과제는 다음과 같이 크게 두 가지로 나눌 수 있으며, 독립형 과제와 달리 읽기 지문 및 청취 내용 모두에 초점을 맞추거나 청취 내용에 초점을 맞춰서 답변해야 하는 것이 특징이다.
– 읽고, 들은 내용에 대해 말하는 과제 (2문제)
  대학 생활과 관련된 글이나 학문적인 주제에 대한 지문을 읽고 나서 이에 대한 짧은 대화나 강의를 들은 후 읽고 들은 정보를 종합해 문제에 답변한다.
– 들은 내용에 대해 말하는 과제 (1문제)
  대학 생활과 관련된 짧은 대화를 들은 후 대화에서 제시된 대안 중 하나를 선택해 그 이유를 설명하거나, 학문적 주제에 대한 강의를 들은 후 내용을 요약해 말한다.

채점 방식과 평가 요소

채점 기준은 문제에 따라 다소 다르지만 대체로 다음과 같은 요소가 반영된다. 채점자들은 완벽한 답변을 기대하지 않으며 아래 세 가지 요소 중 하나에서 경미한 실수가 있어도 높은 점수를 주는 경우가 있다는 것에 주목하자. 말하기 영역 채점 기준표(115-116쪽)를 보면 수험자의 답변이 어떤 기준으로 채점되는지 알 수 있다.

- **언어 구사력**
  얼마나 명확하게 말하는가를 평가한다. 유창하고, 명확하게 정확한 발음과 적당한 속도, 자연스러운 억양으로 답변을 해야 높은 점수를 받는다.

- **언어 사용**
  자신의 생각을 전달하기 위해 문법과 어휘를 얼마나 효과적으로 사용하는지 평가한다. 채점자는 수험자가 문법에 맞게 말하고 적절한 어휘를 사용할 때 높은 점수를 준다.

- **주제의 전개**
  질문에 얼마나 충실히 답하며 자신의 생각을 얼마나 일관성 있게 전개해 나가는지 평가한다. 또한 통합형 과제에서는 수험자가 정보를 얼마나 잘 종합하고 요약하는지 평가한다.

TIP | 1. 모든 문제의 답변 시간은 45초에서 60초이므로 답변 시간을 측정하면서 연습해 보도록 하자.
2. 채점 기준을 잘 숙지하자. 자신의 답변이 어떻게 평가될지 파악하는 데 도움이 될 것이다.

The Independent Task: Question 1_독립형 과제

> **Question 1** 이 문제에서는 두 가지 가능한 행동, 상황, 의견 등을 제시한 뒤 그 중 어떤 것이 더 좋은지, 어떤 의견이 더 정당하다고 생각하는지 답하고 그 이유와 세부 사실을 제시하면 된다. 답변 시간은 45초다.

1. 일반적인 관심사들 또는 익숙한 주제에 대한 상반된 의견이 문제로 출제된다.

1) 이 문제에 나오는 주제에는 학생들이 일상생활에서 겪는 일반적인 관심사가 포함된다. 예를 들면, 집에서 공부하는 것이 좋은지, 도서관에서 공부하는 것이 좋은지, 폭넓은 분야의 과목을 수강하는 것이 좋은지, 한 분야의 과목에 집중하는 것이 좋은지, 또는 대학 신입생은 기숙사에서 살아야 하는지, 캠퍼스 밖의 아파트에서 사는 것을 허용해야 하는지 등의 질문이 나온다.

2) 텔레비전이 인류에게 미친 영향 등 특정 의견에 대한 두 개의 상반된 견해가 제시되고 어느 쪽에 동의하는지를 묻는 문제가 나올 수도 있다.

2. 수험자는 명확한 의견과 이유를 말해야 한다.

1) 수험자는 답변의 근거가 되는 이유, 설명, 세부 사실 등을 명확하게 말해야 한다.

2) 두 가지 행동, 상황, 의견 중에 수험자가 어느 쪽을 택하느냐 하는 것은 문제가 되지 않는다. "정답"이나 "오답"은 없다. 다만 선택한 의견에 대해 그 이유와 세부 사실을 근거로 제시하면서 얼마나 잘 설명했느냐에 따라 채점된다.

3. 생각을 정리한 후 메모를 한다.

문제는 컴퓨터 화면에 나타나고 해설자가 이를 읽어 준다. 답변할 준비를 하는 15초 동안 무엇을 말할지 생각하고 정리한 후 필요하다고 생각되면 메모를 한다. 그러나 답변할 내용을 전부 메모할 필요는 없고 어떤 방향으로 답변할 것인지를 상기시켜 주는 단어나 몇개의 구(phrase)만 메모하면 된다.

TIP | 1. 자신이 선호하는 의견이나 상황에 대해 말한 뒤, 그 논거가 되는 이유를 세부 사실과 함께 분명하게 말해보는 연습을 한다.
　　 2. "In my opinion...", "I believe..." 처럼 의견을 말할 때 흔히 사용되는 단어나 표현을 공부하고 연습한다.

ex.

Some students study for classes individually. Others study in groups. Which method of studying do you think is better for students and why?

Preparation Time: 15 Seconds
Response Time: 45 Seconds

PREPARATION TIME

00:00:07

문제 어떤 학생들은 혼자 학과 공부를 하고, 다른 학생들은 그룹 스터디를 한다. 어떤 공부 방법이 학생들에게 더 좋다고 생각하는가? 그리고 그 이유는 무엇인가?

해설 자신의 의견이 무엇인지 먼저 분명히 말한다. 이런 문제에 답변하기 위해서는 자신의 의견이 무엇인지 먼저 분명히 밝히는 것이 중요하다. 처음부터 자신의 의견을 분명히 말하지 않으면 채점자는 수험자가 제시하는 이유를 이해하기가 어려울 것이다. 어떤 입장을 선택하든 타당한 이유는 얼마든지 제시할 수 있다.

예제 답안 독학을 하는 것이 더 효과적이라고 생각할 경우, 그룹 스터디를 하면 수업과는 무관한 내용을 토의하는 데 시간을 낭비하는 일이 자주 있다는 식으로 말할 수 있을 것이다. 수험자는 그룹 스터디의 비효율성과 개별 학습의 성과를 대비시킴으로써 자신의 입장에 대한 설명을 계속해 나갈 수 있다. 그룹 스터디가 효과적이라고 생각한다면, 그룹 스터디의 장점과 개별 학습의 단점을 설명하면 될 것이다. 그룹을 이뤄 공부하면 좀 더 뛰어난 학생들이 뒤처진 학생들을 도와줄 수 있다는 식의 생각을 전개할 수도 있다. 또는 그룹을 이뤄 공부하는 학생들은 서로 강의 노트를 바꿔 보기도 하므로 강의에서 다룬 모든 내용들을 더 잘 이해할 수 있다는 사실을 말할 수도 있다.

The Integrated Tasks: Question 2_통합형 과제

1. 읽기 지문의 주제들은 이해하기 쉬운 내용들이다.

대학의 정책, 규정과 절차, 대학의 계획, 대학 내 편의시설 또는 학교 생활의 만족도 등이 주제로 등장한다. 이 주제들은 수험자 모두가 쉽게 이해하도록 구성되어 있으며 북미 지역에서 대학 생활을 한 경험이 없어도 답변이 가능하다.

2. 읽기 지문은 여러 가지 유형이 있을 수 있다.

대학의 새로운 주차 규정에 관한 안내문일 수도 있고, 기숙사에서의 라디오 사용을 금지하는 대학의 규정에 대한 견해를 학보 편집장에게 보내는 편지일 수도 있고, 미식축구 경기장을 신축하자는 제안에 대해 논평하는 학보 논설일 수도 있다. 읽기 지문은 일반적으로 이러한 제안들에 대해 기술하고 나서 이 제안에 대한 찬반 양론의 논거를 두 가지 정도 제시한다. 90~115단어 정도의 짧은 분량이므로 읽을 시간은 충분하다.

3. 읽기 지문을 읽은 다음에는 짧은 대화를 듣게 된다.

읽기 지문을 읽은 다음에 나오는 대화 또는 한 사람의 독백에서는 한 명 또는 두 명이(대개 학생들임) 앞서 수험자가 읽은 기사, 편지, 발표 등에 대해 얘기하는 것을 듣게 된다. 두 사람이 등장할 경우, 그 중 한 사람은 특정 제안에 대해 찬성하거나 반대하는 주장을 강하게 펼치고 자신의 의견에 대한 근거를 제시한다. 대화는 통상 60~80초 동안 진행된다.

4. 대화를 듣고 나면 읽고 들은 내용을 바탕으로 문제가 나온다.

지문과 대화 내용을 바탕으로 문제가 나온다. 예를 들면, 대학의 새로운 규정 마련 계획에 대한 읽기 지문과 이에 대해 교수와 학생이 논의하는 대화가 나올 수 있다. 대화에서 학생이 새 규정에 반대하는 경우, 수험자는 읽기 지문과 들은 대화 내용을 바탕으로 학생의 입장과 이유를 설명해야 한다.

1. 다음과 같은 해설자의 말을 듣는다.

ex.

Narrator

Now you will read a passage about a campus situation and then listen to a conversation about the same topic. You will then answer a question, using information from both the reading passage and the conversation. You will have 30 seconds to prepare and 60 seconds to speak.

Narrator

City University is planning to increase tuition and fees. Read the announcement about the increase from the president of City University. You will have 45 seconds to read the announcement. Begin reading now.

2. 읽기 지문은 컴퓨터 화면에 나타난다. 컴퓨터 화면 상단의 시계가 남은 시간을 알려준다.

Announcement from the President

The university has decided to increase tuition and fees for all students by approximately 8% next semester. For the past 5 years, the tuition and fees have remained the same, but it is necessary to increase them now for several reasons. The university has many more students than we had 5 years ago, and we must hire additional professors to teach these students. We have also made a new commitment to research and technology and will be renovating and upgrading our laboratory facilities to better meet our students' needs.

---

3. 읽기 시간이 끝나면 화면에서 지문이 사라지고 대화를 하는 두 학생의 모습이 나타난다.

4. 해설자의 설명이 끝나면 다음과 같은 대화를 듣게 된다.

> **Narrator** Now listen to two students as they discuss the announcement.
>
> **M** Oh, great, now we have to come up with more money for next semester.
>
> **W** Yeah, I know, but I can see why. When I first started here, classes were so much smaller than they are now. With this many students, it's hard to get the personal attention you need...
>
> **M** Yeah, I guess you're right. You know, in some classes I can't even get a seat. And I couldn't take the math course I wanted to because it was already full when I signed up.
>
> **W** And the other thing is, well, I am kind of worried about not being able to get a job after I graduate.
>
> **M** Why? I mean you're doing really well in your classes, aren't you?
>
> **W** I'm doing OK, but the facilities here are so limited. There are some great new experiments in microbiology that we can't even do here... there isn't enough equipment in the laboratories, and the equipment they have is out of date. How am I going to compete for jobs with people who have practical research experience? I think the extra tuition will be a good investment.

5. 대화가 끝나면 학생들 사진이 화면에서 사라지고 다음과 같은 문구가 나타난다.

> # Now get ready to answer
> # the question.

6. 이제 컴퓨터 화면에 문제가 나타나고 해설자가 문제를 읽어 준다.

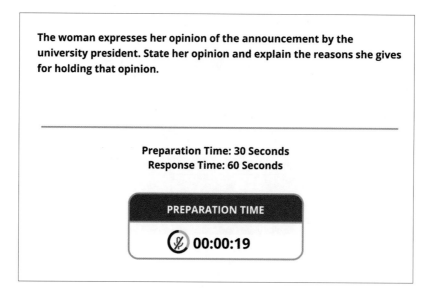

The woman expresses her opinion of the announcement by the university president. State her opinion and explain the reasons she gives for holding that opinion.

Preparation Time: 30 Seconds
Response Time: 60 Seconds

PREPARATION TIME
00:00:19

문제 여학생은 대학 총장의 공지사항에 관해 자신의 견해를 표명한다. 여학생의 견해를 밝히고, 그 견해를 뒷받침하는 근거를 설명하시오.

해설 수업료 인상에 대한 여학생의 의견을 말하고 난 뒤, 여학생이 왜 그렇게 생각하는지 이유를 설명해야 한다. 대화를 들어 보면, 여학생이 총
      장의 발표에 동의하고 있음을 알 수 있다. 수험자는 답변을 할 때 대화와 대학 공지사항에 나온 정보를 연관시켜 말해야 한다.

예제 여학생이 총장의 발표에 동의하고 있으며 대학 측이 수업료를 인상하는 조치가 옳다고 생각한다는 식으로 대답을 시작할 수 있다. 수험자
답안 는 여학생의 의견을 설명할 때, 대학 측이 더 많은 교수를 추가 임용할 수 있기 때문에 등록금 인상이 필요하다고 생각한다고 말할 수 있다.
      또한 강의실이 너무 붐비고, 교수로부터 개별적인 지도를 받기가 어려워졌다고 생각한다는 사실도 언급할 수 있다.
      그리고 마지막으로 실험실 시설을 개선하기 위해서는 투자가 이뤄져야 한다고 생각하고 있는데, 그 이유는 실험실 시설이 낙후돼서 취업
      에 필요한 실습 경험을 쌓기가 어렵기 때문이라는 점을 지적할 수도 있다.

TIP | 화자의 억양, 강세, 단어의 선택에 주의를 기울여 화자가 어떤 입장을 취하고 있는지 파악해 보자. 그러면 화자의 관점을 이해하고 적절한
       답변을 구상하는 데 도움이 될 것이다.

The Integrated Tasks: Question 3_통합형 과제

1. 다양한 분야의 주제가 나온다.

이 문제에 나오는 주제들은 생명과학, 자연과학, 사회과학, 인문과학 등 다양한 분야에서 출제된다. 주제의 성격은 학문적이지만 읽기 지문 및 강의 내용은 어떤 특정 학문 분야의 사전 지식을 요구하지는 않는다. 문제에서 사용된 어휘와 내용들은 수험자들의 전공에 관계없이 이해할 수 있도록 구성된다.

2. 읽기 지문은 이어지는 강의 내용의 배경 정보를 제공한다.

읽기 지문은 대체로 90~115단어 분량으로 이어지는 강의 내용을 이해할 수 있도록 배경지식을 제공한다. 읽기 지문은 주제를 다소 일반적이고 추상적으로 다루는 반면, 강의는 좀 더 구체적인 예들이나 읽기 지문에서 소개된 내용의 적용 사례 등을 제시함으로써 주제를 좀 더 자세하게 다룬다.

3. 강의뿐만 아니라 읽기 지문도 참조해야 질문에 답을 할 수 있다.

1) 강의에 이어서 나오는 문제에 답하기 위해서는 강의뿐만 아니라 읽기 지문도 참조해야 하고, 이 두 자료들로부터 핵심 정보를 종합하여 전달해야 한다.

2) 다음에 나오는 예제는 Question 3의 전형적인 문제다. 이 문제는 가축화하기 쉬운 동물 종의 두 가지 특성을 다룬 읽기 지문으로 시작한다. 이어서 가축화하기 쉬운 동물과, 가축화되지 않은 일반적인 동물의 습성에 대한 교수의 강의가 이어진다. 그리고 이 두 가지 동물의 행동이 가축화의 가능성과 어떻게 관련되는지 설명하라는 문제가 나온다.

TIP | 자신이 좋아하는 주제를 다룬 청취 및 읽기 자료를 찾아 본다. 그 자료들은 서로 유사하거나 상이한 관점을 제시할 수 있다. 읽고 들은 내용을 메모하고 개요를 적은 후 그것을 이용하여 청취 및 읽기 자료들이 제시하는 정보와 개념을 요약하여 말해 본다. 다양한 어휘와 문법 구조를 사용하여 읽고 들은 내용을 자신만의 언어로 표현해 보도록 하자.

1. 다음과 같은 해설자의 말을 듣는다.

Narrator

Now you will read a passage about an academic subject and then listen to a lecture on the same topic. You will then answer a question, using information from both the reading passage and the lecture. You will have 30 seconds to prepare and 60 seconds to speak.

Narrator

Now read the passage about animal domestication. You have 45 seconds to read the passage. Begin reading now.

2. 읽기 지문이 화면에 나타난다. 컴퓨터 화면 상단의 시계가 남은 시간을 나타낸다.

> ### Animal Domestication
>
> For thousands of years, humans have been able to domesticate, or tame, many large mammals that in the wild live together in herds. Once tamed, these mammals are used for agricultural work and transportation. Yet some herd mammals are not easily domesticated.
>
> A good indicator of an animal's suitability for domestication is how protective the animal is of its territory. Nonterritorial animals are more easily domesticated than territorial animals because they can live close together with animals from other herds. A second indicator is that animals with a hierarchical social structure, in which herd members follow a leader, are easy to domesticate, since a human can function as the "leader."

3. 읽기 시간이 끝나면 학생들 앞에 서 있는 교수의 모습이 나타난다.

4. 해설자의 설명이 끝나면 다음과 같은 강의가 이어진다.

Narrator

Now listen to a lecture on this topic in an ecology class.

Professor

So we've been discussing the suitability of animals for domestication... particularly animals that live together in herds. Now, if we take horses, for example... in the wild, horses live in herds that consist of one male and several females and their young. When a herd moves, the dominant male leads, with the dominant female and her young immediately behind him. The dominant female and her young are then followed immediately by the second most important female and her young, and so on. This is why domesticated horses can be harnessed one after the other in a row. They're "programmed" to follow the lead of another horse. On top of that, you often find different herds of horses in the wild occupying overlapping areas—they don't fight off other herds that enter the same territory.

But it's exactly the opposite with an animal like the, uh, the antelope... which... well, antelopes are herd animals too. But unlike horses, a male antelope will fight fiercely to prevent another male from entering its territory during the breeding season; OK—very different from the behavior of horses. Try keeping a couple of male antelopes together in a small space and see what happens. Also, antelopes don't have a social hierarchy—they don't instinctively follow any leader. That makes it harder for humans to control their behavior.

5. 강의가 끝나면 교수의 사진이 사라지고 다음과 같은 문구가 나타난다.

**Now get ready to answer
the question.**

6. 그러고 나서 화면에 문제가 나타나며 해설자가 소리 내어 읽어준다.

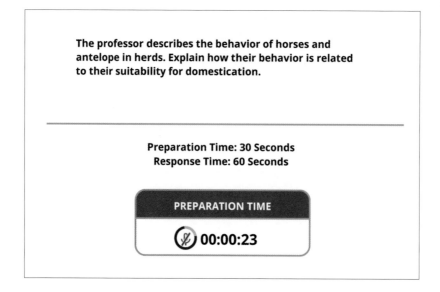

The professor describes the behavior of horses and antelope in herds. Explain how their behavior is related to their suitability for domestication.

Preparation Time: 30 Seconds
Response Time: 60 Seconds

PREPARATION TIME

00:00:23

문제 교수는 무리 생활을 하는 말과 영양의 습성에 관해 설명한다. 이 동물들의 습성이 가축화의 가능성과 어떻게 관련되는지 설명하시오.

해설 수험자는 교수가 강의에서 제시하는 구체적인 정보와 읽기 지문에서 소개된 일반적인 개념을 연결시킬 수 있다. 읽기 지문과 강의에 나오는 모든 정보를 요약하라는 문제가 나오지는 않는다. 그러나 수험자는 답변할 때 읽기 지문을 읽거나 강의를 들은 일이 없는 사람에게 자신의 설명을 이해시킬 수 있을 정도의 충분한 정보를 제공해야 한다.

예제 위계질서를 가지고 있고 영역 다툼을 하지 않는다면 무리 생활을 하는 동물은 쉽게 가축화할 수 있으므로 말이 영양보다 가축화하기 쉽다
답안 는 식으로 대답을 시작할 수 있다. 말의 무리에는 서열이 있기 때문에 상호 간에 지시를 따르려는 경향이 있으므로 인간이 말의 우두머리 역할을 할 수 있다고 설명할 수 있다.
영역을 지키려는 영양의 습성을 말의 습성과 대비시킬 수도 있다. 또 말들과는 달리 수놈 영양들은 함께 있으면 서로 싸우며, 영양들에게는 서열이 없기 때문에 인간이 우두머리가 되어 영양 무리를 통제할 수 없다고 설명할 수 있다.

The Integrated Tasks: Question 4_통합형 과제

Question
4

> Question 4는 학문적인 주제에 관한 교수의 강의 발췌문을 듣고, 이 내용과 관련된 문제에 대해 60초 동안 답변하게 된다. 생명과학, 사회과학, 자연과학, 인문과학 등 다양한 분야의 주제를 다루지만 강의를 이해하고 문제에 답변하기 위해 특정 학문 분야에 관한 사전 지식은 요구되지 않는다.

1. 발췌된 강의는 하나의 주제만 다룬다.

강의 분량은 60~90초 사이로 한 가지 주제를 집중적으로 다룬다. 주로 교수가 어떤 개념을 정의하거나, 어떤 쟁점을 강조하거나 또는 하나의 현상을 소개하는 것으로 강의를 시작한 뒤 이 개념과 관련된 여러 관점들에 대해 논의한다. 대개 강의에 나온 논지나 예들을 사용하여 강의의 주요 개념이나 쟁점들을 설명하라는 문제가 나온다.

2. 강의의 주제는 특정 분야에 한정되지 않는다.

강의는 자연과학, 사회과학, 심리학 등 다양한 분야와 관련된 과정, 방법, 이론, 사상, 또는 현상에 관한 내용이 출제될 수 있다.

1. 수험자는 다음과 같은 해설자의 말을 듣는다.

ex.

Narrator

Now you will listen to a lecture. You will then be asked to summarize the lecture. You will have 20 seconds to prepare and 60 seconds to speak.

2. 학생들 앞에 서 있는 교수의 사진이 화면에 나온다.

3. 그러고 나서 수험자는 다음의 내용을 듣게 된다.

Narrator
Now listen to part of a talk in a United States history class.

Professor
Because the United States is such a large country, it took time for a common national culture to emerge. One hundred years ago there was very little communication among the different regions of the United States. One result of this lack of communication was that people around the United States had very little in common with one another. People in different parts of the country spoke differently, dressed differently, and behaved differently. But connections among Americans began to increase thanks to two technological innovations: the automobile and the radio.

Automobiles began to be mass-produced in the 1920s, which meant they became less expensive and more widely available. Americans in small towns and rural communities now had the ability to travel with ease to nearby cities. They could even take vacations to other parts of the country. The increased mobility provided by automobiles changed people's attitudes and created links that had not existed before. For example, people in small towns began to adopt behaviors, clothes, and speech that were popular in big cities or in other parts of the country.

As more Americans were purchasing cars, radio ownership was also increasing dramatically. Americans in different regions of the country began to listen to the same popular radio programs and musical artists. People repeated things they heard on the radio—some phrases and speech patterns heard in songs and radio programs began to be used by people all over the United States. People also listened to news reports on the radio. They heard the same news throughout the country, whereas in newspapers much news tended to be local. Radio brought Americans together by offering them shared experiences and information about events around the country.

4. 강의가 끝나면 교수의 사진이 사라지고 다음과 같은 문구가 화면에 나타난다.

**Now get ready to answer
the question.**

5. 그리고 나서 문제가 화면에 나타나고 해설자가 소리 내어 읽는다.

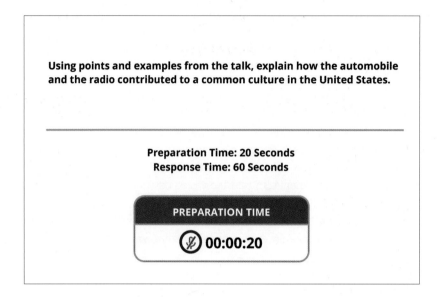

문제 이 강의 내용에 나온 논지와 예를 사용해서 미국의 보편적인 문화 형성에 자동차와 라디오가 어떻게 기여했는지 설명하시오.

해설 약간의 배경 설명을 시작으로, 100년 전 미국에서는 서로 다른 지역에 사는 사람들 간에 교류가 많지 않아 공통된 문화가 없었다고 설명을 한다. 그리고 나서 자동차와 라디오 때문에 이런 상황이 바뀌었으며, 이 두 가지가 어떻게 이런 변화를 야기시켰는지를 설명한 강의 내용을 요약할 수 있다. 강의를 듣지 않은 사람이라도 교수가 설명한 내용을 제대로 이해할 수 있도록 충분히 설명해야 한다.

예제 자동차의 가격이 저렴해지면서 소도시에 사는 사람들이 대도시나 다른 지역으로 여행하기 수월해졌고, 그 결과 사람들은 타지 사람들의
답안 행동과 옷 입는 방식, 말투를 모방하게 되었다는 식으로 대답할 수 있다. 미국의 국민 문화 형성 과정에서 라디오가 했던 역할에 관해 설명할 때는, 라디오가 대중적 인기를 얻게 되자 서로 다른 지역에 사는 사람들이 같은 프로그램과 같은 뉴스를 듣게 되고 말투를 서로 모방하며, 비슷한 경험과 사고 방식을 갖게 되었다는 사실을 지적할 수 있다. 시간이 허용된다면 이렇듯 말투, 옷 입는 방식, 사고 방식이 유사해지면서 미국의 국민 문화가 형성되었다는 결론을 내릴 수 있다.

말하기 영역 채점 기준표

독립형 과제 (Question 1)

4	총평	완결성이 조금 부족하지만 문제가 요구하는 것에 대해 충분히 답변한다. 아주 명료하고, 통일성 있는 답변이다.
	구사력	표현이 유창하고 명확하며, 대체로 속도도 적당하다. 사소한 실수가 있고 발음과 억양에 약간 문제가 있지만 전체적인 의미에는 영향을 끼치지 않는다.
	언어 사용	문법과 어휘를 효과적으로 사용하고 있다. 기본적인 문장 구조와 복잡한 문장 구조 모두 잘 소화하여 매우 자연스러운 답변이 된다. 작은 실수가 있지만 의미를 모호하게 하지는 않는다.
	주제 전개	답변에 일관성이 있고, 과제를 충분히 소화하고 있다. 전반적으로 전개방식이 양호하며 통일성이 있다. 전달하고자 하는 내용 간의 관계가 명확하게 전개되어 있다.
3	총평	문제에 적절하게 답변하였으나 주제의 전개가 불완전하다. 생각을 표현하는 과정에서 실수가 있었으나 대체로 명료하고 일관성이 있으며 유창하게 표현되었다.
	구사력	대체로 명확하고, 자연스럽게 답변하고 있다. 발음과 억양, 끊어 읽기가 다소 취약해 간혹 알아듣기 힘든 부분이 있지만 전체적인 명료성을 해치지는 않는다.
	언어 사용	문법과 어휘를 상당히 자연스럽고 효과적으로 사용하고 있고, 관련 내용들을 일관성 있게 표현하고 있다. 간혹 어휘나 문법을 부정확하게 사용하지만 의사 전달을 심각하게 방해하지는 않는다.
	주제 전개	대체로 일관되고 통일성이 있으며 생각을 적절히 전달한다. 전반적으로 주제의 전개가 다소 미흡하고 상세한 설명과 구체성이 부족하다. 논제들 간의 연결 관계가 명료하지 않은 곳이 종종 눈에 띈다.
2	총평	문제에 적절하게 답변하였으나 주제의 전개가 미흡하다. 의사 전달력이 부족하고 전체적으로 일관성이 결여되어 있으며, 부분적으로 의미가 불분명하기도 하지만 답변 내용을 이해할 수는 있다.
	구사력	전반적으로 알아들을 만하지만 불명확한 발음, 어색한 억양, 끊기는 리듬 때문에 의미가 모호한 곳이 몇 군데 있어서 듣는 사람의 노력이 필요하다.
	언어 사용	문법과 어휘의 사용이 제한적이어서 생각을 충분히 표현하지 못하는 경우가 자주 있다. 전반적으로 가장 기본적인 문장 구조들만 완벽하게 구사한다. 주로 짧거나 일반적인 주장을 펴고 있으며, 논지 간 연결이 단순(계속되는 나열, 접속, 병렬 구조)하고 불명확하다.
	주제 전개	논지를 제시하고 발전시키는 과정이 미흡했으나 제시된 문제에 적절하게 답변한다. 기본적인 생각들은 표현하지만 세부 사실과 근거를 이용한 상세한 설명은 미흡하다.
1	총평	내용면에서나 일관성면에서 매우 미흡하고, 해당 문제에 대한 답변 내용이 부적합하며 이해하기 힘들다.
	구사력	잘못된 발음, 강세, 억양 때문에 알아듣기가 어렵다. 말이 자꾸 끊기거나, 너무 짧게 말하며 중간에 중단하거나 주저하는 경우가 빈번하다.
	언어 사용	문법과 어휘 구사 능력이 상당히 부족해 말하고자 하는 내용 및 내용간 연결 관계를 표현하는 데 어려움을 겪는다. 미리 연습한 표현이나 상투적인 표현에 지나치게 의존하는 경향이 있다.
	주제 전개	적절한 내용을 말하지 못하며, 매우 기본적인 개념 이상의 내용을 표현하지 못한다. 답변을 완성하지 못하거나 제시된 문제를 되풀이하는 데 지나치게 의존한다.
0		답변을 하지 않거나 답변이 주제와 관련이 없는 경우

통합형 과제 (Questions 2, 3, 4)

4	총평	완결성이 조금 부족하지만 문제가 요구하는 것에 충실하게 답변한다. 의사표현이 상당히 명료하며, 지속적이고 통일성이 있다.
	구사력	발음과 억양에서 약간의 실수가 있지만 대체로 명확하고 유창하다. 정보를 기억해 내는 부분에서는 말하는 속도가 달라진다. 전체적으로 매우 명료하게 표현한다.
	언어 사용	기본적인 문장 구조와 복잡한 문장 구조 모두 잘 소화하여 통일성 있고 효과적으로 표현하고, 어휘 선택도 전반적으로 적절하다. 작은 실수가 있지만 의미를 모호하게 하지는 않는다.
	주제 전개	말하고자 하는 내용을 명확하게 전개하고, 문제에서 요구하는 적절한 정보를 전달하고 있다. 사소한 실수나 생략이 눈에 띄지만 세부 사실을 적절히 묘사하고 있다.

3	총평	질문에 적절히 답변하였으나 전개가 충분하지 않다. 대체로 명료하고 일관성이 있으며 표현이 유창하지만, 생각을 표현하는 과정에서 눈에 띄는 실수를 한다.
	구사력	대체로 명확하고 유창한 편이나 발음, 억양, 끊어 읽기가 불완전하여 알아듣기 힘든 부분이 몇 군데 있다.
	언어 사용	문법과 어휘를 상당히 자연스럽고, 효과적으로 사용하고 있으며, 적절한 내용들을 매우 일관되게 표현하고 있다. 부정확한 어휘, 문법, 문장 구조를 사용하였으나 심각하지는 않다.
	주제 전개	대체로 일관성 있게 정보를 전달하고 있다. 그러나 내용면에서 불완전하거나 부정확하고 구체성이 결여된 부분이나, 생각의 전개가 순조롭지 못한 부분이 눈에 띈다.

2	총평	관련된 정보가 다소 누락되거나 부정확하지만 제시된 문제에 어느 정도 답변하고 있다. 명료한 부분도 있지만 가끔 알아듣기 어렵거나 내용 전개에 일관성이 없어서 의미를 모호하게 만들기도 한다.
	구사력	때로는 명료하지만 발음, 억양, 끊어 읽기에 문제가 있어 알아듣기가 상당히 힘들다. 답변에 일관성이 없다. 의미가 명료하지 않아서 내용을 이해하기 힘든 부분이 있다.
	언어 사용	어휘와 문법의 사용이 제한적이다. 일부 복잡한 문장 구조가 사용되고는 있지만 대체로 실수가 동반된다. 그 결과 연결 관계가 제한적이거나 부적절하다.
	주제 전개	완결성이 확실히 부족하다. 논제가 빠져 있고, 핵심적인 생각에 대해 모호하게 언급하거나, 중요한 정보를 잘 전개하지 못한다. 대체로, 표현된 생각들이 연계성과 일관성이 부족하기 때문에 답변 내용을 이해하기 어렵다.

1	총평	답변 내용이 미흡하거나 일관성이 상당히 부족하고, 과제와 연관성도 미미하여 전반적으로 이해하기 힘들다.
	구사력	발음과 억양에 문제가 있어서 알아듣기 상당히 힘들고 의미가 모호하다. 말의 흐름이 순조롭지 못하거나 너무 짧게 말하며 중간에 자주 머뭇거리거나 말을 중단한다.
	언어 사용	문법과 어휘의 수준이 낮아 말하고자 하는 내용 및 내용 간 연결 관계를 제한적으로밖에 표현하지 못한다. 이 수준의 답변은 단순히 단어나 짧은 표현에 의존하여 의미를 전달하려 한다.
	주제 전개	적절한 내용을 전달하지 못하고 있다. 개념들이 부정확하거나 모호하거나 반복되고 있다(제시된 문제 반복 포함).

0	답변을 하지 않거나 답변이 주제와 관련이 없는 경우

Frequently Asked Questions

🖉 왜 말하기 영역이 필요한가?

TOEFL iBT®의 시행 목적은 학문적인 상황에서 영어로 효과적으로 의사소통 할 수 있는지를 평가하는 것이다. 말하기는 듣기, 읽기, 쓰기와 함께 중요한 의사소통 능력의 하나이고, TOEFL iBT® 평가에서 중요한 위치를 차지하고 있다.

🖉 말하기 영역에는 왜 통합형 과제가 사용되는가?

읽기와 듣기 지문을 말하기와 결합해서 출제하는 통합형 과제는 학생들이 대학에서 학업 성취도를 높이기 위해서는 읽기, 듣기, 말하기, 쓰기 네 가지 영역을 통합할 수 있는 능력을 갖출 필요가 있다는 인식에 따른 것이다.

🖉 통합형 과제에 나오는 읽기와 듣기 지문의 분량은 어느 정도인가?

분량은 다양하지만 대체로 짧고 난이도도 높지 않다. 읽기 지문은 약 90~115단어이고 듣기 지문은 대체로 60~90초 길이다. 읽기와 듣기 지문들은 수험자가 말하기 문제에 답변하기 위해 사용할 수 있는 명확하고, 이해 가능한 정보를 제공하기 위한 것이다.

🖉 말하기 영역 테스트 중에 메모를 해도 되나?

그렇다. 말하기 영역 테스트 중 언제라도 메모가 가능하다. 읽기 지문을 읽거나, 대화나 강의를 듣거나, 대답을 준비하는 동안 모두 메모가 가능하다. 대화나 강의를 듣고 메모를 하는 동안 모든 내용을 다 받아 적어서는 안된다. 그렇게 하면 중요한 정보를 놓칠 수 있다. 답변을 준비하는 동안 말할 내용을 미리 다 쓰려고 해서도 안된다. 답변 전체를 쓸 시간도 없을 뿐더러, 준비 시간은 메모한 것을 검토하고 생각을 정리하는 데 할애해야 한다.

🖉 답변은 어떻게 채점되나?

각각의 답변은 채점자와 ETS 자동 채점 엔진이 말하기 영역 채점 기준표(본책 115~116페이지)를 사용하여 채점한다. 채점자는 수험자의 답변을 듣고 주제 전개, 구사력, 언어 사용 능력 등을 채점 기준표를 이용해 채점한다. *SpeechRater®*는 주로 언어 사용 능력과 구사력을 채점 기준표를 기준으로 측정한다.

🖉 말하기 점수의 총점은 어떻게 결정되나?

채점자가 채점한 점수와 *SpeechRater* 기계가 채점한 점수를 합산하여 가중치를 최적으로 적용해 원점수를 산출한다. 이 점수를 환산점수 0-30으로 변환한다. 환산된 점수는 수험자가 요청한 기관으로 통보된다.

실수가 점수에 어떤 영향을 주나?

채점자는 수험자가 실수를 얼마나 많이 했는지에 초점을 맞추지 않고, 답변의 전체적인 수준을 채점한다. 사소한 실수가 있더라도 고득점을 받을 수 있다.

답변을 끝낼 시간이 부족할 때는 어떻게 해야 하나?

얼마나 많은 정보를 전달하느냐 하는 것만큼 얼마나 명확하고 일관되게 정보를 전달하느냐 하는 것도 중요하다는 것을 기억하자. 따라서 말하려고 했던 내용을 남은 시간 동안 다 말하지 못할 것 같다고 해서 부자연스럽게 빠른 속도로 말하는 것은 피해야 한다. 시간을 측정해 가면서 연습한다면 많은 도움이 될 것이다.

시간이 다 되기 전에 답변을 끝내면 어떻게 해야 하나?

시간이 다 되기 전에 답변이 끝나면 답변을 좀 더 완벽하게 하기 위해 어떤 정보를 추가로 말할지 생각해 볼 수도 있다. 시간이 남았을 때 이미 말한 것을 되풀이하는 것은 바람직하지 않다. 그보다는 어느 부분을 좀 더 명확하고 상세하게 이야기할까, 또는 답변을 좀 더 완벽하게 만들기 위해 어떤 말을 더 할까를 생각하자. 시간을 측정해 가면서 연습한다면 많은 도움이 될 것이다.

앞으로 되돌아가서 답변을 수정할 수 있는가?

안 된다. 이미 녹음이 끝난 뒤에 되돌아가서 재녹음하는 것은 불가능하다. 답변은 완벽할 필요는 없다는 사실을 기억하자. 어떤 부분을 틀리게 말했다면 마치 수험자가 모국어를 사용할 때 실수를 바로잡는 것처럼 주저하지 말고 실수를 정정하거나, 실수를 무시하고 답변을 계속할 수도 있다. 대신 나머지 부분을 가능한 명료하고, 일관되고, 정확하게 말하면 된다.

강세와 발음이 점수에 어떤 영향을 주는가?

모든 수험자의 강세와 발음은 정도의 차이는 있겠지만 원어민과 같은 수준은 될 수 없다. 실력이 월등한 수험자도 실수가 있으며, 답변의 명료성을 해치지 않는다면 점수에 불리하게 작용하지 않는다.

말하기 영역 점수 향상 전략

1) 말하기 영역 실전 연습문제를 풀 때 자신의 답변을 녹음하여 주의 깊게 들어 보자. 그리고 자신의 답변을 점검해 볼 수 있는 다음과 같은 평가 기준을 만들자.
   · 문제의 요구대로 과제를 수행했는가?
   · 명확하게 말했는가?
   · 문법적 오류는 없었는가?
   · 단어는 정확히 사용했는가?
   · 나의 생각을 명확하고 적절하게 정리했는가?
   · 완결된 대답을 했는가?
   · 시간을 효과적으로 사용했는가?
2) 평가가 끝나면 답변의 어느 곳을 수정해야 할지에 대해 생각해 보고 답변을 재녹음해 본다. 두 가지 녹음을 비교해 보고 추가로 수정이 필요한지 판단한다.
3) 자신의 강점과 약점을 분석한다. 잘 할 수 있는 부분과 그렇지 않은 부분을 이해하고, 왜 그런지 이유를 생각해 본다.
4) 연습 일지를 기록해 실력 향상을 점검해 볼 수 있다. 또는 친구나 교수로부터 평가를 받아볼 수도 있다. 연습한 것을 녹음해서 스스로 평가할 때에는, 말하는 속도를 체크해 본다. 연습이 하나씩 끝날 때마다 스스로 다음과 같은 질문을 해 보자.
   · 너무 빨리 말했는가?
   · 너무 느리게 말했는가?
   · 중간에 말을 너무 자주 멈췄는가?

■ 시험 당일을 위한 TIP
   1) 통합형 과제에서는 필기가 허용된다는 점을 기억한다.
   2) 문제의 의도가 무엇인지 정확하게 이해하기 위해 지시 사항을 주의 깊게 듣는다.
   3) 준비시간을 가능한 효과적으로 사용한다. 전달하고자 하는 중심 내용들을 단순명료하고 체계적인 방식으로 대답할 수 있도록 준비한다.
   4) 말하라는 지시가 있기 전에는 답변을 시작하지 않는다.
   5) 마이크에 대고 적당한 볼륨으로 말한다. 입을 마이크에 직접 대거나 너무 작은 소리로 말하면, 채점자는 수험자가 하는 말을 이해하기 어려울 수도 있다.

Chapter 5

Writing Section

Writing Section

이 장의 구성_ TOEFL iBT® 쓰기 문제 2가지 유형
유형별 예제 답안과 작문 요령
유형별 채점 기준표
점수 향상 전략

TOEFL iBT® 쓰기 영역에는 통합형과 학술 토론에 관한 쓰기의 두 가지 과제가 있다. 통합형 과제는 동일한 주제의 지문을 읽고 강의를 들은 후, 읽고 들은 내용을 관련지어 종합해 답안을 작성한다. 학술 토론에 관한 쓰기 과제는 제시된 문제에 맞게 자신의 생각을 정리하는 논리적인 에세이를 작성해야 한다.

쓰기 영역에 대한 소개

TOEFL iBT® 쓰기 영역은 통합형 과제와 학술 토론에 관한 쓰기 과제로 구성된다. 실제 영어권 대학에서 공부할 때 필요한 능력을 평가하고자 하는 것이며, 읽기 자료와 듣기 자료에 제시되는 내용도 이 취지에 걸맞게 강의 내용을 바탕으로 구성된다.

문제 유형

1. The Integrated Writing Task_통합형 과제: 지문 읽고 강의 들은 후 요약하기

강의는 보통 읽기 지문에 제시된 정보에 반하는 내용이 나온다. 강의의 내용을 요약할 때 유의할 점은 다음과 같다.

– 그 내용이 읽기 지문에 제시된 특정 내용에 어떻게 이의를 제기하는지/의구심을 제기하는지/반대하는지/응답하는지 설명한다. (반대 또는 모순)
– 강의의 내용이 읽기 지문에 제시된 특정 이론들에 어떻게 이의를 제기하는지 설명한다. (이론과 이론의 약점)
– 강의의 내용이 읽기 지문에 언급된 특정 문제들에 대해 어떻게 해결책을 제시하는지 설명한다. (문제와 해결책)
– 강의의 내용이 읽기 지문에 제안된 특정 해결책들에 대해 어떻게 의심을 제기하는지 설명한다. (해결책과 해결책의 약점)

2. Writing for an Academic Discussion_학술 토론에 관한 쓰기 과제: 어떤 주제에 관해 교수가 게시한 질문과 다른 학생들이 이미 토론에 기여해 답변한 온라인 토론 글을 읽은 후 에세이 작성하기

영역의 두 번째 과제는 학술적 토론에 관한 쓰기 과제이다. 수험자는 교수가 어떤 주제에 관해 질문을 게시하고 몇몇 학생들이 의견을 답해 놓은 온라인 토론 글을 읽게 된다. 수험자는 토론에 참여하여 답안을 쓰게 된다. 교수의 질문과 학생들의 글을 읽고 자신의 글을 쓰는 데 주어지는 시간은 10분이다.

The Integrated Writing Task_통합형 과제

학문적 주제에 관한 지문을 읽고 동일 주제에 관련된 강의를 듣게 된다. 이어서 강의에 나온 요점들을 요약하고, 그것이 독해 지문의 특정 요점들과 어떤 관계가 있는지 설명하라는 문제가 나온다.

1. 다음과 같은 독해 지문이 컴퓨터 화면에 나타나며, 지문을 읽는 시간은 3분이다.

Vitrified Forts

A number of hill forts (fortified defensive structures) built in Scotland during the Middle Ages have an unusual feature: they are what researchers call "vitrified," which means that their stones have been exposed to extreme heat and have melted or fused together, becoming hard and glass-like. Several theories have been offered to explain how and why the forts were vitrified.

One theory holds that vitrification was part of a religious or ceremonial ritual. The ancient myths and folktales of Scotland are full of references to cities and castles made of glass, so glass must have had some special significance to the people of the area. Vitrification could have been their way of trying to create glass castles. Perhaps they believed that the vitrified forts had supernatural powers or benefits.

According to a second theory, the stones of the fort walls became vitrified accidentally by fires set by people who attacked the forts. Supporters of this theory point out that fire was used as a weapon to ignite the wood beams that were used as structural support for the fort walls. Attackers used flaming arrows and other projectiles in an attempt to start a fire. As the wood beams were being burned up by the fire, the heat from the fire could have vitrified the stone parts of the walls.

Other researchers think that it is more probable that the forts' builders purposefully vitrified the walls in order to strengthen them. When a wall becomes vitrified, the stones fuse together so that there are no gaps or openings between them. In other words, vitrification produces a solid, continuous wall surface. This makes it very hard for arrows to penetrate the walls, and so this could have been an effective defensive measure.

While the theories about vitrified forts sound convincing, unfortunately none of them adequately explain the phenomenon.

2. 지문을 읽은 후 다음과 같은 강의를 듣는다.

Narrator
Now listen to part of a lecture on the topic you just read about.

Professor

First, glass may have had special significance for the people of ancient Scotland. But a problem with the reading's theory is that by the time most of the forts were built, Christianity had taken hold in the area. By 900 C.E., when the last forts were being constructed, Christianity had been adopted by most people in the area, to the point that the native religious and ceremonial traditions of the area were almost completely wiped out. And the Christian religion as it was practiced at that time did not attribute any supernatural or magical powers to glass.

Second, re-creations of the vitrification process by scientists have shown that the temperatures needed for vitrification are extremely high—over one thousand degrees Celsius.

A fire that was started by attackers would never reach this temperature. To reach it, a fire would have to be enclosed, blown toward the wall, and maintained, like fires in pottery ovens. There just wasn't enough wood used as structural support for the walls for this to happen. The attackers could not have maintained a fire that was hot enough to vitrify stone.

Third, it's true that the glassy substance produced by vitrification is strong, but it's also very brittle, meaning it can shatter on impact. Scottish defenders knew that the strongest forts are flexible, not brittle— that's why, when building forts, they often tended to pack the stones loosely together. Loosely packed stones would have allowed the walls to bend slightly and thus to absorb the impact of weapons beating against the walls. The brittle walls created by vitrification are actually easier to break down than non-vitrified walls are, so it hardly seems likely that vitrification was deliberately done by fort defenders wanting to strengthen their fort against attack.

3. 강의가 종료되면 독해 지문이 다시 나타나고, 지시 사항과 작문 과제가 제시된다.

> You have **20 minutes** to plan and write your response. Your response will be judged on the basis of the quality of your writing and on how well your response presents the points in the lecture and their relationship to the reading passage. Typically, an effective response will contain a minimum of 150 words.

Summarize the points made in the lecture, being sure to explain how they challenge the specific theories proposed in the reading passage.

Sample Scored Responses_예제 답안

Score 5 Response

The lecture suggests that theories regarding the origin of the vitrification of forts in the passage are all inadequate.

The first theory in the passage, which proposes that vitrification was part of a religious ritual to create glass castles, is deemed highly improbable by the lecturer because by the time these forts were vitrified, Christianity has well-spread into Scotland. Christianity does not attribute any supernatural power over glass or glass forts, which the first theory in the passage states as the main reason for vitrification. Moreso, the lecturer also indicated that by the time the last Scottish fort was vitrified in 900 C.E., most people in the area had adopted Christianity and old religious customs have almost been entirely wiped-out.

The second theory in the passage, which states that the forts have been vitrified due to acciddental fires set by attackers, also seems impossible to the lecturer. This is due to the fact that vitrification requires an extremely high temperature. Fire produced by soldiers at the time did not even come close to the required temperature. Even if it did, the fire needed to be enclosed, blown, and maintained over the stone walls of the fort for it to be vitrified. There was not enough wood available at the fort for this to happen.

The third theory in the passage states that vitrification was done to strengthen the walls of the fort. The lecturer opposes this final theory by claiming that vitrification causes stone to be brittle. Every Scottish war expert at the time would have known that brittle forts were bad as they are easier to break down over impact. Flexible walls were preffered. In this way, the lecturer challenged the last theory used in the reading passage.

Rater Comments

읽기 지문에 제시된 이론들에 이의를 제기하는 강의의 요점을 훌륭하게 제시했으므로 5점을 받을 수 있었다.

- ▬ 강의의 논지가 명확하게 제시되었으며, 모든 중요한 추가 설명이 포함되어 있다. 각 단락을 시작할 때 읽기 지문에서 제시된 이론을 간단히 요약한 후 강의에서 해당 이론에 어떻게 이의를 제기하는지 설명한다. 이는 글을 구성하는 매우 효과적인 방법이다.
- ▬ 몇 가지 작은 실수, 예를 들어 to glass를 over glass로 쓴다거나, old religious customs have almost been entirely wiped-out은 old religious customs had been almost entirely wiped out으로 써야 맞지만, 이런 실수는 전반적으로 드문 편이고, 뛰어난 영어 실력을 가진 비영어권 사람이 에세이의 초안을 제출할 때 흔히 보이는 실수에 해당한다.

Score 4 Response

The lecture main purpose is to cast doubt into the original theories that explained why the walls built in Scotland during the Middle Ages were vitrified.

First, the lecturer describes why vitrification could not be a ceremonial ritual as it is stated in the reading. The reason he uses is that, by the time that the last wall was constructed (around ninth century), christianity was already wiped out the rest of the religions. Christians do not attribute any magical powers to glass. Hence, there would be no reason to use vitrification as a part of a religious ritual.

After that, the lecturer explains that the temperatures needed by the rock to vitrify were really high. In order to get this temperature, a fire should be enclosed and maintained for a while. In the forts there were no enough wood to get that temperture, even if it would get close enough an open air fire can not maintain that temperature for a long time. That is why vitrification could not have been originated accidentally by fire as the reading passage states.

At last, it is not probable that defenders vitrify their walls on purpose because the material could break with impacts. Obviously, this is not intended for a wall, in fact, some walls were made in a way that they can bend to support the impacts.

Rater Comments

전반적으로, 과제에서 요구하는 내용과 대부분의 중요한 정보를 잘 전달하고 있다. 그러나 가끔씩 정확성이 떨어지므로, 이 답안은 4점을 받았다.

- 이 답안은 단어 선택에 문제가 있다. 예를 들어, 첫 단락에 christianity was already wiped out the rest of the religions라는 표현이 나오는데, 강의를 듣지 않은 사람에게는 '기독교가 다른 종교들을 소멸시켰다고 말한 것인가?' 아니면 '다른 종교들에 의해 소멸된 것인가?'라는 의문을 갖게 한다.
- 세 번째 단락에서는 어떤 곳에서 불이 정말 뜨거워지려면 enclosed되어야 한다고 말하고, 다음 문장에서는 open air fire에 대해 언급한다. 이 두 가지 아이디어가 어떻게 의미가 통하는지 명확하지 않다. 마지막 단락에서는 material(물질)이 부서질 수 있다고 지적하지만, 무엇이 물질인지 확실하지 않다(아마도 유리화된 바위를 말하는 것일 텐데, 그렇다면 더 명확하게 표현해야 한다).
- 마지막 문장에서 필자는 impacts를 support하는 walls에 대해 말하는데, 의도된 단어는 아마도 resisting(저항)일 것이다. there were no enough wood와 같은 작지만 눈에 띄는 문법적 오류들도 있다(no는 not으로 바뀌어야 한다).

Score 3 Response

There are three theorie of virtifications of the stones used to build some of the hill forts in scotland. The theories in the lecture were challenged in the reading passage.

First theory according to the passage was that virtifying the stones to a glassy material was a part of a religious ritual, But the lecture opposed this point by mentioning that during that time all religious beleives were all wieped out and didn't exist anymore !!

Second theory mentioned in the passage was that the vitrivaction of the stones happened accidentally by predatores who used to attack the forts using fires, But the professor in the lecture mentioned that the current researches don't approve this theory because the tempreture needed to vitrify the stone should be very high and the stone should be exposed to it for a long time and such thing would not be possible to happen using the traditional methods of predatores fire attacks back in those days.

The third and last theory mentioned in the reading passage was that the people who built the forts did this stone vitrification to a more glassy structre on purpose !! why ?? to mak the stone more stronger so it would provide more protection, However the professor in the lecture contracted this theroy by pointing out that actually although vitrifying the stone to a glassy material will make it fuse together which might make it appear stronger, but actually it will make it more brittle, loose and easy to break down.

Rater Comments

이 답안은 문제가 요구하는 내용을 다루고 있고 전반적으로 잘 구성되었지만, 4점을 받은 답안에서 나타난 문제들보다 더 심각한 문제가 있다.

▨ 우선, 두 번째 단락에서 강의와 읽기 지문의 관계를 왜곡한다. 사실, 강의는 읽기 지문에서 소개된 이론들에 이의를 제기하는 것이지 부정하고 반대하는 것이 아니다. 첫 번째 이론에 대해 언급할 때, 필자는 all religious beleives were all wieped out(모든 종교적 신념이 사라졌다)라고 말한다. 이는 (오류와 오타를 무시하더라도) 기존의 신앙들이 기독교에 의해 대체되었다는 강의의 주장을 크게 과장한 것이다.

▨ 세 번째 단락에서는 '요새를 공격한 predatores'라고 언급한다. predator는 보통 포식 동물을 의미하며, 인간 전사를 의미하지 않는다. 따라서 필자는 요새가 동물에 의해 공격당했다는 잘못된 인상을 준다.

▨ 용법과 문법 오류도 자주 눈에 띄는데 예를 들면, 마지막 단락의 more stronger(more가 없어야 함), contracted(contradicted를 잘못 표현), 그리고 although와 but을 모두 사용하는 복합 문장(while만 사용해야 함) 등이 있다. 이 답안은 3점을 받게 되는 여러 특징을 잘 보여준다.

Score 2 Response

In the lecture the professor made several points about the reasons why the stones in Scotland have been vitrified.

But the lecture cast doubt on the reading.

First of all the professor talks about religious ceremonies. But after some researches we know that the people didn't believe in supernatural power.

On the other hand the reading argues that the vitrification was part of such an ceremonial ritual and that the people of the area believed in supernatural power.

The second point in the reading is that they thougt that the stones became vitrified because of fire.

But the professor in the lecture offeres that the walls were too high to fire them down. So the attacers couldn't use fire to enter the village.

The last point in the reading is that they vitrified the stones to strengthen them. In contrast the professor argues that the walls were britterly. If you vitrifie the wall it is very easy to braek them down.

To sum up the lecture cast doubt on the reading because all the points are different.

Rater Comments

답안은 강의에 나온 몇 가지 관련 정보를 전달하지만, 중요한 부분을 크게 생략하거나 왜곡하며, 주요 부분에서 의미를 불명확하게 만드는 언어적 실수를 보이고 있다. 전형적인 2점 수준의 답안이다.

- 강의의 첫 번째 주장을 전달할 때, people didn't believe in supernatural power(사람들이 초자연을 믿지 않았다)라고 말하고 있는데, 이는 기독교, 다른 종교, 지역 신앙이 변화했다는 중요한 세부 정보를 완전히 무시한다.
- 두 번째 주장에 관해서는 the walls were too high to fire them down이라고 했는데, 이는 이해하기 어려우며, 어떤 의미를 부여하려 해도 강의에서 말한 바를 분명히 전달하지 않는다.
- 세 번째 주장을 요약할 때는, 유리화된 벽이 very easy to braek ... down(매우 쉽게 부술 수 있다)이라고 언급했는데, 강의의 요지를 전달하고 있는 것은 맞지만 추가 설명이 없다. 그리고 britterly가 brittle을 의미한다는 것을 쉽게 알아채기 힘들다. 대다수의 독자가 이해하지 못할 것이기 때문에 추가 설명으로 뒷받침되지 않는다.

Score 1 Response

in the Scotland during the mild age they call " vitrified" . in the past their ancient think a glass need made sothing special in their world. so they created a lot of glass and they think glass have a magic or power and vitrified could have been their way of trying to create glass castles that is the first theory.

Second they think the forrt wall become accidenttally by a fire set by a people who attacked the forts. so they support use a wepond is the wood beam because that can destroy the stucture of the forts wall because the the wood beam can be burn up by the fire. so the heat from the fire could have vitrified the stone parts of the walls.

Scotland make the vitrified very important with their life they think it can protect from everything and vitrified will give them have more powers. So that why in Scotland they have a number of hill forts build in the structure

Rater Comments

이 답안에서 필자는 읽기 지문의 일부를 요약하려 하고 있다. 문법과 용법에 많은 오류가 있으며, 의미는 종종 흐려진다. 그러나 가장 중요한 것은 강의로부터의 정보가 전혀 포함되어 있지 않다는 점이다. 혹여 이 읽기 지문의 요약이 더 완전하고 오류가 적다 해도, 1점보다 더 높은 점수는 받을 수 없다. 강의에서 나온 관련성 있고 중요한 정보를 전달하는 것이 1점보다 많은 점수를 받는 필수 요소임을 기억하자.

통합형 과제 채점 기준표

SCORE	DESCRIPTION
5	이 수준의 답안은 강의의 중요한 논지를 잘 선택하여 이를 읽기 지문의 내용과 연결시켜, 일관되고 정확하게 나타낸다. 간혹 어법상의 실수가 있기도 하지만 내용을 이해하는 데는 아무런 지장을 주지 않는다.
4	이 수준의 답안은 전반적으로 강의의 중요한 정보를 선택하여 이를 읽기 지문의 내용과 연결해서 일관되고 정확하게 잘 나타낸다. 일부 강의 내용이 누락되거나, 부정확하거나, 모호하게 표현되지만 심각한 수준은 아니다. 사소한 어법상의 오류가 자주 눈에 띄어도 표현의 명확성과 개념의 연결에서 가끔 실수가 있는 정도인 경우에 한하여 이 수준의 점수를 받는다.
3	이 수준의 답안은 강의의 일부 중요한 정보가 포함되었고, 읽기 지문과 어느 정도 관련 있는 내용을 전달하지만 다음 중 하나 또는 그 이상의 특징을 나타낸다. · 전체적으로 답안이 과제를 올바르게 파악하고 있는 것으로 보이지만 강의의 요점과 읽기 지문의 요점 사이의 관계를 단지 막연하거나 포괄적으로 또는 애매하거나 다소 부정확하게 전달하고 있다. · 강의의 중요한 핵심 내용 중 하나가 빠져 있다. · 강의나 읽기 지문의 일부 핵심 내용 또는 그 요점들 간의 연결 관계가 불완전하거나 부정확하다. · 어법이나 문법상의 오류가 잦거나 개념 및 전후 관계를 전달할 때 눈에 띄게 모호한 표현이나 분명하지 않은 의미가 사용되었다.
2	이 수준의 답안은 일부 강의 내용을 담고 있지만 어법상 중대한 오류를 범하거나 강의 내용과 읽기 지문을 연결할 때 중요한 개념들이 누락되거나 부정확하게 표현된다. 이 수준의 답안은 다음 중 하나 또는 그 이상의 특징을 포함한다. · 강의와 읽기 지문 간의 전반적인 연결 관계가 상당 부분 잘못 전개되었거나 완전히 누락되었다. · 강의의 주요 내용들이 상당 부분 왜곡되거나 누락되었다. · 주요 연결부의 전후 관계 또는 의미가 상당 부분 모호하거나 읽기 지문이나 강의 내용의 이해를 방해하는 어법상의 오류나 표현들이 있다.
1	이 수준의 답안은 다음 중 하나 또는 그 이상의 특징을 나타낸다. · 강의의 중요한 내용이나 관련된 내용을 거의 또는 전혀 전달하지 못한다. · 어휘 수준이 너무 낮아 의미를 전달하지 못한다.
0	이 수준의 답안은 읽기 지문의 문장을 단순히 베끼거나 주제를 제대로 이해하지 못하며 때로 주제와 무관한 내용이 포함된다. 답란이 공백인 경우도 0점 처리된다.

통합형 과제 점수 향상 전략

■ 읽기 지문을 읽을 때

1) 연습장에 노트 필기를 한다.
2) 읽기 지문의 주제를 파악한다. 주제는 어떤 정책이나 관행 또는 쟁점에 대한 특정한 입장일 수 있다. 혹은 어떤 과정이나 절차가 진행되는 방식이나, 자연 현상에 관한 일반적인 가설을 제기하는 것과 관련될 수도 있다.
3) 주제가 어떻게 전개되는지 살펴본다.
4) 읽기 지문의 내용이 기억나지 않을까 봐 걱정하지 말 것. 답안 작성시 읽기 지문이 컴퓨터 화면에 다시 나온다.
5) 주제를 뒷받침하거나 상반된 내용이 나오면 필기한다. 주제는 보통 세 가지 요점으로 전개된다.

■ 듣기 지문을 들을 때

1) 연습장에 노트 필기를 한다.
2) 읽기 지문의 논지와 상충되는 정보, 사례, 설명을 주의해서 듣는다.

■ 답안을 작성할 때

1) 원한다면 헤드셋을 벗어도 되며, 통합형 문제가 끝나면 헤드셋이 필요없다.
2) 답안을 작성하기 전에 지문을 훑고난 뒤, 필기한 것을 참고하여 쓰고자 하는 중심 내용을 바탕으로 간략한 개요를 작성한다. 이 개요를 연습장에 적거나 답란에 바로 타자하고 답안을 작성할 때 이를 문장이나 문단으로 바꿔 쓰는 방법도 있다.
3) 통합형 과제는 응시자의 의견을 말하는 것이 아님을 기억해야 한다. 문제는 듣기 내용의 논지와 읽기 지문의 논지가 어떤 관계인지 묻는 것이다.
4) 완전한 문장으로 답안을 쓴다. 답안을 가장 잘 구성하는 방법은 독해 지문과 강의에 나오는 주제를 설명하는 간단한 소개 단락을 쓰고 읽기 지문의 각 요점을 요약한 후 해당 강의 내용이 어떻게 대응하거나 관련되는지 설명하는 몇 개(일반적으로 세 개)의 본문 단락을 작성하는 것이다.
5) 강의 내용에서 중요한 정보를 취하여 이를 읽기 지문의 내용에 연결시켜 일관되고 정확하게 표현해야 한다.
6) 분량은 최소한 150단어를 포함해야 한다. 이는 최소한의 기준으로, 많은 고득점 답안이 더 많은 단어로 이루어져 있다. 주어진 과제를 해결하는 한 답변 길이에 상한 제한은 없다.
7) 읽기 지문에 나오는 말을 그대로 베껴서 답안을 작성한 경우에는 0점 처리되며 읽기 지문의 내용에 대해서만 답을 쓰면 1점을 받는다. 고득점을 위해서는 강의의 요점들과 읽기 지문의 구체적인 요점들을 연결시켜 최선을 다해 답안을 작성해야 한다.

채점이 이루어지는 방식

채점자들은 내용의 완성도 및 정확성, 구성, 그리고 언어 사용이라는 세 가지 주요 측면에 주목한다. 내용의 완성도 및 정확성은 고득점 답안의 가장 중요한 특징이다. 이 쓰기 과제에서는 강의에서 제시된 내용을 요약하고, 이것이 읽기 지문과 어떤 관계를 가지는지 설명해야 한다. 전개의 정확성을 평가할 때, 채점자들은 수험자가 강의에서 중요한 정보를 얼마나 잘 선택하고, 명확하고 정확하게 제시하며, 읽기 지문에 담긴 정보와의 관계를 얼마나 잘 설명하는지 살펴본다. 강의에서 가장 중요한 정보만이 아니라, 주요 세부 사항들을 모두 포함하는 것이 중요하다. 즉, 주요 강의 내용을 뒷받침하는 모든 정보가 답안에 포함되어야 한다. 강의를 요약해야 하는 것은 맞지만, 그 요약에서 강의의 주요 세부 사항이 빠져서는 안 된다는 뜻이다. 강의의 중요한 세부 사항을 생략하면 낮은 점수를 받을 수 있다. 자신의 말로 강의를 요약할 때는, 복잡하거나 미묘한 내용도 최대한 명확하게 표현해야 한다. 정확성도 마찬가지다. 답안에서 강의의 주요 세부 사항이나 견해를 잘못 전달하면 낮은 점수를 받을 수 있다. 마지막으로, 강의의 정보가 읽기 지문의 정보와 어떻게 관련되는지(보통 상반됨) 설명해야 한다. 이 관계를 설명하지 않거나 잘못된 설명을 한다면 받는 점수는 낮아질 것이다.

답안은 또한 잘 구성되어야 한다. 어떤 독자도 처음부터 끝까지 쉽게 읽고 주요 논지를 이해하고, 서로 어떻게 뒷받침되고 관련되는가를 이해할 수 있도록 정보를 제시해야 한다. 글을 단락별로 구성하도록 하고, 도입 단락에는 읽기 지문의 주제와 해당 주제에 대해 강의에서 어떻게 말하는지를 포함시킨다. 일반적으로 읽기 지문에는 세 가지 주요 논지가 있고 강의가 그에 응답하기 때문에, 답안을 구성하는 성공적인 방법은 도입 단락 다음에 각각 주요 논지를 다루는 본문 단락 세 개를 구성하는 것이다. 각 본문 단락 내에서는 읽기 지문에서 제시하는 논지를 요약하는 문장을 한 두 개 작성한 후, 강의가 해당 내용에 어떠한 의견을 제시하는지 자세히 설명한다. 읽기 지문의 주요 내용과 세부 사항을 모두 요약할 필요는 없으므로, 각 단락의 대부분은 강의의 주요 정보를 전달하는 데 할애해야 한다. 마지막 단락은 일반적으로 필요하지 않다. 마지막으로, 단락 내에서 아이디어 간 및 단락 간에 명확한 전환이 이루어지도록 하는 것이 중요하다. 답안을 잘 구성하지 않으면 점수가 낮아질 수 있다.

채점자가 점수를 매길 때 매우 중요시하는 것 중 하나가 언어 사용이다. 수험자의 임무는 강의와 읽기 지문에서 제시된 논지와 견해에 대해 요약해서 수험자 자신의 말로 글을 쓰는 것이다. 위에서 설명한 대로, 일부 내용은 복잡하거나 미묘하여 다양한 문법 구조 및 광범위하고 정확한 어휘 사용이 필요할 수 있다. 답안의 문장 구조, 단어 선택 및 어휘는 일관되게 올바르고 정확하며 명확해야 한다. 문법 및 어휘의 오류, 특히 표현하려는 내용의 명확성에 방해가 되는 오류들은 낮은 점수를 받는 요소이다. 읽기 지문에서 많은 내용을 베끼는 것은 좋은 점수를 받는 데 도움이 되지 않는다는 것을 기억하자. 강의를 듣는 동안 단어, 구문 및 논지들에 대한 메모를 작성한 후 답안 작성 시 해당 메모를 사용할 수 있다. 수험자는 글을 쓸 때 자신의 올바른 문법 및 어휘 사용 능력에 의존해야 하며, 채점자는 그것을 판단할 것이다.

글이 완벽하지 않아도 최상의 점수를 받을 수 있다. 그러나 실수는 최소한도로, 크게 하지 않는 것이 좋다.

Writing for an Academic Discussion Task_학술적 토론에 관한 쓰기 과제

쓰기 영역의 두 번째 과제는 학술적 토론에 관한 쓰기 과제이다. 수험자는 교수가 어떤 주제에 관해 질문을 게시하고 몇몇 학생들이 의견을 답해 놓은 온라인 토론 글을 읽게 된다. 그리고 수험자는 토론에 참여하여 답안을 쓰게 된다. 교수의 질문과 학생들의 글을 읽고 자신의 글을 쓰는 데 주어지는 시간은 10분이다.

효과적인 답안은 최소한 100단어를 포함해야 한다. 100단어보다 짧은 답안은 보통 5점을 받기 위해 필요한 의견의 발전과 문법 구조 및 어휘의 다양성을 보여 주지 않는다. 단어 수의 상한 제한은 없다. 수험자는 주어진 시간 안에 원하는 만큼 쓸 수 있지만, 쓴 내용을 검토하고 오류가 있을 경우 수정하는 데 쓸 시간을 남겨두는 것이 좋다. 또한, 쓰기만을 위한 쓰기가 아니라, 명확하고 효과적으로 토론에 기여하는 글쓰기를 해야 한다. 제시하는 의견의 수도 중요하지만, 얼마나 좋은 의견인가, 의견을 효과적으로 표현하고 있는 가가 채점자들이 가장 주안점을 두는 부분이다.

---

ex.

Your professor is teaching a class on education. Write a post responding to the professor's question.

In your response, you should do the following.
- Express and support your opinion.
- Make a contribution to the discussion in your own words.

An effective response will contain at least 100 words.

Dr. Achebe

This week we analyzed some aspects of current educational systems. One type of school system we discussed was boarding schools, which, as the name suggests, is a type of school where students live during the school year. I would like you to discuss whether you consider boarding schools beneficial for students' education or whether you think day schools, or schools where students do not live at the schools, are better for most students. Explain why you think so.

Claire

I would have loved to have attended a boarding school. I feel like boarding schools would have helped me establish a strict daily routine and helped me become more disciplined. Also, being in a boarding school means that you are with friends and classmates around the clock, and I would have loved such an opportunity.

Andrew

I personally do not support the boarding school system as I believe it can lead to many psychological problems. In fact, I have heard about what is referred to as "boarding school syndrome," which, in simple terms, suggests that some students who attend boarding schools at a very young age can have long-term emotional or behavioral challenges. So why take that risk if most students can just go to day schools?

당신의 교수는 교육 과목 수업을 하고 있다. 교수가 하는 질문에 답하는 게시글을 쓰라.

게시글에는 다음을 포함한다.

- 자신의 의견을 표현하고 뒷받침하라.
- 자신만의 언어로 토론에 기여하라.

답안은 최소한 100단어 이상으로 쓴다.

아체베 박사 이번 주에 우리는 현 교육 시스템의 몇 가지 측면을 분석했습니다. 우리가 논의한 한 가지 학교 시스템이 기숙학교인데요, 이름에서 알 수 있듯이, 학생들이 학년 내내 생활하는 학교입니다. 기숙학교가 학생들의 교육에 도움이 되는지, 아니면 대부분의 학생들에게 통학학교나 학교에서 생활하지 않는 학교가 더 나은지 토론해 보길 바랍니다. 그 이유를 설명해주세요.

클레어 저라면 기숙학교에 다녔다면 너무 좋았을 거예요. 기숙학교에 다녔다면 엄격한 일상 루틴을 정하고 좀더 자기 규율을 갖추는 데 도움이 되었을 것 같아요. 또한 기숙학교에 다닌다는 건 친구와 동급생들과 24시간 내내 같이 있는다는 뜻이고, 그런 기회를 저라면 매우 좋아했을 거예요.

앤드루 저는 개인적으로 기숙학교 시스템을 지지하지 않는데 이것이 많은 심리적 문제를 야기할 수 있다고 생각하기 때문입니다. 사실, 저는 '기숙학교 증후군'이라고 불리는 것에 대해 들어봤는데요, 간단히 말해서, 아주 어린 나이에 기숙학교에 다닌 학생들 중 일부는 장기간의 감정적 또는 행동적인 저항을 겪을 수 있다는 주장입니다. 그렇다면 대부분의 학생들이 통학학교에 다닐 수 있는데 왜 그런 위험을 감수해야 할까요?

해설 이 토론 모델에서 교수는 수강생들에게 기숙학교와 통학학교 중 어느 것이 학생들에게 더 나은지 묻고, 두 토론 참가자가 의견을 제시하고 있다. 첫 번째 사람은 기숙학교를 옹호하며, 그들이 학생들에게 규율을 가르치고 동료애를 갖게 한다는 점을 지적한다. 두 번째 사람은 기숙학교에 반대하며, 그들이 학생들에게 심리적 문제를 가져온다고 설명한다.

수험자들은 이 토론에 참여해 기숙학교와 통학학교에 대한 의견을 제시하여야 하는데, 이미 주어진 다른 학생이 쓴 포스팅을 참고해도 되고 완전히 새로운 아이디어를 제시해도 된다. 예를 들어, 어떤 수험자는 클레어가 언급한 규율과 동료애 아이디어를 발전시킬 수 있고, 어떤 수험자는 앤드루가 언급한 심리적 저항에 대해 자세히 설명할 수 있다. 또 다른 수험자는 기숙학교와 통학학교에 다니는 데 필요한 경제적 비용에 관해, 또는 두 유형의 학교 교육의 질에 관해, 또는 기숙학교에 적합한 연령대에 의견의 초점을 맞출 수 있다.

답안 작성 팁

- 교수가 학생들에게 요구하는 과제가 무엇인지 주의 깊게 읽어 본다. 또한 다른 학생의 게시물에서 언급된 내용도 주의 깊게 살펴본다. 이는 토론에 기여할 아이디어를 생각해 내는 데 도움을 줄 것이다. 몇 초 동안 자신이 쓰고 싶은 것에 대해 머릿속으로 아이디어를 떠올리는 시간을 갖는 것도 좋지만, 너무 많은 시간을 쓰지 않는다. 무엇을 쓸지 결정하면 글쓰기를 시작한다.
- 답안에서 교수의 질문에 대한 자신의 견해를 명확하게 밝힌다. 다른 게시물의 의견에 동의하거나 반대할 수 있으며, 토론 주제와 관련된 완전히 새로운 의견을 발전시킬 수도 있지만, 가능한 한 자신의 언어와 목소리를 내도록 한다. 다른 게시물에서 단어와 구문을 많이 복사하는 것은 감점의 요인이 된다.
- 너무 일반적인 단어보다는 정확한 단어를 사용한다. 또한, 이전에 (예를 들어 학교에서) 단어 그대로 암기한 예나 근거를 사용하지 않는다. 채점자들은 완전히 암기된 언어로 표현된 예나 근거를 수험자의 글로 여기지 않을 것이며, 낮은 점수를 받게 될 것이다.
- 약간의 시간을 남겨 답안을 검토하도록 한다.

Sample Scored Responses_예제 답안

Score 5 Essay

I am more inclined to agree that a boarding school system is beneficial. Firstly, a boarding school is a place where you can make friends with your classmates The "roommate" relationship is somewhat strong that you may remember forever, as you wake up, eat meals, study, and go to sleep together with your roommates on every school days. Secondly, a boarding school is usually close to your school campus, which means that you do not need to commute to and from school every day. Thirdly, a boarding school is not a place merely for a disciplined life; it often conducts various activities to help you get immersed in the living environment and make your life more colorful, which cannot be experienced at home. I personally do not agree with Andrew's point that boarding school places high mental pressure on students, as boarding schools are not prisons and students are still free to leave on weekends to bond with their family and pursue their interests.

Rater Comments

필자는 매우 명확하게 표현된 온라인 토론글을 작성하였고 언어 사용에 일관된 재능을 보여 주었다. 이 답변은 5점을 받았다.

- 필자는 명백하게 기숙학교를 선호하며 그 이유를 몇 가지 제시하고 있다. 기숙학교가 제공하는 진한 우정을 칭찬하며, 학생에게 일생 동안 기억될 추억을 남겨 준다고 칭송했다. 또한 기숙학교가 통학 문제를 해결하고, 학생들에게 다양한 활동 기회를 제공한다고 언급한다. 마지막으로, 앤드루가 제기한 심리적 문제에 대해 이의를 제기하며, 기숙학교 학생들은 죄수가 아니고 주말에 가족을 만나고 그들과 함께 시간을 보낼 수 있다고 했다.
- 필자는 효과적인 다양한 구조와 정확한 단어 선택을 사용하고 있으며, 특히 답변이 두 번째 문장으로 넘어갈 때 이러한 구조와 선택이 더욱 명확해진다. 앞 부분의 몇 가지 오류(is somewhat strong that you remember와 on every school days)는 실력이 뛰어난 비영어권 필자가 시간의 압박 속에서 답안을 작성한 후 모든 실수를 검토하고 수정하는 데 시간이 부족해서 생길 수 있는 것으로 예상 가능한 것이다.
- 이 답안이 그렇듯, 고득점을 얻기 위해 다양한 주장이나 이유를 제시할 필요는 없다. 많은 성공적인 답안들이 잘 설명된 하나의 확장된 주장과 이유를 제시하고 있다.

Score 4 Essay

I personally do not support the idea of boarding school. I believe that the boarding school system would cause more problems in their future. The idea of being away from your family would definitely effect of connectivity amongst them. Sending your child to a boarding school would just mean that you're leaving them with someone else, and anything can happen and the parents won't know about it, also I think that being confined into the same environment could effect the child's creativity and also social skills. making new friends, having new personalities around you and exploring new hobbies that children should experience are what makes them grow into a more mature and also diffren

Rater Comments

이 답안은 4점을 받았는데, 토론 기여 의견으로서 성공적이고 관련성도 있으며 이해하기도 쉽다.

▬▬ 필자의 주장이 완전히 정립된 것처럼 보이지 않게 하는 몇 가지 오류가 있다. 필자는 기숙학교에 부정적인 입장을 취하며, 기숙학교에 다님으로써 학생들과 가족 간의 유대관계가 어떻게 위협받고, 어떻게 학생들을 위험에 노출시킬 수 있으며, 어떻게 기숙학교의 제한된 환경이 아이의 창의력과 사회적 기술 발달에 부정적인 영향을 미칠 수 있는지 설명한다. 실력이 뛰어난 사람이 제한된 시간 내에 쓰는 답변이라고 하기엔 도를 지나치는 실수(The idea... would definitely effect of connectivity amongst them)가 있고, 5점 획득에 필요한 만큼의 완전하고 명확한 생각의 전개를 보여 주지 못한다. 예를 들어, anything can happen은 다소 모호하고, 그 다음 주장(also I think)은 명확하게 분리되지 않으며, 마지막 주장인 새 친구 사귀기에 관한 생각은 기숙학교의 상황과 명확하게 대비되지 않는다(기숙학교에서도 새로운 친구를 사귈 수 있다).
▬▬ 문법 구조가 다양하고, 단어 선택은 대부분 적절하며, 오류는 적은 편이다.

Score 3 Essay

I personally do not support the idea of boarding school. I believe that the boarding school system would cause more problems in their future. The idea of being away from your family would definitely effect of connectivity amongst them. Sending your child to a boarding school would just mean that you're leaving them with someone else, and anything can happen and the parents won't know about it, also I think that being confined into the same environment could effect the child's creativity and also social skills. making new friends, having new personalities around you and exploring new hobbies that children should experience are what makes them grow into a more mature and also diffren

Rater Comments

이 응답은 3점을 받았다.

▬▬ 대부분 관련성이 있고 이해하기 쉽다는 점에서 부분적으로는 성공이지만, 3점보다 더 높은 점수를 받을 만한 충분한 능숙함, 다양성 및 자세한 논의가 없어 3점을 넘지 못한다.
▬▬ 필자는 기숙학교를 옹호하며 교육적으로도 충실하고 우정에 대한 감각도 길러줄 뿐 아니라 일상, 공유 관심사, 문화 교류를 제공한다고 주장한다. 하지만, 이러한 주장 중 일부는 충분히 설명되지 않았으며(some good routine이 무엇인지, 기숙학교가 통학학교보다 왜 더 많은 것을 공유하기에 적합한지), 답안 전체적으로 눈에 띄는 어휘 및 문법적 오류가 있다(is in the most interest, cause, interest for commun things, discover other culture, can be more focus, they can count one on each other 등). 이 글은 어느 정도의 어휘 및 문법적 다양성과 능숙도를 보여 주지만 4점을 받기에는 충분하지 않다.

Score 2 Essay

For my own opinion, i would loved to have attended a boarding school too.so that you can make a lot of friends in a short time and experince a whole new things you never done before. boarding is very good learning opportunity to catch new world and also open mind to making friends

Rater Comments

이 답안은 2점을 받았다.

- 토론에 기여하려고 노력은 하지만 필자가 제시하는 의견이 제대로 설명되지 않아 거의 실패한 답안이다. 필자는 기숙학교에 다녀보고 싶었고, 거기서 친구를 사귀고 새로운 경험을 하고 싶어했다고 말한다. 그러나 이러한 아이디어들을 더 발전시키지 않았으며, 기숙학교가 왜 이러한 것들을 경험하기에 통학학교보다 더 나은 곳인지 명확히 밝히지 않았다.
- 필자는 문장 구조, 표현, 어휘 형태 등에서 여러 오류를 범했다(for my own opinion, i would loved, experince a whole new things 등).

Score 1 Essay

I'm partially support the boarding school system. If the term not apart from school, some students may think the boarding school is so strict and not independent. We need relea.

Rater Comments

이 답안은 1점을 받았다.

- 필자는 토론에 기여하려 노력했지만 답 전체에 심각한 오류가 있어 자신의 주장이 일관되게 표현되지 않았는데, 특히 두 번째 문장이 그렇다.

학술적 토론에 관한 글쓰기 과제 채점 기준표

SCORE	DESCRIPTION
5	**완전히 성공적인 답안** 이 수준의 답안은 온라인 토론 주제와 관련이 있고 표현이 매우 명확하며 일관적인 언어 사용 능력을 보여 준다. 전형적인 답안은 다음과 같은 특징이 있다. · 관련성이 높고 잘 상술된 설명, 사례, 또는 세부 사항이 담겨 있다. · 다양한 문법 구조의 효과적인 사용 및 정확하고 관용적인 단어 선택을 보인다. · 실력이 뛰어난 수험자가 제한된 시간 내에 글쓰기를 할 때 보일 수 있는 일반적인 타이핑 오류(흔한 오타, 철자 오류 또는 비슷한 철자의 단어(there/their와 같은))를 제외하고 거의 어휘나 문법적 오류가 없다.
4	**대체로 성공적인 답안** 이 수준의 답안은 온라인 토론 주제와 관련이 있고, 이해하기 쉽도록 능숙하게 언어를 사용한다. 전형적인 답안은 다음과 같은 특징이 있다. · 관련성 있고 충분히 설명된 설명, 예시, 또는 세부 사항 · 다양한 문법 구조 및 적절한 어휘 선택 · 소수의 어휘 또는 문법적 오류
3	**부분적으로 성공적인 답안** 이 수준의 답안은 대체로 온라인 토론 주제와 관련성이 있고, 대체로 이해하기 쉬우며, 언어 사용에 일부 능숙함을 보인다. 전형적인 답안은 다음과 같은 특징이 있다. · 설명, 예시 또는 세부 사항 중 일부가 누락되거나 분명하지 않거나 관련이 없는 설명 · 문법 구조의 약간의 다양성 및 여러 어휘 사용 · 문장 구조, 단어 형태 또는 관용어 사용에서 몇 가지 눈에 띄는 어휘 및 문법적 오류
2	**대체로 성공적이지 않은 답안** 이 수준의 답안은 온라인 토론에 기여하려는 시도를 반영하지만, 언어 사용의 한계로 인해 주장을 이해하기 어렵다. 전형적인 답안은 다음과 같은 특징이 있다. · 부적절하게 설명되거나 일부분만 관련성이 있는 의견 · 제한된 문법 구조 및 어휘 · 다수의 문장 구조, 단어 형태 또는 사용상의 오류
1	**성공적이지 않은 답안** 이 수준의 답안은 온라인 토론 주제에 맞춰 의견을 내는 듯하지만 효과적이지 않고, 언어 사용의 한계로 인해 표현을 제대로 하지 못한다. 전형적인 답안은 다음과 같은 특징이 있다. · 과제를 풀려는 의도가 담긴 단어와 구문이지만 일관된 의견이 아주 조금 있거나 전혀 없다. · 심각하게 제한된 문법 구조 및 어휘 · 언어 사용의 심각하고 빈번한 오류 · 최소한의 창의성; 어떤 일관된 언어라도 대부분 문제로 제시된 온라인 토론글을 베낀 것이다.
0	해당 답안은 공백이거나 주제를 거부하며, 영어가 아니거나, 문제로 제시된 온라인 토론글을 베꼈거나, 토론 과제와 전혀 관련이 없거나, 무작위로 입력된 글자로 이루어져 있다.

에세이 채점 방식

토론에 기여하는 것이 수험자의 답안을 평가하는 매우 중요한 기준이다. 교수의 질문과 다른 학생들의 게시물을 포함한 제시된 온라인 토론글을 기억하라. 다른 학생들의 게시물에 대해 반드시 답을 할 필요는 없지만, 다른 게시물의 내용을 무시해서도 안 된다. 예를 들어, 이미 언급된 다른 학생들의 아이디어를 사용하려는 경우, 자신이 토론에서 처음으로 그것들을 제기한 사람인 것처럼 보이지 않도록 한다. 동시에, 토론에 기여하는 것이 반드시 많은 새로운 아이디어를 내는 것을 의미하지는 않는다. 누군가가 이미 쓴 내용에 동의하는 것도 토론에 기여하는 방식이다. 그러나 그 경우에도 다른 사람이 이미 쓴 내용을 그대로 반복하지 않도록 주의한다. 자신의 말과 자신의 목소리로, 자신만의 생각을 발전시킨다. 물론, 토론에 자신만의 기여도를 높이는 매우 효과적인 다른 방법들도 있다. 다른 게시물의 내용에 반대한다거나, 토론 주제에서 벗어나지 않는 한 완전히 새로운 아이디어를 내는 것도 있다.

채점자들은 근거와 예시로 명확하게 잘 뒷받침된 주장을 원한다. 수험자의 답안은 온라인 게시물을 표방하기 때문에 별도의 단락으로 구성될 필요는 없다. 하지만 잘 연결되고 일관적이며 명확해야 한다. 서로 연결되지 않거나 받쳐주지 않는 단어와 문장을 많이 사용하거나 명확한 견해로 나아가지 않거나 의미 없는 주장을 펼친다면, 낮은 점수를 받게 될 것이다.

채점자들이 사용하는 또 다른 중요한 기준은 언어 사용의 다양성이다. 채점자들은 답안에서 수험자가 다양한 문장 구조와 어휘를 사용하고 있다는 증거를 찾고자 한다. 아주 간단한 문장과 기본적인 어휘를 사용한다면, 매우 복합적이거나 정확한 생각은 표현할 수 없을 것이다. 그러나 문법 구조와 어휘의 다양성은 자연스러워야 하며 주장을 뒷받침해야 한다. 목적 없이 다양한 구조나 어휘를 사용한다면, 높은 점수를 받지 못할 것이다. 마지막 기준은 올바른 언어 사용이다. 올바른 문법과 정확한 단어 선택, 올바른 철자, 구두점, 대문자의 사용도 중요하다. 최고 점수를 받는 데 완벽한 작문까지는 필요 없지만, 실수가 있더라도 제한된 시간 안에 영어 실력이 뛰어난 사람이 글을 쓰다 흔히 저지를 수 있는 종류의 것으로 한정된다. 만약 많은 문법적 오류를 범하고 그로 인해 독자가 자신의 주장을 이해하기 어렵다면, 낮은 점수를 받게 될 것이다. 대체로 글이 쉽게 이해되지 않고, 문장이 지나치게 간단하며, 어휘가 제한적이라면, 수험자의 주장이 얼마나 인상적이든 3점보다 더 높은 점수는 받을 수 없을 것이다.

마지막으로 주의해야 할 것은 암기하거나 정형화된 글을 쓰지 않아야 한다는 점이다. 도입 글이나 클로징 멘트로 긴 암기문을 추가하지 말자. 이러한 시도는 진정한 글쓰기도 아니고 온라인 토론에서 사용되는 글쓰기 방식도 아니다.

학술적 토론을 위한 에세이 연습 주제

학술 토론을 위한 글쓰기 과제는 온라인 토론 포럼에서 교수의 질문에 답하는 것을 포함한다. 다음 목록의 내용들은 교수가 학술적 토론에서 물어볼 수 있는 질문과 유사하다. 시험에서는 교수님과 학생의 게시물을 잘 읽고 자신의 게시물에 무엇을 쓸지 계획해야 하며, 토론에 기여할 수 있는 답변을 작성한다. 이때 학생의 의견이 교수의 질문에 어떻게 반응하는지 고려해야 한다.

학술적 토론을 위한 글쓰기는 전문 지식에 대한 참조를 요구하지 않는다. 시험에서 교수의 질문과 대부분의 주제는 일반적이며, 일반적인 응시생들의 공통된 경험을 기반으로 한다.

시험을 준비하기 위해서, 목록에서 주제를 고르고 답을 쓰는 연습을 하되, 질문을 읽고 답을 계획하고 작성하며 확인하는데 10분을 넘지 않게 시간을 분배하여라.

1) "절대 포기하지 마세요"라는 표현은 계속 노력하고 목표를 위해 일하는 것을 멈추지 않는 것을 의미합니다. 당신은 이 진술에 동의하나요, 반대하나요? 당신의 대답을 뒷받침하기 위해 구체적인 이유와 예시를 작성하세요.

2) 당신은 왜 어떤 사람들이 위험한 스포츠나 다른 위험한 활동에 끌린다고 생각하나요? 당신의 대답을 뒷받침하기 위해 구체적인 이유와 예시를 작성하세요.

3) 당신은 다음 진술에 동의하나요, 반대하나요?
성적(점수)은 학생들이 학습하도록 장려한다.
당신의 의견을 뒷받침하기 위해 구체적인 이유와 예시를 작성하세요.

4) 다른 나라의 사람들이 채택하기 바라는 당신의 나라의 관습을 설명하세요. 구체적인 이유와 예를 들어, 당신의 선택을 설명하세요.

5) 당신은 다음 진술에 동의하나요, 반대하나요?
기술은 세상을 살기 더 나은 곳으로 만들었다.
당신의 의견을 지지하기 위해 구체적인 이유와 예를 작성하세요.

6) 당신은 다음 진술에 동의하나요, 반대하나요?
특정 국가의 광고 내용은 당신에게 그 나라에 대해 많은 것을 말해줄 수 있다.
당신의 대답을 뒷받침하기 위해 구체적인 이유와 예시를 작성하세요.

7) 외국 방문객은 당신의 나라에서 하루만 보낼 수 있습니다. 이 방문객은 하루동안 어디를 방문해야 하는가요? 왜인가요? 당신의 선택을 뒷받침하기 위해 구체적인 이유와 예시를 작성하세요.

8) 다음 진술에 동의하나요, 반대하나요?
춤은 문화에서 중요한 역할을 한다.
당신의 대답을 뒷받침하기 위해 구체적인 이유와 예시를 작성하세요.

9) 어떤 선생님들은 학생들이 한 달 혹은 그 이상의 큰 과제를 학생들에게 줍니다. 3일 혹은 4일 동안 집중적으로 일을 해서 빨리 일을 끝내는 것에 비해, 매일 조금씩 일을 해서 점진적으로 과제를 완성하는 것의 장점은 무엇일까요? 왜일까요?

Chapter 6

Practice Test 1

Reading

Listening

Speaking

Writing

Reading

Listening

Speaking

Writing

Test 1

Test 2

Test 3

Test 4

READING

In this section, you will be able to demonstrate your ability to understand academic passages in English. You will read and answer questions about **two passages**.

In the actual test, you will have 36 minutes total to read both passages and answer the questions. A clock will indicate how much time remains.

Some passages may include one or more notes explaining words or phrases. The words or phrases are marked with footnote numbers and the notes explaining them appear at the end of the passage.

Most questions are worth 1 point, but the last question for each passage is worth 2 points.

You may review and revise your answers in this section as long as time remains.

At the end of this practice test, you will find an answer key, information to help you determine your score, and explanations of the answers.

NINETEENTH-CENTURY POLITICS IN THE UNITED STATES

The development of the modern presidency in the United States began with Andrew Jackson, who swept to power in 1829 at the head of the Democratic Party and served until 1837. During his administration he immeasurably enlarged the power of the presidency. "The President is the direct representative of the American people," he lectured the Senate when it opposed him. "He was elected by the people, and is responsible to them." With this declaration, Jackson redefined the character of the presidential office and its relationship to the people.

During Jackson's second term, his opponents had gradually come together to form the Whig Party. **(A)** Whigs and Democrats held different attitudes toward the changes brought about by the market, banks, and commerce. **(B)** The Democrats tended to view society as a continuing conflict between "the people"—farmers, planters, and workers—and a set of greedy aristocrats. **(C)** This "paper money aristocracy" of bankers and investors manipulated the banking system for their own profit, Democrats claimed, and sapped the nation's virtue by encouraging speculation and the desire for sudden, unearned wealth. **(D)** The Democrats wanted the rewards of the market without sacrificing the features of a simple agrarian republic. They wanted the wealth that the market offered without the competitive, changing society; the complex dealing; the dominance of urban centers; and the loss of independence that came with it.

Whigs, on the other hand, were more comfortable with the market. For them, commerce and economic development were agents of civilization. Nor did the Whigs envision any conflict in society between farmers and workers on the one hand and businesspeople and bankers on the other. Economic growth would benefit everyone by raising national income and expanding opportunity. The government's responsibility was to provide a well-regulated economy that guaranteed opportunity for citizens of ability.

Whigs and Democrats differed not only in their attitudes toward the market but also about how active the central government should be in people's lives. Despite Andrew Jackson's inclination to be a strong President, Democrats as a rule believed in limited government. Government's role in the economy was to promote competition by destroying monopolies[1] and special privileges. In keeping with this philosophy of limited government, Democrats also rejected the idea that moral beliefs were the proper sphere of government action. Religion and politics, they believed, should be kept clearly separate, and they generally opposed humanitarian legislation.

The Whigs, in contrast, viewed government power positively. They believed that it should be used to protect individual rights and public liberty, and that it had a special role where individual effort was ineffective. By regulating the economy and competition, the government could ensure equal opportunity. Indeed, for Whigs the concept of government promoting the general welfare went beyond the economy. In particular, Whigs in the northern sections of the United States also believed that government power should be used to foster the moral welfare of the country. They were much more likely to favor social-reform legislation and aid to education.

Reading

Listening

Speaking

Writing

Test 1

Test 2

Test 3

Test 4

In some ways the social makeup of the two parties was similar. To be competitive in winning votes, Whigs and Democrats both had to have significant support among farmers, the largest group in society, and workers. Neither party could win an election by appealing exclusively to the rich or the poor. The Whigs, however, enjoyed disproportionate strength among the business and commercial classes. Whigs appealed to planters who needed credit to finance their cotton and rice trade in the world market, to farmers who were eager to sell their surpluses, and to workers who wished to improve themselves. Democrats attracted farmers isolated from the market or uncomfortable with it, workers alienated from the emerging industrial system, and rising entrepreneurs who wanted to break monopolies and open the economy to newcomers like themselves. The Whigs were strongest in the towns, cities, and those rural areas that were fully integrated into the market economy, whereas Democrats dominated areas of semisubsistence farming that were more isolated and languishing economically.

---

1. monopolies: companies or individuals that exclusively own or control commercial enterprises with no competitors

Paragraph 1

The development of the modern presidency in the United States began with Andrew Jackson, who swept to power in 1829 at the head of the Democratic Party and served until 1837. During his administration he immeasurably enlarged the power of the presidency. "The President is the direct representative of the American people," he lectured the Senate when it opposed him. "He was elected by the people, and is responsible to them." With this declaration, Jackson redefined the character of the presidential office and its relationship to the people.

1. According to paragraph 1, the presidency of Andrew Jackson was especially significant for which of the following reasons?

Ⓐ The President granted a portion of his power to the Senate.

Ⓑ The President began to address the Senate on a regular basis.

Ⓒ It was the beginning of the modern presidency in the United States.

Ⓓ It was the first time that the Senate had been known to oppose the President.

During Jackson's second term, his opponents had gradually come together to form the Whig Party. Whigs and Democrats held different attitudes toward the changes brought about by the market, banks, and commerce. The Democrats tended to view society as a continuing conflict between "the people"—farmers, planters, and workers—and a set of greedy aristocrats. This "paper money aristocracy" of bankers and investors manipulated the banking system for their own profit, Democrats claimed, and sapped the nation's virtue by encouraging speculation and the desire for sudden, unearned wealth. The Democrats wanted the rewards of the market without sacrificing the features of a simple agrarian republic. They wanted the wealth that the market offered without the competitive, changing society; the complex dealing; the dominance of urban centers; and the loss of independence that came with it.

2. The author mentions "bankers and investors" in the passage as an example of which of the following?

Ⓐ The Democratic Party's main source of support

Ⓑ The people that Democrats claimed were unfairly becoming rich

Ⓒ The people most interested in a return to a simple agrarian republic

Ⓓ One of the groups in favor of Andrew Jackson's presidency

Whigs, on the other hand, were more comfortable with the market. For them, commerce and economic development were agents of civilization. Nor did the Whigs envision any conflict in society between farmers and workers on the one hand and businesspeople and bankers on the other. Economic growth would benefit everyone by raising national income and expanding opportunity. The government's responsibility was to provide a well-regulated economy that guaranteed opportunity for citizens of ability.

3. According to paragraph 3, Whigs believed that commerce and economic development would have which of the following effects on society?

Ⓐ They would promote the advancement of society as a whole.

Ⓑ They would cause disagreements between Whigs and Democrats.

Ⓒ They would supply new positions for Whig Party members.

Ⓓ They would prevent conflict between farmers and workers.

4. According to paragraph 3, which of the following describes the Whig Party's view of the role of government?

Ⓐ To regulate the continuing conflict between farmers and businesspeople

Ⓑ To restrict the changes brought about by the market

Ⓒ To maintain an economy that allowed all capable citizens to benefit

Ⓓ To reduce the emphasis on economic development

Paragraph 4

Whigs and Democrats differed not only in their attitudes toward the market but also about how active the central government should be in people's lives. Despite Andrew Jackson's inclination to be a strong President, Democrats as a rule believed in limited government. Government's role in the economy was to promote competition by destroying monopolies[1] and special privileges. In keeping with this philosophy of limited government, Democrats also rejected the idea that moral beliefs were the proper sphere of government action. Religion and politics, they believed, should be kept clearly separate, and they generally opposed humanitarian legislation.

5. According to paragraph 4, a Democrat would be most likely to support government action in which of the following areas?

   Ⓐ Creating a state religion

   Ⓑ Supporting humanitarian legislation

   Ⓒ Destroying monopolies

   Ⓓ Recommending particular moral beliefs

Paragraph 5

The Whigs, in contrast, viewed government power positively. They believed that it should be used to protect individual rights and public liberty, and that it had a special role where individual effort was ineffective. By regulating the economy and competition, the government could ensure equal opportunity. Indeed, for Whigs the concept of government promoting the general welfare went beyond the economy. In particular, Whigs in the northern sections of the United States also believed that government power should be used to foster the moral welfare of the country. They were much more likely to favor social-reform legislation and aid to education.

6. The word "concept" in the passage is closest in meaning to

   Ⓐ power

   Ⓑ reality

   Ⓒ difficulty

   Ⓓ idea

7. Which of the following can be inferred from paragraph 5 about variations in political beliefs within the Whig Party?

   Ⓐ They were focused on issues of public liberty.

   Ⓑ They caused some members to leave the Whig Party.

   Ⓒ They were unimportant to most Whigs.

   Ⓓ They reflected regional interests.

In some ways the social makeup of the two parties was similar. To be competitive in winning votes, Whigs and Democrats both had to have significant support among farmers, the largest group in society, and workers. Neither party could win an election by appealing exclusively to the rich or the poor. The Whigs, however, enjoyed disproportionate strength among the business and commercial classes. Whigs appealed to planters who needed credit to finance their cotton and rice trade in the world market, to farmers who were eager to sell their surpluses, and to workers who wished to improve themselves. Democrats attracted farmers isolated from the market or uncomfortable with it, workers alienated from the emerging industrial system, and rising entrepreneurs who wanted to break monopolies and open the economy to newcomers like themselves. The Whigs were strongest in the towns, cities, and those rural areas that were fully integrated into the market economy, whereas Democrats dominated areas of semisubsistence farming that were more isolated and languishing economically.

8. Which of the sentences below best expresses the essential information in the highlighted sentence in the passage? Incorrect choices change the meaning in important ways or leave out essential information.

   Ⓐ Whigs were able to attract support only in the wealthiest parts of the economy because Democrats dominated in other areas.

   Ⓑ Whig and Democratic areas of influence were naturally split between urban and rural areas, respectively.

   Ⓒ The semisubsistence farming areas dominated by Democrats became increasingly isolated by the Whigs' control of the market economy.

   Ⓓ The Democrats' power was greatest in poorer areas, while the Whigs were strongest in those areas where the market was already fully operating.

Paragraph 2

During Jackson's second term, his opponents had gradually come together to form the Whig Party. **(A)** Whigs and Democrats held different attitudes toward the changes brought about by the market, banks, and commerce. **(B)** The Democrats tended to view society as a continuing conflict between "the people"—farmers, planters, and workers—and a set of greedy aristocrats. **(C)** This "paper money aristocracy" of bankers and investors manipulated the banking system for their own profit, Democrats claimed, and sapped the nation's virtue by encouraging speculation and the desire for sudden, unearned wealth. **(D)** The Democrats wanted the rewards of the market without sacrificing the features of a simple agrarian republic. They wanted the wealth that the market offered without the competitive, changing society; the complex dealing; the dominance of urban centers; and the loss of independence that came with it.

9. **Directions:** Look at the part of the passage that is displayed above. The letters **(A)**, **(B)**, **(C)**, and **(D)** indicate where the following sentence could be added.

   This new party argued against the policies of Jackson and his party in a number of important areas, beginning with the economy.

   Where would the sentence best fit?

   Ⓐ Choice A
   Ⓑ Choice B
   Ⓒ Choice C
   Ⓓ Choice D

10. **Directions:** An introductory sentence for a brief summary of the passage is provided below. Complete the summary by selecting the THREE answer choices that express the most important ideas in the passage. Some sentences do not belong in the summary because they express ideas that are not presented in the passage or are minor ideas in the passage. **This question is worth 2 points.**

The political system of the United States in the mid-nineteenth century was strongly influenced by the social and economic circumstances of the time.

◆

◆

◆

Answer Choices

A The Democratic and Whig Parties developed in response to the needs of competing economic and political constituencies.

B During Andrew Jackson's two terms as President, he served as leader of both the Democratic and Whig Parties.

C The Democratic Party primarily represented the interests of the market, banks, and commerce.

D In contrast to the Democrats, the Whigs favored government aid for education.

E A fundamental difference between Whigs and Democrats involved the importance of the market in society.

F The role of government in the lives of the people was an important political distinction between the two parties.

BIRD SONGS AND CALLS

Birds use song both in courtship and to define areas of territory. Both of these are communicative purposes: the bird is passing specific messages to other members of its species. Birds communicate for other reasons as well: a blackbird, for instance, will make a sharp "pink-pink" sound when there is a cat nearby, which warns other birds in the neighborhood of the danger.

William Thorpe (1961) studied the behavior of gannets in a colony containing many thousands of birds. **(A)** Thorpe found that when a bird was returning to its nest, it would drift on an updraft of air from the bottom of the cliff upwards, calling as it went. **(B)** When the bird on the nest heard its mate calling, it would call in reply, showing that each bird's call could act as an identification signal. **(C)** Thorpe also discovered that a bird might have as many as fifteen or sixteen different kinds of calls, each serving a different function. **(D)**

J. R. Krebs (1976) realized that birds often sing more intensively in the early morning—the "dawn chorus." By investigating what the birds actually did during each day, and how much time they spent on each activity, Krebs found that the dawn chorus serves a largely territorial function. The early morning is not a particularly good time for gathering food, because it is dark, so visibility is lower, and it is also cold, so many insects are still inactive. On the other hand, at this time many birds move around looking for living space, so establishing and defending a territory is necessary. Birdsong is not just territorial, of course. A bird's song can serve a dual purpose: it can be used to defend a territory and, by indicating to a prospective mate that the singer has a territory to defend, can also attract a female bird.

P. J. B. Slater (1981) suggested that bird calls and birdsong are partly learned from other birds. He found that chaffinches which had been hand-reared and had not heard other wild birds made an entirely different kind of "chink" call from that of wild birds. In another case, Slater observed a laboratory chaffinch in a duet with a wild sparrow outside the window of the laboratory. The chaffinch imitated the sparrow's "cheep" whenever the sparrow produced it. Slater concluded that learning through copying is an important part of the way in which birds acquire their songs. Slater also found that individual chaffinches can have up to five different types of song. Some of these are personal, sung by that bird alone. Others are shared by several birds. In some cases too, Slater observed chaffinches singing songs which were almost identical to those sung by others, but with just a note or two different—possibly because the bird had made an error in copying the song from another.

Slater studied a population of 40 chaffinches on the Orkney Islands and found that among them they had seventeen different song types. So it was not a matter of each bird having its own individual songs—there was a considerable amount of sharing. Slater found that this sharing related to geographical distribution, but that the boundaries were not distinct enough for it to be accurately described as a dialect, or regional variety of a song. Instead, there was considerable overlap between the songs sung in one area and those sung in an adjoining one, but gradually the overlap would become less, until birds a long distance away from one another would be singing entirely different songs.

In 1970, Peter Marler proposed that birdsong and human speech were directly comparable in certain key respects, and that the study of birdsong might provide psychologists with some useful indicators as to the nature and development of speech in human beings. One of the parallels which Marler identified was the way that both humans and birds show a strong genetic predisposition to pick up and imitate certain sounds rather than others. Marler showed that young birds will learn the songs of their own species if they are played to them when young, but they will ignore songs of birds from other species. Similarly, young human beings are surrounded by all kinds of sounds and noises, but it is the human voice to which they listen most closely and human speech which they imitate.

Paragraph 1

William Thorpe (1961) studied the behavior of gannets in a colony containing many thousands of birds. Thorpe found that when a bird was returning to its nest, it would drift on an updraft of air from the bottom of the cliff upwards, calling as it went. When the bird on the nest heard its mate calling, it would call in reply, showing that each bird's call could act as an identification signal. Thorpe also discovered that a bird might have as many as fifteen or sixteen different kinds of calls, each serving a different function.

11. The word "discovered" in the passage is closest in meaning to
   Ⓐ reported
   Ⓑ found
   Ⓒ estimated
   Ⓓ showed

Paragraph 3

J.R. Krebs (1976) realized that birds often sing more intensively in the early morning—the "dawn chorus." By investigating what the birds actually did during each day, and how much time they spent on each activity, Krebs found that the dawn chorus serves a largely territorial function. The early morning is not a particularly good time for gathering food, because it is dark, so visibility is lower, and it is also cold, so many insects are still inactive. On the other hand, at this time many birds move around looking for living space, so establishing and defending a territory is necessary. Birdsong is not just territorial, of course. A bird's song can serve a dual purpose: it can be used to defend a territory and, by indicating to a prospective mate that the singer has a territory to defend, can also attract a female bird.

12. The word "realized" in the passage is closest in meaning to
   Ⓐ indicated
   Ⓑ established
   Ⓒ understood
   Ⓓ argued

13. Which of the following can be inferred from paragraph 3 about birds and food gathering?

   Ⓐ Birds become very territorial while they are gathering food.

   Ⓑ Birds are more likely to sing when gathering food is easy than when it is difficult.

   Ⓒ Most birds gather enough food for the day before they begin singing.

   Ⓓ Birds are less likely to sing intensively when they are looking for food.

14. According to paragraph 3, why are birds concerned with defending territory during the early morning?

   Ⓐ This is the time of day when male birds without mates try to take away living space and mates of other males.

   Ⓑ This is the time of day birds and other animals hunt for insects.

   Ⓒ This is the time of day birds have to defend their homes from predators who attack in darkness.

   Ⓓ This is the time of day when other birds are looking for new places to live.

Paragraph 4

P.J.B. Slater (1981) suggested that bird calls and birdsong are partly learned from other birds. He found that chaffinches which had been hand-reared and had not heard other wild birds made an entirely different kind of "chink" call from that of wild birds. In another case, Slater observed a laboratory chaffinch in a duet with a wild sparrow outside the window of the laboratory. The chaffinch imitated the sparrow's "cheep" whenever the sparrow produced it. Slater concluded that learning through copying is an important part of the way in which birds acquire their songs. Slater also found that individual chaffinches can have up to five different types of song. Some of these are personal, sung by that bird alone. Others are shared by several birds. In some cases too, Slater observed chaffinches singing songs which were almost identical to those sung by others, but with just a note or two different—possibly because the bird had made an error in copying the song from another.

15. Why does the author discuss the behavior of a "chaffinch in a duet with a wild sparrow outside the window of the laboratory"?

   Ⓐ To explain why Slater's hand-reared birds made an entirely different call than that made by wild birds

   Ⓑ To indicate how Slater arrived at the view that imitation plays an important role in how birds learn songs

   Ⓒ To explain why Slater thought that it would be advantageous for birds to sing multiple types of songs

   Ⓓ To provide evidence that there are many different ways in which birds acquire new songs and calls

16. Which of the sentences below best expresses the essential information in the highlighted sentence in the passage? Incorrect choices change the meaning in important ways or leave out essential information.

   Ⓐ Slater observed that all but one or two chaffinches were able to sing nearly identical copies of the songs of other birds.

   Ⓑ Slater observed that chaffinches sang the songs of other birds, with just a wrong note or two that may have been due to copying errors.

   Ⓒ Slater observed that chaffinches learned the songs of other birds, while sometimes adding a wrong note or two they may have learned from a different group of birds.

   Ⓓ Slater observed that chaffinches used one or two notes from their own songs when singing the songs of other birds.

Slater studied a population of 40 chaffinches on the Orkney Islands and found that among them they had seventeen different song types. So it was not a matter of each bird having its own individual songs—there was a considerable amount of sharing. Slater found that this sharing related to geographical distribution, but that the boundaries were not distinct enough for it to be accurately described as a dialect, or regional variety of a song. Instead, there was considerable overlap between the songs sung in one area and those sung in an adjoining one, but gradually the overlap would become less, until birds a long distance away from one another would be singing entirely different songs.

17. According to paragraph 5, the chaffinches of the Orkney Islands were not considered to sing different regional variations of songs because
    Ⓐ each bird had its own individual songs that were not shared by any other birds
    Ⓑ the birds' different songs were not based on geographical location
    Ⓒ even the birds that lived some distance apart shared many of the same songs
    Ⓓ there were no clear divisions to mark the places where differences in songs occurred

In 1970, Peter Marler proposed that birdsong and human speech were directly comparable in certain key respects, and that the study of birdsong might provide psychologists with some useful indicators as to the nature and development of speech in human beings. One of the parallels which Marler identified was the way that both humans and birds show a strong genetic predisposition to pick up and imitate certain sounds rather than others. Marler showed that young birds will learn the songs of their own species if they are played to them when young, but they will ignore songs of birds from other species. Similarly, young human beings are surrounded by all kinds of sounds and noises, but it is the human voice to which they listen most closely and human speech which they imitate.

18. In paragraph 6, why does the author discuss Marler's finding that young birds ignore the songs of other species and young humans listen most closely to human speech?
    Ⓐ To show that listening skills are relatively poorly developed in young birds and young humans
    Ⓑ To argue that the genetic predisposition to pick up and imitate sounds is more sophisticated in humans than in birds
    Ⓒ To explain why Marler thought that birdsong might be helpful in understanding the development of human speech
    Ⓓ To show that surrounding noises and sounds increase the difficulty that birds have learning songs and that humans have learning language

William Thorpe (1961) studied the behavior of gannets in a colony containing many thousands of birds. **(A)** Thorpe found that when a bird was returning to its nest, it would drift on an updraft of air from the bottom of the cliff upwards, calling as it went. **(B)** When the bird on the nest heard its mate calling, it would call in reply, showing that each bird's call could act as an identification signal. **(C)** Thorpe also calculated that a bird might have as many as fifteen or sixteen different kinds of calls, each serving a different function. **(D)**

    J.R. Krebs (1976) investigated how birds seem to sing more intensively in the early morning—the "dawn chorus." By investigating what the birds actually did during each day, and how much time they spent on each activity, Krebs found that the dawn chorus serves a largely territorial function. The early morning is not a particularly good time for gathering food, because it is dark, so visibility is lower, and it is also cold, so many insects are still inactive. On the other hand, at this time many birds move around looking for living space, so establishing and defending a territory is necessary. Birdsong is not just territorial, of course. A bird's song can serve a dual purpose: it can be used to defend a territory and, by indicating to a prospective mate that the singer has a territory to defend, can also attract a female bird.

19 **Directions:** Look at the part of the passage that is displayed above. The letters **(A)**, **(B)**, **(C)**, and **(D)** indicate where the following sentence could be added.

These include flight calls used to coordinate the flock as well as distress calls and begging calls, which are used specifically by chicks to communicate with their parents.

Where would the sentence best fit?

  Ⓐ Choice A

  Ⓑ Choice B

  Ⓒ Choice C

  Ⓓ Choice D

20. **Directions:** : An introductory sentence for a brief summary of the passage is provided below. Complete the summary by selecting the THREE answer choices that express the most important ideas in the passage. Some sentences do not belong in the summary because they express ideas that are not presented in the passage or are minor ideas in the passage. **This question is worth 2 points.**

Birds sing to communicate with other birds.

- ◆
- ◆
- ◆

Answer Choices

A   The number of different songs and calls a bird has varies by species, with blackbirds having some of the smallest collections of songs and calls and chaffinches having some of the largest.

B   Birds that live in dense forests or other places where visibility is poor are especially dependent on songs and calls from other birds to locate sources of food and danger.

C   Many birds sing to establish territory—and attract mates—during hours in which food gathering is difficult, while other birds, such as gannets, use calls to identify themselves.

D   Bird songs and calls may be unique to one bird, shared among several birds, or even learned from other species.

E   Although hand-reared chaffinches at first were slow to correctly copy the calls and songs of their own species in the wild, over time their copying skill improved.

F   Because birds and humans have similar genetic ability to imitate certain sounds, birdsong can help explain the development of speech in humans.

STOP. This is the end of the Reading section of TOEFL iBT® Practice Test 1.

Reading

Listening

Speaking

Writing

Test 1

Test 2

Test 3

Test 4

LISTENING

In this section, you will be able to demonstrate your ability to understand conversations and lectures in English.

In the actual test, the section is divided into two separately timed parts. You will hear each conversation or lecture only one time. A clock will indicate how much time remains. The clock will count down only while you are answering questions, not while you are listening. You may take up to 16.5 minutes to answer the questions.

In this practice test, there is no time limit for answering questions.

You may take notes while you listen. You may use your notes to help you answer the questions. Your notes will not be scored.

Answer the questions based on what is stated or implied by the speakers.

In some questions, you will see this icon: . This means that you will hear, but not see, part of the question.

In the actual test, you must answer each question. You cannot return to previous questions.

At the end of this practice test, you will find an answer key, information to help you determine your score, and explanations of the answers.

Reading

Listening

Speaking

Writing

Test 1

Test 2

Test 3

Test 4

Questions

1. Why does the student go to see the professor?

    Ⓐ To prepare for her graduate school interview
    Ⓑ To get advice about her graduate school application
    Ⓒ To give the professor her graduate school application
    Ⓓ To find out if she was accepted into graduate school

2. According to the professor, what information should the student include in her statement of purpose?
    Select 2 answers.

    Ⓐ Her academic motivation
    Ⓑ Her background in medicine
    Ⓒ Some personal information
    Ⓓ The ways her teachers have influenced her

3. What does the professor consider unusual about the student's background?

    Ⓐ Her work experience
    Ⓑ Her creative writing experience
    Ⓒ Her athletic achievements
    Ⓓ Her music training

4. Why does the professor tell a story about his friend who went to medical school?

    Ⓐ To warn the student about how difficult graduate school can be
    Ⓑ To illustrate a point he is making
    Ⓒ To help the student relax
    Ⓓ To change the subject

5. What does the professor imply about the people who admit students to graduate school?

    Ⓐ They often lack expertise in the fields of the applicants.
    Ⓑ They do not usually read the statement of purpose.
    Ⓒ They are influenced by the appearance of an application.
    Ⓓ They remember most of the applications they receive.

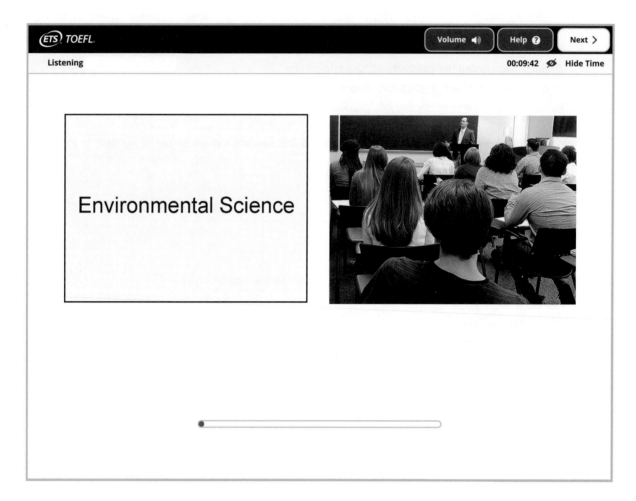

6. What is the talk mainly about?

    Ⓐ A common method of managing water supplies

    Ⓑ The formation of underground water systems

    Ⓒ Natural processes that renew water supplies

    Ⓓ Maintaining the purity of underground water systems

7. What is the professor's point of view concerning the method of "safe yield"?

    Ⓐ It has helped to preserve the environment.

    Ⓑ It should be researched in states other than Arizona.

    Ⓒ It is not an effective resource policy.

    Ⓓ It ignores the different ways people use water.

8. According to the professor, what are two problems associated with removing water from an underground system?

    Select 2 answers.

    Ⓐ Pollutants can enter the water more quickly.

    Ⓑ The surface area can dry and crack.

    Ⓒ The amount of water stored in the system can drop.

    Ⓓ Dependent streams and springs can dry up.

9. What is a key feature of a sustainable water system?

    Ⓐ It is able to satisfy short-term and long-term needs.

    Ⓑ It is not affected by changing environmental conditions.

    Ⓒ It usually originates in lakes, springs, or streams.

    Ⓓ It is not used to supply human needs.

10. What does the professor imply about water systems managed by the "safe-yield" method?

    Ⓐ They recharge at a rapid rate.

    Ⓑ They are not sustainable.

    Ⓒ They must have large storage areas.

    Ⓓ They provide a poor quality of water.

11. *Listen to Track 13 to answer the question.*

    Why does the professor say this?

    Ⓐ To find out whether the students are familiar with the issue

    Ⓑ To introduce a new problem for discussion

    Ⓒ To respond to a student's question

    Ⓓ To encourage the students to care about the topic

12. What are the students mainly discussing?

    Ⓐ Drugs that are harmful to the human body
    Ⓑ Bacteria that produce antibiotics
    Ⓒ DNA that is related to athletic performance
    Ⓓ Genes that protect bacteria from antibiotics

13. According to the conversation, why are transposons sometimes called "jumping genes"?

    Ⓐ They are able to move from one bacteria cell to another.
    Ⓑ They are found in people with exceptional jumping ability.
    Ⓒ They occur in every other generation of bacteria.
    Ⓓ Their movements are rapid and unpredictable.

14. According to the conversation, what are two ways in which bacteria cells get resistance genes?
    Select 2 answers.

    Ⓐ The resistance genes are carried from nearby cells.
    Ⓑ The resistance genes are carried by white blood cells.
    Ⓒ The resistance genes are inherited from the parent cell.
    Ⓓ The resistance genes are carried by antibiotics.

15. What can be inferred about the resistance genes discussed in the conversation?

    Ⓐ They are found in all bacteria cells.
    Ⓑ They are not able to resist antibiotics.
    Ⓒ They make the treatment of bacterial diseases more difficult.
    Ⓓ They are essential to the body's defenses against bacteria.

16. *Listen to Track 15 to answer the question.*
    Why does the woman say this?

    Ⓐ To find out if the man has done his assignment
    Ⓑ To ask the man to find out if the library is open
    Ⓒ To let the man know that she cannot study much longer
    Ⓓ To ask if the man has ever met her roommate

17. What is the main topic of the lecture?

   Ⓐ The size of root systems

   Ⓑ Various types of root systems

   Ⓒ The nutrients required by rye plants

   Ⓓ Improving two types of plant species

18. According to the professor, why did one scientist grow a rye plant in water?

   Ⓐ To expose the roots to sunlight

   Ⓑ To be able to fertilize it with gas

   Ⓒ To be able to see its entire root system

   Ⓓ To see how minerals penetrate its roots

19. The professor mentions houseplants that receive too much water. Why does she mention them?

   Ⓐ To show that many different types of plants can grow in water

   Ⓑ To explain why plants grown in water should have a gas bubbled through them

   Ⓒ To remind the students of the importance of their next experiment

   Ⓓ To make a point about the length of houseplants' roots

20. According to the professor, what similarity is there between crabgrass and rye plants?

   Ⓐ Both start growing in the month of May.

   Ⓑ Both have root systems that require a lot of water.

   Ⓒ Both have more shoot surface than root surface.

   Ⓓ Both produce many shoots from a single seed.

21. *Listen again to part of the lecture by playing Track 17.*
Then answer the question.

Why did the professor say this?

   Ⓐ She wanted to correct the wording of a previous statement.

   Ⓑ She wishes she did not have to bubble gas through it.

   Ⓒ She realized the odor of gas could be unpleasant.

   Ⓓ She forgot to tell the students about a step in the experiment.

22. *Listen again to part of the lecture by playing Track 18.*
Then answer the question.

What does the professor intend to explain?

   Ⓐ Why a mistake made in textbooks was never corrected

   Ⓑ Why she does not believe that the roots of rye plants extend to 1,000 kilometers

   Ⓒ How the roots of rye plants develop to such a great length

   Ⓓ How plants grown in water make use of fertilizer

23. What is the lecture mainly about?

    Ⓐ Technological innovations in the automobile industry
    Ⓑ The organizational structure of companies
    Ⓒ Ways to improve efficiency in an engineering department
    Ⓓ Methods of resolving conflicts in organizations

24. Why does the professor talk about a construction company that has work in different cities?

    Ⓐ To give an example of functional organization
    Ⓑ To give an example of organization around projects
    Ⓒ To illustrate problems with functional organization
    Ⓓ To illustrate the types of conflict that can arise in companies

25. What is an example of a violation of the "unity of command" principle?

    Ⓐ More than one person supervises the same employee.
    Ⓑ A company decides not to standardize its products.
    Ⓒ Several project managers are responsible for designing a new product.
    Ⓓ An employee does not follow a supervisor's instructions.

26. According to the professor, where might there be a conflict in an organizational structure based on both projects and function?

    Ⓐ Between architects and finance experts
    Ⓑ Between the need to specialize and the need to standardize
    Ⓒ Between two engineers who work on the same project
    Ⓓ Between the needs of projects in different cities

27. Indicate whether each sentence below describes functional organization or project organization. Place a check mark in the correct box.

	Functional Organization	Project Organization
A. It encourages people with similar expertise to work closely together.		
B. It helps the company to adapt quickly and meet changing needs.		
C. It helps to achieve uniformity in projects.		

28. *Listen again to part of the lecture by playing Track 20.*
    Then answer the question.

    Why does the professor say this?

    Ⓐ He does not understand why the student is talking about engineers.
    Ⓑ He wants to know how the engineers will communicate with their coworkers.
    Ⓒ The student has not provided a complete answer to his question.
    Ⓓ He wants the student to do more research on the topic.

STOP. This is the end of the Listening section of TOEFL iBT® Practice Test 1.

Reading

Listening

Speaking

Writing

Test 1

Test 2

Test 3

Test 4

SPEAKING

In this section, you will be able to demonstrate your ability to speak about a variety of topics.

In the actual test, the Speaking section will last approximately 16 minutes. You will answer four questions by speaking into the microphone. You may use your notes to help you answer the questions. Your notes will not be scored. For each question, you will have time to prepare before giving your response. You should answer the questions as completely as possible in the time allowed.

For this practice test, you may want to use a personal recording device to record and play back your responses.

For each question, play the audio track listed and follow the directions to complete the task. You may take notes while you listen.

At the end of this Practice Test, you will find scripts for the audio tracks, Important Points for each question, sample responses, and comments on those responses by official raters.

1. You will now give your opinion about a familiar topic. After you hear the question, you will have 15 seconds to prepare and 45 seconds to speak..

Now play Track 21 to hear Question 1.

Some people who unexpectedly receive a large amount of money spend it on practical things, while others spend it for pleasure only. Which do you think is better and why?

Preparation Time: 15 Seconds

Response Time: 45 Seconds

2. Now you will read a passage about a campus situation and then listen to a conversation about the same topic. You will then answer a question, using information from both the reading passage and the conversation. You will have 30 seconds to prepare and 60 seconds to speak.

Now play Track 22 to hear Question 2.

Reading Time: 50 Seconds

Student Health Services Need Improvement

The situation at the health center is unacceptable: you sit in a crowded waiting room for hours waiting to get treatment for minor ailments. Then when it's your turn, you get about three minutes with an overworked doctor. I have two suggestions: first, the health center needs to hire more doctors so that each patient receives quality treatment. And as far as the wait time issue is concerned, the health center is currently open only Monday through Fridays, which means that people who get sick over the weekend wait until the following week to get treatment. So, opening the health center on weekends should solve that problem too.

Sincerely,

Megan Finch

The man expresses his opinion about the student's suggestions that are made in the letter. State the man's opinion and explain the reasons he gives for holding that opinion.

Preparation Time: 30 Seconds

Response Time: 60 Seconds

Reading

Listening

Speaking

Writing

Test 1

Test 2

Test 3

Test 4

3. Now you will read a passage about an academic subject and then listen to a lecture on the same topic. You will then answer a question, using information from both the reading passage and the lecture. You will have 30 seconds to prepare and 60 seconds to speak.

Now play Track 23 to hear Question 3.

Reading Time: 45 Seconds

Social Loafing

When people work in groups to perform a task, individual group members may feel less motivated to contribute, since no one person is held directly responsible for completing the task. The result is that people may not work as hard, or accomplish as much, as they would if they were working alone and their individual output were being measured. This decrease in personal effort, especially on a simple group task, is known as social loafing. While it is not a deliberate behavior, the consequence of social loafing is less personal efficiency when working in groups than when working on one's own.

Using the example from the lecture, explain what social loafing is and how it affects people's behavior.

Preparation Time: 30 Seconds

Response Time: 60 Seconds

4. Now you will listen to a lecture. You will then be asked to summarize the lecture. You will have 20 seconds to prepare and 60 seconds to speak.

Now play Track 24 to hear Question 4.

Using points and examples from the talk, explain internal and external locus of control.

Preparation Time: 20 Seconds

Response Time: 60 Seconds

STOP. This is the end of the Speaking section of TOEFL iBT® Practice Test 1.

Reading

Listening

Speaking

Writing

Test 1

Test 2

Test 3

Test 4

Reading

Listening

Speaking

Writing

Test 1

Test 2

Test 3

Test 4

WRITING

In this section, you will be able to demonstrate your ability to use writing to communicate in an academic environment. There will be two writing tasks.

At the end of this Practice Test, you will find a script for the audio track, topic notes, sample responses, and comments on those responses by official raters.

Turn the page to see the directions for the first writing task.

Integrated Writing

For this task, you will read a passage about an academic topic. Then you will listen to a lecture about the same topic. You may take notes while you listen.

In your response, provide a detailed summary of the lecture and explain how the lecture relates to the reading passage.

In the actual test, you will have 3 minutes to read the passage and 20 minutes to write your response. While you write, you will be able to see the reading passage. If you finish your response before time is up, you may go on to the second writing task.

Now you will see the reading passage. It will be followed by a lecture.

Reading Time: 3 minutes

Some fuels, known as biofuels, can be extracted from plants that produce natural oils. One kind of biofuel comes from algae, the simplest plant organisms. Some people believe that fuel derived from algae could replace other kinds of fuel as our main source of energy. However, manufacturing fuel from algae creates some unique problems.

To get enough oil from algae, algae would have to be farmed on a large scale; this would require a good deal of land and water. In many parts of the world, however, there are dangerous shortages of farmable land, usable water, and agricultural food products. Since algae farming uses up land and water without producing food, building large-scale algae farming operations could make food shortages worse.

A second problem with using algae as a fuel source is that the equipment required to grow and extract oil from the algae is expensive. The cost of starting an algae farm is high. Companies would have to invest in large facilities to contain the algae and expose them to sunlight, in complicated machines to squeeze oil out of the algae, and in other equipment necessary to make the oil usable as fuel.

Third, farming algae is problematic because algae require a large quantity of carbon dioxide gas to grow. All plants need some carbon dioxide (CO_2), which they generally pull directly from the air. Algae, however, do not thrive without a very high concentration of this gas in their environment. To grow large amounts of algae, farmers would have to pump pure CO_2 into algae-growing tanks. Not all of this CO_2 would be absorbed by the algae; a significant amount would pass into the atmosphere. Since CO_2 is considered a pollutant, this would be harmful to the environment.

Now play Track 25.

Question 1

Summarize the points made in the lecture, being sure to explain how they respond to the specific concerns presented in the reading passage. You have 20 minutes to plan and write your response.

Some fuels, known as biofuels, can be extracted from plants that produce natural oils. One kind of biofuel comes from algae, the simplest plant organisms. Some people believe that fuel derived from algae could replace other kinds of fuel as our main source of energy. However, manufacturing fuel from algae creates some unique problems.

To get enough oil from algae, algae would have to be farmed on a large scale; this would require a good deal of land and water. In many parts of the world, however, there are dangerous shortages of farmable land, usable water, and agricultural food products. Since algae farming uses up land and water without producing food, building large-scale algae farming operations could make food shortages worse.

A second problem with using algae as a fuel source is that the equipment required to grow and extract oil from the algae is expensive. The cost of starting an algae farm is high. Companies would have to invest in large facilities to contain the algae and expose them to sunlight, in complicated machines to squeeze oil out of the algae, and in other equipment necessary to make the oil usable as fuel.

Third, farming algae is problematic because algae require a large quantity of carbon dioxide gas to grow. All plants need some carbon dioxide (CO_2), which they generally pull directly from the air. Algae, however, do not thrive without a very high concentration of this gas in their environment. To grow large amounts of algae, farmers would have to pump pure CO_2 into algae-growing tanks. Not all of this CO_2 would be absorbed by the algae; a significant amount would pass into the atmosphere. Since CO_2 is considered a pollutant, this would be harmful to the environment.

Response Time: 20 minutes

Writing for an Academic Discussion

For this task, you will read an online discussion. A professor has posted a question about a topic, and some classmates have responded with their ideas.

In the actual test, you will have 10 minutes to write a response that contributes to the discussion.

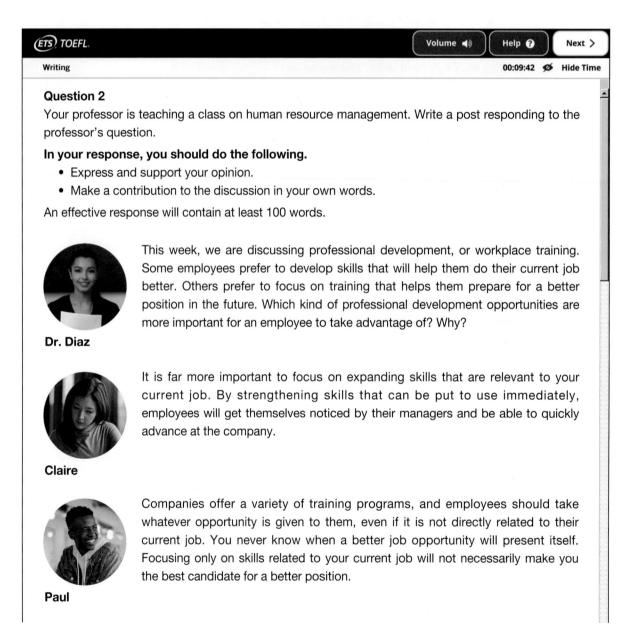

Question 2

Your professor is teaching a class on human resource management. Write a post responding to the professor's question.

In your response, you should do the following.

• Express and support your opinion.
• Make a contribution to the discussion in your own words.

An effective response will contain at least 100 words.

Dr. Diaz

This week, we are discussing professional development, or workplace training. Some employees prefer to develop skills that will help them do their current job better. Others prefer to focus on training that helps them prepare for a better position in the future. Which kind of professional development opportunities are more important for an employee to take advantage of? Why?

Claire

It is far more important to focus on expanding skills that are relevant to your current job. By strengthening skills that can be put to use immediately, employees will get themselves noticed by their managers and be able to quickly advance at the company.

Paul

Companies offer a variety of training programs, and employees should take whatever opportunity is given to them, even if it is not directly related to their current job. You never know when a better job opportunity will present itself. Focusing only on skills related to your current job will not necessarily make you the best candidate for a better position.

Reading

Listening

Speaking

Writing

Test 1

Test 2

Test 3

Test 4

STOP. This is the end of the Writing section of TOEFL iBT® Practice Test 1.

Chapter 7

Practice Test 2

Reading

Listening

Speaking

Writing

READING

In this section, you will be able to demonstrate your ability to understand academic passages in English. You will read and answer questions about **two passages**.

In the actual test, you will have 36 minutes total to read both passages and answer the questions. A clock will indicate how much time remains.

Some passages may include one or more notes explaining words or phrases. The words or phrases are marked with footnote numbers and the notes explaining them appear at the end of the passage.

Most questions are worth 1 point, but the last question for each passage is worth 2 points.

You may review and revise your answers in this section as long as time remains.

At the end of this practice test, you will find an answer key, information to help you determine your score, and explanations of the answers.

Reading

Listening

Speaking

Writing

Test 1

Test 2

Test 3

Test 4

LOIE FULLER

The United States dancer Loie Fuller (1862–1928) found theatrical dance in the late nineteenth century artistically unfulfilling. She considered herself an artist rather than a mere entertainer, and she, in turn, attracted the notice of other artists.

Fuller devised a type of dance that focused on the shifting play of lights and colors on the voluminous skirts or draperies she wore, which she kept in constant motion principally through movements of her arms, sometimes extended with wands concealed under her costumes. She rejected the technical virtuosity of movement in ballet, the most prestigious form of theatrical dance at that time, perhaps because her formal dance training was minimal. Although her early theatrical career had included stints as an actress, she was not primarily interested in storytelling or expressing emotions through dance; the drama of her dancing emanated from her visual effects.

Although she discovered and introduced her art in the United States, she achieved her greatest glory in Paris, where she was engaged by the Folies Bergère in 1892 and soon became "La Loie," the darling of Parisian audiences. Many of her dances represented elements or natural objects—Fire, the Lily, the Butterfly, and so on—and thus accorded well with the fashionable Art Nouveau style, which emphasized nature imagery and fluid, sinuous lines. Her dancing also attracted the attention of French poets and painters of the period, for it appealed to their liking for mystery, their belief in art for art's sake, a nineteenth-century idea that art is valuable in itself rather than because it may have some moral or educational benefit, and their efforts to synthesize form and content.

Fuller had scientific leanings and constantly experimented with electrical lighting (which was then in its infancy), colored gels, slide projections, and other aspects of stage technology. She invented and patented special arrangements of mirrors and concocted chemical dyes for her draperies. Her interest in color and light paralleled the research of several artists of the period, notably the painter Seurat, famed for his Pointillist technique of creating a sense of shapes and light on canvas by applying extremely small dots of color rather than by painting lines. One of Fuller's major inventions was underlighting, in which she stood on a pane of frosted glass illuminated from underneath. This was particularly effective in her *Fire Dance* (1895), performed to the music of Richard Wagner's "Ride of the Valkyries." The dance caught the eye of artist Henri de Toulouse-Lautrec, who depicted it in a lithograph.

As her technological expertise grew more sophisticated, so did the other aspects of her dances. **(A)** Although she gave little thought to music in her earliest dances, she later used scores by Gluck, Beethoven, Schubert, Chopin, and Wagner, eventually graduating to Stravinsky, Fauré Debussy, and Mussorgsky, composers who were then considered progressive. **(B)** She began to address more ambitious themes in her dances such as *The Sea*, in which her dancers invisibly agitated a huge expanse of silk, played upon by colored lights. **(C)** Always open to scientific and technological innovations, she befriended the scientists Marie and Pierre Curie upon their discovery of radium and created a *Radium Dance*, which simulated the phosphorescence of that element. **(D)** She both appeared in films—then in an early stage of development—and made them herself; the hero of her fairy–tale film *Le Lys de la Vie* (1919) was played by René Clair, later a leading French film director.

At the Paris Exposition in 1900, she had her own theater, where, in addition to her own dances, she presented pantomimes by the Japanese actress Sada Yacco. She assembled an all-female company at this time and established a school around 1908, but neither survived her. Although she is remembered today chiefly for her innovations in stage lighting, her activities also touched Isadora Duncan and Ruth St. Denis, two other United States dancers who were experimenting with new types of dance. She sponsored Duncan's first appearance in Europe. Her theater at the Paris Exposition was visited by St. Denis, who found new ideas about stagecraft in Fuller's work and fresh sources for her art in Sada Yacco's plays. In 1924 St. Denis paid tribute to Fuller with the duet *Valse à la Loie*.

Paragraph 1
- -

The United States dancer Loie Fuller (1862–1928) found theatrical dance in the late nineteenth century artistically unfulfilling. She considered herself an artist rather than a mere entertainer, and she, in turn, attracted the notice of other artists.

1. What can be inferred from paragraph 1 about theatrical dance in the late nineteenth century?
   Ⓐ It influenced many artists outside of the field of dance.
   Ⓑ It was very similar to theatrical dance of the early nineteenth century.
   Ⓒ It was more a form of entertainment than a form of serious art.
   Ⓓ It was a relatively new art form in the United States.

Fuller devised a type of dance that focused on the shifting play of lights and colors on the voluminous skirts or draperies she wore, which she kept in constant motion principally through movements of her arms, sometimes extended with wands concealed under her costumes. She rejected the technical virtuosity of movement in ballet, the most prestigious form of theatrical dance at that time, perhaps because her formal dance training was minimal. Although her early theatrical career had included stints as an actress, she was not primarily interested in storytelling or expressing emotions through dance; the drama of her dancing emanated from her visual effects.

2. According to paragraph 2, all of the following are characteristic of Fuller's type of dance EXCEPT

  Ⓐ experimentation using color

  Ⓑ large and full costumes

  Ⓒ continuous movement of her costumes

  Ⓓ technical virtuosity of movement

3. Which of the sentences below best expresses the essential information in the highlighted sentence in the passage? Incorrect choices change the meaning in important ways or leave out essential information.

  Ⓐ Fuller was more interested in dance's visual impact than in its narrative or emotional possibilities.

  Ⓑ Fuller used visual effects to dramatize the stories and emotions expressed in her work.

  Ⓒ Fuller believed that the drama of her dancing sprang from her emotional style of storytelling.

  Ⓓ Fuller's focus on the visual effects of dance resulted from her early theatrical training as an actress.

Paragraph 3

Although she discovered and introduced her art in the United States, she achieved her greatest glory in Paris, where she was engaged by the Folies Bergère in 1892 and soon became "La Loie," the darling of Parisian audiences. Many of her dances represented elements or natural objects—Fire, the Lily, the Butterfly, and so on—and thus accorded well with the fashionable Art Nouveau style, which emphasized nature imagery and fluid, sinuous lines. Her dancing also attracted the attention of French poets and painters of the period, for it appealed to their liking for mystery, their belief in art for art's sake, a nineteenth-century idea that art is valuable in itself rather than because it may have some moral or educational benefit, and their efforts to synthesize form and content.

4. The word "synthesize" in the passage is closest in meaning to

   Ⓐ improve

   Ⓑ define

   Ⓒ simplify

   Ⓓ integrate

5. According to paragraph 3, why was Fuller's work well received in Paris?

   Ⓐ Parisian audiences were particularly interested in artists and artistic movements from the United States.

   Ⓑ Influential poets tried to interest dancers in Fuller's work when she arrived in Paris.

   Ⓒ Fuller's work at this time borrowed directly from French artists working in other media.

   Ⓓ Fuller's dances were in harmony with the artistic values already present in Paris.

Paragraph 4

Fuller had scientific leanings and constantly experimented with electrical lighting (which was then in its infancy), colored gels, slide projections, and other aspects of stage technology. She invented and patented special arrangements of mirrors and concocted chemical dyes for her draperies. Her interest in color and light paralleled the research of several artists of the period, notably the painter Seurat, famed for his Pointillist technique of creating a sense of shapes and light on canvas by applying extremely small dots of color rather than by painting lines. One of Fuller's major inventions was underlighting, in which she stood on a pane of frosted glass illuminated from underneath. This was particularly effective in her *Fire Dance* (1895), performed to the music of Richard Wagner's "Ride of the Valkyries." The dance caught the eye of artist Henri de Toulouse-Lautrec, who depicted it in a lithograph.

6. According to paragraph 4, Fuller's *Fire Dance* was notable in part for its

   Ⓐ use of colored gels to illuminate glass

   Ⓑ use of dyes and paints to create an image of fire

   Ⓒ technique of lighting the dancer from beneath

   Ⓓ draperies with small dots resembling the Pointillist technique of Seurat

As her technological expertise grew more sophisticated, so did the other aspects of her dances. Although she gave little thought to music in her earliest dances, she later used scores by Gluck, Beethoven, Schubert, Chopin, and Wagner, eventually graduating to Stravinsky, Faure, Debussy, and Mussorgsky, composers who were then considered progressive. She began to address more ambitious themes in her dances such as *The Sea*, in which her dancers invisibly agitated a huge expanse of silk, played upon by colored lights. Always open to scientific and technological innovations, she befriended the scientists Marie and Pierre Curie upon their discovery of radium and created a *Radium Dance*, which simulated the phosphorescence of that element. She both appeared in films—then in an early stage of development—and made them herself; the hero of her fairy–tale film *Le Lys de la Vie* (1919) was played by René Clair, later a leading French film director.

7. Why does the author mention Fuller's "*The Sea*"?
   Ⓐ To point out a dance of Fuller's in which music did not play an important role
   Ⓑ To explain why Fuller sometimes used music by progressive composers
   Ⓒ To illustrate a particular way in which Fuller developed as an artist
   Ⓓ To illustrate how Fuller's interest in science was reflected in her work

At the Paris Exposition in 1900, she had her own theater, where, in addition to her own dances, she presented pantomimes by the Japanese actress Sada Yacco. She assembled an all-female company at this time and established a school around 1908, but neither survived her. Although she is remembered today chiefly for her innovations in stage lighting, her activities also touched Isadora Duncan and Ruth St. Denis, two other United States dancers who were experimenting with new types of dance. She sponsored Duncan's first appearance in Europe. Her theater at the Paris Exposition was visited by St. Denis, who found new ideas about stagecraft in Fuller's work and fresh sources for her art in Sada Yacco's plays. In 1924 St. Denis paid tribute to Fuller with the duet *Valse à la Loie*.

8. According to paragraph 6, what was true of Fuller's theater at the Paris Exposition?
   Ⓐ It presented some works that were not by Fuller.
   Ⓑ It featured performances by prominent male as well as female dancers.
   Ⓒ It became a famous school that is still named in honor of Fuller.
   Ⓓ It continued to operate as a theater after Fuller died.

Paragraph 5

As her technological expertise grew more sophisticated, so did the other aspects of her dances. **(A)** Although she gave little thought to music in her earliest dances, she later used scores by Gluck, Beethoven, Schubert, Chopin, and Wagner, eventually graduating to Stravinsky, Fauré, Debussy, and Mussorgsky, composers who were then considered progressive. **(B)** She began to address more ambitious themes in her dances such as *The Sea*, in which her dancers invisibly agitated a huge expanse of silk, played upon by colored lights. **(C)** Always open to scientific and technological innovations, she befriended the scientists Marie and Pierre Curie upon their discovery of radium and created a *Radium Dance*, which simulated the phosphorescence of that element. **(D)** She both appeared in films—then in an early stage of development—and made them herself; the hero of her fairy–tale film *Le Lys de la Vie* (1919) was played by René Clair, later a leading French film director.

9. **Directions:** Look at the part of the passage that is displayed above. The letters **(A)**, **(B)**, **(C)**, and **(D)** indicate where the following sentence could be added.

   For all her originality in dance, her interests expanded beyond it into newly emerging artistic media.

   Where would the sentence best fit?
   - Ⓐ Choice A
   - Ⓑ Choice B
   - Ⓒ Choice C
   - Ⓓ Choice D

10. **Directions:** An introductory sentence for a brief summary of the passage is provided below. Complete the summary by selecting the THREE answer choices that express the most important ideas in the passage. Some sentences do not belong in the summary because they express ideas that are not presented in the passage or are minor ideas in the passage. **This question is worth 2 points.**

Loie Fuller was an important and innovative dancer.

- ◆
- ◆
- ◆

Answer Choices

A Fuller believed that audiences in the late nineteenth century had lost interest in most theatrical dance.

B Fuller transformed dance in part by creating dance interpretations of works by poets and painters.

C Fuller's work influenced a number of other dancers who were interested in experimental dance.

D Fuller introduced many technical innovations to the staging of theatrical dance.

E Fuller continued to develop throughout her career, creating more complex works and exploring new artistic media.

F By the 1920s, Fuller's theater at the Paris Exposition had become the world center for innovative dance.

GREEN ICEBERGS

Icebergs are massive blocks of ice, irregular in shape; they float with only about 12 percent of their mass above the sea surface. They are formed by glaciers—large rivers of ice that begin inland in the snows of Greenland, Antarctica, and Alaska—and move slowly toward the sea. The forward movement, the melting at the base of the glacier where it meets the ocean, and waves and tidal action cause blocks of ice to break off and float out to sea.

Icebergs are ordinarily blue to white, although they sometimes appear dark or opaque because they carry gravel and bits of rock. They may change color with changing light conditions and cloud cover, glowing pink or gold in the morning or evening light, but this color change is generally related to the low angle of the Sun above the horizon. **(A)** However, travelers to Antarctica have repeatedly reported seeing green icebergs in the Weddell Sea and, more commonly, close to the Amery Ice Shelf in East Antarctica.

(B) One explanation for green icebergs attributes their color to an optical illusion when blue ice is illuminated by a near-horizon red Sun, but green icebergs stand out among white and blue icebergs under a great variety of light conditions. **(C)** Another suggestion is that the color might be related to ice with high levels of metallic compounds, including copper and iron. **(D)** Recent expeditions have taken ice samples from green icebergs and ice cores—vertical, cylindrical ice samples reaching down to great depths—from the glacial ice shelves along the Antarctic continent. Analyses of these cores and samples provide a different solution to the problem.

The ice shelf cores, with a total length of 215 meters (705 feet), were long enough to penetrate through glacial ice—which is formed from the compaction of snow and contains air bubbles—and to continue into the clear, bubble-free ice formed from seawater that freezes onto the bottom of the glacial ice. The properties of this clear sea ice were very similar to the ice from the green iceberg. The scientists concluded that green icebergs form when a two-layer block of shelf ice breaks away and capsizes (turns upside down), exposing the bubble-free shelf ice that was formed from seawater.

A green iceberg that stranded just west of the Amery Ice Shelf showed two distinct layers: bubbly blue-white ice and bubble-free green ice separated by a one-meter-long ice layer containing sediments. The green ice portion was textured by seawater erosion. Where cracks were present, the color was light green because of light scattering; where no cracks were present, the color was dark green. No air bubbles were present in the green ice, suggesting that the ice was not formed from the compression of snow but instead from the freezing of seawater. Large concentrations of single-celled organisms with green pigments (coloring substances) occur along the edges of the ice shelves in this region, and the seawater is rich in their decomposing organic material. The green iceberg did not contain large amounts of particles from these organisms, but the ice had accumulated dissolved organic matter from the seawater. It appears that unlike salt, dissolved organic substances are not excluded from the ice in the freezing process. Analysis shows that the dissolved organic material absorbs enough blue wavelengths from solar light to make the ice appear green.

Chemical evidence shows that platelets (minute flat portions) of ice form in the water and then accrete and stick to the bottom of the ice shelf to form a slush (partially melted snow). The slush is compacted by an unknown mechanism, and solid, bubble-free ice is formed from water high in soluble organic substances. When an iceberg separates from the ice shelf and capsizes, the green ice is exposed.

The Amery Ice Shelf appears to be uniquely suited to the production of green icebergs. Once detached from the ice shelf, these bergs drift in the currents and wind systems surrounding Antarctica and can be found scattered among Antarctica's less colorful icebergs.

Paragraph 1

Icebergs are massive blocks of ice, irregular in shape; they float with only about 12 percent of their mass above the sea surface. They are formed by glaciers—large rivers of ice that begin inland in the snows of Greenland, Antarctica, and Alaska—and move slowly toward the sea. The forward movement, the melting at the base of the glacier where it meets the ocean, and waves and tidal action cause blocks of ice to break off and float out to sea.

11. According to paragraph 1, all of the following are true of icebergs EXCEPT:

Ⓐ They do not have a regular shape.

Ⓑ They are formed where glaciers meet the ocean.

Ⓒ Most of their mass is above the sea surface.

Ⓓ Waves and tides cause them to break off glaciers.

Paragraph 2

Icebergs are ordinarily blue to white, although they sometimes appear dark or opaque because they carry gravel and bits of rock. They may change color with changing light conditions and cloud cover, glowing pink or gold in the morning or evening light, but this color change is generally related to the low angle of the Sun above the horizon. However, travelers to Antarctica have repeatedly reported seeing green icebergs in the Weddell Sea and, more commonly, close to the Amery Ice Shelf in East Antarctica.

12. According to paragraph 2, what causes icebergs to sometimes appear dark or opaque?

    Ⓐ A heavy cloud cover

    Ⓑ The presence of gravel or bits of rock

    Ⓒ The low angle of the Sun above the horizon

    Ⓓ The presence of large cracks in their surface

Paragraph 4

The ice shelf cores, with a total length of 215 meters (705 feet), were long enough to penetrate through glacial ice—which is formed from the compaction of snow and contains air bubbles—and to continue into the clear, bubble-free ice formed from seawater that freezes onto the bottom of the glacial ice. The properties of this clear sea ice were very similar to the ice from the green iceberg. The scientists concluded that green icebergs form when a two-layer block of shelf ice breaks away and capsizes (turns upside down), exposing the bubble-free shelf ice that was formed from seawater.

13. The word "penetrate" in the passage is closest in meaning to

    Ⓐ collect

    Ⓑ pierce

    Ⓒ melt

    Ⓓ endure

14. According to paragraph 4, how is glacial ice formed?

    Ⓐ By the compaction of snow

    Ⓑ By the freezing of seawater on the bottom of ice shelves

    Ⓒ By breaking away from the ice shelf

    Ⓓ By the capsizing of a two-layer block of shelf ice

15. According to paragraph 4, ice shelf cores helped scientists explain the formation of green icebergs by showing that

    Ⓐ the ice at the bottom of green icebergs is bubble-free ice formed from frozen seawater

    Ⓑ bubble-free ice is found at the top of the ice shelf

    Ⓒ glacial ice is lighter and floats better than sea ice

    Ⓓ the clear sea ice at the bottom of the ice shelf is similar to ice from a green iceberg

Reading

Listening

Speaking

Writing

Test 1

Test 2

Test 3

Test 4

A green iceberg that stranded just west of the Amery Ice Shelf showed two distinct layers: bubbly blue-white ice and bubble-free green ice separated by a one-meter-long ice layer containing sediments. The green ice portion was textured by seawater erosion. Where cracks were present, the color was light green because of light scattering; where no cracks were present, the color was dark green. No air bubbles were present in the green ice, suggesting that the ice was not formed from the compression of snow but instead from the freezing of seawater. Large concentrations of single-celled organisms with green pigments (coloring substances) occur along the edges of the ice shelves in this region, and the seawater is rich in their decomposing organic material. The green iceberg did not contain large amounts of particles from these organisms, but the ice had accumulated dissolved organic matter from the seawater. It appears that unlike salt, dissolved organic substances are not excluded from the ice in the freezing process. Analysis shows that the dissolved organic material absorbs enough blue wavelengths from solar light to make the ice appear green.

16. Why does the author mention that "The green ice portion was textured by seawater erosion"?

    Ⓐ To explain why cracks in the iceberg appeared light green instead of dark green

    Ⓑ To suggest that green ice is more easily eroded by seawater than white ice is

    Ⓒ To support the idea that the green ice had been the bottom layer before capsizing

    Ⓓ To explain how the air bubbles had been removed from the green ice

17. The word "excluded" in the passage is closest in meaning to

    Ⓐ kept out

    Ⓑ compressed

    Ⓒ damaged

    Ⓓ gathered together

18. Paragraph 5 supports which of the following statements about the Amery Ice Shelf?

    Ⓐ The Amery Ice Shelf produces only green icebergs.

    Ⓑ The Amery Ice Shelf produces green icebergs because its ice contains high levels of metallic compounds such as copper and iron.

    Ⓒ The Amery Ice Shelf produces green icebergs because the seawater is rich in a particular kind of soluble organic material.

    Ⓓ No green icebergs are found far from the Amery Ice Shelf.

Icebergs are ordinarily blue to white, although they sometimes appear dark or opaque because they carry gravel and bits of rock. They may change color with changing light conditions and cloud cover, glowing pink or gold in the morning or evening light, but this color change is generally related to the low angle of the Sun above the horizon. **(A)** However, travelers to Antarctica have repeatedly reported seeing green icebergs in the Weddell Sea and, more commonly, close to the Amery Ice Shelf in East Antarctica.

(B) One explanation for green icebergs attributes their color to an optical illusion when blue ice is illuminated by a near-horizon red Sun, but green icebergs stand out among white and blue icebergs under a great variety of light conditions. **(C)** Another suggestion is that the color might be related to ice with high levels of metallic compounds, including copper and iron. **(D)** Recent expeditions have taken ice samples from green icebergs and ice cores—vertical, cylindrical ice samples reaching down to great depths—from the glacial ice shelves along the Antarctic continent. Analyses of these cores and samples provide a different solution to the problem.

19. **Directions:** Look at the part of the passage that is displayed above. The letters **(A)**, **(B)**, **(C)**, and **(D)** indicate where the following sentence could be added.

Scientists have differed as to whether icebergs appear green as a result of light conditions or because of something in the ice itself.

Where would the sentence best fit?

Ⓐ Choice A
Ⓑ Choice B
Ⓒ Choice C
Ⓓ Choice D

20. **Directions:** An introductory sentence for a brief summary of the passage is provided below. Complete the summary by selecting the THREE answer choices that express the most important ideas in the passage. Some sentences do not belong in the summary because they express ideas that are not presented in the passage or are minor ideas in the passage. **This question is worth 2 points.**

Several suggestions, ranging from light conditions to the presence of metallic compounds, have been offered to explain why some icebergs appear green.

- ◆
- ◆
- ◆

Answer Choices

[A] Ice cores were used to determine that green icebergs were formed from the compaction of metallic compounds, including copper and iron.

[B] All ice shelves can produce green icebergs, but the Amery Ice Shelf is especially well suited to do so.

[C] Green icebergs form when a two-layer block of ice breaks away from a glacier and capsizes, exposing the bottom sea ice to view.

[D] Ice cores and samples revealed that both ice shelves and green icebergs contain a layer of bubbly glacial ice and a layer of bubble-free sea ice.

[E] Green icebergs are white until they come into contact with seawater containing platelets and soluble organic green pigments.

[F] In a green iceberg, the sea ice contains large concentrations of organic matter from the seawater.

STOP. This is the end of the Reading section of TOEFL iBT® Practice Test 2.

Reading

Listening

Speaking

Writing

Test 1

Test 2

Test 3

Test 4

LISTENING

In this section, you will be able to demonstrate your ability to understand conversations and lectures in English.

In the actual test, the section is divided into two separately timed parts. You will hear each conversation or lecture only one time. A clock will indicate how much time remains. The clock will count down only while you are answering questions, not while you are listening. You may take up to 16.5 minutes to answer the questions.

In this practice test, there is no time limit for answering questions.

You may take notes while you listen. You may use your notes to help you answer the questions. Your notes will not be scored.

Answer the questions based on what is stated or implied by the speakers.

In some questions, you will see this icon: 🎧 . This means that you will hear, but not see, part of the question.

In the actual test, you must answer each question. You cannot return to previous questions.

At the end of this practice test, you will find an answer key, information to help you determine your score, and explanations of the answers.

Listen to Track 34.

1. Why does the student go to see the professor?

    Ⓐ For suggestions on how to write interview questions
    Ⓑ For assistance in finding a person to interview
    Ⓒ To ask for advice on starting a business
    Ⓓ To schedule an interview with him

2. Why does the student mention her high school newspaper?

    Ⓐ To inform the professor that she plans to print the interview there
    Ⓑ To explain why the assignment is difficult for her
    Ⓒ To show that she enjoys writing for school newspapers
    Ⓓ To indicate that she has experience with conducting interviews

3. How does the professor help the student?

    Ⓐ He gives her a list of local business owners.
    Ⓑ He allows her to interview business owners in her hometown.
    Ⓒ He suggests that she read the business section of the newspaper.
    Ⓓ He gives her more time to complete the assignment.

4. What does the professor want the students to learn from the assignment?

    Ⓐ That starting a business is risky
    Ⓑ Why writing articles on local businesses is important
    Ⓒ How to develop a detailed business plan
    Ⓓ What personality traits are typical of business owners

5. *Listen again to part of the conversation by playing Track 35.*
   Then answer the question.

   What does the student imply?

    Ⓐ She is surprised by the professor's reaction.
    Ⓑ The professor has not quite identified her concern.
    Ⓒ The professor has guessed correctly what her problem is.
    Ⓓ She does not want to finish the assignment.

Reading

Listening

Speaking

Writing

Test 1

Test 2

Test 3

Test 4

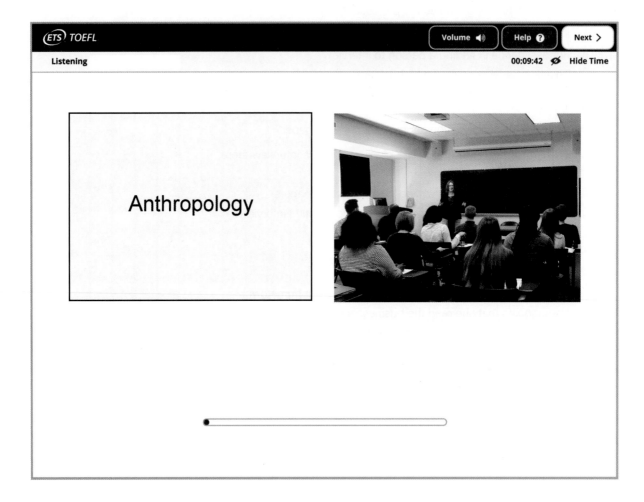

6. What does the professor mainly discuss?

    Ⓐ Various errors in early calendars

    Ⓑ Why people came to believe that Earth moves around the Sun

    Ⓒ Examples of various types of calendars used in different cultures

    Ⓓ The belief that the position of planets and stars can predict future events

7. The professor discusses various theories on how Stonehenge was used. What can be inferred about the professor's opinion?

    Ⓐ She is sure Stonehenge was used as a calendar.

    Ⓑ She believes the main use for Stonehenge was probably as a temple or a tomb.

    Ⓒ She thinks that the stones were mainly used as a record of historical events.

    Ⓓ She admits that the purpose for which Stonehenge was constructed may never be known.

8. According to the professor, how was the Mayan calendar mainly used?

    Ⓐ To keep track of long historical cycles

    Ⓑ To keep track of the lunar months

    Ⓒ To predict the outcome of royal decisions

    Ⓓ To allow priests to compare the orbits of Earth and Venus

9. According to the professor, what was the basis of the ancient Chinese astrological cycle?

    Ⓐ The cycle of night and day

    Ⓑ The orbit of the Moon

    Ⓒ The cycle of the seasons

    Ⓓ The orbit of the planet Jupiter

10. How did the Romans succeed in making their calendar more precise?

    Ⓐ By changing the number of weeks in a year

    Ⓑ By adding an extra day every four years

    Ⓒ By carefully observing the motion of the planet Jupiter

    Ⓓ By adopting elements of the Chinese calendar

11. How does the professor organize the lecture?

    Ⓐ By mentioning the problem of creating a calendar, then describing various attempts to deal with it

    Ⓑ By speaking of the modern calendar first, then comparing it with earlier ones

    Ⓒ By discussing how a prehistoric calendar was adapted by several different cultures

    Ⓓ By emphasizing the advantages and disadvantages of using various time cycles

Listen to Track 37.

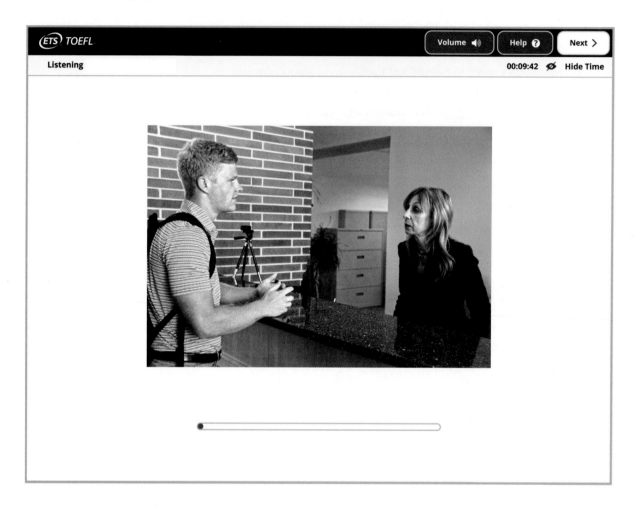

12. Why does the student go to Professor Kirk's office?

    Ⓐ To find out if he needs to take a certain class to graduate

    Ⓑ To respond to Professor Kirk's invitation

    Ⓒ To ask Professor Kirk to be his advisor

    Ⓓ To ask Professor Kirk to sign a form

13. Why is the woman surprised at the man's request?

    Ⓐ He has not tried to sign up for Introduction to Biology at the registrar's office.

    Ⓑ He has waited until his senior year to take Introduction to Biology.

    Ⓒ A journalism student should not need a biology class.

    Ⓓ Professor Kirk no longer teaches Introduction to Biology.

14. What does the man say about his advisor?

    Ⓐ She encouraged the man to take a science class.

    Ⓑ She encouraged the man to major in journalism.

    Ⓒ She is not aware of the man's problem.

    Ⓓ She thinks very highly of Professor Kirk.

15. How will the man probably try to communicate his problem to Professor Kirk?

    Ⓐ By calling her

    Ⓑ By sending an e-mail to her

    Ⓒ By leaving her a note

    Ⓓ By visiting her during office hours

16. *Listen to Track 38 to answer the question.*

    Why does the man say this to the woman?

    Ⓐ To thank the woman for solving his problem

    Ⓑ To politely refuse the woman's suggestion

    Ⓒ To explain why he needs the woman's help

    Ⓓ To show that he understands that the woman is busy

Listen to Track 39.

17. What is the lecture mainly about?

    Ⓐ Various theories explaining why Mars cannot sustain life

    Ⓑ Various causes of geological changes on Mars

    Ⓒ The development of views about the nature of Mars

    Ⓓ Why it has been difficult to obtain information about Mars

18. According to the professor, what was concluded about Mars after the first spacecraft flew by it in 1965?

    Ⓐ It had few geological features of interest.

    Ⓑ It was similar to Earth but colder.

    Ⓒ It had at one time supported life.

    Ⓓ It had water under its surface.

19. What does the professor imply about conditions on Mars billions of years ago?
Select 2 answers.

    Ⓐ Mars was probably even drier than it is today.

    Ⓑ The atmospheric pressure and the temperature may have been higher than they are today.

    Ⓒ Mars was inhabited by organisms that have since become fossilized.

    Ⓓ Large floods were shaping the planet's surface.

20. What is the possible significance of the gullies found on Mars in recent years?

    Ⓐ They may indicate current volcanic activity on Mars.

    Ⓑ They may indicate that the surface of Mars is becoming increasingly drier.

    Ⓒ They may indicate the current existence of water on Mars.

    Ⓓ They may hold fossils of organisms that once existed on Mars.

21. *Listen to Track 40 to answer the question.*

    Why does the professor say this?

    Ⓐ To stress that Mars is no longer interesting to explore

    Ⓑ To describe items that the spacecraft brought back from Mars

    Ⓒ To share his interest in the study of fossils

    Ⓓ To show how much the view of Mars changed based on new evidence

22. *Listen again to part of the lecture by playing Track 41.*
Then answer the question.

    Why does the student say this?

    Ⓐ To ask for clarification of a previous statement

    Ⓑ To convey his opinion

    Ⓒ To rephrase an earlier question

    Ⓓ To express his approval

23. What does the professor mainly discuss?

    Ⓐ The design and creation of the Statue of Liberty

    Ⓑ The creators of two colossal statues in the United States

    Ⓒ The purpose and symbolism of colossal statues

    Ⓓ The cost of colossal statues in ancient versus modern times

24. What evidence does the professor give that supports the idea that modern-day colossal statues are valued social and political symbols?

    Ⓐ They are very costly to build.

    Ⓑ They are studied in classrooms around the world.

    Ⓒ They are designed to last for thousands of years.

    Ⓓ They are inspired by great poetry.

25. According to the professor, what was one result of the Great Depression of the 1930s?

    Ⓐ International alliances eroded.

    Ⓑ Immigration to the United States increased.

    Ⓒ The public experienced a loss of confidence.

    Ⓓ The government could no longer provide funds for the arts.

26. According to the professor, why did the state of South Dakota originally want to create a colossal monument?

    Ⓐ To generate income from tourism

    Ⓑ To symbolize the unity of society

    Ⓒ To commemorate the Great Depression

    Ⓓ To honor United States Presidents

27. Why does the professor discuss the poem by Emma Lazarus?

    Ⓐ To emphasize the close relationship between literature and sculpture

    Ⓑ To illustrate how the meaning associated with a monument can change

    Ⓒ To stress the importance of the friendship between France and the United States

    Ⓓ To point out a difference between Mount Rushmore and the Statue of Liberty

28. *Listen again to part of the lecture by playing Track 43.*
Then answer the question.

    What does the professor imply about the poem by Emma Lazarus?

    Ⓐ It is one of his favorite poems.

    Ⓑ Few people have read the entire poem.

    Ⓒ He does not need to recite the full text of the poem.

    Ⓓ Lazarus was not able to complete the poem.

STOP. This is the end of the Listening section of TOEFL iBT® Practice Test 2.

Reading

Listening

Speaking

Writing

Test 1

Test 2

Test 3

Test 4

SPEAKING

In this section, you will be able to demonstrate your ability to speak about a variety of topics.

In the actual test, the Speaking section will last approximately 16 minutes. You will answer four questions by speaking into the microphone. You may use your notes to help you answer the questions. Your notes will not be scored. For each question, you will have time to prepare before giving your response. You should answer the questions as completely as possible in the time allowed.

For this practice test, you may want to use a personal recording device to record and play back your responses.

For each question, play the audio track listed and follow the directions to complete the task. You may take notes while you listen.

At the end of this Practice Test, you will find scripts for the audio tracks, Important Points for each question, sample responses, and comments on those responses by official raters.

1. You will now be asked to give your opinion about a familiar topic. After you hear the question, you will have 15 seconds to prepare your response and 45 seconds to speak.

Now play Track 44 to hear Question 1.

Some students would prefer to live with roommates. Others would prefer to live alone. Which option would you prefer and why?

> **Preparation Time: 15 Seconds**
> **Response Time: 45 Seconds**

2. Now you will read a passage about a campus situation and then listen to a conversation about the same topic. You will then answer a question, using information from both the reading passage and the conversation. You will have 30 seconds to prepare and 60 seconds to speak.

Now play Track 45 to hear Question 2.

> **Reading Time: 50 Seconds**

University May Build New Student Apartments Off Campus

The Department of Student Housing is considering whether to build new student housing off campus in a residential area of town. Two of the major factors influencing the decision will be parking and space. Those who support building off campus argue that building new housing on campus would further increase the number of cars on and around campus and consume space that could be better used for future projects that the entire university community could benefit from. Supporters also say that students might even have a richer college experience by being connected to the local community and patronizing stores and other businesses in town.

The woman expresses her opinion of the university's plan. State her opinion and explain the reasons she gives for holding that opinion.

Preparation Time: 30 Seconds

Response Time: 60 Seconds

3. Now you will read a passage about an academic subject and then listen to a lecture on the same topic. You will then answer a question, using information from both the reading passage and the lecture. You will have 30 seconds to prepare and 60 seconds to speak.

Now play Track 46 to hear Question 3.

Reading Time: 45 Seconds

Actor-observer

People account for their own behavior differently from how they account for the behavior of others. When observing the behavior of others, we tend to attribute their actions to their character or their personality rather than to external factors. In contrast, we tend to explain our own behavior in terms of situational factors beyond our own control rather than attributing it to our own character. One explanation for this difference is that people are aware of the situational forces affecting them but not of situational forces affecting other people. Thus, when evaluating someone else's behavior, we focus on the person rather than the situation.

Explain how the two examples discussed by the professor illustrate differences in the ways people explain behavior.

Preparation Time: 30 Seconds

Response Time: 60 Seconds

4. Now you will listen to a lecture. You will then be asked to summarize the lecture. You will have 20 seconds to prepare your response and 60 seconds to speak.

Now play Track 47 to hear Question 4.

Using points and examples from the talk, explain how learning art can impact a child's development.

Preparation Time: 20 Seconds

Response Time: 60 Seconds

STOP. This is the end of the Speaking section of TOEFL iBT® Practice Test 2.

Reading
Listening
Speaking
Writing
Test 1
Test 2
Test 3
Test 4

WRITING

In this section, you will be able to demonstrate your ability to use writing to communicate in an academic environment. There will be two writing tasks.

At the end of this Practice Test, you will find a script for the audio track, topic notes, sample responses, and comments on those responses by official raters.

Turn the page to see the directions for the first writing task.

Integrated Writing

For this task, you will read a passage about an academic topic. Then you will listen to a lecture about the same topic. You may take notes while you listen.

In your response, provide a detailed summary of the lecture and explain how the lecture relates to the reading passage.

In the actual test, you will have 3 minutes to read the passage and 20 minutes to write your response. While you write, you will be able to see the reading passage. If you finish your response before time is up, you may go on to the second writing task.

Now you will see the reading passage. It will be followed by a lecture.

Reading

Listening

Speaking

Writing

Test 1

Test 2

Test 3

Test 4

Reading Time: 3 minutes

Professors are normally found in university classrooms, offices, and libraries doing research and lecturing to their students. More and more, however, they also appear as guests on television news programs, giving expert commentary on the latest events in the world. These television appearances are of great benefit to the professors themselves as well as to their universities and the general public.

Professors benefit from appearing on television because by doing so they acquire reputations as authorities in their academic fields among a much wider audience than they have on campus. If a professor publishes views in an academic journal, only other scholars will learn about and appreciate those views. But when a professor appears on TV, thousands of people outside the narrow academic community become aware of the professor's ideas. So when professors share their ideas with a television audience, the professors' importance as scholars is enhanced.

Universities also benefit from such appearances. The universities receive positive publicity when their professors appear on TV. When people see a knowledgeable faculty member of a university on television, they think more highly of that university. That then leads to an improved reputation for the university. And that improved reputation in turn leads to more donations for the university and more applications from potential students.

Finally, the public gains from professors' appearing on television. Most television viewers normally have no contact with university professors. When professors appear on television, viewers have a chance to learn from experts and to be exposed to views they might otherwise never hear about. Television is generally a medium for commentary that tends to be superficial, not deep or thoughtful. From professors on television, by contrast, viewers get a taste of real expertise and insight.

Now play Track 48.

Question 1

Summarize the points made in the lecture, being sure to explain how they respond to the specific concerns presented in the reading passage. You have 20 minutes to plan and write your response.

Response Time: 20 minutes

Professors are normally found in university classrooms, offices, and libraries doing research and lecturing to their students. More and more, however, they also appear as guests on television news programs, giving expert commentary on the latest events in the world. These television appearances are of great benefit to the professors themselves as well as to their universities and the general public.

Professors benefit from appearing on television because by doing so they acquire reputations as authorities in their academic fields among a much wider audience than they have on campus. If a professor publishes views in an academic journal, only other scholars will learn about and appreciate those views. But when a professor appears on TV, thousands of people outside the narrow academic community become aware of the professor's ideas. So when professors share their ideas with a television audience, the professors' importance as scholars is enhanced.

Universities also benefit from such appearances. The universities receive positive publicity when their professors appear on TV. When people see a knowledgeable faculty member of a university on television, they think more highly of that university. That then leads to an improved reputation for the university. And that improved reputation in turn leads to more donations for the university and more applications from potential students.

Finally, the public gains from professors' appearing on television. Most television viewers normally have no contact with university professors. When professors appear on television, viewers have a chance to learn from experts and to be exposed to views they might otherwise never hear about. Television is generally a medium for commentary that tends to be superficial, not deep or thoughtful. From professors on television, by contrast, viewers get a taste of real expertise and insight.

Writing for an Academic Discussion

For this task, you will read an online discussion. A professor has posted a question about a topic, and some classmates have responded with their ideas.

In the actual test, you will have 10 minutes to write a response that contributes to the discussion.

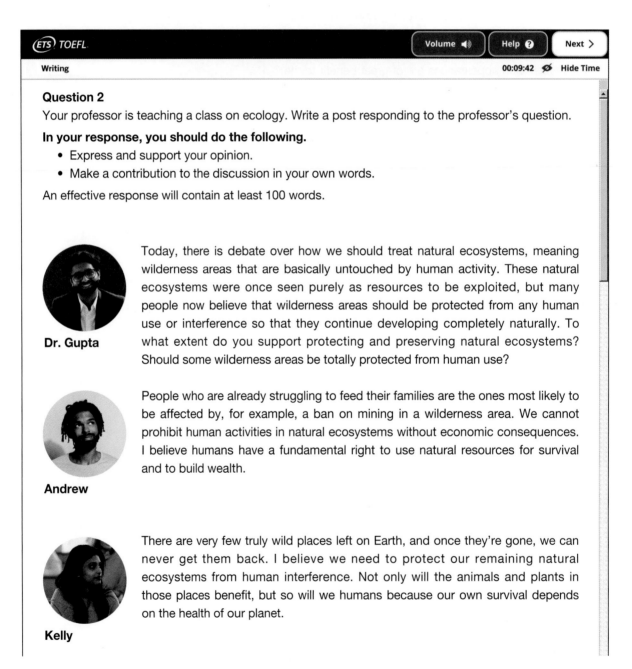

(ETS) TOEFL. | Volume ◀) | Help ❓ | Next >
Writing | 00:09:42 ✍ Hide Time

Question 2
Your professor is teaching a class on ecology. Write a post responding to the professor's question.

In your response, you should do the following.
- Express and support your opinion.
- Make a contribution to the discussion in your own words.

An effective response will contain at least 100 words.

Dr. Gupta
Today, there is debate over how we should treat natural ecosystems, meaning wilderness areas that are basically untouched by human activity. These natural ecosystems were once seen purely as resources to be exploited, but many people now believe that wilderness areas should be protected from any human use or interference so that they continue developing completely naturally. To what extent do you support protecting and preserving natural ecosystems? Should some wilderness areas be totally protected from human use?

Andrew
People who are already struggling to feed their families are the ones most likely to be affected by, for example, a ban on mining in a wilderness area. We cannot prohibit human activities in natural ecosystems without economic consequences. I believe humans have a fundamental right to use natural resources for survival and to build wealth.

Kelly
There are very few truly wild places left on Earth, and once they're gone, we can never get them back. I believe we need to protect our remaining natural ecosystems from human interference. Not only will the animals and plants in those places benefit, but so will we humans because our own survival depends on the health of our planet.

STOP. This is the end of the Writing section of TOEFL iBT® Practice Test 2.

Chapter 8

Practice Test 3

Reading

Listening

Speaking

Writing

READING

In this section, you will be able to demonstrate your ability to understand academic passages in English. You will read and answer questions about **two passages**.

In the actual test, you will have 36 minutes total to read both passages and answer the questions. A clock will indicate how much time remains.

Some passages may include one or more notes explaining words or phrases. The words or phrases are marked with footnote numbers and the notes explaining them appear at the end of the passage.

Most questions are worth 1 point, but the last question for each passage is worth 2 points.

You may review and revise your answers in this section as long as time remains.

At the end of this practice test, you will find an answer key, information to help you determine your score, and explanations of the answers.

Reading

Listening

Speaking

Writing

Test 1

Test 2

Test 3

Test 4

ARCHITECTURE

Architecture is the art and science of designing structures that organize and enclose space for practical and symbolic purposes. Because architecture grows out of human needs and aspirations, it clearly communicates cultural values. Of all the visual arts, architecture affects our lives most directly for it determines the character of the human environment in major ways.

Architecture is a three-dimensional form. It utilizes space, mass, texture, line, light, and color. To be architecture, a building must achieve a working harmony with a variety of elements. Humans instinctively seek structures that will shelter and enhance their way of life. It is the work of architects to create buildings that are not simply constructions but also offer inspiration and delight. Buildings contribute to human life when they provide shelter, enrich space, complement their site, suit the climate, and are economically feasible. The client who pays for the building and defines its function is an important member of the architectural team. The mediocre design of many contemporary buildings can be traced to both clients and architects.

In order for the structure to achieve the size and strength necessary to meet its purpose, architecture employs methods of support that, because they are based on physical laws, have changed little since people first discovered them—even while building materials have changed dramatically. The world's architectural structures have also been devised in relation to the objective limitations of materials. Structures can be analyzed in terms of how they deal with downward forces created by gravity. They are designed to withstand the forces of *compression* (pushing together), *tension* (pulling apart), *bending*, or a combination of these in different parts of the structure.

Every development in architecture has been the result of major technological changes. Materials and methods of construction are integral parts of the design of architectural structures. In earlier times it was necessary to design structural systems suitable for the materials that were available, such as wood, stone, or brick. Today technology has progressed to the point where it is possible to invent new building materials to suit the type of structure desired. Enormous changes in materials and techniques of construction within the last few generations have made it possible to enclose space with much greater ease and speed and with a minimum of material. Progress in this area can be measured by the difference in weight between buildings built now and those of comparable size built one hundred years ago.

(A) Modern architectural forms generally have three separate components comparable to elements of the human body: a supporting *skeleton* or frame, an outer *skin* enclosing the interior spaces, and *equipment*, similar to the body's vital organs and systems. **(B)** The equipment includes plumbing, electrical wiring, hot water, and air-conditioning. **(C)** Of course in early architecture—such as igloos and adobe structures—there was no such equipment, and the skeleton and skin were often one. **(D)**

Much of the world's great architecture has been constructed of stone because of its beauty, permanence, and availability. In the past, whole cities grew from the arduous task of cutting and

Reading

Listening

Speaking

Writing

Test 1

Test 2

Test 3

Test 4

piling stone upon stone. Some of the world's finest stone architecture can be seen in the ruins of the ancient Inca city of Machu Picchu high in the eastern Andes Mountains of Peru. The doorways and windows are made possible by placing over the open spaces thick stone beams that support the weight from above. A structural invention had to be made before the physical limitations of stone could be overcome and new architectural forms could be created. That invention was the *arch*, a curved structure originally made of separate stone or brick segments. The arch was used by the early cultures of the Mediterranean area chiefly for underground drains, but it was the Romans who first developed and used the arch extensively in aboveground structures. Roman builders perfected the semicircular arch made of separate blocks of stone. As a method of spanning space, the arch can support greater weight than a horizontal beam. It works in compression to divert the weight above it out to the sides, where the weight is borne by the vertical elements on either side of the arch. The arch is among the many important structural breakthroughs that have characterized architecture throughout the centuries.

Paragraph 1

Architecture is the art and science of designing structures that organize and enclose space for practical and symbolic purposes. Because architecture grows out of human needs and aspirations, it clearly communicates cultural values. Of all the visual arts, architecture affects our lives most directly for it determines the character of the human environment in major ways.

1. According to paragraph 1, all of the following statements about architecture are true EXCEPT:

   Ⓐ Architecture is a visual art.

   Ⓑ Architecture reflects the cultural values of its creators.

   Ⓒ Architecture has both artistic and scientific dimensions.

   Ⓓ Architecture has an indirect effect on life.

Paragraph 2

Architecture is a three-dimensional form. It utilizes space, mass, texture, line, light, and color. To be architecture, a building must achieve a working harmony with a variety of elements. Humans instinctively seek structures that will shelter and enhance their way of life. It is the work of architects to create buildings that are not simply constructions but also offer inspiration and delight. Buildings contribute to human life when they provide shelter, enrich space, complement their site, suit the climate, and are economically feasible. The client who pays for the building and defines its function is an important member of the architectural team. The mediocre design of many contemporary buildings can be traced to both clients and architects.

2. The word "enhance" in the passage is closest in meaning to
   - Ⓐ protect
   - Ⓑ improve
   - Ⓒ organize
   - Ⓓ match

Paragraph 3

In order for the structure to achieve the size and strength necessary to meet its purpose, architecture employs methods of support that, because they are based on physical laws, have changed little since people first discovered them—even while building materials have changed dramatically. The world's architectural structures have also been devised in relation to the objective limitations of materials. Structures can be analyzed in terms of how they deal with downward forces created by gravity. They are designed to withstand the forces of *compression* (pushing together), *tension* (pulling apart), *bending*, or a combination of these in different parts of the structure.

3. Which of the sentences below best expresses the essential information in the highlighted sentence in the passage? Incorrect choices change the meaning in important ways or leave out essential information.
   - Ⓐ Unchanging physical laws have limited the size and strength of buildings that can be made with materials discovered long ago.
   - Ⓑ Building materials have changed in order to increase architectural size and strength, but physical laws of structure have not changed.
   - Ⓒ When people first started to build, the structural methods used to provide strength and size were inadequate because they were not based on physical laws.
   - Ⓓ Unlike building materials, the methods of support used in architecture have not changed over time because they are based on physical laws.

Reading

Listening

Speaking

Writing

Test 1

Test 2

Test 3

Test 4

Paragraph 4

Every development in architecture has been the result of major technological changes. Materials and methods of construction are integral parts of the design of architectural structures. In earlier times it was necessary to design structural systems suitable for the materials that were available, such as wood, stone, or brick. Today technology has progressed to the point where it is possible to invent new building materials to suit the type of structure desired. Enormous changes in materials and techniques of construction within the last few generations have made it possible to enclose space with much greater ease and speed and with a minimum of material. Progress in this area can be measured by the difference in weight between buildings built now and those of comparable size built one hundred years ago.

4. The word "integral" is closest in meaning to

Ⓐ essential

Ⓑ variable

Ⓒ practical

Ⓓ independent

5. According to paragraph 4, which of the following is true about materials used in the construction of buildings?

Ⓐ Because new building materials are hard to find, construction techniques have changed very little from past generations.

Ⓑ The availability of suitable building materials no longer limits the types of structures that may be built.

Ⓒ The primary building materials that are available today are wood, stone, and brick.

Ⓓ Architects in earlier times did not have enough building materials to enclose large spaces.

6. In paragraph 4, what does the author imply about modern buildings?

Ⓐ They occupy much less space than buildings constructed one hundred years ago.

Ⓑ They are not very different from the buildings of a few generations ago.

Ⓒ They weigh less in relation to their size than buildings constructed one hundred years ago.

Ⓓ They take a long time to build as a result of their complex construction methods.

Much of the world's great architecture has been constructed of stone because of its beauty, permanence, and availability. In the past, whole cities grew from the arduous task of cutting and piling stone upon stone. Some of the world's finest stone architecture can be seen in the ruins of the ancient Inca city of Machu Picchu high in the eastern Andes Mountains of Peru. The doorways and windows are made possible by placing over the open spaces thick stone beams that support the weight from above. A structural invention had to be made before the physical limitations of stone could be overcome and new architectural forms could be created. That invention was the *arch*, a curved structure originally made of separate stone or brick segments. The arch was used by the early cultures of the Mediterranean area chiefly for underground drains, but it was the Romans who first developed and used the arch extensively in aboveground structures. Roman builders perfected the semicircular arch made of separate blocks of stone. As a method of spanning space, the arch can support greater weight than a horizontal beam. It works in compression to divert the weight above it out to the sides, where the weight is borne by the vertical elements on either side of the arch. The arch is among the many important structural breakthroughs that have characterized architecture throughout the centuries.

7. Why does the author include a description of how the "doorways and windows" of Machu Picchu were constructed?

    Ⓐ To indicate that the combined skeletons and skins of the stone buildings of Machu Picchu were similar to igloos and adobe structures

    Ⓑ To indicate the different kinds of stones that had to be cut to build Machu Picchu

    Ⓒ To provide an illustration of the kind of construction that was required before arches were invented

    Ⓓ To explain how ancient builders reduced the amount of time necessary to construct buildings from stone

8. According to paragraph 6, which of the following statements is true of the arch?

    Ⓐ The Romans were the first people to use the stone arch.

    Ⓑ The invention of the arch allowed new architectural forms to be developed.

    Ⓒ The arch worked by distributing the structural load of a building toward the center of the arch.

    Ⓓ The Romans followed earlier practices in their use of arches.

Progress in this area can be measured by the difference in weight between buildings built now and those of comparable size built one hundred years ago.

(A) Modern architectural forms generally have three separate components comparable to elements of the human body: a supporting *skeleton* or frame, an outer *skin* enclosing the interior spaces, and *equipment*, similar to the body's vital organs and systems. **(B)** The equipment includes plumbing, electrical wiring, hot water, and air-conditioning. **(C)** Of course in early architecture—such as igloos and adobe structures—there was no such equipment, and the skeleton and skin were often one. **(D)**

Much of the world's great architecture has been constructed of stone because of its beauty, permanence, and availability.

9. **Directions:** Look at the part of the passage that is displayed above. The letters **(A)**, **(B)**, **(C)**, and **(D)** indicate where the following sentence could be added.

However, some modern architectural designs, such as those using folded plates of concrete or air-inflated structures, are again unifying skeleton and skin.

Where would the sentence best fit?

    Ⓐ Choice A
    Ⓑ Choice B
    Ⓒ Choice C
    Ⓓ Choice D

10. **Directions:** An introductory sentence for a brief summary of the passage is provided below. Complete the summary by selecting the THREE answer choices that express the most important ideas in the passage. Some sentences do not belong in the summary because they express ideas that are not presented in the passage or are minor ideas in the passage. **This question is worth 2 points.**

Architecture uses forms and space to express cultural values.

◆

◆

◆

Answer Choices

A Architects seek to create buildings that are both visually appealing and well suited for human use.

B Both clients and architects are responsible for the mediocre designs of some modern buildings.

C Over the course of the history of building, innovations in materials and methods of construction have given architects ever greater freedom to express themselves.

D Modern buildings tend to lack the beauty of ancient stone buildings such as those of Machu Picchu.

E Throughout history buildings have been constructed like human bodies, needing distinct "organ" systems in order to function.

F The discovery and use of the arch typifies the way in which architecture advances by developing more efficient types of structures.

THE LONG-TERM STABILITY OF ECOSYSTEMS

Plant communities assemble themselves flexibly, and their particular structure depends on the specific history of the area. Ecologists use the term "succession" to refer to the changes that happen in plant communities and ecosystems over time. The first community in a succession is called a pioneer community, while the long-lived community at the end of succession is called a climax community. Pioneer and successional plant communities are said to change over periods from 1 to 500 years. These changes—in plant numbers and the mix of species—are cumulative. Climax communities themselves change but over periods of time greater than about 500 years.

An ecologist who studies a pond today may well find it relatively unchanged in a year's time. Individual fish may be replaced, but the number of fish will tend to be the same from one year to the next. We can say that the properties of an ecosystem are more stable than the individual organisms that compose the ecosystem.

At one time, ecologists believed that species diversity made ecosystems stable. They believed that the greater the diversity the more stable the ecosystem. Support for this idea came from the observation that long-lasting climax communities usually have more complex food webs and more species diversity than pioneer communities. Ecologists concluded that the apparent stability of climax ecosystems depended on their complexity. To take an extreme example, farmlands dominated by a single crop are so unstable that one year of bad weather or the invasion of a single pest can destroy the entire crop. In contrast, a complex climax community, such as a temperate forest, will tolerate considerable damage from weather or pests.

The question of ecosystem stability is complicated, however. The first problem is that ecologists do not all agree what "stability" means. Stability can be defined as simply lack of change. In that case, the climax community would be considered the most stable, since, by definition, it changes the least over time. Alternatively, stability can be defined as the speed with which an ecosystem returns to a particular form following a major disturbance, such as a fire. This kind of stability is also called *resilience*. In that case, climax communities would be the most fragile and the *least* stable, since they can require hundreds of years to return to the climax state.

Even the kind of stability defined as simple lack of change is not always associated with maximum diversity. At least in temperate zones, maximum diversity is often found in mid-successional stages, not in the climax community. Once a redwood forest matures, for example, the kinds of species and the number of individuals growing on the forest floor are reduced. In general, diversity, by itself, does not ensure stability. Mathematical models of ecosystems likewise suggest that diversity does not guarantee ecosystem stability—just the opposite, in fact. A more complicated system is, in general, more likely than a simple system to break down. (A fifteen-speed racing bicycle is more likely to break down than a child's tricycle.)

(A) Ecologists are especially interested in knowing what factors contribute to the resilience of communities because climax communities all over the world are being severely damaged or destroyed by human activities. **(B)** The destruction caused by the volcanic explosion of Mount St. Helens, in the northwestern United States, for example, pales in comparison to the destruction caused by humans. **(C)** We need to know what aspects of a community are most important to the community's resistance to destruction, as well as its recovery. **(D)**

Many ecologists now think that the relative long-term stability of climax communities comes not from diversity but from the "patchiness" of the environment; an environment that varies from place to place supports more kinds of organisms than an environment that is uniform. A local population that goes extinct is quickly replaced by immigrants from an adjacent community. Even if the new population is of a different species, it can approximately fill the niche vacated by the extinct population and keep the food web intact.

Paragraph 1

Plant communities assemble themselves flexibly, and their particular structure depends on the specific history of the area. Ecologists use the term "succession" to refer to the changes that happen in plant communities and ecosystems over time. The first community in a succession is called a pioneer community, while the long-lived community at the end of succession is called a climax community. Pioneer and successional plant communities are said to change over periods from 1 to 500 years. These changes—in plant numbers and the mix of species—are cumulative. Climax communities themselves change but over periods of time greater than about 500 years.

11. The word "particular" in the passage is closest in meaning to

    Ⓐ natural

    Ⓑ final

    Ⓒ specific

    Ⓓ complex

Paragraph 2

An ecologist who studies a pond today may well find it relatively unchanged in a year's time. Individual fish may be replaced, but the number of fish will tend to be the same from one year to the next. We can say that the properties of an ecosystem are more stable than the individual organisms that compose the ecosystem.

12. According to paragraph 2, which of the following principles of ecosystems can be learned by studying a pond?

    Ⓐ Ecosystem properties change more slowly than individuals in the system.

    Ⓑ The stability of an ecosystem tends to change as individuals are replaced.

    Ⓒ Individual organisms are stable from one year to the next.

    Ⓓ A change in the numbers of an organism does not affect an ecosystem's properties.

Reading

Listening

Speaking

Writing

Test 1

Test 2

Test 3

Test 4

Paragraph 4

The question of ecosystem stability is complicated, however. The first problem is that ecologists do not all agree what "stability" means. Stability can be defined as simply lack of change. In that case, the climax community would be considered the most stable, since, by definition, it changes the least over time. Alternatively, stability can be defined as the speed with which an ecosystem returns to a particular form following a major disturbance, such as a fire. This kind of stability is also called *resilience*. In that case, climax communities would be the most fragile and the *least* stable, since they can require hundreds of years to return to the climax state.

13. According to paragraph 4, why is the question of ecosystem stability complicated?

ⓐ The reasons for ecosystem change are not always clear.

ⓑ Ecologists often confuse the word "stability" with the word "resilience."

ⓒ The exact meaning of the word "stability" is debated by ecologists.

ⓓ There are many different answers to ecological questions.

14. According to paragraph 4, which of the following is true of climax communities?

ⓐ They are more resilient than pioneer communities.

ⓑ They can be considered both the most and the least stable communities.

ⓒ They are stable because they recover quickly after major disturbances.

ⓓ They are the most resilient communities because they change the least over time.

Paragraph 5

Even the kind of stability defined as simple lack of change is not always associated with maximum diversity. At least in temperate zones, maximum diversity is often found in mid-successional stages, not in the climax community. Once a redwood forest matures, for example, the kinds of species and the number of individuals growing on the forest floor are reduced. In general, diversity, by itself, does not ensure stability. Mathematical models of ecosystems likewise suggest that diversity does not guarantee ecosystem stability—just the opposite, in fact. A more complicated system is, in general, more likely than a simple system to break down. (A fifteen-speed racing bicycle is more likely to break down than a child's tricycle.)

15. Which of the following can be inferred from paragraph 5 about redwood forests?

ⓐ They become less stable as they mature.

ⓑ They support many species when they reach climax.

ⓒ They are found in temperate zones.

ⓓ They have reduced diversity during mid-successional stages.

16. In paragraph 5, why does the author provide the information that "A fifteen-speed racing bicycle is more likely to break down than a child's tricycle"?

ⓐ To illustrate a general principle about the stability of systems by using an everyday example

ⓑ To demonstrate that an understanding of stability in ecosystems can be applied to help understand stability in other situations

ⓒ To make a comparison that supports the claim that, in general, stability increases with diversity

ⓓ To provide an example that contradicts mathematical models of ecosystems

Many ecologists now think that the relative long-term stability of climax communities comes not from diversity but from the "patchiness" of the environment; an environment that varies from place to place supports more kinds of organisms than an environment that is uniform. A local population that goes extinct is quickly replaced by immigrants from an adjacent community. Even if the new population is of a different species, it can approximately fill the niche vacated by the extinct population and keep the food web intact.

17. Which of the sentences below best expresses the essential information in the highlighted sentence in the passage? Incorrect choices change the meaning in important ways or leave out essential information.

     Ⓐ Ecologists now think that the stability of an environment is a result of diversity rather than patchiness.

     Ⓑ Patchy environments that vary from place to place do not often have high species diversity.

     Ⓒ Uniform environments cannot be climax communities because they do not support as many types of organisms as patchy environments.

     Ⓓ A patchy environment is thought to increase stability because it is able to support a wide variety of organisms.

18. The word "adjacent" in the passage is closest in meaning to

     Ⓐ foreign

     Ⓑ stable

     Ⓒ fluid

     Ⓓ neighboring

A more complicated system is, in general, more likely than a simple system to break down. (A fifteen-speed racing bicycle is more likely to break down than a child's tricycle.)

(A) Ecologists are especially interested in knowing what factors contribute to the resilience of communities because climax communities all over the world are being severely damaged or destroyed by human activities. **(B)** The destruction caused by the volcanic explosion of Mount St. Helens, in the northwestern United States, for example, pales in comparison to the destruction caused by humans. **(C)** We need to know what aspects of a community are most important to the community's resistance to destruction, as well as its recovery. **(D)**

Many ecologists now think that the relative long-term stability of climax communities comes not from diversity but from the "patchiness" of the environment; an environment that varies from place to place supports more kinds of organisms than an environment that is uniform.

19. **Directions:** Look at the part of the passage that is displayed above. The letters **(A)**, **(B)**, **(C)**, and **(D)** indicate where the following sentence could be added.

In fact, damage to the environment by humans is often much more severe than by natural events and processes.

Where would the sentence best fit?

Ⓐ Choice A

Ⓑ Choice B

Ⓒ Choice C

Ⓓ Choice D

20. **Directions:** An introductory sentence for a brief summary of the passage is provided below. Complete the summary by selecting the THREE answer choices that express the most important ideas in the passage. Some sentences do not belong in the summary because they express ideas that are not presented in the passage or are minor ideas in the passage. **This question is worth 2 points.**

The process of succession and the stability of a climax community can change over time.

- ◆
- ◆
- ◆

Answer Choices

A The changes that occur in an ecosystem from the pioneer to the climax community can be seen in one human generation.

B Ecologists agree that climax communities are the most stable types of ecosystems.

C A high degree of species diversity does not always result in a stable ecosystem.

D Disagreements over the meaning of the term "stability" make it difficult to identify the most stable ecosystems.

E The level of resilience in a plant community contributes to its long-term stability.

F The resilience of climax communities makes them resistant to destruction caused by humans.

STOP. This is the end of the Reading section of TOEFL iBT® Practice Test 3.

Reading
Listening
Speaking
Writing
Test 1
Test 2
Test 3
Test 4

LISTENING

In this section, you will be able to demonstrate your ability to understand conversations and lectures in English.

In the actual test, the section is divided into two separately timed parts. You will hear each conversation or lecture only one time. A clock will indicate how much time remains. The clock will count down only while you are answering questions, not while you are listening. You may take up to 16.5 minutes to answer the questions.

In this practice test, there is no time limit for answering questions.

You may take notes while you listen. You may use your notes to help you answer the questions. Your notes will not be scored.

Answer the questions based on what is stated or implied by the speakers.

In some questions, you will see this icon: ∩. This means that you will hear, but not see, part of the question.

In the actual test, you must answer each question. You cannot return to previous questions.

At the end of this practice test, you will find an answer key, information to help you determine your score, and explanations of the answers.

Listen to Track 57.

Reading

Listening

Speaking

Writing

Test 1

Test 2

Test 3

Test 4

Questions

1. Why does the student go to see the man?

    Ⓐ To get information for a class project

    Ⓑ To discuss her participation in an upcoming event

    Ⓒ To request a letter of recommendation for a job

    Ⓓ To offer input on a new construction project

2. What do the speakers say about Lightstone Dormitory? *Select 2 answers*

    Ⓐ It uses unconventional power sources.

    Ⓑ It is located next to the engineering library.

    Ⓒ It is equipped to harvest rainwater.

    Ⓓ It was built with recycled materials.

3. According to the man, why is the Green Buildings Tour taking place in winter?

    Ⓐ More tour guides are available in winter.

    Ⓑ It allows visitors to experience the effectiveness of radiant heat.

    Ⓒ New construction projects are usually completed before cold weather sets in.

    Ⓓ The university offers courses on green design during the winter months.

4. What does the man imply about the fitness center?

    Ⓐ He was not aware that the treadmills there use no electricity.

    Ⓑ Only a few of the treadmills there use no electricity.

    Ⓒ The building that houses the fitness center lacks sustainable features.

    Ⓓ The fitness center was included in a previous tour.

5. *Listen again to part of the conversation by playing Track 58.*
    Then answer the question.

    Why does the man say this?

    Ⓐ To remind the woman that more tour guides are needed for the open house

    Ⓑ To suggest that some information might only be interesting to engineers

    Ⓒ To discourage the woman from gathering more information than she will have time to share

    Ⓓ To suggest that many visitors might already be familiar with the heat-pump technology

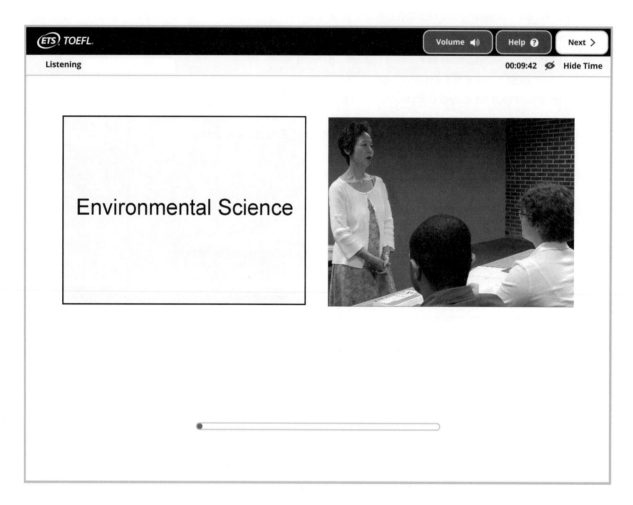

6. What does the professor mainly discuss?

    Ⓐ Major changes in the migratory patterns of hummingbirds
    Ⓑ The adaptation of hummingbirds to urban environments
    Ⓒ Concern about the reduction of hummingbird habitat
    Ⓓ The impact of ecotourism on hummingbird populations

7. What does the professor imply might cause a decrease in the hummingbird population?

    Ⓐ An increase in the ecotourism industry
    Ⓑ An increase in the use of land to raise crops and cattle
    Ⓒ A decrease in banding studies
    Ⓓ A decrease in the distance traveled during migration

8. What does the professor say people have done to help hummingbirds survive?

    Ⓐ They have built a series of hummingbird feeding stations.
    Ⓑ They have supported new laws that punish polluters of wildlife habitats.
    Ⓒ They have replanted native flowers in once polluted areas.
    Ⓓ They have learned to identify various hummingbird species.

9. What way of collecting information about migrating hummingbirds does the professor mention?

    Ⓐ Receiving radio signals from electronic tracking devices
    Ⓑ Being contacted by people who recapture banded birds
    Ⓒ Counting the birds that return to the same region every year
    Ⓓ Comparing old and young birds' migration routes

10. What does the professor imply researchers have learned while studying hummingbird migration?

    Ⓐ Hummingbirds have totally disappeared from some countries due to recent habitat destruction.
    Ⓑ Programs to replant flowers native to hummingbird habitats are not succeeding.
    Ⓒ Some groups of hummingbirds have changed their migration patterns.
    Ⓓ Some plant species pollinated by hummingbirds have become extinct.

11. *Listen again to part of the lecture by playing Track 60.*
    Then answer the question.

    What does the professor imply when she says this?

    Ⓐ There is disagreement about the idea she has presented.
    Ⓑ She does not plan to discuss all the details.
    Ⓒ Her next point may seem to contradict what she has just said.
    Ⓓ The point she will make next should be obvious to the students.

Reading

Listening

Speaking

Writing

Test 1

Test 2

Test 3

Test 4

Questions

12. What is the main purpose of the lecture?

   Ⓐ To discuss the style of an early filmmaker

   Ⓑ To describe different types of filmmaking in the 1930s

   Ⓒ To discuss the emergence of the documentary film

   Ⓓ To describe Painlevé's influence on today's science-fiction films

13. Why are Painlevé's films typical of the films of the 1920s and 1930s?

   Ⓐ They do not have sound.

   Ⓑ They are filmed underwater.

   Ⓒ They are easy to understand.

   Ⓓ They are difficult to categorize.

14. According to the professor, how did Painlevé's films confuse the audience?

   Ⓐ They show animals out of their natural habitat.

   Ⓑ They depict animals as having both human and animal characteristics.

   Ⓒ The narration is scientific and difficult to understand.

   Ⓓ The audiences of the 1920s and 1930s were not used to films shot underwater.

15. Why does the professor mention sea horses?

   Ⓐ To explain that they were difficult to film in the 1930s

   Ⓑ To point out that Cousteau made documentaries about them

   Ⓒ To illustrate Painlevé's fascination with unusual animals

   Ⓓ To explain why Painlevé's underwater films were not successful

16. Why does the professor compare the film styles of Jacques Cousteau and Jean Painlevé?

   Ⓐ To explain how Painlevé influenced Cousteau

   Ⓑ To emphasize the uniqueness of Painlevé's filming style

   Ⓒ To emphasize the artistic value of Cousteau's documentary films

   Ⓓ To demonstrate the superiority of Painlevé's filmmaking equipment

17. *Listen to Track 62 to answer the question.*

   What does the student imply when he says this?

   Ⓐ He does not like Jean Painlevé's films.

   Ⓑ He thinks that the professor should spend more time discussing Jacques Cousteau's films.

   Ⓒ He believes that high-quality filmmakers are usually well known.

   Ⓓ He believes that Jean Painlevé's films have been unfairly overlooked.

Listen to Track 63.

18. Why does the student go to see the professor?

    Ⓐ To ask about a class assignment

    Ⓑ To find out about a mid-semester project

    Ⓒ To get information about summer jobs

    Ⓓ To discuss ways to improve his grade

19. What was originally located on the site of the lecture hall?

    Ⓐ A farmhouse

    Ⓑ A pottery factory

    Ⓒ A clothing store

    Ⓓ A bottle-manufacturing plant

20. What is mentioned as an advantage of working on this project?

    Ⓐ Off-campus travel is paid for.

    Ⓑ Students can leave class early.

    Ⓒ The location is convenient.

    Ⓓ It fulfills a graduation requirement.

21. What is the professor considering doing to get more volunteers?

    Ⓐ Offering extra class credit

    Ⓑ Paying the students for their time

    Ⓒ Asking for student volunteers from outside her class

    Ⓓ Providing flexible work schedules

22. What information does the student still need to get from the professor?

    Ⓐ The name of the senior researcher

    Ⓑ What book he needs to read before the next lecture

    Ⓒ When the training session will be scheduled

    Ⓓ Where the project is located

Reading

Listening

Speaking

Writing

Test 1

Test 2

Test 3

Test 4

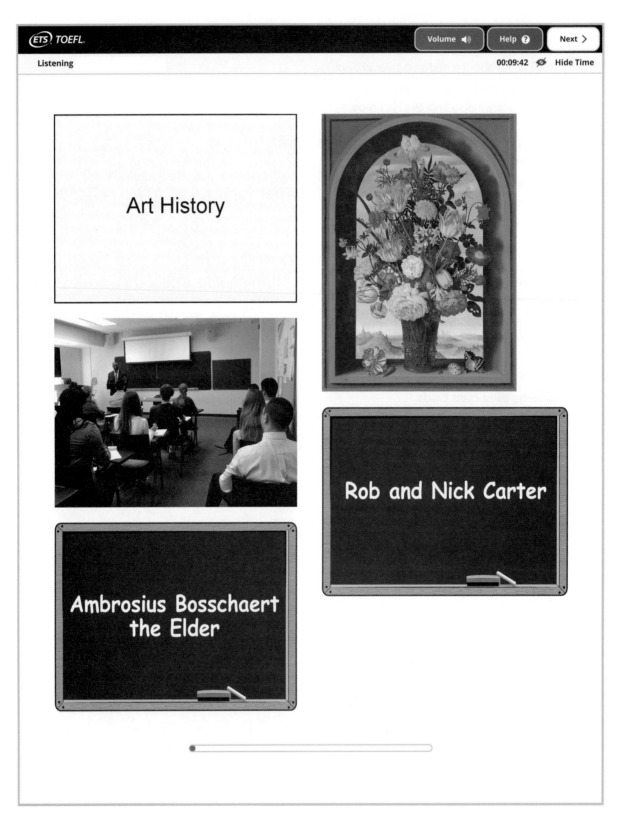

23. What is the lecture mainly about?

   Ⓐ A Dutch painter's method of painting still lifes

   Ⓑ A theory about why still lifes are scarce in contemporary art

   Ⓒ A new discovery about an old painting

   Ⓓ A new way of approaching a traditional art form

24. According to the professor, why could some of the bouquets in Bosschaert's paintings not have existed in real life?

   Ⓐ The flowers grow in widely separated regions of the world.

   Ⓑ Some of the flowers are too toxic to pick.

   Ⓒ The flowers bloom at different times of the year.

   Ⓓ The cost of such exotic bouquets would have been prohibitive.

25. Why does the professor mention the average length of time that people view a work of art?

   Ⓐ To introduce one of the Carters' goals in creating their piece

   Ⓑ To explain a technological problem with the Carters' piece

   Ⓒ To illustrate how ideas about still lifes have changed over time

   Ⓓ To introduce several reasons that children like the Carters' piece

26. Why does the professor mention that the Carters made video recordings of real flowers?

   Ⓐ To emphasize a similarity between their artistic technique and that of Bosschaert

   Ⓑ To stress that technology cannot be used as a substitute for artistic ability

   Ⓒ To argue that the Carters' work should not be considered a still life

   Ⓓ To show how technology can be used to improve an artistic process

27. According to the professor, why does a gust of wind blow in the animated video?

   Ⓐ To make the video seem more realistic

   Ⓑ To ensure that viewers do not lose interest toward the end of the video

   Ⓒ To allow a smoother transition from the end of the video to the beginning

   Ⓓ To symbolize the destructive power of nature

28. What is the professor's opinion about the Carters' treatment of Bosschaert's work?

   Ⓐ It damages Bosschaert's reputation as a painter.

   Ⓑ It highlights the quality of the original painting.

   Ⓒ It demonstrates a lack of familiarity with still lifes.

   Ⓓ It is superior to other attempts at animating still lifes.

STOP. This is the end of the Listening section of TOEFL iBT® Practice Test 3.

Reading

Listening

Speaking

Writing

Test 1

Test 2

Test 3

Test 4

SPEAKING

In this section, you will be able to demonstrate your ability to speak about a variety of topics.

In the actual test, the Speaking section will last approximately 16 minutes. You will answer four questions by speaking into the microphone. You may use your notes to help you answer the questions. Your notes will not be scored. For each question, you will have time to prepare before giving your response. You should answer the questions as completely as possible in the time allowed.

For this practice test, you may want to use a personal recording device to record and play back your responses.

For each question, play the audio track listed and follow the directions to complete the task. You may take notes while you listen.

At the end of this Practice Test, you will find scripts for the audio tracks, Important Points for each question, sample responses, and comments on those responses by official raters.

1. You will now be asked to give your opinion about a familiar topic. After you hear the question, you will have 15 seconds to prepare your response and 45 seconds to speak.

Now play Track 65 to hear Question 1.

Some students prefer to work on class assignments by themselves. Others believe it is better to work in a group. Which do you prefer? Explain why.

Preparation Time: 15 Seconds

Response Time: 45 Seconds

2. Now you will read a passage about a campus situation and then listen to a conversation about the same topic. You will then answer a question, using information from both the reading passage and the conversation. You will have 30 seconds to prepare and 60 seconds to speak.

Now play Track 66 to hear Question 2.

Reading Time: 45 Seconds

Hot Breakfasts Eliminated

Beginning next month, Dining Services will no longer serve hot breakfast foods at university dining halls. Instead, students will be offered a wide assortment of cold breakfast items in the morning. These cold breakfast foods, such as breads, fruit, and yogurt, are healthier than many of the hot breakfast items that we will stop serving, so health-conscious students should welcome this change. Students will benefit in another way as well, because limiting the breakfast selection to cold food items will save money and allow us to keep our meal plans affordable.

The woman expresses her opinion of the change that has been announced. State her opinion and explain her reasons for holding that opinion.

Preparation Time: 30 Seconds

Response Time: 60 Seconds

3. Now you will read a passage about an academic subject and then listen to a lecture on the same topic. You will then answer a question, using information from both the reading passage and the lecture. You will have 30 seconds to prepare and 60 seconds to speak.

Now play Track 67 to hear Question 3.

Reading Time: 50 Seconds

Cognitive Dissonance

Individuals sometimes experience a contradiction between their actions and their beliefs—between what they are doing and what they believe they should be doing. These contradictions can cause a kind of mental discomfort known as *cognitive dissonance*. People experiencing cognitive dissonance often do not want to change the way they are acting, so they resolve the contradictory situation in another way: they change their interpretation of the situation in a way that minimizes the contradiction between what they are doing and what they believe they should be doing.

Using the example discussed by the professor, explain what cognitive dissonance is and how people often deal with it.

Preparation Time: 30 Seconds

Response Time: 60 Seconds

4. Now you will listen to a lecture. You will then be asked to summarize the lecture. You will have 20 seconds to prepare your response and 60 seconds to speak.

Now play Track 68 to hear Question 4.

Using the examples from the talk, explain how persuasive strategies are used in advertising.

Preparation Time: 20 Seconds

Response Time: 60 Seconds

STOP. This is the end of the Speaking section of TOEFL iBT® Practice Test 3.

Reading

Listening

Speaking

Writing

Test 1

Test 2

Test 3

Test 4

WRITING

In this section, you will be able to demonstrate your ability to use writing to communicate in an academic environment. There will be two writing tasks.

At the end of this Practice Test, you will find a script for the audio track, topic notes, sample responses, and comments on those responses by official raters.

Turn the page to see the directions for the first writing task.

Integrated Writing

For this task, you will read a passage about an academic topic. Then you will listen to a lecture about the same topic. You may take notes while you listen.

In your response, provide a detailed summary of the lecture and explain how the lecture relates to the reading passage.

In the actual test, you will have 3 minutes to read the passage and 20 minutes to write your response. While you write, you will be able to see the reading passage. If you finish your response before time is up, you may go on to the second writing task.

Now you will see the reading passage. It will be followed by a lecture.

Reading Time: 3 minutes

Rembrandt is the most famous of the seventeenth-century Dutch painters. However, there are doubts whether some paintings attributed to Rembrandt were actually painted by him. One such painting is known as *Portrait of an Elderly Woman in a White Bonnet*. The painting was attributed to Rembrandt because of its style, and indeed the representation of the woman's face is very much like that of portraits known to be by Rembrandt. But there are problems with the painting that suggest it could not be a work by Rembrandt.

First, there is something inconsistent about the way the woman in the portrait is dressed. She is wearing a white linen cap of a kind that only servants would wear—yet the coat she is wearing has a luxurious fur collar that no servant could afford. Rembrandt, who was known for his attention to the details of his subjects' clothing, would not have been guilty of such an inconsistency.

Second, Rembrandt was a master of painting light and shadow, but in this painting these elements do not fit together. The face appears to be illuminated by light reflected onto it from below. But below the face is the dark fur collar, which would absorb light rather than reflect it. So the face should appear partially in shadow—which is not how it appears. Rembrandt would never have made such an error.

Finally, examination of the back of the painting reveals that it was painted on a panel made of several pieces of wood glued together. Although Rembrandt often painted on wood panels, no painting known to be by Rembrandt uses a panel glued together in this way from several pieces of wood.

For these reasons the painting was removed from the official catalog of Rembrandt's paintings in the 1930s.

Now play Track 69.

Question 1

Summarize the points made in the lecture, being sure to explain how they respond to the specific concerns presented in the reading passage. You have 20 minutes to plan and write your response.

Rembrandt is the most famous of the seventeenth-century Dutch painters. However, there are doubts whether some paintings attributed to Rembrandt were actually painted by him. One such painting is known as *Portrait of an Elderly Woman in a White Bonnet*. The painting was attributed to Rembrandt because of its style, and indeed the representation of the woman's face is very much like that of portraits known to be by Rembrandt. But there are problems with the painting that suggest it could not be a work by Rembrandt.

First, there is something inconsistent about the way the woman in the portrait is dressed. She is wearing a white linen cap of a kind that only servants would wear—yet the coat she is wearing has a luxurious fur collar that no servant could afford. Rembrandt, who was known for his attention to the details of his subjects' clothing, would not have been guilty of such an inconsistency.

Second, Rembrandt was a master of painting light and shadow, but in this painting these elements do not fit together. The face appears to be illuminated by light reflected onto it from below. But below the face is the dark fur collar, which would absorb light rather than reflect it. So the face should appear partially in shadow—which is not how it appears. Rembrandt would never have made such an error.

Finally, examination of the back of the painting reveals that it was painted on a panel made of several pieces of wood glued together. Although Rembrandt often painted on wood panels, no painting known to be by Rembrandt uses a panel glued together in this way from several pieces of wood.

For these reasons the painting was removed from the official catalog of Rembrandt's paintings in the 1930s.

Response Time: 20 minutes

Writing for an Academic Discussion

For this task, you will read an online discussion. A professor has posted a question about a topic, and some classmates have responded with their ideas.

In the actual test, you will have 10 minutes to write a response that contributes to the discussion.

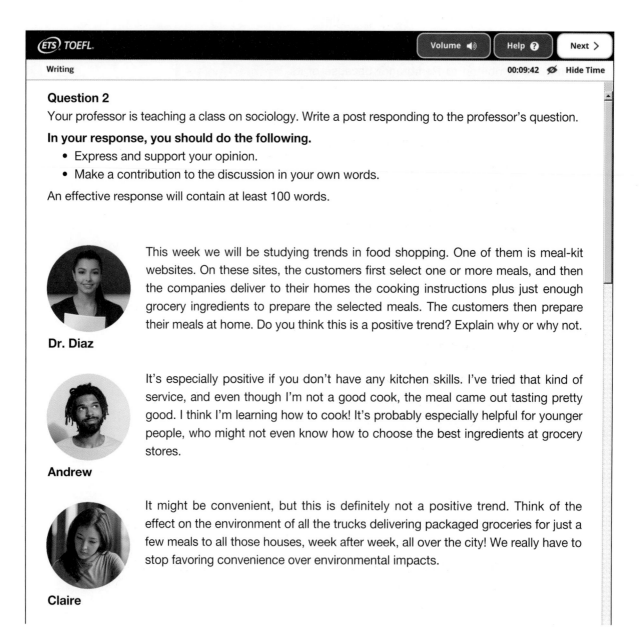

Question 2

Your professor is teaching a class on sociology. Write a post responding to the professor's question.

In your response, you should do the following.

- Express and support your opinion.
- Make a contribution to the discussion in your own words.

An effective response will contain at least 100 words.

Dr. Diaz

This week we will be studying trends in food shopping. One of them is meal-kit websites. On these sites, the customers first select one or more meals, and then the companies deliver to their homes the cooking instructions plus just enough grocery ingredients to prepare the selected meals. The customers then prepare their meals at home. Do you think this is a positive trend? Explain why or why not.

Andrew

It's especially positive if you don't have any kitchen skills. I've tried that kind of service, and even though I'm not a good cook, the meal came out tasting pretty good. I think I'm learning how to cook! It's probably especially helpful for younger people, who might not even know how to choose the best ingredients at grocery stores.

Claire

It might be convenient, but this is definitely not a positive trend. Think of the effect on the environment of all the trucks delivering packaged groceries for just a few meals to all those houses, week after week, all over the city! We really have to stop favoring convenience over environmental impacts.

STOP. This is the end of the Writing section of TOEFL iBT® Practice Test 3.

Reading

Listening

Speaking

Writing

Test 1

Test 2

Test 3

Test 4

Chapter 9

Practice Test 4

Reading

Listening

Speaking

Writing

Reading

Listening

Speaking

Writing

Test 1

Test 2

Test 3

Test 4

READING

In this section, you will be able to demonstrate your ability to understand academic passages in English. You will read and answer questions about **two passages**.

In the actual test, you will have 36 minutes total to read both passages and answer the questions. A clock will indicate how much time remains.

Some passages may include one or more notes explaining words or phrases. The words or phrases are marked with footnote numbers and the notes explaining them appear at the end of the passage.

Most questions are worth 1 point, but the last question for each passage is worth 2 points.

You may review and revise your answers in this section as long as time remains.

At the end of this practice test, you will find an answer key, information to help you determine your score, and explanations of the answers.

INDUSTRIALIZATION IN THE NETHERLANDS AND SCANDINAVIA

While some European countries, such as England and Germany, began to industrialize in the eighteenth century, the Netherlands and the Scandinavian countries of Denmark, Norway, and Sweden developed later. **(A)** All four of these countries lagged considerably behind in the early nineteenth century. **(B)** However, they industrialized rapidly in the second half of the century, especially in the last two or three decades. **(C)** In view of their later start and their lack of coal— undoubtedly the main reason they were not among the early industrializers—it is important to understand the sources of their success. **(D)**

All had small populations. At the beginning of the nineteenth century, Denmark and Norway had fewer than 1 million people, while Sweden and the Netherlands had fewer than 2.5 million inhabitants. All exhibited moderate growth rates in the course of the century (Denmark the highest and Sweden the lowest), but all more than doubled in population by 1900. Density varied greatly. The Netherlands had one of the highest population densities in Europe, whereas Norway and Sweden had the lowest. Denmark was in between but closer to the Netherlands.

Considering human capital as a characteristic of the population, however, all four countries were advantaged by the large percentages of their populations who could read and write. In both 1850 and 1914, the Scandinavian countries had the highest literacy rates in Europe, or in the world, and the Netherlands was well above the European average. This fact was of enormous value in helping the national economies find their niches in the evolving currents of the international economy.

Location was an important factor for all four countries. All had immediate access to the sea, and this had important implications for a significant international resource, fish, as well as for cheap transport, merchant marines, and the shipbuilding industry. Each took advantage of these opportunities in its own way. The people of the Netherlands, with a long tradition of fisheries and mercantile shipping, had difficulty in developing good harbors suitable for steamships; eventually they did so at Rotterdam and Amsterdam, with exceptional results for transit trade with Germany and central Europe and for the processing of overseas foodstuffs and raw materials (sugar, tobacco, chocolate, grain, and eventually oil). Denmark also had an admirable commercial history, particularly with respect to traffic through the Sound (the strait separating Denmark and Sweden). In 1857, in return for a payment of 63 million kronor from other commercial nations, Denmark abolished the Sound toll dues, the fees it had collected since 1497 for the use of the Sound. This, along with other policy shifts toward free trade, resulted in a significant increase in traffic through the Sound and in the port of Copenhagen.

The political institutions of the four countries posed no significant barriers to industrialization or economic growth. The nineteenth century passed relatively peacefully for these countries, with progressive democratization taking place in all of them. They were reasonably well governed, without notable corruption or grandiose state projects, although in all of them the government gave some aid to railways, and in Sweden the state built the main lines. As small countries dependent on foreign markets, they had few or low barriers to foreign trade in the main, though a protectionist movement developed in Sweden. In Denmark and Sweden agricultural reforms took place gradually from the late eighteenth century through the first half of the nineteenth, resulting in a new class of peasant landowners with a definite market orientation.

The key factor in the success of these countries (along with high literacy, which contributed to it) was their ability to adapt to the international division of labor determined by the early industrializers and to stake out areas of specialization in international markets for which they were especially well suited. This meant a great dependence on international commerce, which had notorious fluctuations; however, it also meant high returns to those aspects of production that were fortunate enough to be well placed in times of prosperity. In Sweden exports accounted for 18 percent of the national income in 1870, and in 1913, 22 percent of a much larger national income. In the early twentieth century, Denmark exported 63 percent of its agricultural production: butter, pork products, and eggs. It exported 80 percent of its butter, almost all to Great Britain, where it accounted for 40 percent of British butter imports.

Paragraph 1

While some European countries, such as England and Germany, began to industrialize in the eighteenth century, the Netherlands and the Scandinavian countries of Denmark, Norway, and Sweden developed later. All four of these countries lagged considerably behind in the early nineteenth century. However, they industrialized rapidly in the second half of the century, especially in the last two or three decades. In view of their later start and their lack of coal—undoubtedly the main reason they were not among the early industrializers—it is important to understand the sources of their success.

1. Paragraph 1 supports which of the following ideas about England and Germany?
   Ⓐ They were completely industrialized by the start of the nineteenth century.
   Ⓑ They possessed plentiful supplies of coal.
   Ⓒ They were overtaken economically by the Netherlands and Scandinavia during the early nineteenth century.
   Ⓓ They succeeded for the same reasons that the Netherlands and Scandinavia did.

All had small populations. At the beginning of the nineteenth century, Denmark and Norway had fewer than 1 million people, while Sweden and the Netherlands had fewer than 2.5 million inhabitants. All exhibited moderate growth rates in the course of the century (Denmark the highest and Sweden the lowest), but all more than doubled in population by 1900. Density varied greatly. The Netherlands had one of the highest population densities in Europe, whereas Norway and Sweden had the lowest. Denmark was in between but closer to the Netherlands.

Considering human capital as a characteristic of the population, however, all four countries were advantaged by the large percentages of their populations who could read and write. In both 1850 and 1914, the Scandinavian countries had the highest literacy rates in Europe, or in the world, and the Netherlands was well above the European average. This fact was of enormous value in helping the national economies find their niches in the evolving currents of the international economy.

2. According to paragraphs 2 and 3, which of the following contributed significantly to the successful economic development of the Netherlands and of Scandinavia?

   Ⓐ The relatively small size of their populations

   Ⓑ The rapid rate at which their populations were growing

   Ⓒ The large amount of capital they had available for investment

   Ⓓ The high proportion of their citizens who were educated

Location was an important factor for all four countries. All had immediate access to the sea, and this had important implications for a significant international resource, fish, as well as for cheap transport, merchant marines, and the shipbuilding industry. Each took advantage of these opportunities in its own way. The people of the Netherlands, with a long tradition of fisheries and mercantile shipping, had difficulty in developing good harbors suitable for steamships; eventually they did so at Rotterdam and Amsterdam, with exceptional results for transit trade with Germany and central Europe and for the processing of overseas foodstuffs and raw materials (sugar, tobacco, chocolate, grain, and eventually oil). Denmark also had an admirable commercial history, particularly with respect to traffic through the Sound (the strait separating Denmark and Sweden). In 1857, in return for a payment of 63 million kronor from other commercial nations, Denmark abolished the Sound toll dues, the fees it had collected since 1497 for the use of the Sound. This, along with other policy shifts toward free trade, resulted in a significant increase in traffic through the Sound and in the port of Copenhagen.

3. The word "abolished" in the passage is closest in meaning to

   Ⓐ ended

   Ⓑ raised

   Ⓒ returned

   Ⓓ lowered

4. According to paragraph 4, because of their location, the Netherlands and the Scandinavian countries had all of the following advantages when they began to industrialize EXCEPT

   Ⓐ low-cost transportation of goods

   Ⓑ access to fish

   Ⓒ shipbuilding industries

   Ⓓ military control of the seas

Reading

Listening

Speaking

Writing

Test 1

Test 2

Test 3

Test 4

Paragraph 5

The political institutions of the four countries posed no significant barriers to industrialization or economic growth. The nineteenth century passed relatively peacefully for these countries, with progressive democratization taking place in all of them. They were reasonably well governed, without notable corruption or grandiose state projects, although in all of them the government gave some aid to railways, and in Sweden the state built the main lines. As small countries dependent on foreign markets, they had few or low barriers to foreign trade in the main, though a protectionist movement developed in Sweden. In Denmark and Sweden agricultural reforms took place gradually from the late eighteenth century through the first half of the nineteenth, resulting in a new class of peasant landowners with a definite market orientation.

5. The author includes the information that "a protectionist movement developed in Sweden" in order to

Ⓐ support the claim that the political institutions of the four countries posed no significant barriers to industrialization or economic growth

Ⓑ identify an exception to the general trend favoring few or low barriers to trade

Ⓒ explain why Sweden industrialized less quickly than the other Scandinavian countries and the Netherlands

Ⓓ provide evidence that agriculture reforms take place more quickly in countries that have few or low barriers to trade than in those that do not

6. According to paragraph 5, each of the following contributed positively to the industrialization of the Netherlands and Scandinavia EXCEPT

Ⓐ a lack of obstacles to foreign trade

Ⓑ huge projects undertaken by the state

Ⓒ relatively uncorrupt government

Ⓓ relatively little social or political disruption

The key factor in the success of these countries (along with high literacy, which contributed to it) was their ability to adapt to the international division of labor determined by the early industrializers and to stake out areas of specialization in international markets for which they were especially well suited. This meant a great dependence on international commerce, which had notorious fluctuations; but it also meant high returns to those factors of production that were fortunate enough to be well placed in times of prosperity. In Sweden exports accounted for 18 percent of the national income in 1870, and in 1913, 22 percent of a much larger national income. In the early twentieth century, Denmark exported 63 percent of its agricultural production: butter, pork products, and eggs. It exported 80 percent of its butter, almost all to Great Britain, where it accounted for 40 percent of British butter imports.

7. Which of the sentences below best expresses the essential information in the highlighted sentence in the passage? Incorrect choices change the meaning in important ways or leave out essential information.

   Ⓐ The early industrializers controlled most of the international economy, leaving these countries to stake out new areas of specialization along the margins.

   Ⓑ Aided by their high literacy rates, these countries were able to claim areas of specialization within established international markets.

   Ⓒ High literacy rates enabled these countries to take over international markets and adapt the international division of labor to suit their strengths.

   Ⓓ The international division of labor established by the early industrializers was well suited to these countries, a key factor in their success.

8. According to paragraph 6, a major problem with depending heavily on international markets was that they

   Ⓐ lacked stability

   Ⓑ were not well suited to agricultural products

   Ⓒ were largely controlled by the early industrializers

   Ⓓ led to slower growth of local industries

While some European countries, such as England and Germany, began to industrialize in the eighteenth century, the Netherlands and the Scandinavian countries of Denmark, Norway, and Sweden developed later. **(A)** All four of these countries lagged considerably behind in the early nineteenth century. **(B)** However, they industrialized rapidly in the second half of the century, especially in the last two or three decades. **(C)** In view of their later start and their lack of coal—undoubtedly the main reason they were not among the early industrializers—it is important to understand the sources of their success. **(D)**

All had small populations.

9. **Directions:** Look at the part of the passage that is displayed above. The letters **(A)**, **(B)**, **(C)**, and **(D)** indicate where the following sentence could be added.

During this period, Sweden had the highest rate of growth of output per capita of any country in Europe, and Denmark was second.

Where would the sentence best fit?

Ⓐ Choice A

Ⓑ Choice B

Ⓒ Choice C

Ⓓ Choice D

10. **Directions:** An introductory sentence for a brief summary of the passage is provided below. Complete the summary by selecting the THREE answer choices that express the most important ideas in the passage. Some sentences do not belong in the summary because they express ideas that are not presented in the passage or are minor ideas in the passage. **This question is worth 2 points.**

Although the Netherlands and Scandinavia began to industrialize relatively late, they did so very successfully.

- ◆
- ◆
- ◆

Answer Choices

- [A] Although these countries all started with small, uneducated populations, industrialization led to significant population growth and higher literacy rates.
- [B] Thanks to their ready access to the sea, these countries enjoyed advantages in mercantile shipping, fishing, and shipbuilding.
- [C] Because they all had good harbors for steamships, these countries started with an important advantage in the competition for transit trade.
- [D] These countries were helped by the fact that their governments were relatively stable and honest and had policies that generally encouraged rather than blocked trade.
- [E] These countries were successful primarily because their high literacy rates helped them fill specialized market niches.
- [F] Because they were never fully dependent on international commerce, these countries were able to survive notorious fluctuations in international markets.

THE MYSTERY OF YAWNING

According to conventional theory, yawning takes place when people are bored or sleepy and serves the function of increasing alertness by reversing, through deeper breathing, the drop in blood oxygen levels that are caused by the shallow breathing that accompanies lack of sleep or boredom. Unfortunately, the few scientific investigations of yawning have failed to find any connection between how often someone yawns and how much sleep they have had or how tired they are. About the closest any research has come to supporting the tiredness theory is to confirm that adults yawn more often on weekdays than at weekends, and that school children yawn more frequently in their first year at primary school than they do in kindergarten.

Another flaw of the tiredness theory is that yawning does not raise alertness or physiological activity, as the theory would predict. When researchers measured the heart rate, muscle tension and skin conductance of people before, during and after yawning, they did detect some changes in skin conductance following yawning, indicating a slight increase in physiological activity. However, similar changes occurred when the subjects were asked simply to open their mouths or to breathe deeply. Yawning did nothing special to their state of physiological activity. Experiments have also cast serious doubt on the belief that yawning is triggered by a drop in blood oxygen or a rise in blood carbon dioxide. **(A)** Volunteers were told to think about yawning while they breathed either normal air, pure oxygen, or an air mixture with an above-normal level of carbon dioxide. **(B)** If the theory was correct, breathing air with extra carbon dioxide should have triggered yawning, while breathing pure oxygen should have suppressed yawning. **(C)** In fact, neither condition made any difference to the frequency of yawning, which remained constant at about 24 yawns per hour. **(D)** Another experiment demonstrated that physical exercise, which was sufficiently vigorous to double the rate of breathing, had no effect on the frequency of yawning. Again, the implication is that yawning has little or nothing to do with oxygen.

A completely different theory holds that yawning assists in the physical development of the lungs early in life, but has no remaining biological function in adults. It has been suggested that yawning and hiccupping might serve to clear out the fetus's airways. The lungs of a fetus secrete a liquid that then mixes with its mother's amniotic fluid. Babies with congenital blockages that prevent this fluid from escaping from their lungs are sometimes born with deformed lungs. It might be that yawning helps to clear out the lungs by periodically lowering the pressure in them. According to this theory, yawning in adults is just a developmental fossil with no biological function. But, while accepting that not everything in life can be explained by Darwinian evolution, there are sound reasons for being skeptical of theories like this one, which avoid the issue of what yawning does for adults. Yawning is distracting, consumes energy, and takes time. It is almost certainly doing something significant in adults as well as in fetuses. What could it be?

The empirical evidence, such as it is, suggests an altogether different function for yawning—namely, that yawning prepares us for a change in activity level. Support for this theory came from a study of yawning behavior in everyday life. Volunteers wore wrist-mounted devices that automatically recorded their physical activity for up to two weeks; the volunteers also recorded their yawns by pressing a button on the device each time they yawned. The data showed that yawning tended to occur about 15 minutes before a period of increased behavioral activity. Yawning bore no relationship to sleep patterns, however. This accords with anecdotal evidence that people often yawn in situations where they are neither tired nor bored, but are preparing for impending mental and physical activity. Such yawning is often referred to as "incongruous" because it seems out of place, at least in the tiredness view: soldiers yawning before combat, musicians yawning before performing, and athletes yawning before competing. Their yawning seems to have nothing to do with sleepiness or boredom—quite the reverse—but it does precede a change in activity level.

Paragraph 1

According to conventional theory, yawning takes place when people are bored or sleepy and serves the function of increasing alertness by reversing, through deeper breathing, the drop in blood oxygen levels that are caused by the shallow breathing that accompanies lack of sleep or boredom. Unfortunately, the few scientific investigations of yawning have failed to find any connection between how often someone yawns and how much sleep they have had or how tired they are. About the closest any research has come to supporting the tiredness theory is to confirm that adults yawn more often on weekdays than at weekends, and that school children yawn more frequently in their first year at primary school than they do in kindergarten.

11. Which of the sentences below best expresses the essential information in the highlighted sentence in the passage? Incorrect choices change the meaning in important ways or leave out essential information.

   Ⓐ It is the conventional theory that when people are bored or sleepy, they often experience a drop in blood oxygen levels due to their shallow breathing.

   Ⓑ The conventional theory is that people yawn when bored or sleepy because yawning raises blood oxygen levels, which in turn raises alertness.

   Ⓒ According to conventional theory, yawning is more likely to occur when people are bored or sleepy than when they are alert and breathing deeply.

   Ⓓ Yawning, according to the conventional theory, is caused by boredom or lack of sleep and can be avoided through deeper breathing.

12. In paragraph 1, what point does the author make about the evidence for the tiredness theory of yawning?

   Ⓐ There is no scientific evidence linking yawning with tiredness.

   Ⓑ The evidence is wide-ranging because it covers multiple age-groups.

   Ⓒ The evidence is reliable because it was collected over a long period of time.

   Ⓓ The evidence is questionable because the yawning patterns of children and adults should be different.

Another flaw of the tiredness theory is that yawning does not raise alertness or physiological activity, as the theory would predict. When researchers measured the heart rate, muscle tension and skin conductance of people before, during and after yawning, they did detect some changes in skin conductance following yawning, indicating a slight increase in physiological activity. However, similar changes occurred when the subjects were asked simply to open their mouths or to breathe deeply. Yawning did nothing special to their state of physiological activity. Experiments have also cast serious doubt on the belief that yawning is triggered by a drop in blood oxygen or a rise in blood carbon dioxide. Volunteers were told to think about yawning while they breathed either normal air, pure oxygen, or an air mixture with an above-normal level of carbon dioxide. If the theory was correct, breathing air with extra carbon dioxide should have triggered yawning, while breathing pure oxygen should have suppressed yawning. In fact, neither condition made any difference to the frequency of yawning, which remained constant at about 24 yawns per hour. Another experiment demonstrated that physical exercise, which was sufficiently vigorous to double the rate of breathing, had no effect on the frequency of yawning. Again, the implication is that yawning has little or nothing to do with oxygen.

13. The word "flaw" in the passage is closest in meaning to

Ⓐ fault

Ⓑ aspect

Ⓒ confusion

Ⓓ mystery

14. In paragraph 2, why does the author compare the physiological changes that occur when subjects simply opened their mouths or breathed deeply with those that occur when people yawned?

Ⓐ To present an argument in support of the tiredness theory

Ⓑ To cast doubt on the reliability of the tests that measured heart rate, muscle tension, and skin conductance

Ⓒ To argue against the hypothesis that yawning provides a special way to improve alertness or raise physiological activity

Ⓓ To support the idea that opening the mouth or breathing deeply can affect blood oxygen levels

15. Paragraph 2 answers all of the following questions about yawning EXCEPT:

Ⓐ Does yawning increase alertness or physiological activity?

Ⓑ Does thinking about yawning increase yawning over not thinking about yawning?

Ⓒ Does the amount of carbon dioxide and oxygen in the air affect the rate at which people yawn?

Ⓓ Does the rate of breathing affect the rate at which people yawn?

A completely different theory holds that yawning assists in the physical development of the lungs early in life, but has no remaining biological function in adults. It has been suggested that yawning and hiccupping might serve to clear out the fetus's airways. The lungs of a fetus secrete a liquid that then mixes with its mother's amniotic fluid. Babies with congenital blockages that prevent this fluid from escaping from their lungs are sometimes born with deformed lungs. It might be that yawning helps to clear out the lungs by periodically lowering the pressure in them. According to this theory, yawning in adults is just a developmental fossil with no biological function. But, while accepting that not everything in life can be explained by Darwinian evolution, there are sound reasons for being skeptical of theories like this one, which avoid the issue of what yawning does for adults. Yawning is distracting, consumes energy and takes time. It is almost certainly doing something significant in adults as well as in fetuses.

16. According to the development theory of yawning presented in paragraph 3, what is the role of yawning?
    Ⓐ It causes hiccups, which aid in the development of the lungs.
    Ⓑ It controls the amount of pressure the lungs place on other developing organs.
    Ⓒ It prevents amniotic fluid from entering the lungs.
    Ⓓ It removes a potentially harmful fluid from the lungs.

The empirical evidence, such as it is, suggests an altogether different function for yawning—namely, that yawning prepares us for a change in activity level. Support for this theory came from a study of yawning behavior in everyday life. Volunteers wore wrist-mounted devices that automatically recorded their physical activity for up to two weeks; the volunteers also recorded their yawns by pressing a button on the device each time they yawned. The data showed that yawning tended to occur about 15 minutes before a period of increased behavioral activity. Yawning bore no relationship to sleep patterns, however. This accords with anecdotal evidence that people often yawn in situations where they are neither tired nor bored, but are preparing for impending mental and physical activity. Such yawning is often referred to as "incongruous" because it seems out of place, at least on the tiredness view: soldiers yawning before combat, musicians yawning before performing, and athletes yawning before competing. Their yawning seems to have nothing to do with sleepiness or boredom—quite the reverse—but it does precede a change in activity level.

17. The word "empirical" in the passage is closest in meaning to
    Ⓐ reliable
    Ⓑ based on common sense
    Ⓒ relevant
    Ⓓ based on observation

18. The study of yawning behavior discussed in paragraph 4 supports which of the following conclusions?
    Ⓐ Yawning is associated with an expectation of increased physical activity.
    Ⓑ Yawning occurs more frequently when people are asked to record their yawning.
    Ⓒ People tend to yawn about fifteen minutes before they become tired or bored.
    Ⓓ Mental or physical stress tends to make people yawn.

Reading

Listening

Speaking

Writing

Test 1

Test 2

Test 3

Test 4

Paragraph 2

Another flaw of the tiredness theory is that yawning does not raise alertness or physiological activity, as the theory would predict. When researchers measured the heart rate, muscle tension and skin conductance of people before, during and after yawning, they did detect some changes in skin conductance following yawning, indicating a slight increase in physiological activity. However, similar changes occurred when the subjects were asked simply to open their mouths or to breathe deeply. Yawning did nothing special to their state of physiological activity. Experiments have also cast serious doubt on the belief that yawning is triggered by a drop in blood oxygen or a rise in blood carbon dioxide. **(A)** Volunteers were told to think about yawning while they breathed either normal air, pure oxygen, or an air mixture with an above-normal level of carbon dioxide. **(B)** If the theory was correct, breathing air with extra carbon dioxide should have triggered yawning, while breathing pure oxygen should have suppressed yawning. **(C)** In fact, neither condition made any difference to the frequency of yawning, which remained constant at about 24 yawns per hour. **(D)** Another experiment demonstrated that physical exercise, which was sufficiently vigorous to double the rate of breathing, had no effect on the frequency of yawning. Again, the implication is that yawning has little or nothing to do with oxygen.

19. **Directions:** Look at the part of the passage that is displayed above. The letters **(A)**, **(B)**, **(C)**, and **(D)** indicate where the following sentence could be added.

   This, however, was not the case.

   Where would the sentence best fit?
   Ⓐ Choice A
   Ⓑ Choice B
   Ⓒ Choice C
   Ⓓ Choice D

20. Directions: An introductory sentence for a brief summary of the passage is provided below. Complete the summary by selecting the THREE answer choices that express the most important ideas in the passage. Some sentences do not belong in the summary because they express ideas that are not presented in the passage or are minor ideas in the passage. **This question is worth 2 points.**

The tiredness theory of yawning does not seem to explain why yawning occurs.

- ◆
- ◆
- ◆

Answer Choices

A Although earlier scientific studies strongly supported the tiredness theory, new evidence has cast doubt on these findings.

B Evidence has shown that yawning is almost completely unrelated to the amount of oxygen in the blood and is unrelated to sleep behavior.

C Some have proposed that yawning plays a role in the development of the lungs before birth, but it seems unlikely that yawning serves no purpose in adults.

D Fluids in the lungs of the fetus prevent yawning from occurring, which disproves the development theory of yawning.

E New studies, along with anecdotal evidence, have shown that the frequency of yawning increases during extended periods of inactivity.

F There is some evidence that suggests that yawning prepares the body and mind for a change in activity level.

STOP. This is the end of the Reading section of TOEFL iBT® Practice Test 4.

Reading

Listening

Speaking

Writing

Test 1

Test 2

Test 3

Test 4

LISTENING

In this section, you will be able to demonstrate your ability to understand conversations and lectures in English.

In the actual test, the section is divided into two separately timed parts. You will hear each conversation or lecture only one time. A clock will indicate how much time remains. The clock will count down only while you are answering questions, not while you are listening. You may take up to 16.5 minutes to answer the questions.

In this practice test, there is no time limit for answering questions.

You may take notes while you listen. You may use your notes to help you answer the questions. Your notes will not be scored.

Answer the questions based on what is stated or implied by the speakers.

In some questions, you will see this icon: 🎧 . This means that you will hear, but not see, part of the question.

In the actual test, you must answer each question. You cannot return to previous questions.

At the end of this practice test, you will find an answer key, information to help you determine your score, and explanations of the answers.

Listen to Track 78.

Reading

Listening

Speaking

Writing

Test 1

Test 2

Test 3

Test 4

Questions

1. Why does the student go to the university office?

   Ⓐ To apply for a position at the university library

   Ⓑ To get information about hosting an exchange student

   Ⓒ To find out if there are any jobs available on campus

   Ⓓ To find out the hours of the computer lab

2. Why did the student transfer to Central University?

   Ⓐ To take advantage of an academic program

   Ⓑ To participate in a student exchange program

   Ⓒ To attend a smaller university than the one he was at before

   Ⓓ To benefit from Central University's international reputation

3. Why does the student mention hosting foreign-exchange students?

   Ⓐ To explain his interest in a particular field of study

   Ⓑ To explain why he is looking for a job so late in the semester

   Ⓒ To explain why he would like to be an exchange student the following year

   Ⓓ To explain how he learned his computer skills

4. What can be inferred about students who apply for the open position at the technology-support help desk?

   Ⓐ They must be enrolled in a computer course.

   Ⓑ They will only be able to work on weekends.

   Ⓒ They are willing to work many hours each day they work.

   Ⓓ They are willing to work irregular hours.

5. *Listen again to part of the conversation by playing Track 79.*
   Then answer the question.

   Why does the woman say this?

   Ⓐ To dissuade the student from starting a job right away

   Ⓑ To suggest looking for an off-campus job

   Ⓒ To imply that the student might not like the job that is available

   Ⓓ To encourage the student to apply to a work-study program

6. What is the lecture mainly about?

    Ⓐ Different views of a type of sculpture popular in ancient Roman times

    Ⓑ Evidence that Romans had outstanding artistic ability

    Ⓒ The differences between Greek sculpture and Roman sculpture

    Ⓓ The relationship between art and politics in ancient Roman times

7. According to traditional art historians, why did the Romans copy Greek sculpture?

    Ⓐ The Roman public was not interested in original works of art.

    Ⓑ The Roman government did not support other forms of art.

    Ⓒ Roman artists did not have sufficient skill to create original sculpture.

    Ⓓ Romans wanted to imitate the art they admired.

8. What is Gazda's view of the Roman copies of Greek statues?

    Ⓐ The copies represented the idea that Roman society was similar to Greek society.

    Ⓑ The copies introduced the citizens of the Roman Empire to Greek history.

    Ⓒ The copies were inferior to the original statues.

    Ⓓ The copies had both artistic and political functions.

9. Why does the professor mention Roman coins?

    Ⓐ To show the similarity between the likenesses of the emperor in statues and on coins

    Ⓑ To illustrate the Roman policy of distributing the emperor's image throughout the empire

    Ⓒ To imply that the citizens of the Roman Empire became quite wealthy

    Ⓓ To suggest that the Romans also copied Greek art on their coins

10 According to the professor, why did the Romans sometimes remove the emperor's head from a statue? *Select 2 answers.*

    Ⓐ The head made the statue too heavy to transport.

    Ⓑ The head was placed on the body of a different statue.

    Ⓒ The emperor was no longer in power.

    Ⓓ The emperor was not satisfied with the quality of the statue.

11. *Listen again to part of the lecture by playing Track 81.*
    Then answer the question.

    What does the professor imply when he says this?

    Ⓐ Art historians frequently change their views.

    Ⓑ The contemporary view is not easy to understand.

    Ⓒ It is not difficult to determine why the Romans copied Greek sculptures.

    Ⓓ The view of traditional art historians is probably incorrect.

Listen to Track 82.

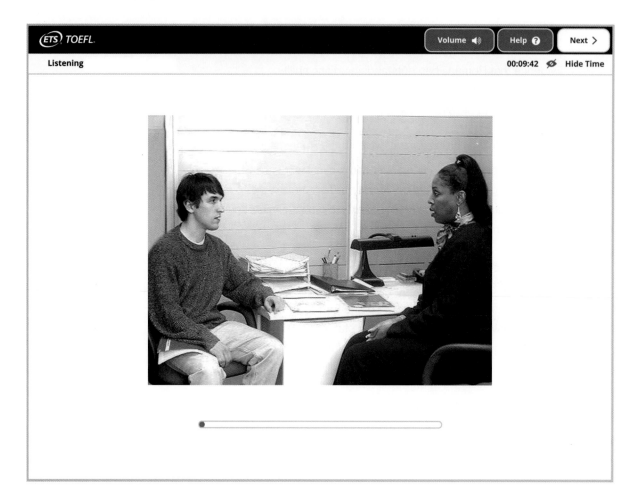

280

12. What is the conversation mainly about?

    (A) The topic of the man's research paper

    (B) Some current research projects in sociology

    (C) Effective ways of conducting sociology research

    (D) The man's possible participation in a research project

13. What does the professor imply about the man's outline?

    (A) It has revealed that he should limit the focus of his paper.

    (B) It does not provide enough information for him to write the paper.

    (C) It will help him write clearly about a complex topic.

    (D) It overstates the connection between sociology and marketing.

14. What is the main goal of the study that the professor's colleague is conducting?

    (A) To find out if some television shows will be popular with people in a certain age range

    (B) To collect information about food products that college students like

    (C) To generate ideas for new television shows

    (D) To determine sociological factors that are related to people's television-viewing preferences

15. What does the professor imply about the owners of Fox's Diner?

    (A) They would probably do a favor for her.

    (B) They are unlikely to grant the man's request.

    (C) They would enjoy participating in the research study.

    (D) They often advertise on television.

16. *Listen again to part of the conversation by playing Track 83.* *Then answer the question.*

What does the professor mean when she says this?

    (A) The student could probably find a marketing professor who has an interest in sociology.

    (B) The student's marketing professor might not be aware of the television study.

    (C) No more students are needed to participate in the television study.

    (D) The marketing department needs students for several research studies.

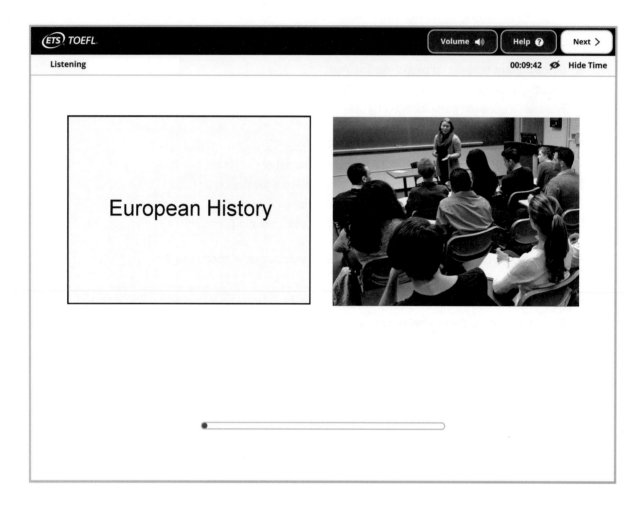

Questions

17. What is the main purpose of the lecture?

Ⓐ To explore the use of spices in cooking in the Middle Ages

Ⓑ To explain the significance of spices for medieval society

Ⓒ To describe how the spice trade evolved in medieval Europe

Ⓓ To examine changes in the role that spices played in the Middle Ages

18. Based on the lecture, indicate whether each of the following is true about spices in medieval Europe.

Mark your answers with an "X" below.

	YES	NO
A. They had to be imported.		
B. They were unaffordable for many people.		
C. They were used to preserve meat during the winter.		
D. They were believed to have medicinal properties.		
E. Their sale in public markets was closely regulated.		

19. What two factors explain why medieval Europeans did not use spices to cover the taste of spoiled meat? *Select 2 answers.*

    A   Fresh meat was less expensive than spices were.

    B   Spices were mainly used in incense and perfume.

    C   The sale of spoiled food was prohibited.

    D   Salt was cheaper than most spices were.

20. Why does the professor mention the collapse of the Roman Empire?

    Ⓐ   To indicate that the spice trade became more direct

    Ⓑ   To explain why the price of pepper suddenly increased

    Ⓒ   To indicate that spices were not available in Europe for centuries

    Ⓓ   To explain why the origins of spices became more mysterious

21. What does the professor say about European explorers during the age of discovery?

    Ⓐ   Their discoveries caused the price of certain spices to increase.

    Ⓑ   They were responding to the demand for spices.

    Ⓒ   They did not expect to find spices during their explorations.

    Ⓓ   Their main goal was to discover unknown lands.

22. *Listen again to part of the lecture by playing Track 85. Then answer the question.*

Why does the professor say this?

    Ⓐ   To indicate that pepper was commonly used as payment

    Ⓑ   To indicate where pepper could be found at the time

    Ⓒ   To emphasize the high value of pepper at the time

    Ⓓ   To suggest that pepper was nearly as plentiful as gold

Reading

Listening

Speaking

Writing

Test 1

Test 2

Test 3

Test 4

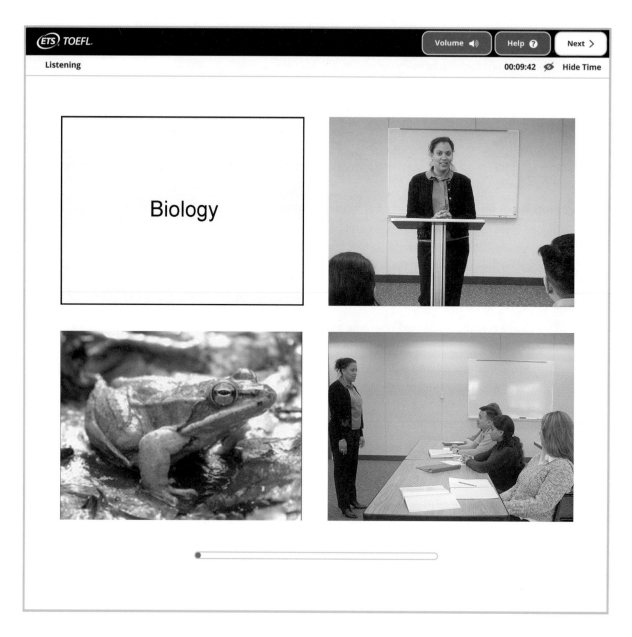

23. What is the main purpose of the lecture?

Ⓐ To explain the biological advantages of a physical change that occurs in North American wood frogs

Ⓑ To explain why the North American wood frog's habitat range has expanded

Ⓒ To describe the functioning of the circulatory system of the North American wood frog

Ⓓ To introduce students to an unusual phenomenon affecting North American wood frogs

24. Why does the professor first mention the arrival of spring?

Ⓐ To encourage students to look for thawing wood frogs

Ⓑ To point out the time period when frogs begin mating

Ⓒ To explain why the class will soon be doing experiments with wood frogs

Ⓓ To emphasize the speed of the thawing process

25. What happens to a wood frog as it begins to freeze?

Ⓐ Blood is concentrated in the center of its body.

Ⓑ Blood stops producing sugar.

Ⓒ Water moves out of its internal organs.

Ⓓ Water from just beneath the skin begins to evaporate.

26. What are two points the professor makes about the thawing process of the wood frog?
Select 2 answers.

Ⓐ The thawing process is not fully understood.

Ⓑ The thawing process takes longer than the freezing process.

Ⓒ The frog's internal organs thaw before its outer skin thaws.

Ⓓ Thawing occurs when the frog's heart begins pumping glucose through its body.

27. What impact does freezing have on some thawed wood frogs?

Ⓐ It increases their reproductive success.

Ⓑ It decreases their life span.

Ⓒ It causes them to be more vocal and active.

Ⓓ It reduces their ability to recognize potential mates.

28. *Listen again to part of the lecture by playing Track 87.*
Then answer the question.

What does the professor imply when she says this?

Ⓐ She wants the student to clarify his question.

Ⓑ She wants the student to draw his own conclusions.

Ⓒ She thinks the student does not understand how car antifreeze works.

Ⓓ She thinks the student has misunderstood her point.

STOP. This is the end of the Listening section of TOEFL iBT® Practice Test 4.

Reading

Listening

Speaking

Writing

Test 1

Test 2

Test 3

Test 4

SPEAKING

In this section, you will be able to demonstrate your ability to speak about a variety of topics.

In the actual test, the Speaking section will last approximately 16 minutes. You will answer four questions by speaking into the microphone. You may use your notes to help you answer the questions. Your notes will not be scored. For each question, you will have time to prepare before giving your response. You should answer the questions as completely as possible in the time allowed.

For this practice test, you may want to use a personal recording device to record and play back your responses.

For each question, play the audio track listed and follow the directions to complete the task. You may take notes while you listen.

At the end of this Practice Test, you will find scripts for the audio tracks, Important Points for each question, sample responses, and comments on those responses by official raters.

1. You will now be asked to give your opinion about a familiar topic. After you hear the question, you will have 15 seconds to prepare your response and 45 seconds to speak.

Now play Track 88 to hear Question 1.

Do you agree or disagree with the following statement?
It is important to learn about other cultures.
Use details and examples to explain your opinion.

Preparation Time: 15 Seconds

Response Time: 45 Seconds

2. Now you will read a passage about a campus situation and then listen to a conversation about the same topic. You will then answer a question, using information from both the reading passage and the conversation. You will have 30 seconds to prepare your response and 60 seconds to speak.

Now play Track 89 to hear Question 2.

Reading Time: 50 Seconds

University Choir to Enter Off-Campus Singing Competitions

Currently, the university choir gives singing concerts only on campus. Next year, however, the choir will add competitive events at other locations to its schedule. The choir's new director feels that entering singing competitions will make the quality of the choir's performance even better than it is now. "Competitions will motivate students in the choir to pursue a higher standard of excellence in singing," he said. In addition, it is hoped that getting the choir off campus and out in the public will strengthen the reputation of the university's music program. This in turn will help the program grow.

The man expresses his opinion about the change described in the article. Briefly summarize the change. Then state his opinion about the change and explain the reasons he gives for holding that opinion.

Preparation Time: 30 Seconds

Response Time: 60 Seconds

Reading

Listening

Speaking

Writing

Test 1

Test 2

Test 3

Test 4

3. Now you will read a passage about an academic subject and then listen to a lecture on the same topic. You will then answer a question, using information from both the reading passage and the lecture. You will have 30 seconds to prepare your response and 60 seconds to speak.

Now play Track 90 to hear Question 3.

Reading Time: 50 Seconds

Relict Behaviors

In general, animals act in ways that help them to survive within their specific habitats. However, sometimes an animal species may display a behavior that no longer serves a clear purpose. The original purpose for the behavior may have disappeared long ago, even thousands of years before. These behaviors, known as *relict behaviors*, were useful to the animal when the species' habitat was different; but now, because of changed conditions, the behavior no longer serves its original purpose. Left over from an earlier time, the behavior remains as a relict, or remnant, long after the environmental circumstance that influenced its evolution has vanished.

Using the example of the pronghorn and lion, explain the concept of a relict behavior.

Preparation Time: 30 Seconds
Response Time: 60 Seconds

4. Now you will listen to a lecture. You will then be asked to summarize the lecture. You will have 20 seconds to prepare your response and 60 seconds to speak.

Now play Track 91 to hear Question 4.

Using points and examples from the lecture, explain how the characteristics of target customers influence marketing strategy for products.

> Preparation Time: 20 Seconds
>
> Response Time: 60 Seconds

STOP. This is the end of the Speaking section of TOEFL iBT® Practice Test 4.

Reading

Listening

Speaking

Writing

Test 1

Test 2

Test 3

Test 4

Reading

Listening

Speaking

Writing

Test 1

Test 2

Test 3

Test 4

WRITING

In this section, you will be able to demonstrate your ability to use writing to communicate in an academic environment. There will be two writing tasks.

At the end of this Practice Test, you will find a script for the audio track, topic notes, sample responses, and comments on those responses by official raters.

Turn the page to see the directions for the first writing task.

Integrated Writing

For this task, you will read a passage about an academic topic. Then you will listen to a lecture about the same topic. You may take notes while you listen.

In your response, provide a detailed summary of the lecture and explain how the lecture relates to the reading passage.

In the actual test, you will have 3 minutes to read the passage and 20 minutes to write your response. While you write, you will be able to see the reading passage. If you finish your response before time is up, you may go on to the second writing task.

Now you will see the reading passage. It will be followed by a lecture.

Reading Time: 3 minutes

In the 1950s *Torreya taxifolia*, a type of evergreen tree once very common in the state of Florida, started to die out. No one is sure exactly what caused the decline, but chances are good that if nothing is done, *Torreya* will soon become extinct. Experts are considering three ways to address the decline of *Torreya*.

The first option is to reestablish *Torreya* in the same location in which it thrived for thousands of years. *Torreya* used to be found in abundance in the northern part of Florida, which has a specific microclimate. A microclimate exists when weather conditions inside a relatively small area differ from the region of which that area is a part. Northern Florida's microclimate is very favorable to *Torreya*'s growth. This microclimate is wetter and cooler than the surrounding region's relatively dry, warm climate. Scientists have been working to plant *Torreya* seeds in the coolest, dampest areas of the microclimate.

The second option is to move *Torreya* to an entirely different location, far from its Florida microclimate. *Torreya* seeds and saplings have been successfully planted and grown in forests further north, where the temperature is significantly cooler. Some scientists believe that *Torreya* probably thrived in areas much further north in the distant past, so by relocating it now, in a process known as assisted migration, humans would simply be helping *Torreya* return to an environment that is more suited to its survival.

The third option is to preserve *Torreya* in research centers. Seeds and saplings can be moved from the wild and preserved in a closely monitored environment where it will be easier for scientists both to protect the species and to conduct research on *Torreya*. This research can then be used to ensure the continued survival of the species.

Now play Track 92.

the black locust tree

Question 1

Summarize the points made in the lecture, being sure to explain how they respond to the specific concerns presented in the reading passage. You have 20 minutes to plan and write your response.

In the 1950s *Torreya taxifolia*, a type of evergreen tree once very common in the state of Florida, started to die out. No one is sure exactly what caused the decline, but chances are good that if nothing is done, *Torreya* will soon become extinct. Experts are considering three ways to address the decline of *Torreya*.

The first option is to reestablish *Torreya* in the same location in which it thrived for thousands of years. *Torreya* used to be found in abundance in the northern part of Florida, which has a specific microclimate. A microclimate exists when weather conditions inside a relatively small area differ from the region of which that area is a part. Northern Florida's microclimate is very favorable to *Torreya*'s growth. This microclimate is wetter and cooler than the surrounding region's relatively dry, warm climate. Scientists have been working to plant *Torreya* seeds in the coolest, dampest areas of the microclimate.

The second option is to move *Torreya* to an entirely different location, far from its Florida microclimate. *Torreya* seeds and saplings have been successfully planted and grown in forests further north, where the temperature is significantly cooler. Some scientists believe that *Torreya* probably thrived in areas much further north in the distant past, so by relocating it now, in a process known as assisted migration, humans would simply be helping *Torreya* return to an environment that is more suited to its survival.

The third option is to preserve *Torreya* in research centers. Seeds and saplings can be moved from the wild and preserved in a closely monitored environment where it will be easier for scientists both to protect the species and to conduct research on *Torreya*. This research can then be used to ensure the continued survival of the species.

Response Time: 20 minutes

Writing for an Academic Discussion

For this task, you will read an online discussion. A professor has posted a question about a topic, and some classmates have responded with their ideas.

In the actual test, you will have 10 minutes to write a response that contributes to the discussion.

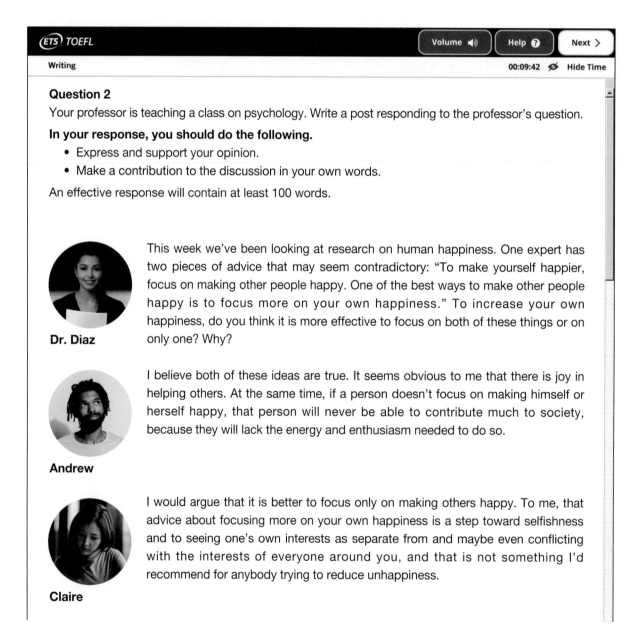

Question 2

Your professor is teaching a class on psychology. Write a post responding to the professor's question.

In your response, you should do the following.
- Express and support your opinion.
- Make a contribution to the discussion in your own words.

An effective response will contain at least 100 words.

Dr. Diaz

This week we've been looking at research on human happiness. One expert has two pieces of advice that may seem contradictory: "To make yourself happier, focus on making other people happy. One of the best ways to make other people happy is to focus more on your own happiness." To increase your own happiness, do you think it is more effective to focus on both of these things or on only one? Why?

Andrew

I believe both of these ideas are true. It seems obvious to me that there is joy in helping others. At the same time, if a person doesn't focus on making himself or herself happy, that person will never be able to contribute much to society, because they will lack the energy and enthusiasm needed to do so.

Claire

I would argue that it is better to focus only on making others happy. To me, that advice about focusing more on your own happiness is a step toward selfishness and to seeing one's own interests as separate from and maybe even conflicting with the interests of everyone around you, and that is not something I'd recommend for anybody trying to reduce unhappiness.

Response Time: 10 minutes

Reading

Listening

Speaking

Writing

Test 1

Test 2

Test 3

Test 4

STOP. This is the end of the Writing section of TOEFL iBT® Practice Test 4.

Chapter 10

Writer's Handbook for English Language Learners

Writer's Handbook for English Language Learners

이 장의 구성_   Grammar_문법
Usage_용법
Mechanics_철자법과 구두법
Style_문체
Organization and Development_조직화와 전개
Advice to Writers_에세이 작성자들을 위한 조언
Revising, Editing, and Proofreading_수정, 편집, 교열
Glossary_용어

Grammar_문법

Sentence Errors

1. Fragments_미완결문

미완결문은 앞뒤에 오는 문장을 읽어야 그 뜻을 파악할 수 있는 불완전한 문장을 말한다. 즉 대문자로 시작해서 마침표로 끝나지만 하나의 완전한 내용을 표현하지 못하는 문장이다. 이런 문장에는 주어나 동사 중 하나 또는 둘 다 빠져 있다. 다음은 완전한 문장이 될 수 없는 미완결문의 세 가지 예이다. 이런 미완결문들을 교정하는 방법에는 두 가지가 있다. 미완결문을 완전한 문장과 결합하거나 주어와 동사를 명확히 해주는 단어들을 추가하면 된다.

Where the neighbors were too noisy.

→ <u>Peter left the apartment</u> where the neighbors were too noisy.

→ <u>This is</u> where there were mice and cockroaches.

A movie that inspires deep emotions.

→ <u>I went to see "The Silver Star,"</u> a movie that inspires deep emotions.

→ A movie that inspires deep emotions <u>is rare.</u>

Analyzing the characters' motives.

→ Analyzing the characters' motives <u>is important.</u>

2. Run-On sentence_접속사 없이 이어진 두 문장

접속사나 구두점 없이 두 개의 문장이 연결된 경우에는 대개 구두점이나 접속사를 넣어 교정한다.

1) 두 개의 독립된 문장으로 분리한다.

My sister loves to dance she is very good at it.

→ My sister loves to dance. She is very good at it.

Jim showed us his ticket someone gave it to him.

→ Jim showed us his ticket. Someone gave it to him.

2) 각 부분을 등위접속사와 쉼표로 연결한다.

for, and, nor, but, or, yet, so (앞글자를 따서 FANBOYS로 기억하자.)

My sister loves to dance she is very good at it.

→ My sister loves to dance, <u>and</u> she is very good at it.

She agreed to chair the meeting she didn't come.

→ She agreed to chair the meeting, <u>but</u> she didn't come.

3) 각 부분을 종속접속사로 연결한다.

after, although, as, because, before, if, since, unless, until, when, where, while

My sister loves to dance she is very good at it.

→ My sister loves to dance <u>because</u> she is very good at it.

Maria and John like skiing Karen does not.

→ <u>Although</u> Maria and John like skiing, Karen does not.

4) 각 부분을 세미콜론(;)으로 나눈다.

Gordon laughed at Sandy's joke it was funny.

→ Gordon laughed at Sandy's joke<u>;</u> it was funny.

I thought he was here I was wrong.

→ I thought he was here<u>;</u> I was wrong.

Word Errors

1. Noun Forms_명사

1) 명사는 사람, 장소, 또는 사물을 나타낸다.

> 사람: man, woman, waiter, John
> 장소: home, office, town, station, Hong Kong
> 사물: table, car, apple, money, music, love, dog, monkey

2) 가산명사는 셀 수 있는 명사를 뜻한다. 즉, house처럼 한 채, 두 채, 세 채 등으로 셀 수 있다.

> dog, cat, animal, man, person, bottle, box, pound, coin,
> dollar, bowl, plate, fork, table, chair, suitcase, bag

3) 가산명사는 단수 혹은 복수의 형태를 띤다.
I have a friend.
I have two friends.

4) 대개 명사의 복수형은 명사에 s를 붙여서 만든다. 그러나 예외적인 경우들도 있다.
· −ch, −s, −sh, −ss 또는 −x로 끝나는 단어들은 −es를 붙인다.
benches, gases, dishes, dresses, taxes
· 자음(b, d, m, n, p) 뒤에 −y로 끝나는 단어들은 −ies를 붙인다.
parties, bodies, policies
· 모음 뒤에 −y로 끝나는 단어들은 −s를 붙인다.
trays, joys, keys
· −o로 끝나는 단어들은 −es를 붙이는 경우가 많다.
tomatoes, potatoes, heroes
· 모음 뒤에 o로 끝나는 단어는 −s를 붙인다.
videos, studios
· f로 끝나는 단어의 복수는 −s를 붙이거나 f를 v로 바꾸고 −es를 붙인다.
beliefs, puffs, wives, leaves, loaves
· −ex 또는 −ix로 끝나는 단어는 −es를 붙인다.
appendixes, indexes
· 단수와 복수의 형태가 같은 경우도 있다.
deer, sheep, fish, series

5) 셀 수 없는 물건들을 표현하는 불가산명사는 'cups of coffee' 또는 'pounds of coffee'의 형태로 셀 수 있다.

> music, art, love, happiness, advice, information, news, furniture, luggage, rice, sugar, butter, water, electricity, gas, money

6) 불가산명사는 보통 단수로 취급한다.
These <u>furnitures are</u> beautiful. → This <u>furniture is</u> beautiful.

7) 생각이나 감정을 표현하는 추상명사는 물리적으로 만질 수 없으므로 불가산명사에 속한다.
madness, health, justice

8) 추상명사는 셀 수 없으므로 언제나 단수다.
<u>Healths are</u> more important than <u>wealths.</u> → <u>Health is</u> more important than <u>wealth.</u>
Have <u>funs</u> at the reunion. → Have <u>fun</u> at the reunion.

9) paper, room, hair, noise, time 등 일부 명사는 가산명사, 불가산명사로 모두 쓰이며 단 · 복수에 따라 뜻이 달라진다.
The Diwali <u>lights</u> make the mall very pretty.
This room does not get enough <u>light.</u>

Othello is one of Shakespeare's most famous <u>works.</u>
I have a lot of <u>work</u> to do tonight.

10) 단수 가산명사는 대개 관사나 한정사(a, an, the, this, my, such) 뒤에 온다.
His mother is doctor. → His mother is <u>a</u> doctor.
Boy standing over there is brother. → <u>The</u> boy standing over there is <u>my</u> brother.
We saw child in playground. → We saw <u>a</u> child in <u>the</u> playground.

2. Verb Forms_동사

1) 조동사는 본동사 앞에 온다.

> be, am, is, are, was, were, being, been, has, have, had, do, does,
> did, can, will, shall, should, could, would, may, might, must

Many people don`t know what they <u>are</u> going to do after college.
I <u>am</u> going to give you step-by-step instructions.

2) might, must, can, would, should 같은 조동사들은 능력, 허락, 가능, 필요 등 여러 가지 다양한 의미를 나타낸다.

Tom <u>might</u> have gone to the party if he had been invited.
If I had a million dollars, I <u>would</u> buy a house for my parents.

3) 부정사는 동사 원형에 to를 붙여서 만들 수 있다.

He is too tired <u>to go</u> to the barbecue.
The manager wants <u>to hire</u> a new secretary.

4) 부정사는 문장에서 주어나 목적어로도 사용될 수 있다.

<u>To invest</u> now seems risky.
The teacher told him <u>to leave.</u>

5) 부정사는 동시적인 행위와 뒤에 일어날 행위 모두를 나타낸다.

We like <u>to play</u> video games. like는 play와 동시에 일어나고 있다.
My best friend wants <u>to shop</u> at that mall. shop은 want보다 뒤에 일어날 것이다.

3. Subject Verb Agreement_주어와 동사의 수 일치

1) 단수주어는 단수동사를 취한다.

The <u>teacher was</u> happy with my answer.
My <u>cell phone is</u> not working.

2) 복수주어는 복수동사를 취한다.

My <u>parents were</u> happy with my grades.
Many <u>television stations have</u> reported that story.

3) 복수주어에 단수동사를 사용해서는 안 된다.

Many <u>students thinks</u> tomorrow is a holiday. → Many <u>students think</u> tomorrow is a holiday.
The <u>student think</u> tomorrow is a holiday. → The <u>student thinks</u> tomorrow is a holiday.

4) 주어와 동사가 단어나 구로 분리되는 경우, 수 일치에 유념한다.

Your <u>suggestions</u> about the show <u>was</u> excellent.
→ Your <u>suggestions</u> about the show <u>were</u> excellent.

The <u>use</u> of cell phones during concerts <u>are</u> not allowed.
→ The <u>use</u> of cell phones during concerts <u>is</u> not allowed.

5) 복합주어에는 복수동사가 필요하다. 작문을 교열할 때 문장에서 주어가 무엇인지 정확히 파악한다.

<u>The camcorder and the tripod were</u> returned yesterday.
<u>Both Chantel and Rochelle are</u> nice names.

4. Pronouns_대명사

대명사는 명사를 대신하는 품사로 다음 몇 가지 규칙을 익히면 정확하고 효과적으로 사용할 수 있다.

> he, his, she, her, hers, it, they, their, them, these, that, this, those, who, whom, which, what, whose

1) 대명사는 지시하는 명사와 일치해야 한다.

대명사가 여성을 가리킨다면 여성형 대명사(she, her, hers)를, 남성을 가리킨다면 남성형 대명사(he, his, him)를 사용한다. 그런데 사람의 성별을 알지 못하거나 그 사람이 어떤 성별에도 속하지 않을 수 있다. 영어에는 사람을 지칭할 수 있는 성 중립적인 단수 대명사가 없기 때문에 의미가 명확하다면 복수대명사(they, their)를 사용하는 것이 허용된다. 대명사는 일반적으로 지시하는 명사와 수가 일치해야 한다. 단수명사를 지시하기 위해 사용한다면 단수대명사를, 복수명사를 대체하기 위해서 사용한다면 복수대명사를 사용한다.

Julia reminded us that that <u>she</u> would not stay late.

Bob bought two computers and had <u>them</u> delivered to his office.

The person who answered the phone said <u>they</u> would leave a message for Miguel.

2) 일부 부정대명사는 대부분의 경우 단수로 취급한다.

<u>Neither</u> of the boys sent in <u>his</u> report.

그러나 때로는 포괄성을 위해 예외를 둘 수 있는데, 아래 예문을 보면 모든 티켓 구매자의 성별을 알 수 없기 때문에, 비록 복수형이지만 중립적인 대명사 'their'를 사용하는 것이 허용된다. (다른 표현으로 Everyone must buy his or her ticket. 또는 간단히 Everyone must buy a ticket.으로 쓸 수 있다.)

<u>Everyone</u> must buy <u>their</u> own ticket.

3) both나 many 같은 일부 부정대명사는 항상 복수이며 them을 가리키는 다른 대명사들도 복수다.

<u>Both</u> of <u>them</u> are here tonight.

<u>Many</u> of the managers have moved into <u>their</u> new offices.

4) 일부 부정대명사는 단수이거나 복수일 수 있다.

> all, any, more, most, none, some

<u>Most</u> of my time <u>is</u> spent reviewing for the test.

most는 단수명사 time을 가리키므로 단수동사 is를 취함

<u>Most</u> of the students <u>have</u> turned in <u>their</u> reports.

most는 복수명사 students를 가리키므로 복수동사 have, 복수대명사 their를 취함

5) 대명사를 지나치게 많이 사용하면 혼동을 초래할 수 있다.

다음 문장의 지지자는 대통령의 지지자인가, 부통령의 지지자인가? 그들은 누구와 만나는가?

The President informed the Vice President that all of <u>his</u> supporters should be meeting <u>with him</u>.

→ The President informed the Vice President that all of <u>the President's</u> supporters should be meeting with <u>the President</u>.

6) it을 지나치게 많이 사용하면 의미가 약해진다.

We were visiting the museum. I saw <u>it</u>. <u>It</u> was interesting and unusual. I was amazed by <u>it</u>.

→ We were visiting the museum. I saw <u>the space exhibit</u>. It was interesting and unusual. I was amazed by it. 첫 번째 it이 무엇을 나타내는지 설명함으로써 문장을 개선할 수 있다.

Although the car hit the tree, <u>it</u> was not damaged. 여기서 it은 차를 지칭하는가, 나무를 지칭하는가?

→ <u>The car</u> was not damaged, although it hit the tree.

7) 접속사(and, or, nor)로 연결된 명사를 쓸 때는 명사를 가리키는 대명사와 그 명사의 수가 일치해야 한다.

If <u>Bob and Rick</u> want to go, <u>they</u> will need to take the bus because I don't have room in my car.

Bob과 Rick이 접속사 and로 연결되어 있으므로 복수대명사 they를 사용

Whether I buy a <u>dishwasher</u> or <u>dryer</u>, <u>it</u> will have to go in the kitchen.

명사는 단수(dishwasher 또는 dryer)이므로 단수대명사 it을 사용

8) who, whom, which, that 등이 언제 사용되는지 알고 있어야 한다.

The committee interviewed all the candidates <u>who</u> applied. who는 사람들(candidates)을 지칭한다.

Do you still have the magazine <u>that</u> I lent you last week? that은 사물(magazine)을 지칭한다.

<u>Which</u> courses should I take in the fall? which는 사물(courses)을 지칭한다.

5. Possessive pronouns_소유대명사

1) 점유나 소유를 나타내는 his, hers, mine, theirs, yours, our 같은 소유대명사를 사용할 때는 지시하는 명사의 수와 일치하도록 해야 한다.

I have my ticket, and my husband has <u>theirs</u>. → I have my ticket, and my husband has <u>his</u>.

This is the children's room. All those toys are <u>hers</u>. → This is the children's room. All those toys are <u>theirs</u>.

2) 소유대명사는 이미 소유의 의미를 가지고 있는 대명사들이므로 아포스트로피를 사용하지 않는다.

> his, hers, its , ours, yours, theirs, whose

Each art room has <u>it's</u> own sink. → Each art room has <u>its</u> own sink.

it is를 의미하는 it's를 쓰는 것이 아니라 소유대명사(its)를 써야 한다.

<u>His'</u> office is on the third floor. → <u>His</u> office is on the third floor.

소유대명사 his를 써야 한다. his'라는 표현은 쓸 수 없다.

6. Other ways to show possession_소유를 나타내는 기타 방법

1) –s로 끝나는 명사에 '소유'의 의미를 담고자 할 때는 아포스트로피를 붙인다.

I like Jame<u>s'</u> company.

This is Harri<u>s'</u> wife, Anna.

2) 아포스트로피는 적당한 곳에 붙여야 한다. 단수인 경우 –s 앞에 붙인다.

The teacher<u>'s</u> desk is right in front.

My sister<u>'s</u> haircut cost $70 dollars.

My neighbor<u>'s</u> house is bigger than mine.

Henry<u>'s</u> cat likes to play with our baby.

3) 복수인 경우에는 –s 뒤에 아포스트로피를 붙인다.

We borrowed our parents<u>'</u> car.

I went to a party at my friend<u>s'</u> house.

4) 두 사람 이상이 공동으로 소유하면 마지막 명사에 아포스트로피 –s를 붙이고, 각자 소유하고 있는 경우에는 각각 's를 붙인다.

John and Jack's room is very messy. 존과 잭이 방을 같이 소유하고 있다.

Ian's and George's dreams are very different, even though the two boys come from the same family.
이언과 조지는 다른 꿈을 가지고 있다.

5) 명사를 복수로 만들 때 아포스트로피를 붙이는 실수를 하지 않도록 유의하자.

The new student's look confused. (틀린 문장)

There are too many car's on our street's. (틀린 문장)

7. Prepositions_전치사

전치사는 문장에서 좀 더 자세한 정보를 제공하기 위해 명사(또는 명사구) 앞에 쓰이는 품사로 사물의 위치나 어떤 일이 일어난 시간을 나타낼 때 주로 쓰인다.

> in, among, between, across, at, with, beside, behind, into, from, during, before, after

1) 전치사는 다음과 같은 것을 나타내기 위해 사용한다.
- 장소

The main office is in New York.

I'm meeting my colleagues at the coffee shop.
- 시간

Let's try to get there by 3:30.

Please do not talk during the show.
- 행위 또는 동작

He jumped into the river.

We flew from Los Angeles to Toronto.

2) 일부 동사와 형용사 뒤에는 특정 전치사들이 온다. 특정 단어와 짝을 이루는 전치사의 예는 다음과 같다.

> familiar with, afraid of, far from, close to, believe in, borrow from, lend to, absent from,
> nice to, argue with, made of, take off, turn on, happy with, sad about, famous for

They always argue about money.

I borrowed a book from the library.

I am afraid of losing my textbooks.

The student argued with the teacher.

Other Errors

1. Wrong or Missing Word_철자 오류

글을 빨리 쓰거나 타자를 빨리 칠 때, 잘못된 단어를 사용하거나 철자가 틀린 단어를 사용하는 경우가 있다. 문장을 수정, 편집, 교열할 때는 잘못된 단어나 빠뜨린 단어가 있는지 잘 살펴본다. 틀리거나 빠뜨린 단어는 문장을 꼼꼼히 검토하면 쉽게 고칠 수 있으며 컴퓨터의 자동 맞춤법 검사 기능도 이런 오류들을 잡아낼 수 있다.

1) 가장 자주 발생하는 문제는 흔히 they대신 the를 사용하는 것이다.
   <u>The</u> went to the store each Monday. → <u>They</u> went to the store each Monday.

2) 또 다른 오류는 흔히 the 다음에 명사를 빠뜨리는 것이다.
   <u>The</u> go to the store each Monday. → <u>The brothers</u> go to the store each Monday.

2. Keyboard Errors or Typos_오타 또는 오탈자

에세이의 초안을 작성할 때 문법, 용법, 어법상의 오류는 물론 단어를 빠뜨리거나 오타를 범하는 경우도 있다. 이런 오류들을 바로잡기 위해 에세이를 편집하고 수정할 때 세심하게 교열해야 한다.

Usage_용법

Article Errors / Determiner Errors

1. 관사는 무엇인가?

관사(a, an, the)는 명사나 명사의 수식어 앞에 위치하며 a와 an은 부정관사, the는 정관사라고 한다.

> a thinker, an apple, the house, a car, an old house, the newspapers

1) a/an은 불특정한 것을 가리킬 때 단수명사 앞에 사용된다.

James must write <u>an essay</u> for his writing class today.

<u>A newspaper</u> is good source of information on current events.

I received <u>a letter</u> from my sister.

Sending <u>an e-mail</u> is a fast way to communicate with classmates.   a/an은 가산명사 앞에 위치한다.

<u>a</u> basketball, <u>a</u> new automobile   관사 뒤에 오는 명사나 수식어가 자음으로 시작되면 a를 써야 한다.

<u>an</u> elephant, <u>an</u> old truck   명사나 그 수식어가 모음으로 시작되면 an을 써야 한다.

This will be <u>a</u> one-time charge to your account.   간혹 명사나 수식어가 모음으로 시작되지만 음가가 모음이 아닌 경우도 있다. 예를 들면 one이라는 단어에서 모음 o는 won의 w와 비슷하게 발음된다.

2) a/an은 셀 수 없는 명사 앞에는 사용되지 않는다.

I like to drink milk.   milk는 셀 수 없다.

I like to drink <u>a glass of milk</u> before I go to bed.   우유의 형태가 구체화되면 관사를 사용할 수 있다.

· 간혹 추상적이고 일반적인 개념(분노, 아름다움, 사랑, 가난, 고용 등)을 표현하기 위해 사용되는 명사 앞에는 a나 an을 쓰지 않는다.

Love is a difficult emotion to describe in words.

Money alone cannot buy happiness.

· 복수 명사가 일반적인 의미로 사용될 때는 the를 쓰지 않는다.

<u>Computers</u> are helpful tools for student writers.   Computers는 특정한 컴퓨터가 아니라 일반적인 컴퓨터를 말한다.

<u>The computers</u> in that classroom are used for writing class.   The computers는 특정한 컴퓨터들을 의미한다.

3) the는 특정하거나 구체적인 명사 앞에서 사용된다.

<u>The art class</u> that I want to take is taught by a famous painter.

<u>The students</u> in Mrs. Jones' class do not want to participate in <u>the debate</u>.

또한, 다음과 같은 경우에도 정관사 the를 사용한다.

· 모두가 알고 있는 사물을 가리킬 때(the sun, the stars)

· 유일한 사물을 가리킬 때(the White House)

· 시간을 나타낼 때(the past, the present, the future)

2. 그 밖의 한정사(Determiner) 오류들

this, that, these, those 같은 형용사는 뒤에 오는 명사를 한정 수식한다. 따라서 이 형용사들은 수식을 받는 명사들과 수가 일치해야 한다. this와 that은 단수명사를, these와 those는 복수명사를 한정하기 위해 사용된다.

I would buy these house for those reason.

→ I would buy <u>this house for that reason</u>.

This kinds of technologies will affect people's behavior.

→ <u>These kinds</u> of technologies will affect people's behavior.

Homonyms

'동음이의어'는 발음은 같으나 뜻, 철자 또는 용법이 다른 단어로, 철자가 같은 단어와 발음이 같은 단어가 있다. 철자는 같지만 의미가 다른 단어를 동형이의어(homograph)라고 하며(예: '곰'을 뜻하는 명사 bear와 '운반하다'를 뜻하는 동사 bear), 발음은 같지만 의미와 철자가 다른 단어를 동음이자(homophone)라고 한다(예: '완전하다'는 뜻의 형용사 whole 과 '구멍'을 의미하는 명사 hole).

다음은 흔히 볼 수 있는 동음이의어의 예이다.

here	'이곳'을 의미하는 부사 We have been waiting **here** for an hour.
hear	'듣다'를 뜻하는 동사 Do you **hear** the birds singing?
hole	'구멍'을 의미하는 명사 The children dug a big **hole** in their sandbox.
whole	'완전한, 전체의'라는 뜻의 형용사 Our **whole** project will involve cooperation from everyone.
its	대명사 it의 소유격 The kitten hurt **its** paw.
it's	it is의 축약형 **It's** not fair to leave her behind.
know	'알다, 인식하다'를 의미하는 동사 Do you **know** how to get to the subway?
no	'부인, 거절'을 의미하는 부사 The employee said **no** to the job offer.
knew	동사 know의 과거형 The boy **knew** how to count ten.
new	'새로운'을 의미하는 형용사 At the start of the school year, the students bought **new** books.

desert	'사막'을 의미하는 명사
	It rarely rains in the **desert**.
desert	'버리다'를 의미하는 동사
	The officer commanded the troops not to **desert** their posts.
dessert	'디저트'를 의미하는 명사
	After a big meal, I enjoy a simple **dessert** of vanilla ice cream.
to	'~쪽으로'를 의미하는 전치사
	The man pointed **to** the sky.
two	'숫자 2'를 의미하는 형용사 또는 대명사
	Five is **two** more than three.
too	'또한'을 의미하는 부사
	Tom and Eleanor wanted to go with them **too**.
they're	'They are'의 축약형
	They're both coming to the party.
their	'그들의'라는 뜻의 소유대명사
	That is **their** blue house on the corner.
there	'그곳에'를 의미하는 부사
	Did you see anyone you knew **there**?
through	'~을 지나' 또는 '~을 끝내고'를 의미하는 부사
	When she was **through** eating, she put her plate in the sink.
threw	'던지다'를 의미하는 동사 throw의 과거형
	The boy **threw** the ball to his sister.

Other Confused Words

동음이의어 이외에 철자, 발음, 의미가 비슷해서 혼동하기 쉬운 단어들이 있다. 흔히 혼동하기 쉬운 단어들로는 accept/except, advice/advise, affect/effect, loose/lose 등이 있으며 이런 단어들을 잘못 사용하면 컴퓨터의 자동 맞춤법 검사 기능도 잡아내지 못한다. 원어민들도 작문할 때, 특히 서둘러서 작문할 때 이런 혼동하기 쉬운 단어들에서 실수하는 경우가 많다. 작문을 검토할 때 정확한 단어를 썼는지 확인하기 위해 다음의 단어들에 주의한다. 하지만 이것들은 영어에서 자주 혼동되는 단어들 중 몇 가지에 불과하므로, 어떤 단어의 용법이 무엇인지 확실치 않다면 영어 사전을 찾아 보도록 한다.

accept	'받다, 인정하다', '~을 받아들이다'를 의미하는 동사
	I **accept** your kind invitation.
except	'~외에는, ~을 제외하고는'을 의미하는 전치사
	Everyone **except** Phil can attend the conference.
advice	'충고, 조언, 권고'를 의미하는 명사
	He has always given me valuable **advice** regarding my future plans.
advise	'권하다, 충고[조언]하다'를 의미하는 동사
	I **advise** you to stay in school and study hard.

affect	'~에 영향을 미치다' 또는 '작용하다'를 의미하는 동사
	The weather can **affect** a person's mood.
effect	'결과'를 의미하는 명사
	When students study for tests, they see a positive **effect** on their test results.
effect	'~을 가져오다, 초래하다'를 의미하는 동사
	The governor can **effect** change in state education policies.

loose	'풀린, 묶이지 않은', '느슨한'을 의미하는 형용사
	She lost her bracelet because it was too **loose** on her wrist.
lose	'잃다, 상실하다', '지다'를 의미하는 동사
	If you don't pay attention to the signs, you might **lose** your way.

quiet	'조용한, 고요한'을 의미하는 형용사
	Please be **quiet** when other people are speaking.
quit	'포기하다, 단념하다', '그만두다'를 의미하는 동사
	The boys will **quit** their jobs the week before school starts.
quite	'꽤, 상당히'를 의미하는 부사
	Moving to a new city will be **quite** a change for my family.

sense	'의식, 지각', '감각'을 의미하는 명사
	My brother had the good **sense** to keep out of trouble.
	The doctor explained that my **sense** of smell is not functioning well.
since	'~이래 줄곧'을 의미하는 부사, '~한 때부터'를 의미하는 접속사
	Ginny has lived in the same house ever **since** she moved to town.
	Karl has worked as an accountant **since** graduating from college.

than	두 가지 요소를 비교할 때 사용하는 접속사
	Her puppy is smaller **than** mine.
then	'그때 당시, 그 다음에, 그러고 나서'를 의미하는 부사
	First I will stop at the store, and **then** I will go home.

<u>Wrong Form of Word</u>

1) 작문한 것을 검토할 때 다음의 예와 같은 오류들은 없는지 잘 읽어 본다. 아니면 다른 사람에게 작문한 것을 읽게 하고 확실치 않은 부분을 지적해 달라고 한다.

But certain types of businesses will continue to grow to an <u>extend</u>, he thinks.

→ But certain types of businesses will continue to grow to an <u>extent</u>, he thinks.

Traffic has stopped because a truck is <u>disable</u> in the middle of the road.

→ Traffic has stopped because a truck is <u>disabled</u> in the middle of the road.

2) 각각의 품사가 문장에서 어떤 역할을 하는지 알아야 한다. 자신이 쓴 것을 교정해 보면 이런 오류들도 바로잡을 수 있다.

Faulty Comparison

비교의 오류는 문장에서 more가 -er로 끝나는 단어와 함께 사용될 때와 most가 -est로 끝나는 단어와 함께 사용되는 경우이다. 이런 종류의 오류를 피하기 위해 다음과 같은 규칙들에 유의해야 한다.

1) 하나의 사물을 다른 것과 비교할 때 짧은 단어에는 끝에 -er을 붙인다.

   The boy with the red hair is more taller than the girl with the black hair.

   → The boy with the red hair is <u>taller</u> than the girl with the black hair.

   Today it is hot, but yesterday it was even more hotter.

   → Today it is hot, but yesterday it was even <u>hotter</u>.

2) 셋 이상을 비교할 때 짧은 단어에는 -est를 붙인다.

   The girl in the back of the room is the <u>tallest</u> girl in her entire class.

   Yesterday was the <u>hottest</u> day ever recorded by the National Weather Service.

3) 두 개 이상의 음절로 이루어진 단어에는 -er이나 -est를 붙이지 않는다. 대신 둘을 비교할 때는 앞에 more를 붙이고, 셋 이상을 비교할 때는 most를 붙인다.

   The judges must decide which of the two remaining singers is <u>more talented</u>.

   Of the three new students, Amancia is the <u>most accomplished</u>.

4) 부정적인 비교의 경우 둘을 비교할 때는 less를 쓰고, 셋 이상을 비교할 때는 least를 쓴다.

   The third floor apartment is <u>less costly</u> than the first floor apartment.

   Of the three colleges that I've visited, this one is the <u>least expensive</u>.

Nonstandard Verb or Word Form

일상 대화에서 사용하는 단어들은 일반적으로 작문에서 사용하는 단어들과 다른 경우가 많다. 읽는 사람이 이러한 구어체 단어(gotta, gonna, wanna, kinda)를 이해할 수는 있겠지만 작문할 때는 사용하지 않도록 한다.

I told her I gotta go to school now. → I told her I <u>have got to</u> go to school now.

Do you wanna go to college? → Do you <u>want to</u> go to college?

Capitalization

1) 모든 문장의 첫 단어는 대문자로 쓴다.

She is the most famous director. There is no doubt about it.

Give it to me. It looks like mine.

2) 사람, 물건, 제목, 장소의 명칭 같은 모든 고유명사는 대문자로 쓴다.

Francis Lloyd Mantel lives on Moore Street. Francis Lloyd Mantel(사람 이름) Moore Street(장소 이름) 대문자로 시작

The class is reading *Adventure of Huckleberry Finn*. 책 제목

3) 모든 명칭은 고유명사이므로 대문자로 시작한다.

· 기관, 장소, 지명

She is a new faculty member at Webler University.

Their main office is in New Delhi, India.

· 역사적 사건, 날짜, 요일

Independence Day is a school holiday.

Classes don't meet until October.

· 언어명, 고유 형용사

He speaks Spanish and Italian fluently.

They teach Korean dances at the academy.

4) 일인칭 대명사 I는 문장 중간에 나와도 언제나 대문자로 쓴다.

It is I who sent you that letter.

They told me that I should call for an appointment.

5) father, mother, aunt, uncle 같은 단어들이 고유명사와 함께 쓰이거나 특정한 사람을 가리킬 때는 대문자로 쓴다. 그러나 my와 their 같은 소유대명사와 함께 쓰이면 고유명사가 아니므로 대문자로 시작하지 않는다.

Uncle Ruofan and Aunt Shanshan just moved into their new apartment.

Yes, Mom, I'm going after dinner.

My father is not at home.

Their mother is my aunt.

Spelling

1) fiery, friend, dried처럼 e 앞에 i를 쓴다. 단, 다음과 같은 예외가 있다.

· c 다음 (receive)

· neighbor처럼 a로 발음될 때(weigh, heir, foreign)

All applicants will receive a response within three weeks.

The breakfast special is fried eggs and sausage.

2) 단어가 묵음 e로 끝나면, 모음으로 시작되는 접미사를 붙일 때 e를 탈락시킨다. 단, 접미사가 자음으로 시작되면 탈락시키지 않는다.

I like to skate, I enjoy skating. 접미사 -ing가 모음 i로 시작되었으므로 e가 탈락되었다.

I could use a dictionary. A dictionary is very useful. 접미사 -ful이 자음 f로 시작되므로 e는 탈락되지 않았다.

3) 어떤 단어가 y로 끝나고 y앞에 오는 글자가 자음일 경우 접미사를 붙이기 전에 y를 탈락시키고 i를 붙인다.

The beaches in Thailand are extremely <u>beautiful</u>.

They <u>hurried</u> to the gate because they were so late.

4) 어떤 단어가 y로 끝나고 앞에 모음이 올 경우 복수형을 만들 때는 s만 붙이면 된다. 단 y 앞에 자음이 올 경우 y를 탈락시키고 ie를 붙인 후 s를 붙인다.

Funkidz is a popular <u>toy</u> store. It sells all kinds of toy<u>s</u>.

The <u>babies</u> started to crawl.

5) 단어가 자음으로 끝나고 그 앞에 모음이 올 경우, 모음으로 시작되는 접미사를 붙일 때는 그 단어의 마지막 자음을 한 번 더 쓴다. e로 끝나면 자음을 두 번 쓰는 대신 e를 탈락시키고 접미사를 붙인다.

The children <u>swim</u> at the community pool. They love <u>swimming</u>.

You should <u>begin</u> at the <u>beginning</u>. Start by writing the title.

The children go <u>skating</u> in the winter.

6) 다음 문장들에는 철자 오류의 예가 포함되어 있다.

We visited the monkey house at the zoo. There were monkies from all over the world.

→ We visited the monkey house at the zoo. There were <u>monkeys</u> from all over the world.

monkey의 복수형은 monkeys이다. y로 끝나고 그 앞에 모음이 오는 단어의 복수형은 s만 붙이면 된다.

My neice is a student in your class. → My <u>niece</u> is a student in your class.

niece가 맞는 철자다. "c 다음이 아니라면 e 앞에 i를 쓴다."라는 규칙이 적용됐다.

7) 철자 규칙에는 일부 예외들이 있으며, 키보드를 너무 빨리 치다가 실수를 하는 경우도 있다. 이런 경우를 대비한 전략 중 하나는 컴퓨터의 자동 맞춤법 검사 기능을 사용하는 것이다.

A letter <u>frrom</u> her former neighbor came in the mail today.

<u>Becuase</u> I lost my homework, I had to do it again.

8) 자동 맞춤법 검사 기능으로 잡아내기 어려운 실수도 있으므로 문장을 읽고 그 의미를 파악하면서 실수를 찾아내야 한다.

Would you know <u>weather</u> he is at work today?

Are <u>their</u> any good Indian restaurant in this area?

Punctuation

구두법은 문장 부호를 사용하는 것을 말한다. 아포스트로피 같은 문장 부호는 각각의 단어와 함께 사용되며, 쉼표 등은 문장의 부분을 나누거나 숫자의 단위를 표시하기 위해 쓴다. 마침표, 물음표, 느낌표 등은 문장을 구별하기 위해 사용한다. 이처럼 문장 부호는 문장의 의미를 명확하게 한다.

1. Apostrophe

1) 축약형을 쓸 때 아포스트로피를 사용한다.

축약은 일부 단어를 탈락시키고 아포스트로피를 붙여 두 단어를 합치는 것을 말한다. 예를 들면 can't는 cannot의 축약형, shouldn't는 should not의 축약형, let's는 let us의 축약형이다. 이 외에도 won't, it's, wouldn't, couldn't 등이 있다.

They <u>won't</u> be able to enter without their tickets. won't는 will not의 축약형

We could hear them, but we <u>couldn't</u> see them. couldn't는 could not의 축약형

2) 아포스트로피 없이 축약형을 쓰는 것은 잘못된 것이다.

Lets go to the park tomorrow. → <u>Let's</u> go to the park tomorrow.

She <u>lets</u> us use the computer when she's not using it. 이 문장에서는 아포스트로피 없이 "allow"라는 뜻으로 쓰였다.

3) 정확한 사용을 위해 아포스트로피는 적절한 위치에 있어야 한다.

We could'nt understand the lecture. → We <u>couldn't</u> understand the lecture.

Students were'nt in school in the summer. → Students <u>weren't</u> in school in the summer.

4) 아포스트로피는 탈락되는 모음을 대체하는 것임을 기억해야 한다.

2. Comma

쉼표는 읽는 사람에게 잠시 멈추라는 신호 기능을 하는 가장 흔하게 나오는 문장 부호다. 다음 예문을 주의 깊게 읽어 보면 쉼표가 있는 곳에서 자연스럽게 쉬어 읽는 것을 알 수 있다. 몇 가지 기본적인 규칙을 익히면 쉼표를 좀 더 효과적으로 사용할 수 있다.

1) 두 개의 절을 중문으로 결합시키기 위해 쉼표와 접속사를 사용한다.

The causes of the Civil War were many, <u>and</u> the effects of the war were numerous.

The experiment was incomplete, <u>but</u> the lessons learned were important.

2) 단어들을 문장의 앞 또는 뒤쪽으로 연결하기 위해 쉼표를 사용한다.

하나 이상의 단어를 문장의 앞 또는 뒤쪽에 붙임으로써 정보를 추가하는 경우 읽는 사람이 주요 메시지를 파악할 수 있도록 쉼표를 사용할 수 있다. 다음 두 문장은 시간을 나타내는 구로 시작되며, 쉼표에 의해 주제 문장과 분리되어 있다.

Last night, my friend and I celebrated his 58th birthday.

Many years ago, I studied French and German.

3) 한 문장에서 세 개 이상의 항목을 나열할 때 그 항목들 사이에 쉼표를 사용한다.

The flag was red, white, and blue.

I bought milk, bread, cheese, and butter.

4) 수식되는 명사 앞에 두 개의 형용사가 올 때 이들을 분리하기 위해 쉼표를 사용한다.

The <u>cold, wintry</u> wind chilled me to my bones.

The <u>complex, diverse</u> cultures in the city add to its excitement.

5) 세부 사실을 묘사하는 정보는 문장의 핵심 부분(동사와 목적어)과 구별되어야 하므로 이 단어들 앞뒤에 쉼표를 사용한다.

Ms. Johnson, <u>the company president</u>, will announce the winner.

My brother, <u>who loves to read</u>, uses the library every day.

Conrad Redding, the father of the bride, cried at the wedding.

In conclusion, I believe that technology will be the main factor affecting life in the 21st century.

6) 인용된 부분을 구별하기 위해 쉼표를 사용한다.

"Take a break," said the instructor.

Yeonsuk announces, "I am going to a job interview tomorrow."

7) 도시, 군 또는 이에 상당하는 지명 뒤에 주나 국가의 이름이 나오면 쉼표를 사용해서 구별한다.

The newspaper is based in Chicago, Illinois.

Her flight to Beijing, China, took twelve hours.

8) 4자리 이상의 숫자와 연, 월, 일을 표기할 때 쉼표를 사용한다.

He won $1,000,000 in the lottery.

The date is March 15, 2024.

3. Hyphen

하이픈은 복합어를 만들기 위해 두 단어 사이를 연결할 때 사용하는 문장 부호다. 형용사구의 일부로서 숫자에 사용되거나 접두사와 함께 사용되는 경우가 가장 보편적이다. 복합어를 만들기 위해 하이픈을 사용하지만 항상 그런 것은 아니며, 미국식 영어에서는 하이픈을 점점 더 적게 쓰는 경향이 있다. 정확한 하이픈 사용을 위해 항상 최신 사전을 참조할 것을 권한다.

1) 명사 앞에서 하나의 형용사 역할을 하는 단어들을 결합하기 위해 하이픈을 쓴다.

His uncle is a <u>well-known</u> author. The author is <u>well known</u> for his mystery stories.

복합형용사가 명사 뒤에 올 때는 하이픈으로 연결하지 않는다.

2) 분수나 21 이상의 수를 표기할 때 하이픈을 사용한다.

The cup is <u>three-quarters</u> full.

Our teacher is <u>sixty-three</u> years old.

3) 접두사는 단어에 덧붙여 의미를 변화시키는 음절이나 단어를 말한다. self-, ex-, great- 등의 접두사는 언제나 하이픈을 써야 한다. 그러나 dis-, pre-, re-, un- 같은 접두사의 경우는 통상 하이픈을 사용하지 않는다.

The instructions are <u>self-explanatory</u>.

The children are with their <u>great-grandparents</u>.

My aunt <u>dislikes</u> loud music.

The answer to that question is <u>unknown</u>.

4. Final Punctuation

문장을 끝마칠 때 사용하는 구두점들에는 물음표, 마침표, 느낌표 등이 있다.

1) 직접의문문 뒤에 물음표를 사용한다.

When did Second World War begin<u>?</u>

What were the key stages in the Romantic Art movement<u>?</u>

Have you called Mrs. Han yet<u>?</u>

2) 마침표는 문장의 종료를 나타내기 위해 사용하며 간접의문에서도 사용한다.

I just completed the project<u>.</u>

Cindy asked me who would be taking notes at the meeting<u>.</u>

3) 강한 감정을 표현하거나 강조가 필요한 문장 뒤에는 느낌표를 사용한다.

That was utter nonsense<u>!</u>

What absolutely gorgeous flowers<u>!</u> Thank you<u>!</u>

Oh, that's an amazing story<u>!</u>

Other Errors

1. Compound Words

복합어는 두 개 이상으로 이뤄진 단어들이다. 예를 들면 everywhere는 every와 where라는 뚜렷이 구별되는 두 개의 단어로 구성되어 있다. 그러나 복합어인 everywhere는 every와 where와는 다른 새로운 의미를 가진다. 어떤 단어가 복합어인지에 대해서는 전문가들도 의견이 일치하지 않지만 대부분의 경우 명확한 규칙이 있다.

I work to support my self and my family. → I work to support <u>myself</u> and my family.

You can learn from every thing happening today. → You can learn from <u>everything</u> happening today.

TIP | 영어에서 형용사나 명사 같은 단어들은 다양한 방식으로 결합되어 복합어가 되며 복합어를 구성하는 각각의 단어와는 다른 의미를 가진다. 모든 단어들이 이런 식으로 결합될 수 있는 것은 아니다. 그러므로 어떤 단어의 복합어 여부를 확인할 때 사전을 참조하도록 한다.

2. Fused Words

작문할 때 두 개의 단어를 결합해서 틀린 복합어를 만들지 않도록 주의해야 한다.

Some people say that highschool is the best time of your life.

→ Some people say that <u>high school</u> is the best time of your life.

I like to play soccer alot. → I like to play soccer <u>a lot</u>.

3. Duplicate Words

작문의 초안을 쓸 때 입력하는 속도가 생각하는 속도를 못 따라가기 때문에 실수를 할 수도 있다. 그 결과 같은 단어를 두 번 쓰게 되거나 간혹 서로 형태는 다르지만 같은 역할을 하는 두 개의 단어를 이어 쓰는 경우가 생긴다. 초안을 작성할 때 흔히 다음과 같이 두 개의 동사, 대명사, 관사를 쓰기도 한다.

Sally's older sister can may help her pay for college.

→ Sally's older sister <u>can help</u> her pay for college.

→ Sally's older sister <u>may help</u> her pay for college.

He was as silly as a the clown.

→ He was as silly as <u>a</u> clown.

→ He was as silly as <u>the</u> clown.

TIP | 같은 단어를 두 번 쓰거나 같은 기능을 하는 단어들을 잇달아 쓰면 중복되게 된다. 중복된 철자는 자동 맞춤법 검사 기능으로 바로잡기가 쉽다. 또한 같은 기능을 하는 두 단어 중 어느 것을 사용하는지 확실하지 않은 경우에는 사전을 참조하도록 한다.

318

Word Repetition

핵심 주제를 강조하기 위해 단어를 반복하는 것은 좋은 작문 기법의 하나다. 그러나 같은 단어를 여러 번 자주 반복해서 사용하면 미숙한 문체로 보이거나 에세이를 지루하게 만들 수 있다. 효과적인 작문을 위한 다양한 어휘 사용에 도움이 되는 아이디어들을 소개한다.

1) 반복되는 단어를 대체하기 위해 동의어를 사용한다. 예를 들면 make 같은 흔한 단어 대신 다음 동의어 중 적절한 것을 함께 쓸 수 있다.

> create, produce, perform, do, execute, bring about, cause, form, manufacture,
> construct, build, put up, set up, put together, compose

2) 다음 문단에서는 명사 student가 너무 자주 반복되고 있다.

> Think about this situation. A <u>student</u> interviewed many <u>students</u> about what it is like to be an only child. If the teachers in charge of the school paper did not edit names of <u>students</u> from the paper or facts that would give that particular <u>student</u> away to other <u>students</u>, then serious problems could be caused for the <u>students</u> who gave their information.

⬇

> Think about this situation. <u>A reporter</u> interviewed many <u>students</u> about what it is like to be an only child. If the teachers in charge of the school paper did not edit the <u>individuals'</u> names from the paper or facts that would give <u>each person</u> away to the <u>readers</u>, then serious problems could be caused for the <u>students</u> who gave their information.

3) 같은 단어의 반복을 피하기 위해 the former, the latter, the first one, the other 같은 표현을 사용한다. 다양한 표현을 사용해서 다음과 같이 바꿔 쓸 수 있다.

> Of the two sisters, <u>Grace</u> is confident and at ease with everyone. <u>Lily</u> is shy and cautious. <u>Grace</u> always gets what she wants. <u>Lily</u> waits patiently for whatever comes her way. <u>Grace</u> never misses a chance to show off her many talents. <u>Lily</u> never says a word unless someone asks her a question.

⬇

> Of the two sisters, <u>Grace</u> is confident and at ease with everyone. <u>Lily</u> is shy and cautious. <u>The former</u> always gets what she wants. <u>The latter</u> waits patiently for whatever comes her way. <u>Grace</u> never misses a chance to show off her many talents. <u>Her sister</u> never says a word unless someone asks her a question.

TIP | 작문한 것을 검토할 때 지나치게 자주 사용된 단어나 구를 어떻게 대체할 수 있을지 생각해 보자. 또한 동의어 사전을 참조하면 작문을 좀 더 다양하게 할 수 있다.

Inappropriate Words or Phrases

속어와 같이 지나치게 구어체적인 표현은 작문에 사용하기 부적절하다. 그러나 어떤 표현이 구어체적인지 알기 쉬운 것은 아니다. 자주 쓰이기 때문에 작문할 때 사용해도 무방하다고 생각되는 구어체 표현들도 있기 때문이다.

No way would she ever say a thing like that. → She would never say that.

People need to get it all together and step up for the picnic.

→ We need people to get organized and set up the picnic.

Too Many Passive Sentences

1) 문장에서 주어가 행위자인 경우를 능동태 문장, 주어가 행위를 받는 경우를 수동태 문장이라고 한다.

Only a few hundred people saw the movie. 주어(only a few hundred people)는 행위자

The movie was seen by 200 million people. 주어(the movie)는 행위를 받는 것

2) 수동태 문장은 대개 길이가 길고, 읽기 어렵기 때문에 너무 많이 사용하면 작문이 느슨하고 지루해질 수 있다. 반면에 능동태 문장은 일반적으로 더 명확하고 직접적이며, 강한 느낌을 준다.

전문가들은 작문할 때 수동태 문장의 비중을 5% 정도로 두는 것이 적당하다고 말한다. 즉, 수동태 문장을 적재적소에 사용하면 작문에 힘을 실을 수 있다.

3) 수동태를 쓰는 것이 더 효과적인 경우는 다음과 같다.

· 행위 자체가 행위자보다 중요할 때

The theater was opened last month.

New students are invited to meet the dean in room 226.

극장이 개장하고 학생들이 초대된다는 사실이 '행위자'(극장을 개장한 사람들 또는 학생들을 초대한 사람들)보다 중요하다.

· 행위의 객체가 행위자보다 중요한 경우

Everyone was given a key to the gym. 열쇠를 준 사람들보다 열쇠를 받은 사람들이 더 중요하다.

The letters were sent this morning. 편지를 보낸 사람들보다 보내진 편지가 더 중요하다.

· 행위의 결과가 행위자보다 중요한 경우

Our advice was followed by our clients. 충고를 하는 사람들보다 고객이 충고를 따르는 행위 자체가 더 중요하다.

The new computers were installed by the systems staff. 컴퓨터를 설치한 사람들보다 컴퓨터의 설치가 더 중요하다.

· 행위를 누가 했는지 모르거나, 관심이 없거나, 몰라도 되는 경우

A mistake was made, and all the scholarship application files were lost.

This report was written at the last minute.

· 객관적인 느낌을 주고 싶을 때

수동태 문장은 과학 기술 분야의 글에서 흔하게 쓰인다. 어떤 실험 결과를 보고하거나 연구에 대해 기술하는 경우 객관적이고 공정하게 보이는 것이 좋기 때문이다. 또한 실험 보고서에 수동태 문장을 쓰면 읽는 사람이 연구자보다는 실험 자체에 관심을 더 가질 수 있다.

The pigeons were observed over a period of three weeks.

The subjects were divided into three groups.

TIP | 작문한 내용을 검토할 때 수동태 문장을 너무 많이 사용하지 않았는지 생각해 보자. 수동태 문장은 능동태 문장보다 길이가 길고 이해하기 어렵다. 따라서 중요한 부분을 강조할 필요가 있을 때 수동태를 사용하도록 한다.

Too Many Long Sentences

1) 전문가들은 문장의 평균 길이는 15~20단어가 되어야 한다고 생각한다. 이 정도의 길이는 읽는 사람이 글쓴이의 생각을 더 쉽게 이해하도록 해준다.

> My favorite place to visit is my grandparents' house near the lake where we love to fish and swim, and we often take the boat out on the lake.

> My favorite place to visit is my grandparents' house near the lake. We love to fish and swim, and we often take the boat out on the lake.

2) 작문을 잘 하는 사람은 효과적인 글 쓰기를 위해 긴 문장 사이사이에 짧은 문장을 섞어 쓴다. 긴 문장을 몇 개 쓰고 나서 짧은 문장을 쓰면 자신의 논지를 강조하는 데 효과적이다.

> Benjamin Franklin, who was one of the Founding Fathers of the United States, helped write the Declaration of Independence. He also invented many things such as bifocals and the Franklin stove, and he discovered electricity, which became very important to modern life.

> Benjamin Franklin, who was one of the Founding Fathers of the United States, helped write the Declaration of Independence. He also invented many things such as bifocals and the Franklin stove, and he discovered electricity. Think about that discovery. Where would we be without electricity?

Too Many Short Sentences

작문에서 짧은 문장을 너무 많이 사용하는 경우가 있는데 효과적인 작문을 위해서는 읽기에 지루하지 않도록 문장의 길이를 다양화해야 한다. 짧은 문장이 너무 많으면 글의 맥이 끊기는 것처럼 보이므로 부드럽게 연결하기 위해서 접속사와 전치사를 이용해 일부 짧은 문장을 결합할 수 있다.

> I knew my friends would throw me a party. It was for my birthday. There was something in the air. I felt it for a whole week before that. I was nervous. I was also very excited. I got home that night. My friends didn't disappoint me. I walked in my house. All my friends yelled, "Surprise!"

> <u>Because</u> it was my birthday, I knew my friends would throw me a party. There was something in the air <u>for</u> a whole week before that. I was nervous <u>but</u> excited <u>when</u> I got home that night. I wasn't disappointed. <u>When</u> I walked in my house, all my friends yelled, "Surprise!"

Sentences Beginning with Coordinating Conjunctions

1) and, but, as, or, yet, for, nor 같은 등위접속사는 문장 중간에서 내용을 연결하고 결합해 준다.

   I love pizza, <u>so</u> I eat it for breakfast.

   Mother drove to town to buy groceries, <u>but</u> she came home with a present for me.

2) 등위접속사는 문장을 시작할 때도 쓸 수 있다.

   <u>And</u> I didn't like parties.

   <u>So</u> I did not do well on that test.

3) 그러나 등위접속사로 시작되는 문장이 너무 많으면 글의 흐름이 끊기는 것처럼 보인다.

> Baseball is the great American sport. <u>And</u> it is thought of as a summer pastime. <u>So</u> as soon as the weather turns warm, all the neighborhood kids find a field to toss a ball around. <u>And</u> soon they form teams and play each other. <u>But</u> all summer, they always find time to watch professional games on TV. <u>Or</u> they go see them at a ballpark.

⬇

> Baseball, the great American sport, is thought of as a summer pastime. As soon as the weather turns warm, the neighborhood kids find a field to toss a ball around. Soon, they form teams to play each other, but all summer, they always find time to watch professional games on TV or go see them at a ballpark.

TIP | 등위접속사는 문장 중간에서 내용들을 결합하는 데 매우 유용하게 쓰이지만 작문할 때 문장을 등위접속사로 시작하는 것은 피해야 한다.

Organization and Development_조직화와 전개

Introduction

1. 서론이란 무엇인가?

서론은 읽는 사람에게 에세이가 무엇에 관한 글인지, 어떤 내용을 논의할 것인지에 대한 배경 지식을 제공한다. 잘 쓴 서론은 다음과 같은 몇 가지 특징이 있다.
- 에세이를 읽고 싶게 만든다.
- 에세이의 전체 주제가 무엇인지 드러낸다.
- 읽는 사람에게 에세이의 논제를 알려 준다.

2. 서론을 어떻게 쓸 것인가?

여러 가지 다양한 방법으로 서론을 쓸 수 있다. 다음은 서론을 효과적으로 구성하기 위해 활용할 수 있는 몇 가지 아이디어와 해당 예문이다. 굵게 표시된 부분이 에세이의 논제(thesis)가 되는 문장이다.

- **Background about the Topic_배경 설명하기**

  Since the beginning of time, there have been teachers. The "classroom" teacher has many important tasks to do. A teacher has to teach information while keeping things interesting. She also sometimes has to be a referee, a coach, and a secretary. At times, a teacher has to be a nurse or just a good listener. **This career demands a lot, but it's the career I most want to have.**

  유사 이래 교사라는 직업은 존재해 왔다. '강단'의 교사들은 많은 중요한 직무들을 담당하고 있다. 교사는 지식을 전달함과 동시에 학생들이 흥미를 느끼도록 해야 한다. 교사는 때로는 심판, 코치, 비서가 되어야 한다. 간혹 교사는 간호사 또는 이야기를 경청하는 사람이 되어야 한다. 이 직업에는 요구되는 것이 많지만 교사는 내가 가장 선택하고 싶은 직업이다.

- **Narrative_설명하기**

  My fourth-grade teacher, Mr. Sanchez, was not an imposing person. He was quiet-spoken and always calm. Even though he never raised his voice, he had no trouble controlling his students. He could quiet us down with just a glance. We always wanted to please him because we knew how much he wanted us to succeed. He expected us to do the best we could... **Mr. Sanchez was the kind of teacher I want to be.**

  내가 4학년 때 담임이셨던 산체스 선생님은 위압적인 분은 아니었다. 그는 말수가 적고 항상 침착했다. 비록 한 번도 목소리를 높이지 않으셨지만, 학생들을 통제하는 데 어려움이 없었다. 선생님은 그냥 시선을 주는 것만으로도 우리를 조용하게 만드셨다. 우리는 선생님이 우리가 성공하기를 얼마나 바라셨는지 알고 있었기 때문에 항상 선생님을 기쁘게 해드리고 싶어 했다. 선생님은 우리가 최선을 다하기를 기대하셨… 산체스 선생님은 내가 되고 싶었던 교사였다.

- **Quotation_인용하기**

  "Teaching is better than tossing a pebble into a pond of water and watching those ripples move out from the middle. With teaching, you never know where those ripples will end." I remember those words of my fourth grade teacher. Ms. Vela once told me that years after they left her class, her students would come back to tell her how much she had helped them. Ms. Vela's students said that it was because of her that they learned to work hard and to feel proud of what they did. **I would like to teach because I would like to make that kind of difference.**

  "누군가를 가르치는 것은 연못에 조약돌을 던지고 난 뒤 가운데서부터 물결이 퍼져 나가는 것을 보는 것보다 낫습니다. 가르침으로 인한 물결의 파문은 어디서 끝날지 알 수 없습니다." 나는 4학년 때 선생님이 하신 이 말씀을 기억하고 있다. 벨라 선생님은 학생들이 졸업 후 몇 년 뒤 다시 찾아와 선생님에게 얼마나 큰 도움을 받았는지 말하곤 했다고 말씀하셨다. 벨라 선생님의 제자들은 열심히 공부하고, 자부심을 느끼게 된 것은 벨라 선생님 덕분이라고 말했다. 나는 그런 의미 있는 일을 하고 싶기 때문에 교사가 되고자 한다.

- **Dramatic Statistics/Facts**_통계자료나 사실 이용하기

Three out of four people said that they thought it didn't matter how many students were taught in one class. However, our class researched this and found that the opposite is true. Studies completed at a university show that having small class sizes, especially in the primary grades, makes a big difference in how much students learn. **Before we decide how many students to assign to a primary school teacher, we need to think more carefully about how important smaller class size is.**

4명 중 3명이 한 학급의 학생수가 얼마나 되든지 문제가 되지 않는다고 말했다. 그러나 우리 학급이 이 문제에 대해 조사한 결과, 사실은 그 반대라는 것을 알아냈다. 대학에서 행한 연구를 통해 밝혀진 바에 따르면, 학급 규모가 작은 것이, 특히 초등 학년에서, 학생들의 학습량에 큰 영향을 준다고 한다. 초등학교 교사에게 얼마나 많은 학생들을 배정할 것인지를 결정하기 전에 학급의 규모가 작은 것이 얼마나 중요한지에 대해 좀 더 주의 깊게 생각해 볼 필요가 있다.

- **Controversial**_논란이 되는 내용 삽입하기

Some people believe that good teaching is more of an art than a science and something of a mystery when it comes to trying to explain how it comes about. **However, research has shown that a particular set of strategies is common to all effective teachers and can be successfully adopted by struggling teachers who practice them regularly.**

일부 사람들은 좋은 가르침이 과학보다는 예술에 가깝고, 어떻게 좋은 가르침이 이루어지는지를 설명하려고 할 때 다소 불가사의한 면이 있다고 믿는다. 그러나 연구에 따르면, 성공적인 교사들에게 공통적으로 나타나는 특정한 전략들이 있으며, 어려움을 겪었던 교사도 이를 정기적으로 훈련하여 효과를 볼 수 있었다고 한다.

- **Questions That Lead to the Thesis**_논제 유도를 위해 질문하기

What exactly is "voice"? Is it a speaking voice or singing voice? When someone says that they have a voice in their head but no way to get it out, what does that mean? **"Voice" has less to do with throats and mouths than it has to do with being human, being alive.**

'음성'이란 정확히 무엇인가? 말소리인가, 노래 소리인가? 어떤 사람이 머릿속에 어떤 소리가 맴도는데 그것을 꺼낼 방법이 없다고 말한다면, 그것은 무슨 뜻인가? '음성'은 목구멍이나 입보다는 인간이라는 것, 살아 있다는 것과 더 관계가 있다.

Thesis

1. 논제란 무엇인가?

논제를 진술하는 것은 에세이의 요지 또는 가장 핵심적인 내용을 밝히는 것이다. 이는 주제에 관한 글쓴이의 논지를 강조하며, '어떤 중요한 사실, 또는 흥미로운 것을 이야기할 것인가' 라는 질문에 대한 답이 된다. 논제를 효과적으로 전개하는 방법을 터득한다면 에세이의 나머지 부분에서 어떤 정보를 제공하고 어떤 정보를 생략해야 하는지 결정하는 데 도움이 될 것이다. 좋은 논제는 다음과 같은 특징을 가지고 있다.

1) 글쓴이가 주제에 관해 어떤 이야기를 할 것인지에 대한 힌트를 준다.

Abraham Lincoln was an interesting man.

→ Abraham Lincoln was a person of contradictions.

Television is a total waste of time.

→ Parents should carefully choose appropriate, educational television shows for their children to watch.

2) 단순한 사실이나 관찰 내용이 아닌 주제에 대한 글쓴이의 의견이 제시된다.

London is the capital of England.

→ For tourists interested in British history, London is an ideal travel destination.

Many movies today are violent.

→ The violence in movies today makes children less sensitive to other people's suffering.

3) 완전한 의미 파악이 가능하다.

Should something be done about bad drivers?

→ Bad drivers should have to take a driving course before being allowed to drive again.

There is a problem with the information on the Internet.

→ To make sure information found on the Internet is valid, computer users must make sure the sources of the information are credible.

4) 주제에 대한 자신의 '주관적' 견해를 밝힌다.

In my paper, I will write about whether schools should require uniforms.

→ Public schools should not require uniforms.

The subject of this essay is drug testing.

→ Drug testing is needed for all professional athletes.

2. 글을 읽는 사람이 논제를 이해했는지 어떻게 알 수 있는가?

가끔 서론이나 논제를 쓸 때 단어를 정의하거나 설명해야 할 때가 있다. 예를 들면, '영웅은 누구인가?' 라는 주제에 대해 글을 쓴다면 먼저 영웅이란 단어가 무슨 뜻이라고 생각하는지를 설명해야 할 것이다. 영웅은 다른 사람을 구하기 위해 자신의 목숨을 버리는 사람인가? 이유를 막론하고 사람들로부터 존경을 받는 사람인가? 이처럼 자신이 생각하는 대로 단어를 정의해 주면 읽는 사람이 글쓴이가 의미하는 바를 더 잘 이해할 수 있다.

3. 논제를 뒷받침할 수 있을 정도로 주장이 충분히 전개되고 있는가?

주장은 글쓴이가 자신의 생각을 강하게 피력하고자 하는 부분으로 읽는 사람들이 이 주장을 이해할 수 있도록 에세이를 전개해야 한다. 에세이마다 주장의 수는 다를 수 있으며, 중요한 것은 글쓴이가 주장하는 바가 논제를 충분히 뒷받침해야 한다는 것이다. 효과적인 주장 전개를 위한 요령은 다음과 같다.

1) 어떤 특정한 주제에 대해 스스로 다음과 같은 질문들을 해본다.

   · Who?
   · What?
   · When?
   · Where?
   · Why?
   · How?
   · What if? Why not?

2) 다른 사람들과 주제에 관해 이야기한다.

   많은 사람들은 자신이 알고 있는 것을 남에게 말하기를 좋아한다. 다른 사람들의 이야기를 잘 메모해 두었다가 에세이에 활용해 보도록 한다.

   · 주변 사람들은 특정 주제에 관해 각자 의견을 가지고 있을 것이다.
   · 어떤 쟁점이나 주제에 대한 지식이 있는 교사들이 의견을 제공해줄 수 있을 것이다.
   · 전문가들은 귀중한 정보와 의견을 가지고 있을 수 있다.
   · 인터넷이나 도서관에서 주제에 대해 조사해본다.
   · 전문가에게 주제와 관련된 e-mail을 보낸다.

3) 어떤 종류의 글을 쓰고 있는지 스스로 생각해 본다.

   아래 질문들에 대해 생각해 보면, 어떤 논지를 더해야 하는지, 그 논지들을 어떻게 전개해야 하는지 판단하는 데 도움이 된다.

   · 대상들이 어떻게 비슷한지(비교) 또는 어떻게 다른지(대조)를 설명하고 있는가?
     어떤 것에 대해 묘사할 때 또는 서로 다른 관점들을 분석할 때 이런 질문을 활용할 수 있다.
   · 아이디어를 범주화하고 있는가?
     일반적으로 어떤 것을 묘사하고 나서 그 구체적인 특성을 설명할 수 있다. 예를 들면, 좋은 교사에 대한 글을 쓸 때 좋은 교사가 되기 위해 갖춰야 할 자질에 대해 이야기한 후에 어떤 특정 선생님의 자질에 대해 이야기할 수 있다.
   · 어떤 문제가 어떻게 발생하게 되었는지와 그 문제의 결과에 대한 이유를 밝히고 있는가?
     예를 들어 학생들의 태도가 환경으로부터 어떤 영향을 받는지에 대해 논하고 있다면 우선 그 특정한 태도가 형성된 원인이 무엇인지에 대해 설명한 뒤, 그러한 태도의 결과에 대해 이야기할 수 있다.
   · 누군가에게 당신의 생각을 설득하려 하는가 아니면 당신이 원하는 방향으로 상황을 개선하려고 하는가?
     예를 들어 친구에게 어떤 쟁점에 대해 당신의 의견을 설득하려고 한다면 그 쟁점이 무엇인지와 왜 자신의 의견이 옳다고 생각하는지를 먼저 이야기하면서 작문을 시작할 수도 있다.

4) 처음부터 다시 시작해서 작문이 어떤 방향으로 진행되는지 살펴본다.

   글 쓰는 사람들 중 상당수가 어떤 대상에 대해 여러 번 쓰면서 참신하고 좋은 아이디어를 얻게 되므로 처음부터 다시 써보는 것에 너무 부담을 갖지 않도록 한다.

5) 초안을 다시 읽어 본다.

   · 이전에 쓴 초안을 검토해 보고 흥미로운 부분이나 주장 전개에 있어서 가장 중요하다고 생각되는 부분을 다시 살펴본다.
   · 주장을 뒷받침하는 문장을 세 개 정도 더 써 본다.
   · 추가로 쓴 문장들을 살펴보고, 가장 나은 것을 골라 그 문장의 요지를 설명하는 문장을 세 개 더 써 본다.

Main Ideas

1. 주장하고자 하는 주요 논지들이 모두 주제문으로 시작되는가?

주요 논지란 아이디어를 설명하는 문장의 한 요소로서 각각의 주요 논지들은 에세이에서 충분히 논의되어야 한다. 주요 논지를 포함하는 문장을 주제문이라고 하며, 독자가 주제에 관련된 질문에 대해 생각하도록 만드는 것이 주제문의 목표라 할 수 있다.

1) 주제문은 무엇에 관한 글인지 글을 읽는 사람이 이해할 준비를 하도록 해준다.

<u>Teachers don't get paid for every hour that they work.</u> Teachers sometimes do work even when they are not in the classroom. Sometimes my mother grades papers and projects all day on Sunday. Even though she does not get paid, she says the weekend is the only time she can grade all of her students' work. My neighbor spends three weeks of his summer vacation on a ship that does scientific experiments. He doesn't get paid for any of that work, but he says the things that he learns help him be a better teacher.

교사들은 근무하는 모든 시간에 대해 임금을 받지 않는다. 교사들은 교실에 있지 않을 때도 근무를 한다. 나의 어머니는 가끔 일요일에 하루 종일 답안지와 연구 과제를 채점한다. 비록 보수를 받지는 않지만 어머니는 주말이 모든 학생들의 과제를 채점할 수 있는 유일한 시간이라고 말씀하신다. 나의 이웃은 3주간의 여름 휴가를 과학 실험을 하는 배에서 보낸다. 그는 그에 대한 보수를 받지 않지만 거기서 배우는 것들이 더 좋은 교사가 되는 데 도움이 된다고 말한다.

2) 주제문은 두 개의 문단이나 두 개의 주요 논지를 연결하는 역할을 한다. 다음 글의 첫 번째 문장은 주제문이며, 두 번째 단락의 주제문과 함께 두 개의 다른 논지를 연결하고 있다.

<u>Teachers get many benefits in their careers.</u> My neighbor has children and likes having the summer off when his children are home. Some teachers say their work is very enjoyable. At least that's what my mom says when she mixes up her magic bubble formula for science class. My mom also says that one of the benefits of teaching is that she is using her college education every day. She also gets paid to take refresher courses. But she works hard.

<u>In fact, teachers don't get paid for every hour that they work, but the teachers that I know say that they love their work.</u>

교사는 업무에서 많은 혜택을 얻는다. 자녀가 있는 내 이웃은 아이들이 집에 있을 때 여름 휴가 가는 것을 좋아한다. 어떤 교사들은 일을 매우 즐기고 있다고 말한다. 최소한 우리 어머니는 과학 수업에 쓰일 마술 비누 방울 용액을 섞으면서 그렇게 말씀하신다. 우리 어머니는 가르치는 일이 주는 혜택 중의 하나는 대학에서 공부한 내용을 매일 활용하는 것이라고도 하신다. 어머니는 또한 재교육 과정 수강료를 지원 받으신다. 그러나 어머니는 열심히 일하신다.

사실 교사들은 근무하는 모든 시간에 대해 보수를 받지는 않지만 내가 아는 교사들은 자기 일을 좋아한다고 말한다.

2. 각각의 주요 논지를 충분히 논의했는가?

좋은 글은 글쓴이와 독자로 하여금 글쓴이가 모든 문제를 논의한 것처럼 느끼게 만드는 글이므로 작문할 때 각각의 논지를 충분히 논해야 한다. 효과적인 논지 작성을 위한 몇 가지 방법들을 소개한다.

1) 각 핵심 논지마다 하나의 단락을 할애한다.

그러나 핵심 주제가 너무 광범위하다면 하나의 단락으로 만들기 복잡하므로 두 개 이상의 단락으로 구성해야 한다.

2) 논지를 체계적인 방식으로 전개하도록 한다.

논지를 전개하는 방법은 많다. 다음은 흔히 쓰이는 두 가지 전개 방식이다.

· 예를 들면 시간 순서, 즉 사건이 발생한 순서대로 전개할 수 있다. 가장 먼저 일어난 일부터 시작하여 그 이후에 일어난 일들을 각 단락에서 설명할 수 있다. 다음 글은 두 개의 논지를 두 개의 단락으로 전개했다.

I have wanted to be a teacher ever since I failed a test in Miss Vela's class in fourth grade.

나는 4학년 때 벨라 선생님 반에서 시험에 낙제하고 난 이후 교사가 되기로 결심했다.

Then in eighth grade I had an assignment to teach a science lesson to a class in my former primary school, and that experience showed me how good I felt when the students didn't want the class to be over.

그리고 8학년 때 나는 모교인 초등학교에서 과학 과목을 가르치라는 과제를 부여 받았고 그때의 경험을 통해 학생들이 수업이 끝나지 않기를 바랐을 때 기분이 얼마나 좋은지 알게 되었다.

· 중요도가 높은 것에서 낮은 순으로 논지를 전개하거나 그 반대로 할 수 있다.

짧은 시간 안에 작문을 마쳐야 한다면 가장 중요한 논지나 이유부터 설명해야 한다. 다음 두 명의 글쓴이가 각각 어떤 것을 가장 중요한 논지로 생각하는지 살펴보자.

The most important reason to be a science teacher is to help the next generation learn about the Earth.

과학 교사가 되려는 가장 중요한 이유는 다음 세대가 지구에 대해 배우는 것을 돕기 위해서다.

Getting to do fun activities is the reason why I want to be a science teacher.

재미있는 활동을 할 수 있다는 것이 내가 과학 교사가 되려는 이유다.

Supporting Ideas

1. 뒷받침하는 논지를 전개하는 방법에는 어떤 것들이 있는가?

뒷받침하는 논지는 독자들에게 주요 논지가 합당하다는 확신을 심어 주는 역할을 한다. 논지를 뒷받침하는 효과적인 방법들은 다음과 같다.

– 주요 논지를 명백하게 전달하는 이야기를 한다.
– 주요 논지에 관한 예를 제시해 무엇에 대한 단락인지 설명한다.
– 논지를 뒷받침하는 논거를 제시한다. 여기에는 사실, 논리적 주장, 또는 전문가 의견 등이 포함된다.
– 어떤 논지가 다른 논지들과 어떻게 다른지 독자가 이해할 수 있도록 아주 구체적인 사실들을 활용한다.
– 보고, 듣고, 냄새 맡고, 만지고, 느끼고, 경험할 수 있는 것들을 이야기한다.
– 다양한 각도에서 논지를 보도록 한다.
– 사건, 사람, 사물들이 주요 논지에 어떤 영향을 줄 수 있는지를 이야기한다.
– 독자가 하나의 논지를 다른 논지와 비교하여 이해할 수 있도록 은유나 유추를 사용한다.

2. 논지를 뒷받침하고 발전시키기 위해 최선을 다했는가?

독자가 어떤 주제에 대해 모든 것을 알고 싶어 하는 호기심 많은 사람이라고 가정하고 다음과 같이 질문해 보자.

1) 어떤 문제 또는 쟁점에 관해 써야 할 경우
   · 어떤 종류의 문제 또는 쟁점인가?
   · 어떤 문제나 쟁점이 존재하는 징후는 무엇인가?
   · 그 문제나 쟁점 때문에 영향을 받는 사람이나 사물은 무엇인가?
   · 그 문제나 쟁점의 역사는 무엇인가?(어떤 인물 혹은 사물 때문에 그것이 야기되었으며 현재는 어떤 상태인가?)
   · 그 문제나 쟁점은 왜 중요한가? 이것을 중요하거나 덜 중요하게 만드는 요인은 무엇인가?

2) 독자가 자신의 견해에 동의하도록 주장을 펼치거나 설득할 경우
   · 뒷받침 자료로 어떤 사실이나 통계자료를 언급할 수 있는가?
   · 논지를 입증하기 위해 어떤 내용을 논할 수 있는가?
   · 독자들이 쟁점을 이해하도록 돕기 위해 어떤 비교를 할 수 있는가?
   · 어떤 전문적인 견해가 논지에 타당성을 부여하는가?
   · 사례들을 통해 논지를 뒷받침할 수 있는가?
   · 다른 견해를 가진 사람의 입장을 설명할 수 있는가?

TIP | 설득력 있는 주장을 펼치기 위해 자신의 주장과 상반된 견해의 좋은 점을 언급할 수도 있다. 이 경우 although that is a point well taken, granted, while it is true that, 또는 I agree that 등의 표현을 사용하면 효과적이다.

3) 문학 평론이나 영화의 평을 쓸 경우

　·무슨 일이 일어났는지 독자들이 이해할 수 있게 이야기를 요약할 수 있는가?

　·독자가 이야기의 맥락을 이해하도록 장소나 시간에 대한 구체적 사실을 제시할 수 있는가?

　·독자가 주인공들이 왜 특별하고 흥미로운지 이해할 수 있도록 주인공들의 어떤 점을 이야기할 수 있는가?

　·위기에 처한 주인공들이 힘겨운 선택을 해야 하는 대목을 묘사할 수 있는가?

　·등장인물들이 나누는 대화와 그들의 경험에 대해 말하는 것을 인용할 수 있는가?

　·논의할 만한 심오한 주제가 있는가?

　·이야기를 전개하는 방식이나 영화의 카메라 앵글에 대해 설명할 수 있는가?

　·흥미로운 이미지나 상징이 있는가?

4) 어떤 것에 대해 묘사하거나 정의를 내릴 경우

　·그 사물이 어떤 모습을 하고 있고, 그 부분들은 무엇인지 말할 수 있는가?

　·그 사물이 무엇을 하는지 또는 무엇을 의미하는지 말할 수 있는가?

　·그 사물의 역할이나 의미하는 바가 시간이 지남에 따라 변했다면, 전에는 어떠했고 현재는 어떠한지 말할 수 있는가?

　·묘사하려는 것의 명칭과 의미가 알려진 것과 다르다면 독자에게 그 이름과 의미를 설명할 수 있는가?

5) 어떤 일을 하는 방법이나 만드는 방법에 대해 말할 경우

　·적당한 부분에서 시작하고, 논리적으로 진행했는가?

　·글을 읽는 사람들을 위해 생소한 용어를 설명했는가?

　·내용을 이해하는 데 도움이 되는 예를 제시했는가?

　·지시 내용을 명확히 설명했는가? 읽는 사람이 순서를 잘 알 수 있도록 번호를 붙였는가?

TIP | 독자들이 잘 이해할 수 있도록 글의 내용을 구성하는 방법을 생각해 보자. 예를 들면, 요리책에서 재료들은 페이지 상단에 나열하고, 조리방법은
짧은 단락으로 만들거나 조리 순서대로 번호를 매긴다.

Conclusion

1. 결론이란 무엇인가?

결론 문단은 에세이를 끝내는 문단으로 다음과 같은 특징이 있다.

– 논지의 중요성에 대해 이야기한다.

– 새로운 용어를 사용해 논제를 다시 언급한다.

– 주요 논지를 요약한다.

– 일화, 인용, 통계, 제의 등을 포함하는 경우도 있다.

2. 결론을 쓰는 방법

결론 문단을 쓸 때 다음과 같이 접근할 수 있다.

– 중요한 요점들을 요약한다.

– 요약문을 제공한다.

– 흥미를 유발하거나 기억에 남는 인용구를 포함시킨다.

– 예측하거나 제안한다.

– 독자에게 생각할 여지를 준다.

서로 다른 두 개의 결말 단락을 보자.

Good teaching requires flexibility, compassion, organization, knowledge, energy, and enthusiasm. A good teacher must decide when a student needs to be prodded and when that student needs mercy. Good teaching requires knowing when to listen and reflect and when to advise or correct. It requires a delicate balance of many skills, and often a different mix of approaches for different students and different situations. Is this profession demanding? Yes! Boring? Never! Exciting? Absolutely!

바람직한 교수법에는 융통성, 열정, 조직화, 지식, 활력, 열의 등이 요구된다. 좋은 교사는 학생에게 언제 채찍질하고 언제 관용을 베풀어야 하는지를 결정해야 한다. 좋은 교사는 언제 남의 이야기를 듣고 호응해야 하며, 언제 충고하고 고쳐줘야 할지를 알아야 한다. 그러려면 여러 가지 능력들을 학생들과 상황에 따라 다르게 조합하여 접근해야 한다. 이처럼 교사라는 직업은 많은 것을 요구하는가? 그렇다. 교사라는 직업은 따분한가? 전혀 그렇지 않다! 교사라는 직업은 흥미로운가? 물론 그렇다!

When I become a teacher, I want fourth graders like Ms. Vela's. We adored her and wanted to please her. But more importantly, I want to be a Ms. Vela for my students. I want to challenge my students to become good citizens. When the river in our town flooded its banks and some classmates had to be evacuated, Ms. Vela asked us to think about what we could do. We came up with three decisions. We packed lunches for our classmates, we shared our books and pencils in class, and we gave them clothing. Later when we studied civics, we realized that we were taking care of our classmates the way the local or federal government does in a disaster. Ms. Vela was helping her fourth graders become more civic minded. I'm hoping to help my students think like that when I'm a teacher.

내가 교사가 되면 벨라 선생님처럼 4학년을 맡고 싶다. 우리는 선생님을 존경했고 그분을 기쁘게 해 드리고 싶었다. 그러나 그보다 더 중요한 것은 내가 가르치는 학생들에게 벨라 선생님과 같은 존재가 되고 싶다는 것이다. 나는 학생들에게 훌륭한 시민이 되라고 요구하고 싶다. 우리 마을의 강물이 강둑을 넘쳐 몇몇 급우들이 대피해야 했을 때 벨라 선생님은 우리가 무엇을 할 수 있을지에 대해 생각해 보라고 하셨다. 우리는 세 가지 결정을 내렸다. 급우들을 위해 점심 도시락을 쌌고, 교실에서 책과 연필을 같이 썼으며, 옷을 나눠 주었다. 나중에 국민윤리(civics)에 대해 공부해 보니 우리가 재난 시에 주 또는 연방 정부가 하는 방식으로 급우들을 도왔다는 것을 알았다. 벨라 선생님은 자신이 맡은 4학년 학생들의 시민의식을 드높이고자 하셨다. 내가 교사가 되면 나의 학생들도 그런 생각을 갖도록 돕고 싶다.

Transitional Words and Phrases

1. 독자를 하나의 논지에서 다음 논지로 유도하기 위해 전환어를 사용하는가?

전환하는 단어와 구는 이미 읽은 내용과 앞으로 읽을 내용을 연결시켜 다양한 논지와 부수적인 내용들 간의 관계를 알 수 있게 해 준다. 또한 문장들 간의 관계를 보여 주는 데도 도움을 주므로 에세이를 읽는 사람들에게 길잡이가 된다.

1) 시간 순서 및 사건들 간의 관계에 대해 말할 수 있도록 도와준다.

today, tomorrow, next week, yesterday, meanwhile, about, before, during, at, after, soon, immediately, afterward, later, finally, then, when, next, simultaneously, as a result

2) 논지들의 순서를 나타낼 수 있다.

first, second, third, finally, lastly, most importantly, of least importance

3) 위치를 설명할 수 있다.

above, over, below, beneath, behind, in front of, in back of, on top of, inside, outside, near, between, beside, among, around, against, throughout, off, onto, into, beyond

4) 유사점을 비교하거나 보여 준다.

also, as, similarly, in the same way, likewise, like

5) 차이점을 강조하거나 보여 준다.

in contrast, however, although, still, even though, on the other hand, but

6) 내용을 추가할 때 도움이 된다.

in addition, for instance, for example, moreover, next, likewise, besides, another, additionally, again, also, in fact

7) 논지를 명확히 하는 데 도움이 된다.

in other words, for instance, that is, in summary

8) 논지를 강조하는 데 도움이 된다.

truly, in fact, for this reason, again, to reiterate

9) 결론을 내리거나 요약할 때 도움이 된다.

all in all, lastly, as a result, in summary, therefore, finally

2. 각 단락이 주요 논지를 뒷받침하고 발전시키거나 설명하는가?

하나의 단락은 문장이 모여 이루어지며 이 단락 속에는 특정 주제에 대한 내용을 담고 있는 문장들이 있다. 하나의 단락에는 보통 하나의 논지가 있고, 단락의 길이는 다양하다. 한 문장으로만 이루어진 단락도 있는 반면 어떤 단락은 내용을 충분히 전달하기 위해 반드시 여러 개의 문장이 있어야 하는 경우도 있다. 주요 쟁점을 다루는 단락들도 있고, 논지 간 전환부 역할을 하는 단락들도 있다. 다음은 단락을 제대로 작성했는지 점검하기 위한 항목들이다.

1) 각 단락의 내용이 완전히 전달되도록 충분히 논했는가?

각 단락에 제목을 붙이고 그것을 읽고 단락의 의미가 통하는지 살펴본다. 읽는 사람이 구체적인 질문을 하는 경우 이 단락에서 답을 찾을 수 있을 것인가? 질문에 대한 대답으로 맞지 않는 문장들이 있다면 그 문장들은 삭제하거나 다른 단락으로 옮겨야 한다.

2) 설명이나 정의가 필요한 단어들을 사용했는가?

잘 쓰이지 않는 단어를 쓰고 그 의미를 자세히 설명하지 않았다면 독자는 실망할 것이다. 무언가에 대해 정의하고 설명할 때는 두세 개 이상의 문장으로 논지를 충분히 설명해야 한다.

3) 증거를 제시했는가? 말하고자 하는 것에 대한 예를 들었는가?

글쓴이가 이야기하고 있는 것이 사실임을 나타내는 견실한 예를 드는 것이 중요하다.

4) 말하고자 하는 것을 입증할 개인적인 경험이나 다른 자료에서 인용한 것이 있는가?

어떤 에세이에서는 개인적인 경험을 쓰는 것이 적절할 수 있으나 그렇지 않은 경우도 있다. 에세이에서 어떤 유형의 정보를 요구하는지 유념해야 한다. 다른 출처에서 내용을 인용할 경우 그 내용은 정확한지, 인용부호는 제대로 사용했는지 확인한다.

5) 논지의 내용을 연결하는 명확한 전환어를 썼는가?

단락을 기차로, 문장은 그 기차의 각 칸으로 그리고 주제문을 엔진으로 생각해 보자. 단락의 모든 부분이 연결되거나 서로 잘 들어맞는가?

Advice to Writers_에세이 작성자들을 위한 조언

1. Persuasion

설득은 독자가 글쓴이의 생각에 동의하도록 만드는 것이므로 견해를 뒷받침하는 타당한 논거를 제시하고, 대립되는 견해를 언급해야 하며, 가능하면 그에 대한 대안까지 제시해야 한다.

시작하는 방법

a. 자신의 견해를 지지하거나 반박하는 구체적인 주장들을 나열한다.

b. 보충할 내용을 좀 더 찾아야 하는지 결정한다. (주장을 뒷받침하는 통계, 전문가의 말, 아이디어를 구체화하는 사례, 개인적인 경험, 사실들)

c. 반대 의견을 가진 사람들이 주장한 내용 중에서 차용할 만한 것이 있는지 생각해 본다. 그 사람들에게 어떤 식으로 대응할 것인가?

TIP | 설득하는 에세이를 쓸 때는 확신에 차 있어야 하며, 이런 유형의 글에서는 가장 설득력 있는 내용을 마지막에 쓰는 것도 한 가지 방법이다. 어떤 종류의 글이건 간에 연습을 하면 실력이 향상된다. 글을 쓰고 고치는 연습을 반복하면서 설득하는 에세이들을 가급적 많이 접하도록 하자.

2. Informative Writing

독자들이 어떤 주제를 이해하는 데 도움이 되도록 정보를 제공하는 글을 말한다. 지구온난화, 재즈 음악, 공해 등에 관한 정보를 제공하는 에세이는 객관적인 조사 자료(문서, 인터뷰, 인터넷 검색)를 근거로 할 수 있으며, 때로는 개인적인 경험이나 관찰 내용에 대해 써야 할 때도 있다.

시작하는 방법

a. 구체적으로 초점을 맞춘다.

　　예　일반적인 재활용이 아니라 종이의 재활용

b. 논의되어야 할 중요한 논지를 몇 개 선택한다.

　　예　종이는 어떻게 재활용되는가, 재활용된 종이는 어떻게 쓰이는가?

c. 각 논지를 뒷받침하는 세부 사실에 대해 생각해 본다. 여기에는 사실, 관찰, 묘사, 예시 문장 등이 속한다.

　　예　재생지를 이용한 제품에는 페이퍼 타올, 연하장 등이 있다.

3. Comparison/Contrast

비교·대조는 두 개의 대상을 비교하고 대조하는 것이다. '비교'는 두 개의 대상이 얼마나 비슷한가를, '대조'는 두 개의 대상이 어떻게 다른가를 보여 준다. 묘사, 정의, 분석 등의 글에서 비교와 대조가 많이 사용되며 사실상 글의 종류에 관계없이 쓸 수 있다.

시작하는 방법

a. 기본적인 유사점이나 차이점을 가진 두 개의 대상을 고른다.

b. 이 두 대상이 어떻게 비슷하고 다른지 찾아본다.

c. 정보를 어떻게 제공할 것인지 결정한다. 한 가지 방법을 선택해 에세이 전체에 걸쳐 그 방법을 고수한다.

· 한 대상에 대한 논지를 전개하고 나서 두 번째 대상에 대해서도 같은 논지를 펴고 싶은가?

· 하나의 대상에 대한 모든 중요한 논지를 펴고 나서 두 번째 대상에 대해서도 모든 중요한 논지를 펴고 싶은가?

· 두 대상이 어떻게 같은지 논한 다음 어떻게 다른지 논하고 싶은가?

d. 어떤 점에 대해 비교 또는 대조하고서 또 다른 점을 비교하거나 대조할 때 독자가 확실히 알 수 있도록 해야 한다. 다음과 같은 전환어를 쓰는 것이 도움이 된다.

· 유사점　similarly, likewise, furthermore, besides

· 차이점　in contrast, in comparison, on the other hand, although, however, nevertheless, whereas, yet

4. Description

묘사를 할 때는 사람, 장소, 물건, 특정 시기, 이론 등에 대한 내용을 머릿속에 그릴 수 있을 정도로 구체적인 사실을 제시해야 한다. 폭넓은 어휘, 상상력이 풍부한 표현, 흥미로운 비교, 감각에 호소하는 이미지들을 사용하는 것이 효과적인 묘사에 도움이 된다.

시작하는 방법

a. 독자가 글의 내용을 보고, 듣고, 냄새 맡고, 맛보고 느낄 수 있도록 오감을 사용하여 글을 쓴다.
  - 예 The ancient driver nervously steered the old car down the red mud road, with me bouncing along on the backseat.
b. 구체적으로 쓴다.
  - 예 단순히 'This dessert is good.' 이 아니라 'The fudge brownie is moist, chewy, and very tasty.' 로 표현할 수 있다.
c. 글쓴이의 관점에서 독자에게 사물들이 어떻게 배치되어 있는지를 보여 준다.
  - 예 As I passed through the wooden gates, I heard a cough. A tiny woman came out from behind the trees.
d. 주관적인 견해를 말할 것인지 객관적인 견해를 말할 것인지 결정한다.

TIP | 흔하지 않거나 모순되는 내용은 대상에 흥미를 더할 수 있다.
  (Martin Luther King probably contributed more than anyone else to changes in civil rights, but he hardly earned any money for his speeches and work.)

5. Narration

이 유형의 에세이는 자기 자신, 사건, 추억, 경험 등에 관한 이야기를 구상하고 쓸 기회를 준다. 해설 또는 이야기에는 보통 플롯, 이야기의 배경, 등장인물, 절정, 결말 등이 포함된다.
서술은 대개 'I' 를 사용해 1인칭으로 쓰는 것이 보통이지만 이야기를 좀 더 재미있게 만들기 위해 자신이 아닌 다른 사람이 '화자' 가 될 수도 있다.

시작하는 방법

a. 친구와의 싸움에 대해 쓸 때
  · 싸움의 원인이 무엇이었는지 생각한다.
  · 누가 어떻게 관련되었는지 생각한다.
  · 싸움이 어떻게 전개되고, 해결되었는지, 또는 친구와 현재 친하게 지내고 있는지 등을 생각한다.
b. 사건을 실감나게 만드는 세부 내용을 기억한다. (예: 친구가 당신에게 무슨 말을 어떤 어조로 했는지 등)
c. '이 일은 나에게 어떤 의미였는가?' 라는 질문에 답해 본다.
d. 시작하는 방법을 선택한다. 다음 중 하나를 선택할 수 있다.
  · 이야기를 영화에서처럼 장면으로 구성한다.
  · 일어난 일을 요약하고, 가장 중요한 장면만 이야기한다.
  · 이 일이 왜 그렇게 중요한 사건이었는지에 대해 이야기한다.

6. Cause and Effect

원인과 결과에 관한 에세이는 어떤 일들이 왜 일어나는지, 그리고 그 결과 어떤 일이 일어나는지에 대한 것이다. 원인과 결과 에세이에서는 이성적인 어조로 사실에 입각하여 신뢰감을 주는 것이 중요하다.

시작하는 방법

a. 쓰고자 하는 사건이나 쟁점을 생각해 본다.

b. 아이디어를 브레인스토밍한다.

c. 주요 논지를 소개한다.

d. 주요 논지를 뒷받침하기 위한 타당하고 적절한 세부 내용을 찾아서 다음과 같은 방법으로 구성한다.

· 시간순(chronological): 사물·사건이 일어난 순서로 쓴다.

· 중요도 순(order of importance): 가장 중요한 것 또는 가장 덜 중요한 것부터 쓴다.

· 범주화(categorical): 주제를 부분이나 범주로 나눈다.

· 다음 예처럼 적절한 전환어와 구를 사용한다.

because, thus, therefore, due to, one cause is, another is, since, for, first, second, consequently, as a result, resulted in, one result is, another is

7. Problem and Solution

문제 해결 에세이에서는 어떤 문제를 파악한 뒤, 하나 이상의 해결책을 제시한다. 이런 에세이는 대개 글쓴이와 독자 모두가 관심을 갖는 주제들에 바탕을 두고 있다.

시작하는 방법

a. 문제의 원인을 생각해 본다.

· 왜 일어났는가?

· 어떻게 시작되었는가?

· 왜 지금 그런 문제가 생겼는가?

b. 가능성이 가장 낮은 해결책부터 나열한다.

c. 어떤 해결책이 가장 효과가 있을지 평가한다.

d. 하나 이상의 좋은 해결책에 대한 찬반 의견을 써 본다. 그러나 에세이의 대부분은 최선의 해결책에 할애한다.

e. 가장 좋은 해결책을 선택한 이유를 설명한다.

8. Description of a Process ("HOW-to")

이런 에세이는 어떤 일을 하는 방법(예: 가장 좋아하는 케이크를 굽는 법) 또는 어떤 일이 일어나는 방식(예: 영화는 어떻게 만드는가) 등을 설명한다.

어떤 일을 하는 방법에 대한 에세이를 시작하는 방법

a. 필요한 모든 장비, 기술, 소재를 생각해 본다.

b. 이 과정에는 몇 개의 단계가 있는가? 단계를 올바른 순서대로 배열한다. 각 단계는 왜 중요한가?

c. 각 단계에는 어떤 어려움들이 있는가?

d. 이 과정은 얼마나 걸리는가?

어떤 일이 일어나는 방식에 관한 에세이를 시작하는 방법

a. 독자가 과정을 이해할 수 있도록 배경을 상세히 설명한다.

b. 어떤 일이 일어나는 단계별로 이야기한다.

과정에 관한 에세이는 대개 시간에 따라 구성되며, 다음은 이런 종류의 에세이에서 보편적으로 사용되는 전환어와 어구들이다.

first of all, first, second, third, next, soon after, after a few hours, afterward, initially, at the same time, in the meantime, before, before this, immediately before, in the meanwhile, currently, during, meanwhile, later, then, previously, at last, eventually, finally, last, last but not least, lastly

9. Writing as Part of an Assessment

이런 유형의 작문은 특정 장소에서 한정된 시간 내에 효과적인 글을 써야 하므로 어려울 수 있지만 다음과 같이 몇 가지 요령을 활용할 수 있다.

시작하는 방법

a. 질문을 이해하고 떠오르는 아이디어를 메모한다.

b. 쓰기 전에 주요 논지와 이를 뒷받침하는 세부 사실을 어떻게 구성할 것인지 잠시 계획을 세운다. 개요를 만들어 보는 것이 유용한 전략이 될 수도 있다.

c. 글을 쓰는 도중 더 좋은 아이디어가 떠오르면 그것을 쓴다.

d. 제한 시간을 유념하되 당황하지 않는다.

e. 독자의 관점에서 글을 보며, 필요할 경우 수정 · 재구성하고 설명을 덧붙인다.

f. 글을 교정할 시간을 남겨 둔다.

10. Response to Literature

이것은 어떤 문학작품(이야기, 영화, 시, 희곡)이 왜 흥미로우며, 그것을 효과적으로 만드는 요소가 무엇인지 이야기하는 것이다. (예: 왜 웃음이 나오는가, 왜 등장인물에 관심을 갖는가)

이런 작문에서는 왜 문학작품이 진실되게 보이는지 등장인물이나 행위를 분석하거나 문학작품이 어떻게 효과를 달성하는지를 분석할 수 있다.

문학작품에 대해 쓰는 방법

a. 문학에 대한 개인적인 느낌에 대해 쓴다. 작품의 배경, 상황, 등장인물 또는 분위기 중 어느 것에 가장 관심이 있는가? 이런 것들은 작문할 내용에 대한 몇 가지 단서들이다.

b. 상황이나 심리상태는 어떠한가?

c. 글쓴이는 이야기, 시, 또는 영화의 진정한 의미에 대해 어떤 단서를 제공하고 있는가? (예를 들면, 세상에 존재하는 많은 '신데렐라' 이야기들은 아무리 가난하더라도 친절한 행위는 보상받는다는 식의 의미구조를 가지고 있다.)

d. 자신의 생각을 구성하고, 문학작품에 나오는 사례로 이를 뒷받침한다. 쓰려고 하는 이야기나 영화에 대해 독자가 알고 있다고 가정하면서 쓰는 것은 바람직하지 않다.

11. Writing in the Workplace

편지, 메모, 보고서 등은 사업상 거래를 할 때 가장 많이 쓰는 유형의 작문이다. 이런 글을 쓸 때는 가능하면 신속하고 명확하게 논지를 전개하는 것이 좋다. 따라서 간결하고 직접적으로 글을 쓴다.

작문을 시작하는 방법

a. 생각을 조직화한다. 대부분의 비즈니스 서신은 한 페이지 분량이다.

b. 정해진 양식이 있는지 생각해 본다.

c. 상대방이 조치를 취하기를 원하는지(설득), 어떤 문제를 이해하기를 원하는지(정보 제공), 또는 무언가를 해결하기를 원하는지(문제 해결)를 결정한다.

d. 명확하고 정중하게 글을 쓴다.

e. 관련되는 인용어구를 넣는다.

f. 상대방이 생각할 수 있는 여지를 준다.

Revising, Editing, and Proofreading_수정, 편집, 교열

1. The Writing Process

작문의 절차에는 계획, 초안 작성, 글쓰기, 수정, 편집, 교열 등 여러가지 단계가 있으며, 이 중 에세이 실력을 향상시키는 데 수정, 편집, 교열의 세 가지 단계가 중요하다.

- Step1 Organization and Development
  주제에 대해 생각해 보고 에세이의 구성과 전개 방식에 변화를 준다.

- Step 2 Style
  자신의 아이디어를 이해하기 쉬운지 보기 위해 각 문장을 살핀다.

- Step 3 Grammar, Usage, Mechanics
  각 단어와 문장을 검토하고 오류를 찾아 본다.

- Step 4 Proofreading
  최종 원고를 읽을 때 철자와 오타를 점검한다.

생각을 명확하게 전개하기 위해 에세이를 몇 번에 걸쳐 수정하고 편집할 수도 있다. 최종 원고가 완성된 후에는 주의 깊게 교열해야 한다. 각 단계를 완전하게 이해하기 위해 다음 표의 내용을 살펴보자.

	수 정	편 집	교 열
목적	개념이 완전한지 살펴본다. 본래 전달하고자 하는 내용을 썼는지 살펴본다. 아이디어를 덧붙인다.	문법과 어법을 고친다. 단어 선택이나, 문체, 자신의 생각을 설명하는 방법을 바꾸어 본다.	오타, 철자 및 구두점 오류가 있는 부분을 고친다.
언제	초안을 쓴 후, 바로 수정한다.	주요 내용을 완성하고 구조를 수정한 후 고치기 시작한다.	글을 제출하기 전 마지막 단계에서 한다.
무엇을	처음부터 끝까지 다 읽어 본다.	각 문장을 읽을 때, 앞 문장을 먼저 읽고 고친 후, 다음 문장을 고친다.	단어와 문장을 하나하나 꼼꼼히 읽으면서 고친다.
전략	· 글의 각 부분에 서론, 주제, 논지, 뒷받침하는 내용, 그리고 결론이 들어가 있는지 확인한다. · 내용이 연결되는 방식과 문단의 순서를 신중히 검토한다. · 과감하게 새로운 내용을 덧붙이거나 삭제한다.	· 교사나 친구에게 아이디어와 조언을 구한다. · 먼저 문법과 어법이 틀린 부분을 종류별로 분류해 본다. · 문장이 적절하다고 생각되면 수정을 하지 않는다. 단, 문제가 있을 것 같은 부분에 대해 생각해 본다. · 참고서 등을 사용하여 오류를 고치고 문장을 다시 쓰는 데 도움이 되도록 한다.	· 출력하여 교정을 본다. · 영어 실력이 뛰어난 사람에게 자신의 글을 큰 소리로 읽어 주고, 틀린 내용을 표시해 본다. · 영어 실력이 뛰어난 사람에게 글을 거꾸로, 즉 마지막 문장부터 읽어 보게 한다. · 사전, 참고서, 철자 검사 기능을 사용하여 오류를 고치는 데 도움이 되도록 한다.

2. Using a Computer to Write

TOEFL iBT 시험에서, 수험자는 컴퓨터와 거의 동일한 기능을 제공하는 화면에 답변을 작성하게 된다. 텍스트 잘라내기 및 붙여넣기, 선택 취소 및 다시 실행, 단어 수 추적이 가능하다. 그러나 응답 화면에는 철자 검사 기능이 없다. 만약 단어의 철자가 확실하지 않다면, 제시된 읽기 자료에 해당 단어 또는 변형된 단어가 있는지 확인하여 이를 철자 가이드로 사용하자.

· **active voice**_능동태

영어 문장은 능동태 또는 수동태로 쓸 수 있으며, 능동태에서 주어는 행위자를 뜻한다. 예를 들어 Sam kicked the ball. 이라는 문장에서 행위자는 Sam이고 행위는 kicked이다. 능동태 문장은 행위자를 강조한다.

· **adjective**_형용사

형용사는 명사 앞에서 명사를 수식한다.
a red umbrella, a rainy day, a dull party

· **adverb**_부사

quickly, happily, carefully 같은 단어들로, 형용사나 부사, 동사를 수식한다.
very big, very quietly, walk slowly

· **antecedent**_선행사

대명사가 지시하는 명사를 의미한다. John was late for school because he missed the bus.에서 John은 대명사 he의 선행사다.

· **apostrophe**_아포스트로피

축약형에서 글자의 탈락(cannot-can't), 또는 소유(the girl's saxophone, the parents' input)를 나타낸다.

· **article**_관사

관사는 a, an, the처럼 명사 앞에 오는 품사를 의미한다. 정관사 the는 하나 이상의 특정한 사물(the house on the hill), 동물, 사람을 지칭하기 위해 쓴다. 부정관사 a, an은 일반적인 방식으로 사물(a house), 동물(an elephant), 사람을 지칭할 때 사용된다.

· **clause**_절

절은 주어와 동사를 포함하는 요소들의 집합으로 종속절과 독립절 두 가지 종류가 있다.

· **collective noun**_집합명사

집합명사는 일단의 사람 또는 동물을 의미한다.
population, family, troop, committee

· **comma**_쉼표

쉼표는 단어들을 구별하기 위해 사용하거나(She bought apples, oranges, and grapes) 문장의 각 부분을 구별하기 위해 사용한다(He was here, but he left.).

· **compound subject**_복합주어

주어가 복수인 경우, 즉 하나 이상의 요소로 구성된 주어를 의미한다.
Lions, tigers, and bears are top predators.

· **compound verb**_복합동사

하나 이상의 요소로 구성된 동사를 의미한다.
The baby started crying.

· **compound words**_복합어

두 개의 단어로 구성된 단어를 의미한다.
everywhere, keyboard, himself, weekend

· **conclusion**_결론

에세이를 끝내는 단락으로 논제를 다시 언급하거나 요약할 수 있다.

· **conjunction**_접속사

접속사는 단어, 구, 문장들을 연결하는 품사로 단어, 구, 문장 사이의 관계를 나타내는 역할을 한다. 접속사는 등위접속사와 종속접속사가 있다. 등위접속사는 and, but, or, nor, for와 같이 대등한 요소들을 연결하는 접속사다. 반면에 although, because, if, since, when 같은 종속접속사는 대등하지 않은 요소들을 연결한다.

She bought a desk and a chair.

Because he missed the trains, he was late for work.

· **contraction**_축약

두 개의 단어를 결합하여 그중 하나를 짧게 만들고 아포스트로피를 붙이면 축약형이 된다.

cannot → can't   does not → doesn't   should not → shouldn't   it is → it's

· **dependent clause**_종속절

종속절(When he swept the floor)은 문장의 일부로서 자립할 수 없으며, 완전한 문장(When he swept the floor, he whistled.)이 되려면 독립절이 필요하다.

· **exclamation point**_느낌표

문장 끝에 오는 느낌표는 놀라움이나 강한 감정을 나타낸다.

· **fragment**_미완결문

미완결문은 대문자로 시작하여 문장 부호로 끝나고, 대개 주어와 동사를 포함하지만 완전한 문장이 되지 못하는 요소들의 집합이다.

· **helping verb**_조동사

Auxiliary verb라고도 하며 동사구에서 본동사와 함께 사용된다.

is going, were singing, can talk, may leave, must tell, will see

· **hyphen**_하이픈

하이픈(–)은 복합어의 각 부분들을 구별하기 위해 사용된다.

mother-in-law, self-motivated student.

· **independent clause**_독립절

독립절(She saw him.)은 주어와 동사를 갖추고 완전한 생각을 표현하는 문장으로 간주되며, 다른 독립절과 결합해 중문(She saw him, so she called him over.)을 만들거나 종속절을 취해 복문(She saw him even though it was dark.)을 만든다.

· **infinitive verb**_부정사

부정사는 to+동사(to go, to swim, to wish)로 구성되며 명사, 형용사, 부사의 역할을 한다. 예를 들면 To swim the English Channel is my friend's strongest dream.에서 부정사 to swim은 문장의 주어로서 명사 역할을 한다.

· **intransitive verb**_자동사

목적어 없이 스스로 의미를 완성하는 동사다.

John ran. Bob left. Jane slept.

· **introduction**_서론

서론은 에세이의 첫 단락으로 효과적인 서론은 독자의 주의를 끌고, 에세이 전체가 무엇에 관한 것인지를 알려 준다. 그러므로 서론에는 대개 주제와 글쓴이의 주장을 명확히 밝히는 논제가 포함되어 있다.

- **main idea**_주요 논지

주요 논지를 통해 각 단락에서(분량이 긴 에세이의 경우에는 단락의 집합에서) 어떤 내용을 논할지에 대해 진술한다. 주요 논지는 주장을 뒷받침하는 세부 사실에 의해 전개된다.

- **modal verb**_법조동사

일종의 조동사로 허용(may), 의무(must), 예측(will, shall), 능력(can) 등을 표현한다.

- **noun phrase**_명사구

명사구는 몇 개의 단어들로 구성되어 문장에서 명사 역할을 한다. Talking to my mother made me feel better.라는 문장에서 "Talking to my mother"는 주어 역할을 하는 명사구다.

- **paragraph**_단락

에세이는 단락이라고 하는 작은 부분들로 구성된다. 각각의 단락은 하나의 주요 논지에 초점을 맞춰야 한다. 그리고 주제문을 사용해서 그 주요 논지가 무엇인지 나타내야 한다. 좋은 단락은 그 안에 포함된 모든 문장들이 주제문을 뒷받침하는 단락이다.

- **passive voice**_수동태

수동태에서 동사 to be는 동사의 과거 분사형과 결합한다. (예: John was introduced.) 수동태 문장은 행위를 당하는 자나 행위의 결과를 강조한다.

- **period**_마침표

평서문의 종료를 나타내거나 축약(Mr., St., Ave.)을 나타내기 위해 사용된다.

- **phrase**_구

하나의 문법적 기능을 하는 단어의 집합이다. The girl in the corner is Mary.에서 명사구(The girl in the corner)는 명사 또는 주어의 역할을 한다.

- **plural**_복수

복수는 '둘 이상'을 의미한다. 영어 문법에서 명사, 대명사, 동사는 복수형을 가질 수 있다. 예를 들면 cars는 복수명사, we나 they는 복수대명사, climb은 복수동사다.

- **possessive pronoun**_소유대명사

소유관계를 나타내는 대명사(my, our, his, her, their, whose)를 의미하며 어떤 소유대명사는 명사 역할을 할 수 있다. Is this yours? That book is mine.

- **prefix**_접두사

접두사는 co-star의 co처럼 단어의 앞에 붙어서 새로운 단어를 만드는 역할을 한다. 또 다른 예로 접두사 re를 sell에 붙이면 resell이 되고 이것은 '되판다(sell again)'는 뜻이 된다.

- **preposition**_전치사

전치사는 in, of, by, from 같은 단어들로 문장에서 단어 사이의 관계를 나타낸다. The professor sat on the desk.에서 전치사 on은 책상을 기준으로 교수의 상대적인 위치를 나타낸다.

- **pronoun**_대명사

대명사는 명사나 다른 대명사를 대체할 수 있다. 작문할 때 반복을 줄이기 위해 she, it, which, they 같은 대명사를 쓸 수 있다.

- **question mark**_물음표

직접의문문 뒤에 쓰이는 문장 부호다. Is David coming to the party?

· **sentence combining**_문장 결합

짧은 문장을 두 개 이상 결합하여 하나의 긴 문장을 만들 수 있는데 이는 짧은 문장을 너무 많이 썼을 때 글의 흐름이 끊기는 것처럼 보이는 것을 방지한다. 수정 단계에서 문장 결합 기법을 사용하면 에세이의 문체를 개선할 수 있다.

· **singular**_단수

명사, 대명사, 동사는 단수 형태를 취할 수 있다. 예를 들면 car는 단수명사, he 또는 she는 단수대명사, climbs는 현재 시제의 단수동사다.

· **subject**_주어

문장의 주어는 문장이 무엇 또는 누구에 관한 것인지를 말해 준다. 예를 들면 Stephen ran into the parking lot.에서 Stephen이 문장의 주어다.

· **supporting idea**_뒷받침하는 논지

단락의 주요 논지를 전개하는 세부 사실들로 여기에는 정의, 설명, 예시, 의견, 증거, 사례 등이 포함된다. 보통 주제문 뒤에 오며 단락의 본문을 구성한다.

· **tense**_시제

시간을 의미하는 것으로 어떤 경우에는 He sings.(현재 시제) / He sang.(과거 시제)처럼 동사의 변화로 나타내고, 어떤 경우에는 법조동사 또는 조동사를 덧붙여 나타낸다.(He will give me fifty dollars. / He has given me fifty dollars.)

· **thesis**_논제

논제 또는 논제의 진술을 통해 전체 에세이에서 논할 내용을 표현하며 독자에게 에세이에 대한 요약 정보를 제공해 준다. 논제는 보통 주제, 그리고 그 주제에 관해 글쓴이가 무엇을 말하고자 하는가로 나뉘며 주요 논지에 의해 뒷받침된다.

· **topic sentence**_주제문

주제문은 단락이 무엇에 관한 것인지를 말해 준다. 독자가 단락의 주제를 이해하도록 하는 쉬운 방법은 주제문을 단락 시작 부분에 넣는 것이다. (이것은 유일한 방법은 아니지만 경험이 적은 사람들에게 유용한 일반적인 규칙이다.)

· **transition word or phrase**_전환어와 구

논지들을 연결하고 각 논지 간 관계를 먼저 알리는 역할을 한다. 예를 들면 First는 여러 개의 논지들 중 첫 번째 것이라는 신호를 주기 위해 사용된다. 어떤 결과를 보여 주려면 Thus를 쓸 수 있다.

· **transitive verb**_타동사

타동사는 목적어가 필요한 동사다. 예를 들면 He mailed the letter.에서 mailed는 타동사, letter는 목적어다.

· **verb**_동사

동사는 '행위'를 나타내는 품사다. 영어 동사(climb, jump, run, eat)는 시간을 표현하기도 하는데 과거시제 동사인 climbed, jumped, ran, ate 등은 어떤 행위가 과거에 일어났음을 나타낸다.

· **verb phrase**_동사구

동사구는 본동사(climb, jump, run, eat)와 하나 이상의 조동사(may, can, has, is, are)로 이루어진 단어의 집합이다.(She may go. / The students will receive certificates.)

Appendix

Performance Feedback for Test Takers

TOEFL iBT® 점수는 수험자의 읽기, 듣기, 말하기, 쓰기 영역의 능력 수준을 알려 준다. 다음은 성적표에 기재되는 점수대별 수험자의 능력 수준에 대한 설명이다.

TOEFL iBT® Test Reading Section Performance Descriptors

Advanced
(Score range 24–30, CEFR Level C1)

읽기 영역에서 **ADVANCED** 레벨을 받은 수험자는 대체로 영어로 된 대학 입문 수준의 학술 지문을 이해한다. 이런 지문에는 명제와 정보가 촘촘하게 응축되어 있고 어려운 어휘, 장황하고 복잡한 문장과 단락, 그리고 복합적 방식으로 제시되는 추상적이고 미묘한 개념이 포함되기도 한다.

Test takers who score at the Advanced level typically can

- Understand a range of academic and low-frequency vocabulary as well as less common meanings of words.
- Understand explicit connections among pieces of information and make appropriate inferences, even when the passage is conceptually dense and the language is complex.
- Recognize the expository organization of a passage and the purpose that specific information serves within the larger context, even when the purpose of the information is not marked and the passage is conceptually dense.
- Follow a paragraph-length argument involving speculation, qualifications, counterevidence, and subtle rhetorical shifts.
- Synthesize information in passages that contain complex language and are conceptually dense.

수험자 능력

ADVANCED 레벨 수험자의 능력은 다음과 같다.

- 어휘에 담긴 드문 의미뿐만 아니라 다양한 학술 어휘와 자주 쓰이지 않는 어휘들을 이해한다.
- 개념이 난해한 복잡한 글이라도 단편적인 정보들 간의 명시적 연관성을 이해하고 적절한 추론이 가능하다.
- 정보의 목적이 따로 표시되지 않고 개념이 난해한 글이라도 글의 설명 구조와 특정 정보가 더 큰 맥락에서 하는 역할을 인지한다.
- 추측, 단서, 반증, 미묘한 어조 변화가 포함된 단락 길이의 논지를 이해한다.
- 개념이 난해한 복잡한 글로 이루어진 단락들에서 정보를 통합한다.

능력 향상을 위한 조언

가능한 한 많은 글을 자주 읽는다. 장르와 개념 응축도가 다른 다양한 주제의 학술 자료를 읽는다.

- 뉴욕타임스, 사이언스타임스 같은 주요 신문과 웹사이트(National Public Radio [NPR], BBC) 기사를 읽는다.

– 원문의 구성 양식을 통합해 글을 요약하고, 꾸준히 어휘력을 기른다.

글을 읽다가 접하는 새로운 단어들을 활용하는 연습을 하면 단어의 의미와 정확한 용법을 익히는 데 도움이 된다.

High-Intermediate
(Score range 18–23, CEFR Level B2)

읽기 영역에서 HIGH-INTERMEDIATE 레벨을 받은 수험자는 대체로 영어로 된 대학 입문 수준의 학술 지문에서 주요 개념과 중요한 세부 내용을 이해하지만, 명제와 정보가 난해하고 개념과 정보의 제시 방식이 복잡한 일부 지문은 완벽하고 정확하게 이해할 수 없다.

Test takers who score at the High-Intermediate level typically can

– Understand common academic vocabulary, but sometimes have difficulty with low-frequency words or less common meanings of words.
– Understand explicit connections among pieces of information and make appropriate inferences, but may have difficulty in parts of a passage that contain low-frequency vocabulary or that are conceptually dense, rhetorically complex, or abstract.
– Distinguish important ideas from less important ones.
– Often recognize the expository organization of a passage and the purpose of specific information within a passage, even when such information is not explicitly marked.
– Synthesize information in a passage, but may have difficulty doing so when the passage is conceptually dense, rhetorically complex, or abstract.

수험자 능력

HIGH-INTERMEDIATE 레벨 수험자의 능력은 다음과 같다.

– 흔히 쓰이는 학술 어휘는 이해하지만 드물게 쓰이는 어휘나 의미가 나오면 종종 어려움을 겪는다.
– 단편적인 정보들 간의 명시적 연관성을 이해해 적절한 추론이 가능하지만, 드물게 쓰이는 어휘가 있거나 개념이 난해하고 수사학적으로 복잡하거나 추상적인 글을 파악하는 데는 어려움을 겪는다.
– 중요한 개념과 중요도가 떨어지는 개념을 구별한다.
– 글의 설명 구조를 인식하며 특정 정보가 분명하게 강조되지 않더라도 특정 정보의 목적을 인지한다.
– 글에 담긴 정보를 통합할 수 있지만 개념이 난해한 글, 수사학적으로 복잡하거나 추상적인 글을 파악하는 데는 어려움을 겪는다.

능력 향상을 위한 조언

가능한 한 많은 글을 자주 읽는다. 학술문의 구성과 지문의 전반적 구조를 익히되 처음부터 끝까지 읽는다.

– 주요 개념과 이를 뒷받침하는 세부 사항의 관계에 유의한다.
– 개요를 작성해 보면서 독해 지문의 구조를 얼마나 이해하고 있는지 점검한다.
– 전체 지문의 요약문을 작성한다.
– 비교하는 글이라면 요약문에도 이를 반영해야 한다. 두 가지 관점에 대해 논쟁하는 글이라면 요약문에도 두 가지 관점 모두 반영해야 한다. 생소한 어휘를 기록하는 시스템을 만들어 꾸준히 어휘력을 기른다. 주제나 의미에 따라 단어를 분류하고 관련 단어들을 한 묶음으로 익힌다.

– 어근, 접두사, 접미사, 어족(語族)을 학습한다.
– 동의어 사전, 연어(흔히 함께 쓰이는 단어) 사전 등 다양한 어휘 교재를 활용한다.

Low-Intermediate
(Score range 4–17, CEFR Level B1)

읽기 영역에서 LOW-INTERMEDIATE 레벨을 받은 수험자는 대체로 영어로 된 학술 지문에 제시된 주요 개념 일부와 중요한 정보 일부를 이해하지만, 전반적인 이해력에는 한계가 있다. 예를 들어 어떤 주장 뒤에 뒷받침하는 예가 바로 이어지는 글처럼 문장들 사이의 관계가 명료하고 단순하면 둘 이상 문장들의 연관성을 이해할 수 있지만 난해한 글이나 복잡한 글은 파악하는 데 어려움을 겪는다.

Test takers who score at the Low-Intermediate level typically can

– Understand texts with basic grammar, but have inconsistent understanding of texts with complex grammatical structures.
– Understand high-frequency academic vocabulary, but often have difficulty with lower-frequency words.
– Locate information in a passage by matching words or relying on high-frequency vocabulary, but their limited ability to recognize paraphrases results in incomplete understanding of the connections among ideas and information.
– Identify an author's purpose when that purpose is explicitly stated or easy to infer from the context.
– Recognize major ideas in a passage when the information is clearly presented, memorable, or illustrated by examples but have difficulty doing so when the passage is more demanding.

수험자 능력

LOW-INTERMEDIATE 레벨 수험자의 능력은 다음과 같다.
– 기본적인 문법이 쓰인 지문은 이해하지만 문법 구조가 복잡한 지문은 간혹 이해하지 못하는 경우도 있다.
– 자주 쓰이는 학술 어휘는 이해하지만 흔하지 않은 어휘가 나오면 어려움을 겪는다.
– 어구를 서로 맞춰 보거나 흔히 쓰이는 어휘들에 의존해 지문에 담긴 정보를 찾아내지만 바꾸어 쓴 표현을 인지하는 능력이 부족해 개념과 정보의 연관성을 충분히 이해하지 못한다.
– 저자의 목적이 분명하게 진술되거나 맥락에서 추론하기 쉬운 경우 저자의 목적을 파악한다.
– 정보가 명확히 제시되고 기억하기 쉽거나 예시를 통해 설명된 경우 지문의 주요 개념을 인지하지만 글이 더 어려워지면 어려움을 겪는다.

능력 향상을 위한 조언

가능한 한 많은 글을 자주 읽는다. 생소한 어휘를 기록하는 시스템을 만든다.
– 주제나 의미에 따라 단어를 분류해 이를 기억하도록 정기적으로 복습하고 학습한다.
– 어근, 접두사, 접미사, 어족 등 단어를 부분별로 분석하고 익혀 어휘력을 기른다.
– 학술문의 구성과 독해 지문의 전반적인 구조를 연구하되 지문을 처음부터 끝까지 읽는다.
– 문장들의 연관성을 살펴본다. 즉 한 문장의 끝 부분이 다음 문장의 첫 부분과 어떻게 연결되는지 살펴본다.
– 주요 개념과 이를 뒷받침하는 세부 사항을 찾아보고 둘의 관계에 유의한다.
– 개요를 작성해 보면서 독해 지문의 구조를 얼마나 이해하고 있는지 점검한다. 먼저 동일한 개념을 다루는 단락들끼리 묶는다. 동일한 개념을 논하는 단락들을 한 문장으로 요약한다.

- 전체 지문을 요약한다.

Below Low-Intermediate
(Score range 0–3)

읽기 영역에서 4점 이하를 받은 수험자는 아직 LOW-INTERMEDIATE 레벨의 실력을 갖추지 못했다.

TOEFL iBT® Test Listening Section Performance Descriptors

Advanced
(Score range 22–30, CEFR Level C1)

듣기 영역에서 **ADVANCED** 레벨을 받은 수험자는 대체로 교육 현장에서 일어나는 대화와 강의를 이해한다. 즉 어려운 어휘, 추상적이거나 복잡한 개념, 복잡한 문법 구조, 다양한 억양과 복잡한 방식으로 구성된 다량의 정보가 포함된 대화와 강의를 이해할 수 있다.

Test takers who score at the Advanced level typically can

- Understand main ideas and explicitly stated important details, even if not reinforced.
- Distinguish important ideas from less important points.
- Keep track of conceptually complex (and sometimes conflicting) information over extended portions of a lecture.
- Understand how information or examples are being used (for example, to provide evidence for or against a claim, to make comparisons or draw contrasts, or to express an opinion or a value judgment) and how pieces of information are connected (for example, in a cause-effect relationship).
- Understand different ways that speakers use language for purposes other than to give information (for example, to express an emotion, to emphasize a point, to convey agreement or disagreement, or to communicate an intention).
- Synthesize information, even when it is not presented in sequence, and make appropriate inferences on the basis of that information.

수험자 능력

ADVANCED 레벨 수험자의 능력은 다음과 같다.
- 주요 개념과 분명하게 진술된 중요한 세부 사항은 특별히 강조하지 않아도 이해한다.
- 중요한 개념과 덜 중요한 요점을 구별한다.
- 긴 강의에서 개념이 복잡하고 종종 모순되는 정보를 추적해 파악한다.
- 정보나 예시가 이용되는 방식(예를 들어 어떤 주장에 찬성 혹은 반박하기 위해 증거 제시하기, 비교하기, 대조하기, 의견이나 가치 판단 표명하기)과 단편적인 정보들이 연결되는 방식(예를 들어 인과관계)을 이해한다.
- 정보 전달 이외의 목적(예를 들어 감정 표현하기, 요점 강조하기, 찬성 또는 반대 나타내기, 의도 전달하기)을 위해 화자

가 말하는 다양한 방식을 이해한다.

– 순서대로 제시되지 않더라도 정보들을 통합하고 이러한 정보를 토대로 적절하게 추론한다.

매일 청취 연습을 하되 청취 분량을 점점 늘리고 난이도를 점차 높이면서 청취력을 더욱 탄탄하게 기른다.

– 주제가 다양한 여러 종류의 학습자료를 듣는다.

- 생소한 주제에 집중한다.
- 학술 강의와 대중 강연을 듣는다.
- TV, 라디오, 인터넷 등 시청각 자료를 듣는다.
- NOVA, BBC, NPR 같은 학술 콘텐츠가 있는 프로그램을 듣는다.
- 대화, 전화 통화, 전화 녹음을 듣는다.
- 가이드 투어나 음성 가이드 투어(박물관 투어 등)를 한다.

– 능동적인 자세로 듣는다.

- 주요 개념과 중요한 세부 사항을 귀담아들으며 메모한다.
- 다음에 들을 내용을 예측한다.
- 요약한다.
- 새로운 단어와 표현을 적는다.

선택한 자료의 난이도가 높다면 여러 번 듣는다.

1. 먼저 주요 개념과 핵심 세부 사항을 유의해서 듣는다.
2. 그런 다음 다시 들으면서 이해하지 못한 부분을 메운다. 즉 개념들 간의 연관성, 담화 구조, 화자의 태도를 이해하고 사실과 의견을 구분한다.

High-Intermediate

(Score range 17–21, CEFR Level B2)

듣기 영역에서 **HIGH-INTERMEDIATE** 레벨을 받은 수험자는 대체로 교육 현장에서 일어나는 대화와 강의의 주요 개념과 중요한 세부 사항을 이해한다. 즉 어려운 어휘, 추상적이거나 복잡한 개념, 복잡한 문장 구조, 다양하게 활용된 억양, 일련의 발언을 통해 추적해야 하는 정보들이 포함된 대화와 강의를 이해할 수 있다. 그러나 강조되지 않은 정보가 응축된 형태로 제시되는 강의와 대화를 파악하는 데는 어려움을 겪는다.

Test takers who score at the High-Intermediate level typically can

– Understand main ideas and explicitly stated important details that are reinforced (by repetition, paraphrase, or indirect reference).

– Distinguish main ideas from other information.

– Keep track of information over an extended portion of an information-rich lecture or conversation, and recognize multiple, possibly conflicting, points of view.

– Understand how information or examples are being used (for example, to provide support for a claim) and how pieces of information are connected (for example, in a narrative explanation, a compare-and-contrast relationship, or a cause-effect chain).

– Understand, though perhaps not consistently, ways that speakers use language for purposes other than to give information (for example, to emphasize a point, express agreement or disagreement, express opinions, or convey intentions indirectly), especially when the purpose is supported by intonation.

– Synthesize information from adjacent parts of a lecture or conversation and make appropriate inferences on the basis of that information, but may have difficulty synthesizing information from separate parts of a lecture or conversation.

수험자 능력

HIGH-INTERMEDIATE 레벨 수험자의 능력은 다음과 같다.

– 주요 개념과 강조(반복, 바꾸어 말하기, 간접 언급)를 통해 분명하게 진술된 중요한 세부 사항을 이해한다.

– 주요 개념과 기타 정보를 구별한다.

– 정보가 다량 포함된 긴 강의나 대화에서 정보를 추적하고, 다양하고 종종 모순되는 관점들을 인식한다.

– 정보나 예시가 이용되는 방식(예를 들어 어떤 주장을 뒷받침하기 위해 이용)과 단편적인 정보들이 연결되는 방식(예를 들어 서술적 설명, 비교–대조 관계, 인과관계)을 이해한다.

– 정보 제공 이외의 목적(예를 들어 요점 강조, 찬성이나 반대 표명, 의견 표명, 또는 간접적으로 의도 전달하기)을 위해 화자가 말하는 방식을 간혹 이해하지 못하는 경우도 있다.

– 강의나 대화에서 인접하여 제시되는 정보들을 통합하고 이 정보를 토대로 적절하게 추론한다. 그러나 따로 떨어져서 제시되는 정보를 통합하는 데는 어려움을 겪는다.

능력 향상을 위한 조언

매일 청취 연습을 하되 듣기 시간과 분량을 늘리고 난이도를 점차 높인다.

– 주제가 다양한 여러 종류의 학습자료를 듣는다.

  • 익숙한 주제로 시작해 생소한 주제로 넘어간다.

  • 팟캐스트, 스트리밍되는 라디오 및 TV 프로그램, 인터넷 비디오 등, 일시 정지하고 다시 재생할 수 있는 오디오 및 비디오 자료를 들어 본다.

  • NOVA, BBC, NPR 같은 학술 콘텐츠가 있는 프로그램을 듣는다.

  • 대화와 전화 녹음을 듣는다.

– 능동적인 자세로 듣는다.

  • 주요 개념과 중요한 세부 사항을 귀담아들으며 메모한다.

  • 기본 정보(누가? 무엇을? 언제? 어디서? 왜? 어떻게?)에 관해 스스로에게 질문한다.

  • 다음에 들을 내용을 예측한다.

  • 요약한다.

  • 새로운 단어와 표현을 적는다.

자료의 난이도가 높다면 여러 번 듣는다.

1. 먼저 가능하면 영어 자막을 보면서 듣는다.

2. 그런 다음 자막 없이 들으면서 주요 개념과 핵심 세부 사항을 귀담아든는다.

3. 그런 다음 다시 들으면서 기본적인 내용 중 이해하지 못한 부분을 메우고 개념들 간의 연관성을 이해한다.

Low-Intermediate

(Score range 9–16, CEFR Level B1)

듣기 영역에서 **LOW-INTERMEDIATE** 레벨을 받은 수험자는 대체로 교육 현장에서 일어나는 대화와 강의의 주요 개념과 중요한 세부 사항 일부를 이해한다. 즉 기본적인 학술어, 두드러지게 강조된 추상적이거나 복잡한 개념, 복잡한 문장 구조, 일부 억양 활용, 반복되거나 두드러지게 강조된 다량의 정보를 이해한다.

Test takers at the Low-Intermediate level typically can

- Understand main ideas, even in complex discussions, when the ideas are repeatedly referred to, extensively elaborated on, or illustrated with multiple examples.
- Understand explicitly stated important details but may have difficulty understanding details if they are not reinforced (such as through repetition or with an example) or marked as important, or if they are conveyed over several exchanges among different speakers.
- Understand some ways that speakers use language to express an opinion or attitude (for example, agreement, disagreement, surprise), especially when the opinion or attitude is related to a central theme, clearly marked as important, or supported by intonation.
- Understand connections between important ideas, particularly if the ideas are related to a central theme or are repeated and can make appropriate inferences from information expressed in one or two sentences, especially when that information is reinforced.

수험자 능력

LOW-INTERMEDIATE 레벨 수험자의 능력은 다음과 같다.
- 개념이 반복하여 상세하게 언급되거나 다양한 예를 통해 설명된 경우 복잡한 논지라도 주요 개념을 이해한다.
- 명시적으로 진술된 중요한 세부 사항은 이해하지만, (반복이나 예를 통해) 강조되지 않거나 중요하다고 언급되지 않은 경우, 여러 사람이 주고받는 대화 속에서 전달될 경우에는 세부 사항을 파악하는 데 어려움을 겪기도 한다.
- 특히 의견이나 태도(예를 들어 찬성, 반대, 놀라움)가 중심 주제와 연관되거나 중요하다고 언급되거나 억양으로 강조된 경우에 화자가 의견이나 태도를 표명하기 위해 언어를 사용하는 방식을 이해한다.
- 특히 개념이 중심 주제와 관련이 있거나 반복될 때 중요한 개념들의 연관성을 이해하며 특히 정보가 강조된 경우 한두 문장 속에 표명된 정보를 통해 적절하게 추론할 수 있다.

능력 향상을 위한 조언

매일 청취 연습을 하되 듣기 시간과 개별 청취 자료의 분량을 늘린다.
- 주제가 다양한 여러 종류의 학습자료를 듣는다.
  - 익숙한 주제에 관한 녹음자료
  - 녹음된 영어 강의
  - 팟캐스트, 스트리밍되는 라디오 및 TV 프로그램, 인터넷 비디오 등, 일시 정지하고 다시 재생할 수 있는 오디오 및 비디오 자료를 들어 본다.
  - 학술 대담 콘텐츠가 있는 짧은 프로그램
- 능동적인 자세로 듣는다.
  - 주요 개념과 중요한 세부 사항을 귀담아들으며 메모한다.
  - 기본 정보(누가? 무엇을? 언제? 어디서? 왜? 어떻게?)에 관해 스스로에게 질문한다.
  - 다음에 들을 내용을 예측한다.
  - 요약한다.
  - 새로운 단어와 표현을 적는다.

녹음 자료를 여러 번 듣는다.

1. 먼저 가능하면 영어 자막을 보면서 듣는다.
2. 그런 다음 자막 없이 들으면서 주요 개념과 핵심 세부 사항을 귀담아듣는다.
3. 그런 다음 다시 들으면서 기본적인 내용 중 이해하지 못한 부분을 메우고 개념들 간의 연관성을 이해한다.

Below Low-Intermediate
(Score range 0–8)

듣기 영역에서 9점 이하를 받은 수험자는 아직 LOW-INTERMEDIATE 레벨의 실력을 갖추지 못했다.

TOEFL iBT® Test Speaking Section Performance Descriptors

Advanced
(Score range 25–30, CEFR Level C1)

말하기 영역에서 **ADVANCED** 레벨을 받은 수험자는 대체로 어려움 없이 다양한 주제에 관해 유창하고 효과적으로 소통할 수 있다.

Test takers who score at the Advanced level typically can

- Speak clearly and use intonation to support meaning so that speech is generally easy to understand and follow; any minor lapses do not obscure meaning.
- Speak with relative ease on a range of general and academic topics, demonstrating control of an appropriate range of grammatical structures and vocabulary; any minor errors may be noticeable, but do not obscure meaning.
- Convey mostly well-supported summaries, explanations, and opinions, including both concrete and abstract information, with generally well-controlled organization and cohesion; lapses may occur, but they rarely impact overall comprehensibility.

수험자 능력

ADVANCED 레벨 수험자의 능력은 다음과 같다.
- 분명하게 말하고 억양을 활용해 의미가 뚜렷하게 드러나게 하므로 전반적으로 이해하고 알아듣기 쉽다. 사소한 실수가 있어도 의미가 흐려지지는 않는다.
- 문법 구조와 어휘를 적절하게 구사해 일반 및 학술 주제에 관해 비교적 쉽게 말한다. 사소한 오류가 눈에 띄지만 의미가 흐려지지는 않는다.
- 구체적이고 추상적인 정보를 포함해 요약, 설명 및 의견을 대체로 잘 뒷받침해 짜임새 있고 조리 있게 전달한다. 실수가 있지만 전반적인 내용을 이해하는 데 방해가 되지는 않는다.

능력 향상을 위한 조언

영어를 더욱 유창하게 말할 수 있는 기회를 찾는다.

- 언제든 과감하게 영어로 대화하는 사람들과 어울린다.
- 영화, 음악, 여행 등 일상 주제에 대해 영어로 대화하는 영어 말하기 모임에 가입한다. 모임 가입이 여의치 않으면 직접 시작하고 유창하게 영어로 말할 수 있는 실력자들을 초대해보자.

자신의 말을 녹음한 뒤 들으면서 기록한다.
- 신문이나 교재에 나온 짧은 기사를 읽는다. 기사를 요약해 말하는 것을 녹음한다.
- 녹음한 내용을 글로 적은 뒤 다시 읽어 본다. 같은 내용을 다르게 말할 수 있는 방법을 생각해 본다.

High-Intermediate
(Score range 20–24, CEFR Level B2)

말하기 영역에서 **HIGH-INTERMEDIATE** 레벨을 받은 수험자는 일반적이거나 친숙한 대다수 주제에 대해 대체로 효과적으로 소통할 수 있으며 좀 더 복잡하거나 학술적인 주제를 논할 때도 상대방이 알아듣도록 말할 수 있다.

Test takers who score at the High-Intermediate level typically can

- Speak clearly and without hesitancy on general or familiar topics, with overall good intelligibility; pauses and hesitations (to recall or plan information) are sometimes noticeable when more demanding content is produced, and any mispronunciations or intonation errors only occasionally cause problems for the listener.
- Produce stretches of speech that demonstrate control of some complex structures and a range of vocabulary, although occasional lapses in precision and accuracy may obscure meaning at times.
- Convey sufficient information to produce mostly complete summaries, explanations, and opinions, but some ideas may not be fully developed or may lack elaboration; any lapses in completeness and cohesion may at times affect the otherwise clear progression of ideas.

수험자 능력

HIGH-INTERMEDIATE 레벨 수험자의 능력은 다음과 같다.
- 일반적이거나 친숙한 주제에 관해 대체로 알아듣기 쉽게 머뭇거리지 않고 분명하게 말한다. 까다로운 내용을 말할 때 (정보를 기억하거나 구상하느라) 멈칫하고 발음이나 억양 오류 때문에 소통에 문제가 생기지만 가끔일 뿐이다.
- 때로는 정밀함과 정확성이 떨어져 의미가 흐려지기는 하지만, 복잡한 구조와 다양한 어휘를 구사할 수 있다.
- 대체로 완벽하게 요약하고 설명 및 의견을 개진하기에 충분한 정보를 전달하지만, 일부 개념은 완전히 전개되지 않거나 정교함이 결여되기도 한다. 때때로 완벽성과 논리적 일관성이 떨어져 개념을 명확하게 개진하는 데 지장을 준다.

능력 향상을 위한 조언

학창생활에서 중요한 일상 주제에 관해 영어로 말하는 연습을 하면 더 유창하고 자신감 있게 말할 수 있다.
- 대화 상대를 찾아 매주 시간을 정해 영어로 말하는 연습을 한다.
- 유창하게 영어로 말하는 사람을 찾을 수 없으면 영어로 말하기 연습을 원하는 친구를 찾아서 특정 기간 동안 영어로만 말하기로 약속한다.
- 인터넷에서 학보 기사를 찾아 읽는다.

다양한 학술 주제에 관해 말하는 연습을 한다.
- 신문이나 교재에 나온 짧은 기사를 읽는다. 기사의 주요 내용어를 기록한다.
- 기사에 관한 두세 가지 질문을 적되 내용어가 포함되도록 한다.

- 질문에 큰 소리로 대답하는 연습을 하되 답변에 내용어가 포함되도록 노력한다.
- 연습 후 질문에 대한 답변을 녹음한다.

Low-Intermediate
(Score range 16–19, CEFR Level B1)

말하기 영역에서 **LOW-INTERMEDIATE** 레벨을 받은 수험자는 대체로 일반적이거나 친숙한 주제에 대해 비교적 수월하게 말할 수 있다.

Test takers who score at the Low-Intermediate level typically can

- Speak clearly with minor hesitancies about general or familiar topics; longer pauses are noticeable when speaking about more complex or academic topics, and mispronunciations may obscure meaning at times.
- Produce short stretches of speech consisting of basic grammatical structures connected with "and," "because," and "so;" attempts at longer utterances requiring more complex grammatical structures may be marked by errors and pauses for grammatical planning or repair.
- Use vocabulary that is sufficient to discuss general or familiar topics, but limitations in range of vocabulary sometimes result in vague or unclear expression of ideas.
- Convey some main points and other relevant information but summaries, explanations, and opinions are sometimes incomplete, inaccurate, and/or lack detail; long or complex explanations may lack coherence.

수험자 능력

LOW-INTERMEDIATE 레벨 수험자의 능력은 다음과 같다.
- 조금 머뭇거리기는 하지만 일반적이거나 친숙한 주제는 분명하게 말한다. 더 복잡하거나 학술적인 주제는 멈추는 시간이 더 길고 발음 오류 때문에 이따금 의미가 모호해진다.
- 'and', 'because', 'so'로 연결된 기초적인 문법 구조를 사용해 짧게 말한다. 복잡한 문법 구조가 요구되는 긴 문장을 말하려고 하면 오류를 범하고 문법을 구상하거나 고치느라 머뭇거린다.
- 일반적이거나 친숙한 주제에 대해 논의하기에 충분한 어휘를 사용하지만, 어휘 범위의 제한으로 때때로 개념이 모호하거나 불분명하게 표현될 수 있다.
- 중요한 요점과 관련 정보를 일부 전달하지만 요약, 설명, 의견이 때때로 불완전, 부정확하고 또는 세부 내용이 부족하다. 길고 복잡한 설명에 일관성이 부족하다.

Basic
(Score range 10–15 CEFR Level A2)

말하기 영역에서 BASIC 레벨을 받은 수험자는 대체로 친숙하고 일상적인 주제에 대해 제한된 정보를 전달할 수 있다.

Test takers who score at the Basic level typically can

- Speak slowly and carefully so that they make themselves understood, but pronunciation may be strongly influenced by the speaker's first language and at times be unintelligible; speech may be marked by frequent pauses, reformulations, and false starts.
- Produce mostly short utterances, connecting phrases with simple linking words (such as "and") to make themselves understood; grammar and vocabulary are limited, and frequent pauses may occur while searching for words.
- Convey some limited information about familiar topics; supporting points and/or details are generally missing, and main ideas may be absent, unclear, or not well connected.

BASIC 레벨 수험자의 능력은 다음과 같다.
- 천천히, 조심스럽게 말하지만 발음에 모국어의 영향이 강해 이따금 알아들을 수 없을 때도 있다. 말을 자주 멈추고 바꾸며 시작하는 말이 부적절하다.
- 간단한 연결어("and" 등)로 어구를 연결해 짧게 말한다. 문법과 어휘에 한계가 있으며 단어를 찾느라 자주 멈춘다.
- 친숙한 주제라면 제한된 정보를 전달하지만 대체로 뒷받침하는 요점 또는 세부 내용이 누락되며 주요 개념이 없거나 불명확하고 연결이 느슨하다.

Low-Intermediate & Basic 레벨 수험자들을 위한 능력 향상을 위한 조언

영어로 대화하려는 사람과 친하게 지낸다. 다른 사람들과 교류하다 보면 말하기 실력이 는다. 유창하게 영어로 말하는 사람을 찾을 수 없다면 영어 말하기 연습을 원하는 친구를 찾아 일정 기간 영어로만 말하자고 약속한다.
- 신문이나 교재에 나온 짧은 기사를 읽는다. 기사의 주요 내용어를 기록한다.
- 기사에 관한 두세 가지 질문을 적되 내용어가 포함되도록 한다.
- 질문에 큰 소리로 대답하는 연습을 하되 답변에 내용어가 포함되도록 노력한다.
- 연습 후 질문에 대한 답변을 녹음한다.

시사에 관해 말하는 연습을 한다.
- 영어로 작성된 신문기사, 사설, 문화행사 정보를 읽는다. 읽은 정보를 친구에게 영어로 말한다.
- 대학 수업을 청강하면서 필기한다. 그 다음 필기를 참고해 들은 정보를 친구에게 영어로 말한다.
- 학술 어휘력을 기른다. 읽거나 들을 때 새로운 단어가 나오면 적어 두고 발음을 연습한다.
- 일기예보를 들으며 필기한 다음 친구에게 영어로 일기예보를 말한다.

Basic
(Score range 10–15, CEFR Level A)

말하기 영역에서 **Basic** 레벨을 받는 사람들은 일반적으로 친숙한 일상 주제에 대해 제한된 정보를 전달할 수 있다.

Test takers who score at the Basic level typically can

- Speak slowly and carefully so that they make themselves understood, but pronunciation may be strongly influenced by the speaker's first language and at times be unintelligible; speech may be marked by frequent pauses, reformulations, and false starts.

- Produce mostly short utterances, connecting phrases with simple linking words (such as "and") to make themselves understood; grammar and vocabulary are limited, and frequent pauses may occur while searching for words.
- Convey some limited information about familiar topics; supporting points and/or details are generally missing, and main ideas may be absent, unclear, or not well connected.

수험자 능력

BASIC 레벨 수험자의 능력은 다음과 같다.

- 말하는 속도가 느리고 조심스럽게 말하여 이해할 수는 있지만, 말하는 사람의 모국어에 발음이 크게 영향을 받을 수 있으며 때로는 알아들을 수 없을 때도 있다. 말하다가 자주 멈추고, 재구성하고, 애초에 시작부터 틀리게 말하는 특징을 보인다.
- 대부분 짧게 말하며, 간단한 연결어(and 같은)로 구문을 연결한다. 문법과 어휘가 제한적이며, 단어를 생각해 내기 위해 자꾸 말을 멈춘다.
- 친숙한 주제에 대해 일부 제한된 정보를 전달한다. 뒷받침하는 요점과 세부 사항이 일반적으로 누락되며, 주요 개념이 없거나, 불분명하거나, 잘 연결되지 않을 수 있다.

능력 향상을 위한 조언

회화 수업을 들으면 더 유창하게 말할 수 있고 발음도 개선된다.
어휘력을 기르고 문법 실력을 키운다.

- 말할 때 문법을 정확하게 활용할 수 있도록 기초 문법 규칙을 학습한다.
- 새로운 단어와 표현을 익힐 때 또렷하게 발음하도록 연습하고 발음한 것을 녹음한다.

Below Basic
(Score range 0–9)

말하기 영역에서 10점 이하를 받은 수험자는 아직 **Basic** 레벨의 실력을 갖추지 못했다.

TOEFL iBT® Test Writing Section Performance Descriptors

Advanced
(Score range 24–30, CEFR Level C1)

쓰기 영역에서 **ADVANCED** 레벨을 받은 수험자는 대체로 광범위한 학술, 비학술 주제에 대해 영어로 명료하고 자신 있게 글을 쓸 수 있다.

Test takers who score at the Advanced level typically can

- Produce clear, well-developed, and well-organized text; ungrammatical, unclear, or unidiomatic use of English is rare.
- Express an opinion on a controversial issue and support that opinion with appropriate details and explanations in writing, demonstrating variety and range of vocabulary and grammatical structures.
- Select important information from multiple sources, integrate it, and present it coherently and clearly in writing, with only occasional minor imprecision in the summary of the source information.

수험자 능력

ADVANCED 레벨 수험자의 능력은 다음과 같다.
- 명확하며 정돈된 글로 논지를 충분히 전개한다. 문법에 어긋나거나 불명확하거나 관용어법에 맞지 않은 영어를 사용하는 경우가 드물다.
- 쟁점에 대한 의견을 표명하고 다양한 어휘와 문법 구조를 통해 적절한 세부 사항과 설명으로 의견을 뒷받침한다.
- 출처 정보를 요약할 때 이따금 정확성이 조금 떨어지지만 복수의 출처에서 중요한 정보를 선택하고 통합해 조리 있고 명확하게 글로 제시한다.

능력 향상을 위한 조언

둘 이상의 출처에서 정보를 전달하고 연결하는 능력을 꾸준히 기른다. 예를 들어 영어로 된 독해 지문을 분석하는 연습을 한다.
- 같은 주제나 쟁점을 논한 두 가지 기사나 글을 읽고, 각각 요약한 다음 비슷한 점과 다른 점을 설명한다.
- 교사의 강의나 친구의 대화와 관련된 글을 검색해 듣기와 읽기를 결합하는 연습을 한다.

기성 저자들이 의견을 표명하는 방식을 연구해 의견 표현력을 꾸준히 기른다.
- 전문 저자들이 쟁점(예를 들어, 사회 · 환경 · 교육 문제)에 관해 의견을 표명하기 위해 작성한 기사와 에세이를 읽는다.
- 저자의 의견을 파악한다.
- 저자가 반박 논리에 대처하는 방법에 주목한다.

High-Intermediate
(Score range 17–23, CEFR Level B2)

쓰기 영역에서 **HIGH-INTERMEDIATE** 레벨을 받은 수험자는 대체로 일반적이거나 친숙한 주제에 대해 영어로 글을 잘 작성할 수 있다. 학술 주제의 복잡한 개념에 관해 쓸 때는 주요 개념 대부분을 전달할 수 있다.

Test takers who score at the High-Intermediate level typically can

– Produce summaries of multiple sources that include most of the main ideas; some important ideas from the sources may be missing, unclear, or inaccurate.

– Express an opinion on an issue clearly; some ideas and explanations may not be fully developed and lapses in cohesion may at times affect a clear progression of ideas.

– Write with some degree of facility; grammatical mistakes or vague/incorrect uses of words may make the writing difficult to follow in some places.

수험자 능력

HIGH-INTERMEDIATE 레벨 수험자의 능력은 다음과 같다.

– 복수의 출처를 요약할 때 주요 개념 대부분이 포함된다. 출처에서 나온 중요한 개념 일부가 누락되거나 불분명, 또는 부정확할 수 있다.

– 쟁점에 관한 의견을 명확하게 표현한다. 일부 개념과 설명은 논지 전개가 불완전할 수도 있고 일관성에 문제가 있어 이따금 개념이 명확하게 개진되지 못한다.

– 일정 수준 매끄럽게 글을 작성하지만 문법 오류나 모호하고 잘못된 단어 사용으로 글을 이해하기 어려운 부분도 있다.

능력 향상을 위한 조언

요점을 찾아내는 연습을 한다.

– 텔레비전이나 라디오에서 영어로 된 뉴스와 정보 프로그램을 녹음하거나 인터넷에서 대화 또는 강의를 다운로드한다.

– 들으면서 메모한다. 약 30초마다 듣기를 중지하고 들은 내용을 간략히 요약해 적는다.

– 다시 들으면서 요약문을 점검한다. 녹음된 내용을 이해했는지 또는 자신의 의견을 잘 표현했는지 미심쩍은 부분을 표시한다.

기사나 에세이에 대해 상반된 관점의 답변을 영어로 작성한다.

– 답변 개요를 작성한다.

– 개념을 뒷받침하기 위해 자신이 사용한 방식에 유의한다. 자신이 작성한 글을 다시 읽는다.

– 뒷받침하는 개념들이 핵심 요점과 명확하게 연결됐는지 확인한다.

– 뒷받침하는 각 개념의 논지를 전개하는 데 사용한 방식에 유의한다.

– 요점을 분명히 하기 위해 추가했어야 할 내용이 있는지 점검하며 각 요점을 상세하게 전개했는지 확인한다.

Low-Intermediate
(Score range 13–16, CEFR Level B1)

쓰기 영역에서 **LOW-INTERMEDIATE** 레벨을 받은 수험자는 대체로 일반적이거나 친숙한 주제에 대해 영어로 간단한 글을 작성할 수 있다.

Test takers who score at the Low-Intermediate level typically can

– Produce a simple text that expresses some ideas on an issue, but the development of ideas is limited because of insufficient or inappropriate details and explanations.

– Summarize some relevant information from multiple sources, but important ideas from the sources are omitted or significantly misrepresented, especially ideas that require unfamiliar vocabulary or are complex.

– Write with limited facility, with language errors obscuring connections or meaning at key junctures between ideas in the text.

LOW-INTERMEDIATE 레벨 수험자의 능력은 다음과 같다.

– 쟁점에 관한 생각을 표현하는 간단한 글을 작성하지만 세부 내용과 설명이 미흡하거나 부적절해 논지 전개에 제약이 있다.
– 복수의 출처에서 적절한 정보 일부를 요약하지만 특히 복잡하거나 생소한 어휘가 필요한 개념일 경우 출처에 있는 중요한 개념이 빠지거나 현저하게 잘못 전달된다.
– 일정 수준 매끄럽게 글을 작성하지만 오류 때문에 개념들이 연결되는 중요한 지점에서 의미나 연결이 모호해진다.

능력 향상을 위한 조언

모국어로 된 학술 지문과 기타 자료를 읽고 듣는다. 읽고 들은 내용을 적는다.

– 먼저 모국어로 적은 뒤 영어로 적는다.
– 완전한 영어 문장으로 요점을 요약한다.
– 적은 글을 검토하고 오류를 정정해 달라고 교사에게 요청한다.
– 자료를 읽고 요약하는 시간을 점차 줄여 나간다.
– 표준형(쿼티 배열) 키보드로 타자 연습을 한다.

잘 작성된 단락이나 에세이를 연구한다. 잘 쓴 단락 하나에는 한 가지 주요 개념이 논의된다. 이 개념은 대체로 첫 문장으로 표현되는데 이를 주제문이라고 한다. 에세이를 작성할 때 한 단락에는 주제의 한 측면에 관해 논해야 한다.

– 하나의 중심 개념에 초점을 두고 해당 개념을 설명하거나 뒷받침하는 다수의 완전한 문장이 포함된 단락을 영어로 써 본다.
– 교사에게 단락을 검토하고 교정해 달라고 요청한다.

Basic

(Score range 7–12, CEFR Level A2)

쓰기 영역에서 BASIC 레벨을 받은 수험자는 영어로 작성된 글을 통해 대체로 매우 기초적인 정보를 전달할 수 있다.

Test takers who score at the Basic level typically can

– Produce some text that is related to the topic, but with little detail and/or lack of organization.
– Convey some information from the sources or some ideas on an issue, but grammatical errors, unclear expressions, and/or poor sentence structure make their writing difficult to comprehend.

BASIC 레벨 수험자의 능력은 다음과 같다.

– 주제와 관련된 글을 작성할 수 있지만 세부 사항이 거의 없거나 체계가 부족하다.
– 출처에서 일부 정보나 쟁점 관련 개념 일부를 전달할 수 있지만 문법 오류, 명확하지 못한 표현과 빈약한 문장 구조 때문에 이해하기 어렵다.

– 영어 독해력과 작문 기술을 연습하고 어휘력과 문법 실력을 기른다.

– 독해력과 작문 기술이 향상되면 위에 언급한 Low-Intermediate 레벨을 위한 조언을 따른다.

Below Basic

(Score range 0–6)

쓰기 영역에서 7점 이하를 받은 수험자는 아직 **Basic** 레벨의 실력을 갖추지 못했다.

Notes

Notes

Notes

The Official Guide to the TOEFL iBT® Test 7TH EDITION

해설 및 정답

McGraw Hill · YBM

The Official Guide to the TOEFL iBT® Test

Test SEVENTH EDITION ⑦

········· 해설 및 정답 ·········

Contents

QUESTION TYPES

Type 1 예제	p. 37

"...Sculptures must, for example, be stable, which requires an understanding of the properties of mass, weight distribution, and stress. Paintings must have rigid stretchers so that the canvas will be taut, and the paint must not deteriorate, crack, or discolor. These are problems that must be overcome by the artist because they tend to intrude upon their conception of the work. For example, in the early Italian Renaissance, bronze statues of horses with a raised foreleg usually had a cannonball under that hoof. This was done because the cannonball was needed to support the weight of the leg. In other words, the demands of the laws of physics, not the sculptor's aesthetic intentions, placed the ball there. That this device was a necessary structural compromise is clear from the fact that the cannonball quickly disappeared when sculptors learned how to strengthen the internal structure of a statue with iron braces (iron being much stronger than bronze)..."

According to paragraph 2, sculptors in the Italian Renaissance stopped using cannonballs in bronze statues of horses because
Ⓐ they began using a material that made the statues weigh less
Ⓑ they found a way to strengthen the statues internally
Ⓒ the aesthetic tastes of the public had changed over time
Ⓓ the cannonballs added too much weight to the statues

"…예를 들면, 조각상들은 안정감이 있어야 하는데, 이를 위해서는 질량, 무게의 분산 그리고 응력의 속성에 대한 이해가 필수적이다. 회화에서는 캔버스를 팽팽하게 해 줄 단단한 캔버스 틀이 필요하고 물감은 부패하거나, 갈라지거나, 변색되어서는 안 된다. 이런 문제들은 작품에 대한 미술가의 구상에 방해가 되기 때문에 미술가 자신이 극복해야 한다. 예를 들면, 이탈리아 르네상스 초기에 앞다리를 쳐든 모습을 한 청동 말 조각상의 말발굽 아래에는 흔히 포탄이 놓여 있었다. 말 다리의 무게를 지탱하기 위해 포탄이 필요했기 때문이었다. 다시 말해서 미술가의 미적인 의도가 아니라 물리법칙 때문에 포탄을 그곳에 놓아둔 것이었다. 이러한 장치가 불가피한 구조적 절충안이었다는 것은 조각가들이 쇠로 만든 버팀대로 조각의 내부 구조를 강화하는 방법을 터득하고 난 후 포탄이 바로 사라졌다는 사실을 보면 명백히 알 수 있다. (쇠가 청동보다 훨씬 강하다)…"

두 번째 단락에 따르면, 이탈리아 르네상스 시대의 조각가들이 청동 말 조각상에 포탄을 더 이상 사용하지 않게 된 이유는?
Ⓐ 조각상의 무게를 가볍게 할 수 있는 재료를 사용하기 시작했기 때문에
Ⓑ 조각상을 내부적으로 강화할 수 있는 방법을 발견했기 때문에
Ⓒ 대중의 미적인 취향이 시간이 흐르면서 변했기 때문에
Ⓓ 포탄이 조각상에 너무 많은 하중을 주었기 때문에

material 재료   statue 동상   strengthen 강화하다

해설 두 번째 단락에서 답을 찾을 것을 요구하고 있으므로 관련 정보를 찾기 위해 지문 전체를 다 훑어볼 필요는 없다. 보기 A는 조각가들이 조각상의 무게를 줄이는 재료를 사용하기 시작했기 때문에 들린 말의 다리에 포탄을 받치는 것을 그만두었다고 했지만 읽기 지문에는 조각상의 무게를 줄이는 것에 대한 내용이 없다. 대신 조각가들이 조각상의 무게를 지탱할 더 좋은 방법을 터득했다고 나와 있다. 보기 C는 대중의 취향이 바뀌었기 때문에 그런 변화가 일어났다는 내용이므로 지문의 내용과 모순된다. 보기 D는 포탄이 조각상의 무게를 가중시켰다는 내용으로, 이 역시 지문의 내용과 모순된다. 보기 B는 조각의 변화에 대해 지문이 제시하는 이유를 정확하게 짚어냈으므로 정답이다. 조각가들이 조각상의 내부를 강화할 방법을 개발했기 때문에 포탄이 필요 없게 되었다는 것이다.

어휘 sculpture 조각, 조각품   stable 안정된, 튼튼한   property 고유의 성질, 특성, 재산, 소유(권)   stress 응력, 압력, 강조   rigid 단단한, 엄격한   stretcher 캔버스 틀, 들것   taut (밧줄, 돛이) 팽팽한, 긴장된   deteriorate (질 등이) 나빠지다, 악화되다   crack 깨지다, 금이 가다, 갈라지다   discolor 변색[퇴색]하다, 더러워지다   overcome 극복하다, 압도하다   intrude 참견하다, 침입하다   bronze 청동   cannonball 포탄   hoof (소, 말 따위의) 발굽   sculptor 조각가   aesthetic 심미적인   compromise 절충안, 타협   internal 내부의, 내재적인   brace 버팀대

Type 2 예제

p. 38

"The United States in the 1800s was full of practical, hardworking people who did not consider the arts—from theater to painting—useful. In addition, the public's attitude that European art was better than American art both discouraged and infuriated American artists. In the early 1900s there was a strong feeling among artists that the United States was long overdue in developing art that did not reproduce European traditions. Everybody agreed that the heart and soul of the new country should be reflected in its art. But opinions differed about what this art would be like and how it would develop."

According to paragraph 1, all of the following were true of American art in the late 1800s and early 1900s EXCEPT:

Ⓐ Most Americans thought art was unimportant.

Ⓑ American art generally copied European styles and traditions.

Ⓒ Most Americans considered American art inferior to European art.

Ⓓ American art was very popular with European audiences.

"1800년대 미국에는 (연극에서부터 회화까지) 예술이 쓸모 있지 않다고 생각한 현실적이고, 근면한 사람들이 아주 많았다. 게다가 미국 예술보다 유럽 예술이 더 낫다는 대중의 태도는 미국 예술가들의 사기를 꺾었고, 그들을 분노하게 만들었다. 1900년대 초에는 미국이 유럽의 전통을 모방하지 않는 예술을 발전시킬 때가 무르익었다는 인식이 예술가들 사이에 강하게 자리잡고 있었다. 신대륙의 감정과 영혼이 예술에 반영되어야 한다는 데 모두가 동의했다. 그러나 그런 예술이 어떤 모습이어야 하며, 어떻게 발전되어야 하는지에 대해서는 의견이 분분했다."

첫 번째 단락에 따르면, 1800년대 말과 1900년대 초, 미국 예술에 대한 다음 설명 중 사실이 아닌 것은?

Ⓐ 대부분의 미국인은 예술이 중요하지 않다고 생각했다.

Ⓑ 미국 예술은 대체로 유럽의 양식과 전통을 모방했다.

Ⓒ 대부분의 미국인은 미국 예술이 유럽 예술보다 못하다고 생각했다.

Ⓓ 미국 예술은 유럽의 애호가들에게 아주 인기가 높았다.

copy 모방하다　**consider** 여기다, 간주하다　**popular** 인기 있는

해설　틀린 정보 찾기 문제에서는 응시자가 고른 답이 지문에서 언급되지 않았는지 확인하기 위해 지문 전체를 검토해야 하는 경우가 있다. 그러나 이 예제에서는 문제가 하나의 단락에 국한되어 있으므로 그 단락에 있는 문장만을 근거로 답을 찾으면 된다. 보기 A는 단락의 첫 번째 문장을 바꿔 말한 것이다. 대부분의 미국인은 예술을 쓸모 있다고 생각하지 않았기 때문에 중요하게 여기지 않았다. 보기 B는 세 번째 문장과 같은 뜻이다. "미국이 유럽의 전통을 모방하지 않는 예술을 발전시킬 때가 무르익었다"는 것은 이 시점까지 미국 예술은 유럽 전통을 모방했다는 뜻이 된다. 보기 C는 지문의 두 번째 문장에 해당된다. 미국 예술가들은 "미국 예술보다 유럽 예술이 더 낫다는 대중의 태도" 때문에 좌절했다. 보기 D는 지문 어디에도 언급되지 않은 내용이므로 정답은 D다.

어휘　**practical** 실용적인, 현실적인　**hardworking** 근면한, 열심히 일하는　**infuriate** 격분[격앙]시키다　**overdue** 늦은, 기한이 지난, 과도한　**heart and soul** 마음과 영혼, (사물의) 핵심, 몸과 마음을 다하여　**differ** 다르다, 틀리다　**inferior to** ~보다 열등한

"In the animal world the task of moving about is fulfilled in many ways. For some animals locomotion is accomplished by changes in body shape..."

The word "locomotion" in the passage is closest in meaning to
Ⓐ evolution
Ⓑ movement
Ⓒ survival
Ⓓ escape

"동물의 세계에서 이동하는 일은 여러 가지 방식으로 수행된다. 어떤 동물들의 경우에는 몸의 형태를 바꿈으로써 이동이 이뤄진다…"

지문의 단어 locomotion과 의미상 가장 가까운 것은?
Ⓐ 진화
Ⓑ 이동
Ⓒ 생존
Ⓓ 탈출

해설　locomotion은 '장소와 장소 사이를 이동하는 능력'을 의미한다. 지문에서 이 단어는 앞 문장에 있는 "이동하는 일(the task of moving)"과 같은 뜻으로 쓰였다. 따라서 정답은 B다.

어휘　task 일, 과제　fulfill 이행하다, 달성하다　locomotion 이동, 운동

"Some poisonous snake bites need to be treated immediately or the victim will suffer paralysis..."

In stating that the victim will "suffer paralysis" the author means that the victim will
Ⓐ lose the ability to move
Ⓑ become unconscious
Ⓒ undergo shock
Ⓓ feel great pain

"일부 독사에게 물리면 즉시 치료해야 한다. 그렇지 않으면 환자가 마비 증세를 겪게 된다 …"

글쓴이가 말한 suffer paralysis는 환자가 어떻게 된다는 것을 의미하는가?
Ⓐ 움직일 수 있는 능력을 잃는다.
Ⓑ 의식을 잃는다.
Ⓒ 쇼크를 겪는다.
Ⓓ 심한 통증을 느낀다.

해설　문제로 나온 단어와 보기는 모두 구의 형태로 제시되었다. paralysis(마비)란 "움직일 수 없음"이라는 뜻으로 독사에게 물려서 독이 퍼지고 "마비 증세를 겪으면(suffer paralysis)", 그 사람은 움직일 수는 있는 능력을 잃게 될 것이다. 따라서 정답은 보기 A다.

어휘　poisonous snake 독사　paralysis 마비　become unconscious 의식을 잃다　undergo 겪다

"...The first weekly newspaper in the colonies was the *Boston Gazette*, established in 1719, the same year that marked the appearance of Philadelphia's first newspaper, the *American Mercury*, where the young Benjamin Franklin worked. By 1760 Boston had 4 newspapers and 5 other printing establishments; Philadelphia, two newspapers and three other presses; and New York, three newspapers. The distribution, if not the sale, of newspapers was assisted by the establishment of a postal service in 1710, which had a network of some 65 offices by 1770, serving all 13 colonies..."

The word "which" in the passage refers to

Ⓐ distribution   Ⓑ sale

Ⓒ newspaper   Ⓓ postal service

"…동부 13개 주에서 발행된 최초의 주간 신문은 1719년에 창간된 〈보스턴 가제트〉지다. 1719년은 필라델피아 주에서 발행된 최초의 신문이자, 벤자민 프랭클린이 젊은 시절에 일했던 〈아메리칸 머큐리〉 지가 발행된 해이기도 하다. 1760년에 보스턴에서는 4개의 신문과 5개의 다른 간행물이 발간되고 있었다. 필라델피아에서는 2개의 신문과 3개의 다른 출판물들이 발간되었으며, 뉴욕에서는 3개의 신문이 발행되었다. 신문의 판매는 아니더라도 그 보급은 1710년 우편 서비스의 확립으로 지원을 받았는데, 이것은 1770년까지 65개의 지국망을 가졌고, 동부 13개 주에 보급되어 …"

지문에서 which가 가리키는 것은?

Ⓐ 배포   Ⓑ 판매

Ⓒ 신문   Ⓓ 우편 서비스

해설 이 예제에서 음영 처리된 단어는 관계대명사로, 관계사절인 "which had a network of some 65 offices…"의 주어다. which는 바로 앞에 있는 우편 서비스(postal service)를 가리킨다. 따라서 정답은 D다.

어휘 colony 동부 13주; 미국 독립 때 합중국을 형성했던 13개주   establish 설립하다, 창설하다   press 출판물   distribution 배포, 보급   postal service 우편 서비스

"...Roots anchor the plant in one of two ways or sometimes by a combination of the two. The first is by occupying a large volume of shallow soil around the plant's base with a *fibrous root system*, one consisting of many thin, profusely branched roots. Since these kinds of roots grow relatively close to the soil surface, they effectively control soil erosion. Grass roots are especially well suited to this purpose. Fibrous roots capture water as it begins to percolate into the ground and so must draw their mineral supplies from the surface soil before the nutrients are leached to lower levels..."

The phrase "this purpose" in the passage refers to

Ⓐ combining two root systems

Ⓑ feeding the plant

Ⓒ preventing soil erosion

Ⓓ leaching nutrients

"…뿌리는 두 가지 방법 중 하나 또는 두 방법의 조합으로 식물을 고정시킨다. 첫 번째 방법은 식물의 아래쪽 둘레에 있는 많은 양의 얕은 토층에 가는 잔뿌리로 구성된 수염뿌리 계를 분포시키는 것이다. 이런 뿌리들은 상대적으로 지표면 근처에서 자라기 때문에 토양의 침식을 효과적으로 제어한다. 풀뿌리가 특히 이 목적에 잘 부합된다. 수염뿌리는 물이 땅에 스며들 때 물을 흡수하기 때문에, 영양소가 걸러져 함량이 적어지기 전에 지표면의 토양으로부터 공급되는 무기물을 흡수해야 한다…"

지문에서 this purpose가 가리키는 것은?

Ⓐ 두 개의 뿌리계를 결합하는 것

Ⓑ 식물에 영양소를 공급하는 것

Ⓒ 토양의 침식을 막는 것

Ⓓ 양분을 걸러내는 것

해설 이 예제에서 음영 처리된 구에는 지시어(this)와 명사(purpose)가 있다. 수염뿌리계는 흙을 일정 장소에 고정시킬 수 있으므로 침식을 막을 수 있는데 풀뿌리가 바로 수염뿌리계이다. 이 문장은 "Grass roots are especially well suited to preventing soil erosion.(풀뿌리는 특히 토양의 침식을 막는 데 적합하다)"로 고쳐 쓸 수 있으므로 정답은 C다.

어휘 **anchor** 고정시키다, 정박시키다   **occupy** 차지하다, 거주하다   **shallow** 얕은   **fibrous root** 수염뿌리   **profusely** 아낌없이, 풍부하게   **branch** 가지를 뻗다   **relatively** 상대적으로   **erosion** 침식   **be suited to** ~에 부합되다, 적합하다   **percolate** 스며들다, 침투하다   **nutrient** 영양소

"... Although we now tend to refer to the various crafts according to the materials used to construct them—clay, glass, wood, fiber, and metal—it was once common to think of crafts in terms of function, which led to their being known as the "applied arts." Approaching crafts from the point of view of function, we can divide them into simple categories: containers, shelters, and supports. There is no way around the fact that containers, shelters, and supports must be functional. The applied arts are thus bound by the laws of physics, which pertain to both the materials used in their making and the substances and things to be contained, supported, and sheltered. These laws are universal in their application, regardless of cultural beliefs, geography, or climate.

"…우리는 공예품을 제작에 사용된 재료(점토, 유리, 나무, 섬유, 금속)를 기준으로 부르는 경향이 있지만, 한때는 공예품을 기능의 관점에서 생각하는 것이 보편적이었기 때문에 공예품들을 '응용 미술'로 부르게 됐다. 기능의 관점에서 공예품에 접근하면, 용기, 덮개, 지지대 등 단순한 범주로 분류할 수 있다. 용기, 덮개, 지지대가 기능적이어야 한다는 것은 부인할 수 없다. 따라서 응용 미술은 물리 법칙에 지배되며, 물리 법칙은 공예품을 만드는 데 사용된 재료, 그리고 용기에 담기거나, 지지되거나, 차폐되는 물질이나 물건에 적용된다. 이 법칙들은 문화적 신념, 지리, 또는 기후와 무관하게 보편적으로 적용된다. 어떤 항아리에 바닥이 없거나 측면에 커다란 구멍이 있다면 그 항아리는 어떠한 전통적인 관념에서도

If a pot has no bottom or has large openings in its sides, it could hardly be considered a container in any traditional sense. Since the laws of physics, not some arbitrary decision, have determined the general form of applied-art objects, they follow basic patterns, so much so that functional forms can vary only within certain limits. Buildings without roofs, for example, are unusual because they depart from the norm. However, not all functional objects are exactly alike; that is why we recognize a Shang Dynasty vase as being different from an Inca vase. What varies is not the basic form but the incidental details that do not obstruct the object's primary function..."

Which of the following best expresses the essential information in the highlighted sentence in the passage? Incorrect answer choices change the meaning in important ways or leave out essential information.

Ⓐ Functional applied-art objects cannot vary much from the basic patterns determined by the laws of physics.

Ⓑ The function of applied-art objects is determined by basic patterns in the laws of physics.

Ⓒ Since functional applied-art objects vary only within certain limits, arbitrary decisions cannot have determined their general form.

Ⓓ The general form of applied-art objects is limited by some arbitrary decision that is not determined by the laws of physics.

용기로 생각하기 힘들다. 응용 미술 작품은 어떤 자의적 결정이 아니라 물리 법칙에 의해 일반적인 형태가 결정되므로, 이들은 기본적인 패턴을 따르는 경향이 강하여 기능적 형태는 어떤 한도 내에서만 변화가 가능하다. 예를 들면, 지붕이 없는 건물은 규범에서 벗어나는 것이므로 흔치 않다. 그러나 모든 기능적 사물들이 똑같지는 않다. 우리가 중국 상 왕조의 꽃병을 잉카 문명의 꽃병과 다른 것으로 인식할 수 있는 것은 이런 이유때문이다. 차이가 나는 것은 기본적인 형태들이 아니라 공예품의 주요 기능을 방해하지 않는 부수적인 세부 묘사다…"

다음 중 음영으로 표시된 문장이 담고 있는 핵심 정보를 가장 잘 표현한 것은? 정답 외의 보기들은 의미가 상당히 왜곡되거나 필수적인 정보가 빠져 있다.

Ⓐ 기능적인 응용 미술품들은 물리 법칙에 의해 결정된 기본 패턴을 크게 벗어날 수 없다.

Ⓑ 응용 미술품의 기능은 물리 법칙의 기본 패턴에 의해 결정된다.

Ⓒ 기능적인 응용 미술품은 일정 한도 내에서만 변하기 때문에 자의적인 결정에 의해 일반적인 형태를 결정할 수 없다.

Ⓓ 응용 미술품의 일반적인 형태는 물리 법칙을 따르지 않는 어떤 자의적 결정에 의해 제한된다.

determine 결정하다   vary 변하다, 바뀌다   arbitrary 자의적인

해설 문제에서 오답들이 문장의 원래 의미를 바꾸거나 중요한 정보를 누락한다고 말하고 있다는 점에 주목해야 한다. 보기 D는 기능적인 작품의 형태는 절대로 자의적이지 않다고 말한, 지문에 표시된 문장과는 달리 기능적인 작품들이 자의적이라고 말했다. B도 응용 미술 작품의 기능은 물리 법칙에 의해 결정된다고 했으므로 맞지 않는다. 지문에 표시된 문장에서 "작품의 형태"는 물리 법칙에 의해 결정되지만 그 기능은 사람이 결정하는 것이라고 했기 때문이다. C는 기능적인 작품의 형태는 자의적이지 않다고 말했지만, 기본적인 형태를 결정하는 것이 물리 법칙이라는 사실을 언급하지 않아 중요한 정보를 빠뜨렸다. A는 문제에 제시된 문장과 의미가 같고, 핵심 내용도 모두 담고 있다.

어휘 refer to ~라고 일컫다   craft 공예품   in terms of ~의 관점에서   divide into ~로 분류하다   container 용기   shelter 피난처   support 덮개, 지지대   there is no way around the fact that~ ~라는 사실은 부인할 수 없다   be bound by ~에 의해 지배되다, 제한되다   pertain to ~에 포함하다, 속하다   depart from ~에서 벗어나다   norm 규범   incidental 부수적인, 우연히 일어나는   obstruct 방해하다, 차단하다

"...The nineteenth century brought with it a burst of new discoveries and inventions that revolutionized the candle industry and made lighting available to all. In the early-to-mid-nineteenth century, a process was developed to refine tallow (fat from animals) with alkali and sulfuric acid. The result was a product called stearin. Stearin is harder and burns longer than unrefined tallow. This breakthrough meant that it was possible to make tallow candles that would not produce the usual smoke and rancid odor. Stearins were also derived from palm oils, so vegetable waxes as well as animal fats could be used to make candles..."

Which of the following can be inferred from paragraph 1 about candles before the nineteenth century?

Ⓐ They did not smoke when they were burned.

Ⓑ They produced a pleasant odor as they burned.

Ⓒ They were not available to everyone.

Ⓓ They contained sulfuric acid.

"…19세기에는 양초 산업에 혁명을 가져온 새로운 발견과 발명품들이 쏟아져 나와 모든 사람들이 조명을 이용할 수 있게 되었다. 19세기 초에서 중반까지 알칼리와 황산으로 수지(동물에서 뽑아낸 지방)를 정제하는 공정이 개발되었다. 그 결과 스테아린이라는 제품이 만들어졌다. 스테아린은 정제되지 않은 수지보다 더 단단하고 오래 탄다. 이러한 획기적인 기술 덕분에 기존의 양초에서 뿜어 나오던 연기와 독한 냄새가 나지 않는 수지 양초를 만들 수 있었다. 스테아린은 야자유에서도 추출할 수 있어서 동물의 지방뿐만 아니라 식물 밀랍으로도 양초를 만들 수 있었다 …"

첫 번째 단락에서 19세기 이전의 양초에 대해 어떤 추론을 할 수 있는가?

Ⓐ 탈 때 연기가 나지 않았다.

Ⓑ 탈 때 좋은 향기가 났다.

Ⓒ 모든 사람이 사용할 수 없었다.

Ⓓ 황산이 포함되어 있었다.

pleasant 기분 좋은　contain 포함하다

해설 지문의 첫 번째 문장에서 글쓴이는 "새로운 발견과 발명 덕에 모든 사람이 조명을 이용할 수 있었다"고 말하고 있다. 이 글에서 얘기하고 있는 유일한 조명은 양초다. 새로운 발견이 모든 사람이 양초를 이용할 수 있게 할 정도로 중요한 것이었다면, 그러한 발견이 있기 전에는 모든 사람이 양초를 이용할 수 있었던 것은 아니라는 사실을 추론할 수 있다. 따라서 정답은 보기 C다. 보기 A와 B는 지문의 내용("흔히 발생하는 연기와 독한 냄새")과 명백히 상충되기 때문에 답에서 제외된다. 황산은 19세기 이전이 아니라, 19세기에 스테아린을 만들기 위해 최초로 사용되었으므로 보기 D도 제외된다.

어휘 burst 돌발, (갑작스러운) 활동, 폭발하다　revolutionize 혁명을 일으키다, 대변혁을 가져오다　refine 정제하다, 불순물을 없애다, 세련되게 하다　tallow 수지, 쇠기름　alkali 알칼리, 염기성 물질　sulfuric acid 황산　stearin 스테아린, 경유(지방의 주성분)　breakthrough (과학 등의) 획기적 발전, 타개책　rancid 악취가 나는, 고약한, 불쾌한　odor 냄새, 악취　derive from ~로부터 끌어내다, ~에서 나오다　palm oil 야자유　vegetable wax 목랍

Fossils—the mineralized remains of plants and animals—provide important clues to life in the past. The fossils collected by Mary Anning (1799–1847) along the southwest coast of England helped shape modern science. Some fossils found or excavated by Anning were truly spectacular. While still a girl, Anning recovered the body of a large, strange animal whose skull was discovered by her brother in 1810. Thought to be a crocodile when only its head had been found, the fossil set off years of debate, with the animal eventually identified as an Ichthyosaurus, a previously unknown reptile. In 1824, she discovered the first intact skeleton of Plesiosaurus, a four-limbed swimming creature with a small head, and in 1828, the remains of the first flying reptile located outside of Germany. Finds such as these were rare and dangerous to unearth. The cliffs rising above Lyme Regis beaches were unstable with frequent mudslides in winter and during storms, yet these were best times for collecting fossils—the crumbling and washing away of parts of the cliffs left fossils newly exposed. Unless such fossils were collected right away, they would be washed out to sea. Given these conditions, it is hardly surprising that Anning narrowly escaped severe injury several times.

Which of the following can be inferred about Mary Anning from her efforts to search for fossils on the cliffs of Lyme Regis?

Ⓐ She was brave and was not easily discouraged.

Ⓑ She stopped searching for fossils when conditions became stormy.

Ⓒ She suffered serious injuries multiple times as a result of her searches.

Ⓓ She sometimes waited for fossils to wash out to sea before collecting them.

식물과 동물의 유해가 광물화된 형태인 화석은 과거의 생명체에 관한 중요한 단서를 제공한다. 메리 애닝(1799- 1847)이 영국 남서부 해안에서 수집한 화석은 현대 과학을 형성하는 데 중요한 역할을 했다. 애닝이 발견하거나 발굴해낸 화석 일부는 실로 놀라운 것이었다. 애닝이 아직 소녀였을 때 그녀는 크고 이상한 동물의 시체를 발견했는데, 그 동물의 두개골은 1810년에 그녀의 오빠에 의해 발견되었다. 처음 화석의 머리만 발견되었을 때는 악어로 여겨졌지만, 이후 수년간 논쟁이 이어졌으며 결국 그 동물은 이전에는 잘 알려지지 않은 파충류인 이크티오사우루스로 확인되었다. 1824년에 그녀는 작은 머리의 네 발 달린 수중 생물 플레시오사우루스의 온전한 형태를 갖춘 최초의 해골을 발견했으며, 1828년에는 독일 이외의 곳에서 최초의 비행 파충류의 유해를 발견했다. 이러한 발견들은 드물었고 발굴 작업은 위험했다. 라임 레지스 해변 위로 솟아오른 절벽은 겨울철과 폭풍우가 몰아칠 때 발생하는 잦은 산사태로 불안정했지만, 바로 이 때 절벽의 일부가 무너지고 씻겨 나가면서 화석이 새롭게 노출되었기 때문에 화석을 수집하기에는 최적기였다. 이러한 화석들은 즉시 수집되지 않으면 바다로 씻겨 나가곤 했다. 이러한 상황들을 고려할 때, 애닝이 여러 번 심각한 부상을 입을 뻔한 위기에서 간신히 벗어났다는 사실은 그리 놀랍지 않다.

라임 레지스의 절벽에서 화석을 발굴하기 위해 노력했던 애닝에게서 추론 가능한 것은 다음 중 무엇인가?

Ⓐ 그녀는 용감했고 쉽게 좌절하지 않았다.

Ⓑ 비바람이 몰아치는 상태가 되면 그녀는 화석 발굴을 멈추었다.

Ⓒ 그녀는 발굴 작업의 결과로 여러 번 심각한 부상을 입었다.

Ⓓ 그녀는 때때로 화석을 수집하기 전에 화석이 바다로 씻겨 나가는 것을 기다렸다.

해설 메리 애닝은 '용감했고 쉽게 좌절하지 않았다'는 올바른 추론인 보기 A는 그녀가 화석 발굴을 할 때의 상황에 대해 묘사한 지문의 마지막 세 문장에 기반한다. 이들은 그녀가 화석을 찾기 위해 처해야 하는 조건을 설명한다. 문장에 따르면 폭풍이 불면 절벽 일부가 물에 씻겨 나가 이전에 묻혀 있던 화석을 새롭게 노출시켜주기 때문에 화석이 가장 잘 발견되었다. 또한 새롭게 노출된 화석은 바로 수집하지 않으면 바다로 씻겨 나가서 사라질 수 있기 때문에 화석을 찾는 사람들은 바로 발굴 작업을 해야 한다고 써 있다. 따라서 발굴에 관해 제공된 자세한 정보에서 애닝이 용기와 결연함을 가진 사람이라는 것을 명백히 알 수 있다.

어휘 mineralize 광물화하다   shape (어떤 학문을) 형성하다   excavate 발굴하다   spectacular 놀라운   reptile 파충류   intact 온전한 형태의   four-limbed 네 발 달린   unearth 발굴하다   mudslide 산사태   crumbling 바스러짐

"...Sensitivity to physical laws is thus an important consideration for the maker of applied-art objects. It is often taken for granted that this is also true for the maker of fine-art objects. This assumption misses a significant difference between the two disciplines. Fine-art objects are not constrained by the laws of physics in the same way that applied-art objects are. Because their primary purpose is not functional, they are only limited in terms of the materials used to make them. Sculptures must, for example, be stable, which requires an understanding of the properties of mass, weight distribution, and stress. Paintings must have rigid stretchers so that the canvas will be taut, and the paint must not deteriorate, crack, or discolor. These are problems that must be overcome by the artist because they tend to intrude upon his or her conception of the work. For example, in the early Italian Renaissance, bronze statues of horses with a raised foreleg usually had a cannonball under that hoof. This was done because the cannonball was needed to support the weight of the leg..."

Why does the author discuss the "bronze statues of horses" created by artists in the early Italian Renaissance?

Ⓐ To provide an example of a problem related to the laws of physics that a fine artist must overcome

Ⓑ To argue that fine artists are unconcerned with the laws of physics

Ⓒ To contrast the relative sophistication of modern artists in solving problems related to the laws of physics

Ⓓ To note an exceptional piece of art constructed without the aid of technology

"…그러므로 물리 법칙에 대한 민감도는 응용 미술 작품의 제작자들이 고려해야 할 중요한 요소다. 순수 미술 작품의 제작자들 역시 마찬가지라는 생각이 당연시되곤 한다. 이러한 주장은 두 분야 간의 중요한 차이를 간과하고 있다. 순수 미술 작품은 응용 미술 작품과 같은 방식으로 물리 법칙의 제약을 받지 않는다. 순수 미술 작품의 주된 목적은 기능적인 것이 아니기 때문에 그 작품을 제작하는 데 사용되는 재료에 의해서만 제약을 받는다. 예를 들면, 조각상들은 안정감이 있어야 하는데, 이를 위해서는 질량, 무게의 분산 그리고 응력의 속성에 대한 이해가 필수적이다. 회화에서는 캔버스를 팽팽하게 해 줄 단단한 캔버스 틀이 필요하고 물감은 부패하거나, 갈라지거나, 변색되어서는 안 된다. 이런 문제들은 작품에 대한 미술가의 구상에 방해가 되기 때문에 미술가 자신이 극복해야 한다. 예를 들면, 이탈리아 르네상스 초기에 앞다리를 쳐든 모습을 한 청동 말 조각상의 말발굽 아래에는 흔히 포탄이 놓여 있었다. 말 다리의 무게를 지탱하기 위해 포탄이 필요했기 때문이었다…"

글쓴이는 왜 이탈리아 초기 르네상스 예술가들이 만든 청동 말 조각상에 대해 이야기하고 있는가?

Ⓐ 순수 미술가가 극복해야 할 물리 법칙과 관련된 문제의 예를 보여 주기 위해

Ⓑ 순수 미술가는 물리 법칙에 관심이 없음을 주장하기 위해

Ⓒ 물리 법칙과 관련된 문제를 해결하는 데 현대 미술가들이 상대적으로 더 정교하다는 사실을 대조하기 위해

Ⓓ 기술의 도움 없이 제작된 예외적인 예술 작품을 언급하기 위해

be unconcerned with ~에 관심이 없다
sophistication 정교함, 세련됨　exceptional 예외적인

해설　'청동 말 조각상'에 대해 언급한 문장이 "예를 들면(For example)"으로 시작되는 것에 주목해야 한다. 글쓴이는 이 단락의 앞 부분에서 자신이 소개한 내용을 예를 들어 설명하고 있다. 이 단락은 물리 법칙에 의한 제약이 응용 미술이나 공예와 달리 순수 미술에 어떤 영향을 끼치는가를 대조해서 보여 주고 있다. 순수 미술가들은 실용적인 물건을 만드는 데 관심이 있는 것이 아니므로 응용 미술보다는 제약을 덜 받는다. 그러나 순수 미술 작품도 특정 재료로 제작되므로 순수 미술가는 그 재료의 물리적 성질을 고려해야 한다. 위 글에서 글쓴이는 미술가들이 청동의 물리적 특성 때문에 말 조각상의 들린 앞다리를 지탱할 수 있는 받침대를 사용했다는 얘기를 하기 위해 청동 말 조각상을 예로 든 것이다. 따라서 정답은 A다.

어휘　sensitivity 민감도, 감수성　consideration 고려할 사항, 고려　applied-art 응용 미술　object 작품, 물건　It is taken for granted that ~을 당연시하다　fine-art 순수 미술　assumption 주장, 가정　significant 중요한, 상당한　discipline 분야, 학과, 훈련　constrain 억누르다, 강요하다　primary 주된, 첫째의

Type 8 예제
p. 46

One of the most puzzling aspects of the paintings is their location. Other rock paintings—for example, those of Bushmen in South Africa—are either located near cave entrances or completely in the open. **(A)** Cave paintings in France and Spain, however, are in recesses and caverns far removed from original cave entrances. **(B)** This means that artists were forced to work in cramped spaces and without sources of natural light. **(C)** It also implies that whoever made them did not want them to be easily found. **(D)** Since cave dwellers normally lived close to entrances, there must have been some reason why so many generations of Lascaux cave dwellers hid their art.

Directions: Look at the part of the passage that is displayed above. The letters **(A)**, **(B)**, **(C)**, and **(D)** indicate where the following sentence could be added.

This made it easy for the artists to paint and display them for the rest of the cave dwellers.

Where would the sentence best fit?

Ⓐ Choice A   Ⓑ Choice B   Ⓒ Choice C   Ⓓ Choice D

그림의 가장 이해하기 어려운 부분 중 하나는 그 위치이다. 다른 암각화들—예를 들면, 남아프리카의 부시맨의 그림들—은 동굴 입구 근처에 있거나 완전히 바깥 쪽에 위치해 있다. **(A)** 그러나 프랑스와 스페인의 동굴 벽화들은 원래의 동굴 입구에서 멀리 떨어진 안쪽에 위치해 있다. **(B)** 이는 예술가들이 좁은 공간에서 자연광원 없이 작업해야 했다는 것을 의미한다. **(C)** 이것은 또한 작품을 만든 사람들이 타인에게 쉽게 발견되길 원치 않았음을 시사한다. **(D)** 헐거인들은 일반적으로 입구 가까이 살았기 때문에, 라스코 헐거인들이 수대에 걸쳐 그들의 예술을 숨겼던 이유가 있었을 것이다.

지시문: 위에 제시된 지문의 일부를 보시오. 지문에 표시된 **(A), (B), (C), (D)** 중 하나에 다음 문장이 삽입될 수 있다.

이것은 예술가들이 다른 헐거인들을 위해 벽화를 그리고 전시하는 것을 용이하게 해 주었다.

이 문장이 들어갈 가장 적당한 위치는?

Ⓐ   Ⓑ   Ⓒ   Ⓓ

해설 이 예제의 정답은 A이다. 제시된 문장은 두 번째 문장 뒤에 있을 때만 의미가 통한다. 글쓴이는 동굴 입구 근처나 외부에 위치한 남아프리카의 암각화와, 동굴 깊숙한 곳에 위치한 스페인과 프랑스의 암각화를 대조하여 설명하고 있다. 삽입될 문장은 암각화를 "예술가들이 그림을 그리고 다른 사람들에게 전시하기 쉽게" 만드는 요인(This)에 관해 말한다. 동굴 입구 근처나 외부에 있다는 사실이 이러한 요인이며 삽입된 문장은 암각화의 그러한 위치에 관한 내용 뒤에 와야 한다.

어휘 puzzling 이해하기 어려운   entrance 입구   in recess 깊숙한 곳에   cavern (큰) 동굴   cramped space 좁은 공간   imply 시사하다   dweller 주거인   generation 세대   display 전시하다

Type 9 예제
p. 47

Applied Arts and Fine Arts

Although we now tend to refer to the various crafts according to the materials used to construct them—clay, glass, wood, fiber, and metal—it was once common to think of crafts in terms of function, which led to their being known as the "applied arts." Approaching crafts from the point of view of function, we can divide them into simple categories: containers, shelters, and supports. There is no way around the fact that containers, shelters, and supports must be functional. The applied arts are thus bound by the laws of physics, which pertain to both the materials used in their making and the substances and things to be contained, supported, and sheltered. These laws are universal in their application, regardless of cultural beliefs, geography, or

응용 미술과 순수 미술

우리는 공예품을 제작에 사용된 재료(점토, 유리, 나무, 섬유, 금속)를 기준으로 부르는 경향이 있지만, 한때는 공예품을 기능의 관점에서 생각하는 것이 보편적이었기 때문에 공예품들을 '응용 미술'로 부르게 됐다. 기능의 관점에서 공예품에 접근하면, 용기, 덮개, 지지대 등 단순한 범주로 분류할 수 있다. 용기, 덮개, 지지대가 기능적이어야 한다는 것은 부인할 수 없다. 따라서 응용 미술은 물리 법칙에 지배되며, 물리 법칙은 공예품을 만드는 데 사용된 재료, 그리고 용기에 담기거나, 지지되거나, 차폐되는 물질이나 물건에 적용된다. 이 법칙들은 문화적 신념, 지리, 또는 기후와 무관하게 보편적으로 적용된다. 어떤 항아리에 바닥이 없거나 측면에 커다란 구멍이 있다면 그 항아리는 어떠한 전통적인 관념에서도 용

climate. If a pot has no bottom or has large openings in its sides, it could hardly be considered a container in any traditional sense. Since the laws of physics, not some arbitrary decision, have determined the general form of applied-art objects, they follow basic patterns, so much so that functional forms can vary only within certain limits. Buildings without roofs, for example, are unusual because they depart from the norm. However, not all functional objects are exactly alike; that is why we recognize a Shang Dynasty vase as being different from an Inca vase. What varies is not the basic form but the incidental details that do not obstruct the object's primary function.

Sensitivity to physical laws is thus an important consideration for the maker of applied-art objects. It is often taken for granted that this is also true for the maker of fine-art objects. This assumption misses a significant difference between the two disciplines. Fine-art objects are not constrained by the laws of physics in the same way that applied-art objects are. Because their primary purpose is not functional, they are only limited in terms of the materials used to make them. Sculptures must, for example, be stable, which requires an understanding of the properties of mass, weight distribution, and stress. Paintings must have rigid stretchers so that the canvas will be taut, and the paint must not deteriorate, crack, or discolor. These are problems that must be overcome by the artist because they tend to intrude upon their conception of the work. For example, in the early Italian Renaissance, bronze statues of horses with a raised foreleg usually had a cannonball under that hoof. This was done because the cannonball was needed to support the weight of the leg. In other words, the demands of the laws of physics, not the sculptor's aesthetic intentions, placed the ball there. That this device was a necessary structural compromise is clear from the fact that the cannonball quickly disappeared when sculptors learned how to strengthen the internal structure of a statue with iron braces (iron being much stronger than bronze).

Even though the fine arts in the twentieth century often treat materials in new ways, the basic difference in attitude of artists in relation to their materials in the fine arts and the applied arts remains relatively constant. It would therefore not be too great an exaggeration to say that practitioners of the fine arts work to overcome the limitations of their materials, whereas those engaged in the applied arts work in concert with their materials.

An introductory sentence for a brief summary of the passage is provided below. Complete the summary by selecting the THREE answer choices that express the most important ideas in the passage. Some sentences do not belong in the summary because they express ideas that are not presented in the passage or are minor ideas in the passage. **This question is worth 2 points.**

기로 생각하기 힘들다. 응용 미술 작품은 어떤 자의적 결정이 아니라 물리 법칙에 의해 일반적인 형태가 결정되므로, 이들은 기본적인 패턴을 따르는 경향이 강하여 기능적 형태는 어떤 한도 내에서만 변화가 가능하다. 예를 들면 지붕이 없는 건물은 규범에서 벗어나는 것이므로 흔치 않다. 그러나 모든 기능적 사물들이 똑같지는 않다. 우리가 중국 상 왕조의 꽃병을 잉카 문명의 꽃병과 다른 것으로 인식할 수 있는 것은 이런 이유 때문이다. 차이가 나는 것은 기본적인 형태들이 아니라 공예품의 주요 기능을 방해하지 않는 부수적인 세부 묘사다.

그러므로 물리 법칙에 대한 민감도는 응용 미술 작품의 제작자들이 고려해야 할 중요한 요소다. 순수 미술 작품의 제작자들 역시 마찬가지라는 생각이 당연시되곤 한다. 이러한 주장은 두 분야 간의 중요한 차이를 간과하고 있다. 순수 미술 작품은 응용 미술 작품과 같은 방식으로 물리 법칙의 제약을 받지 않는다. 순수 미술 작품의 주된 목적은 기능적인 것이 아니기 때문에, 그 작품을 제작하는 데 사용되는 재료에 의해서만 제약을 받는다. 예를 들면, 조각상들은 안정감이 있어야 하는데, 이를 위해서는 질량, 무게의 분산 그리고 응력의 속성에 대한 이해가 필수적이다. 회화에서는 캔버스를 팽팽하게 해 줄 단단한 캔버스 틀이 필요하고 물감은 부패하거나, 갈라지거나, 변색되어서는 안 된다. 이런 문제들은 작품에 대한 미술가의 구상에 방해가 되기 때문에 미술가 자신이 극복해야 한다. 예를 들면, 이탈리아 르네상스 초기에 앞다리를 쳐든 모습을 한 청동 말 조각상의 말발굽 아래에는 흔히 포탄이 놓여 있었다. 말 다리의 무게를 지탱하기 위해 포탄이 필요했기 때문이었다. 다시 말해서 미술가의 미적인 의도가 아니라 물리 법칙 때문에 포탄을 그곳에 놓아둔 것이었다. 이러한 장치가 불가피한 구조적 절충안이었다는 것은 조각가들이 쇠로 만든 버팀대로 조각의 내부 구조를 강화하는 방법을 터득하고 난 후 포탄이 바로 사라졌다는 사실을 보면 명백히 알 수 있다. (쇠가 청동보다 훨씬 강하다)

20세기 순수 미술에서 재료를 새로운 방식으로 다루는 일이 종종 있지만, 순수 미술과 응용 미술에서 재료와 관련해 미술가들이 갖는 태도의 기본적인 차이는 비교적 변함이 없다. 따라서 순수 미술을 하는 사람들은 그들이 사용하는 재료의 한계를 극복하기 위해 작업하고, 응용 미술을 하는 사람들은 사용하는 재료와 조화를 이뤄 작업한다는 것이 과장된 말은 아니다.

이 지문을 간단히 요약하기 위한 도입 문장이 아래에 제시되어 있다. 아래 보기들 중에서 지문의 가장 중요한 개념을 표현한 문장 3개를 골라 요약을 완성하라. 보기들 중에는 지문에 나오지 않았거나 중요하지 않은 개념이기 때문에 요약문으로 적절치 않은 것들도 있다. 이 문제의 배점은 2점이다.

This passage discusses fundamental differences between applied-art objects and fine-art objects.

이 지문은 응용 미술 작품과 순수 미술 작품의 근본적인 차이를 논하고 있다.

Answer Choices

Ⓐ Applied-art objects fulfill functions, such as containing or sheltering, and objects with the same function have similar characteristics because they are constrained by their purpose.

Ⓑ It is easy to recognize that Shang Dynasty vases are different from Inca vases.

Ⓒ Fine-art objects are not functional, so they are limited only by the properties of the materials used.

Ⓓ Renaissance sculptors learned to use iron braces to strengthen the internal structures of bronze statues.

Ⓔ In the twentieth century, fine artists and applied artists became more similar to one another in their attitudes toward their materials.

Ⓕ In all periods, fine artists tend to challenge the physical limitations of their materials while applied artists tend to cooperate with the physical properties of their materials.

Ⓐ 응용 미술 작품은 보관 또는 차폐 등 기능에 충실하다. 그리고 같은 기능의 작품은 특성도 비슷한데 이는 용도의 제약이 있기 때문이다.

Ⓑ 중국 고대 상 왕조의 꽃병은 잉카 문명의 꽃병과 다르다는 것을 쉽게 알아볼 수 있다.

Ⓒ 순수 미술 작품은 기능적이지 않아서, 사용되는 재료의 속성에 따른 제약만을 받는다.

Ⓓ 르네상스 시대의 조각가들은 청동 조각상의 내부 구조를 강하게 지지하기 위해 쇠 버팀대를 사용할 줄 알게 되었다.

Ⓔ 20세기에는 재료에 대한 태도에 있어 순수 미술가들과 응용 미술가들 간의 상호 유사성이 더 높아졌다.

Ⓕ 모든 시대를 통틀어 순수 미술가들은 재료의 물리적 한계에 도전하는 성향을 보인 반면 응용 미술가들은 재료의 물리적 속성에 맞추어 작업하는 성향을 보인다.

해설 보기 A 도입 문장을 보면 알 수 있듯, 본문은 주로 응용 미술 작품과 순수 미술 작품의 대조적 차이를 논하고 있다. 비교의 핵심 관점은 기능성으로, 응용 미술 작품은 기능성을 갖고 있는 반면 순수 미술작품은 그렇지 않다는 것이다. 본문의 첫 번째 부분은 본연의 기능성으로 인해 생길 수밖에 없는 응용 미술 작품들의 '기본 형태'에 대하여 설명하였고, 두 번째 부분에서는 기능성으로부터는 자유로우나 재료의 제약을 받는 순수 미술 작품의 형태에 대해 설명하였다. 본문을 제대로 요약한 것이라면 응용 미술 작품에 대한 정의와 "같은 기능의 작품은 유사한 형태를 갖는다"는 결과적 고찰을 포함하고 있어야 하는데, 보기 A는 이에 해당된다.

보기 B 보기 자체의 내용은 사실이나, 본문 전체 또는 첫 문단의 주요 논지가 아니다. 오히려 "기능이 같은 작품은 모두 비슷하다"는 본문 요점에 상반된다. 첫 문단 마지막 문장을 보면 상 왕조의 꽃병은 잉카문명의 꽃병과는 세부적으로는 다르지만 기본형은 동일하다고 되어 있다. 그러므로 보기 B는 잘못된 요약이다.

보기 C 본문은 응용 미술 작품과 순수 미술 작품을 대조 비교하고 있으므로 제대로 된 요약이라면 두 작품 간의 기본적인 차이점을 담고 있어야 한다. 보기 C를 요약에 추가하면, "응용 미술 작품은 기능성을 갖는 반면 순수 미술 작품은 그렇지 않다. 순수 미술 작품은 기능성을 갖지 않아도 되기 때문에 응용 미술 작품만큼 제약을 받지는 않는다"는 본문의 의도한 요점을 포함할 수 있게 된다.

보기 D 이 보기는 두 번째 문단의 아홉 번째에서 열한 번째 문장까지 담긴 내용에 대한 요약이다. 이 부분은 본문의 전체 맥락 상 순수 미술 작품이 재료 때문에 어떠한 제약을 받는지를 이해하는 데 도움이 된다. 그러나 본문에서 가장 중요한 내용을 발췌하여야 한다는 문장선택 요령을 상기할 때, 이 보기는 두 작품의 차이점에 대하여 일반적으로 논하는 것 보다는 덜 중요한 내용을 담고 있다.

보기 E 이 보기는 본문에 근거가 제시되어 있지 않으므로 선택될 수 없다. 재료에 대한 태도에 있어 순수 미술가와 응용 미술가의 태도 차이가 여전하다는 세 번째 문단을 잘못 이해한 것이다. 본문의 내용이나 논점과는 모순이 되는 보기는 요약의 일부로 선택될 수 없다.

보기 F 본문의 마지막 문단에서는 이제까지 제시한 응용 미술 작품과 순수 미술 작품의 근본적인 차이점에 근거한 추론으로 결론을 내리고 있다. 즉 응용 미술가와 순수 미술가의 재료에 대한 태도 차이를 논한 것으로서 제대로 된 요약이라면 이 마지막 논점이 포함되어 있어야 한다.

어휘 refer to 지칭하다, 언급하다 crafts 공예작품 applied arts 응용 미술 from the point of view of ~라는 관점에서 볼 때 supports 지지대, 버팀대 pertain to ~와 관련되다 be bound by ~에 속박되다, 제한을 받다 the laws of physics 물리학의 법칙 Shang Dynasty 중국 고대의 상 왕조 arbitrary 임의적, 자의적 depart from the norm 규범에서 벗어나다 sensitivity to ~에 대한 민감도 consideration 고려 대상 is taken for granted that …라는 사실이 당연한 것으로 간주된다 fine arts 순수 미술 discipline 지식, 학문 등의 분야 be constrained by ~의 제약을 받는다 properties 사물의 속성 mass 질량, 양감 weight distribution 무게 분산 stress 응력 rigid 단단한 stretcher 캔버스틀 taut 팽팽한 aesthetic 미적인, 미학적인 deteriorate 상태가 악화되다 crack 균열이 생기다 discolor 변색되다, 퇴색되다 intrude upon 침범하다, 방해하다 bronze statue 청동 조각상 foreleg 앞다리 cannonball 포탄 hoof 발굽 braces 버팀대, 죔쇠 compromise 타협, 절충 relatively 상대적으로 constant 지속적인 exaggeration 과장 practitioner 실천가 whereas 반면에 engage in ~에 종사하다 in concert with ~에 맞춰, ~와 협력하여 fundamental 기본적인, 근본적인

READING PRACTICE SETS

IMPACT OF RAILROAD TRANSPORTATION IN THE UNITED STATES

Both the steamboat and the railroad system with its steam-powered trains revolutionized transport in the United States in the nineteenth century. Entire regions that would hardly have been touched, especially in the West, were opened up to settlement and exploitation. In a geographic sense, the impact of the steamboat and railroad was simply immense. Some historians have argued further that they were the key to the rapid economic growth experienced by the United States in the middle decades of the century. The railroad, especially, not only lowered transport costs but caused a surge in the output of the iron, coal, and engineering sectors. It thus was a driving force in economic development.

In recent decades economic historians have attempted to quantify the economic impact of railroads. Both Robert Fogel and Albert Fishlow found that, with appropriate investments in canals and roads, the total of railroad services for a typical year in the late nineteenth century could have been provided by other means, at a cost of just a couple years' worth of economic growth. Moreover, the effect of railroads on the iron and coal industries had been greatly exaggerated.

Still, Fogel recognized that he could not measure the *dynamic* effects that railroads might have had. By tying markets together, they allowed firms to operate at a much larger scale than previously. By facilitating personal travel, they increased the flow of ideas and likely had a significant impact on the rate of innovation, because technological innovation generally involves the synthesis of diverse ideas. The fact that firms were exposed to a wider range of raw materials and new marketing opportunities must also have spurred innovative activity.

The railroad also speeded up the decline in travel times that had been underway for decades with improved roads, stagecoaches[1], canals, and steamboats. In 1790, it took one week to reach Maine from New York City and two weeks to reach Florida, and no stagecoaches crossed the Appalachian Mountains (courageous travelers would spend at least five weeks reaching the present site of Chicago). **(A)** By 1860, a New Yorker could reach Maine in a day, and Florida in three; most dramatic was the fact that by rail Chicago was now only two days away. **(B)** Soon, rail travel between East Coast and West Coast cities would occur at speeds that would have amazed earlier generations. **(C)** Although automobiles and airplanes would further reduce travel times in the next century, the impact of the railroad was arguably

미합중국 철도 수송의 영향

증기선과, 증기 기관을 탑재한 철도망이 19세기 미국의 교통에 혁신을 일으켰다. 아직 사람들의 발길이 닿지 않았던 모든 지역, 특히 서부 지역에 이주와 개척의 문이 열렸다. 지리적인 측면에서 볼 때, 증기선과 철도의 영향은 실로 어마어마했다. 일부 역사학자들은 더 나아가 이러한 교통 수단이 19세기 중반 10년간 미국이 경험한 빠른 경제 성장의 열쇠였다고 주장했다. 특히 철도는 운송 비용을 낮출 뿐만 아니라 철, 석탄 및 공학 부문의 생산량도 급증시켰다. 따라서 경제 발전의 주요 동력이었다.

최근 몇십 년간 경제 역사학자들은 철도의 경제적 영향을 양적으로 측정하려고 노력했다. 로버트 포겔과 앨버트 피시로우 두 사람은 운하와 도로에 적절한 투자가 이루어졌다면, 19세기 후반의 평년 대비 철도가 제공한 총 서비스가 단지 2년치의 경제 성장 비용으로 다른 수단으로 대체될 수 있었다는 것을 알아냈다. 또한, 철도가 철과 석탄 산업에 미친 영향이 크게 과장되었다.

그럼에도 불구하고, 포겔은 철도가 가질 수 있는 동적 효과는 측정할 수 없다고 인정했다. 철도는 시장을 결속시켜 기업들이 이전보다 훨씬 큰 규모로 사업을 운영할 수 있게 했다. 개인 여행을 용이하게 함으로써, 철도는 아이디어의 흐름을 증가시켰고, 이는 혁신 속도에 상당한 영향을 미쳤을 것이다. 왜냐하면 기술 혁신은 일반적으로 다양한 아이디어의 융합을 포함하기 때문이다. 기업들이 보다 다양한 원자재와 새로운 마케팅 기회에 노출되었다는 사실도 혁신 활동을 촉진했을 것이다.

철도는 또한 개선된 도로, 합승 마차, 운하 및 증기선과 더불어 수십 년 동안 여행 시간의 감소를 가속화했다. 1790년에는 뉴욕시에서 메인 주까지 1주일이 걸렸고, 플로리다까지는 2주가 걸렸으며, 애팔래치아 산맥을 통과하는 합승 마차는 한 대도 없었다(용감한 여행자들은 최소 5주는 걸려 현재의 시카고의 위치에 도달하곤 했다). 1860년이 되자 뉴욕 시민들이 하루만에 메인 주에 도착할 수 있었고, 플로리다까지는 3일만에 도착했다. 가장 인상적인 것은 철도를 통해 이틀만에 시카고에 도착할 수 있게 된 것이었다. 곧 동부 해안과 서부 해안 도시 간의 철도 여행은 이전 세대를 놀라게 할 속도로 진행될 것이었다. 다음 세대에는 자동차와 비행기가 여행 시간을 더욱 감소시킬 예정이었지만, 단언컨대 철도의 영향은 훨씬 지대했다. 고립되었던 많은 지역들이 이제 국가 경제권 안으로 들어왔다.

more profound. **(D)** Many regions that had previously been isolated were now enveloped in the national economy.

The social effects went beyond the strictly economic. Travel for pleasure became a possibility for many, given the high speed and low cost of railroad travel. With the freedom to travel came a greater sense of national identity and a reduction in regional cultural diversity. Farm children could more easily acquaint themselves with the big city, and easterners could readily visit the West. It is hard to imagine a United States of continental proportions without the railroad. Arguably, because of its speed, the railroad also changed the way that people from the United States viewed nature: as a distant and passing scene, rather than as an immediate experience.

The impact on local economies could be huge. Many towns began as division points where trains changed their crews and steam locomotives were resupplied with water. Others became industrial centers because the railroad linked them to materials and markets. On the other hand, those towns and regions without access by rail to coal suffered competitively in the age of steam. Farmers who would otherwise have been limited to a local market were able to specialize in crops best suited to their soil and climate. Local manufacturers based on local resources were affected in the same way.

Finally, the railroad had major impacts on how goods were distributed: first wholesalers, in the 1850s, and then department stores, chain stores, and mail-order companies from the 1870s created large national markets for goods. As happened with changes in distribution ushered in by improvements to roads in the eighteenth century, these developments changed the way that producers operated. In the final decades of the nineteenth century, some major companies created large hierarchical organizations to manage both large-scale production and national marketing of their goods.

1. Stagecoaches: passenger carriages pulled by horses for long-distance transportation

사회적 영향은 경제적인 것을 훨씬 넘어섰다. 빠른 속도와 저비용의 기차 여행으로 많은 사람들에게 유람 여행이 가능해졌다. 여행의 자유가 생기면서 국민 정체성이 강화되었고 지역적 문화의 다양성은 줄어들었다. 농장 아이들은 대도시에 익숙해졌고 동부 사람들은 서부를 손쉽게 방문할 수 있었다. 철도 없는 거대한 미대륙을 상상하기란 어려웠다. 이견이 있을 수도 있지만, 철도는 그 속도 때문에 미국인들이 자연을 보는 방식도 바꾸었다. 즉 직접적인 경험의 대상이 아닌 저 멀리 지나쳐가는 풍경으로 보게 되었다.

지역 경제에 미치는 영향은 엄청날 수 있었다. 많은 마을들이 기차가 승무원을 교체하고 증기 기관에 물을 보충하는 분기점이 되기 시작했다. 다른 곳들은 기차가 자원과 시장으로 연결시켜 주었기 때문에 산업 중심지가 되었다. 한편, 철도가 없어 석탄을 얻을 수 없었던 마을과 지역들은 증기 시대의 경쟁에서 고전을 면치 못했다. 반면 지역 시장에만 한정되어 있었을 농부들은 자신들의 토양과 기후에 가장 적합한 작물을 특산품으로 키워낼 수 있었다. 지역 자원에 기반한 지방 제조업자들도 같은 방식으로 영향을 받았다.

마지막으로, 철도는 상품 유통 방식에 큰 영향을 미쳤다. 도매상들은 먼저 1850년대에, 그리고 그 이후로는 백화점, 체인점 및 우편 주문 회사들이 1870년대부터 국내 상품 시장을 형성했다. 18세기에 도로 개선으로 유통 방식의 변화가 시작된 것처럼, 이러한 발전들은 생산업자들의 사업 운영 방식을 변경시켰다. 19세기의 마지막 10년간 일부 대형 기업들은 대규모 생산과 국내 상품 마케팅 관리를 위해 대규모의 계층적 조직을 만들었다

1. stagecoach(역마차): 장거리 수송을 위해 말이 끄는 객차

어휘

steamboat 증기선 revolutionize 혁신을 일으키다 settlement 이주 exploitation 개척 immense 엄청난 rapid 급속한 surge in 급증 output 생산량 driving force 추진력 원동력 attempt to ~하려고 시도하다 canal 운하 exaggerate 과장하다 facilitate 가능하게 하다 synthesis 종합, 합성 spur 원동력을 주다, 박차를 가하다 automobile 자동차 arguably 거의 틀림없이 profound 엄청난 be enveloped in 휩싸이다 go beyond ~를 넘어서다 diversity 다양성 acquaint oneself ~를 알다 continental 대륙의 local economy 지역 경제 locomotive 기관의, 운동의 resupply 다시 공급하다 competitively 경쟁적으로 distribute 나누어주다, 유통시키다 wholesaler 도매업자 usher in ~이 시작되게 하다 hierarchical 계층의

1. 지문의 단어 immense와 의미상 가장 가까운 것은?

Ⓐ 필적할 수 없는
Ⓑ 믿기 힘든
Ⓒ 이해하기 힘든
Ⓓ 거대한

어휘 문제
해설 지문에서 immense는 '거대한'이라는 의미로 쓰였다.

2. 다음 중 세 번째 단락에 음영으로 표시된 문장이 담고 있는 핵심 정보를 가장 잘 표현한 것은? 정답 외의 보기들은 의미가 상당히 왜곡되거나 본질적인 정보가 빠져 있다.

Ⓐ 대부분의 기술적 혁신과 마찬가지로, 다양한 아이디어가 융합된 결과로 개인 여행을 용이하게 해 주는 수단들이 나타났다.
Ⓑ 철도는 사람들이 손쉽게 다른 장소에서 만나고 의견을 나누게 해줌으로써 기술적 혁신의 속도를 높였을 것이다.
Ⓒ 기술적 혁신의 결과로 나타난 아이디어의 흐름은 철도 여행에 대한 관심을 증가시켰다.
Ⓓ 기술적 혁신은 보통 다양한 아이디어의 결합을 포함하며, 따라서 정보의 흐름이 증가함에 따라 증가한다.

문장 재구성 문제
해설 개인 여행을 용이하게 함으로써, 아이디어의 흐름을 증가시키고 혁신 속도에 중요한 영향을 끼쳤을 것으로 추측된다고 했으므로 B가 가장 타당하다.

3. 지문의 단어 courageous와 의미상 가장 가까운 것은?

Ⓐ 참을성 있는
Ⓑ 용감한
Ⓒ 경험이 없는
Ⓓ 준비된

어휘 문제
어휘 inexperienced 경험이 부족한
해설 지문에서 courageous는 '용감한'이라는 의미로 쓰였다.

4. 네 번째 단락에 따르면, 철도가 확실히 미국에 자동차나 비행기보다 더 큰 영향을 미친 것은 왜인가?

Ⓐ 철도 여행은 자동차나 비행기 여행보다 저렴했다.
Ⓑ 철도는 전국적인 경제 시스템 안에서 공동체들을 연결했다.
Ⓒ 철도는 국내 경제에서 더 큰 비율을 차지했다.
Ⓓ 철도 여행으로의 전환은 더 빨리 일어났다.

세부 사항 찾기 문제
어휘 countrywide 전국의 proportion 부분
해설 네 번째 단락 마지막 두 문장의 정보를 잘 결합해야 한다. 철도의 영향이 훨씬 지대했다고 말하고 이어 고립된 지역이 국가 경제권 안으로 들어왔다고 했으므로 B가 타당하다.

5. 다섯 번째 단락에 따르면, 다음 중 철도가 미친 사회적 영향이 아닌 것은?

Ⓐ 나라의 넓게 떨어진 지역들이 문화적 유사성을 띄게 되었다.
Ⓑ 재미로 다니는 여행이 훨씬 더 흔해졌다.
Ⓒ 많은 사람들이 자연 세계의 변화를 걱정하기 시작했다.
Ⓓ 사람들이 미국 시민으로서의 정체성을 더 강하게 느끼기 시작했다.

틀린 정보 찾기 문제
어휘 identify 정체성을 느끼다
해설 미국인들이 자연을 보는 방식을 바꾸어 저 멀리 지나쳐가는 풍경으로 보게 되었다고 했으므로 정답은 C다.

6. 다음 중 여섯 번째 단락에서 철도가 지역 경제에 미친 영향으로 언급된 것은?

Ⓐ 철도는 많은 도시를 산업 중심지와 주거지로 양분시켰다.
Ⓑ 지역 자원을 이용한 생산자들은 더 큰 시장에서의 경쟁력을 잃고 도산했다.
Ⓒ 곳곳에서 새로운 승무원이 기차에 탑승하고 기차에서 작동할 증기 기관이 준비된 뉴타운들이 생겨났다.
Ⓓ 철도 접근성이 없었던 마을과 지역들이 증기력을 사용하는 대체 수단을 개발했다.

세부 사항 찾기 문제
어휘 divide A in half 양분시키다 go out of business 도산하다 fresh 새로운 alternative 대체의
해설 많은 마을들이 기차가 승무원을 교체하고 증기 기관에 물을 보충하는 분기점이 되기 시작했다고 했으므로 C가 정답이다.

7. 여섯 번째 단락에서 철도의 도입 이전에 일부 농민들이 지역 토양과 기후에 가장 적합한 작물을 길러내지 못했다고 한 이유는?

Ⓐ 그들에게 가장 생산적인 영농법 지식이 부족했기 때문에
Ⓑ 필요한 도구와 용품를 얻을 수 없었기 때문에
Ⓒ 노동력이 부족했기 때문에
Ⓓ 자신들의 작물을 지역 시장에만 판매할 수 있었기 때문에

내용 추론 문제
해설 지역 시장에만 한정되었을 농부들이 자신들의 토양과 기후에 가장 적합한 작물을 특산품으로 키워낼 수 있었다는 설명에서 D를 유추할 수 있다.

8. 일곱 번째 단락에서 글쓴이는 일부 대형 기업들이 왜 대규모의 계층적 조직을 만들었다고 했는가?

Ⓐ 이러한 조직 형태가 철도 회사의 비즈니스 모델을 토대로 했다는 것을 주장하기 위해

Ⓑ 이 시대에 일어난 철도와 관련이 없는 변화의 예를 제공하기 위해

Ⓒ 일부 생산업자들이 철도의 영향에 대응하여 상품의 유통을 변화시킨 구체적 방식을 설명하기 위해

Ⓓ 백화점, 체인점, 우편 주문 회사들이 왜 1870년대에 확장될 수 있었는지 설명하기 위해

수사학적 의도 찾기 문제

어휘 in response to ~에 대응하여

해설 글쓴이가 일부 대형 기업들이 대규모의 계층적 조직을 만들었다고 말한 이유는 바로 이전 문장, 18세기에 도로 개선으로 유통 방식의 변화가 있었던 것처럼, 철도의 발전이 생산업자들의 사업 운영 방식을 변경시켰는데, 그 구체적 예를 들기 위해서이다. 정답은 C가 된다. 대규모 계층적 조직을 만들고 난 후 백화점, 체인점, 우편 주문 회사들이 확장된 것은 아니기 때문에 D는 정답이 아니다.

9. **지시문:** 위에 제시된 지문의 일부를 보시오. 지문에 표시된 **(A)**, **(B)**, **(C)**, **(D)** 중 하나에 다음 문장이 삽입될 수 있다.

On June 4, 1876, a train arrived in San Francisco, California, only 83 hours and 39 minutes after leaving New York City.

(1876년 6월 4일, 뉴욕시를 출발한 기차가 캘리포니아 주 샌프란시스코에 83시간 39분만에 도착했다.)

이 문장이 들어갈 가장 적당한 위치는?

The railroad also speeded up the decline in travel times that had been underway for decades with improved roads, stagecoaches1 , canals, and steamboats. In 1790, it took one week to reach Maine from New York City and two weeks to reach Florida, and no stagecoaches crossed the Appalachian Mountains (courageous travelers would spend at least five weeks reaching the present site of Chicago). **(A)** By 1860, a New Yorker could reach Maine in a day, and Florida in three; most dramatic was the fact that by rail Chicago was now only two days away. **(B)** Soon, rail travel between East Coast and West Coast cities would occur at speeds that would have amazed earlier generations. **(C)** On June 4, 1876, a train arrived in San Francisco, California, only 83 hours and 39 minutes after leaving New York City. Although automobiles and airplanes would further reduce travel times in the next century, the impact of the railroad was arguably more profound. **(D)** Many regions that had previously been isolated were now enveloped in the national economy.

Ⓐ   Ⓑ   Ⓒ   Ⓓ

문장 삽입 문제

해설 뉴욕시에서 출발한 기차가 캘리포니아 주 샌프란시스코에 도착했다는 것에서 동부에서 서부로의 기차 여행에 관한 이야기임을 알 수 있다. 따라서 곧 동부 해안과 서부 해안 도시 간의 철도 여행은 이전 세대를 놀라게 할 속도로 진행될 것이라고 말한 다음, 즉 (C)에 삽입되어야 문맥상 가장 적합하다.

10. **지시문:** 지문을 간단히 요약하기 위한 도입 문장이 아래에 제시되어 있다. 아래 보기들 중에서 지문의 가장 중요한 개념을 표현한 문장 3개를 골라 요약을 완성하라. 보기들 중에는 지문에 나오지 않았거나 중요하지 않은 개념이기 때문에 요약문으로 적절치 않은 것들도 있다. 이 문제의 배점은 2점이다.

19세기 철도 교통 시스템의 발전은 미국의 삶을 크게 바꾸었다.

Ⓐ 산업체들이 필요한 자원과 새로운 시장을 얻게 만들면서 철도는 미국의 경제 성장을 크게 증대시켰다.

Ⓑ 포겔이나 피시로우 같은 학자들의 새로운 연구는 철도가 철이나 석탄 같은 생산재 시장들을 이어주는 데 큰 영향력을 발휘했음을 밝혀냈다.

Ⓒ 철도 시스템이 제공한 빠르고 저렴한 개인 여행은 사람들이 나라 곳곳을 다니면서 사회적인 교류를 할 수 있도록 해 주었다.

Ⓓ 철도가 결국 먼 서부와 다른 지역들을 연결해 주기는 했지만, 개인의 유람 여행은 주로 동부 지역에서만 이루어졌다.

Ⓔ 철도가 지역 생산업자들을 먼 시장까지 연결해 주어 그들이 재배하거나 생산해낸 것들을 특화할 수 있게 해 주었고 대규모 제조 회사가 나타났다.

Ⓕ 19세기 후반, 생산과 유통 모두에 관여하는 대형 계층 구조 기업들의 등장으로 철도의 영향력은 감소했다.

지문 요약하기 문제

어휘 significantly 유의미하게   inexpensive 저렴한   allow A to B A가 B할 수 있게 해 주다   distant 먼   specialize 특화하다   distribution 유통

해설 A는 첫 번째와 두 번째 단락의 정보를 요약하고 있다. B는 철도가 철과 석탄 산업에 미친 영향이 크게 과장되었다고 했으므로 적절치 않다. C는 세 번째, 네 번째, 다섯 번째 단락을 잘 요약하고 있다. D는 언급되지 않았다. E는 철도 시스템이 농부와 제조업자, 공산품 회사들에 미친 영향에 대한 여섯 번째와 일곱 번째 단락의 내용을 요약하고 있다. F는 대형 계층 구조 기업들의 등장 이후 이야기는 나오지 않으므로 알 수 없다.

DESERT FORMATION

The deserts, which already occupy approximately a fourth of the Earth's land surface, have in recent decades been increasing at an alarming pace. The expansion of desertlike conditions into areas where they did not previously exist is called **desertification**. It has been estimated that an additional one-fourth of the Earth's land surface is threatened by this process.

Desertification is accomplished primarily through the loss of stabilizing natural vegetation and the subsequent accelerated erosion of the soil by wind and water. In some cases the loose soil is blown completely away, leaving a stony surface. In other cases, the finer particles may be removed, while the sand-sized particles are accumulated to form mobile hills or ridges of sand.

Even in the areas that retain a soil cover, the reduction of vegetation typically results in the loss of the soil's ability to absorb substantial quantities of water. The impact of raindrops on the loose soil tends to transfer fine clay particles into the tiniest soil spaces, sealing them and producing a surface that allows very little water penetration. Water absorption is greatly reduced, consequently runoff is increased, resulting in accelerated erosion rates. The gradual drying of the soil caused by its diminished ability to absorb water results in the further loss of vegetation, so that a cycle of progressive surface deterioration is established.

In some regions, the increase in desert areas is occurring largely as the result of a trend toward drier climatic conditions. Continued gradual global warming has produced an increase in aridity for some areas over the past few thousand years. The process may be accelerated in subsequent decades if global warming resulting from air pollution seriously increases.

There is little doubt, however, that desertification in most areas results primarily from human activities rather than natural processes. The semiarid lands bordering the deserts exist in a delicate ecological balance and are limited in their potential to adjust to increased environmental pressures. Expanding populations are subjecting the land to increasing pressures to provide them with food and fuel. In wet periods, the land may be able to respond to these stresses. During the dry periods that are common phenomena along the desert margins, though, the pressure on the land is often far in excess of its diminished capacity, and desertification results.

Four specific activities have been identified as major contributors to the desertification processes: overcultivation, overgrazing, firewood gathering, and overirrigation. The cultivation of crops has expanded into progressively drier regions as population densities have grown. These regions are especially likely to have periods of

사막화 현상

이미 지구 표면의 4분의 1 정도를 덮고 있는 사막은 지난 수십 년에 걸쳐 엄청난 속도로 증가했다. 예전에는 존재하지 않았던 사막 환경이 점차 확산되는 현상을 '사막화'라고 한다. 지구 표면의 또 다른 4분의 1이 사막화의 위험에 처한 것으로 추산되고 있다.

사막화가 일어나는 주요 원인으로는 안정된 자연 식생이 손실되고, 이에 따라 바람과 물에 의해 토양 침식이 가속화되기 때문이다. 어떤 경우에는 푸석푸석해진 토양이 완전히 바람에 쓸려가 지표면을 돌투성이로 남겨놓기도 한다. 또 다른 경우에는 미세한 토양 입자들이 사라지고 모래 굵기의 입자들만이 축적되어 쉽게 변화되는 모래 능선이나 둔덕을 형성하기도 한다.

토양 표면이 그대로 유지되어 있는 지역에서도 식생이 감소하면 대개 토양이 충분한 양의 물을 흡수할 수 없게 된다. 푸석푸석한 토양에 빗물이 떨어지면 미세한 점토 입자들이 토양 사이의 세밀한 공간에 침투하여 그곳을 메워버려 소량의 물도 흡수될 수 없게 만든다. 흡수되는 물의 양이 크게 감소하면, 결국 지표수가 급증하여 토양 침식이 가속화된다. 물의 흡수력이 떨어져 토양이 점차 건조해지면 식생은 더욱 손실되고 점진적인 지표면의 사막화 과정이 시작된다.

일부 지역에서 사막화가 확대되는 것은 기후가 점차 건조해지고 있기 때문이다. 지난 수천 년에 걸쳐 지구온난화가 계속되면서 어떤 지역에서는 건조화가 심해졌다. 대기 오염으로 지구온난화가 더욱 악화되면서 앞으로 수십 년에 걸쳐 이런 과정이 가속화될 것으로 보인다.

그렇지만 대부분 지역에서 사막화는 분명 자연 현상보다는 인간의 활동 때문에 발생하고 있다. 사막과 경계를 이루고 있는 반건조 지대는 생태학적으로 불안정한 상태에 처해 있으며, 점차 가중되고 있는 환경 압박에 대한 잠재적 적응력도 한계를 갖게 되었다. 인구팽창에 따른 식량과 연료 공급 문제로 토양은 더욱 몸살을 앓고 있다. 우기에 이런 지대는 그런 문제에 대처할 수 있다. 하지만 사막과 경계를 이루는 지대의 흔한 현상인 건기에 토양에 대한 압박은 취약해진 지력을 훨씬 뛰어넘게 되어 결과적으로 사막화가 발생하게 된다.

사막화를 발생시키는 구체적인 활동으로는 네 가지가 밝혀져 있다. 즉 지나친 경작, 과도한 방목, 땔감 채취, 지나친 관개이다. 인구 밀도가 높아지면서 작물 경작은 점차 건조한 지역으로 확대되어 왔다. 특히 이런 지역은 극심한 건기가 찾아오기 때문에 경작의 실패는 흔한 일이다. 작물을 경작하려면 대개 사전에 천연 식생을 제거해야 하는데, 경작에 실패하는 경우 광활한 토양에 보호막 구실을 하는 식물이 없기 때문에 바람과 물의 침식에 취약해진다.

severe dryness, so that crop failures are common. Since the raising of most crops necessitates the prior removal of the natural vegetation, crop failures leave extensive tracts of land devoid of a plant cover and susceptible to wind and water erosion.

(A) The raising of livestock is a major economic activity in semiarid lands, where grasses are generally the dominant type of natural vegetation. **(B)** The consequences of an excessive number of livestock grazing in an area are the reduction of the vegetation cover and the trampling and pulverization of the soil. **(C)** This is usually followed by the drying of the soil and accelerated erosion. **(D)**

Firewood is the chief fuel used for cooking and heating in many countries. The increased pressures of expanding populations have led to the removal of woody plants so that many cities and towns are surrounded by large areas completely lacking in trees and shrubs. The increasing use of dried animal waste as a substitute fuel has also hurt the soil because this valuable soil conditioner and source of plant nutrients is no longer being returned to the land.

The final major human cause of desertification is soil salinization resulting from overirrigation. Excess water from irrigation sinks down into the water table. If no drainage system exists, the water table rises, bringing dissolved salts to the surface. The water evaporates and the salts are left behind, creating a white crustal layer that prevents air and water from reaching the underlying soil.

The extreme seriousness of desertification results from the vast areas of land and the tremendous numbers of people affected, as well as from the great difficulty of reversing or even slowing the process. Once the soil has been removed by erosion, only the passage of centuries or millennia will enable new soil to form. In areas where considerable soil still remains, though, a rigorously enforced program of land protection and cover-crop planting may make it possible to reverse the present deterioration of the surface.

반건조 지대에서 목축은 인간의 주요 경제 활동이다. 그런 지대에서의 대표적인 자연 식생은 초지다. 그런 곳에서 많은 수의 가축을 방목하게 되면 초지가 감소될 뿐 아니라 토양이 파괴되고 분쇄되는 결과가 초래된다. 그리고 이는 대체로 토양의 건조화와 침식의 가속화로 이어지게 된다.

땔감은 많은 나라들에서 요리와 난방을 위한 주요 연료이다. 인구 팽창의 압박으로 수목이 제거되면서 많은 도시들과 마을들이 나무와 관목이 절대적으로 부족한 지대로 둘러싸이게 되었다. 동물들의 마른 배설물을 대체 연료로 자주 사용하는 것도 토양에 심각한 해를 미치게 되었는데, 토양에 중요한 자양분이자 식물의 영양소인 배설물이 더 이상 땅으로 환원되지 못하기 때문이다.

마지막으로 인간의 활동 때문에 사막화가 되는 주요 원인으로는 지나친 관개로 토양이 염류화되는 현상이다. 지나친 관개 사업은 많은 물을 지하수면으로 스며들게 만든다. 아무런 배수 시설이 없는 상태에서 지하수면이 상승하면 용해된 염수가 지표면으로 부상한다. 그리고 물이 증발하면 염분이 남게 되는데, 이것이 지표면을 하얗게 덮어버리면서 공기와 물이 저층의 토양으로 도달하는 것을 막는다.

사막화의 심각성은 원상복구나 그 과정을 늦추는 문제가 매우 까다롭다는 사실뿐 아니라, 폐해 지역의 방대함과 엄청난 피해자 수 때문이다. 토양이 침식에 의해 파괴된다면 수백 년 혹은 수천 년이 지나야만 새로운 토양이 형성될 수 있을 것이다. 아직 상당한 토양이 남아 있는 지역에서는 토양 보호 프로그램이나 지피(地被)식물 재배 등의 계획을 강력히 추진한다면, 현재 진행 중인 지표면의 황폐화를 되돌릴 수 있을지도 모른다.

어휘

desertlike 사막 같은 **desertification** 사막화 **primarily** 주로 **stabilize** 안정시키다 **natural vegetation** 자연 식생 **subsequent** 이어진, 그 이후의 **accelerate** 가속화하다 **erosion** 침식 **loose** (흙 따위가) 푸석푸석한, 헐렁헐렁한 **fine** 미세한 **particle** 입자 **accumulate** 축적하다 **mobile** 움직이기 쉬운, 위치가 변하는 **ridge** 산등성이, 둔덕 **penetration** 침투 **absorption** 흡수, 병합 **runoff** 땅 위를 흐르는 빗물, 지표수 **result in** ~의 결과를 가져오다 **diminished** 줄어든, 감소한 **deterioration** 상태의 악화, 황폐화 **aridity** 건조, 불모 **subsequent** 그후의, 수반하는 **global warming** 지구온난화 **semiarid** 반건조성의 **margin** 가장자리, 경계 **phenomenon** 현상 **overgrazing** 지나친 방목 **overirrigation** 지나친 관개 **population** 인구, 집단 **susceptible to** ~의 영향을 받기 쉬운 **dominant** 우세한, 주된 **trample** 짓밟다, 유린하다 **pulverization** 가루가 됨, 분쇄됨 **firewood** 장작, 땔나무 **substitute fuel** 대체 연료 **animal waste** 동물 배설물 **soil conditioner** 토양 개량제 **salinization** 염류화 **drainage system** 배수시설 **evaporate** 증발하다 **crustal** 외피의, 지각의 **tremendous** 광장한, 거대한 **millennia** (millennium의 복수형) 수천년 **rigorously** 엄격하게, 혹독하게 **cover-crop** 지피(地被)식물

1. 지문의 단어 threatened와 의미상 가장 가까운 것은?

Ⓐ 제한된
Ⓑ 위험에 처한
Ⓒ 방지된
Ⓓ 거절당한

어휘 문제

해설 'be동사 + 과거분사' 형태의 수동태 문장에 쓰인 것으로, 동사 원형은 threaten(위협하다)이다. 보기 중 의미가 가장 유사한 어휘는 endangered 밖에 없다.

2. 세 번째 단락에 따르면, 자연 식생의 손실은 토양에 어떤 결과를 초래하는가?

Ⓐ 돌이 많아짐
Ⓑ 물의 흡수력 약화
Ⓒ 토양 속 공간의 증가
Ⓓ 지표수 감소

세부 사항 찾기 문제

어휘 stony 돌이 많은, 돌처럼 단단한   content 면적, 체적, 범위

해설 세 번째 단락 첫 번째 문장에 식생의 손실이 물의 흡수력을 약화시킨다는 내용이 나와 있다. 보기 C와 D는 이 단락의 내용과는 상반되며, 보기 A는 언급되지 않았다.

3. 지문의 단어 delicate와 의미상 가장 가까운 것은?

Ⓐ 취약한
Ⓑ 예측 가능한
Ⓒ 복잡한
Ⓓ 귀중한

어휘 문제

해설 delicate에는 여러 가지 의미가 있지만, 여기서는 '취약하다(fragile)'는 의미로 쓰였다.

4. 다섯 번째 단락에 따르면, 건기에 사막과의 경계 지역은 어떤 어려움을 안고 있는가?

Ⓐ 정착지가 유발시킨 압박에 적응하는 것
Ⓑ 사막화 이후에 비옥도를 유지하는 것
Ⓒ 작물의 관개를 위해 물을 제공하는 것
Ⓓ 식량과 연료를 구하는 인구를 유입시키는 것

세부 사항 찾기 문제

어휘 settlement 정착, 해결   fertility 비옥함, 번식력

해설 인구 팽창으로 더 많은 식량과 연료가 필요하지만, 토양이 그런 압박에 제대로 대처하지 못한다는 사실이 언급되어 있다. 보기 B와 C는 이 단락에서 다루지 않고 있으며, 보기 D는 '인구팽창'이 아니라 '인구 유입' 문제를 언급하고 있으므로 답이 될 수 없다.

5. 지문의 단어 progressively와 의미상 가장 가까운 것은?

Ⓐ 공개적으로
Ⓑ 인상적으로
Ⓒ 객관적으로
Ⓓ 점진적으로

어휘 문제

해설 progressively는 어떤 일이 '점진적으로' 혹은 '점차적으로' 진행되는 상황을 표현하는 부사다.

6. 여섯 번째 단락에 따르면, 다음 보기 중 어떤 일이 작물 경작과 깊은 관련이 있는가?

Ⓐ 적절한 관개 기술의 부족
Ⓑ 특정 지역에 알맞은 작물 경작의 실패
Ⓒ 자연적인 식생의 제거
Ⓓ 동물의 마른 배설물의 과도한 이용

세부 사항 찾기 문제

어휘 suited ~에 적당한, 적합한

해설 여섯 번째 단락의 마지막 문장에 작물 경작을 위해 자연 식생을 파괴한다는 내용이 나와 있으므로 보기 C가 정답이다. 여기서는 적절한 관개 기술이 아니라 지나친 관개를 문제 삼고 있으므로 보기 A는 틀렸고, 보기 B와 D는 언급되지 않은 내용이다.

7. 아홉 번째 단락에 따르면, 어떤 이유로 토양이 과도한 양의 물을 흡수하는 것이 사막화의 요인이 되는가?

Ⓐ 토지의 관개를 방해하기 때문에
Ⓑ 물의 증발을 억제하기 때문에
Ⓒ 토양에 더 많은 양의 공기를 유입시킬 수 있기 때문에
Ⓓ 염분이 지표면으로 올라오게 만들기 때문에

세부 사항 찾기 문제

어휘 interfere 방해하다, 간섭하다

해설 이 단락의 요지는 지나친 관개 때문에 지하 수면이 상승, 염분이 지표면으로 올라오게 되어 토양이 물과 공기를 제대로 흡수하지 못한다는 것이다. 따라서 보기 D가 정답이다. 보기 A, B, C는 언급되어 있지 않다.

8. 다음 중 마지막 단락에 음영으로 표시된 문장이 담고 있는 핵심 정보를 가장 잘 표현한 것은? 정답 외의 보기들은 의미가 상당히 왜곡되거나 본질적인 정보가 빠져 있다.

Ⓐ 사막화는 복구시키기가 어렵고 상당히 넓은 지역과 많은 사람들에게 영향을 미치기 때문에 심각한 문제다.

Ⓑ 광범위한 지역으로 점차 확산되고 있는 인구 성장 때문에 사막화의 과정을 지연시키는 것은 어려운 일이다.

Ⓒ 사막화는 여러 국가들에서 많은 사람들이 공조해야만 해결될 수 있는 심각한 문제로 간주되고 있다.

Ⓓ 폐해 지역의 인구가 감소되지 않는 한 사막화된 곳을 복구시키기는 대단히 어려운 일이다.

문장 재구성 문제

해설 사막화가 심각한 이유를 설명한 것인데, 보기 A는 해당 문장의 as well as 앞뒤 내용의 순서를 바꾸어 놓은 것으로 의미를 변화시키거나 정보를 빠뜨리지 않았으므로 정답이다.

9. 지시문: 위에 제시된 지문의 일부를 보시오. 지문에 표시된 **(A)**, **(B)**, **(C)**, **(D)** 중 하나에 다음 문장이 삽입될 수 있다.

This economic reliance on livestock in certain regions makes large tracts of land susceptible to overgrazing.

(이렇듯 경제를 가축에 의존하는 곳에서는 상당히 넓은 땅이 지나친 방목의 영향을 받을 수 있다.)

이 문장이 들어갈 가장 적당한 위치는?

(A) The raising of livestock is a major economic activity in semiarid lands, where grasses are generally the dominant type of natural vegetation. **(B)** This economic reliance on livestock in certain regions makes large tracts of land susceptible to overgrazing. The consequences of an excessive number of livestock grazing in an area are the reduction of the vegetation cover and the trampling and pulverization of the soil. **(C)** This is usually followed by the drying of the soil and accelerated erosion. **(D)**

Ⓐ   Ⓑ   Ⓒ   Ⓓ

문장 삽입 문제

어휘 reliance 의지, 신뢰   susceptible 영향받기 쉬운

해설 삽입될 문장은 '경제를 가축에 의존하는 곳'의 문제점에 대해 기술하고 있으므로, 그 앞의 문장은 전제가 될 만한 내용이 나와야 한다. 즉 이 단락의 논리 전개는 이렇다. "반건조 지대에서는 목축이 주요 경제활동이다. → 그런 지역에서는 상당히 넓은 땅이 방목의 영향을 받는다 → 과도한 가축 방목의 결과는…" 그러므로 이 문장은 (B)에 삽입되어야 한다.

10. 지시문: 이 지문을 간단히 요약하기 위한 도입 문장이 아래에 제시되어 있다. 아래 보기들 중에서 지문의 가장 중요한 개념을 표현한 문장 3개를 골라 요약을 완성하라. 보기들 중에는 지문에 나오지 않았거나 중요하지 않은 개념이기 때문에 요약문으로 적절치 않은 것들도 있다. 이 문제의 배점은 2점이다.

최근 수십 년에 걸쳐 많은 요인들이 사막화를 확산시켰다.

Ⓐ 어떤 지역에서는 인구 증가와 그에 따른 경작지의 확대로 생태학적 균형이 깨져 사막화가 확산되었다.

Ⓑ 심각한 건기가 보편적인 현상이 되면서 많은 작물들의 경작 실패 사례가 늘어났다.

Ⓒ 지나친 가축 수와 연료용 땔감 채취로 초지와 수목이 감소되어 토양이 황폐해지고 취약해졌다.

Ⓓ 배수 시설을 제대로 갖추지 않고 지나치게 관개 사업을 벌여 염분이 토양으로 올라와 토양이 물과 공기를 제대로 흡수하지 못하게 되었다.

Ⓔ 동물의 배설물은 식물의 성장에 필요한 영양분을 제공해 토양을 비옥하게 만들어 준다.

Ⓕ 반건조 지대에서 초지는 자연 식생의 대표적인 형태다.

지문 요약하기 문제

어휘 cattle 가축   dung 비료   enrich 비옥하게 하다
      vulnerable 상처받기 쉬운, 취약한

해설 사막화를 확산시키는 원인을 찾는 문제로 인간 활동에 기인한 네 가지 요소들, 즉 지나친 경작, 과도한 방목, 땔감 채취, 지나친 관개를 떠올리면 쉽게 답을 찾을 수 있다. 따라서 보기 A, C, D를 골라야 한다. 보기 B는 단편적인 사실에 불과할 뿐 주요개념이 될 수 없고, 보기 E는 여덟 번째 단락의 내용과는 상반되며, 보기 F는 일곱 번째 단락에서 논점을 전개하기 위해 소개한 한 가지 사소한 정보일 뿐이다.

EARLY CINEMA

The cinema did not emerge as a form of mass consumption until its technology evolved from the initial "peepshow" format to the point where images were projected on a screen in a darkened theater. In the peepshow format, a film was viewed through a small opening in a machine that was created for that purpose. Thomas Edison's peepshow device, the Kinetoscope, was introduced to the public in 1894. It was designed for use in Kinetoscope parlors, or arcades, which contained only a few individual machines and permitted only one customer to view a short, 50-foot film at any one time. The first Kinetoscope parlors contained five machines. For the price of 25 cents (or 5 cents per machine), customers moved from machine to machine to watch five different films (or, in the case of famous prizefights, successive rounds of a single fight).

These Kinetoscope arcades were modeled on phonograph parlors, which had proven successful for Edison several years earlier. In the phonograph parlors, customers listened to recordings through individual ear tubes, moving from one machine to the next to hear different recorded speeches or pieces of music. The Kinetoscope parlors functioned in a similar way. Edison was more interested in the sale of Kinetoscopes (for roughly $1,000 apiece) to these parlors than in the films that would be run in them (which cost approximately $10 to $15 each). He refused to develop projection technology, reasoning that if he made and sold projectors, then exhibitors would purchase only one machine—a projector—from him instead of several.

(A) Exhibitors, however, wanted to maximize their profits, which they could do more readily by projecting a handful of films to hundreds of customers at a time (rather than one at a time) and by charging 25 to 50 cents admission. **(B)** About a year after the opening of the first Kinetoscope parlor in 1894, showmen such as Louis and Auguste Lumière, Thomas Armat and Charles Francis Jenkins, and Orville and Woodville Latham (with the assistance of Edison's former assistant, William Dickson) perfected projection devices. **(C)** These early projection devices were used in vaudeville theaters, legitimate theaters, local town halls, makeshift storefront theaters, fairgrounds, and amusement parks to show films to a mass audience. **(D)**

With the advent of projection in 1895-1896, motion pictures became the ultimate form of mass consumption. Previously, large audiences had viewed spectacles at the theater, where vaudeville, popular dramas, musical shows, classical plays, lec-tures, and slide-and-lantern shows had been presented to several hundred

초창기 영화

영화가 대중의 소비 매체로 부각되기까지는 초창기 '핍쇼' 형태로부터 시작되어 어두운 극장에서 스크린에 이미지를 투영시키는 방식에 이르기까지 기술 발달의 과정이 있었다. 핍쇼는, 엿보기 위한 목적으로 발명된 기계의 작은 구멍을 통해 영화를 들여다보는 방식이다. 토머스 에디슨이 발명한 핍쇼 장치인 키네토스코프는 1894년 일반 대중에게 소개되었다. 이것은 키네토스코프 전용 감상실(아케이드)용으로 만든 것인데, 감상실에는 기계가 몇 대 배치되어 있고 고객 한 명이 한 번에 50피트짜리 짤막한 영화를 관람할 수 있었다. 최초의 키네토스코프 감상실에는 5대의 기계가 있었다. 고객은 25센트(기계 한 대당 5센트)를 내고 이 기계에서 저 기계로 옮겨 다니며 각기 다른 5편의 영화를 관람했다.(유명한 프로 권투시합의 경우에는 라운드별로 기계를 바꿔가며 관람했다.)

이런 키네토스코프 감상실은 이 기계가 나오기 몇 해 전 에디슨에게 성공을 안겨준 축음기 감상실을 본뜬 것이다. 축음기 감상실에서 개인은 기계를 바꿔가며 청음기를 통해 다른 녹음된 연설이나 음악을 들었다. 키네토스코프 감상실도 이와 비슷한 방식으로 운영되었다. 에디슨은 키네토스코프를 통해 상영되는 필름(편당 대략 10~15달러)보다는 키네토스코프 기계(대당 약 1,000달러)를 이런 감상실에 판매하는 데 더 관심이 많았다. 그는 영사 기술을 개발하려고 하지 않았는데, 그 이유는 만일 영사기를 만들어 판다면 흥행업자들이 영사기를 여러 대가 아니라 단 한 대만을 구입할 것이라고 생각했기 때문이었다.

하지만 흥행업자들은 자신들의 이익을 극대화시키길 원했다. 그들은 (한 번에 한 사람이 아니라) 한 번에 25~50센트의 입장료를 받고 수백 명의 고객들에게 여러 편의 영화를 보여 준다면 수입을 쉽게 올릴 수 있다고 보았다. 1894년 첫 번째 키네토스코프 감상실이 문을 연 지 1년쯤 후에 루이와 오거스트 뤼미에르 형제, 토머스 아매트, 찰스 프란시스 젠킨스, 오르빌, 그리고 (에디슨의 과거 조수였던 윌리엄 딕슨의 도움을 받아) 우드빌 라담 등과 같은 흥행업자들이 영사기를 완성시켰다. 이런 초창기 영사기들은 희가극 극장, 정통극 극장, 지역 공회당, 임시 상점 앞 극장, 장터, 놀이공원 등에서 대중들에게 영화를 보여 주기 위해 사용되었다.

1895~1896년 영사 기술의 등장으로 영화는 본격적인 대중 소비 매체가 되었다. 그 전에 대규모 관람객들이 극장에서 구경거리를 관람했다. 이런 극장에서는 한 번에 수백 명의 관람객을 모아 놓고 희가극, 대중극, 뮤지컬, 고전극, 강연, 슬라이드 랜턴쇼 등을 보여 주었다. 하지만 이런 유흥 양식들과 영화는 근본적으로 달랐다. 다른 유흥 양식들은 라이브 공연이나 (슬라이드 랜턴쇼에서처럼) 최종 프로그램을

spectators at a time. But the movies differed significantly from these other forms of entertainment, which depended on either live performance or (in the case of the slide-and-lantern shows) the active involvement of a master of ceremonies who assembled the final program.

Although early exhibitors regularly accompanied movies with live acts, the substance of the movies themselves is mass-produced, prerecorded material that can easily be reproduced by theaters with little or no active participation by the exhibitor. Even though early exhibitors shaped their film programs by mixing films and other entertainments together in whichever way they thought would be most attractive to audiences or by accompanying them with lectures, their creative control remained limited. What audiences came to see was the technological marvel of the movies; the lifelike reproduction of the commonplace motion of trains, of waves striking the shore, and of people walking in the street; and the magic made possible by trick photography and the manipulation of the camera.

With the advent of projection, the viewer's relationship with the image was no longer private, as it had been with earlier peepshow devices such as the Kinetoscope and the Mutoscope, which was a similar machine that reproduced motion by means of successive images on individual photographic cards instead of on strips of celluloid. It suddenly became public—an experience that the viewer shared with dozens, scores, and even hundreds of others. At the same time, the image that the spectator looked at expanded from the minuscule peepshow dimensions of 1 or 2 inches (in height) to the life-size proportions of 6 or 9 feet.

짜는 사회자의 적극적인 개입에 의존하고 있었다.

초창기 흥행업자들은 영화에다 라이브 공연을 곁들이곤 했지만, 영화는 본질적으로 대량생산이 가능하며 상영 전에 이미 녹화된 매체이므로, 흥행업자들의 특별한 개입이 없이도 극장에서 손쉽게 재생될 수 있었다. 초기의 흥행업자들은 최대한 관람객들의 흥미를 끌기 위해 영화에 다른 오락 요소를 가미한다거나 강연 등을 곁들이는 시도를 했지만, 그들의 창조적 관리에는 한계가 있을 수밖에 없었다. 관람객들이 감탄한 것은 영화 기술의 경이로움이었다. 일상적인 기차의 움직임, 해안에 부딪치는 파도, 그리고 거리를 걷는 사람들의 모습을 똑같이 재현한 광경이나, 촬영의 트릭과 카메라 조작을 통해 가능해진, 마술 같은 장면에 놀라워했다.

영사 기술이 등장하면서 관람자와 영상과의 관계는 키네토스코프나 뮤토스코프 같은 초기 핍쇼 장치의 개인적인 차원을 벗어났다. 뮤토스코프는 키네토스코프와 비슷한 기계지만, 셀룰로이드 조각 대신에 낱장의 사진 카드에 새긴 연속적인 이미지를 통해 동작을 재생했다. 관람자와 영상과의 관계는 갑자기 공적인 것이 되면서 이제 수십, 아니 수백 명의 관람객들이 모두 공유하는 경험이 되었다. 동시에 관람객이 보는 영상도 높이 1인치나 2인치의 자그마한 핍쇼 필름에서 6피트나 9피트의 실물 크기의 비율로 크게 확대되었다.

어휘

emerge 나타나다, 부각되다   consumption 소비, 소모   evolve 발전하다, 진화하다   peepshow 들여다보는 구경거리, 음란쇼   project 투영하다, 영사하다   opening 트인 구멍, 틈   parlor 응접실, 휴게실   prizefight 프로 권투 시합   successive 연속되는   round (권투의) 1회, 1라운드   model 본받다, 본보기로 삼다   phonograph 축음기   ear tube 청음기   apiece 각각에게, 하나에   approximately 대략   projector 영사기   exhibitor 영화관 경영자, 출품자   maximize 극대화시키다   readily 즉석에서, 쉽사리   a handful of 소량의   admission 입장료   vaudeville 가벼운 희가극, 보드빌   legitimate 정통극   makeshift storefront theater 임시로 만든 상점 앞 극장   fairground 장터, 박람회   amusement park 놀이공원   with the advent of ~의 도래로, ~의 출현으로   ultimate 최종의   lifelike 실물 그대로의   participation 참여   marvel 놀라운 일   manipulation 조작   celluloid 셀룰로이드, 영화 필름   minuscule 소문자인, 대단히 작은   life-size 실제 크기의   proportion 비율

1. 첫 번째 단락에 따르면, 키네토스코프 감상실에서 영화를 볼 때 해당되지 않는 내용은?

Ⓐ 한 번에 한 사람씩 영화를 관람했다.
Ⓑ 고객은 영화를 한 편씩 차례대로 관람할 수 있었다.
Ⓒ 프로 권투시합이 가장 인기 있는 영화였다.
Ⓓ 영화 길이는 짧았다.

틀린 정보 찾기 문제

해설 프로 권투시합은 영화의 주제 가운데 하나로 언급되어 있지만, 가장 인기 있는 것이라고 하지는 않았다.

2. 두 번째 단락에서 필자는 축음기 감상실에 대해 설명했는데 그 이유는?

Ⓐ 에디슨의 경제적 성공을 설명하기 위해
Ⓑ 키네토스코프 감상실을 만드는 데 사용되었던 모델을 설명하기위해
Ⓒ 축음기 감상실과 키네토스코프 감상실의 인기를 비교하기 위해
Ⓓ 키네토스코프 감상실의 기술적인 발달을 설명하기 위해

수사학적 의도 파악 문제

어휘 financial success 경제적 성공 illustrate 설명하다

해설 에디슨은 과거에 축음기 감상실로 성공을 거두었기 때문에, 키네토스코프 감상실을 만들 때 축음기 감상실을 모델로 삼았다는 내용이 이 단락의 첫 번째 문장에 나와 있다. 그러므로 보기 B가 정답. 보기 A의 에디슨의 경제적 성공은 이 단락의 주요 포인트가 아니며, 보기 C, D는 전혀 언급되지 않았다.

3. 다음 중 두 번째 단락에 음영으로 표시된 문장이 담고 있는 핵심 정보를 가장 잘 표현한 것은? 정답 외의 보기들은 의미가 상당히 왜곡되거나 본질적인 정보가 빠져 있다.

Ⓐ 에디슨은 단 하나의 기계를 위한 기술보다는 여러 가지 기계를 개발하는 데 관심이 있었다.
Ⓑ 에디슨은 흥행업자들이 자신들의 영사기를 새로운 기계로 대체하지 않을 것이라고 생각했기 때문에 영사 기술을 개발하려고 하지 않았다.
Ⓒ 에디슨은 영사 기술이 등장하면 자신이 팔 수 있는 기계의 수가 줄어들기 때문에 그 기술을 개발하려고 하지 않았다.
Ⓓ 흥행업자들이 자신으로부터 영사기를 한 대 이상 구입하겠다고 동의하지 않는 한, 에디슨은 영사 기술을 개발하려고 하지 않았을 것이다.

문장 재구성 문제

해설 보기 A와 B는 사실이 아니며, 보기 D는 원래의 의미를 왜곡시킨 것이다. 에디슨은 한 대의 영사기보다는 여러 대의 키네토스코프를 팔고 싶기 때문에 영사 기술을 개발하려고 하지 않았다는 의미이므로 보기 C가 정답이다.

4. 지문의 단어 readily와 의미상 가장 가까운 것은?

Ⓐ 빈번히   Ⓑ 쉽게   Ⓒ 총명하게   Ⓓ 명백히

어휘 문제

해설 readily는 '쉽게', '용이하게' 라는 뜻이다.

5. 네 번째 단락에 따르면, 초창기 영화는 예전에 대규모 관중이 관람하던 구경거리와 어떤 점에서 다른가?

Ⓐ 값비싼 오락 매체였다.
Ⓑ 대규모 관중이 관람했다.
Ⓒ 더 교육적이었다.
Ⓓ 라이브 공연자가 필요 없었다.

세부 사항 찾기 문제

어휘 educational 교육적인

해설 이 단락의 마지막 문장에 영화와 다른 구경거리의 차이점이 설명되어 있다. 예전의 구경거리는 라이브 공연이거나 사회자가 등장한다는 점이 영화와 크게 다른 점이다. 따라서 보기 D가 정답이다.

6. 다섯 번째 단락에 따르면, 초기 흥행업자들은 극장에서 영화를 상영하는 데 어떤 역할을 했는가?

Ⓐ 영화 프로그램에 다양한 요소들을 결합시켰다.
Ⓑ 영화제작자들에게 적절한 영화 소재를 제공했다.
Ⓒ 종종 라이브 공연에 직접 참가했다.
Ⓓ 극장에서 보여 줄 구경거리를 제작하거나 사전에 녹화해 두었다.

세부 사항 찾기 문제

어휘 filmmaker 영화제작자

해설 Even though로 시작하는 문장에서 영화에 다른 오락거리를 결합시켰다는 내용이 나와 있다. 따라서 정답은 보기 A. 나머지 보기들은 흥행업자들의 역할로 기술되어 있지 않다.

7. 지문에서 It이 가리키는 것은?

Ⓐ 영사 기술의 도래
Ⓑ 관람자와 영상과의 관계
Ⓒ 비슷한 기계
Ⓓ 셀룰로이드

지시 대상 찾기 문제

해설 앞 문장이 길기 때문에 It이 무엇을 가리키는지 헷갈리기 쉽다. 하지만 앞 문장의 주요 포인트가 '관람자와 영상과의 관계가 더 이상 개인적인 것이 아니다' 이므로, 문맥의 흐름상 It은 당연히 '관람자와 영상과의 관계' 가 되어야 한다.

8. 여섯 번째 단락에 따르면, 초창기 핍쇼에서 관람객이 구경한 영상은 스크린에 영사된 영상과 비교해 볼 때 어떤 점에서 다른가?

Ⓐ 크기가 작다.

Ⓑ 제작비가 많이 든다.

Ⓒ 초점이 맞지 않는다.

Ⓓ 소재 선택에 한계가 있다.

세부 사항 찾기 문제

어휘 subject 주제, 과목

해설 이 단락의 마지막 문장에서 영상 크기의 차이가 설명되어 있다.

9. 지시문: 위에 제시된 지문의 일부를 보시오. 지문에 표시된 **(A)**, **(B)**, **(C)**, **(D)** 중 하나에 다음 문장이 삽입될 수 있다.

When this widespread use of projection technology began to hurt his Kinetoscope business, Edison acquired a projector developed by Armat and introduced it as "Edison's latest marvel, the Vitascope."

(영사 기술이 널리 이용되면서 자신의 키네토스코프 사업이 타격을 입기 시작하자, 에디슨은 아매트가 개발한 영사기를 취득하여 그것을 '에디슨의 최신 발명품 비타스코프'라고 소개했다.)

이 문장이 들어갈 가장 적당한 위치는?

(A) Exhibitors, however, wanted to maximize their profits, which they could do more readily by projecting a handful of films to hundreds of customers at a time (rather than one at a time) and by charging 25 to 50 cents admission. **(B)** About a year after the opening of the first Kinetoscope parlor in 1894, showmen such as Louis and Auguste Lumière, Thomas Armat and Charles Francis Jenkins, and Orville and Woodville Latham (with the assistance of Edison's former assistant, William Dickson) perfected projection devices. **(C)** These early projection devices were used in vaudeville theaters, legitimate theaters, local town halls, makeshift storefront theaters, fairgrounds, and amusement parks to shown films to a mass audience. **(D)** When this widespread use of projection technology began to hurt his Kinetoscope business, Edison acquired a projector developed by Armat and introduced it as "Edison's latest marvel, the Vitascope."

Ⓐ   Ⓑ   Ⓒ   Ⓓ

문장 삽입 문제

어휘 widespread 널리 보급된   acquire 획득하다, 습득하다

해설 삽입될 문장은 영사기가 발명되어 널리 인기를 얻은 후에 나타난 결과다. 즉 에디슨은 처음에는 영사기를 개발하지 않으려고 했지만, 다른 사람들에 의해 개발된 영사기가 보편화되면서 어쩔수 없이 현실을 받아들이고 새로운 대안을 찾을 수밖에 없는 상황을 기술한 것이다. 따라서 삽입될 문장은 (D)에 들어가야 문맥의 흐름이 자연스럽다.

10. 지시문: 이 지문을 간단히 요약하기 위한 도입 문장이 아래에 제시되어 있다. 아래 보기들 중에서 지문의 가장 중요한 개념을 표현한 3개를 골라 요약을 완성하라. 보기들 중에는 지문에 나오지 않았거나 중요하지 않은 개념이기 때문에 요약문으로 적절치 않은 것들도 있다. 이 문제의 배점은 2점이다.

현대 영화 기술은 19세기 말에 발달했다.

Ⓐ 영화 관람을 위한 키네토스코프 감상실은 축음기 감상실을 모델 삼아 만들어졌다.

Ⓑ 토머스 에디슨이 키네토스코프를 발명함으로써 대형 스크린 영사 기술의 발달이 촉진되었다.

Ⓒ 초창기 영화는 개인이 특별한 기계를 이용해 혼자서 영화를 볼 수 있도록 만들어졌다.

Ⓓ 랜턴 슬라이드쇼는 수백 명의 관람객들을 대상으로 펼쳐졌다.

Ⓔ 영사 기술의 발달로 대형스크린에 영상을 영사하는 것이 가능해졌다.

Ⓕ 필름 영상을 영사할 수 있게 되면서 영화는 대중 소비매체가 되었다.

지문 요약하기 문제

해설 보기 C, E, F가 정답이다. 보기 C는 키네토스코프와 영사기의 주요 차이점에 대한 설명이고, 첫 번째, 세 번째, 네 번째, 여섯 번째 단락에서 반복적으로 기술하고 있는 주요 개념이다. 보기 E는 영화가 대중 소비 매체로 자리 잡게 된 이유인데, 세 번째, 네 번째, 다섯 번째, 여섯 번째 단락에서 그 과정이 자세히 설명되어 있다. 보기 F는 이 글의 중심 주제다. 보기 A, D는 지엽적인 사실에 불과하고, 보기 B는 이 글의 내용과는 다르다.

WATER AND OCEAN LIFE

The physical and chemical properties of water, unsurprisingly, determine much about life in the ocean. Water is dense (high mass per unit of volume), about 840 times as dense as air—roughly as dense as most life forms, as they are primarily made of water. This means that marine organisms fight no battle with gravity and possess none of the structures that we need on land to combat it. In the ocean, there are no tree trunks. The closest analogy would be the stipes (stalks) of the large seaweeds known as kelp, allowing kelp to form "forests." But these stipes do not hold the kelp up—they just hold it in place. At low tide the kelp collapses. Likewise, marine animals can have flexible skeletons or no skeleton at all. This makes it much easier to become large. The major problem with the density of the ocean comes in the depths, where the weight of all that seawater bears down, creating enormous pressures.

Related to density is viscosity—or, basically, thickness due to internal friction. It is about sixty times easier to move through air than water. The importance of this friction depends on how big one is and how fast one is moving. It is much more significant for the little creatures. As a result, while a killer whale can cruise at about ten kilometers per hour, krill, weighing about 0.2 grams, can achieve only about 0.2 kilometers per hour. So, in the viscous ocean the little animals move slowly, giving the big ones a significant advantage. There are no darting ocean insects. Some medium-sized animals, like flying fish and leaping dolphins, leave the water when they want to move really fast.

Water dissolves other substances better than any other common liquid. This allows it to function as the medium for chemical communication using hormones within animal bodies. Seawater includes all kinds of dissolved substances, including, of course, salt. Many of these substances are important for marine life, but none has the significance of oxygen, which all animals need to power their bodies. Seawater is about 0.5–0.9 percent oxygen at the surface. Most marine animals use gills to get oxygen from seawater into their bodies. A few, including the marine mammals, come to the surface and breathe the air. Coming to the surface may have costs in time, energy, or vulnerability to predators, but it has benefits, too, primarily that air is 21 percent oxygen.

Few animals just sit, or move aimlessly along, waiting for good things, like food or mates, or dangerous things, like predators, to come their way. They sense their environment and change their physiology or behavior, and they communicate with each other.

물과 바다 생물

물의 물리적 및 화학적 특성은 당연하게도 바다의 생명체에 많은 영향을 미친다. 물은 공기의 약 840배에 달할 정도로 밀도(단위 부피당 높은 질량)가 높은데, 대부분의 생물이 물로 이루어져 있기 때문에 대부분의 생물과 거의 비슷한 밀도를 가진다. 이것은 해양 생물들이 중력과 싸우지 않으며 우리가 땅 위에서 중력과 싸우기 위해 필요한 구조를 그들은 가지고 있지 않음을 뜻한다. 바닷속에는 나무 줄기가 없다. 가장 유사한 형태라면 '켈프'라고 알려진 큰 해조류의 줄기인데, 덕분에 켈프는 '숲'을 형성한다. 그런데 이 줄기는 켈프를 지탱해서 세워주는 것이 아니라, 제자리에 있게 해준다. 썰물 때에는 켈프가 쓰러진다. 마찬가지로 해양 동물들은 유연한 뼈를 가지거나 아예 뼈가 없을 수 있고 이로 인해 몸집이 커질 수 있다. 바다의 밀도의 가장 큰 문제는 심해에서 발생하는데, 그곳에서는 모든 해수의 무게가 아래로 내리눌러 엄청난 압력을 발생시킨다.

밀도와 관련된 것은 점성인데, 이는 기본적으로 내부 마찰로 인한 진한 농도를 의미한다. 공기 속에서 움직이는 것이 물속에서 움직이는 것보다 약 60배 더 쉽다. 이 마찰의 중요성은 대상이 얼마나 큰가, 또 얼마나 빠른가에 따라 다르다. 이것은 작은 생물들에게 훨씬 더 중요하다. 결과적으로, 범고래는 시간당 약 10킬로미터를 헤엄쳐 갈 수 있지만, 약 0.2그램인 크릴 새우는 시간당 0.2킬로미터만 헤엄칠 수 있다. 따라서 점성이 높은 바다에서 작은 동물들은 느리게 이동하며, 큰 동물들에게 상당한 이점을 제공한다. 바다에는 쏜살같이 움직이는 곤충은 없다. 날치나 도약하는 돌고래 같은 중간 크기의 동물들은 정말 빠르게 움직이고자 할 때 물 밖으로 나간다.

물은 어떤 일반적인 액체보다 다른 물질들을 잘 녹인다. 이런 성질이 물이 동물의 체내에서 분비되는 호르몬을 이용한 화학적 소통의 매개체로서 작용할 수 있게 한다. 바닷물에는 온갖 종류의 용해된 물질이 포함되어 있는데, 물론 그 중에는 소금도 들어있다. 이러한 물질들 대다수가 해양 생물에게 중요하지만 산소만큼 중요한 것은 없는데, 모든 동물이 몸을 활성화하는 데 산소를 필요로 한다. 바닷물은 표면에 약 0.5-0.9%의 산소를 포함하고 있다. 대부분의 해양 동물은 바닷물에서 몸 속으로 산소를 얻기 위해 아가미를 사용한다. 해양 포유류를 포함한 몇몇 해양 동물들은 표면으로 올라와 공기를 마신다. 수면으로 올라오는 것은 시간, 에너지, 또는 포식자에 대한 취약성과 같은 기회 비용이 들 수 있지만, 공기에는 산소가 21퍼센트나 포함되어 있기 때문에 우선적인 이득이 있다.

그저 그 자리에서 먹이나 짝짓기 대상 같은 좋은 것들이 나타나기를 기다리거나, 포식자와 같은 위험한 것들이 오는

One can sense and communicate through a variety of channels, primarily what we call the five senses: touch, taste, smell, hearing, and sight. Moving from the air to water changes the relative benefit of each of the senses. Chemical signals are not dispersed as widely or as predictably under water as in air, so taste and smell have less value for marine animals. Some penguins seem to be able to smell areas with high concentrations of organisms and swim toward them over large ranges, but, tellingly, they do so by smelling the air that they breathe, not by tasting the water that they swim through, even though the organisms they are aiming for are in the water. Sight is also degraded in the ocean because light is absorbed by water. At depths of a few hundred meters there is virtually no light, even in the middle of the day, and even just beneath the surface one can rarely see more than about twenty meters, less than the length of a blue whale.

(A) One sense that does do better underwater is sound. (B) Sound travels about four times faster than in air. (C) More important, and in contrast to light, sound is less weakened by water than air. (D) While there are a few sounds of terrestrial mammals that travel over kilometers—the roars of lions, the rumbles of elephants, and the howls of wolves—most sounds of most terrestrial mammals are lost at much shorter ranges. Many underwater sounds of marine mammals, on the other hand, can be heard in quiet conditions at a kilometer and some travel very much farther.

걸 기다리는 동물들은 거의 없다. 그들은 주변 환경을 감지하고 자신들의 생리나 행동을 변경시키며 서로 소통한다. 동물은 다양한 채널, 주로 우리가 오감이라고 부르는 것, 즉 촉각, 미각, 후각, 청각 및 시각을 통해 느끼고 교류한다. 공기 중에서 물속으로 이동하면 각 감각의 상대적 이익이 변한다. 화학적 신호는 물속에서는 공기 중에서처럼 넓게 또는 예측 가능하게 퍼져 나가지 않기 때문에 해양 생물에게는 미각과 후각이 덜 중요하다. 일부 펭귄들은 유기체가 잔뜩 모여 있는 지역을 냄새로 감지하고 멀리까지 헤엄쳐 이동할 수 있는 것처럼 보이는데, 그들은 헤엄치면서 물의 맛을 보고 이렇게 하는 것이 아니라 그들이 숨쉬는 공기 속 냄새를 맡으면서 그렇게 한다. 그들이 노리는 유기체가 물속에 있어도 말이다. 또한 바닷속에서는 물이 빛을 흡수하기 때문에 시력이 저하된다. 깊이가 수백 미터인 곳에서는 낮에도 거의 빛이 없고, 표면 바로 아래에서도 보통 약 20미터밖에 볼 수 없다. 이는 흰긴수염고래보다 짧은 길이다.

바닷속에서 더 힘을 발휘하는 것은 소리이다. 소리는 공기 중에서보다 4배 빠른 속도로 이동한다. 빛과는 다르면서 더 중요한 성질은, 소리가 공기에서보다 물속에서 더 오래 멀리 퍼진다는 것이다. 몇몇 육지 포유류들의 소리—사자의 포효, 코끼리의 울음, 늑대의 울부짖음—는 수 킬로미터를 이동하지만 거의 대부분의 육지 포유류의 소리 대부분은 훨씬 짧은 범위 내에서 사라진다. 반면에 해양 포유류들이 수중에서 내는 소리는, 조용한 환경에서일 경우 1킬로미터 밖에서도 들리고 어떤 소리는 훨씬 멀리까지 이동한다.

어휘

physical 물리적   chemical 화학적   determine 결정하다   dense 밀도가 높은   primarily 주로   tree trunk 나무의 큰 줄기   analogy 유사점   stipe 줄기   in place 제자리에   tide 조수   collapse 쓰러지다   bear down 쓰러지다   viscosity 점도   friction 마찰   killer whale 범고래   krill 크릴새우   dart 쏜살같이 움직이다   flying fish 날치   dissolve 녹다   gill 아가미   vulnerability 취약함   predator 포식자   aimlessly 목적 없이   physiology 생리   channel 경로, 수단   disperse 흩어지다   high concentration 고농도   organism 유기체   tellingly 효과적으로, 강력하게   degraded 퇴화한, 저하된   terrestrial 육상의   rumble 덜컹거리며 나아가다   howl (짐승의) 울음소리

1. 첫 번째 단락에서 글쓴이가 켈프가 썰물 때 쓰러진다고 말한 이유는?

Ⓐ 바닷속 유기체는 중력을 극복하기 위한 구조가 결여돼 있다는 견해를 설명하기 위해

Ⓑ 켈프는 주로 물로 이루어져 있다는 증거를 제공하기 위해

Ⓒ 켈프가 제자리에 있을 수 있도록 지탱해 주는 줄기가 필요한 이유를 설명하기 위해

Ⓓ 심해의 어마어마한 압력이 어떻게 큰 문제를 발생시키는지 입증하기 위해

수사학적 의도 파악 문제

어휘 overcome 극복하다

해설 썰물 때 물이 거의 빠져나가면 켈프가 쓰러진다는 사실은 켈프에 중력을 극복하기 위한 구조가 결여되어 있음을 뜻한다. 따라서 정답은 A. 대부분의 생명체가 물로 이루어져 있다는 말이 단락에 나오지만 썰물에 쓰러지는 켈프가 이 주장에 대한 증거는 아니므로 B는 오답. 지문에 켈프가 가진 줄기에 관한 이야기가 나오긴 하지만 줄기는 제자리에 있게 해 줄 뿐 지탱해주는 것이 아니라고 했으므로 C도 정답이 아니다. 마찬가지로 보기 D의 내용도 관계가 없으므로 오답이다.

2. 첫 번째 단락에 따르면, 다음 중 해양 동물이 매우 거대해지는 이유는?

Ⓐ 바다의 생명체 개체 수가 거대한 압력을 형성하여 동물이 거대하게 자라도록 만든다.

Ⓑ 거대한 바다 동물들은 단단한 뼈가 필요 없다.

Ⓒ 켈프 숲은 거대한 동물들에게 유연한 서식지를 제공한다.

Ⓓ 심해에는 거대한 동물을 위한 공간이 많이 있다.

세부 사항 찾기 문제

어휘 rigid 단단한　habitat 서식지　room 공간

해설 첫 번째 단락에서 해양 동물들이 유연한 뼈를 가지거나 아예 뼈가 없을 수 있으며, 이는 그들이 커지기 쉽게 만든다고 했다. '유연한' 것은 '딱딱하지 않은(not rigid)'의 뜻이므로 정답은 B. 보기 A, C 및 D는 해양 동물의 큰 크기에 대한 설명에 해당하지 않는다.

3. 두 번째 단락에서, 글쓴이가 범고래와 크릴 새우의 헤엄치는 속도를 비교한 이유는?

Ⓐ 공기를 통해 이동하는 것이 물을 통해 이동하는 것보다 훨씬 빠르다는 생각을 뒷받침하기 위해

Ⓑ 고래의 일반적인 먹이가 크릴 새우인 이유를 설명하기 위해

Ⓒ 물의 점성이 큰 동물보다 작은 동물에게 더 큰 영향을 미친다는 주장을 뒷받침하기 위해

Ⓓ 작은 크기가 바다에서는 큰 장점임을 입증하기 위해

수사학적 의도 파악 문제

해설 글쓴이는 마찰의 중요성이 해양 동물의 크기와 속도에 따라 달라지며, 이는 특히 작은 동물들에게 더 중요하다고 설명한다. 그리고 큰 동물인 범고래와 작은 동물인 크릴의 수영 속도를 비교하여 이 주장을 뒷받침한다. 정답은 C가 된다. 보기 A의 물보다 공기를 통해 이동하는 것이 더 쉽다는 내용도 나오지만 이를 위

해 무언가 비교를 하지는 않았다. B는 언급되지 않았고 D는 상반되는 내용이다.

4. 세 번째 단락에 따르면, 다음 중 바닷물에 대한 옳은 설명 2가지는 무엇인가? 점수를 얻기 위해서 반드시 2가지를 고르시오.

Ⓐ 바다에 포함된 소금은 바닷속에 있지 않을 때보다 더 많은 산소를 녹이도록 돕는다.

Ⓑ 바닷물은 동물의 호르몬 분비를 방해하여 그들의 소통 능력을 제한한다.

Ⓒ 바닷물에는 동물이 필요로 하는 많은 물질이 포함되어 있다.

Ⓓ 바닷물에 포함된 산소는 많은 해양 동물들의 아가미를 통해 흡입된다.

세부 사항 찾기 문제

어휘 otherwise 그렇지 않으면　interfere with 방해하다

해설 바닷물에는 온갖 종류의 용해된 물질이 포함되어 있는데, 이러한 물질들 대다수가 해양 생물에게 중요하다는 내용과 대부분의 해양 동물은 바닷물에서 몸 속으로 산소를 얻기 위해 아가미를 사용한다는 내용이 나와 있다. 물이 물질을 녹인다고 했을 뿐 소금이나 산소의 언급은 없었고, 물질을 녹이는 물의 성질이 동물의 체내에서 분비되는 호르몬을 이용한 화학적 소통의 매개체로서 작용할 수 있게 한다고 했으므로 A와 B는 틀렸다.

5. 지문의 단어 primarily와 의미상 가장 가까운 것은?

Ⓐ 보통　　　　　Ⓑ 흔히

Ⓒ 특히　　　　　Ⓓ 주로

어휘 문제

해설 primarily는 '주로'라는 뜻의 부사이다.

6. 다음 중 네 번째 단락에 음영으로 표시된 문장이 담고 있는 핵심 정보를 가장 잘 표현한 것은? 정답 외의 보기들은 의미가 상당히 왜곡되거나 본질적인 정보가 빠져 있다.

Ⓐ 넓은 범위에 걸쳐 유기체가 많이 모여 있는 곳을 감지할 수 있는 펭귄들은 물을 맛보는 것에서가 아닌 공기로 냄새를 감지하고 그렇게 하는 것처럼 보인다.

Ⓑ 일부 펭귄은 많은 유기체가 모여 있는 지역을 감지하고 멀리까지 헤엄칠 수 있다.

Ⓒ 일부 펭귄은 숨쉬는 공기를 맡아서 유기체를 감지하는 반면 다른 펭귄들은 헤엄치면서 물의 맛을 보고 감지한다.

Ⓓ 일부 펭귄은 유기체와 자신들이 물속에 있을 때만 유기체들이 모여 있는 지역을 감지할 수 있는 것으로 보인다.

문장 재구성 문제

해설 해당 문장의 주요 정보와 내용을 전부 포함하고 있는 보기는 A이다. B는 물맛을 통해서가 아니라 공기중에서 냄새를 맡고 감지한다는 제일 중요한 정보가 빠져 있다. C와 D는 틀린 내용이다.

7. 지문의 in contrast to와 의미상 가장 가까운 것은?

Ⓐ ~보다 많은

Ⓑ ~을 제외하고

Ⓒ ~을 따라서

Ⓓ ~와 달리

어휘 문제

해설 in contrast to는 '~와는 대조적으로'라는 뜻의 숙어이다.

8. 다섯 번째 단락에서 사자의 울음소리, 코끼리의 포효소리, 늑대의 울부짖음으로부터 유추할 수 있는 것은?

Ⓐ 그것들은 때때로 해양 동물에게 들리기도 한다.

Ⓑ 그것들은 육지 동물이 만드는 소리 중에서 가장 멀리 이동하는 소리에 포함된다.

Ⓒ 그것들은 대부분의 해양 동물이 내는 소리보다 약 4배 빠르게 이동한다.

Ⓓ 그것들은 해양 동물이 만드는 소리보다 훨씬 더 넓은 범위에서 들을 수 있다.

내용 추론 문제

해설 지문에서 육지 동물들이 내는 소리 중에 수 킬로미터를 넘어서는 것은 거의 없다고 언급하고 있으며, 사자의 포효, 코끼리의 울음, 늑대의 울부짖음을 이런 소리의 예로 들고 있다. 또한 대부분의 육지 동물들의 소리가 짧은 범위 내에서 소멸된다고 말하고 있다. 즉 사자의 포효, 코끼리의 울음, 늑대의 울부짖음이 육지 동물이 내는 소리 중에서 가장 멀리 들리는 소리임을 추론할 수 있다.

9. 지시문: 위에 제시된 지문의 일부를 보시오. 지문에 표시된 **(A)**, **(B)**, **(C)**, **(D)** 중 하나에 다음 문장이 삽입될 수 있다.

There are a couple of reasons for this.
(여기엔 두 가지의 이유가 있다.)

이 문장이 들어갈 가장 적당한 위치는?

(A) One sense that does do better underwater is sound. **(B)** There are a couple of reasons for this. Sound travels about four times faster than in air. **(C)** More important, and in contrast to light, sound is less weakened by water than air. **(D)** While there are a few sounds of terrestrial mammals that travel over kilometers—the roars of lions, the rumbles of elephants, and the howls of wolves—most sounds of most terrestrial mammals are lost at much shorter ranges. Many underwater sounds of marine mammals, on the other hand, can be heard in quiet conditions at a kilometer and some travel very much farther.

Ⓐ   Ⓑ   Ⓒ   Ⓓ

문장 삽입 문제

어휘 couple of 두 가지의

해설 제시된 문장에서 앞으로 두 가지 이유에 대해 설명할 예정임을 알 수 있다. 바닷속에서 더 힘을 발휘하는 것은 소리라고 하고 이후에 그 이유인 소리의 속도와 강도에 대해 설명하고 있다. 따라서 (B)의 위치에 들어가야 맥락이 자연스럽다. (A)는 앞 단락이 바닷속에서의 시야에 대해 설명하고 있으므로 오답. (C)가 답이 되려면 다음에 소리가 빠른 속도로 이동하는 이유가 나와야 하는데, 그렇지 않으므로 틀렸다. 마찬가지로 (D)가 답이 되려면 다음에 왜 바닷속에서 소리가 덜 약해지는지 이유가 나와야 한다.

10. 지시문: 지문을 간단히 요약하기 위한 도입 문장이 아래에 제시되어 있다. 아래 보기들 중에서 지문의 가장 중요한 개념을 표현한 문장 3개를 골라 요약을 완성하라. 보기들 중에는 지문에 나오지 않았거나 중요하지 않은 개념이기 때문에 요약문으로 적절치 않은 것들도 있다. 이 문제의 배점은 2점이다.

물의 성질이 바다에 사는 생명체들의 성질을 결정한다.

Ⓐ 물의 밀도 때문에 해양 생물들은 중력을 이겨내지 않아도 되지만, 깊은 바다에서 물의 밀도는 극심한 압력을 유발하여 생명체에 문제가 될 수 있다.

Ⓑ 해양 동물들은 소금, 다른 동물의 호르몬, 그리고 해수에 용해된 다른 유해 물질들을 상대해야 하며, 이 과정을 위해 산소가 필요하다.

Ⓒ 바닷속에 있는 산소는 농도는 낮지만, 해양 생물들에게 가장 중요한 용해 물질이며, 대부분의 해양 동물들은 아가미를 통해 산소를 들이마신다.

Ⓓ 바닷속의 산소는 표면 근처에 훨씬 더 농축되어 있어서, 많은 생물들이 빠르게 움직이는 데 필요한 에너지를 얻기 위해 표면 쪽으로 올라간다.

Ⓔ 육지 동물들에게는 결여되어 있지만 해양 동물들은 가지고 있는 한 가지 감각은 화학 신호인데, 화학 물질이 물에 쉽게 용해되고 넓은 영역에 분포될 수 있기 때문이다.

Ⓕ 수중에서는 감각의 상대적인 중요성이 다른데, 시각, 후각, 미각이 육지에서보다 덜 유용하며, 청각이 훨씬 더 효과적이다.

지문 요약하기 문제

어휘 property 성질   deal with 상대하다   signaling 신호
distribute 분포하다

해설 A는 첫 번째 단락을 요약하고 있다. 해양 동물들이 소금, 호르몬, 용해 물질을 상대해야 한다는 내용은 지문에 없으므로 B는 적절치 않다. C는 세 번째 단락을 요약하고 있다. D는 산소량 비교를 하고 있지 않고, 해양 동물이 해수면쪽으로 가는 것은 산소를 호흡하고자 하는 것이고, 빨리 움직이고 싶으면 물밖으로 나간다고 했으므로 적절치 않다. E는 화학적 신호에 대해 전혀 다른 설명을 하고 있다. F는 네 번째와 다섯 번째 단락을 요약하고 있다.

FREDERICK TAYLOR AND UNITED STATES INDUSTRY

By the twentieth century, making workers more "cost-efficient" had become the single most important management goal in large-scale industries. Everywhere in industrial America managers were drafting work rules and designing tasks with an eye to increasing worker output.

The leading supporter of productivity was Frederick Winslow Taylor, whose time-and-motion studies revolutionized the industrial workplace and whose writings, especially *The Principles of Scientific Management*, had unquestionable authority among industrial engineers and factory managers. Taylor was obsessed with order and efficiency. Taylor also grew up at a time when the processes of motion were fascinating to many Americans. Artists such as Thomas Eakins were painting the human form in ways that showed its dexterity. **(A)** In the 1870s, in California, the English-born photographer Eadweard Muybridge was developing a multiple-camera technique to record an animal in motion. **(B)** Muybridge's experiments, which laid the groundwork for motion pictures, started out to settle a bet whether all four of a racehorse's hooves simultaneously left the ground at some point during its stride (he showed that they did), but they attracted national attention for demonstrating that machines could measure movement. **(C)** Picture frame by picture frame, Muybridge revealed what the naked eye could not see, and by breaking down complex movement his cameras made it understandable and potentially subject to control. **(D)**

In the iron and steel factories that Taylor visited during the 1870s and 1880s, he saw only disorder and inefficiency on shop floors where skilled workers controlled the rhythms and division of labor. Taylor believed that scientific study could break down the industrial process into its simplest parts, which, once understood, would allow managers to increase production and lower costs by reducing unnecessary motion and workers. Stopwatch in hand, he recorded the time workers spent on each particular task and then suggested changes in the jobs to improve efficiency. In his most famous demonstration, at the Bethlehem Steel Company in 1898, Taylor designed fifteen kinds of ore shovels, each for a specific task and each to be used in a specific way. He was able to show that 140 men could do the work of 600. The company thereupon fired the "excess" shovelers, cutting its ore-shoveling costs by half. It also gave the remaining shovelers a raise in salary.

The other side of Taylor's plan was to provide motivations for workers to exceed production goals by rewarding them with extra pay when they did so. Under Taylor's proposal, however, workers

프레드릭 테일러와 미국의 산업

20세기에 들어서면서 대규모 산업에서 노동자들을 보다 '비용 효율적'으로 만드는 것이 가장 중요한 단일 경영 목표가 되었다. 미국의 산업 현장 어디에서나, 관리자들이 노동자의 생산성을 높일 목적으로 작업 규칙을 작성하고 작업을 설계했다.

생산성을 지지하는 주요 인물은 프레드릭 윈슬로 테일러였다. 그의 시간과 동작에 관한 연구는 산업 현장을 혁명했고, 특히 〈과학적 관리법〉이라는 저서는 산업 기술자와 공장 경영자들 사이에서 의문의 여지가 없는 권위를 지니고 있었다. 테일러는 질서와 효율에 집착했다. 테일러는 또한 미국인들에게 동작의 과정이 매혹적이었던 시대에 자라났다. 토머스 에이킨스와 같은 화가들은 인간을 그들의 민첩성을 보여 주는 방식으로 그렸다. 1870년대, 캘리포니아에서, 영국 출신의 사진작가 에드워드 머이브리지는 동물의 움직임을 기록하기 위해 다중 카메라 기법을 개발하고 있었다. 영화의 기초를 마련하는 데 기여한 머이브리지의 실험은 경주마의 네 발이 동시에 땅에서 떨어지는 순간이 있는지에 대한 내기를 해결하기 위해 시작되었다(그는 그렇다는 것을 보여 줬다). 그런데 이 실험은 기계가 움직임을 측정할 수 있다는 것을 입증한 사실로 전국민적 관심을 끌었다. 머이브리지는 사진 한 장 한 장 사람의 맨눈으로는 볼 수 없는 것을 보여 주었으며, 복잡한 움직임을 분해함으로써 그의 카메라는 이를 이해하기 쉽게 해 주었고 제어할 수도 있음을 시사했다.

1870년대와 1880년대 테일러가 방문한 철강 공장에서, 그는 숙련된 노동자들이 업무의 리듬과 분담을 통제하는 작업장에서 오직 무질서와 비효율성만을 보았다. 테일러는 과학적 연구가 산업 공정을 가장 간단한 부분들로 나눌 수 있으며, 한번 이를 이해한 후에는 관리자들이 불필요한 움직임과 노동자 수를 줄여서 생산량을 늘리고 비용을 절감할 수 있게 할 것이라고 믿었다. 스톱워치를 들고, 그는 각각의 특정 작업에 노동자들이 소요한 시간을 기록한 다음 효율성을 개선하기 위해 작업에서 변경할 사항들을 제안했다. 그의 가장 유명한 시범은 1898년 베슬리헴 철강회사에서 이루어졌는데, 테일러는 각 특정 작업에 특정 방식으로 사용하도록 한 15종류의 광석 삽을 고안했다. 그는 140명의 노동자가 600명 분의 일을 할 수 있다는 것을 보여 줄 수 있었다. 그러자 회사는 '과잉' 삽 작업자들을 해고하여 광석 삽 작업 비용을 절반으로 줄였다. 또한 남은 삽 작업자들의 월급을 인상해 주었다.

테일러의 계획의 다른 부분은 노동자들에게 생산 목표를 초과할 경우 추가 보상을 제공하여 그들에게 동기 부여를 하는 것이었다. 그러나 테일러의 제안 속에서 노동자들은 갈 곳을 잃었다. 작업은 더 지루하고 단조로워졌으며, 작업의

lost. Jobs became more tedious and monotonous, and the character and speed of work were defined by management rather than the workers themselves. Skill and tradition yielded to "scientifically" ordained rules from which workers could not deviate. Managers, the "white shirts" in workers' parlance, were not able to be on the floor all the time observing work, so they measured output instead. They weighed the tonnage of coal, for example, in determining the "efficiency" of miners, rather than going into the mines themselves. By evaluating workers mainly by looking at their output, managers lost effective contact with the work culture and failed to grasp and respect the difficulties or skills involved in producing. Managers also adopted Taylor's ideas piecemeal, preferring the emphasis on worker productivity while ignoring his calls for higher wages. Indeed, most managers looked for ways to cut wages for poor work rather than raising them for better work.

"Taylorism," as Taylor's ideas came to be known, did not take hold everywhere. His program called for redesigning the physical layout and work patterns of the whole factory and for precise record keeping and cost accounting to watch over every aspect of the flow of goods and work. Few manufacturers could bear the costs of complete retooling and reorganization of heavy industries, and workers fought against management's efforts to reduce them to robots. Also, the mechanization of industry itself was an uneven process. Such basic industries as logging, for example, continued to rely on manual labor and horse-drawn transportation into the early twentieth century. The widespread adoption of Taylorism waited until the twentieth century, especially the 1920s, when a "cult of productivity" and the widespread replacement of steam power with electricity encouraged fuller mechanization of both capital and finished goods industries.

특성과 속도는 노동자 자신이 아닌 관리자에 의해 결정되었다. 기술과 전통은 노동자가 벗어날 수 없는 '과학적으로' 정해진 규칙에 양보되었다. 노동자들 사이에서 '흰 셔츠'로 불리던 관리자들은 항상 현장에서 작업을 관찰하고 있을 수 없었으므로 대신 생산량을 측정했다. 예를 들어, 광부들의 '효율성'을 결정할 때 광산에 직접 들어가는 게 아니라 석탄의 톤 수를 측정했다. 주로 생산량을 보고 노동자를 평가함으로써, 관리자들은 작업 문화에 대한 효과적인 접촉 기회를 상실하고 생산과 관련된 어려움이나 기술을 이해하거나 존중하지 못했다. 또한, 관리자들은 테일러의 아이디어를 단편적으로 채택하였으며, 노동자 생산성에 중점을 두는 반면에 더 높은 임금을 주어야 한다는 그의 요구를 무시했다. 실제로 대부분의 관리자들은 일을 잘하면 임금을 올려 주는 게 아니라 일을 못하면 임금을 삭감할 방법을 찾았다

'테일러리즘'으로 알려진 테일러의 아이디어가 모든 곳에서 받아들여지는 않았다. 그의 프로그램은 전체 공장의 물리적 배치와 작업 패턴을 재설계하고 각 상품과 작업 흐름의 모든 측면을 감시하기 위한 정확한 기록 및 비용 회계 처리를 요구했다. 소수의 제조업자들만이 중공업 산업의 전면적 설비 교체와 재조직의 비용을 감당할 수 있었으며, 노동자들은 자신들을 로봇으로 만들려는 관리자들의 노력에 반발했다. 또한, 산업의 기계화 자체가 불균등한 과정이었다. 예를 들어, 벌목과 같은 기간 산업은 20세기 초기까지 수작업과 마부가 끌어 주는 운송에 의존했다. 테일러리즘이 널리 받아들여진 것은 20세기, 특히 '생산성 숭배'와 증기 동력에서 전기로의 광범위한 교체가 자본재와 완제품 산업의 더 완전한 기계화를 촉진시켰던 1920년대에 이르러서였다.

어휘

cost-efficient 비용 효율적 management goal 경영 목표 draft 설계하다 revolutionize 변화를 일으키다 unquestionable 의심할 여지없는 authority 권한 be obsessed with ~에 사로잡힌 fascinating 매력적인 dexterity 재주 groundwork 준비 작업, 기초 공사 hoof (말 등의) 발굽 simultaneously 동시에 stride 달리기 naked eye 육안 shop floor 작업 현장 division of labor 분업 break down ~을 나누다 ore 광석 shovel 삽, 삽질하다 thereupon 곧바로 reward A with B A에게 B로 보답하다 tedious 지루한 monotonous 단조로운 yield 산출량 산출하다 ordain 미리 정하다 deviate 벗어나다 일탈하다 parlance 용어 tonnage (무게)총 톤수 miner 광부 emphasis on 강조하다 wage 임금 retool 개편하다 uneven 불균등한, 고르지 못한 basic industry 기간 산업 logging 벌목 manual 육체노동의, 수동의 mechanization 기계화 capital goods 자본재 finished goods 완제품

1. 첫 번째 단락에 따르면, 20세기 들어 대규모 산업체 관리자들의 주요 목적은?

  Ⓐ 더 나은 업무 규칙을 수립하는 것
  Ⓑ 작업을 재설계하는 것
  Ⓒ 노동자 생산성을 높이는 것
  Ⓓ 경영 목표를 수정하는 것

세부 사항 찾기 문제
어휘 aim 목적   revise 수정하다
해설 20세기에 들어서면서 대규모 산업에서 노동자들을 보다 '비용 효율적'으로 만드는 것이 가장 중요한 단일 경영 목표가 되었다고 말하고 있으므로 C가 정답이다.

2. 두 번째 단락에 따르면, 에드워드 머이브리지의 실험으로 알게 된 사실이 아닌 것은?

  Ⓐ 경주마가 달릴 때 네 발이 한꺼번에 모두 땅에서 떨어지는 순간이 있다.
  Ⓑ 움직임은 기계로 측정할 수 있다.
  Ⓒ 카메라는 맨눈으로 볼 수 없는 복잡한 움직임의 측면을 드러낼 수 있다.
  Ⓓ 복잡한 움직임은 관찰할 수 있지만 제어할 수 없다.

틀린 정보 찾기 문제
해설 마지막 문장에서 머이브리지는 사진 한 장 한 장 사람의 육안으로는 볼 수 없는 것을 보여 주었으며, 복잡한 움직임을 분해함으로써 그의 카메라는 이를 이해하기 쉽게 해 주었고 제어할 수도 있음을 시사했다고 말했으므로 D가 정답이다.

3. 세 번째 단락에 따르면, 1870년대와 1880년대의 철강 공장에 대한 테일러의 인상은?

  Ⓐ 그들의 작업장은 잘 조직되지 않았으며 효율적이지 않았다.
  Ⓑ 업무 리듬과 분담을 통제하지 않았다.
  Ⓒ 그들은 산업체 관리자들에게 너무 많은 권력을 부여했다.
  Ⓓ 그들의 작업장에는 충분히 숙련된 노동자가 없었다.

세부 사항 찾기 문제
어휘 impression 인상
해설 단락의 첫 문장에 테일러가 철강 공장을 방문했을 때, 작업장에서 무질서와 비효율성을 보았다고 나와 있으므로 A가 정답이다. 같은 문장에서 숙련된 노동자들이 업무 리듬과 분담을 통제했다고 언급되었으므로 B는 오답. 관리자와 숙련된 노동자에 대한 언급이 있긴 하지만, C나 D를 뒷받침하는 내용은 없다.

4. 세 번째 단락에 따르면, 140명이 600명의 일을 할 수 있게 만든 것은?

  Ⓐ 더 많은 날 동안 평소 시간의 반만 일하기
  Ⓑ 더 많은 돈을 받기
  Ⓒ 테일러가 스톱워치로 시간을 재는 것
  Ⓓ 서로 다른 작업을 위해 다르게 고안된 삽 사용

세부 사항 찾기 문제
해설 단락의 후반부에 테일러가 140명이 600명의 일을 할 수 있게 만든 방법에 대한 설명이 있다. 그는 15종류의 광석 삽을 고안했는데, 각각은 특정 작업을 위해 만들어졌으며, 덕분에 회사가 광석 삽 작업 비용을 절반으로 줄일 수 있게 했다.

5. 지문의 단어 contact with와 의미상 가장 가까운 것은?

  Ⓐ ~와의 연결
  Ⓑ ~에 대한 인내력
  Ⓒ ~에 대한 통제
  Ⓓ ~에 대한 믿음

어휘 문제
해설 contact with는 '~와의 접촉[연결]'이라는 뜻이다.

6. 네 번째 단락에 따르면, 테일러의 제안 하에서 더 나빠진 작업 조건이 아닌 것은?

  Ⓐ 일의 다양성이 줄어들었다.
  Ⓑ 생산에 필요한 기술에 대한 존중이 줄었다.
  Ⓒ 경영진은 엉터리 작업에 대한 임금을 줄이는 방법을 모색했다.
  Ⓓ 관리들은 작업 중인 노동자들을 끊임없이 감시했다.

틀린 정보 찾기 문제
해설 테일러의 제안 아래서 작업 조건이 악화된 방식이 아닌 것을 묻고 있다. 작업이 단조로워져서 작업의 다양성이 줄어들었고, 관리자들은 생산과 관련된 어려움이나 기술을 이해하거나 존중하지 못했다고 했으며, 마지막 문장에서 대부분의 관리자들이 엉터리 일에 대한 임금을 줄이는 방법을 찾았다고 언급되므로 A, B, C는 단락과 일치한다. 관리자들이 항상 현장에서 작업을 관찰하고 있을 수 없었으므로 대신 생산량을 측정했다는 내용에서 D의 내용이 틀린 것을 알 수 있다.

7. 네 번째 단락에 따르면, 노동 생산성을 측정하기 위해 관리자들이 생산성에 의존한 결과 나타난 영향은?

  Ⓐ 관리자들은 작업 과정에 실제로 어떤 것들이 포함되어 있는지 이해하지 못했다.
  Ⓑ 관리자들은 생산 과정을 관찰하기 위해 더 많은 시간을 작업장에서 보내야 했다.
  Ⓒ 관리자들은 전통적이라고 강조하며 업무 규칙의 시행을 정당화하기 시작했다.
  Ⓓ 관리자들은 생산 목표 초과를 위해 노동자들에게 더 많은 임금을 지불해야 했다.

세부 사항 찾기 문제
어휘 justify 정당화하다   enforcement 시행   exceed 초과하다
해설 해당 단락에서 관리자들은 주로 생산량을 보고 노동자를 평가함으로써, 작업 문화에 대한 효과적인 접촉 기회를 상실하고 생산과 관련된 어려움이나 기술을 이해하거나 존중하지 못했다고 언급하고 있다. B의 내용은 단락과 모순된다. C는 기술과 전통은 노동자가 벗어날 수 없는 '과학적으로' 정해진 규칙에 양보되었다고 했으므로 틀렸다. 또한 관리자들이 더 높은 임금을 요구하

는 테일러의 요구를 무시하고 일을 잘하면 임금을 올려주는 방식이 아닌 일을 못하면 임금을 삭감할 방법을 찾았다고 했으므로 D도 답이 아니다.

8. 다섯 번째 단락에서 글쓴이가 벌목 업계 운영 방식에 관한 정보를 제공하는 이유는?

Ⓐ 테일러리즘이 널리 채택되는 일이 20세기까지 이루어지지 않은 이유를 설명하기 위해서

Ⓑ 테일러리즘을 채택한 후 생산성이 더 높아진 산업의 예시로 벌목 산업을 주장하기 위해서

Ⓒ 벌목 산업이 정확한 기록 보관과 비용 회계 처리의 전통이 없었다는 점을 강조하기 위해서

Ⓓ 완전한 기계화가 증기 동력을 전기로 교체하는 것에 의존한다는 생각을 지지하기 위해서

수사학적 의도 파악 문제

어휘 adoption 채택   cost accounting 회계 처리

해설 특정 정보가 제공되는 이유를 묻는 수사학적 의도 파악 문제이다. 글쓴이는 산업의 기계화가 불균등한 과정임을 언급하고, 벌목 산업을 비롯한 다른 산업이 20세기 초까지 전통적인 방법에 의존했다고 지적한다. 이것은 당시 테일러의 아이디어가 많은 산업에서 받아들여지지 않은 이유를 설명하는 데 도움이 된다. B, C, D는 모두 단락에 있는 정보를 기반으로 하지만, 글쓴이가 벌목 산업을 논의하는 목적에 해당되지 않는다.

9. 지시문: 위에 제시된 지문의 일부를 보시오. 지문에 표시된 **(A)**, **(B)**, **(C)**, **(D)** 중 하나에 다음 문장이 삽입될 수 있다.

Taylor was determined to apply this new understanding of motion to the improvement of industrial processes.
(테일러는 이러한 새로운 동작에 대한 이해를 산업 공정 개선에 적용하기로 결심했다.)

이 문장이 들어갈 가장 적당한 위치는?

The leading supporter of productivity was Frederick Winslow Taylor, whose time-and-motion studies revolutionized the industrial workplace and whose writings, especially *The Principles of Scientific Management*, had unquestionable authority among industrial engineers and factory managers. Taylor was obsessed with order and efficiency. Taylor also grew up at a time when the processes of motion were fascinating to many Americans. Artists such as Thomas Eakins were painting the human form in ways that showed its dexterity. **(A)** In the 1870s, in California, the English-born photographer Eadweard Muybridge was developing a multiple-camera technique to record an animal in motion. **(B)** Muybridge's experiments, which laid the groundwork for motion pictures, started out to settle a bet whether all four of a racehorse's hooves simultaneously left the ground at some point during its stride (he showed that they did), but they attracted national attention for demonstrating that machines could measure movement.

(C) Picture frame by picture frame, Muybridge revealed what the naked eye could not see, and by breaking down complex movement his cameras made it understandable and potentially subject to control. **(D)** Taylor was determined to apply this new understanding of motion to the improvement of industrial processes.

In the iron and steel factories that Taylor visited during the 1870s and 1880s, he saw only disorder and inefficiency on shop floors where skilled workers controlled the rhythms and division of labor. Taylor believed that scientific study could break down the industrial process into its simplest parts, which, once understood, would allow managers to increase production and lower costs by reducing unnecessary motion and workers. Stopwatch in hand, he recorded the time workers spent on each particular task and then suggested changes in the jobs to improve efficiency. In his most famous demonstration, at the Bethlehem Steel Company in 1898, Taylor designed fifteen kinds of ore shovels, each for a specific task and each to be used in a specific way. He was able to show that 140 men could do the work of 600. The company thereupon fired the "excess" shovelers, cutting its ore-shoveling costs by half. It also gave the remaining shovelers a raise in salary.

Ⓐ   Ⓑ   Ⓒ   Ⓓ

문장 삽입 문제

해설 해설 보기가 두 번째 문단의 끝에 있기 때문에 두 번째 문단의 뒷부분이나 세 번째 문단도 고려해야 한다. 첨부된 문장은 산업 프로세스 개선에 관한 세 번째 단락의 주제를 언급하고 있다. 따라서 삽입 문장은 두 번째 단락의 끝에 어울리고 두 단락을 연결하는 역할을 한다.

10. 지시문: 이 지문을 간단히 요약하기 위한 도입 문장이 아래에 제시되어 있다. 아래 보기들 중에서 지문의 가장 중요한 개념을 표현한 문장 3개를 골라 요약을 완성하라. 보기들 중에는 지문에 나오지 않았거나 중요 하지 않은 개념이기 때문에 요약문으로 적절치 않은 것들도 있다. 이문제의 배점은 2점이다.

프레드릭 테일러의 시간과 동작 연구를 통한 생산성 증가 프로그램은 산업의 작업장을 혁명화했다.

Ⓐ 테일러는 산업 공정을 최대한 간략화하여 불필요한 동작을 식별하고 줄일 수 있으며, 따라서 필요한 노동자 수를 줄여 비용을 절감할 수 있다고 주장했다.

Ⓑ 테일러는 사진작가 에드워드 머이브리지와 함께 기계를 사용하여 육안으로는 할 수 없는 정확하게 동작을 측정하는 기술을 개발했다.

Ⓒ 테일러의 생산 목표 초과 시 더 많은 임금을 지불하는 아이디어는 관리자들에 의해 채택되지 않았으며, 그의 과학적으로 정의된 업무 프로세스는 대부분의 대규모 산업체에서 즉시 채택하기에는 비용이 너무 많이 들었다.

Ⓓ 테일러는 노동자 생산성을 높이는 유일한 방법은 노동자들이 더 발전된 도구를 사용하도록 요구하기 이전에 더 높은 임금을 지급하는 것이라고 믿었다.

E 테일러의 제안 하에서, 관리자들은 기록 보관과 비용 회계 처리에 더 많은 시간을 할애하고 작업 현장에서 감독하는 시간은 줄어들 것이기 때문에 노동자들은 더 기술적으로 숙련되어야 했다.

F 테일러리즘은 '생산성의 숭배'와 증기 동력의 전기로의 교체가 생산의 기계화를 촉진시킨1920년대에 이르러서야 대부분의 산업 분야에서 완전히 채택되었다.

지문 요약하기 문제

해설 A는 산업 생산성을 개선하는 데 있어 테일러의 믿음과 성과에 대한 두 번째와 세 번째 단락의 핵심 내용을 요약하고 있으므로 적절하다. B는 머이브리지와 테일러가 함께 기술을 개발했다는 내용은 없으므로 적절치 않다. C는 네 번째 단락의 핵심 내용인 테일러의 노동자 동기부여 방안과 그의 아이디어가 채택되지 않은 이유들을, 그리고 다섯 번째 단락에서 테일러의 산업 공정 재설계 아이디어가 몇몇 산업에서 즉각 채택되지 않은 것에 대한 내용을 요약하고 있다. D는 언급되지 않았다. E는 기술이 과학적으로 정해진 규칙에 양보되어야 한다, 즉 기술이 덜 중요시되었다는 내용에 오히려 위배된다. F는 마지막 단락에 나오는 테일러리즘의 채택과 회사들이 이를 가능하게 해 준 조건들에 대해 요약하고 있다.

Practice Set 6   p. 68

THE DISTRIBUTION OF PLANTS AND ANIMALS

There is a much greater similarity between the flowering plant floras of different continents—South America, Africa, Asia, and Australia—than between the mammalian faunas (animals) of these regions. Only in the case of the African/Asian comparison are the plant and animal figures at a similar level. Three factors seem to have caused these differences.

First, the families of flowering plants evolved and dispersed earlier than the families of mammals. Recent palaeobotanical techniques have made it possible to retrieve and identify complete and partial flowers from sediments from the middle Cretaceous (144 to 65 million years ago). These demonstrate that several currently existing families had appeared by the middle Cretaceous, about 120 million years ago, and at least a dozen by 95 to 5 million years ago. Therefore, the angiosperms (flowering plants) commenced their dispersal across the world much earlier than the mammals, and thus had a much greater chance of reaching the different continents before they drifted far apart. In contrast, the diversification and dispersal of modern mammals only began in the earliest Cenozoic, 66 to 65 million years ago, by which time the continents had drifted farther apart and were more difficult to reach. However, those mammals that did succeed as colonists were able, in the isolation of each continent, to diverge into a number of unique, native groups that show little similarity to those in other continents, for example New World monkeys in South America, elephants and aardvarks in Africa, and marsupials like the kangaroo in Australia.

Secondly, there has been more extinction and replacement during the history of mammals than during that of flowering plants. For example, in addition to the approximately 100 living families of mammals, over 300 other families evolved and became extinct during the Cenozoic—some 70 percent of the families of mammals died out completely. Some of these were previously widespread families, which were replaced in the now-separate continents by new families found only in those particular regions. In other cases, the family became extinct only in some areas, so that it now had a disjunct distribution, with widely separated subgroups, as in the camel-llama group. Another example of the influence of extinction is seen if one compares the similarities between the mammal faunas of North and South America before and after a wave of extinctions in the Pleistocene (1.8 million to 10,000 years ago). **(A)** All these phenomena reduced the levels of similarity between the faunal regions. **(B)** In the flowering plants, in

식물 및 동물의 분포

남아메리카, 아프리카, 아시아 및 오스트레일리아와 같은 다양한 대륙의 현화식물 식물군 사이에는 같은 지역 포유류 동물군보다 훨씬 큰 유사성이 존재한다. 식물과 동물의 수치가 유사한 수준을 보이는 경우는 아프리카와 아시아를 비교할 때뿐이다. 세 가지 요인이 이러한 차이를 일으킨 것으로 보인다.

첫째로, 현화식물과는 포유류과보다 먼저 진화하고 퍼져 나갔다. 최근의 고식물학 기술로 중생대(약 1억 4,400만~6,500만 년 전)의 퇴적물에서 완전하거나 부분적인 꽃을 수습하고 식별할 수 있게 되었다. 이러한 자료는 현존하는 몇 가지 현화식물과들이 약 1억 2000만 년 전인 중생대 중기에, 그리고 최소한 12종의 과가 9,500만~500만 년 전에 등장했음을 보여 준다. 따라서 속씨식물(꽃식물)은 포유류보다 훨씬 더 일찍 세계적으로 확산을 시작했고, 대륙들이 서로 멀어지기 전에 다양한 대륙에 도달할 수 있는 기회가 훨씬 더 많았다. 반면, 현대 포유류의 다양화와 확산은 신생대 초기인 6,600만~6,500만 년 전에 겨우 시작되었으며, 그 시점에 대륙들은 더 멀리 이동해 있었고 도달하기가 더 어려웠다. 어쨌든 각 대륙이 고립된 상태에서 성공적으로 대량 서식을 성취한 포유류들은 각 대륙에서 고유의 토착종으로 다양화될 수 있었고 다른 대륙의 포유류와 유사성을 거의 보이지 않았다. 예를 들면, 남미의 광비 원숭이, 아프리카의 코끼리와 땅돼지, 그리고 호주의 캥거루와 같은 유대류들이 그것이다.

둘째로, 포유류의 역사에서는 현화식물의 역사에서보다 더 많은 멸종과 교체가 있었다. 예를 들어, 현존하는 약 100개의 포유류과에 더하여 신생대 동안 약 300개 이상의 다른 포유류과가 진화하고 멸종되어 포유류과의 약 70%가 완전히 사라졌다. 이 중 일부는 이전에 널리 분포하던 과들이며, 분리된 대륙에서 해당 지역에서만 발견되는 새로운 과들에 의해 교체되었다. 다른 경우로는 일부 지역에서만 과가 멸종되어 격리 분포가 이루어졌으며, 크게 갈라진 하위 집단을 가지게 되었는데, 예를 들면 낙타-라마 종들에서 이를 볼 수 있다. 멸종이 미치는 영향의 또 다른 예는, 홍적세(약 180만~1만 년 전)에 발생한 멸종의 물결 이전과 이후의 북미와 남미의 포유류 동물군 간 유사성을 비교해 보면 알 수 있다. 이 모든 현상은 동물군 지역 간의 유사성 수준을 낮추었다. 이에 반해, 현화식물에서는 훨씬 적은 멸종이 있었다. 게다가, 식물군은 포유류군보다 훨씬 오랜 기간 존속했다. 예를 들어, 남방 너도밤나무인 노토파구스의 분포는 적어도 7,000만 년 전인 후기 백악기에 진화했다는 것을 보여 준다. 반면 포유류군의 평균적인 수명은 단 800만 년이다.

contrast, there has been much less extinction. **(C)** Furthermore, groups of plants are much longer-lived than are those of mammals. **(D)** For example, the distribution of the southern beech tree, Nothofagus, shows that it evolved in the Late Cretaceous, at least 70 million years ago, while the average longevity of mammalian groups is only eight million years.

Finally, of course, not all floral similarities were merely the result of early dispersal across insignificant barriers rather than a later colonization across wider gaps. The extent of the spread of flowering plants across the Pacific (over 200 different immigrant flowering plants have reached the most isolated island group, Hawaii) shows clearly that they can cross even quite wide stretches of ocean, especially where intermediate island steppingstones were available.

For all these reasons, it is not surprising that the flora of the different continents shows more similarities to one another than do their mammalian faunas. However, there is one exception: the almost identical levels of similarity for the two groups when the African and Asian regions are compared. The floral similarity here is not surprising, for it is at the same general level as the similarities between the other tropical regions. It is therefore the faunal similarity between the African and Asian regions that is unexpectedly high. This is probably because of the faunal exchange that took place between Africa and Eurasia after the two continents became connected in the Miocene era (28.3 to 5.3 million years ago) and before deserts spread through the Middle East.

마지막으로, 물론, 모든 현화식물의 유사성이 초기에 큰 의미가 없는 장벽을 횡단한 조기 확산의 결과인 것만은 아니다. 후기에 보다 넓은 간격의 거리를 횡단하여 대량 서식이 이루어진 결과이기도 하다. 태평양을 횡단하는 꽃 식물의 확산 정도(200여 종 이상의 이주 현화식물이 가장 고립된 섬 군락인 하와이에까지 도착했다)는 이들이 특히 중간에 징검다리처럼 섬이 있는 경우에는 꽤 넓게 뻗어 있는 바다를 횡단할 수 있다는 것을 명확히 보여 준다.

이러한 모든 이유로 인해, 다른 대륙의 식물군들끼리 동물군보다 서로 더 많은 유사성을 보이는 것은 놀라운 일이 아니다. 다만 한 가지 예외가 있는데, 아프리카와 아시아 지역을 비교할 때 두 그룹 간은 거의 동일한 수준의 유사성을 보인다. 여기서의 꽃식물의 유사성은 놀랍지 않다. 왜냐하면 그것은 다른 열대 지역들 간의 유사성과 동일한 일반적인 수준에 있기 때문이다. 그러므로 예상 외로 높은 것은 아프리카와 아시아 지역 간의 동물군 유사성이다. 이것은 아마도 중신세 시대(약 2,830만~530만 년 전)에 두 대륙이 연결된 이후와 중동을 통해 사막이 퍼져 나가기 이전에 아프리카와 유라시아 간에 발생한 동물 교환 때문일 것이다.

어휘

flowering plant 현화식물, 꽃식물, 종자식물 **flora** 식물군 **continent** 대륙 **mammalian fauna** 포유류의 동물군 **comparison** ~와 비교 **evolve** 진화하다 **disperse** 흩어지다 **palaeobotanical** 고식물학의 **retrieve** 되찾다 **partial** 부분적인 **sediment** 퇴적물 **Cretaceous** 백악기의 **angiosperms** 속씨 식물 **commence** 시작되다 **drift** 이동, 표류 **diversification** 다양화 **Cenozoic** 신생대(의) **diverge into** 다양화되다 **aardvarks** 땅돼지 **marsupial** 유대류 **extinction** 멸종 **disjunct** 격리 **subgroup** 하위 집단 **Pleistocene** 홍적세 **phenomenon** 현상 **Nothofagus** 너도밤나무(식물) **steppingstone** 징검다리

1. 지문의 단어 demonstrate와 의미상 가장 가까운 것은?

Ⓐ 토론하다

Ⓑ 보여 주다

Ⓒ 강조하다

Ⓓ 결론짓다

어휘 문제

해설 demonstrate는 '증거를 들어가며 보여 주다', '입증하다'라는 뜻이다.

2. 두 번째 단락에 따르면, 현화식물이 대륙이 서로 분리되기 전에 나타났다는 것을 어떻게 알 수 있는가?

Ⓐ 신생대까지 기원을 거슬러 올라갈 수 있는 현존하는 많은 현화식물들로부터

Ⓑ 중생대의 퇴적물에서 발견된 꽃들로부터

Ⓒ 초기 현화식물들이 바다를 횡단하여 대량 서식하는 데 성공하지 못했다는 사실로부터

Ⓓ 현화식물이 포유류보다 먼저 모든 대륙에 도달했다는 사실로부터

세부 사항 찾기 문제

어휘 track back 거슬러 올라가다   colonize 대량으로 서식하다

해설 중생대의 퇴적물에서 완전하거나 부분적인 꽃을 발굴할 수 있게 되면서 현화식물과들이 중생대 중기에 등장했음을 알 수 있다고 했다. 그리고 현화식물이 포유류보다 훨씬 더 일찍 세계적으로 확산을 시작했고, 대륙들이 서로 멀어지기 전에 다양한 대륙에 도달할 수 있는 기회가 많았다고 하고 있다. 따라서 정답은 B. 신생대는 포유류의 확산이 시작된 시기이며, 현화식물이 나타난 시기가 아니므로 A는 오답이다. C와 D는 현화식물이 나타난 시기와는 상관이 없다.

3. 글쓴이는 왜 '남미의 광비 원숭이'를 언급하였는가?

Ⓐ 대륙 내 격리된 지역에서만 발견되는 포유류의 범위를 예로 들기 위해서

Ⓑ 포유류가 일반적으로 현화식물보다 나중에 확산되었다는 점을 뒷받침하기 위해서

Ⓒ 포유류들이 다양화로 인해 각 대륙에서 성공적으로 정착할 수 있었던 과정을 설명하기 위해서

Ⓓ 고립된 환경에서 진화한 포유류 그룹이면서 다른 대륙에 사는 가장 가까운 동족과는 매우 다른 모습을 지닌 포유류의 예를 보여 주기 위해서

수사학적 의도 파악 문제

어휘 relative 동족

해설 글쓴이는 대륙이 멀리 떨어진 후에 각 대륙에서 다양화된 동물 그룹의 예시를 들고 있다. 포유류는 다른 대륙과 격리되어 있으며, 대륙 내부에서 격리되어 있는 것이 아니므로 A는 올바르지 않다. B는 꽃이 퍼져나가는 것보다 포유류가 나중에 퍼졌다고 하더라도, 이것이 글쓴이가 광비 원숭이를 언급한 이유는 아니다. 포유류가 대륙에 성공적으로 정착한 방법을 설명하거나 다양성이 성공의 원인이었다고 말하지 않으므로 C는 올바르지 않다.

4. 지문의 단어 Furthermore와 의미상 가장 가까운 것은?

Ⓐ 하지만

Ⓑ 그러므로

Ⓒ 게다가

Ⓓ 사실상

어휘 문제

해설 furthermore는 '더욱이', '게다가'의 뜻으로 쓰이는 부사이다.

5. 세 번째 단락에 따르면 다음 중 포유류에 관해 사실인 것은?

Ⓐ 현존하는 포유류과는 신생대 초기까지 진화했다.

Ⓑ 아직 존재하는 포유류과는 크게 갈라진 하위 그룹으로 구성되어 있다.

Ⓒ 대부분의 포유류과는 신생대 동안 멸종했다.

Ⓓ 신생대 동안 멸종한 포유류과가 생존한 포유류과보다 더 널리 분포했었다.

세부 사항 찾기 문제

해설 신생대에 포유류과의 약 70%가 완전히 사라졌다고 했으므로 정답은 C가 된다. 대부분의 포유류과는 신생대 초기부터 진화했으므로 A는 틀렸다. 크게 갈라진 하위 그룹은 일부 포유류들이므로 B도 틀렸다. D는 언급되지 않았다.

6. 세 번째 단락에 따르면, 북미와 남미의 포유류 사이의 유사성이 눈에 띄게 줄어든 것은?

Ⓐ 홍적세에 많은 포유류가 멸종해서이다.

Ⓑ 다른 포유류과의 희생으로 일부 포유류과의 확산이 이루어져서이다.

Ⓒ 대륙을 횡단하는 서로 다른 포유류과들의 확산 속도가 달라서이다.

Ⓓ 각 대륙에서 발달한 하위 그룹의 수가 달라서이다.

세부 사항 찾기 문제

어휘 at the expense of ~의 희생으로

해설 홍적세에 발생한 멸종의 물결 이전과 이후의 북미와 남미의 포유류 동물군 간 유사성을 비교해 보면 이 모든 현상이 동물군 지역 간의 유사성 수준을 낮추었다고 말하고 있으므로 정답은 A이다. B, C, D는 언급되지 않았다.

7. '하와이'에 대한 언급은 다음 보기 중 어떤 것을 가정하더라도 식물과가 포유류과보다 더 널리 퍼졌을 것이라는 생각을 뒷받침하는가?

Ⓐ 포유류의 확산에 중요한 장벽이 없었더라도

Ⓑ 많은 식물과가 어떤 지역에서는 멸종했지만 다른 지역에서는 그렇지 않았다고 하여도

Ⓒ 대륙이 서로 분리되기 전에 식물이 퍼져 나가지 않았다고 하여도

Ⓓ 포유류보다 식물이 더 많이 멸종했다고 하여도

추론 문제

어휘 significant 중요한   barrier 장벽

8. 다섯 번째 단락에 따르면, 다음 중 아프리카와 아시아 지역 간 동물들의 높은 유사성을 설명할 수 있는 것은?

Ⓐ 두 지역 간의 동물 교환은 다른 지역 간의 교환보다 이른 시기에 일어났다.

Ⓑ 아프리카와 유라시아가 연결된 후 잠시 동안 동물들은 비교적 쉽게 한 지역에서 다른 지역으로 이동할 수 있었다.

Ⓒ 두 지역의 식물상은 대륙이 연결되기 이전에 매우 유사했다.

Ⓓ 포유류들은 결국 중동 대부분으로 퍼져 나간 사막에 적응할 수 있었다.

세부 사항 찾기 문제

어휘 adapt to ~ ~에 적응하다

해설 지문에서 두 대륙이 연결되었을 때 발생한 동물교환으로 유사성이 있었을 가능성에 대해 언급한다. A, C, D는 언급되지 않았다.

9. 지시문: 위에 제시된 지문의 일부를 보시오. 지문에 표시된 **(A)**, **(B)**, **(C)**, **(D)** 중 하나에 다음 문장이 삽입될 수 있다.

In fact, there is no record yet of the extinction of a major group of flowering plants.

(사실, 주요 현화식물군의 멸종에 대한 기록은 아직 없다.)

이 문장이 들어갈 가장 적당한 위치는?

Secondly, there has been more extinction and replacement during the history of mammals than during that of flowering plants. For example, in addition to the approximately 100 living families of mammals, over 300 other families evolved and became extinct during the Cenozoic—some 70 percent of the families of mammals died out completely. Some of these were previously widespread families, which were replaced in the now-separate continents by new families found only in those particular regions. In other cases, the family became extinct only in some areas, so that it now had a disjunct distribution, with widely separated subgroups, as in the camel-llama group. Another example of the influence of extinction is seen if one compares the similarities between the mammal faunas of North and South America before and after a wave of extinctions in the Pleistocene (1.8 million to 10,000 years ago). **(A)** All these phenomena reduced the levels of similarity between the faunal regions. **(B)** In the flowering plants, in contrast, there has been much less extinction. **(C)** In fact, there is no record yet of the extinction of a major group of flowering plants. Furthermore, groups of plants are much longer-lived than are those of mammals. **(D)** For example, the distribution of

the southern beech tree, Nothofagus, shows that it evolved in the Late Cretaceous, at least 70 million years ago, while the average longevity of mammalian groups is only eight million years.

Ⓐ   Ⓑ   Ⓒ   Ⓓ

문장 삽입 문제

해설 삽입될 문장의 '사실'이라는 말은 앞으로 나올 말이 앞 문장에서 언급된 아이디어를 발전시킬 것임을 가리킨다. (C)의 앞문장, 이에 반해, 현화식물에서는 훨씬 적은 멸종이 있었다는 말 다음에 들어가면 의미가 통한다. (A)나 (B)에는 이와 같은 연결이 불가능하므로 적절한 위치가 아니다. (D)에 삽입하면 앞 문장의 존속 기간에 대한 언급과 다음의 '예를 들어'라는 구문과 의미가 통하지 않는다.

10. 지시문: 이 지문을 간단히 요약하기 위한 도입 문장이 아래에 제시되어 있다. 아래 보기들 중에서 지문의 가장 중요한 개념을 표현한 문장 3개를 골라 요약을 완성하라. 보기들 중에는 지문에 나오지 않았거나 중요하지 않은 개념이기 때문에 요약으로 적절치 않은 것들도 있다. 이문제의 배점은 2점이다.

다양한 대륙의 포유류는 같은 지역의 현화식물 식물군보다 서로 더 큰 차이점이 있다.

Ⓐ 포유류와는 달리, 대륙이 서로 멀어지기 전에 현화식물이 나타나고 확산되었으며, 이는 대륙 간의 식물 유사성이 동물 유사성보다 더 큰 이유를 설명한다.

Ⓑ 고대 퇴적물에서 발견된 꽃 조각들을 완전한 꽃으로 재구성함으로써, 과학자들은 현존하는 대부분의 현화식물과가 중생대 중기 이전에 아직 나타나지 않았음을 보여 주었다.

Ⓒ 대륙의 분리와 종의 확산에 대한 연구는 가장 오래된 생물군이 남미에서 처음으로 발견되었음을 보여 주었다.

Ⓓ 식물과는 달리, 많은 포유류과가 멸종되고 특정 지역의 고유한 과로 대체되거나 대륙마다 서로 매우 다르게 진화했다.

Ⓔ 하와이와 같은 고립된 섬과 다른 열대 지역 사이의 식물 유사성은 현화식물이 처음 나타났을 때 연결되었던 대륙 간의 유사성만큼 크지 않다.

Ⓕ 식물은 넓은 바다를 통해 퍼져 나갈 수 있지만, 포유류는 일반적으로 중생대에 아프리카와 유라시아 사이에 있었던 것과 같은 연결된 육지가 있을 때만 확산할 수 있다.

지문 요약하기 문제

어휘 reconstruct 재구성하다   die out 멸종되다   be replaced by ~로 대체되다   unique 고유의

해설 A는 두 번째 단락의 핵심 내용을 요약하고 있으므로 적절하다. B는 꽃 조각들을 완전한 꽃으로 재구성했다는 이야기는 나오지 않고 일부 현화식물이 중생대 중기에 나타났다고 말하고 있으므로 적절치 않다. C는 언급되지 않았다. D는 세 번째 단락을 요약하고 있다. E는 식물이 연결되었던 대륙 간보다 고립된 열대 지역 사이에서 덜 유사하다고 언급하지 않았기 때문에 적절치 않다. F는 세 번째, 네 번째 단락에 나오는 정보를 요약하고 있다.

Notes

Reading

Listening

Speaking

Writing

QUESTION TYPES

Type 1 예제 　　　　　　　　　p. 77

Script
Professor

…So the Earth's surface is made up of these huge segments, these tectonic plates. And these plates move, right? But how can, uh, motion of plates, do you think, influence climate on the Earth? Again, all of you probably read this section in the book, I hope, but, uh, uh, how—how can just motion of the plates impact the climate?

…when a plate moves, if there's landmass on the plate, then the landmass moves too, okay? That's why continents shift their positions, because the plates they're on move. So as a landmass moves away from the equator, its climate would get colder. So, right now we have a continent—the landmass Antarctica—that's on a pole.

So that's dramatically influencing the climate in Antarctica. Um, there was a time when most of the landmasses were closer to a pole; they weren't so close to the equator. Uh, maybe 200 million years ago Antarctica was attached to the South American continent; oh, and Africa was attached too, and the three of them began moving away from the equator together.

…in the Himalayas. That was where two continental plates collided. Two continents on separate plates. Um, when this, uh, Indian, uh, uh, plate collided with the Asian plate, it wasn't until then that we created the Himalayas. When we did that, then we started creating the type of cold climate that we see there now. Wasn't there until this area was uplifted.

So again, that's something else that plate tectonics plays a critical role in. Now, these processes are relatively slow; the, uh, Himalayas are still rising, but on the order of millimeters per year. So they're not dramatically influencing climate on your—the time scale of your lifetime. But over the last few thousands of—tens of thousands of years, uh—hundreds of thousands of years—yes, they've dramatically influenced it.

Uh, another important thing—number three—on how plate tectonics have influenced climate is how they've influenced—we talked about how changing landmasses can affect atmospheric circulation patterns, but if you alter where the landmasses are connected, it can impact oceanic, uh, uh, uh, circulation patterns.

…Um, so, uh, these other processes, if, if we were to

…따라서 지구의 표면은 이런 거대한 조각들인 판 구조로 구성됩니다. 그리고 이 판들은 움직입니다, 그렇죠? 그런데 여러분은 판들의 이동이 어떻게 지구의 기후에 영향을 줄 수 있다고 생각합니까? 다시 말하면, 여러분 모두 아마도 책에서 이 장을 읽었을 거라 믿지만 단지 판들이 움직인다는 것이 어떻게 기후에 영향을 미칠 수 있을까요?

…판들이 움직일 때, 그 판 위에 대륙이 있다면 대륙도 함께 움직일 겁니다, 그렇죠? 대륙의 위치가 변하는 것은 대륙이 얹혀 있는 판들이 이동하기 때문입니다. 그러니까 대륙이 적도로부터 멀어지면서 해당 대륙의 기온이 차가워지는 것입니다. 이렇게 해서 현재의 남극대륙이 생긴 것입니다. 극지에 위치한 땅 말이죠.

그래서 그것이 남극 대륙의 기후에 엄청난 영향을 주고 있는 것입니다. 대부분의 대륙들이 극지에 더 가까웠던 때가 있었습니다. 이들은 원래 적도에 그렇게 가깝지 않았습니다. 아마 2억 년 전에 남극 대륙과 아프리카가 남미 대륙에 붙어 있었으며, 이 세 대륙이 함께 적도로부터 멀어지기 시작했을 것입니다.

…히말라야 산맥에서입니다. 그곳에서 대륙 판이 충돌했습니다. 따로 떨어진 판 위에 있던 두 개의 대륙이 충돌한 것이지요. 인도 판이 유라시아 판과 충돌하고 나서 히말라야 산맥이 생겼습니다. 히말라야 산맥이 형성되자 현재 그곳에서 볼 수 있는 유형의 차가운 기후가 나타나기 시작했습니다. 이 지역이 융기하기 전까지는 없었던 일입니다.

다시 말하지만, 이것은 판 구조론이 또 다른 부분에서 아주 중요한 역할을 한다는 것입니다. 현재 이러한 과정은 비교적 느리게 진행됩니다. 그러니까 히말라야 산맥은 지금도 융기하고 있지만 그 속도는 1년에 대략 몇 밀리미터에 불과합니다. 따라서 그것은 여러분이 살아 있는 동안에는 기후에 현저한 영향을 주지 않습니다. 그러나 지난 수천, 수만 년, 수십만 년 넘게 아주 큰 영향을 끼쳐왔습니다.

세 번째로 판 구조론이 기후에 어떤 영향을 미쳤는지에 대해서 또 한 가지 중요한 점은 그것이 어떻게 영향을 주는지 그러니까 우리는 대륙의 변화가 대기의 순환 패턴에 어떤 영향을 줄 수 있는지에 대해 이야기했는데 만약 대륙들이 연결된 부분을 바꾸면 대양의 순환 패턴에 영향을 줄 수 있다는 것입니다.

disconnect North and South America right through the middle—say, through Panama—that would dramatically influence climate in North and South America—probably the whole globe. So suddenly now as the two continents gradually move apart, you can have different circulation patterns in the ocean between the two. So, uh, that might cause a dramatic change in climate if that were to happen, just as we've had happen here in Antarctica to separate, uh, from South America.

1-1. What is the main topic of the lecture?
Ⓐ The differences in climate that occur in different countries
Ⓑ How movement of the Earth's plates can affect climate
Ⓒ Why the ocean has less effect on climate than previously thought
Ⓓ The history of the climate of the region where the university is located

1-2. What is the main topic of the lecture?
Ⓐ A climate experiment and its results
Ⓑ A geologic process and its effect
Ⓒ How a theory was disproved
Ⓓ How land movement is measured

…그래서 이러한 다른 과정들, 만약 우리가 북미 대륙과 남미 대륙을 딱 중간에서, 그러니까, 파나마쯤에서 분리시킨다면, 북남미 기후와, 아마 지구 전체에 막대한 영향을 줄 것입니다. 따라서 갑자기 이 두 대륙이 점차 멀어지면서 두 대륙 사이 대양의 순환 패턴이 달라질 수도 있죠. 따라서, 그러한 상황이 벌어진다면 엄청난 기후 변화를 초래할 것입니다. 남극 대륙이 남미 대륙으로부터 분리되었을 때처럼 말이죠.

1-1. 이 강의의 주제는 무엇인가?
Ⓐ 서로 다른 나라에서 발생하는 기후의 차이
Ⓑ 지구 판의 움직임이 기후에 미치는 영향
Ⓒ 이전에 생각했던 것보다 바다가 기후에 끼치는 영향이 적은 이유
Ⓓ 이 대학이 위치한 지역의 기후의 역사

occur 발생하다, 일어나다   previously 이전에, 그에 앞서

1-2. 이 강의의 주제는 무엇인가?
Ⓐ 기후 실험과 그 결과
Ⓑ 지질학적 과정과 그 영향
Ⓒ 이론이 반증된 방식
Ⓓ 대륙 이동이 측정되는 방식

geologic 지질학(상)의   disprove 논박하다   measure 측정하다

해설 1-1. 지문의 주제를 가장 잘 나타내는 것은 보기 B다. 교수는 지구 판의 움직임, 즉 판 구조론이 기후에 영향을 준다는 강의의 요점을 설명하기 위한 예로 남극 대륙과 히말라야 산맥을 들고 있다.

1-2. 정답은 보기 B로, 표현이 매우 다르기는 하지만 기본적으로 1-1의 보기 B와 같은 내용을 언급하고 있다. 즉 지질학적 과정은 지구 판들의 이동과 같은 것이며, 이것의 영향이란 기후의 변화를 의미한다.

어휘 segment 조각, 부분   tectonic 지질 구조의   plate 판, (납작한) 접시   impact 영향[충격]을 주다   landmass 대륙, 광대한 땅   continent 대륙, 본토   shift 이동하다, 움직이다   equator 적도   Antarctica 남극 대륙   pole 극지, (자석의) 극, 막대기   dramatically 극적으로, 현저하게   be attached to ~에 소속[부속]되다   collide 충돌하다, 부딪히다   uplift ~을 들어올리다, (땅)을 융기시키다   critical 중요한, 결정적인   process 과정, 진행   relatively 비교적, 상대적으로   on the order of 약, 대략   atmospheric 대기(중)의, 공기의   circulation 순환, 유통   pattern 방식, 무늬   alter 바꾸다, 고치다   oceanic 대양의   disconnect (~로부터) 떼어놓다, 분리하다   globe 지구, 구   gradually 점차, 차츰

N Narrator   P Professor   S Student

Script

N Listen to a conversation between a professor and a student.

S I was hoping you could look over my note for my presentation... just to see what you think of it.

P Okay, so refresh my memory: what's your presentation about?

S Two models of decision making...

P Oh, yes—the classical and the administrative model.

S Yeah, that's it.

P And what's the point of your talk?

S I'm gonna talk about the advantages and disadvantages of both models.

P But what's the point of your talk? Are you going to say that one's better than the other?

S Well I think the administrative model's definitely more realistic. But I don't think it's complete. It's kind of a tool... a tool to see what can go wrong.

P Okay, so what's the point of your talk? What are you trying to convince me to believe?

S Well, uh, the classical model—you shouldn't use it by itself. A lot of companies just try to follow the classical model, but they should really use both models together.

P Okay, good. So let me take a look at your notes here... Oh, typed notes,... Wow, you've got a lot packed in here. Are you sure you're going to be able to follow this during your talk?

S I was hoping to get some advice about that.

Why does the student visit the professor?

Ⓐ To get help understanding the difference between two decision-making models

Ⓑ To show her some examples of common errors in research

Ⓒ To review the notes for his presentation with her

Ⓓ To ask for help in finding a topic for his presentation

N 교수와 학생의 대화를 들으시오.

S 제 발표용 노트 자료를 좀 봐 주셨으면 하는데요… 그냥 어떻게 생각하시는지 알고 싶어서요…

P 좋네, 그럼 어디 보자. 무엇에 관한 발표지?

S 의사 결정의 두 가지 모델에 관한 것입니다…

P 아, 그래, 고전적 모델과 행정적 모델이지.

S 네, 맞습니다.

P 자네가 말하고자 하는 요점이 뭔가?

S 두 모델의 장단점에 대해 이야기하려고 합니다.

P 그러니까 자네 이야기의 논지가 뭐지? 어느 하나가 다른 것보다 낫다고 말하려는 건가?

S 글쎄요. 저는 행정적 모델이 분명히 더 현실적이라고 생각합니다. 그것이 완벽하다고 생각하지는 않지만요. 그것은 무엇이 잘못될 수 있는지 보기 위한 일종의 도구입니다.

P 좋아, 그러면 자네 이야기의 요점은 무엇인가? 내게 설득하고자 하는 내용이 뭐지?

S 그러니까, 고전적 모델만 사용해서는 안 된다는 거죠. 많은 회사들이 단지 고전적 모델을 따르려 하고 있지만, 사실은 두 모델을 함께 사용해야 하는 것이죠.

P 좋아, 알겠네. 그럼 자네 노트 자료를 한번 보지. 아 타이핑을 했군. 내용을 아주 꽉 채웠군 그래. 발표할 때 이 내용들을 다 소화할 수 있겠나?

S 그것에 대한 조언을 듣고 싶었습니다.

학생은 왜 교수를 찾아갔는가?

Ⓐ 두 가지 의사 결정 모델 간의 차이를 이해하는 데 도움을 받기 위해서

Ⓑ 조사 때 흔히 할 수 있는 실수의 예를 보여 주기 위해서

Ⓒ 교수와 발표에 쓸 노트 자료를 검토하기 위해서

Ⓓ 발표 주제를 찾는 데 도움을 요청하기 위해서

error 실수, 착오, 오류   **research** 조사, 연구   **review** 검토하다, 복습하다   **note** 메모, 기록

해설 대화의 상당 부분이 학생의 발표 내용과 관련 있지만 "Why does the student visit the professor?"라는 질문에 대한 가장 올바른 답은 C다. 즉 교수와 함께, 발표에 참고할 노트 자료를 검토하기 위해서다.

어휘 **presentation** 발표, 소개   **refresh** (기억을) 되살리다, 원기를 회복시키다   **decision making** 의사 결정   **classical** 고전적인, 전형적인 **administrative** 행정상의, 관리의, 경영상의   **definitely** 분명히, 확실히   **realistic** 현실적, 실제적인   **complete** 완벽한, 전부의   **convince** 설득하다, 확신시키다   **take a look at** ~을 훑어보다   **packed** 꽉 찬, 만원의 *cf.* **pack** ~을 (꽉) 채우다, 포장하다   **otherwise** 그렇지 않으면, (~와는) 다르게   **handwriting** 필적, 서체

Script
Professor

Uh, other things that glaciers can do is, uh, as they retreat, instead of depositing some till, uh, scraped-up soil, in the area, they might leave a big ice block, and it breaks off, and as the ice block melts, it leaves a depression, which can become a lake. These are called kettle lakes. These are very critical ecosystems in this region, um, because, uh, uh, they support some unique biological diversity, these kettle lakes do.

The Great Lakes are kettle lakes; they were left over from the Pleist—from the Pleistocene glaciers. Uh, now, as the glaciers were retreating, the Great Lakes underwent a change. Once the weight of the glacier ice decreased, and the pressure decreased, the land at the bottom of the lakes rose. In some places it rose by as much as one hundred feet.

So I just wanted to tell you a little bit more about glaciers...

1. What are kettle lakes?
Ⓐ Lakes that form in the center of a volcano
Ⓑ Lakes that have been damaged by the greenhouse effect
Ⓒ Lakes formed by unusually large amounts of precipitation
Ⓓ Lakes that form when pieces of glaciers melt

2. What happened to the Great Lakes when the glaciers retreated?
Ⓐ The lakes became less deep.
Ⓑ The lakes became larger.
Ⓓ The biodiversity of the lakes increased.
Ⓓ The amount of soil in the lakes increased.

빙하의 또 다른 작용으로는 후퇴하면서 그 지역에 빙력토 그러니까 그러모은 토양을 퇴적시키는 대신, 커다란 얼음 덩어리가 남아 결국 부서지는데, 이것이 녹으면서 호수가 될 정도로 지각이 함몰됩니다. 이것을 케틀 호수라고 부릅니다. 케틀 호수는 이 지역의 아주 중요한 생태계인데, 왜냐하면 이러한 케틀 호수는 독특하고 다양한 생물체가 서식하도록 해 주기 때문입니다.

오대호는 케틀 호로, 홍적세 빙하가 남긴 호수입니다. 어, 빙하가 후퇴하면서 오대호도 변화를 겪었죠. 일단 빙하의 무게가 줄고 압력이 줄자 호수 바닥에 있는 땅이 융기했습니다. 어떤 곳에서는 땅이 자그마치 100피트나 솟았습니다.

그래서 전 단지 여러분에게 빙하에 대해 조금 더 이야기하고 싶었습니다…

1. 케틀 호수는 무엇인가?
Ⓐ 화산 중심부에서 형성되는 호수
Ⓑ 온실 효과에 의해 파괴된 호수
Ⓒ 비정상적으로 많은 양의 비가 내려 형성된 호수
Ⓓ 빙하 조각이 녹을 때 형성되는 호수

volcano 화산, 분화구   greenhouse effect 온실 효과
precipitation (기상) 강설, 강수(량)   melt 녹다

2. 빙하가 후퇴할 때 오대호에 무슨 일이 일어났는가?
Ⓐ 호수들이 더 얕아졌다.
Ⓑ 호수들이 더 커졌다.
Ⓒ 호수들의 생물학적 다양성이 증가했다.
Ⓓ 호수에 있는 토양의 양이 증가했다.

biodiversity 생물학적 다양성

해설   1. 교수가 주전자 호수에 대해 설명하는 부분에 답이 있다. 세부 정보 찾기 문제에서는 새로운 용어를 묻는 경우가 종종 있음을 기억해야 한다. 정답은 D.

2. 교수가 "the land at the bottom of the lakes rose. In some places it rose by as much as one hundred feet."이라고 설명하는 부분에 답이 있다. 정답은 A.

어휘   glacier 빙하   retreat 후퇴하다, 물러서다   deposit 퇴적시키다, 예금하다   till 빙력토   scrape ~을 그러모으다, 문지르다   break off 부서지다, 갈라지다   depression (지각의) 함몰, 의기소침, 불경기   kettle 주전자, 솥   ecosystem 생태계   biological 생물학(상)의, 생물학적인   diversity 다양성, 차이점   the Great Lakes 오대호   Pleistocene 홍적세, 홍적세의   undergo 겪다   decrease 줄다, 감소하다

N Narrator   S Student   A Administrative Assistant

Script

N Listen again to a part of the conversation. Then answer the question.

S Okay. I'll just pay with a credit card. *[pause]* And where do I do that at?

A At, um, the housing office.

S Housing office, all right.

A Do you know where they are?

What is the woman trying to find out from the man?

Ⓐ Where the housing office is

Ⓑ Approximately how far away the housing office is

Ⓒ Whether she needs to tell him where the housing office is

Ⓓ Whether he has been to the housing office already

N 대화의 일부를 다시 듣고 질문에 답하라.

S 좋습니다. 그냥 신용카드로 결제할게요. [잠시 멈췄다가] 어디서 결제하면 되죠?

A 음, 기숙사 사무실이요.

S 기숙사 사무실이요, 알겠습니다.

A 어디 있는지 알아요?

여자가 남자에게서 알아내고자 하는 것은 무엇인가?

Ⓐ 기숙사 사무실이 어디 있는지

Ⓑ 기숙사 사무실이 대략 어느 정도 거리에 있는지

Ⓒ 남자에게 기숙사 사무실의 위치를 알려줘야 하는지

Ⓓ 남자가 기숙사 사무실에 이미 갔다 왔는지

approximately 대략, 대체로

해설 여직원이 남학생에게 질문을 한 이유는 남학생에게 기숙사 사무실의 위치를 말해줘야 할 필요가 있는지를 알아보기 위한 것이다. 그러므로 이 문제의 정답은 C다.

A Advisor   S Student

Script

A Well, good. So, bookstore isn't working out?

S Oh, bookstore's working out fine. I just, I—this pays almost double what the bookstore does.

A Oh, wow!

S Yeah. Plus credit.

A Plus credit.

S And it's more hours, which... The bookstore's—I mean it's a decent job 'n' all. Everybody I work with... that part's great; it's just... I mean I'm shelving books and kind of hanging out and not doing much else... if it weren't for the people, it'd be totally boring.

A 자, 좋아요. 그러니까 서점 일이 마음에 안 든다는 거죠?

S 아, 서점 일이 좋기는 한데요. 단지 저는 이 일이 서점의 두 배에 가까운 보수를 준다는 겁니다.

A 와, 그렇군요!

S 예. 거기다가 학점도 주고요.

A 학점도요.

S 그리고 시간도 많고… 서점도 괜찮은 일이긴 해요. 저와 함께 일하는 사람들은 다… 그 점은 아주 좋아요. 그냥 … 선반에 책을 정리하고, 그냥 돌아다니기도 하고 그 밖에 할 일은 별로 없죠. 사람들만 아니었다면 아주 지루했을 거예요.

What is the student's attitude toward the people he currently works with?

Ⓐ He finds them boring.

Ⓑ He likes them.

Ⓒ He is annoyed by them.

Ⓓ He does not have much in common with them.

학생은 지금 함께 일하는 사람들에 대해 어떤 태도를 보이고 있는가?

Ⓐ 지루하다고 생각한다.

Ⓑ 좋아한다.

Ⓒ 그들 때문에 언짢다.

Ⓓ 그들과 공통점이 별로 없다.

currently 지금(은), 현재   annoy 짜증나게 하다, 귀찮게 굴다   have in common 공통점이 있다

해설 이 예제에서는 일에 대한 학생의 태도와 함께 일하는 사람들에 대한 태도를 혼동하기 쉽다. 정답은 B로 학생은 함께 일하는 사람들이 아니라, 하는 일에 대해 지루해 하고 있다.

어휘 decent 적당한, 괜찮은   shelve 선반에 얹다   hang out 슬슬 거닐다, ~와 가까이 지내다

Type 6 예제 1
p. 82

N Narrator   P Professor

Script

N Listen again to a statement made by the professor. Then answer the question.

P There's this committee I'm on... Th-the name of the thing, and it's probably, well, you don't have to take notes about this, um, the name of the thing is academic standards.

Why does the professor tell the students that they do not have to take notes?

Ⓐ The information is in their books.

Ⓑ The information may not be accurate.

Ⓒ She is going to tell a personal story.

Ⓓ They already know what she is going to talk about.

N 교수가 하는 말을 다시 듣고 질문에 답하라.

P 제가 속한 위원회가 있는데… 그 이름이 아마, 뭐 이건 적을 필요가 없는데… 음, 그 명칭이 학계의 표준입니다.

교수는 왜 학생들에게 필기할 필요가 없다고 말하는가?

Ⓐ 정보가 책에 있으므로

Ⓑ 정보가 정확하지 않을 수 있으므로

Ⓒ 개인적인 이야기를 하려고 하므로

Ⓓ 학생들이 이미 교수가 무슨 말을 할지 알고 있으므로

accurate 정확한, 틀림없는

해설 반복 재생된 진술의 앞에 나오는 청취 지문은 관료주의가 작용하는 방식에 관한 것이며, 뒤에 나오는 내용은 관료주의에 관한 개인적인 이야기다. 문제를 푸는 실마리는 뒤에 나오는 강의의 일부가 개인적인 이야기임을 알아야 한다는 것이다. 정답은 C로 반복 재생된 부분에서 교수는 이제부터 말하고자 하는 것은 앞서 말한 것과 다르다는 점을 나타내고 있다.

어휘 statement 진술, 의견, 주장   committee 위원회   take notes 메모하다   standard 표준, 기준, 모범

Script
Professor

So we have reproductive parts—the seeds, the fruit walls—we have leaf parts, but the great majority of plant fibers come from vasculature within the stem... fibers that occur in stem material. And what we do is consider these fibers *[false start]*—basically they're what are called *bast* fibers. Bast fibers. Now, basically bast fibers are parts of the plant that the plant uses to maintain vertical structure.

Think about it this way: what's the first thing you see when you see a building being built... uh, what's the first thing they put up? Besides the foundation, of course? The metalwork, right? They put all those steel girders up there, the framework. OK, well, think of *[false start]*—bast fibers basically constitute the structural framework to support the stem of the plant. OK? So as the plant grows, it basically builds a girder system within that plant, like steel, so to speak.

So suppose you cut across the stem of one of these plants... take a look at how the bast fibers are arranged, so you're looking at a cross section... you'll see that the fibers run vertically side by side. Up and down next to each other, forming a kind of tube, which is significant...'cause, which is physically stronger: a solid rod or a tube? The tube—physics tells you that. What's essentially happening—well, the plant is forming a structural ring of these bast fibers all around the stem, and that shape allows for structural rigidity, but also allows for bending and motion.

자, 여기 생식기관인 씨와 과실벽이 있습니다. 잎 부분이 있지만 식물 섬유의 대부분은 줄기 부분에서 생기는 줄기 섬유 내의 맥관 구조로부터 나옵니다. 우리가 하는 일은 이 섬유를 검토하는 (말문을 잘못 엶)-원래 이것은 인피 섬유라고 부르는 것들입니다. 인피 섬유. 인피 섬유는 기본적으로 식물이 수직 구조를 유지하는 데 사용하는 식물의 일부분입니다.

이렇게 생각해 봅시다. 어떤 건물을 지을 때 가장 먼저 보는 부분이 어디… 어떤 부분을 가장 먼저 세웁니까? 물론 기초공사를 다 하고 나서 말입니다. 철골 구조지요? 건물을 지을 때 뼈대가 되는 철 대들보를 세우지요. 자, 그럼 생각해 볼 것은 (말문을 잘못 엶)-인피 섬유는 기본적으로 식물의 줄기를 지탱하는 뼈대를 구성합니다. 따라서 식물이 자랄 때, 요컨대 식물 내에 대들보를 세우는 거죠. 이를테면, 철근처럼요.

그럼 이런 식물들 중 하나의 줄기를 가로로 잘라서 인피 섬유가 어떻게 배열되어 있는지 본다고 가정해 봅시다. 그러니까 단면을 보면… 섬유들이 수직으로 나란히 배열되어 있는 것을 볼 수 있습니다. 위아래로 서로 붙어 일종의 관을 형성하는데, 이것이 중요합니다. 왜냐하면, 어떤 것이 물리적으로 더 강한가요, 단단한 막대인가요? 아니면 관인가요? 관이죠. 물리학으로 밝혀졌잖아요. 본질적으로 무슨 일이 일어나냐 하면 그러니까, 식물은 모든 줄기 주변에 이러한 인피 섬유로 된 구조(상)의 고리를 형성하는데 이 모양은 곧게 서 있을 수 있게 하면서도 구부리거나 움직이는 것 역시 가능하게 해줍니다.

1. Why does the professor talk about steel?

Ⓐ To identify the substance that has replaced fiber products.

Ⓑ To explain a method for separating fibers from a plant.

Ⓒ To compare the chemical structure of fibers to metals.

Ⓓ To illustrate the function of fibers in a plant's stem.

2. Why does the professor mention a tube?

Ⓐ To explain how some fibers are arranged in a plant.

Ⓑ To show how plants carry water to growing fibers.

Ⓒ To describe an experiment involving plant fibers.

Ⓓ To explain why some plant stems cannot bend.

1. 교수는 왜 철에 대해 이야기하고 있는가?

Ⓐ 섬유 제품을 대체한 물질을 확인하기 위해

Ⓑ 식물에서 섬유를 분리하는 방법을 설명하기 위해

Ⓒ 섬유의 화학 구조와 금속의 화학 구조를 비교하려고

Ⓓ 식물의 줄기 안에 있는 섬유의 기능을 설명하려고

substance 물질, 내용   **separate** 분리하다, 떼어놓다
chemical 화학의, 화학적인   **illustrate** 설명[예증]하다

2. 교수가 관을 언급하는 이유는?

Ⓐ 식물의 섬유 배열을 설명하려고

Ⓑ 식물이 성장하고 있는 섬유에 어떻게 물을 공급하는지 보여 주기 위해

Ⓒ 식물 섬유와 관련된 실험을 설명하기 위해

Ⓓ 특정 식물줄기들이 구부러지지 않는 이유를 설명하려고

arrange 배열하다, 정돈하다   **involve** ~와 관계를 맺다, ~을 포함하다

해설 1. 강의는 철근에 관한 것이 아니라 식물과 식물 섬유에 관한 것이다. 교수가 철근을 언급한 이유는 그것을 식물 섬유의 구조적 뼈대와 비교하기 위해서다. 그러므로 첫 번째 질문에 대한 정답은 D.

2. 학생들이 식물의 구조를 좀 더 쉽게 시각화할 수 있도록 하기 위한 것이다. 따라서 정답은 A다.

어휘 **reproductive** 생식의, 번식하는, 재생의   **seed** 씨, 종자   **vasculature** 맥관 구조   **stem** 줄기, 대   **fiber** 섬유 (조직), 섬유질   **bast** 인피(부)   **vertical** (잎의 면이) 수직인, 세로의   **foundation** 토대, 기초   **steel** 강철   **girder** 대들보, 도리   **framework** 구조물, 뼈대, 틀   **so to speak** 말하자면   **suppose** 가정하다, 상상하다   **cross section** 횡단면, 단면도   **side-by-side** 나란히 (서) 있는   **tube** 관, 통   **physically** 물리(학)적으로, 육체적으로   **solid** 단단한, 고체의   **rod** 막대(기), 장대, 지팡이   **physics** 물리학   **essentially** 본질적으로, 본래   **rigidity** 단단함, 강도   **bend** 구부리다, 굽히다

Script
Professor

OK, Neptune and its moons. Neptune has several moons, but there's only... we'll probably only worry about two of them, the two fairly interesting ones. The first one's Triton. So you have this little struggle with the word *Titan*, which is the big moon of Saturn, and the name *Triton*, which is the big moon of *Neptune*. Triton: it's, it's the only *large moon* in the solar system to go backwards, to go around its—what we call its parent planet—in this case Neptune, the wrong way. OK? Every other large moon orbits the *parent planet* in the same counterclockwise direction... same as most of the other bodies in the solar system. But this moon... the reverse direction, which is perfectly OK as far as the laws of gravity are concerned. But it indicates some sort of peculiar event in the early solar system that gave this moon a motion in contrast to the general spin of the raw material that it was formed from.

The other moon orbiting Neptune that I want to talk about is Nereid. Nereid is, Nereid has the most eccentric orbit, the most lopsided, elliptical-type orbit for a large moon in the solar system. The others tend more like circular orbits.

...Does it mean that Pluto and Neptune might have been related somehow in the past and then drifted slowly into their present orbits? If Pluto... did Pluto ever belong to the Neptune system? Do Neptune's moons represent Pluto-type bodies that have been captured by Neptune? Was some sort of... was Pluto the object that disrupted the Neptune system at some point in the past?

It's really hard to prove any of those things. But now we're starting to appreciate that there's quite a few junior Plutos out there: not big enough to really call a planet, but large enough that they're significant in history of the early solar system. So we'll come back to those when we talk about comets and other small bodies in the fringes of the outer solar system.

자, 해왕성과 그 위성들입니다. 해왕성은 여러 개의 위성을 가지고 있지만, 아마도 우리는 그 중에 오직 두 개, 꽤 흥미로운 위성 두 개에 대해서만 생각해 볼 것 같습니다. 첫 번째는 트리톤입니다. 토성의 큰 위성을 가리키는 타이탄이라는 단어와 해왕성의 큰 위성을 나타내는 이름인 트리톤이 약간 혼동될 거예요. 트리톤은 우리가 모성(parent planet)이라고 부르는, 이 경우 모성은 해왕성이죠, 해왕성을 거꾸로 도는, 즉 모성 주위를 역방향 공전하는 태양계의 위성들 중 유일하게 큰 위성입니다. 아시겠죠? 다른 모든 거대한 위성들은 모성 주위의 궤도를 똑같이 반시계 방향으로 돕니다. 태양계에 있는 대부분의 다른 천체들처럼 말이죠. 그렇지만 이 위성은… 반대 방향으로 도는데, 중력 법칙에 관한 한 전혀 문제되지 않습니다. 하지만 그것은 이 위성을 형성했던 원래 구성 물질의 일반적인 회전 운동과는 정반대로 움직이게 될 일종의 특이한 사건이 태양계 초기에 있었음을 의미합니다.

해왕성 주위를 도는 다른 위성으로 제가 말씀드리고 싶은 것은 네레이드입니다. 네레이드는 이심률이 매우 큰 궤도 즉 태양계의 덩치 큰 위성치고는 한쪽으로 매우 일그러진 타원 궤도를 갖고 있습니다. 다른 위성들의 궤도는 좀 더 원형에 가깝지요.

…이것은 명왕성과 해왕성이 과거에 어떤 식으로든 관련되어 있다가 서서히 현재의 궤도로 이동해왔다는 것을 의미할까요? 혹시 명왕성이… 명왕성이 해왕성계에 속해 있었던 것은 아닐까요? 해왕성의 위성들은 해왕성에 붙잡힌 명왕성 형태의 천체에 해당할까요? 명왕성은 과거 어느 때 해왕성계를 흐트러뜨린 일종의 어떤… 천체였을까요?

이 중 어떤 것도 증명하기 아주 힘듭니다. 그러나 현재 우리는 소형 명왕성들이 상당수에 달한다는 것을 인식하기 시작했습니다. 행성이라 부를 정도로 크지는 않지만 태양계 초기 역사에서 중요한 의미를 가질 정도의 크기는 되죠. 그러면 태양계 바깥 주변의 혜성들과 다른 작은 천체들에 대해 이야기할 때 그것들에 대해 다시 살펴보도록 하겠습니다.

What does the professor imply about the orbits of Triton and Nereid?

Ⓐ They used to be closer together.

Ⓑ They might provide evidence of an undiscovered planet.

Ⓒ They might reverse directions in the future.

Ⓓ They might have been changed by some unusual event.

교수는 트리톤과 네레이드의 궤도에 대해 무엇을 암시하고 있는가?

Ⓐ 과거에 서로 더 가까이 있었다.

Ⓑ 미발견 행성에 대한 증거를 제공할 수도 있다.

Ⓒ 미래에 역방향으로 움직일 수 있다.

Ⓓ 어떤 특이한 사건에 의해 변화를 겪었을 수도 있다.

imply 내포하다, 함축하다 **evidence** 증거, 근거

해설 내용 연결 문제에서는 청취 지문의 곳곳에 있는 정보를 활용해야 한다. 교수는 트리톤과 네레이드의 궤도에 관해 설명하면서, 이들의 궤도를 변화시키거나 방해했을 초기 태양계의 사건들을 언급하고 있다. 그러므로 가장 적당한 답은 D다.

어휘 Neptune 해왕성 moon 위성, 달 fairly 꽤, 상당히 Triton 해왕성의 제1위성 Titan 토성의 제6위성 Saturn 토성 solar system 태양계 backward 거꾸로, 뒤쪽으로 orbit 궤도를 돌다, 궤도 counterclockwise 반시계 방향으로 reverse 반대의, 역행하다 gravity 중력, 지구 인력 peculiar 특이한, 이상한 in contrast to ~와는 대조적으로 spin 회전 (운동) raw material 원료, 원자재 Nereid 해양성의 제 2위성 eccentric 이상한, 별난 lopsided 한쪽으로 기운 elliptical 타원(형)의 circular 원형의 Pluto 명왕성 somehow 어떻게든 drift 떠돌다, 표류하다 capture 붙잡다, 획득하다 disrupt 혼란시키다, 붕괴시키다 appreciate 인식하다, 인정하다 junior 소형의 significant 중요한, 상당한 comet 혜성 fringe 가장자리, 주변 outer 외부의, 외계의

Script
Professor

Dada is often considered under the broader category of Fantasy. It's one of the early directions in the Fantasy style. The term "Dada" itself is a nonsense word—it has no meaning... and where the word originated isn't known. The "philosophy" behind the "Dada" movement was to create works that conveyed the concept of *absurdity*—the artwork was meant to shock the public by presenting the ridiculous, absurd concepts. Dada artists rejected reason—or rational thought. They did not believe that rational thought would help solve social problems...

...When he turned to Dada, he quit painting and devoted himself to making a type of sculpture he referred to as a "ready-made"... probably because they were constructed of readily available objects... At the time, many people reacted to Dadaism by saying that the works were not art at all... and in fact, that's exactly how Duchamp and others conceived of it—as a form of "non-art"... or anti-art.

Duchamp also took a reproduction of da Vinci's famous painting the *Mona Lisa*, and he drew a mustache and goatee on the subject's face. Treating this masterpiece with such disrespect was another way Duchamp was challenging the established cultural standards of his day.

다다이즘은 흔히 좀 더 폭넓은 환타지 범주에 해당되는 것으로 생각됩니다. 다다이즘은 환타지 양식의 초기 경향들 중 하나입니다. '다다이즘'이라는 용어 자체는 무의미한 단어로 아무런 뜻이 없고 유래도 알 수 없습니다. '다다이즘' 운동 이면의 철학은 부조리라는 개념을 전달하는 작품을 만드는 것이었습니다. 우스꽝스럽고 부조리한 개념을 나타냄으로써 대중에게 충격을 주는 것이 목적이었죠. 다다이즘 예술가들은 이성 또는 합리적인 사고를 거부했습니다. 그들은 합리적인 사고가 사회 문제를 해결하는 데 도움이 되지 않는다고 생각했습니다.

…그가 다다이즘으로 돌아섰을 때, 그림을 포기하고 자신이 '기성품'이라고 부르던 일종의 조각품을 제작하는 데 전력했는데… 이것은 아마도 그의 작품들이 쉽게 구할 수 있는 물건들로 제작되었기 때문일 것입니다. 그 당시, 다다이즘에 대한 많은 사람들의 반응은 다다이즘 작품들은 전혀 예술이 아니라는 것이었습니다. 그리고 사실, 뒤샹을 비롯한 다른 사람들의 다다이즘에 대한 생각도 마찬가지였습니다. '비(非) 예술' 또는 반(反) 예술의 한 형식으로 본 것이죠.

뒤샹은 다빈치의 유명한 그림인 〈모나리자〉의 모사품을 만들어 모나리자의 얼굴에 콧수염과 턱수염을 그렸습니다. 이 걸작을 이렇듯 무례하게 다루는 것이 다다이즘의 또 다른 방식이었습니다. 뒤샹은 당대의 기성문화 규범에 도전했던 것입니다.

What does the professor imply about the philosophy of the Dada movement?
Ⓐ It was not taken seriously by most artists.
Ⓑ It varied from one country to another.
Ⓒ It challenged people's concept of what art is.
Ⓓ It was based on a realistic style of art.

다다이즘 운동의 철학을 교수는 무엇이라고 하는가?
Ⓐ 대부분의 예술가들은 이를 진지하게 받아들이지 않았다.
Ⓑ 나라마다 그 모습이 달랐다.
Ⓒ 예술이란 무엇인가에 대한 사람들의 관념에 도전했다.
Ⓓ 사실주의적인 예술 양식에 바탕을 두었다.

seriously 진지하게, 심각하게   vary 다르다, 변화하다
realistic 사실적인, 실제적인

해설 지문(첫 번째 단락의 네 번째 문장과 두 번째, 세 번째 단락의 마지막 문장)을 통해 다다이즘은 예술에 대한 대중의 관념에 도전하고자 했음을 알 수 있으므로 가장 적절한 답은 C다.

어휘 Dada 다다이즘   category 범주, 종류   direction 경향, 추세   term 용어, 전문어   nonsense 무의미한   originate 시작되다, 유래하다   philosophy 철학   convey 전달하다, 나르다   concept 개념, 관념   absurdity 부조리, 불합리   ridiculous 우스운, 터무니없는   absurd 불합리한, 모순된   reason 이성, 이유   rational 합리적인, 이성적인   devote oneself to ~에 전념[몰두]하다   sculpture 조각, 조각 작품   refer ~라고 부르다, 참고하다, 지시하다   ready-made 기성품   readily 쉽사리, 손쉽게   available 이용할 수 있는   conceive ~라고 여기다, 생각하다   reproduction 복제(품), 모조(품), 재생산   mustache 콧수염   goatee 턱수염   masterpiece 걸작, 명작   disrespect 무례, 경시   challenge 도전하다, 이의를 제기하다   established 확립된, 확정된

LISTENING PRACTICE SETS

🎧 T-01

Practice Set 1	p. 86

N Narrator　　P Professor　　S Student

Script

N Listen to a conversation between a student and a professor.

S Uh, excuse me, Professor Thompson. I know your office hours are tomorrow, but I was wondering if you had a few minutes free now to discuss something.

P Sure, John. What did you wanna talk about?

S Well, I have some quick questions about how to write up the research project I did this semester—about climate variations.

P Oh, yes. You were looking at variations in climate in the Grant City area, right? How far along have you gotten?

S I've got all my data, so I'm starting to summarize it now, preparing graphs and stuff. But I'm just... I'm looking at it and I'm afraid that it's not enough, but I'm not sure what else to put in the report.

P I hear the same thing from every student. You know, you have to remember now that you're the expert on what you've done. So think about what you'd need to include if you were going to explain your research project to someone with general or casual knowledge about the subject, like... like your parents. That's usually my rule of thumb: would my parents understand this?

S OK. I get it.

P I hope you can recognize by my saying that how much you do know about the subject.

S Right. I understand. I was wondering if I should also include the notes from the research journal you suggested I keep?

P Yes, definitely. You should use them to indicate what your evolution in thought was through time. So, just set up, you know, what was the purpose of what you were doing—to try to understand the climate variability of this area—and what you did, and what your approach was.

S OK. So, for example, I studied meteorological records; I looked at climate charts; I used different methods for analyzing the data, like certain statistical tests; and then I discuss the results. Is that what you mean?

P Yes, that's right. You should include all of that. The statistical tests are especially important. And also be sure you include a good reference section where all your published and unpublished data came from, 'cause you have a lot of unpublished climate data.

N 학생과 교수의 대화를 들으시오.

S 죄송합니다만, 톰슨 교수님. 교수님의 면담 시간은 내일이지만, 상의드릴 게 있는데 잠깐 시간 좀 내주시겠어요?

P 그래, 존. 무슨 얘긴가?

S 이번 학기 제 연구 프로젝트인 기후 변동에 대해 리포트를 써야 하는데 기술 방식에 대해 간단히 여쭤볼 게 좀 있거든요.

P 아 그래. 자네는 그랜트 시티 지역의 기후 변동에 대해 조사하고 있었지? 어느 정도나 진척되었나?

S 데이터는 모두 얻었고요. 이제 그걸 요약하면서 그래프 등을 준비하고 있습니다. 하지만 저는… 제가 보기에는 좀 미진한 부분이 있는 것 같거든요. 리포트에 무엇을 더 추가해야 할지 모르겠어요.

P 모든 학생들이 그런 이야기를 한다네. 자네는 자신이 연구한 것에 대해 전문가라는 사실을 명심해야 하네. 그러니까 그 주제에 대해 일반적인 혹은 단편적인 지식을 가진 사람에게… 이를테면 자네 부모님에게 그 연구 프로젝트를 설명한다면 어떤 것들이 필요한가를 생각해 보게나. 나의 경험법칙은 바로 이것이라네. 나의 부모님이 과연 이걸 이해할 수 있을까?

S 네. 알겠습니다.

P 내 말을 이해한다면, 자네 자신이 그 주제에 대해 얼마나 잘 알고 있는지 깨달을 수 있기를 바라네.

S 네. 알겠습니다. 저는 교수님이 쓰라고 하셨던 연구일지의 메모도 포함시켜야 할지 망설이고 있었습니다.

P 물론이지. 그것을 이용해 시간이 흐르면서 생각이 어떻게 발전되었는가를 파악해야 한다네. 그러므로 이 지역의 기후 변동을 이해하기 위해 자네가 하던 일의 목표를 세우고 해놓은 일과 접근법을 정리해놓게.

S 예. 예를 들어, 기상 기록을 검토하고 기후 차트를 살펴보고, 특정 통계적 실험 같은 데이터 분석에 필요한 여러 방법들을 이용했습니다. 그리고 나서 결과를 검토하라는 말씀이시죠?

P 그렇다네. 그 모든 걸 포함시켜야 한다는 말이지. 통계적 실험은 특히 중요하다네. 그리고 발표되었거나 발표되지 않은 모든 데이터들의 출처를 밝혀 놓은 신뢰할 만한 참고 목록을 포함시키는 것도 잊지 말게. 미발표된 기후 데이터도 상당히 많이 가지고 있을 테니 말이네.

S Hmm... something just came into my mind and went out the other side.

P That happens to me a lot, so I've come up with a pretty good memory management tool. I carry a little pad with me all the time and jot down questions or ideas that I don't wanna forget. For example, I went to the doctor with my daughter and her baby son last week, and we knew we wouldn't remember everything we wanted to ask the doctor, so we actually made a list of five things we wanted answers to.

S A notepad is a good idea. Since I'm so busy now at the end of the semester, I'm getting pretty forgetful these days. OK. I just remembered what I was trying to say before.

P Good. I was hoping you'd come up with it.

S Yes. It ends up that I have data on more than just the immediate Grant City area, so I also included some regional data in the report. With everything else it should be a pretty good indicator of the climate in this part of the state.

P Sounds good. I'd be happy to look over a draft version before you hand in the final copy, if you wish.

S Great. I'll plan to get you a draft of the paper by next Friday. Thanks very much. Well, see ya.

P OK.

S 음… 방금 뭔가 말씀드릴 게 있었는데 잊었어요.

P 나도 그런 일이 종종 있지. 그래서 나는 기억을 유지하는 데 상당히 좋은 한 가지 도구를 이용한다네. 항상 메모장을 가지고 다니면서 잊고 싶지 않은 질문이나 아이디어를 적어놓지. 예를 들면, 나는 지난주 내 딸과 손자와 함께 병원에 갔거든. 그런데 의사에게 물어볼 걸 전부 기억해낼 수 없다는 걸 알기 때문에, 실제로 대답을 듣고 싶은 질문을 다섯 가지 적어가지고 갔다네.

S 메모장이 좋은 방법이 되겠군요. 요새 학기말에는 너무 바빠서 건망증이 심해져요. 아, 아까 말씀 드리려고 했던 게 방금 생각났어요.

P 그래. 나도 그게 뭔가 궁금했네.

S 예. 결국 제가 수집한 데이터는 그랜트 시티 지역에 국한되지 않았어요. 그래서 리포트에 지역별 데이터도 포함시켰어요. 다른 모든 요소들과 함께 그것은 이 지방 기후의 훌륭한 지표가 될 것입니다.

P 훌륭하군. 자네가 원한다면 최종 리포트를 완성해서 제출하기 전에 내가 초안을 한번 검토해 주겠네.

S 좋습니다. 다음 금요일까지 리포트 초안을 보여드리겠습니다. 대단히 감사합니다. 그럼, 안녕히 계세요.

P 그래.

어휘

research 연구, 학술조사   project 프로젝트, 계획   climate variation 기후 변화   summarize 요약하다   expert 전문가, 숙련된, 노련한
include 포함하다   knowledge 지식, 학식   casual 우연의, 되는 대로의   rule of thumb 경험 법칙, 주먹구구   recognize 알아보다, 인지하다
research journal 연구일지   climate variability 기후 변동   approach 접근법, 접근하다   meteorological 기상학의   analyze 분석하다, 검토하다   statistical 통계적, 통계학상의   reference 참고목록, 참조   come up with (아이디어 등을) 생각해 내다   jot down 메모하다   end up that~ 결국 ~가 되다   regional 지역의, 지방의   indicator 지표, 척도, 표시   look over 검토하다   draft version 초안   hand in 제출하다

1. 이 남자는 왜 교수를 만나러 갔는가?

Ⓐ 차트와 도표를 빌리기 위해

Ⓑ 어떤 통계 절차에 관한 설명을 듣기 위해

Ⓒ 자신이 쓰고 있는 리포트에 대해 논의하기 위해

Ⓓ 시험 점수에 대해 이야기하기 위해

내용의 목적을 묻는 문제

어휘 procedure 절차, 순서

해설 남자는 기후 변동에 대한 리포트를 작성하기 위해 교수를 찾아왔다. 정답은 보기 C.

2. 이 남자는 리포트에 어떤 정보를 포함시킬 것인가?
아래 제시된 각각의 정보에 대해 '보고서에 포함되는 것', '보고서에 포함되지 않는 것' 둘 중 하나에 표시를 하라.

	보고서에 포함되는 것	보고서에 포함되지 않는 것
기후 차트	✔	
기상학자와의 인터뷰		✔
연구일지 메모	✔	
통계적 실험	✔	

내용 연결 문제

어휘 meteorologist 기상학자

해설 학생과 교수는 기후 변동을 조사하는 데 필요한 여러 정보 출처에 대해 논의하고 있다. 기상학자와의 인터뷰는 이 대화에서 전혀 언급되지 않는다.

3. 교수가 남자에게 병원에 간 이야기를 한 이유는 무엇인가?

Ⓐ 무언가를 기억해내는 방법을 알려주기 위해

Ⓑ 곧 떠나야 하는 이유를 설명하기 위해

Ⓒ 그의 리포트에 나타난 한 가지 요점을 설명하기 위해

Ⓓ 건강 유지의 중요성을 강조하기 위해

의도 파악 문제

어휘 demonstrate 논증하다, ~의 증거가 되다   emphasize 강조하다, 역설하다

해설 병원에 간 이야기를 한 것은 메모의 중요성을 강조하기 위해 언급한 것이다. 따라서 정답은 보기 A.

4. 교수는 그 남자를 위해 무엇을 해 주겠다고 제의하는가?

Ⓐ 그 주의 다른 지역들에 관한 데이터를 더 수집하는 데 도움을 주겠다고

Ⓑ 출판을 위해 그의 연구 결과를 제출하겠다고

Ⓒ 그에게 의사의 전화번호를 알려주겠다고

Ⓓ 리포트의 초안을 검토해 주겠다고

세부 정보 찾기 문제

어휘 submit 제출[제시]하다   publication 출간, 발행, 출판물

해설 교수는 학생이 리포트를 제출하기 전에 한번 검토해 주겠다고 제의했다. 따라서 정답은 보기 D.

5. 대화의 일부를 다시 듣고 질문에 답하라.   🎧 T-02

> P You know, you have to remember now that you're the expert on what you've done. So think about what you'd need to include if you were going to explain your research project to someone with general or casual knowledge about the subject, like... like your parents. That's usually my rule of thumb: would my parents understand this?
>
> S OK. I get it.
>
> P I hope you can recognize by my saying that how much you do know about the subject.
>
> N *Why does the professor say this?*
>
> P I hope you can recognize by my saying that how much you do know about the subject.

Ⓐ 리포트의 길이에 대해 질문하기 위해

Ⓑ 격려하기 위해

Ⓒ 데이터의 출처를 문제 삼기 위해

Ⓓ 어떤 이론을 설명하기 위해

의도 파악 문제

어휘 encouragement 격려, 장려   dispute 논쟁하다, 반론하다

해설 질문은 '교수는 왜 이 말을 했는가?'이다. 학생은 리포트를 작성할 때 정보를 어떤 식으로 제시해야 하는지 감을 잡지 못하고 있다. 교수는 학생 스스로 자신감을 갖도록 격려하고 있다.

Practice Set 2   p. 88

N Narrator   P Professor

Script

N Listen to part of a lecture in a philosophy class.

P OK. Another ancient Greek philosopher we need to discuss is Aristotle—Aristotle's ethical theory. What Aristotle's ethical theory is all about is this: he's trying to show you how to be happy—what true happiness is.

Now, why is he interested in human happiness? It's not just because it's something that all people want or aim for. It's more than that. But to get there, we need to first make a very important distinction. Let me introduce a couple of technical terms: extrinsic value and intrinsic value.

To understand Aristotle's interest in happiness, you need to understand this distinction.

Some things we aim for and value, not for themselves, but for what they bring about in addition to themselves. If I value something as a means to something else, then it has what we will call "extrinsic value." Other things we desire and hold to be valuable for themselves alone. If we value something not as a means to something else, but for its own sake, let us say that it has "intrinsic value."

Exercise. There may be some people who value exercise for itself, but I don't. I value exercise because if I exercise, I tend to stay healthier than I would if I didn't. So I desire to engage in exercise, and I value exercise extrinsically... not for its own sake, but as a means to something beyond it. It brings me good health.

Health. Why do I value good health? Well, here it gets a little more complicated for me. Um, health is important for me because I can't... do other things I wanna do—play music, teach philosophy—if I'm ill. So health is important to me—has value to me—as a means to a productive life. But health is also important to me because I just kind of like to be healthy—it feels good. It's pleasant to be healthy, unpleasant not to be. So to some degree I value health both for itself and as a means to something else: productivity. It's got extrinsic and intrinsic value for me.

N 철학 강의의 일부를 들으시오.

P 좋습니다. 우리가 논의하고자 하는 또 다른 고대 그리스 철학자는 아리스토텔레스인데, 그의 윤리학 이론에 대해서 살펴봅시다. 아리스토텔레스의 윤리학 이론은 바로 이것입니다. 인간이 어떻게 행복해질 수 있고, 진실한 행복이 무엇인가를 보여 주는 것입니다.

그렇다면, 왜 그는 인간의 행복에 관심을 두었을까요? 행복이 모든 인간이 원하고 목표로 삼고 있는 것이기 때문만이 아닙니다. 행복은 그 이상의 의미가 있습니다. 하지만 그것에 도달하기 위해 우리는 먼저 매우 중요한 차이점을 구별할 필요가 있습니다. 두 가지 전문 용어를 소개하면 바로 비본질적 가치와 본질적 가치라는 것입니다.

아리스토텔레스의 행복론을 이해하려면 이 개념의 차이를 이해해야 합니다.

어떤 것은 그것 자체만으로는 의미가 없고 그것이 초래하는 결과에 의미가 있기 때문에 우리는 그것을 목표로 삼거나 소중히 여깁니다. 내가 어떤 것을 다른 어떤 것의 수단으로 중요하게 여긴다면, 그것은 소위 '비본질적 가치'를 지니고 있는 것입니다. 또 다른 어떤 것은 그것 자체만으로도 의미가 있기 때문에 우리는 그것을 열망하거나 소중히 여깁니다. 우리가 어떤 것을 다른 어떤 것의 수단이 아니라 그것 자체에 가치를 둔다면 그것은 '본질적 가치'를 지니고 있는 것입니다.

운동을 예로 들어 봅시다. 운동 그 자체를 중요시 여기는 사람들이 있습니다. 하지만 저는 그렇지 않습니다. 저는 운동을 하면 하지 않을 때보다 건강해지기 때문에 운동을 가치 있는 것으로 생각합니다. 따라서 운동을 비본질적 가치로서 중요시 여기고 운동을 하려는 것입니다. 즉 운동 자체가 아니라 그것을 넘어선 무언가의 수단으로서 소중히 생각하는 것이죠. 운동이 신체를 건강하게 만들어 준다는 데 의미를 두는 겁니다.

건강에 대해 생각해 봅시다. 나는 왜 건강을 중요하게 생각할까요? 이 문제는 제게는 좀 복잡하군요. 건강은 내게 중요합니다. 왜냐하면 아프면 내가 하고 싶은 다른 일들, 이를 테면 음악 연주나 철학 강의 등을 할 수 없기 때문입니다. 그래서 건강은 생산적인 삶의 수단으로 내게 중요하고 가치가 있는 것입니다. 하지만 내게 건강이 중요한 또 다른 이유는 나 자신이 건강하고 싶기 때문입니다. 기분이 좋은 느낌이 드니까요. 건강하면 기분이 좋고, 건강하지 않으면 기분이 좋지 않습니다. 따라서 어느 정도 나는 건강을 그것 자체만으로 소중히 여기면서도 동시에 어떤 다른 것, 즉 생산성의 수단으로서도 소중히 여깁니다. 내게 건강은 비본질적 가치와 본질적 가치를 모두 지니고 있다고 할 수 있지요.

Then there's some things that are just valued for themselves. I'm a musician, not a professional musician; I just play a musical instrument for fun. Why do I value playing music? Well, like most amateur musicians, I only play because, well, I just enjoy it. It's something that's an end in itself.

Now, something else I value is teaching. Why? Well, it brings in a modest income, but I could make more money doing other things. I'd do it even if they didn't pay me. I just enjoy teaching. In that sense it's an end to itself.

But teaching's not something that has intrinsic value for all people—and that's true generally. Most things that are enjoyed in and of themselves vary from person to person. Some people value teaching intrinsically, but others don't.

So how does all this relate to human happiness? Well, Aristotle asks: is there something that all human beings value... and value only intrinsically, for its own sake and only for its own sake? If you could find such a thing, that would be the universal final good, or truly the ultimate purpose or goal for all human beings. Aristotle thought the answer was yes. What is it? Happiness. Everyone will agree, he argues, that happiness is the ultimate end to be valued for itself and really only for itself. For what other purpose is there in being happy? What does it yield? The attainment of happiness becomes the ultimate or highest good for Aristotle.

The next question that Aristotle raises is: what is happiness? We all want it; we all desire it; we all seek it. It's the goal we have in life. But what is it? How do we find it? Here he notes, with some frustration, people disagree.

But he does give us a couple of criteria, or features, to keep in mind as we look for what true human happiness is. True human happiness should be, as he puts it, complete. Complete in that it's all we require. Well, true human happiness... if you had that, what else do you need? Nothing.

어떤 것들은 그것 자체만으로 소중하게 생각됩니다. 저는 음악을 연주하지만 전문 음악가는 아닙니다. 저는 단지 재미로 악기를 연주합니다. 제가 왜 음악 연주를 소중히 생각할까요? 대부분의 아마추어 연주가들과 마찬가지로 저도 그냥 즐겁기 때문에 악기를 연주합니다. 이런 행위는 그것 자체가 목적이 됩니다.

그리고 제가 소중히 여기는 또 다른 활동은 가르치는 일입니다. 왜냐고요? 적당한 수입이 생기긴 하지만, 아마 다른 일을 하면 더 많은 돈을 벌 수 있을 겁니다. 저는 보수를 받지 못하더라도 이 일을 했을 겁니다. 저는 그저 가르치는 일을 좋아합니다. 그런 점에서 제게는 가르치는 일 자체가 목적입니다.

하지만 가르치는 일이 모든 사람들에게 본질적인 가치를 지니는 것은 아닙니다. 그리고 이는 일반적인 사실입니다. 순수하게 즐기는 것들의 대부분이 개인에 따라 차이가 있습니다. 어떤 사람들은 가르치는 일이 본질적인 가치가 있다고 여기지만 다른 사람들은 그렇게 생각하지 않습니다.

그렇다면 이 모든 것들이 인간의 행복과 어떤 관계가 있을까요? 아리스토텔레스는 이렇게 묻습니다. "모든 인간들이 오로지 그 자체만을 본질적인 가치로 삼는 것이 있을까?" 그런 것을 발견한다면, 그것은 보편적이고 최종적인 선이 될 것이며, 모든 인간들의 궁극적인 목적이자 목표라고 할 수 있을 겁니다. 아리스토텔레스는 그런 것이 있다고 생각했습니다. 그게 무엇일까요? 행복입니다. 모든 사람들은 행복이 그 자체만으로 소중한 궁극적인 목적이라는 데 동의할 것이라고 아리스토텔레스는 주장했습니다. 행복해지는 데 어떤 다른 목적이 있을 수 있겠습니까? 그것으로 어떤 결과가 생겨날까요? 아리스토텔레스에게 행복의 달성은 궁극적인, 최고의 선이었습니다.

아리스토텔레스가 제기한 다음 질문은 이것입니다. "행복은 무엇인가?" 우리 모두 행복을 원합니다. 우리 모두가 행복을 열망합니다. 우리 모두가 행복을 추구합니다. 행복은 우리 인생의 목적입니다. 하지만 무엇이 행복일까요? 우리는 행복을 어떻게 발견할까요? 이 부분에서 그는 약간 좌절하며 사람들의 의견이 분분함을 지적합니다.

하지만 그는 우리가 진정한 행복을 추구할 때 명심해야 할 몇 가지 기준 혹은 주안점을 제시하였습니다. 그는 인간의 진정한 행복은 완전한 것이 되어야 한다고 했습니다. 완전하다는 것은 우리에게 필요한 모든 것이라는 의미입니다. 인간의 진정한 행복을 갖게 된다면 다른 무엇이 필요하겠습니까? 아무것도 없습니다.

And, second, true happiness should be something that I can obtain on my own. I shouldn't have to rely on other people for it. Many people value fame and seek fame. Fame for them becomes the goal. But, according to Aristotle, this won't work either, because fame depends altogether too much on other people. I can't get it on my own, without help from other people.

In the end, Aristotle says that true happiness is the exercise of reason—a life of intellectual contemplation... of thinking. So let's see how he comes to that.

그리고 두 번째로, 진정한 행복은 스스로 얻을 수 있는 것이 되어야 합니다. 그것을 얻기 위해 다른 사람들에게 의존해서는 안 됩니다. 많은 사람들이 명성을 소중히 여기고 명성을 추구합니다. 이 경우에 그들에게는 명성이 목표가 됩니다. 하지만 아리스토텔레스의 말에 따르면, 명성은 행복이 되지 못합니다. 왜냐하면 명성은 전적으로 다른 사람들에게 지나치게 의존해야 하기 때문입니다. 다른 사람들의 도움 없이는 나 스스로 명성을 얻을 수 없습니다.

결국, 아리스토텔레스가 말하는 진정한 행복이란 이성의 활동입니다. 즉 지적인 숙고… 사고하는 삶을 말합니다. 자, 그럼 그가 어떻게 그런 결론에 도달했는지 살펴봅시다.

어휘

philosopher 철학자, 현인   Aristotle 아리스토텔레스   ethical 도덕상의, 윤리적인   be interested in ~에 흥미를 가지다   make a distinction 차이점을 구별하다   extrinsic 비본질적인, 외래의   value 값어치, 소중하게 여기다   intrinsic 본질적인, 고유의   means 수단   for its own sake 그 자체로   human being 인류   complicated 복잡한, 뒤얽힌, (이해하기) 어려운   to some degree 어느 정도   productivity 생산성   moderate 적당한   relate 관련시키다(to), 설명하다   ultimate 궁극적인, 최후의   attainment 달성, 도달   criteria (criterion의 복수형) 기준, 표준   feature 주안점, 특징   keep in mind 명심하다   depend on ~에 달려 있다   reason 이성   contemplation 숙고, 묵상

1. 이 강의의 주요 목적은 무엇인가?

Ⓐ 비본질적인 가치의 중요성을 설명하기

Ⓑ 가르침의 중요성에 대한 아리스토텔레스의 견해를 설명하기

Ⓒ 사람들이 자신들이 소중히 여기는 것을 바꾸는 이유를 설명하기

Ⓓ 인간의 행복에 관한 아리스토텔레스의 견해를 논의하기

내용의 목적을 묻는 문제

어휘 view 관점

해설 서두에서 교수는 강의의 목적을 아리스토텔레스 윤리학의 주제인 행복론이라고 밝히고 있다. 따라서 정답은 보기 D.

2. 교수는 자신이 중요시 여기는 몇 가지 예를 들고 있다. 각각의 예가 그녀에게 어떤 가치가 있는지 지적해 보라.

해당 박스에 표시하라. 이 문제의 배점은 2점이다.

이 문제는 특정 활동이 교수에게 어떤 유형의 가치를 지니는지 묻고 있다. 올바르게 표기된 표는 다음과 같다:

	비본질적 가치	본질적 가치	비본질적 가치와 본질적 가치
가르치기		✓	
운동	✓		
건강			✓
악기 연주하기		✓	

내용 연결 문제

어휘 indicate 지시하다   checkmark 부호

해설 교수는 자신의 여러 활동을 예로 들면서 각각이 어떤 가치 영역에 해당하는지 설명하는데, 운동을 비본질적인 가치로, 가르치기와 악기 연주를 본질적인 가치로, 건강을 두 영역 모두에 해당하는 가치로 지적하고 있다.

3. 행복이 아리스토텔레스의 이론의 핵심 주제인 이유는?

Ⓐ 사람들이 성취하기가 매우 어렵기 때문에

Ⓑ 모든 사람들이 그것 자체만으로도 가치가 있다고 여기기 때문에

Ⓒ 생산적인 삶의 수단이 되기 때문에

Ⓓ 대부분의 사람들이 행복의 개념에 대해 일치된 견해를 갖고 있기 때문에

세부 정보 찾기 문제

해설 아리스토텔레스는 행복이 그 자체만으로 궁극적인 목적이라는 데 모든 사람들이 동의할 것이라고 생각했기 때문이다. 따라서 정답은 보기 B.

4. 교수에 따르면, 아리스토텔레스는 왜 명성이 진정한 행복을 가져다 줄 수 없다고 생각했는가?

Ⓐ 명성은 다른 사람들의 도움 없이는 달성될 수 없다.

Ⓑ 명성은 모든 사람들에 의해 달성될 수는 없다.

Ⓒ 명성은 영원히 지속되지 않는다.

Ⓓ 다른 사람들과 명성을 공유할 수 없다.

세부 정보 찾기 문제

어휘 obtain 얻다, 획득하다

해설 강의 막바지에서 교수는 명성이 다른 사람들에게 지나치게 의존해야 하기 때문에 진정한 행복을 주지 못한다는 아리스토텔레스의 주장을 밝히고 있다. 정답은 보기 A.

5. 강의의 일부를 다시 듣고 질문에 답하라.

🎧 T-04

> P Now, something else I value is teaching. Why? Well, it brings in a modest income, but I could make more money doing other things.
>
> N *What does the professor mean when she says this?*
>
> P Well, it brings in a modest income, but I could make more money doing other things.

Ⓐ 가르치는 일은 사회에서 높이 평가 받는 직업이 아니다.

Ⓑ 그녀는 돈을 더 많이 벌기 위해 직업을 바꿀 수도 있다.

Ⓒ 그녀가 교수직을 택한 이유는 봉급과 관계가 거의 없다.

Ⓓ 봉급이 더 높다면 더 많은 사람들이 교사가 되었을 것이다.

의도 파악 문제

어휘 profession 직업, 전문직

해설 교수는 자신에게 본질적인 가치가 있는 활동으로 가르치는 일을 예로 들고 있다. 그녀가 가르치는 일을 소중히 여기는 것은 봉급 때문이 아니라 그것을 좋아하기 때문이라고 밝히고 있다. 따라서 정답은 보기 C.

Script

N Listen to part of a psychology lecture. The professor is discussing behaviorism.

P Now, many people consider John Watson to be the founder of behaviorism. And like other behaviorists, he believed that psychologists should study only the behaviors they can observe and measure. They're not interested in mental processes. While a person could describe his thoughts, no one else can see or hear them to verify the accuracy of his report. But one thing you can observe is muscular habits. What Watson did was to observe muscular habits because he viewed them as a manifestation of thinking. One kind of habit that he studied are laryngeal habits.

Watson thought laryngeal habits—you know, from *larynx*; in other words, related to the voice box—he thought those habits were an expression of thinking. He argued that for very young children, thinking is really talking out loud to oneself because they talk out loud even if they're not trying to communicate with someone in particular. As the individual matures, that overt talking to oneself becomes covert talking to oneself, but thinking still shows up as a laryngeal habit. One of the bits of evidence that supports this is that when people are trying to solve a problem, they, um, typically have increased muscular activity in the throat region. That is, if you put electrodes on the throat and measure muscle potential—muscle activity—you discover that when people are thinking, like if they're diligently trying to solve a problem, that there is muscular activity in the throat region.

So Watson made the argument that problem solving, or thinking, can be defined as a set of behaviors—a set of responses—and in this case the response he observed was the throat activity. That's what he means when he calls it a laryngeal habit. Now, as I am thinking about what I am going to be saying, my muscles in my throat are responding. So thinking can be measured as muscle activity. Now, the motor theory... yes?

S Professor Blake, um, did he happen to look at people who sign? I mean deaf people?

P Uh, he did indeed, um, and to jump ahead, what one finds in deaf individuals who use sign language when they're given problems of various kinds, they have muscular changes in their hands when they are trying to solve a problem... muscle changes in the hand, just like the muscular changes going on in the throat region for speaking individuals.

N 심리학 강의의 일부를 들으시오. 교수는 행동주의에 대해 논의하고 있다.

P 많은 사람들은 존 왓슨이 행동주의의 창시자라고 생각합니다. 그리고 다른 행동주의자들과 마찬가지로, 그는 심리학자들이 관찰하고 측정할 수 있는 행동만을 연구해야 한다고 생각했습니다. 그들은 정신 활동에는 관심이 없지요. 개인이 자신의 생각을 기술할 수는 있겠지만, 아무도 그 내용의 정확성을 검증할 수 있도록 개인의 생각을 볼 수도 들을 수도 없습니다. 하지만 관찰할 수 있는 한 가지는 바로 근육의 습성입니다. 왓슨은 근육의 습성을 관찰했는데, 그 이유는 그것이 사고의 발현이라고 생각했기 때문입니다. 그가 연구한 한 가지 습성은 후두의 습성입니다.

왓슨은 후두부, 다시 말해서 발성 기관과 관련된 부분에서 생기는 습성을 연구했습니다. 그는 그 습성이 사고의 표현이라고 생각했지요. 그는 아주 어린 아동들의 경우, 사고가 혼잣말을 하는 형태로 나타난다고 주장했습니다. 아동들은 특별히 어떤 사람과 대화를 하지 않는데도 큰 소리로 말하기 때문입니다. 크게 혼잣말을 하는 행위는 성장하면서 조용한 혼잣말로 바뀌게 됩니다. 하지만 사고는 여전히 후두의 습성으로 나타납니다. 이를 뒷받침하는 증거들 중 하나는, 사람들이 문제를 풀려고 할 때 대개 목 부위의 근육 활동이 증가한다는 점이에요. 즉 목에 전극을 부착하고 근육의 전위, 즉 근육 활동을 측정해 보면, 열심히 문제를 풀 때처럼 생각을 할 때 그런 현상이 나타난다는 것이죠. 목 부위에서 근육 활동이 나타난다는 것입니다.

이렇듯 왓슨은 문제 해결 과정 혹은 사고 활동을 일련의 행동, 일련의 반응으로 규정할 수 있다고 주장했습니다. 이 경우에 그가 관찰했던 반응은 목의 활동입니다. 그가 후두의 습성이라고 했던 것이 바로 이런 의미입니다. 자, 내가 지금 말하려는 것에 대해 생각할 때 나의 목 근육은 반응을 나타내고 있습니다. 그러므로 사고는 근육 활동으로 측정될 수 있습니다. 자, 근육 운동 이론은… 네?

S 블레이크 교수님, 그는 혹시 수화를 쓰는 사람들도 관찰했나요? 청각장애인들 말이죠.

P 그렇습니다. 요점만 말하자면, 수화를 사용하는 청각장애인들에게 다양한 종류의 문제를 제시했을 때 나타나는 반응을 알아보았는데요. 그들이 문제를 풀려고 할 때는 손에서 근육의 변화가 있었습니다. 말을 하는 사람들에게서 목 부위에 근육의 변화가 나타났듯이, 이들에게서는 손에서 근육의 변화가 나타났던 것입니다.

So, for Watson, thinking is identical with the activity of muscles. A related concept of thinking was developed by William James. It's called ideomotor action.

Ideomotor action is an activity that occurs without our noticing it, without our being aware of it. I'll give you one simple example. If you think of locations, there tends to be eye movement that occurs with your thinking about that location. In particular, from where we're sitting, imagine that you're asked to think of our university library. Well, if you close your eyes and think of the library, and if you're sitting directly facing me, then according to this notion, your eyeballs will move slightly to the left, to your left, 'cause the library's in that general direction.

James and others said that this is an idea leading to a motor action, and that's why it's called "ideomotor action"—an idea leads to motor activity. If you wish to impress your friends and relatives, you can change this simple process into a magic trick. Ask people to do something such as I've just described: think of something on their left; think of something on their right. You get them to think about two things on either side with their eyes closed, and you watch their eyes very carefully. And if you do that, you'll discover that you can see rather clearly the eye movement—that is, you can see the movement of the eyeballs. Now, then you say, "Think of either one and I'll tell which you're thinking of."

OK. Well, Watson makes the assumption that muscular activity is equivalent to thinking. But given everything we've been talking about here, one has to ask: are there alternatives to this motor theory—this claim that muscular activities are equivalent to thinking? Is there anything else that might account for this change in muscular activity, other than saying that it is thinking? And the answer is clearly yes. Is there any way to answer the question definitively? I think the answer is no.

따라서 왓슨에게 사고는 곧 근육 활동과 동일한 의미입니다. 윌리엄 제임스는 사고와 관련된 또 하나의 개념을 탄생시켰습니다. 그것은 관념 운동이라는 것입니다.

관념 운동은 사람이 깨닫지도 못하고, 의식하지도 않는 상태에서 일어나는 활동입니다. 한 가지 예를 들어보겠습니다. 여러분이 어떤 장소에 대해 생각한다면, 그 장소를 생각하는 과정에서 안구의 움직임이 일어나기 마련입니다. 특히 여러분이 앉아 있는 곳에서 우리 대학의 도서관에 대해 생각한다고 상상해 봅시다. 여러분이 눈을 감고 도서관에 대해 생각하면서 나와 직접 대면한 상태로 앉아 있을 때, 이 개념에 따르면 여러분의 안구는 약간 왼쪽으로, 여러분의 왼쪽으로 움직이게 됩니다. 왜냐하면 도서관이 그쪽 방향에 있기 때문입니다.

제임스를 비롯한 학자들에 따르면, 이 이론의 요지는 어떤 관념이 근육 활동을 유발한다는 것입니다. 관념이 근육 활동으로 이어진다고 해서 이 이론을 '관념 운동'이라고 부르는 거죠. 여러분이 친구나 친척을 놀라게 하고 싶다면, 이런 단순한 과정을 마술처럼 이용해 볼 수도 있습니다. 지금까지 내가 설명한 것을 사람들에게 시켜보십시오. 그들에게 왼쪽에 있는 무언가를 머릿속에 떠올리게 합니다. 그리고 오른쪽에 있는 무언가를 생각해 보게 합니다. 그 다음 그들에게 눈을 감고 양쪽에 위치한 것들을 생각해 보도록 지시합니다. 그리고 눈을 자세히 관찰하는 겁니다. 그러면 눈의 움직임을 좀 분명하게 관찰할 수 있을 것입니다. 즉 안구의 움직임을 알 수 있지요. 그러고 나서 여러분은 이렇게 말하는 겁니다. '어느 한쪽에 있는 것을 생각해 봐요. 그러면 내가 어느 쪽에 있는 것을 생각하는지 맞춰 볼게요.'

그렇습니다. 왓슨은 근육 운동이 사고와 상응한다고 가정했습니다. 그러나 우리가 여기서 논의해 온 모든 점들을 감안하건대, 이런 질문을 던지지 않을 수 없습니다. 이런 근육 운동 이론, 즉 근육 운동이 사고와 상응한다는 이론에 비길 만한 대안 이론들이 있을까요? 근육 운동이 사고와 상응한다고 보지 않고 근육 운동의 변화를 설명할 수 있는 다른 이론이 있을 수 있을까요? 분명히 '그렇다'고 대답할 수 있습니다. 그런데 이 질문에 대해 완벽한 대답을 제시할 수 있는 방안이 있을까요? 저는 없다고 생각합니다.

어휘

founder 창시자, 창립자   behaviorism 행동주의   behaviorist 행동주의자   observe 관찰하다, 목격하다   measure 측정하다, 재다   verify 검증하다   accuracy 정확성, 정밀도   muscular 근육의, 건강한   view A as B A를 B로 간주하다   manifestation 표시, 징후   laryngeal (해부) 후두부   larynx (해부) 후두   voice box 발성기관   overt 공개적인   covert 사적인   electrode 전극   diligently 부지런히   sign language 수화   be identical with ~와 동일하다   ideomotor 관념 운동의   motor 운동근육, 모터   be aware of 의식하다   assumption 가정, 가설   be equivalent to ~에 상응하다   alternative 대안, 양자택일   account for 설명하다

1. 교수가 주로 다루고 있는 내용은?

Ⓐ 아이들의 운동 기능 발달

Ⓑ 심리학자들이 목의 근육 활동을 측정하는 방법

Ⓒ 근육 활동과 사고 사이의 관계에 관한 이론

Ⓓ 청각 장애인들의 문제해결 방법에 관한 연구

내용의 요점을 묻는 문제

어휘 development 발달, 성장 technique 기술, 기교

해설 이 강의의 주제는 근육 활동과 사고와의 관계이다. 다른 보기들의 내용도 언급되어 있지만 주제와는 거리가 멀다. 따라서 정답은 보기 C.

2. 교수는 수화를 사용하는 사람들에 대해 어떤 말을 하는가?

Ⓐ 그들의 사고 습관을 연구하는 것은 가능하지 않다.

Ⓑ 그들은 후두의 습성을 드러낸다.

Ⓒ 그들이 문제를 풀 때 손의 근육이 움직인다.

Ⓓ 그들은 관념 운동을 보여 주지 않는다.

세부 정보 찾기 문제

어휘 exhibit 나타내다, 보이다

해설 교수는 말을 하는 사람들이 목 부위의 움직임을 보이고, 청각 장애인들은 문제를 풀 때, 손 근육의 움직임을 보인다고 설명한다. 정답은 보기 C.

3. 교수는 대학 도서관을 언급하면서 어떤 주장을 하는가?

Ⓐ 문제 해결에 관한 연구가 그곳에서 이루어진다.

Ⓑ 학생들은 행동주의에 관한 책을 더 읽어보려면 그곳에 가야 한다.

Ⓒ 학생들이 그것에 대해 생각할 때 눈은 그곳을 향한다.

Ⓓ 그는 그곳에서 윌리엄 제임스의 사고의 개념에 대해 알았다.

구성 파악 문제

해설 어떤 장소에 대해 생각하면 그곳이 위치한 쪽으로 안구가 움직인다는 것을 설명하기 위해 대학 도서관을 예로 든 것이다. 따라서 정답은 보기 C.

4. 교수는 학생들에게 마술을 이야기한다. 이 마술은 무엇을 표시하는가?

Ⓐ 사람들이 의식하지 않으면서 취하는 행동

Ⓑ 행동주의자들이 실제로 과학자들이 아니라는 것

Ⓒ 심리학자들이 아동을 연구하는 방법

Ⓓ 위치를 기억해내는 방법

내용 연결 문제

어휘 method 방법, 방식

해설 관념 운동의 개념을 묻는 질문인데, 이것은 깨닫지도 못하고, 의식하지도 않았는데 일어나는 활동을 말한다. 정답은 보기 A.

5. 사고에 관한 운동 근육 이론에 대해 교수는 어떤 생각을 가지고 있는가?

Ⓐ 그가 수집한 대부분의 증거는 그것과 상반된다.

Ⓑ 그것은 아이의 행동보다는 성인의 행동을 더 잘 설명해 준다.

Ⓒ 현재로서는 사고에 관한 가장 타당한 이론이다.

Ⓓ 완전히 입증될 수도 없고 반박할 수도 없다.

태도 파악 문제

어휘 evidence 징표, 증거 contradict 모순되다 valid 설득력 있는, 정당한 completely 철저히 proved 입증된 disproved 반증된

해설 마지막 부분에서 이 이론에 대한 교수의 의견이 나와 있다. 그는 이 이론의 대안이 될 만한 이론이 있을 수 있겠지만, 그것을 완전히 뒤집을 만한 이론은 없다고 밝히고 있다. 따라서 정답은 보기 D.

6. 강의의 일부를 다시 듣고 질문에 답하라.

> P Watson thought laryngeal habits — you know, from *larynx*; in other words, related to the voice box — he thought those habits were an expression of thinking.
>
> N *Why does the professor say this?*
>
> P ... you know, from *larynx*; in other words, related to the voice box...

Ⓐ 후두의 습성의 예를 제시하기 위해서

Ⓑ 어떤 용어의 의미를 설명하기 위해서

Ⓒ 후두의 습성을 논의하는 이유를 설명하기 위해서

Ⓓ 그가 이전에 다루었던 논점을 학생들에게 상기시키기 위해서

의도 파악 문제

해설 교수는 후두의 습성(laryngeal habits)이라는 특이한 용어를 소개하면서, 학생들에게 이 용어의 개념을 이해시키고 있다. 정답은 보기 B.

Practice Set 4   p. 92

N Narrator   P Professor   M Male Student   F Female Student

Script

N Listen to part of a lecture in an astronomy class. You will not need to remember the numbers the professor mentions.

P OK. Let's get going. Today I'm going to talk about how the asteroid belt was discovered. And... I'm going to start by writing some numbers on the board. Here they are: we'll start with zero, then 3,... 6,... 12. Uh, tell me what I'm doing.

F Multiplying by 2?

P Right. I'm doubling the numbers, so 2 times 12 is 24, and the next one I'm going to write after 24 would be...

F 48.

P 48. Then 96. We'll stop there for now. Uh, now I'll write another row of numbers under that. Tell me what I'm doing: 4, 7, 10... How am I getting this second row?

M Adding 4 to the numbers in the first row.

P I'm adding 4 to each number in the first row to give you a second row. So the last two will be 52, 100, and now tell me what I'm doing.

F Putting in a decimal?

P Yes, I divided all those numbers by 10 by putting in a decimal point. Now I'm going to write the names of the planets under the numbers. Mercury... Venus... Earth... Mars.

So, what do the numbers mean? Do you remember from the reading?

M Is it the distance of the planets from the Sun?

P Right. In astronomical units—not perfect, but tantalizingly close. The value for Mars is off by... 6 or 7 percent or so. It's... but it's within 10 percent of the average distance to Mars from the Sun. But I kind of have to skip the one after Mars for now. Then Jupiter's right there at 5-point something, and then Saturn is about 10 astronomical units from the Sun. Um, well, this pattern is known as Bode's Law.

Um, it isn't really a scientific law, not in the sense of predicting gravitation mathematically or something, but it's attempting a pattern in the spacing of the planets, and it was noticed by Bode hundreds of years ago. Well, you can imagine that there was some interest in why the 2.8 spot in the pattern was skipped, and um... but there wasn't anything obvious there, in the early telescopes. Then what happened in the late 1700s? The discovery of... ?

N 천문학 강의의 일부를 들으시오. 여러분은 교수가 언급하는 숫자들을 기억할 필요는 없다.

P 자. 이제 강의를 시작합니다. 오늘은 소행성대가 어떻게 발견되었는지 알아봅시다. 그리고… 칠판에 몇몇 숫자를 적어보는 것부터 시작해 봅시다. 자 보세요. 0부터 시작해서 3…6…12. 어, 이 숫자들이 어떤 식으로 배열되었나요?

F 2를 곱한 것 아닌가요?

P 맞습니다. 수에 2배수를 한 겁니다. 12의 2배수는 24죠. 그리고 그 다음 24의…

F 48이요.

P 48이죠. 그 다음은 96이겠죠. 이 숫자들은 여기까지 써 놓고요. 이제 그 밑에 다른 숫자들을 죽 써 보겠습니다. 이 숫자들은 어떤 식으로 배열된 겁니까? 4, 7, 10… 두 번째 수열은 어떻게 만들어진 걸까요?

M 첫 번째 수열에 있는 각 숫자에 4를 더한 것입니다.

P 첫 번째 수열에 있는 각 숫자에 4를 더해서 두 번째 수열을 만든 것입니다. 그래서 마지막 두 숫자는 각각 52와 100이 되겠지요. 자, 지금은 내가 무엇을 하고 있나요?

F 소수점 찍기요?

P 맞습니다. 나는 소수점을 찍어 숫자들을 모두 10으로 나눈 수로 만들었죠. 이제 각 숫자의 밑에 행성의 이름을 적겠습니다. 수성…금성…지구…화성.

자, 이 숫자들은 어떤 의미가 있을까요? 여러분이 책에서 읽은 내용이 기억납니까?

M 그건 태양과 행성의 거리 아닌가요?

P 그렇습니다. 천문 단위로 따지는 것인데 완벽하지는 않지만, 거의 근사치에 해당합니다. 화성의 값은 6퍼센트나 7퍼센트 정도 벗어나 있습니다. 하지만 그것은 태양에서 화성까지의 평균 거리의 10퍼센트 이내에 해당합니다. 화성 다음에는 잠시 천문 단위 하나를 건너뛰겠습니다. 그러면 천문 단위 5점 쯤에 목성이 있지요. 그리고 토성은 천문 단위가 10입니다. 이런 패턴을 보데의 법칙이라고 하죠.

음, 이것은 사실 과학 법칙이 아닙니다. 수학적으로 인력을 예측하는 방식 따위가 아니고, 행성들의 간격 패턴을 파악하려는 것입니다. 이것은 수백 년 전 보데가 알아낸 것입니다. 이 패턴에서 여러분은 왜 천문 단위 2.8을 건너뛰었는지 의문스러울 겁니다… 하지만 초창

F Another planet?

P The next planet out, Uranus—after Saturn.

And look, Uranus fits in the next spot in the pattern pretty nicely, um, not perfectly, but close. And so then people got really excited about the validity of this thing and finding the missing object between Mars and Jupiter. And telescopes, remember, were getting better. So people went to work on finding objects that would be at that missing distance from the Sun, and then in 1801, the object Ceres was discovered.

And Ceres was in the right place—the missing spot. Uh, but it was way too faint to be a planet. It looked like a little star. Uh, and because of its starlike appearance, um, it was called an "asteroid." OK? *Aster* is Greek for "star," as in *astronomy*. Um, and so, Ceres was the first and is the largest of what became many objects discovered at that same distance. Not just one thing, but all the objects found at that distance form the asteroid belt. So the asteroid belt is the most famous success of this Bode's Law. That's how the asteroid belt was discovered.

기 망원경으로는 그 자리에 별다른 것을 찾지 못했습니다. 그러다가 1700년대 말에 무슨 일이 일어났을까요? 하나의 발견이…

F 또 다른 행성이요?

P 다음 행성으로는, 토성 다음에 천왕성이 있지요.

보세요, 천왕성은 이 패턴에 상당히 잘 맞습니다. 완벽하진 않아도 근사치에 해당합니다. 그러자 사람들은 이 패턴의 타당성에 대해 경이롭게 여겼고, 화성과 목성 사이에 빠져 있는 무언가를 찾으려고 했습니다. 여러분도 알다시피, 망원경의 성능이 점차 좋아지고 있었지요. 사람들은 태양계에서 그 위치에 존재할 것으로 추정되는 천체를 찾으려고 했습니다. 그리고 1801년 세레스가 발견되었습니다.

세레스는 공백으로 남아 있던 바로 그 지점에 있었습니다. 하지만 행성으로 보기에는 너무 희미했습니다. 그것은 자그마한 별처럼 보였습니다. 그리고 별처럼 보인다고 해서 '소행성(asteroid)'이라고 부르게 되었지요. 아셨지요? Asteroid의 Aster는 astronomy에서처럼 star(별)를 뜻하는 그리스어입니다. 세레스는 동일한 거리에서 발견된 많은 천체들 중 첫 번째이자 가장 큰 소행성이었습니다. 단 하나의 천체가 아니라 그 위치에서 발견된 모든 천체들이 소행성대를 형성하고 있습니다. 소행성대는 보데의 법칙이 이룩해낸 가장 유명한 성공이라고 할 수 있습니다. 이것이 소행성대가 발견된 과정입니다.

어휘

astronomy 천문학   asteroid 소행성   multiply 곱하다, 증가하다   decimal 소수점, 십진법의   Mercury 수성   Venus 금성   Earth 지구   Mars 화성   Uranus 천왕성   Jupiter 목성   Saturn 토성   astronomical 천문학상의, 천문학적인   tantalizingly close 대단히 근접한   Bode's Law 보데의 법칙; 행성의 평균 거리에 관한 법칙   scientific law 과학 법칙   attempt 시도하다, 기도하다   gravitation 인력   mathematically 수학적으로   telescope 망원경   discovery 발견, 발견물   validity 타당성, 확실(성)   faint 희미한

1. 보데의 법칙이란?

Ⓐ 인력의 법칙

Ⓑ 화성과 목성 간의 거리 산정법

Ⓒ 소행성들의 수를 예측하는 법

Ⓓ 행성들의 간격 패턴

세부 정보 찾기 문제

어휘 estimate 추정, 견적, 평가하다 prediction 예측, 예언

해설 교수는 보데의 법칙이 과학 법칙이 아니며 행성들의 간격 패턴을
파악하려는 시도라고 밝히고 있다. 따라서 정답은 보기 D.

2. 교수는 왜 학생들에게 보데의 법칙을 설명하는가?

Ⓐ 소행성들의 크기를 설명하기 위해

Ⓑ 소행성대가 어떻게 발견되었는가를 설명하기 위해

Ⓒ 인력이 어떻게 행성들에게 영향을 미치는가를 설명하기 위해

Ⓓ 망원경이 천문학에 미친 영향을 설명하기 위해

내용의 목적을 묻는 문제

어휘 gravitational 중력의, 인력(작용)의   influence 영향력, 작용,
영향을 끼치는 사람

해설 교수는 강의 서두에서 소행성대가 어떻게 발견되었는가를 설명
하겠다고 했으며, 맨 마지막에도 이것이 소행성대가 발견된 과
정이라고 언급했다. 따라서 정답은 보기 B.

3. 교수는 보데의 법칙을 어떻게 소개하는가?

Ⓐ 수학적으로 어떻게 도출되었는가를 설명함으로써

Ⓑ 천왕성의 발견에 대해 기술함으로써

Ⓒ 일정한 패턴의 부정확성에 주목함으로써

Ⓓ 여러 소행성들의 이름을 말함으로써

구성 파악 문제

어휘 be derived ~에서 파생되다   inaccuracy 부정확

해설 교수는 우선 숫자들을 나열하고 그 숫자들이 어떤 패턴을 갖고
있는지 설명하면서 보데의 법칙을 도출하고 있다. 따라서 정답
은 보기 A.

4. 교수에 따르면, 소행성 세레스의 발견에 기여했던 두 요소들은?
   두 개의 답을 선택하라.

Ⓐ 발달된 망원경

Ⓑ 수학의 발전

Ⓒ 새로운 별의 발견

Ⓓ 패턴에서 천왕성의 위치

세부 정보 찾기 문제

어휘 factor 요인, 요소   contribute to 기여하다, 기부를 하다
       improved 개선된

해설 교수는 천왕성이 패턴에 잘 들어맞는다는 것과 망원경의 발달을
언급한 후 1801년 세레스가 발견되었다고 밝혔다. 따라서 정답
은 보기 A, D.

5. 교수가 소행성대에 대해 암시하고 있는 것은?

Ⓐ 천왕성보다 태양에서 멀리 떨어져 있다.

Ⓑ 보데는 그것이 작은 별들로 이루어졌다고 믿었다.

Ⓒ 그것은 사람들이 행성이 있을 것이라고 추정했던 위치에 존재했다.

Ⓓ 세레스는 망원경 없이 육안으로 관찰할 수 있는 유일한 소행성
이다.

추론 문제

어휘 farther (거리상으로) 더 멀리

해설 사람들은 화성과 목성 사이 천문 단위 2.8 지점에 행성이 있을
것으로 추정했고, 결국 그 위치에서 소행성대를 발견했다. 정답
은 보기 C.

6. 강의의 일부를 다시 듣고 질문에 답하라.

🎧 T-08

> **P** Um, well, this pattern is known as Bode's Law.
> Um, it isn't really a scientific law, not in the sense
> of predicting gravitation mathematically or
> something, but it's attempting a pattern in the
> spacing of the planets, and it was noticed by
> Bode hundreds of years ago.
>
> **N** *Why does the professor say this?*
> **P** ..., not in the sense of predicting gravitation
> mathematically or something, ...

Ⓐ 보데의 법칙을 대신할 응용 법칙을 소개하기 위해

Ⓑ 보데의 법칙이 설명할 수 없는 것의 예를 제시하려고

Ⓒ 인력 이론의 한계를 기술하려고

Ⓓ 보데의 법칙과 실제적인 과학 법칙을 비교하려고

의도 파악 문제

어휘 alternative 대안, 양자택일   application 적용, 신청
       contrast 대조, 대조하다

해설 교수는 보데의 법칙이 과학 법칙과 어떻게 다른가를 지적하고
있다. 따라서 정답은 보기 D.

Script

N Listen to part of a lecture from a botany class.

P Hi, everyone. Good to see you all today. Actually, I expected the population to be a lot lower today. It typically runs between 50 and 60 percent on the day the research paper is due. Um, I was hoping to have your exams back today, but, uh, the situation was that I went away for the weekend, and I was supposed to get in yesterday at five, and I expected to fully complete all the exams by midnight or so, which is the time that I usually go to bed, but my flight was delayed, and I ended up not getting in until one o'clock in the morning. Anyway, I'll do my best to have them finished by the next time we meet.

OK. In the last class, we started talking about useful plant fibers. In particular, we talked about cotton fibers, which we said were very useful, not only in the textile industry, but also in the chemical industry, and in the production of many products, such as plastics, paper, explosives, and so on. Today we'll continue talking about useful fibers, and we'll begin with a fiber that's commonly known as "Manila hemp."

Now, for some strange reason, many people believe that Manila hemp is a hemp plant. But Manila hemp is not really hemp. It's actually a member of the banana family—it even bears little banana-shaped fruits. The "Manila" part of the name makes sense, because Manila hemp is produced chiefly in the Philippine Islands, and, of course, the capital city of the Philippines is Manila.

Now, as fibers go, Manila hemp fibers are very long. They can easily be several feet in length and they're also very strong, very flexible. They have one more characteristic that's very important, and that is that they are exceptionally resistant to salt water. And this combination of characteristics—long, strong, flexible, resistant to salt water—makes Manila hemp a great material for ropes, especially for ropes that are gonna be used on oceangoing ships. In fact, by the early 1940s, even though steel cables were available, most ships in the United States Navy were not moored with steel cables; they were moored with Manila hemp ropes.

Now, why was that? Well, the main reason was that steel cables degrade very, very quickly in contact with salt water. If you've ever been to San Francisco, you know that the Golden Gate Bridge is red. And it's red because of the zinc paint that goes on those stainless steel cables. That, if they start at one end of the bridge and they work to the other end, by the time they finish, it's already time to go back and start painting the beginning of the bridge again, because the bridge was built with steel cables, and steel cables can't take the salt air unless they're

N 식물학 강의의 일부를 들으시오.

P 여러분 안녕하세요. 오늘 만나서 반갑습니다. 사실 오늘은 강의 출석률이 훨씬 낮을 것이라고 예상했어요. 리포트 제출 마감일에는 보통 출석률이 50~60퍼센트 정도밖에 안 되거든요. 여러분의 시험 결과를 오늘 가져오려고 했는데요. 주말에 어디 좀 갔다 오느라고 가져오지 못했습니다. 원래는 어제 5시에 도착할 예정이어서, 취침 시간인 자정 무렵까지는 시험 채점을 마치려고 했거든요. 하지만 비행기가 연착하는 바람에 결국 새벽 1시에 도착했습니다. 어쨌든, 다음 강의 시간까지는 채점을 끝내도록 최선을 다하겠습니다.

자, 지난번 강의 시간에 우리는 실용적인 식물 섬유에 관한 논의를 시작했지요. 특히 면섬유에 대해 알아보았는데, 이것이 섬유산업뿐 아니라 화학산업에서, 그리고 플라스틱, 종이, 폭발물 같은 많은 제품들의 생산에 매우 유용하다고 말씀드렸습니다. 오늘도 유용한 섬유에 대한 이야기를 계속 나눠 보겠습니다. 우선 흔히 '마닐라삼'이라고 하는 섬유에 대해 알아봅시다.

어떤 이유 때문인지는 몰라도 많은 사람들이 마닐라삼을 삼 식물이라고 믿습니다. 하지만 마닐라삼은 사실 삼이 아닙니다. 실제로는 바나나과의 식물입니다. 심지어는 바나나 모양의 작은 열매를 맺습니다. '마닐라'라는 이름은 타당성이 있습니다. 마닐라삼은 주로 필리핀에서 생산되는데, 필리핀의 수도가 마닐라이기 때문이죠.

섬유가 그렇듯, 마닐라삼 섬유는 매우 깁니다. 이것은 길이가 수 피트나 되며 매우 질기며 유연합니다. 그리고 아주 중요한 또 하나의 특성이 있는데, 바닷물에 특히 강하다는 것입니다. 길고 질기고 유연하고 바닷물에 강한 특성들 때문에 마닐라삼은 로프를 만드는 데 훌륭한 재료가 됩니다. 특히 원양어선에 사용되는 로프의 재료로 많이 쓰이죠. 사실 1940년대 초만 해도, 강철 케이블을 구할 수 있었지만, 대부분의 미 해군 선박들은 강철 케이블을 이용하지 않았습니다. 마닐라삼으로 만든 로프를 사용해 배를 정박했습니다.

그 이유가 무엇이었을까요? 가장 큰 이유는 강철 케이블은 바닷물에 닿으면 대단히 빠르게 부식되기 때문입니다. 샌프란시스코에 가봤다면 금문교가 붉은색이라는 것을 알 수 있습니다. 스테인리스 강철 케이블에 아연 페인트를 칠했기 때문에 붉은색을 띠는 것입니다. 다리의 한쪽 끝에서 페인트 작업을 시작해서 다른 쪽 끝에 도달할 때쯤 되면, 다시 돌아가서 칠을 시작해야 합니다. 왜냐하면 이 다리는 강철 케이블로 만들어졌고, 강철 케이블은 아연 페인트로 되풀이해서 칠하지 않으면 염분이 실린 공기를 견디지 못하기 때문입니다.

treated repeatedly with a zinc-based paint.

On the other hand, plant products like Manila hemp, you can drag through the ocean for weeks on end. If you wanna tie your anchor to it and drop it right into the ocean, that's no problem, because plant fibers can stand up for months, even years, in direct contact with salt water. OK. So how do you take plant fibers that individually you could break with your hands and turn them into a rope that's strong enough to moor a ship that weighs thousands of tons? Well, what you do is you extract these long fibers from the Manila hemp plant, and then you take several of these fibers, and you group them into a bundle, because by grouping the fibers, you greatly increase their breaking strength—that bundle of fibers is much stronger than any of the individual fibers that compose it. And then you take that bundle of fibers and you twist it a little bit, because by twisting it, you increase its breaking strength even more. And then you take several of these little bundles, and you group and twist them into bigger bundles, which you then group and twist into even bigger bundles, and so on, until eventually, you end up with a very, very strong rope.

한편, 마닐라삼 같은 식물 제품은 바다에서 몇 주 동안 계속 끌고 다닐 수 있습니다. 그것을 닻에 묶고 바닷속 깊숙이 떨어뜨려도 아무런 문제가 없습니다. 왜냐하면 식물 섬유는 바닷물에 직접 닿아도 여러 달, 심지어는 여러 해 동안 견딜 수 있기 때문입니다. 그렇다면 낱개로는 손으로도 부러뜨릴 수 있는 식물 섬유로 어떻게 수천 톤짜리 배를 정박시킬 만큼 강한 로프를 만들 수 있을까요? 우선, 마닐라삼에서 기다란 섬유들을 뽑아내고, 여러 가닥들을 가지고 다발로 만듭니다. 섬유들을 다발로 묶으면 파괴 강도가 크게 증가합니다. 섬유다발은 낱개의 섬유보다 훨씬 강합니다. 그 다음에는 섬유다발을 가지고 꼽니다. 다발을 꼬면 파괴 강도가 더욱 증가합니다. 그리고 이런 몇 개의 다발을 다시 뭉쳐 꼬아서 더 큰 다발을 만들고, 그것들을 가지고 다시 뭉쳐 꼬아서 더욱 더 큰 다발을 만듭니다. 결국 이런 과정을 거쳐 아주 강력한 로프를 얻게 됩니다.

어휘

botany 식물학 due 기한이 된 end up ~ing 결국 ~하게 되다 plant fiber 식물 섬유 in particular 특히 explosive 폭발물, 폭발적인 Manila hemp 마닐라삼 hemp plant 삼 식물 flexible 유연한, 유순한 characteristic 특징 exceptionally 특별히, 예외적으로 resistant 방지하는, 저항하는 steel cable 강철 케이블 moor (배를) 정박시키다 degrade 부식되다, 가치가 떨어지다 Golden Gate Bridge 금문교 zinc 아연 stand up 견디다 extract 추출하다 bundle 다발 breaking strength 파괴 강도 end up with~ 결국~이 되다

1. 교수는 마닐라삼의 어떤 측면을 주로 설명하는가?

Ⓐ 면섬유와 마닐라삼 사이의 유사점

Ⓑ 다양한 종류의 마닐라삼 섬유

Ⓒ 마닐라삼 섬유의 경제적 중요성

Ⓓ 마닐라삼 섬유의 용도

내용의 요점을 묻는 문제

어휘 similarity 유사성　various 여러 가지의　economic 경제적인, 경제학의　hemp 삼, 대마

해설 교수는 마닐라삼 섬유의 특성들을 열거하면서, 이런 특성들이 선박 산업에 어떻게 이용되었는가를 자세히 설명하고 있다. 따라서 정답은 보기 D.

2. '마닐라삼'이라는 이름에 대해 교수가 암시하는 것은?

Ⓐ 그것은 상업적인 상표명이다.

Ⓑ 그 이름의 일부는 부적당하다.

Ⓒ 그 이름은 최근에 변경되었다.

Ⓓ 그 이름은 1940년대에 처음 사용되었다.

추론 문제

어휘 inappropriate 타당하지 않은, 부적당한　recently 최근에

해설 교수는 마닐라삼이 필리핀에서 주로 생산되기 때문에 '마닐라'라는 이름이 붙은 것은 타당하지만, 이 식물이 바나나과 식물이기 때문에 '삼'이라는 이름이 붙은 것은 적절치 못하다고 밝히고 있다. 따라서 정답은 보기 B.

3. 교수는 왜 금문교를 언급하는가?

Ⓐ 강철 케이블의 단점을 설명하기 위해

Ⓑ 색깔을 창조적으로 사용한 예를 들기 위해

Ⓒ 강철 케이블이 바닷물에 잘 견딜 수 있음을 보여 주기 위해

Ⓓ 마닐라삼이 사용된 예를 제시하기 위해

구성 파악 문제

어휘 resist ~에 저항하다, 반항하다　salt water 바닷물, 염수

해설 금문교를 언급한 것은 강철 케이블과 마닐라삼 섬유로 만든 로프를 비교하기 위해서다. 강철 케이블은 바닷물에 취약해서 페인트 칠을 되풀이해야 한다는 것이 단점이다. 따라서 정답은 보기 A.

4. 교수에 따르면, 많은 선박들이 강철 케이블 대신에 마닐라삼 섬유로 만든 로프를 사용했던 가장 큰 이유는 무엇인가?

Ⓐ 마닐라삼이 더 쌌다.

Ⓑ 마닐라삼이 생산하기 더 수월했다.

Ⓒ 마닐라삼이 바닷물에 잘 견딘다.

Ⓓ 마닐라삼의 무게가 더 가볍다.

세부 정보 찾기 문제

해설 이 강의에서는 바닷물에 잘 견디는 마닐라삼의 특성이 계속 강조되고 있다. 따라서 정답은 보기 C.

5. 이 강의에 따르면, 마닐라삼 섬유로 만든 로프의 강도를 높이는 두 가지 방법은 무엇인가?

두 개의 답을 선택하라.

Ⓐ 섬유를 아연 페인트로 코팅하기

Ⓑ 섬유를 다발로 묶기

Ⓒ 섬유 다발을 바닷물에 적시기

Ⓓ 섬유 다발을 꼬기

세부 정보 찾기 문제

어휘 bundle 묶음, 덩어리　twist 꼬다

해설 마닐라삼 섬유로 로프를 만드는 과정에서 답을 찾을 수 있다. 다발로 묶어서 꼬는 방식을 되풀이하여 로프의 강도를 높인다고 설명되어 있다. 따라서 정답은 보기 B, D.

6. 강의의 일부를 다시 듣고 질문에 답하라.

🎧 T-10

P Um, I was hoping to have your exams back today, but, uh, the situation was that I went away for the weekend, and I was supposed to get in yesterday at five, and I expected to fully complete all the exams by midnight or so, which is the time that I usually go to bed, but my flight was delayed, and I ended up not getting in until one o'clock in the morning. Anyway, I'll do my best to have them finished by the next time we meet.

N *Why does the professor mention going away for the weekend?*

Ⓐ 학생들에게 농담을 하기 위해

Ⓑ 어떤 작업을 끝내지 못한 것을 사과하기 위해

Ⓒ 강의의 주제를 소개하기 위해

Ⓓ 학생들이 자신의 여행에 대해 질문하도록 유도하기 위해

의도 파악 문제

어휘 apologize 사과하다, 변명하다

해설 교수는 비행기 연착으로 늦게 도착하는 바람에 채점을 끝내지 못했다고 학생에게 사과하고 있다. 그러므로 정답은 보기 B.

QUESTION TYPES

Question 1 예제   p. 101

Narrator

Some students study for classes individually. Others study in groups. Which method of studying do you think is better for students and why?

어떤 학생들은 혼자 학과 공부를 한다. 다른 학생들은 그룹 스터디를 한다. 어떤 공부 방법이 학생들에게 더 좋다고 생각하며, 그 이유는 무엇인가?

Question 2 예제   p. 103

Narrator

City University is planning to increase tuition and fees. Read the announcement about the increase from the president of City University. You will have 45 seconds to read the announcement. Begin reading now.

씨티 대학이 수업료와 입학금 인상을 계획하고 있다. 인상 내용에 관한 씨티 대학 총장의 발표를 45초 동안 읽으시오. 지금 읽으시오.

Announcement from the President

The university has decided to increase tuition and fees for all students by approximately 8% next semester. For the past 5 years, the tuition and fees have remained the same, but it is necessary to increase them now for several reasons. The university has many more students than we had 5 years ago, and we must hire additional professors to teach these students. We have also made a new commitment to research and technology and will be renovating and upgrading our laboratory facilities to better meet our students' needs.

총장 발표

우리 대학은 다음 학기에 전교생을 대상으로 수업료와 입학금을 8% 가량 인상하기로 결정했습니다. 지난 5년 간 수업료와 입학금은 동결되어 왔지만 이제는 몇 가지 이유 때문에 인상이 불가피해졌습니다. 우리 대학은 5년 전보다 학생 수가 훨씬 늘어났고 교수들을 추가 임용해야 합니다. 또한 연구 및 기술 분야에 새롭게 매진하고 있고 학생들의 요구에 더욱 부응하기 위해 대학의 연구소 시설을 보수하고 개선할 것입니다.

Script

M Oh, great, now we have to come up with more money for next semester.

W Yeah, I know, but I can see why. When I first started here, classes were so much smaller than they are now. With this many students, it's hard to get the personal attention you need...

M Yeah, I guess you're right. You know, in some classes I can't even get a seat. And I couldn't take the math course I wanted to because it was already full when I signed up.

W And the other thing is, well, I am kind of worried about not being able to get a job after I graduate.

M Why? I mean you're doing really well in your classes, aren't you?

W I'm doing OK, but the facilities here are so limited. There are some great new experiments in microbiology that we can't even do here... there isn't enough equipment in the laboratories, and the equipment they have is out of date. How am I going to compete for jobs with people who have practical research experience? I think the extra tuition will be a good investment.

Narrator

The woman expresses her opinion of the announcement by the university president. State her opinion and explain the reasons she gives for holding that opinion.

남	야, 이거, 다음 학기에는 돈을 좀 더 마련해야겠군.
여	그래, 알아. 하지만 그 이유를 알 것 같아. 처음 이 학교에 입학했을 때는 지금보다 학생 수가 훨씬 적었거든. 요즘처럼 학생들이 많으면 (교수님으로부터) 개별적인 지도를 받기 힘들어.
남	그래, 네 말이 맞는 것 같다. 어떤 강의 시간에는 빈자리도 없다니까. 게다가 듣고 싶던 수학 강의는 수강 신청할 때 벌써 마감돼 버려서 들을 수도 없었어.
여	또 한 가지는, 음, 나는 졸업 후에 취직을 못할까봐 걱정이 좀 돼.
남	왜? 너는 학업 성적도 좋잖아, 안 그래?
여	좋기는 하지만 우리 학교는 실험 시설이 너무 부족해. 아주 괜찮은 새로운 미생물학 실험들이 있는데 우리 학교에서는 할 수도 없어… 실험실에 장비도 부족하고 지금 있는 장비도 낡았어. 그러니 직접 실험을 해 본 학생들하고 어떻게 취업 경쟁을 할 수 있겠어? 나는 등록금 인상이 좋은 투자라고 생각해.

대학 총장의 발표에 대해 여학생이 자신의 입장을 밝힌다. 여학생의 입장이 무엇인지 말하고, 그런 입장을 취하는 이유를 설명하시오.

어휘

announcement 발표   tuition 수업료   fee 입학금, 요금   approximately 약, 대략   semester 학기   hire 채용하다   additional 추가적인   commitment 약속   renovate 보수하다 *cf.* renovation 보수   facility 시설   limited 부족한, 한정된   experiment 실험   microbiology 미생물학   equipment 장비   laboratory 연구소   investment 투자

Narrator

Now read the passage about animal domestication. You have 45 seconds to read the passage. Begin reading now.

Animal Domestication

For thousands of years, humans have been able to domesticate, or tame, many large mammals that in the wild live together in herds. Once tamed, these mammals are used for agricultural work and transportation. Yet some herd mammals are not easily domesticated.

A good indicator of an animal's suitability for domestication is how protective the animal is of its territory. Nonterritorial animals are more easily domesticated than territorial animals because they can live close together with animals from other herds. A second indicator is that animals with a hierarchical social structure, in which herd members follow a leader, are easy to domesticate, since a human can function as the "leader."

Script

Professor

So we've been discussing the suitability of animals for domestication... particularly animals that live together in herds. Now, if we take horses, for example... in the wild, horses live in herds that consist of one male and several females and their young. When a herd moves, the dominant male leads, with the dominant female and her young immediately behind him. The dominant female and her young are then followed immediately by the second most important female and her young, and so on. This is why domesticated horses can be harnessed one after the other in a row. They're "programmed" to follow the lead of another horse. On top of that, you often find different herds of horses in the wild occupying overlapping areas—they don't fight off other herds that enter the same territory.

But it's exactly the opposite with an animal like the, uh, the antelope... which... well, antelopes are herd animals too. But unlike horses, a male antelope will fight fiercely to prevent another male from entering its territory during the breeding season; OK—very different from the behavior of horses. Try keeping a couple of male antelopes together in a small space and see what happens. Also, antelopes don't have a social hierarchy—they don't instinctively follow any leader. That makes it harder for humans to control their behavior.

동물의 가축화에 대한 읽기 지문을 45초 동안 읽으시오. 지금 읽으시오.

동물의 가축화

인간은 수천 년 동안 야생에서 무리 생활을 하는 많은 대형 포유류들을 가축화하거나 길들일 수 있었다. 이 포유류들은 일단 가축화되면 농사일에나 운송 수단으로 사용된다. 그러나 무리 지어 사는 일부 포유류들은 쉽게 가축화되지 않는다.

어떤 동물이 가축화하기에 적당한지 판단하는 좋은 지표는 그 동물이 자기 영역을 지키려는 성향이 얼마나 강한가이다. 영역이 없는 동물들은 다른 무리의 동물들과 가까이 살 수 있기 때문에 영역이 있는 동물보다 좀 더 쉽게 가축화된다. 두 번째 지표는 무리 구성원들이 우두머리를 따르는 서열 구조를 가진 동물들은 가축화하기 쉽다는 것이다. 인간이 '우두머리' 역할을 할 수 있기 때문이다.

우리는 지금까지 동물의 가축화 가능성에 대해서 토의했습니다… 특히 무리를 이루어 사는 동물들에 관해서였죠. 그럼 말의 경우를 예로 들어 봅시다. 야생에서 말은 수놈 한 마리와 암놈 몇 마리, 그리고 새끼들로 구성된 무리를 이루어 삽니다. 이 무리가 이동하면 우두머리 수놈이 앞장서고 우두머리 암놈과 새끼들이 바로 뒤따라갑니다. 우두머리 암놈과 새끼들 뒤를 이어 서열 2위인 암놈과 새끼들이 따르는 식으로 행렬은 계속 이어집니다. 가축화된 말들을 일렬로 세워 놓고 차례로 마구를 채울 수 있는 이유가 여기에 있습니다. 말들은 다른 말이 인도하는 대로 따르도록 '길들여져' 있는 것입니다. 게다가 야생에서는 서로 다른 여러 말 무리의 영역이 서로 겹치는 경우를 종종 볼 수 있는데, 이 때 말들은 같은 영역 안에 들어온 다른 무리의 말들과 싸워서 쫓아내지 않습니다.

그러나 영양 같은 동물의 경우는 정반대입니다. 영양도 무리 생활을 하는 동물이지만 말들과는 달리 수놈 영양은 번식기 동안 다른 수놈이 자기 영역에 들어오지 못하도록 격렬하게 싸웁니다. 예, 말들의 습성과는 아주 다르죠. 수놈 영양 두 마리를 좁은 공간에 함께 있도록 하면 어떤 일이 벌어질까요. 영양들에게는 또한 집단 서열 구조가 없습니다. 이들은 본능적으로 우두머리를 따르지 않죠. 인간이 영양의 행동을 통제하기 어려운 이유가 여기에 있습니다.

Narrator

The professor describes the behavior of horses and antelope in herds. Explain how their behavior is related to their suitability for domestication.

교수는 무리 생활을 하는 말과 영양의 습성에 대해 설명한다. 이 동물들의 습성이 가축화의 가능성과 어떻게 관련되는지 설명하시오.

어휘

domesticate 길들이다   mammal 포유동물   herd (가축의) 무리, 떼   tame 길들이다   agricultural 농업의   transportation 운송   indicator 지표, 표준   suitability 적합성, 안정성   territory 세력권, 영역   hierarchical 계층의   social structure 사회 구조   consist of ~로 구성되다(= be composed of)   young 새끼   immediately 즉시, 바로   dominant 우두머리인, 우위를 차지하는   harness 마구를 채우다   one after the other 차례로   in a row 일렬로, 연속적으로   program 계획하다, (자연스럽게 특정 행동을 하도록) 길들이다   in the wild 야생에서   occupy (장소를) 차지하다   overlapping 겹치는   antelope (동물) 영양   fiercely 격렬하게, 사납게   prevent A from B A가 B하지 못하게 하다   breeding season 번식기   instinctively 본능적으로, 반사적으로   cf. instinct 본능

Script
Professor

Because the United States is such a large country, it took time for a common national culture to emerge. One hundred years ago there was very little communication among the different regions of the United States. One result of this lack of communication was that people around the United States had very little in common with one another. People in different parts of the country spoke differently, dressed differently, and behaved differently. But connections among Americans began to increase thanks to two technological innovations: the automobile and the radio.

Automobiles began to be mass-produced in the 1920s, which meant they became less expensive and more widely available. Americans in small towns and rural communities now had the ability to travel with ease to nearby cities. They could even take vacations to other parts of the country. The increased mobility provided by automobiles changed people's attitudes and created links that had not existed before. For example, people in small towns began to adopt behaviors, clothes, and speech that were popular in big cities or in other parts of the country.

As more Americans were purchasing cars, radio ownership was also increasing dramatically. Americans in different regions of the country began to listen to the same popular radio programs and musical artists. People repeated things they heard on the radio—some phrases and speech patterns heard in songs and radio programs began to be used by people all over the United States. People also listened to news reports on the radio. They heard the same news throughout the country, whereas in newspapers much news tended to be local. Radio brought Americans together by offering them shared experiences and information about events around the country.

미국은 매우 큰 나라이므로 보편적인 국민 문화가 태동하기까지 시간이 걸렸습니다. 100년 전 미국의 여러 지역들 사이에는 교류가 거의 없었습니다. 이렇게 교류가 적었기 때문에 나타난 결과의 하나가 미국에 사는 사람들 사이에는 공통점이 거의 없었다는 것입니다. 미국 내 서로 다른 지역에 사는 사람들은 서로 말이 다르고, 옷 입는 스타일이 다르고, 행동도 달랐습니다. 그러나 자동차와 라디오라는 두 가지 기술 혁신 덕에 미국인들 사이의 교류가 증가하기 시작했습니다.

1920년대에 자동차가 대량 생산되기 시작했고, 그 결과 자동차 가격이 저렴해져서 더 많은 사람들이 이용할 수 있게 되었습니다. 소도시와 시골에 사는 미국인들은 이제 가까운 도시로 쉽게 여행할 수 있게 되었습니다. 미국의 다른 지역으로 휴가를 떠날 수도 있게 되었습니다. 자동차 덕분에 기동성이 증가하자 사람들의 태도가 달라졌고, 이전에 볼 수 없었던 교류가 이뤄졌습니다. 예를 들면 소도시에 사는 사람들이 대도시나 다른 지역에서 유행하는 행동양식, 옷, 말투를 취하기 시작한 것입니다.

자동차를 구매하는 미국인들이 증가했던 것처럼 라디오 보유 대수도 현저히 증가하고 있었습니다. 미국 내 서로 다른 지역에 사는 미국인들이 같은 인기 라디오 프로그램과 음악을 듣게 되었습니다. 사람들은 라디오에서 들은 것을 따라했습니다. 그러니까 미국 전역에 사는 사람들이 노래나 라디오 프로그램에서 들은 문구나 말투들을 사용하기 시작한 것입니다. 사람들은 라디오에서 뉴스도 들었습니다. 사람들이 라디오를 통해 나라 전역에 걸쳐 같은 뉴스를 들었던 반면 신문의 경우 많은 뉴스들이 지역성을 띠는 경향이 있었습니다. 라디오는 미국 전역에서 일어나는 사건들에 대한 경험과 정보의 공유를 제공함으로써 미국인들을 결집시켰습니다.

Narrator

Using points and examples from the talk, explain how the automobile and the radio contributed to a common culture in the United States.

이 강의 내용에 나온 논지와 예를 사용해서 미국의 보편적인 문화 형성에 자동차와 라디오가 어떻게 기여했는지 설명하시오.

어휘

national culture 국민 문화   emerge 일어나다, 나타나다   region 지역   behave 행동하다   differently 다르게   connection 교류, 연결 thanks to ~ 덕분에   technological innovation 기술 혁신   automobile 자동차   mass produce 대량 생산하다   expensive 값비싼 available 사용 가능한   rural 전원의, 시골의   take a vacation 휴가를 가다   mobility 기동성   attitude 태도   adopt 수용하다, 채택하다 behavior 행동   ownership 소유, 소유권   dramatically 현저하게   news reports 뉴스 보도   whereas ~에 반하여, 그러나   tend (to) ~하는 경향이 있다, ~하기 쉽다   local 지방의, 지역의   share 공유하다   experience 경험

QUESTION TYPES

The Integrated Writing Task   p.121

Vitrified Forts

A number of hill forts (fortified defensive structures) built in Scotland during the Middle Ages have an unusual feature: they are what researchers call "vitrified," which means that their stones have been exposed to extreme heat and have melted or fused together, becoming hard and glass-like. Several theories have been offered to explain how and why the forts were vitrified.

One theory holds that vitrification was part of a religious or ceremonial ritual. The ancient myths and folktales of Scotland are full of references to cities and castles made of glass, so glass must have had some special significance to the people of the area. Vitrification could have been their way of trying to create glass castles. Perhaps they believed that the vitrified forts had supernatural powers or benefits.

According to a second theory, the stones of the fort walls became vitrified accidentally by fires set by people who attacked the forts. Supporters of this theory point out that fire was used as a weapon to ignite the wood beams that were used as structural support for the fort walls. Attackers used flaming arrows and other projectiles in an attempt to start a fire. As the wood beams were being burned up by the fire, the heat from the fire could have vitrified the stone parts of the walls.

Other researchers think that it is more probable that the forts' builders purposefully vitrified the walls in order to strengthen them. When a wall becomes vitrified, the stones fuse together so that there are no gaps or openings between them. In other words, vitrification produces a solid, continuous wall surface. This makes it very hard for arrows to penetrate the walls, and so this could have been an effective defensive measure.

While the theories about vitrified forts sound convincing, unfortunately none of them adequately explain the phenomenon.

Script
Professor

First, glass may have had special significance for the people of ancient Scotland. But a problem with the reading's theory is that by the time most of the forts were built, Christianity had taken hold in the area. By 900 C.E., when the last forts were being constructed, Christianity had been adopted by most people in the

유리화된 요새들

중세 시대에 스코틀랜드에서 건설된 다수의 산성(요새화된 방어 시설)들은 흔치 않은 특징을 가지고 있다. 학자들이 '유리화된'이라고 부르는 특징인데, 돌들이 극도로 높은 열에 노출되어 녹거나 융합하여 단단하고 유리 같은 모습으로 변한 것을 뜻한다. 요새들이 어떻게, 왜 유리화되었는지 설명하기 위해 여러 가지 이론들이 제시되었다. 한 가지 이론에서는 유리화가 종교 또는 제례 의식의 일부였다고 생각한다. 스코틀랜드의 고대 신화와 전설은 유리로 만들어진 도시와 성에 대한 언급들로 가득 차 있으므로, 유리는 그 지역 사람들에게 특별한 의미를 가졌을 것이다. 유리화는 그들이 유리 성을 만들려고 시도한 방식이었을 수도 있다. 아마도 그들은 유리화된 요새들이 초자연적인 힘이나 복을 지니고 있다고 믿었을지도 모른다.

두 번째 이론에 따르면 요새 벽의 돌들은 요새를 공격한 사람들이 지른 불로 우연히 유리화되었다. 이 이론의 지지자들은 불이 요새 벽의 구조적 지지대로 사용되었던 나무 보를 불태우기 위한 무기로 사용되었다고 지적한다. 공격자들은 불을 붙이려고 시도할 때 불화살과 여타 발사체를 사용했다. 나무 보가 불에 타면서, 불로부터 발생한 열이 벽의 돌 부분을 유리화시킬 수 있었을 것이다.

다른 학자들은 요새를 건축한 사람들이 벽을 강화하기 위해 고의로 벽을 유리화했을 가능성이 더 높다고 생각한다. 벽이 유리화되면 돌들이 서로 융합되어 간격이나 틈새가 없어지게 된다. 다시 말해, 유리화는 단단하고 연속적인 벽 표면을 생성한다. 그렇게 되면 화살이 벽을 관통하기가 매우 어려워지므로, 이것이 효과적인 방어 수단이 될 수 있었을 것이다.

유리화된 요새에 관한 이론들은 설득력이 있어 보이지만, 불행히도 이들 중 그 어느 것도 이 현상을 충분히 설명하지 못한다.

첫째로, 유리는 고대 스코틀랜드 사람들에게 특별한 의미를 지녔을 수 있습니다. 그러나 지문의 이론에 대한 문제점은 대부분의 요새들이 건축된 시기에 그 지역은 기독교가 장악하고 있었습니다. 900년경 마지막 요새들이 건설됐을 때 그 지역 대부분의 사람들이 기독교를 받아들이고 있었고,

area, to the point that the native religious and ceremonial traditions of the area were almost completely wiped out. And the Christian religion as it was practiced at that time did not attribute any supernatural or magical powers to glass.

Second, re-creations of the vitrification process by scientists have shown that the temperatures needed for vitrification are extremely high—over one thousand degrees Celsius. A fire that was started by attackers would never reach this temperature. To reach it, a fire would have to be enclosed, blown toward the wall, and maintained, like fires in pottery ovens. There just wasn't enough wood used as structural support for the walls for this to happen. The attackers could not have maintained a fire that was hot enough to vitrify stone.

Third, it's true that the glassy substance produced by vitrification is strong, but it's also very brittle, meaning it can shatter on impact. Scottish defenders knew that the strongest forts are flexible, not brittle—that's why, when building forts, they often tended to pack the stones loosely together. Loosely packed stones would have allowed the walls to bend slightly and thus to absorb the impact of weapons beating against the walls. The brittle walls created by vitrification are actually easier to break down than non-vitrified walls are, so it hardly seems likely that vitrification was deliberately done by fort defenders wanting to strengthen their fort against attack.

Question

Summarize the points made in the lecture, being sure to explain how they challenge the specific theories proposed in the reading passage.

심지어 지역 원주민의 종교 및 제례의식 전통이 거의 완전히 사라지는 상태에까지 이르렀습니다. 그 당시의 기독교 신앙은 유리가 초자연적이거나 마법적인 힘을 가졌다고 생각하지 않았습니다.

둘째로, 과학자들에 의한 유리화 과정의 재현은 유리화에 필요한 온도가 극도로 높다는 것을 보여 주었습니다. 섭씨 1,000도가 넘어야 하죠. 공격자가 붙인 불이 이런 온도에 도달할 수는 없었을 것입니다. 이런 온도까지 올라가려면, 불을 벽 쪽으로 가둬두어야 하고, 벽 쪽으로 바람을 불어, 마치 도자기 가마의 불처럼 유지시켜야 합니다. 이걸 가능하게 할, 벽을 구조적으로 지지할 수 있을 만한 충분한 나무는 한마디로 없었습니다. 공격자들은 돌을 유리화시킬 정도로 뜨거운 불길을 유지할 수 없었을 것입니다.

셋째로, 유리화로 인해 생성된 유리성 물질은 강하긴 하지만 매우 부서지기 쉽습니다. 즉 충격에 산산조각이 날 수 있습니다. 스코틀랜드의 방어자들은 가장 강한 요새는 부서지는 것이 아닌, 유연한 것이어야 함을 알고 있었습니다. 그래서 요새를 건축할 때 돌을 느슨하게 쌓곤 했습니다. 느슨하게 쌓인 돌들은 벽이 살짝 휘어지도록 만들어 벽을 때리는 무기의 충격을 흡수했습니다. 유리화로 인해 부서지기 쉬워진 벽은 실제로 유리화되지 않은 벽보다 쉽게 붕괴될 수 있으므로, 요새 방어자들이 자신들의 요새를 공격에 대비해 강화하고자 의도적으로 유리화한 것으로 보기는 어렵습니다.

강의에서 말하는 요점들이 어떻게 읽기 지문에 제시된 특정 이론에 대해 대응하고 있는지 반드시 설명하면서 요약하시오.

어휘

fort 요새   vitrification 유리화   fuse 융합되다   religious 종교의   ceremonial 의식의   folktale 설화   significance 중요성   supernatural power 초자연적인 힘   point out 가리키다, 지적하다   projectile 발사체   in attempt to ~ ~하기 위해   purposefully ~하려는 목적으로   solid 단단한   continuous 연속적인   convincing 설득력 있는   phenomenon 현상   adequately 적절한   adopt 받아들이다   be wiped out 사라지다   enclose 가두다   pottery oven 도자기 가마   substance 물질   brittle 잘 부서지는   shatter 산산조각나다   slightly 약간   deliberately 의도적으로

Your professor is teaching a class on education. Write a post responding to the professor's question.

In your response, you should do the following.
- Express and support your opinion.
- Make a contribution to the discussion in your own words.

An effective response will contain at least 100 words.

Dr. Achebe

This week we analyzed some aspects of current educational systems. One type of school system we discussed was boarding schools, which, as the name suggests, is a type of school where students live during the school year. I would like you to discuss whether you consider boarding schools beneficial for students' education or whether you think day schools, or schools where students do not live at the schools, are better for most students. Explain why you think so.

Claire

I would have loved to have attended a boarding school. I feel like boarding schools would have helped me establish a strict daily routine and helped me become more disciplined. Also, being in a boarding school means that you are with friends and classmates around the clock, and I would have loved such an opportunity.

Andrew

I personally do not support the boarding school system as I believe it can lead to many psychological problems. In fact, I have heard about what is referred to as "boarding school syndrome," which, in simple terms, suggests that some students who attend boarding schools at a very young age can have long-term emotional or behavioral challenges. So why take that risk if most students can just go to day schools?

교수가 교육에 관한 수업을 가르치고 있다. 교수의 질문에 답하는 게시물을 작성하시오.

답변을 작성할 때, 다음 사항을 수행해야 한다.
- 자신의 의견을 제시하고 뒷받침할 것.
- 자신만의 글로 논의에 기여할 것.

효과적인 답변은 최소 100자의 단어를 포함한다.

아체베 박사

이번 주에 우리는 현 교육 시스템의 몇 가지 측면을 분석했습니다. 우리가 논의한 한 가지 학교 시스템이 기숙학교인데요, 이름에서 알 수 있듯이, 학생들이 학년 내내 숙식하며 학교입니다. 기숙학교가 학생들의 교육에 도움이 되는지, 아니면 대부분의 학생들에게 통학학교나 학교에서 생활하지 않는 학교가 더 나은지 토론해 보길 바랍니다. 자신의 의견에 대한 이유를 설명해 주세요.

클레어

저라면 기숙학교에 다녔다면 너무 좋았을 거예요. 기숙학교에 다녔다면 엄격한 일상 루틴을 정하고 좀더 자기 규율을 갖추는 데 도움이 되었을 것 같아요. 또한 기숙학교에 다닌다는 건 친구와 동급생들과 24시간 내내 같이 있다는 뜻이고, 그런 기회를 저라면 매우 좋아했을 거예요.

앤드루

저는 개인적으로 기숙학교 시스템을 지지하지 않는데 이것이 많은 심리적 문제를 야기할 수 있다고 생각하기 때문입니다. 사실, 저는 '기숙학교 증후군'이라고 불리는 것에 대해 들어 봤는데요, 간단히 말해서, 아주 어린 나이에 기숙학교에 다닌 학생들 중 일부는 장기간의 감정적 또는 행동적인 저항을 겪을 수 있다는 주장입니다. 그렇다면 대부분의 학생들이 통학학교에 다닐 수 있는데 왜 그런 위험을 감수해야 할까요?

어휘

analyze 분석하다   aspect 측면   boarding school 기숙학교   beneficial 도움이 되는   strict 엄격한   disciplined 규율을 지키는, 절제력 있는
around the clock 쉬지 않고   syndrome 증후군   challenge 저항

Notes

READING

NINETEENTH-CENTURY POLITICS IN THE UNITED STATES

p. 142

The development of the modern presidency in the United States began with Andrew Jackson, who swept to power in 1829 at the head of the Democratic Party and served until 1837. During his administration he immeasurably enlarged the power of the presidency. "The President is the direct representative of the American people," he lectured the Senate when it opposed him. "He was elected by the people, and is responsible to them." With this declaration, Jackson redefined the character of the presidential office and its relationship to the people.

During Jackson's second term, his opponents had gradually come together to form the Whig Party. **(A)** Whigs and Democrats held different attitudes toward the changes brought about by the market, banks, and commerce. **(B)** The Democrats tended to view society as a continuing conflict between "the people"—farmers, planters, and workers—and a set of greedy aristocrats. **(C)** This "paper money aristocracy" of bankers and investors manipulated the banking system for their own profit, Democrats claimed, and sapped the nation's virtue by encouraging speculation and the desire for sudden, unearned wealth. **(D)** The Democrats wanted the rewards of the market without sacrificing the features of a simple agrarian republic. They wanted the wealth that the market offered without the competitive, changing society; the complex dealing; the dominance of urban centers; and the loss of independence that came with it.

Whigs, on the other hand, were more comfortable with the market. For them, commerce and economic development were agents of civilization. Nor did the Whigs envision any conflict in society between farmers and workers on the one hand and businesspeople and bankers on the other. Economic growth would benefit everyone by raising national income and expanding opportunity. The government's responsibility was to provide a well-regulated economy that guaranteed opportunity for citizens of ability.

Whigs and Democrats differed not only in their attitudes toward the market but also about how active the central government should be in people's lives. Despite Andrew Jackson's inclination to be a strong President, Democrats as a rule believed in limited government. Government's role in the economy was to promote competition by destroying monopolies[1] and special privileges. In keeping with this philosophy of limited government, Democrats also

19세기 미국의 정치

미국의 현대적인 대통령의 직위는 앤드루 잭슨으로부터 발전하기 시작했다. 민주당 당수로서 1829년 정권을 잡았던 그는 1837년까지 대통령직을 역임했다. 재임 기간 동안 그는 대통령의 권한을 엄청나게 확대했다. 상원이 자신의 의견에 반대하자 그는 이렇게 역설했다. "대통령은 미국 국민의 직접적인 대표입니다. 그는 국민에 의해 선출되었고 그들에게 책임을 지는 인물입니다." 이런 선언을 통해 잭슨은 대통령직의 특성 및 대통령과 국민과의 관계를 재정립했다.

잭슨의 재선 임기 동안에 그의 반대파들이 규합하여 휘그당을 결성하였다. 휘그당과 민주당은 시장, 은행, 상업으로 야기된 여러 변화들에 대해 상반된 견해를 가지고 있었다. 민주당은 사회 안에는 농민, 농장주, 노동자 등 '평민층'과 탐욕스런 귀족층의 지속적인 갈등이 존재한다고 보았다. 은행가나 투자가 등의 '지폐 귀족'이 금융시스템을 조작하여 자신들의 사리사욕을 채우고 있으며, 투기와 일확천금의 욕망을 부추겨 국민의 가치관을 타락시켰다고 생각했다. 민주당은 단순한 농업 공화국의 기능들을 그대로 살리면서 시장의 이점도 얻으려고 했다. 시장이 변화와 경쟁이 심한 사회, 복잡한 거래관계, 도심 시설의 지배, 그로 인한 독립성의 상실 등의 현상을 일으키지 않고 부를 제공해 주기를 원했다.

반면에 휘그당은 시장을 적극적으로 수용했다. 그들에게 상업과 경제개발은 문명의 전도사였다. 휘그당은 농부나 노동자로 이루어진 계층과 사업가와 은행가로 이루어진 계층 사이에 갈등이 존재한다고 생각하지 않았다. 경제성장을 통해 국민소득을 증대하고 기회를 확대하면 모든 사람들에게 혜택이 돌아갈 수 있다고 보았다. 정부의 책임은 능력 있는 시민들에게 기회를 보장해 줄 수 있는 적절한 통제 경제를 마련해주는 것이었다.

휘그당과 민주당은 시장경제에 대한 태도뿐 아니라, 중앙정부가 민생에 개입하는 문제에서도 입장의 차이를 드러냈다. 앤드루 잭슨은 강력한 대통령이 되려는 경향이 있었지만, 민주당은 대체로 제한된 정부 역할을 지지했다. 경제 문제에 있어 정부의 역할은 독점과 특권을 없애 경쟁을 장려하는 것에 국한되었다. 이런 제한된 정부의 역할을 정치 철학으로 삼으면서 아울러 그들은 도덕적 신념을 정부 정책의 타당성으로 여기는 개념에도 반대했다. 그들은 종교와 정치가 명백히 구분되어야 한다고 생각했으며, 대체로 인도적 차원의 법안에 반대했다.

이와는 대조적으로 휘그당은 정부 권력을 긍정적으로 평

rejected the idea that moral beliefs were the proper sphere of government action. Religion and politics, they believed, should be kept clearly separate, and they generally opposed humanitarian legislation.

The Whigs, in contrast, viewed government power positively. They believed that it should be used to protect individual rights and public liberty, and that it had a special role where individual effort was ineffective. By regulating the economy and competition, the government could ensure equal opportunity. Indeed, for Whigs the concept of government promoting the general welfare went beyond the economy. In particular, Whigs in the northern sections of the United States also believed that government power should be used to foster the moral welfare of the country. They were much more likely to favor social-reform legislation and aid to education.

In some ways the social makeup of the two parties was similar. To be competitive in winning votes, Whigs and Democrats both had to have significant support among farmers, the largest group in society, and workers. Neither party could win an election by appealing exclusively to the rich or the poor. The Whigs, however, enjoyed disproportionate strength among the business and commercial classes. Whigs appealed to planters who needed credit to finance their cotton and rice trade in the world market, to farmers who were eager to sell their surpluses, and to workers who wished to improve themselves. Democrats attracted farmers isolated from the market or uncomfortable with it, workers alienated from the emerging industrial system, and rising entrepreneurs who wanted to break monopolies and open the economy to newcomers like themselves. The Whigs were strongest in the towns, cities, and those rural areas that were fully integrated into the market economy, whereas Democrats dominated areas of semisubsistence farming that were more isolated and languishing economically.

1. monopolies: companies or individuals that exclusively own or control commercial enterprises with no competitors

가했다. 그들은 정부가 개인의 권리와 대중의 자유를 보호하기 위해 권력을 행사할 수 있으며, 개인의 노력이 역부족인 분야에서 특별한 역할을 수행할 수 있다고 생각했다. 정부는 경제와 경쟁을 규제함으로써 동등한 기회를 보장해줄 수 있다고 보았다. 사실, 정부가 전반적인 복지를 증진시키는 역할을 수행해야 한다는 휘그당의 개념은 경제적 차원을 넘어서는 것이었다. 특히, 미국 북부 지역의 휘그당원들은 정부 권력이 국가의 도덕적 행복을 증진시키는 데도 이용되어야 한다고 생각했다. 그들은 사회 개혁 법안과 교육 지원에 상당히 찬성하는 것 같았다.

어떤 면에서 두 당의 사회 계층 비율은 비슷했다. 휘그당이든 민주당이든 득표수에 있어서 우위를 차지하려면, 당시 규모가 가장 큰 집단이었던 농민들과 노동자들의 전폭적인 지지를 얻어야만 했다. 어떤 당도 부유층이나 빈곤층 어느 한쪽만 의존해서는 선거에서 승리를 거둘 수 없었다. 하지만 휘그당은 기업과 상업 계층의 압도적인 지지를 얻었다. 휘그당은 세계 시장에서 면화와 쌀 교역 자금을 충당하기 위해 대출이 필요했던 농장주들, 잉여 농산물을 팔고자 했던 농민들, 그리고 좀 더 나은 삶을 추구하는 노동자들의 지지를 받았다. 민주당은 시장으로부터 동떨어져 있으며 그런 체제를 불편하게 여기는 농민들, 점차 부상하고 있는 산업 시스템에서 소외된 노동자들, 그리고 독점이 타파되고 자신들 같은 신참들에게 경제적 기회가 부여되기를 원하는 신흥 기업가들의 마음을 끌었다. 휘그당은 타운, 도시, 그리고 시장 경제에 확고히 편입되어 있는 농촌 지역에서 강세를 보인 반면, 민주당은 고립되어 있고 경제적으로 침체된 반(半) 생계형 경작 지역에서 인기를 얻었다.

1. 독점 기업: 시장에서 특정 상품이나 용역에 대한 공급을 경쟁자 없이 점유하고 있는 기업

어휘

presidency 대통령직 sweep to power 손쉽게 정권을 잡다 immeasurably 엄청나게, 헤아릴 수 없을 정도로 opponent 반대파, 적수 come together 뭉치다, 결집하다 commerce 상업, 교역 Whig 휘그당: 17-18세기에 일어난 민권당으로 Tory당과 대립하여 19세기에 지금의 Liberals(자유당)가 된 정당 Democrat 민주당 planter 농장주, 경작자 aristocrat 귀족층, 귀족정치주의자 manipulate (시장, 가격 등을) 교묘히 조작하다 sap 활력을 잃게 하다, (세력, 체력 등을) 약화시키다 speculation 투기, 사색, 추측 unearned 일하지 않고 얻은 agrarian republic 농업 공화국 envision 상상하다, (장래의 일을) 마음에 그리다 well-regulated 적절히 통제된 monopoly 독점, (상품, 사업 등의) 전매 privilege 특권, (특별한) 혜택 moral belief 도덕적 신념 humanitarian legislation 인도적 차원의 법안 exclusively 배타적으로, 독점적으로 regulate 규제하다, 조절하다 welfare 복지, 복지 사업 social-reform 사회 개혁 disproportionate 압도적인, 불균형의, 과잉의 credit (은행의) 신용 대출, 신용 surplus 잉여 농산물, 나머지 alienate A from B A를 B로부터 소외시키다 emerging 부상하고 있는, 최근에 생겨난 dominate 우위를 차지하다, 지배하다 semisubsistence 반(半) 생계형 languish 약화되다, 침체되다

1. 첫 번째 단락에 따르면, 앤드루 잭슨의 대통령직 역임이 특히 중요한 의미를 지니는 이유가 무엇인가?

Ⓐ 잭슨 대통령이 그의 권력의 일부를 상원에게 양도했기 때문이다.

Ⓑ 잭슨 대통령은 정기적으로 상원 앞에서 연설을 하기 시작했기 때문이다.

Ⓒ 미국에서 현대적인 대통령직의 시작이었기 때문이다.

Ⓓ 상원이 최초로 대통령에게 반기를 들었다고 알려졌기 때문이다.

세부 사항 찾기 문제

어휘 significant 중요한 portion 일부 address 연설하다

해설 첫 번째 문장에 그 이유가 나와 있다. 정답은 보기 C. 보기 A는 본문의 내용과 상반되는데, 잭슨 대통령은 대통령의 권력을 양도한 것이 아니라 확대시켰다. 보기 B는 지문에서 상원에서 정기적으로 연설했는지 여부는 언급되지 않으므로 틀렸다. 보기 D는 지문에 상원이 대통령에게 반대한 경우가 최초인지 나와있지 않으므로 틀렸다.

2. 두 번째 단락에서 필자는 '은행가들과 투자가들'이 어떤 부류에 해당한다고 언급하는가?

Ⓐ 민주당의 주요지지 기반

Ⓑ 부당한 방법으로 부자가 되었다고 민주당원들이 주장하는 사람들

Ⓒ 단순한 농업 공화국으로의 회귀를 가장 바라는 사람들

Ⓓ 앤드루 잭슨의 대통령직 역임을 지지하는 집단

수사학적 의도 파악 문제

어휘 claim 주장하다

해설 민주당원들은 이들이 금융 시스템을 조작하여 사익을 챙긴다고 생각한다. 보기 B를 제외한 나머지 보기들은 모두 지문과 상반되는 내용이다.

3. 세 번째 단락에 따르면, 휘그당원들은 상업과 경제개발이 사회에 어떤 영향을 미칠 것이라고 믿었는가?

Ⓐ 사회 전체의 진보를 촉진시킬 것이다.

Ⓑ 휘그당원들과 민주당원들 사이에 견해 차이를 초래할 것이다.

Ⓒ 휘그당원들에게 새로운 자리를 마련해 줄 것이다.

Ⓓ 농민들과 노동자들 사이의 갈등을 방지할 것이다.

세부 사항 찾기 문제

어휘 disagreement 견해 차이

해설 이 단락은 상업과 경제개발이 사회에 긍정적인 영향을 미칠 것이라는 휘그당의 입장을 설명하고 있다. 보기 B, C는 언급되지 않았으며, 보기 D는 지문의 내용과 다르다.

4. 세 번째 단락에 따르면, 다음 보기들 중 정부의 역할에 대한 휘그당의 관점을 기술한 것은?

Ⓐ 농민들과 사업가들 사이의 지속적인 갈등을 억제하기

Ⓑ 시장에 의해 초래된 여러 변화들을 규제하기

Ⓒ 모든 유능한 시민들이 혜택을 입을 수 있는 경제를 유지하기

Ⓓ 경제개발에 중점을 두지 않기

세부 사항 찾기 문제

어휘 restrict 규제하다 benefit 혜택을 입다

해설 마지막 문장에 정부가 능력 있는 시민들에게 기회를 보장해 주는 경제 정책을 시행해야 한다고 나와 있다. 보기 C가 그와 같은 맥락의 문장이다. 휘그당은 농민들과 사업가들 사이의 갈등 자체를 인정하지 않았으므로 보기 A는 사실이 아니다. 보기 B 역시 휘그당은 시장에 의해 초래된 모든 변화를 지지했기 때문에 틀렸다. 보기 D도 휘그당은 경제개발을 중시했으므로 틀렸다.

5. 네 번째 단락에 따르면, 민주당원이 정부의 조치를 지지하리라 생각되는 분야는 다음 중 어느 것인가?

Ⓐ 국교를 만드는 일

Ⓑ 인도적 차원의 법안을 지지하는 일

Ⓒ 독점을 없애는 일

Ⓓ 특별한 도덕적 신념을 권장하는 일

세부 사항 찾기 문제

어휘 state religion 국가 종교

해설 이 단락의 세 번째 문장을 보면, 민주당원들은 정부가 독점을 없애 경쟁을 촉진시켜야 한다고 생각했다. 따라서 정답은 보기 C. 나머지 보기들은 전부 민주당원들의 관점과 정반대 되는 내용이다.

6. 지문의 단어 concept와 의미상 가장 가까운 것은?

Ⓐ 힘 Ⓑ 현실 Ⓒ 어려움 Ⓓ 개념

어휘 문제

어휘 idea 개념, 생각

해설 concept는 '개념', '관념'이라는 의미다.

7. 다섯 번째 단락으로 보아 휘그당 내부에 존재하는 색다른 정치적 신조들에 대해 다음 중 어떤 점을 추론할 수 있는가?

Ⓐ 그것들은 대중의 자유에 관한 사안들에 초점이 맞춰져 있다.

Ⓑ 그것들 때문에 일부 휘그당원들은 당을 떠났다.

Ⓒ 그것들은 대부분의 휘그당원들에게 중요하지 않았다.

Ⓓ 그것들은 지역적 이해관계를 반영했다.

내용 추론 문제

어휘 reflect 반영하다

해설 다섯 번째 문장을 보면, 휘그당 내에서 북부지역 당원들은 정부의 역할에 대해 더욱 특이한 관점을 가지고 있다는 사실을 지적하고 있다. 이는 당내에서도 지역에 따라서는 정부 역할에 대한 견해 차이가 있는 것으로 볼 수 있다. 따라서 정답은 보기 D.

8. 다음 중 마지막 단락에 음영으로 표시된 문장이 담고 있는 핵심 정보를 가장 잘 표현한 것은? 정답 외의 보기들은 의미가 상당히 왜곡되거나 본질적인 정보가 빠져 있다.

Ⓐ 휘그당은 부유한 지역에서만 지지를 얻을 수 있었는데, 그 이유는 민주당이 그 밖의 다른 지역을 장악하고 있었기 때문이었다.

Ⓑ 휘그당과 민주당의 강세 지역은 애초부터 도시와 농촌으로 각기 분리되어 있었다.

Ⓒ 민주당이 장악해 온 반 생계형 경작 지역은 휘그당의 시장경제 지배로 인해 점차 고립되었다.

Ⓓ 민주당이 빈곤한 지역에서 영향력이 가장 강했던 반면, 휘그당은 시장경제가 충분히 활성화된 지역에서 영향력이 가장 강했다.

문장 재구성 문제

어휘 semisubsistence 반 생계형의   operating 활성화되고 있는

해설 보기 D가 강조된 문장의 핵심을 잘 짚어냈는데, 보기 문장에서는 지문 내용의 순서를 서로 바꾸어 표현했다. 보기 A와 C는 지문에 나와 있지 않다. 휘그당과 민주당의 지지 기반의 차이는 도시나 농촌에 있지 않고, 시장경제가 구축되어 있느냐 그렇지 않느냐에 있으므로 보기 B는 틀렸다.

9. **지시문:** 위에 제시된 지문의 일부를 보시오. 지문에 표시된 **(A)**, **(B)**, **(C)**, **(D)** 중 하나에 다음 문장이 삽입될 수 있다.

This new party argued against the policies of Jackson and his party in a number of important areas, beginning with the economy.

(이 새로운 당은 경제 문제를 비롯하여 많은 주요 분야에서 잭슨과 그의 당이 추진하는 정책에 반대했다.)

이 문장이 들어갈 가장 적당한 위치는?

During Jackson's second term, his opponents had gradually come together to form the Whig Party. **(A)** This new party argued against the policies of Jackson and his party in a number of important areas, beginning with the economy. Whigs and Democrats held different attitudes toward the changes brought about by the market, banks, and commerce. **(B)** The Democrats tended to view society as a continuing conflict between "the people"— farmers, planters, and workers—and a set of greedy aristocrats. **(C)** This "paper money aristocracy" of bankers and investors manipulated the banking system for their own profit, Democrats claimed, and sapped the nation's virtue by encouraging speculation and the desire for sudden, unearned wealth. **(D)** The Democrats wanted the rewards of the market without sacrificing the features of a simple agrarian republic. They wanted the wealth that the market offered without the competitive, changing society; the complex dealing; the dominance of urban centers; and the loss of independence that came with it.

Ⓐ   Ⓑ   Ⓒ   Ⓓ

문장 삽입 문제

해설 주어 This new party는 휘그당을 가리키는데, 문맥상 바로 앞 문장에 이 당을 소개하는 내용이 나와야 한다. (B)는 앞 문장의 주어가 휘그당과 민주당이기 때문에 들어갈 수 없다. (C), (D) 역시 앞 문장의 주어가 휘그당이 아닌 민주당이기 때문에 들어갈 수 없다.

10. **지시문:** 이 지문을 간단히 요약하기 위한 도입 문장이 아래에 제시되어 있다. 아래 보기들 중에서 지문의 가장 중요한 개념을 표현한 문장 3개를 골라 요약을 완성하라. 보기들 중에는 지문에 나오지 않았거나 중요하지 않은 개념이기 때문에 요약문으로 적절치 않은 것들도 있다. 이 문제의 배점은 2점이다.

19세기 중반 미국의 정치체제는 당시의 사회적, 경제적 환경에 의해 강한 영향을 받았다.

Ⓐ 민주당과 휘그당은 서로 경쟁하는 경제적, 정치적 유권자 층의 요구에 대응하면서 발전했다.

Ⓑ 대통령직을 두 차례 역임하는 동안 앤드루 잭슨은 민주당과 휘그당, 두 당의 지도자 역할을 했다.

Ⓒ 민주당은 주로 시장, 은행, 상업 쪽의 이해관계를 대변했다.

Ⓓ 민주당과 달리, 휘그당은 교육에 대한 정부 지원을 지지했다.

Ⓔ 휘그당과 민주당의 근본적 차이는 시장의 사회적 중요성에 대한 인식에 있었다.

Ⓕ 정부의 민생 개입 문제에서 두 당의 중요한 정치적 입장이 명백히 달랐다.

지문 요약하기 문제

어휘 constituency 유권자층   primarily 주로   represent 대변하다   in contrast to ~과는 달리   distinction 구별, 차별

해설 보기 A는 지문 전체에서 다루고 있는 포괄적인 주제이다. 앤드루 잭슨은 민주당 당수였으므로 보기 B는 사실과 다르다. 보기 C에 나온 시장, 은행, 상업 쪽은 민주당이 아닌 휘그당의 지지층이다. 보기 D에서 교육에 대한 정부 지원을 지지한 사람들은 북부 지역의 휘그당원들에게만 해당되는 내용이다. 다른 휘그당원들이나 민주당원들이 그 사안에 대해 어떻게 생각했는지는 언급되어 있지 않다. 보기 E, F는 모두 본문의 핵심 내용이다.

Birds use song both in courtship and to define areas of territory. Both of these are communicative purposes: the bird is passing specific messages to other members of its species. Birds communicate for other reasons as well: a blackbird, for instance, will make a sharp "pink-pink" sound when there is a cat nearby, which warns other birds in the neighborhood of the danger.

William Thorpe (1961) studied the behavior of gannets in a colony containing many thousands of birds. **(A)** Thorpe found that when a bird was returning to its nest, it would drift on an updraft of air from the bottom of the cliff upwards, calling as it went. **(B)** When the bird on the nest heard its mate calling, it would call in reply, showing that each bird's call could act as an identification signal. **(C)** Thorpe also discovered that a bird might have as many as fifteen or sixteen different kinds of calls, each serving a different function. **(D)**

J. R. Krebs (1976) realized that birds often sing more intensively in the early morning—the "dawn chorus." By investigating what the birds actually did during each day, and how much time they spent on each activity, Krebs found that the dawn chorus serves a largely territorial function. The early morning is not a particularly good time for gathering food, because it is dark, so visibility is lower, and it is also cold, so many insects are still inactive. On the other hand, at this time many birds move around looking for living space, so establishing and defending a territory is necessary. Birdsong is not just territorial, of course. A bird's song can serve a dual purpose: it can be used to defend a territory and, by indicating to a prospective mate that the singer has a territory to defend, can also attract a female bird.

P. J. B. Slater (1981) suggested that bird calls and birdsong are partly learned from other birds. He found that chaffinches which had been hand-reared and had not heard other wild birds made an entirely different kind of "chink" call from that of wild birds. In another case, Slater observed a laboratory chaffinch in a duet with a wild sparrow outside the window of the laboratory. The chaffinch imitated the sparrow's "cheep" whenever the sparrow produced it. Slater concluded that learning through copying is an important part of the way in which birds acquire their songs. Slater also found that individual chaffinches can have up to five different types of song. Some of these are personal, sung by that bird alone. Others are shared by several birds. In some cases too, Slater observed chaffinches singing songs which were almost identical to those sung by others, but with just a note or two

---

새의 노래와 울음소리

새들은 구애할 때, 그리고 영역에 해당하는 구역을 규정하는 데 있어 모두 노랫소리를 이용한다. 두 경우 모두 의사 전달의 목적을 지니고 있는데, 같은 종의 다른 구성원들에게 특정한 메시지를 전하는 것이다. 새들은 다른 이유로도 의사소통하며, 예를 들어, 검은지빠귀는 고양이가 가까이 있을 때 날카로운 "핑핑" 소리를 내는데, 이는 근처의 다른 새들에게 위험 요소를 경고하는 것이다.

윌리엄 소프(1961년)는 수천 마리의 새들을 포함하는 군락에 속한 부비새의 행동을 연구했다. 소프는 새 한 마리가 둥지로 돌아갈 때, 절벽 밑에서부터 위쪽으로 공기의 상승 기류를 타고 떠오르며, 이동하면서 울음소리를 낸다는 사실을 발견했다. 보금자리에 있는 새가 짝의 울음소리를 들으면, 대답으로 울음소리를 내는데, 이는 각각의 새 울음소리가 신분 확인용 신호의 역할을 할 수 있음을 보여 주는 것이다. 소프는 새 한 마리가 각각 다른 기능을 하는 15~16가지나 되는 많은 다른 종류의 울음소리를 낼 수도 있다는 점도 알아냈다.

J. R. 크렙스(1976년)는 새들이 흔히 이른 아침에 더 집중적으로 노래한다는 사실을 알게 되었는데, 이를 '이른 아침의 합창'이라고 부른다. 새들이 실제로 매일 하루 중에 무엇을 하는지, 그리고 각 활동에 얼마나 많은 시간을 소비하는지 조사함으로써, 크렙스는 이른 아침의 합창이 주로 영역과 관련된 기능을 한다는 사실을 알았다. 이른 아침은 먹이를 모으기에 특별히 좋은 시간대는 아닌데, 어두워서 가시성이 더 떨어지는데다, 춥기까지 해서 많은 곤충들이 여전히 활동하지 않는 상태이기 때문이다. 반면에, 이 시간대는 많은 새들이 생활 공간을 찾아 이리저리 이동하기 때문에, 영역을 확립하고 방어하는 것이 필수이다. 당연히, 새들의 노랫소리가 영역과 관련된 것만은 아니다. 새 한 마리의 노래는 이중 목적을 지니고 있을 수 있는데, 영역을 방어하는 데 이용될 수 있으며, 노래하는 새가 방어할 영역이 있음을 잠재적인 짝에게 나타냄으로써, 암컷 새를 유혹할 수도 있다.

P. J. B. 슬레이터(1981년)는 새의 울음소리와 노랫소리가 부분적으로 다른 새들을 통해 터득된다고 주장했다. 그는 사람 손에 자라서 야생의 다른 새들이 내는 소리를 듣지 못한 되새가 야생의 새들과 완전히 다른 종류의 "찍찍" 소리를 낸다는 사실을 발견했다. 또 다른 사례로, 슬레이터는 실험실 창문 밖에 있는 야생의 참새와 듀엣을 이룬 실험실 되새도 관찰했다. 이 되새는 참새가 소리를 낼 때마다 그 참새의 "짹짹" 소리를 모사했다. 슬레이터는 모방을 통해 배우는 것이 새들이 노랫소리를 터득하는 방식에 있어 중요한 일부분이라는 결론을 내렸다. 슬레이터는 또한 각각의 되새가 최대 5가지 다른 종류의 노랫소리를 지니고 있을 수 있다는 점도 발견했다. 이 노랫소리들 중 일부는 그 새만 부르는 개별적인 것이다. 다른 소리들은 여러 새들이 공유한다. 몇몇 사례

different—possibly because the bird had made an error in copying the song from another.

Slater studied a population of 40 chaffinches on the Orkney Islands and found that among them they had seventeen different song types. So it was not a matter of each bird having its own individual songs—there was a considerable amount of sharing. Slater found that this sharing related to geographical distribution, but that the boundaries were not distinct enough for it to be accurately described as a dialect, or regional variety of a song. Instead, there was considerable overlap between the songs sung in one area and those sung in an adjoining one, but gradually the overlap would become less, until birds a long distance away from one another would be singing entirely different songs.

In 1970, Peter Marler proposed that birdsong and human speech were directly comparable in certain key respects, and that the study of birdsong might provide psychologists with some useful indicators as to the nature and development of speech in human beings. One of the parallels which Marler identified was the way that both humans and birds show a strong genetic predisposition to pick up and imitate certain sounds rather than others. Marler showed that young birds will learn the songs of their own species if they are played to them when young, but they will ignore songs of birds from other species. Similarly, young human beings are surrounded by all kinds of sounds and noises, but it is the human voice to which they listen most closely and human speech which they imitate.

에서도, 슬레이터는 다른 새들이 부르는 것과 거의 동일한 노래를 부르는 되새를 관찰했지만, 딱 한두 가지 다른 소리가 있었는데, 이는 아마 그 새가 다른 새의 노래를 모방하는 데 실수를 했기 때문일 것이다.

슬레이터는 오크니 제도에서 40마리의 되새 개체군을 연구하면서, 그들 사이에서 17가지의 다른 노래 종류가 있다는 사실을 발견했다. 따라서 각 새에게 자신만의 개별 노래가 있는 것의 문제가 아니었으며, 상당히 많은 공유가 이뤄지고 있었다. 슬레이터는 이러한 공유가 지리적 분포와 관련되어 있다는 점, 하지만 그 경계는 하나의 방언, 즉 노래의 지역별 종류로 정확히 묘사될 수 있을 정도로 충분히 뚜렷하지는 않았다는 점을 발견했다. 대신, 한 구역 내에서 부르는 노래들과 인접한 곳에서 부르는 노래들 사이에 상당한 공통점이 있었지만, 점차적으로 그 공통점은 서로 아주 먼 거리에 있는 새들이 완전히 다른 노래를 부르게 될 때까지 더 줄어들게 되었다.

1970년에, 피터 말러는 새의 노래와 인간의 말이 특정 음조 측면에 있어 직접적으로 비교할 만하다는 점, 그리고 새의 노래 연구가 심리학자들에게 인간의 말이 지닌 특징 및 발달과 관련된 몇몇 유용한 지표를 제공해 줄 수도 있다는 점을 제안했다. 말러가 확인한 유사점들 중의 하나는 인간과 새 둘 모두 다른 것들보다 특정한 소리를 익히고 모방하는 강한 유전적 성향을 보이는 방식이었다. 말러는 어린 새들이 어릴 때 같은 종이 부르는 노래가 들리면 그것을 배우지만, 다른 종의 새들이 부르는 노래는 무시한다는 사실을 보여주었다. 마찬가지로, 인간도 어릴 때 온갖 종류의 소리와 소음에 둘러싸이지만, 가장 크게 주의를 기울여 듣는 것은 인간의 목소리이며, 모방하는 것은 인간의 말이다.

어휘

courtship 구애 define 규정하다 territory 영역 communicative 의사 소통의 specific 특정한, 구체적인 species (동식물의) 종 warn A of B A에게 B를 경고하다 behavior 행동 colony 군락 contain 포함하다 drift 떠 있다 updraft 상승 기류 act as ~의 역할을 하다 identification 신분 확인 function 기능 intensively 집중적으로 investigate 조사하다 territorial 영역의 visibility 가시성 insect 곤충 inactive 활동하지 않는 establish 확립하다 defend 방어하다 indicate to ~에게 나타내다 prospective 잠재적인 hand-reared 사람 손에 길러진 entirely 완전히 observe 관찰하다 imitate 모방하다 acquire 얻다 identical to ~와 동일한 note (새의) 울음소리, 음 population 개체군 individual 각각의, 개별적인 a considerable amount of 상당히 많은 sharing 공유 relate to ~와 관련되다 geographical distribution 지리적 분포 boundary 경계 distinct 뚜렷한 describe 묘사하다 dialect 방언 regional 지역의 variety 종류, 다양(성) overlap 공통점, 겹침 adjoining 인접한 gradually 점차적으로 comparable 비교할 만한 key 음조 respect 측면, 사항 provide A with B A에게 B를 제공하다 psychologist 심리학자 indicator 지표 nature 특징, 본질 parallel 유사점 identify 확인하다 genetic 유전의 predisposition 성향, 경향 pick up 익히다 ignore 무시하다

11. 지문의 단어 discovered와 의미상 가장 가까운 것은?

Ⓐ 보고했다
Ⓑ 알아냈다
Ⓒ 추정했다
Ⓓ 보여 주었다

수사학적 의도 파악 문제

어휘 estimate 추정하다, 추산하다

해설 discover는 어떤 사실을 '알아내다' 라는 의미다.

12. 지문의 단어 realized와 의미상 가장 가까운 것은?

Ⓐ 가리켰다
Ⓑ 확립했다
Ⓒ 이해했다
Ⓓ 주장했다

어휘 문제

어휘 indicate 가리키다, 나타내다   establish 확립하다, 설립하다

해설 realize는 어떤 사실을 '알게 되다, 이해하다' 를 의미한다.

13. 다음 중 세 번째 단락에서 새와 먹이 수집에 관해 추론할 수 있는 것은?

Ⓐ 새들은 먹이를 수집하는 동안 대단히 텃세가 강해진다.
Ⓑ 새들은 먹이 수집이 어려울 때보다 쉬울 때 노래할 가능성이 더 크다.
Ⓒ 대부분의 새들은 하루에 충분한 먹이를 수집한 후에 노래를 시작한다.
Ⓓ 새들은 먹이를 찾고 있을 때 집중적으로 노래할 가능성이 더 적다.

내용 추론 문제

어휘 territorial 텃세를 부리는   be more likely to do ~할 가능성이 더 크다   be less likely to do ~할 가능성이 더 적다

해설 새들이 흔히 이른 아침에 더 집중적으로 노래하는데, 그것이 주로 영역과 관련된 기능을 한다고 언급되어 있다. 또한, 이른 아침은 먹이를 잡기 좋은 시간대가 아니며, 영역을 확립하고 방어하는 것이 필수인 시간대라고 쓰여 있다. 따라서, 먹이를 잡는 다른 시간대에는 덜 집중적으로 노래하는 것으로 볼 수 있으므로 D가 정답이다.

14. 세 번째 단락에 따르면, 새들은 왜 이른 아침에 영역을 방어하는 일에 관심이 있는가?

Ⓐ 하루 중에 짝이 없는 수컷 새들이 생활 공간 및 다른 수컷의 짝들을 빼앗으려 하는 시간대이다.
Ⓑ 하루 중에 새들과 다른 동물들이 곤충을 사냥하는 시간대이다.
Ⓒ 하루 중에 새들이 어둠 속에서 공격하는 포식자들로부터 보금자리를 방어해야 하는 시간대이다.
Ⓓ 하루 중에 다른 새들이 새로 생활할 공간을 찾는 시간대이다.

세부 사항 찾기 문제

어휘 be concerned with ~에 관심이 있다   take away 빼앗다, 없애다   insect 곤충   predator 포식자   attack 공격하다

해설 이른 아침 시간대는 많은 새들이 생활 공간을 찾아 이리저리 이동하기 때문에 영역을 확립하고 방어하는 것이 필수라는 말이 제시되어 있으므로 D가 정답이다.

15. 저자가 왜 "실험실 창문 밖에 있는 야생의 참새와 듀엣을 이룬 실험실 되새"의 행동을 이야기하는가?

Ⓐ 슬레이터의 손에 자란 새들이 왜 야생의 새들이 내는 것과 완전히 다른 울음소리를 냈는지 설명하기 위해
Ⓑ 슬레이터가 어떻게 모방이 새들이 노래를 터득하는 데 있어 중요한 역할을 한다는 견해에 이르게 되었는지 나타내기 위해
Ⓒ 슬레이터가 새들이 많은 종류의 노래를 부르는 것이 왜 이로울 것이라고 생각했는지 설명하기 위해
Ⓓ 새들이 새로운 노래와 울음소리를 터득하는 많은 다른 방식이 있다는 증거를 제공하기 위해

수사학적 의도 파악 문제

어휘 arrive at (확신 등) ~에 이르다   play an important role in ~에 있어 중요한 역할을 하다   advantageous 이로운, 유리한   evidence 증거

해설 실험실 창문 밖에 있는 야생의 참새와 듀엣을 이룬 실험실 되새가 참새의 "짹짹" 소리를 모사하는 모습을 통해, 모방이 새들이 노랫소리를 터득하는 방식에 있어 중요한 일부분이라는 결론을 내렸다고 언급되어 있다. 이는 슬레이터가 그러한 견해를 갖게 된 과정을 말하는 것이므로 B가 정답이다.

16. 다음 중 지문에서 음영으로 표시된 문장이 담고 있는 핵심 정보를 가장 잘 표현한 것은? 정답 외의 보기들은 의미가 상당히 왜곡되거나 필수적인 정보가 빠져 있다.

Ⓐ 슬레이터는 거의 한두 마리의 되새가 다른 새들이 부르는 노래를 거의 동일하게 모방해 부를 수 있다는 점을 관찰했다.
Ⓑ 슬레이터는 되새가 다른 새들의 노래를 부르면서 모방상의 실수로 인한 것이었을 수 있는 한두 가지 틀린 소리를 냈다는 점을 관찰했다.
Ⓒ 슬레이터는 되새가 다른 새들의 노래를 배우는 동안 때때로 다른 집단의 새들에게 배웠을 수 있는 한두 가지 틀린 소리를 추가했다는 점을 관찰했다.
Ⓓ 슬레이터는 되새가 다른 새들의 노래를 부를 때 자신들의 노래에 있는 한두 가지 소리를 활용했다는 점을 관찰했다.

문장 재구성 문제

어휘 all but 거의   be able to do ~할 수 있다   due to ~로 인해   add 추가하다

해설 다른 새들이 부르는 것과 거의 동일한 노래를 부르는 되새를 관찰했다는 점, 한두 가지 다른 소리를 냈다는 점, 그리고 그것이 아마 모방하면서 실수한 것이었을 수 있다는 점을 모두 포함하고 있는 B가 정답이다.

17. 다섯 번째 단락에 따르면, 오크니 제도의 되새들이 다른 지역적 변주곡을 부르는 것으로 여겨지지 않았던 이유는?

Ⓐ 각각의 새에게 다른 어떤 새들과도 공유되지 않은 자신만의 개별 노래가 있었기 때문에
Ⓑ 그 새들의 다른 노래들이 지리적 위치를 기반으로 하지 않았기 때문에
Ⓒ 심지어 어느 정도 멀리 떨어진 곳에 서식하는 새들도 많은 동일한 노래를 공유했기 때문에
Ⓓ 노래의 차이가 발생한 곳들을 나타낼 명확한 구획이 존재하지 않았기 때문에

Reading

Listening

Speaking

Writing

Test 1

Test 2

Test 3

Test 4

수사학적 의도 파악 문제

어휘 be based on ~을 기반으로 하다 division 구획, 구분, 부분 occur 발생하다

해설 오크니 제도에 있는 되새들의 노래 공유가 지리적 분포와 관련되어 있기는 하지만, 지역별 종류로 구분하기에는 그 경계가 충분히 뚜렷하지 않다는 사실이 제시되어 있다. 따라서, 이러한 노래의 차이와 관련된 명확한 구획이 존재하지 않았다는 점을 언급한 D가 정답이다.

18. 여섯 번째 단락에, 저자는 왜 어린 새들은 다른 종의 노래를 무시하고 인간은 어릴 때 인간의 말에 더 귀 기울여 듣는다는 말러의 결과물을 이야기하는가?

Ⓐ 듣는 능력이 어린 새와 어린 아이에게서 상대적으로 저조하게 발달된다는 점을 보여 주기 위해

Ⓑ 소리를 익히고 모방하는 유전적 성향은 새보다 인간이 정교하다고 주장하기 위해

Ⓒ 말러가 왜 새의 노래가 인간이 하는 말의 발달 과정을 이해하는 데 유용할 지도 모른다고 생각했는지 설명하기 위해

Ⓓ 주변의 소음과 소리가 새가 노래를 배우는 데 있어, 그리고 인간이 언어를 배우는 데 있어 그 어려움을 증가시킨다는 점을 보여 주기 위해

세부 정보 찾기 문제

어휘 relatively 상대적으로, 비교적 sophisticated 정교한, 복잡한

해설 새의 노래 연구가 심리학자들에게 인간의 말이 지닌 특징 및 발달과 관련된 몇몇 유용한 지표를 제공해 줄 수도 있다는 점을 제안했다고 언급하면서 어린 새와 어릴 때의 인간이 각각 노래와 말을 습득하는 성향을 이야기하고 있다. 따라서, 새의 노래 연구가 지니는 이러한 유용성을 언급한 C가 정답이다.

19. 지시문: 위에 제시된 지문의 일부를 보시오. 지문에 표시된 **(A)**, **(B)**, **(C)**, **(D)** 중 하나에 다음 문장이 삽입될 수 있다.

These include flight calls used to coordinate the flock as well as distress calls and begging calls, which are used specifically by chicks to communicate with their parents.

(여기에 포함되는 것은 무리를 조직화하는 데 이용되는 비행 울음소리뿐만 아니라 특히 새끼들이 어미들과 의사 소통하기 위해 이용하는 고통 울음소리와 애원 울음소리이다.)

이 문장이 들어갈 가장 적당한 위치는?

William Thorpe (1961) studied the behavior of gannets in a colony containing many thousands of birds. **(A)** Thorpe found that when a bird was returning to its nest, it would drift on an updraft of air from the bottom of the cliff upwards, calling as it went. **(B)** When the bird on the nest heard its mate calling, it would call in reply, showing that each bird's call could act as an identification signal. **(C)**) Thorpe also calculated that a bird might have as many as fifteen or sixteen different kinds of calls, each serving a different function. **(D)** These include flight calls used to coordinate the flock as well as distress calls and begging calls, which are used specifically by chicks to

communicate with their parents.

Ⓐ   Ⓑ   Ⓒ   Ⓓ

문장 삽입 문제

어휘 coordinate 조직화하다 flock 무리 distress 고통, 괴로움 specifically 특히

해설 삽입 문장은 새가 내는 다양한 울음소리의 종류에 포함되는 예시를 언급하고 있다. 따라서, 각각 다른 기능을 하는 15~16가지나 되는 많은 다른 종류의 울음소리를 낼 수도 있다는 점을 알리는 문장 뒤에 위치해 그 예시를 말하는 흐름이 되어야 자연스러우므로 (D)가 정답이다.

20. 지시문: 이 지문을 간단히 요약하기 위한 도입 문장이 아래에 제시되어 있다. 아래 보기들 중에서 지문의 가장 중요한 개념을 표현한 문장 3개를 골라 요약을 완성하라. 보기들 중에는 지문에 나오지 않았거나 중요하지 않은 개념이기 때문에 요약문으로 적절치 않은 것들도 있다. 이 문제의 배점은 2점이다.

새들은 다른 새들과 의사 소통하기 위해 노래한다.

Ⓐ 새 한 마리가 지니고 있는 다른 노래와 울음소리의 숫자는 종에 따라 다양하며, 검은지빠귀는 가장 적은 종류의 노래와 울음소리를 지니고 있고, 되새는 몇몇 가장 많은 것을 지니고 있다.

Ⓑ 가시성이 떨어지는 빽빽한 숲이나 다른 장소에 서식하는 새들은 먹이 공급원과 위험 요소의 위치를 파악하는 데 있어 다른 새들의 노래와 울음소리에 특히 의존한다.

Ⓒ 많은 새들이 먹이 수집이 어려운 시간대에 영역을 확립하고 짝을 유혹하기 위해 노래하는 반면, 부비새 같은 다른 새들은 신분 확인을 위해 울음소리를 이용한다.

Ⓓ 새의 노래와 울음소리는 새 한 마리에게 고유하거나 여러 새들 사이에서 공유될 수 있으며, 심지어 다른 종을 통해 터득할 수 있다.

Ⓔ 사람 손에 길러진 되새가 처음에는 야생의 같은 종이 내는 울음소리와 노래를 정확히 모방하는 데 더뎠지만, 시간이 흐름이 따라 그 모방 능력이 향상되었다.

Ⓕ 새와 인간이 특정 소리를 모방하는 유사한 유전적 능력을 지니고 있기 때문에, 새의 노래는 인간의 말 발달 과정을 설명하는 데 도움이 될 수 있다.

지문 요약하기 문제

어휘 dense 빽빽한, 밀집된 dependent on ~에 의존하는 locate ~의 위치를 찾다 unique 고유한 correctly 정확하게 improve 향상되다

해설 두 번째 단락과 세 번째 단락에 부비새가 신분 확인을 위해 울음소리를 이용한다는 사실과 많은 새들이 먹이 수집이 어려운 이른 아침 시간대에 영역을 확립하고 짝을 유혹하기 위해 노래한다는 점이 요점으로 제시되어 있으므로 C는 핵심 내용이다. D는 새의 노래와 울음소리가 특정 새에게 고유하거나 여러 새들이 공유할 수도 있고, 심지어 다른 새를 통해 터득할 수 있다는 내용이 제시된 네 번째 단락과 다섯 번째 단락을 요약한 문장이다. F는 새와 인간이 지닌 소리 모방 능력의 유사성과 새의 노래가 인간이 하는 말의 발달 과정을 이해하는 데 도움이 될 수 있다고 주장하는 마지막 단락에 대한 핵심 내용이다.

LISTENING

🎧 T-11

Questions 1-5	p. 156

N Narrator P Professor S Student

Script

N Listen to a conversation between a student and a professor.

P Hey, Ellen. How are you doing?

S Oh, pretty good, thanks. How are you?

P OK.

S Did you, um, have a chance to look at my grad school application... you know, the statement of purpose I wrote?

P Well, yeah. In fact, here it is. I just read it.

S Oh, great! What did you think?

P Basically, it's good. What you might actually do is take some of these different points here, and actually break them out into separate paragraphs. So, um, one: your purpose for applying for graduate study—uh, why do you want to go to graduate school—and an area of specialty; and, uh, why you want to do the area you're specifying; um, and what you want to do with your degree once you get it.

S OK.

P So those are... they're pretty clear on those four points they want.

S Right.

P So you might just break them out into, uh... you know, separate paragraphs and expand on each point some. But really what's critical with these is that, um, you've gotta let yourself come through. See, you gotta let them see you in these statements. Expand some more on what's happened in your own life and what shows your... your motivation and interest in this area—in geology. Let 'em see what really, what... what captures your imagination about this field.

S OK. So make it a little more... personal? That's OK?

P That's fine. They look for that stuff. You don't wanna go overboard...

S Right.

P ...but it's critical that... that somebody sees what your passion is—your personal motivation for doing this.

S OK.

P And that's gotta come out in here. Um, and let's see, uh, you might also give a little, uh—since this is your only chance to do it, you might give a little more explanation about your unique undergraduate background. So, you know, how you went through,

N 학생과 교수의 대화를 들으시오.

P 엘렌이구나. 잘 지내지?

S 네, 잘 지내요, 고맙습니다. 안녕하세요?

P 그래.

S 혹시 제 대학원 입학지원서 보셨어요? 제가 작성한 학업계획서요.

P 그래. 실은 여기 있다. 방금 읽었어.

S 그러세요! 어떻게 생각하세요?

P 전체적으로 괜찮구나. 이런 여러 가지 사항들을 단락별로 구분하는 것이 낫겠다는 생각이 드는구나. 우선 대학원에 지원한 목적, 대학원에 가고 싶은 이유와 전공분야, 네가 명시한 분야를 공부하고 싶은 이유, 그리고 학위를 딴 후에 하고 싶은 일 등을 말이지.

S 알겠습니다.

P 그런 것들이… 그들은 요구하는 이런 네 가지 사항들에 중점을 둘 거야.

S 그렇죠.

P 그러니까, 그것들을 별도의 단락으로 나누고 각 사항마다 좀 더 자세히 설명할 필요가 있어. 하지만 이런 사항들을 기술할 때 정말 중요한 것은 네 자신을 충분히 드러내야 한다는 거야. 그들이 이런 문장들 속에서 네 모습을 볼 수 있어야 한다는 말이지. 네가 살아오면서 겪었던 일과 이 분야, 즉 지질학에 대한 너의 동기와 관심에 대해 보다 상세히 기술해야 해. 이 분야에서 정말로 어떤 것이 네 상상력을 자극했는지 알려주도록 해.

S 알겠습니다. 그러니까 좀 더… 개인적인 내용이 되어야 한다는 말씀이죠? 그래도 괜찮을까요?

P 그렇단다. 그들은 그런 걸 원하지. 도가 지나칠까봐 염려하는 것 같은데…

S 그렇습니다.

P 하지만 중요한 건 너의 열정이 얼마나 강하고 이 분야에 대한 너의 개인적인 동기가 무엇인지를 보여줘야 한다는 거야.

S 알겠습니다.

P 그리고 이 부분은 빼야겠구나. 그리고, 또 추가로 약간의… 이번이 네게는 유일한 기회이므로, 학부 시절의 특기 사항에 대해 설명을 추가하는 것이 좋겠다. 그러니까

you know, the music program; what you got from that; why you decided to change. I mean it's kind of unusual to go from music to geology, right?

S Yeah. I was... I was afraid that, you know, maybe the personal-type stuff wouldn't be what they wanted, but...

P No, in fact it's... um, give an example: I... I had a friend, when I was an undergrad, um, went to medical school. And he put on his med school application—and he could actually tell if somebody actually read it 'cause, um, he had asthma and the reason that he wanted to go to med school was he said he wanted to do sports medicine because he, you know, he had this real interest. He was an athlete too, and... and wanted to help athletes who had this physical problem. And he could always tell if somebody actually read his letter, because they would always ask him about that.

S ...Mmm... so something unique.

P Yeah. So see, you know, that's what's good and, and, I think for you probably, you know, your music background's the most unique thing that you've got in your record.

S Right.

P ...Mmm... so you see, you gotta make yourself stand out from a coupla hundred applications. Does that help any?

S Yeah, it does. It gives me some good ideas.

P And... what you might also do too is, you know, uh, you might get a friend to proof it or something at some point.

S Oh, sure... sure.

P Also, think about presentation—how the application looks. In a way, you're actually showing some other skills here, like organization. A lot of stuff that's... that they're not... they're not formally asking for, they're looking at. So your presentation format, your grammar, all that stuff, they're looking at in your materials at the same time.

S Right. OK.

음악 과정을 어떻게 밟아왔는지에 대해서 말이야. 그 과정을 통해 배운 것은 무엇이고 왜 전공을 바꾸려고 결심했는지도 덧붙일 필요가 있지. 음악에서 지질학으로 전공을 바꾸는 건 흔한 경우는 아니니까 말이야.

S 네. 저는… 저는 그들이 사적인 내용을 중심으로 기술하는 방식을 원하지 않을 거라고 생각했어요. 하지만…

P 아니, 사실은… 예를 들어보자. 내가 학부 시절에 사귄 친구 하나는 의과대학에 들어갔어. 그는 의과대학에 입학 지원서를 냈어. 그리고 그는 누군가가 지원서를 정말 읽었는지, 아니면 안 읽었는지 확실히 알 수 있었어. 왜냐하면 그는 천식이 있었는데, 자신이 의과대학에 들어가길 원했던 이유가 스포츠 의학에 관심이 많기 때문이라고 했거든. 그 친구는 운동선수이기도 했어. 그리고 신체적인 결함을 지닌 운동선수들을 돕고 싶다고 했지. 그는 누군가가 자신의 지원서를 정말 읽어봤는지 알 수 있었어. 왜냐하면 읽어 본 사람들은 항상 천식에 대해 물어봤으니까.

S 음… 그렇게 특이한 사항 말이죠.

P 그래. 그런 게 효과적이야. 그리고 내 생각에는 네 경우는 음악을 했다는 것이 가장 특이한 배경인 것 같다.

S 맞아요.

P 음… 너는 수백 개의 지원서들 가운데 자신을 부각시켜야만 하는 거야. 그게 도움이 되지 않겠니?

S 네, 그럴 것 같습니다. 듣고 보니 좋은 생각이 떠오르네요.

P 그리고… 또 할 수 있는 것은 어떤 시점에서 그런 사항들을 검증해 줄 친구의 도움을 받을 수도 있을 거야.

S 아, 네…

P 또 발표를 생각해 봐. 지원서를 잘 보여 주기 위한 방식 말이지. 어떤 점에서 너는 이것을 통해 다른 능력들도 보여 주고 있는 셈이야. 이를테면 짜임새 있게 글을 구성하는 능력 같은 거 말이야. 여러 가지 능력들… 그들이 정식으로 요구하지 않지만 주목하고 있는 능력들이 있거든. 그들은 네가 제출한 자료를 통해 제시하는 형식이나 문법 등도 관찰하고 있단다.

S 잘 알겠습니다.

어휘

statement of purpose 학업계획서 specify 자세한 설명을 하다 expand on ~에 대해 상술하다 critical 중요한 let oneself come through 자신을 충분히 설명하다 motivation 동기부여 geology 지질학, 지질 go overboard 도를 넘다 undergrad 학부생 medical[med] school 의과 대학 asthma 천식 sports medicine 스포츠 의학 athlete 운동선수 stand out 부각되다 proof 증명하다 presentation 발표, 제출

1. 학생은 왜 교수를 만나러 갔는가?

Ⓐ 대학원 인터뷰를 준비하기 위해

Ⓑ 대학원 입학지원서에 대해 조언을 얻기 위해

Ⓒ 교수에게 자신의 대학원 입학지원서를 주기 위해

Ⓓ 대학원 입학이 허용되었는지 알아보기 위해

내용의 목적을 묻는 문제

어휘 graduate school 대학원 　accept (대학, 클럽 등에서) 정식으로 받아들이다

해설 학생은 대학원 입학지원서를 쓰는 방법에 관해 조언을 얻으려고 한다. 교수가 이미 학생의 입학지원서를 읽어본 후 나누는 대화임에 유의해야 한다. 정답은 보기 B.

2. 교수의 말에 따르면, 학생은 학업계획서에 어떤 정보를 포함시켜야 하는가?
두 개의 답을 선택하라.

Ⓐ 자신의 학문적인 동기

Ⓑ 의학을 공부한 배경

Ⓒ 개인적인 정보

Ⓓ 그녀의 교수들이 끼친 영향

세부 정보 찾기 문제

어휘 academic 학구적인 　motivation 동기 부여 　background (사람의) 배경, 경력 　influence 영향을 끼치다

해설 교수는 학업계획서에 포함시켜야 할 두 가지 사항을 강조하고 있다. 하나는 대학원 공부에 관심을 두게 된 동기이고, 다른 하나는 개인적인 배경이다. 따라서 정답은 보기 A, C.

3. 교수는 학생의 배경에 대해 무엇이 특이하다고 생각하는가?

Ⓐ 그녀의 일 경험

Ⓑ 그녀의 창의적인 글쓰기 경험

Ⓒ 그녀의 운동선수로서의 성과

Ⓓ 그녀의 음악 공부

세부 정보 찾기 문제

어휘 athletic 체육의, (운동) 경기의 　achievement 달성, 업적

해설 교수는 학생이 전공을 음악에서 지질학으로 바꾸게 된 것이 특이한 사항이라고 언급하고 있다. 따라서 정답은 보기 D.

4. 교수는 왜 의과대학에 간 자신의 친구 이야기를 하는가?

Ⓐ 학생에게 대학원이 얼마나 힘든지 주의를 주기 위해

Ⓑ 자신의 주장을 설명하기 위해

Ⓒ 학생이 쉴 수 있도록 도와주기 위해

Ⓓ 주제를 바꾸기 위해

의도 파악 문제

어휘 medical school 의과대학

해설 교수는 좋은 입학지원서에는 개인적인 정보가 담겨 있어야 한다는 점을 강조하기 위해 자신의 친구를 예로 들었다. 따라서 정답은 보기 B.

5. 교수가 대학원 입학을 허가하는 사람들에 대해 암시하는 것은?

Ⓐ 그들은 지원자들의 분야에 대해 전문지식이 부족하다.

Ⓑ 그들은 대개 학업계획서를 읽지 않는다.

Ⓒ 그들은 지원서의 겉모습에 의해 영향을 받는다.

Ⓓ 그들은 접수한 지원서들의 대부분을 기억한다.

추론 문제

어휘 lack 부족, 결핍 　appearance 외관, 출현

해설 교수는 마지막에 입학지원서와 학업계획서의 형식도 중요하다는 것을 설명하고 있다. 예를 들면 지원서의 형식은 짜임새 있게 구성하는 능력을 드러낼 수 있으며 오류 없는 문장은 꼼꼼한 자질을 보여 주는 것이라고 암시한다. 이런 것들은 모두 지원서의 겉모습에 해당한다. 따라서 정답은 보기 C.

Question 6-11   p. 158

N Narrator   P Professor   M Male Student   F Female Student

Script

N Listen to part of a talk in an environmental science class.

P So I wanted to discuss a few other terms here... actually, some, uh, some ideas about how we manage our resources.

Let's talk about what that... what that means. If we take a resource like water... well, maybe we should get a little bit more specific here—back up from the more general case—and talk about underground water in particular.

So hydrogeologists have tried to figure out... how much water can you take out from underground sources? This has been an important question. Let me ask you guys: how much water, based on what you know so far, could you take out of, say, an aquifer... under the city?

M As... as much as would get recharged?

P OK. So we wouldn't want to take out any more than naturally comes into it. The implication is that, uh, well, if you only take as much out as comes in, you're not gonna deplete the amount of water that's stored in there, right?

Wrong, but that's the principle. That's the idea behind how we manage our water supplies. It's called "safe yield." Basically what this method says is that you can pump as much water out of a system as naturally recharges... as naturally flows back in.

So this principle of safe yield—it's based on balancing what we take out with what gets recharged. But what it does is, it ignores how much water naturally comes out of the system.

In a natural system, a certain amount of recharge comes in and a certain amount of water naturally flows out through springs, streams, and lakes. And over the long term the amount that's stored in the aquifer doesn't really change much. It's balanced. Now humans come in... and start taking water out of the system. How have we changed the equation?

F It's not balanced anymore?

P Right. We take water out, but water also naturally flows out. And the recharge rate doesn't change, so the result is we've reduced the amount of water that's stored in the underground system.

If you keep doing that long enough—if you pump as much water out as naturally comes in—gradually the underground water levels drop. And when that happens, that can affect surface water. How? Well, in underground systems there are natural discharge points—places where the water flows out of the underground systems, out to lakes and streams. Well, a drop in the water level can mean those discharge points will eventually

N 환경학 수업 내용의 일부를 들으시오.

P 나는 여기서 몇 가지 다른 용어들을 논의해 보고자 하는데… 자원을 관리하는 방법과 관련 있는 몇몇 개념들에 대해서 말이죠.

그게 무슨… 무슨 의미인지 얘기해 봅시다. 물과 같은 자원을 예로 들자면… 여기서는 일반적인 사례에서 한발 물러나 좀 더 구체적으로 살펴봐야겠군요. 특히 지하수 문제에 대해서만 논의해 봅시다.

수문지질학자들은 지하에서 우리가 얼마나 많은 물을 끌어 쓸 수 있는가를 밝혀내려고 했습니다. 이것은 중요한 문제인데요. 여러분에게 질문을 하나 해 보죠. 여러분의 상식으로는 이 도시의 지하 대수층에서 얼마나 많은 양의 물을 끌어올릴 수 있다고 생각합니까?

M 보충되는 만큼 아닌가요?

P 좋습니다. 우리는 자연적으로 유입되는 양 이상의 물을 끌어올리려고 하지 않을 것입니다. 유입되는 양만큼만 끌어올린다면, 지하에 저장된 물의 양이 고갈되지 않는다는 뜻이겠죠. 그렇죠?

틀렸습니다만, 그것이 원칙이기도 합니다. 이 원칙이 바로 물 공급량을 관리하는 방법을 뒷받침하는 개념입니다. 이것을 '안전채수량'이라고 합니다. 기본적으로 이 방식은 자연적으로 보충되는 만큼, 즉 자연적으로 유입되는 만큼 물을 퍼 올릴 수 있다는 것입니다. 안전채수량의 원칙은 물의 보충량과 채수량의 균형을 맞추는 것입니다. 하지만 이 원칙은 지하수로부터 자연적으로 빠져나가는 물의 양을 고려하지 않고 있습니다.

자연계에서는 어느 정도의 수량은 보충되고 어느 정도의 수량은 샘이나 강, 호수를 통해 자연적으로 배출됩니다. 그리고 장기간에 걸쳐 대수층에 저장된 수량은 크게 변하지 않습니다. 균형이 맞춰져 있지요. 그런데 인간이 개입하여 물을 끌어 쓰기 시작했습니다. 우리가 그런 평형 상태를 어떻게 변화시켰을까요?

F 이제는 균형을 잃지 않았나요?

P 그렇습니다. 우리가 물을 끌어내지만, 물은 자연적으로 밖으로 빠져나가기도 합니다. 수량이 보충되는 비율은 변하지 않기 때문에 우리는 결국 지하수계에 저장되어 있는 물의 양을 감소시켰습니다.

그런 일이 오랫동안 계속되다 보면, 즉 자연적으로 유입되는 양만큼 퍼 올리게 되면, 점차 지하수면이 낮아집니다. 그리고 그런 일이 발생하면 지표수에도 영향을 미칠 수 있습니다. 어떻게 그렇게 될까요? 지하수계에는 자연적인 배출 지점이 있습니다. 즉 물이 지하수계에서 밖으로 나와 호

Reading
Listening
Speaking
Writing
Test 1
Test 2
Test 3
Test 4

dry up. That means water's not getting to lakes and streams that depend on it. So we've ended up reducing the surface water supply, too.

You know, in the state of Arizona we're managing some major water supplies with this principle of safe yield, under a method that will eventually dry up the natural discharge points of those aquifer systems.

Now, why is this an issue? Well, aren't some of you going to want to live in this state for a while? Want your kids to grow up here, and your kids' kids? You might be concerned with... does Arizona have a water supply which is sustainable—key word here? What that means... the general definition of *sustainable* is will there be enough to meet the needs of the present without compromising the ability of the future to have the availability... to have the same resources?

Now, I hope you see that these two ideas are incompatible: sustainability and safe yield. Because what sustainability means is that it's sustainable for all systems dependent on the water—for the people that use it and for... uh, for supplying water to the dependent lakes and streams.

So, I'm gonna repeat this: so if we're using a safe-yield method, if we're only balancing what we take out with what gets recharged, but—don't forget, water's also flowing out naturally—then the amount stored underground is gonna gradually get reduced and that's gonna lead to another problem. These discharge points—where the water flows out to the lakes and streams—they're gonna dry up. OK.

수나 강으로 흘러가는 지점 말입니다. 지하수면이 낮아진다는 것은 결국 배출 지점의 물이 고갈될 수 있음을 의미합니다. 이는 지하수에 의존하는 호수나 강으로 물이 흘러 들어가지 못한다는 것을 뜻하죠. 이렇게 해서 우리는 결국 지표수 공급량도 감소시키게 된 것이죠.

애리조나 주에서는 안전채수량의 원칙에 따라 일부 주요 장소의 물 공급량을 관리하고 있습니다. 궁극적으로 대수층의 자연적인 배출 지점을 고갈시키게 될 방식으로 말이죠.

이것이 왜 문제가 될까요? 여러분은 앞으로 얼마 동안 이 주에 살려고 하지 않겠습니까? 여러분의 자녀, 여러분의 자손들이 여기서 성장하길 원합니까? 여러분의 관심은… 애리조나는 지속 가능한 물 공급 정책을 갖고 있을까요? 여기서 '지속 가능한'이란 단어가 핵심어입니다. 그 의미는… '지속 가능한'의 일반적 정의는, 현재의 수요를 충족하면서 미래의 자원 확보 능력, 똑같은 양을 확보할 수 있는 능력을 떨어뜨리지 않는 것입니다.

지속 가능성과 안전채수량, 이 두 개념은 서로 양립할 수 없음을 이해하기 바랍니다. 왜냐하면 지속 가능성이란 바로 물에 의존하는 모든 시스템들과 물을 이용하는 사람들에게 지속 가능한 것이고… 그리고 지하수에 의존하는 호수나 강에 물 공급이 지속 가능하다는 의미이기 때문입니다.

따라서 나는 또 다시 이 점을 강조하고자 합니다. 우리가 안전채수량 방식을 사용하고자 한다면, 채수량과 보충량의 균형을 맞추고자 하다면, 잊지 말아야 할 것이 있습니다. 물은 밖으로도 자연적으로 빠져나가며 지하에 저장된 물의 양이 점차 감소되어 결국 또 다른 문제를 발생시킨다는 점입니다. 물이 호수나 강으로 흘러나가는 배출 지점이 고갈될 것입니다.

어휘

environmental science 환경학 hydrogeologist 수문지질학자 aquifer (지질) 지하 대수층: 지하수를 간직한 다공질 삼투성 지층 recharged 보충되는, 재충전되는 deplete 고갈시키다, 격감시키다 principle 원칙, 원리 safe yield 안전채수량 discharge point 배출지점 dry up 고갈되다 be concerned with ~에 관계가 있다 compromising 위태롭게 하는, 명예를 손상시키는 availability 이용할 수 있음, 이용 가능한 것 incompatible 양립할 수 없는 sustainability 지속 가능성 flow out 흘러나가다 reduce 줄이다, 감소시키다

6. 이 강의의 주제는 무엇인가?

Ⓐ 물 공급을 관리하는 일반적인 방법

Ⓑ 지하수계의 구성

Ⓒ 물 공급을 재개하는 자연적 과정

Ⓓ 지하수계의 청정 상태를 유지하기

내용의 요점을 묻는 문제

어휘 formation 형성, 구성 underground 지하의, 지하 maintain 유지하다 purity 청결, 맑음

해설 강의 시작 부분을 잘 들어보면 교수는 천연자원을 관리하는 방법에 대해 논하고 있으며, 천연자원의 하나로 지하수를 예로 들고 있다. 그리고 계속해서 '안전채수량' 이라는 지하수 관리법을 집중적으로 살펴보고 있다. 따라서 정답은 보기 A.

7. '안전채수량' 방식에 대한 교수의 관점은?

Ⓐ 그것은 환경을 보존하는 데 기여했다.

Ⓑ 그것은 애리조나 주 이외의 주에서도 연구되어야 한다.

Ⓒ 그것은 효과적인 자원 정책이 아니다.

Ⓓ 그것은 사람들이 물을 사용하는 여러 방식들을 고려하지 않는다.

태도 파악 문제

해설 안전채수량 방식은 결코 안전하지 않다고 교수는 지적한다. 이 방식에는 지하수계에서 인간이 퍼 올리는 물 이외에 자연적으로 빠져나가는 물도 있다는 사실이 반영되지 않았기 때문이다. 따라서 정답은 보기 C.

8. 교수에 따르면, 지하수계에서 물을 빼내는 것과 관련된 두 가지 문제점은?

두 개의 답을 선택하라.

Ⓐ 오염물질이 더욱 빠르게 물에 침투할 수 있다.

Ⓑ 표면이 말라서 갈라질 수 있다.

Ⓒ 지하수계에 저장된 물의 양이 감소할 수 있다.

Ⓓ 지하수에 의존하는 강과 샘이 고갈될 수 있다.

세부 정보 찾기 문제

어휘 pollutant 오염, 오염 물질 store 저장하다 dependent 의지하는, ~에 좌우되는

해설 모든 보기들이 지하수 감소로 발생하는 결과가 될 수 있지만, 이 강의에는 C, D에 대해서만 논하고 있다.

9. 지속 가능한 물 공급 시스템의 주요 특징은?

Ⓐ 단기 및 장기 수요를 충족할 수 있다.

Ⓑ 환경 조건의 변화에 영향을 받지 않는다.

Ⓒ 대개 호수, 샘, 강에서 발원된다.

Ⓓ 인간의 수요를 충족하기 위해 이용되지 않는다.

세부 정보 찾기 문제

어휘 short-term 단기간의 long-term 장기간의 originate 유래하다, 시작하다

해설 교수는 '지속 가능성' 이란 현재의 수요는 물론이고, 미래의 수요를 충족할 수 있는 것이라고 정의한다. 이는 보기 A의 단기 및 장기 수요를 충족할 수 있다는 것과 같은 의미다.

10. 교수가 '안전채수량' 방식으로 관리되는 물 공급 시스템에 대해 암시하는 것은?

Ⓐ 빠른 속도로 보충된다.

Ⓑ 지속 가능하지 않다.

Ⓒ 대규모 저장 지대가 있어야 한다.

Ⓓ 수질이 좋지 않은 물을 공급한다.

추론 문제

어휘 recharge 재충전 sustainable 유지할 수 있는, 지탱할 수 있는 storage 저장, 창고

해설 교수는 지속 가능성과 안전채수량이라는 두 개념이 양립할 수 없다고 지적하고 있다. 즉 안전채수량 방식에 의한 물 공급은 지속 가능하지 않다. 따라서 정답은 보기 B.

11. 강의의 일부를 다시 듣고 질문에 답하라.

🎧 T-13

> N *Why does the professor say this?*
> P Now, why is this an issue? Well, aren't some of you going to want to live in this state for a while? Want your kids to grow up here, and your kids' kids?

Ⓐ 학생들이 이 사안에 익숙한지 알아내기 위해

Ⓑ 논의할 새 문제를 소개하기 위해

Ⓒ 한 학생의 질문에 답하기 위해

Ⓓ 그 사안에 대한 학생들의 관심을 촉구하기 위해

의도 파악 문제

해설 교수는 장차 지하수 고갈로 심각한 문제가 발생할 수 있다는 점을 강조하면서, 학생들이 애리조나 주의 미래에 대해 생각해 볼 것을 촉구하고 있다. 따라서 정답은 보기 D.

Questions 12-16   p. 160

N Narrator   M Male Student   F Female Student

Script

N Listen to part of a conversation between two students. The woman is helping the man review for a biology examination.

M OK, so... what do you think we should go over next?

F How about if we go over this stuff about how bacteria become resistant to antibiotics.

M OK.

F Um, but first of all, though, how many pages do we have left? I told my roommate I'd meet her at the library at seven o'clock.

M Ummm... There's only a few pages left. We should be finished in a few minutes.

F OK. So, ummm...

M About how bacteria become resistant to antibiotics.

F Oh yeah, OK. So you know that some bacteria cells are able to resist the drugs we use against them, and that's because they have these special genes that, like, protect them from the drugs.

M Right. If I remember correctly, I think the genes, like... weaken the antibiotics, or, like... stop the antibiotics from getting into the bacteria cell, something like that?

F Exactly. So when bacteria have these genes, it's very difficult for the antibiotics to kill the bacteria.

M Right.

F So do you remember what those genes are called?

M Umm...

F Resistance genes.

M Resistance genes. Right. Resistance genes. OK.

F And that makes sense, right? Because they help the bacteria resist the antibiotics.

M Yeah, that makes sense. OK.

F OK. But the question is: how do bacteria get the resistance genes?

M How do they get the resistance genes? They just inherit them from the parent cell, right?

F OK, yeah, that's true. They can inherit them from the parent cell, but that's not what I'm talking about.

M OK.

F I'm talking about how they get resistance genes from other cells in their environment, you know, from the other cells around them.

M Oh, I see what you mean. Umm, is that that stuff about "hopping genes," or something like that?

F Right. Although actually they're called "jumping genes," not "hopping genes."

M Oh, OK. Jumping genes.

N 두 학생이 주고받는 대화의 일부를 들으시오. 여학생은 남학생의 생물학 시험 준비를 도와주고 있다.

M 좋아, 그럼... 다음 무슨 내용을 볼까?

F 박테리아가 항생제에 대해 내성을 갖게 되는 과정에 대해 알아볼까?

M 그래.

F 음, 우선 지금 몇 페이지나 남았니? 7시에 도서관에서 룸메이트를 만나기로 했거든.

M 음… 몇 페이지 안 남았는데. 몇 분 안에 끝낼 수 있을 거 같아.

F 좋아. 그럼…

M 박테리아가 항생제에 대해 어떻게 내성을 갖게 되는가 알아보자구.

F 그래 좋아. 어떤 박테리아 세포는 우리가 사용하는 약에 대해 견뎌낼 수 있어. 이것은 그것들이 특별한 유전자를 갖고 있어서 약으로부터 보호를 받기 때문이야.

M 그래. 내 기억이 맞는다면, 그런 유전자는 항생제를 약화시키거나, 또는… 항생제가 박테리아 세포로 침투하는 걸 막아준다지 아마?

F 맞아. 그래서 박테리아이 이런 유전자를 가지고 있으면 항생제가 박테리아를 죽이기가 매우 어렵다는 거야.

M 그래.

F 그런 유전자를 뭐라고 부르는지 기억나니?

M 음…

F 내성 유전자.

M 내성 유전자. 맞다. 내성 유전자. 좋아.

F 이해가 되지? 그런 유전자 때문에 박테리아가 항생제에 견뎌낼 수 있으니까 말이야.

M 그래, 이해가 된다. 됐어.

F 좋아. 그렇다면 다음 질문은 이거야. 박테리아가 어떻게 내성 유전자를 갖게 되었을까?

M 박테리아가 어떻게 내성 유전자를 갖게 되었냐구? 그야 모세포로부터 물려받은 거 아냐?

F 그래, 맞아. 모세포로부터 물려받은 거야. 하지만 내가 말하려는 건 그게 아냐.

M 그래.

F 그들이 주변 환경의 다른 세포들로부터 내성 유전자를 얻게 된 과정에 대해 말하려는 거야.

M 아, 네가 뭘 말하려는지 알겠다. '호핑 유전자' 같은 걸 말하는 거지?

F 맞아. 사실은 '호핑 유전자' 아니라 '점핑 유전자' 라는 이름으로 부르기는 하지만 말이야.

Reading

Listening

Speaking

Writing

Test 1

Test 2

Test 3

Test 4

F Yeah, but they have another name, too, that I can't think of. Umm ... lemme see if I can find it here in the book...

M I think it's probably on...

F Oh, OK. Here it is. Transposons. That's what they're called.

M Lemme see. OK. Trans... po... sons... trans... posons. So "transposon" is another name for a jumping gene?

F Right. And these transposons are, you know, like, little bits of DNA that are able to move from one cell to another. That's why they're called "jumping genes." They kind of, you know, "jump" from one cell to another.

M OK.

F And these transposons are how resistance genes are able to get from one bacteria cell to another bacteria cell. What happens is that a resistance gene from one cell attaches itself to a transposon and then, when the transposon jumps to another cell...

M The other cell gets the resistance gene and...

F Right.

M That's how it becomes resistant to antibiotics.

F Right.

M Wow. That's really cool. So that's how it happens.

F That's how it happens.

M 아, 그래. 점핑 유전자.

F 그래, 하지만 또 다른 이름이 있는데 생각이 안 나네. 뭐더라… 여기 책에서 한번 찾아봐야겠다.

M 내 생각에 그건 아마…

F 아, 그래. 여기 있다. 트랜스포존. 이런 이름으로도 불리지.

M 어디 보자. 트랜스…포…존…트랜스…포존. 트랜스포존이 점핑 유전자의 또 다른 이름이라고?

F 그래. 트랜스포존은 한 세포에서 다른 세포로 이동할 수 있는 DNA 조각 같은 거야. 그래서 '점핑 유전자'라는 이름이 붙은 거고. 한 세포에서 다른 세포로 점프한다는 의미지.

M 그렇구나.

F 이 트랜스포존을 통해서 내성 유전자가 하나의 박테리아 세포에서 다른 박테리아 세포로 전파되는 거야. 그런 일이 어떻게 일어나느냐 하면, 한 세포의 내성 유전자가 트랜스포존에 붙은 후에 트랜스포존이 또 다른 세포로 점프하면…

M 다른 세포가 내성 유전자를 얻게 된다는 거지. 그리고…

F 맞아.

M 그래서 항생제에 견뎌낼 수 있는 거구나.

F 그렇지.

M 야. 정말 기막히네. 그래서 그렇게 된 거구나.

F 그래서 그렇게 된 거지.

| 어휘 |

biology 생물학   go over 살펴보다(review), 복습하다   resistant 내성의, 저항력이 있는   antibiotics 항생제, 항생물질   gene 유전자   weaken 묽게 하다, 약해지다   get into 침투하다   resistance gene 내성유전자   resistance 저항, 반대   inherit 물려받다, 상속하다   parent cell 모세포   jumping gene 점핑 유전자   transposon 트랜스포존(움직이는 유전자로 염색체상의 어떤 위치에서 임의의 다른 위치로 자유로이 이동하는 DNA 단위)   cool 신기한, 멋진

12. 학생들은 주로 무엇에 대해 이야기를 나누고 있는가?

Ⓐ 인체에 해로운 약품

Ⓑ 항생제를 만들어내는 박테리아

Ⓒ 운동 능력과 관련 있는 DNA

Ⓓ 박테리아를 항생제로부터 보호하는 유전자

내용의 요점을 묻는 문제

어휘 harmful 유해한   antibiotic 항생의   be related to ~와 관련되어 있다   performance 달성, 실행

해설 남학생은 여학생과의 대화를 통해 박테리아가 항생제에 대해 어떻게 내성을 갖게 되었는지를 공부하고 있다. 그리고 그 원인인 내성 유전자에 대해 논하고 있다. 따라서 정답은 보기 D.

13. 이 대화에 따르면, 왜 트랜스포존을 때때로 '점핑 유전자'라고 부르는가?

Ⓐ 하나의 박테리아 세포에서 다른 박테리아 세포로 이동할 수 있기 때문에

Ⓑ 점프 능력이 매우 뛰어난 사람들에게서 발견되기 때문에

Ⓒ 박테리아에서 한 세대 걸러 나타나기 때문에

Ⓓ 움직임이 빠르고 예측하기 어렵기 때문에

세부 정보 찾기 문제

어휘 cell (생물) 세포   exceptional 예외적인, 특별한   rapid 빠른   unpredictable 예측할 수 없는

해설 대화에서 여학생은 그 유전자가 한 세포에서 다른 세포로 건너뛴다는 사실을 두 차례에 걸쳐 밝히고 있다. 정답은 보기 A.

14. 이 대화에 따르면, 박테리아 세포가 내성 유전자를 얻는 두 가지 방법은 무엇인가?

두 개의 답을 선택하라.

Ⓐ 내성 유전자는 인근 세포로부터 운반된다.

Ⓑ 내성 유전자가 백혈구 세포에 의해 운반된다.

Ⓒ 내성 유전자는 모세포로부터 유전된다.

Ⓓ 내성 유전자는 항생제에 의해 운반된다.

세부 정보 찾기 문제

어휘 carry 운반하다

해설 두 학생은 내성 유전자가 모세포로부터 유전된다는 사실을 간단히 언급한 후, 트랜스포존을 통해 주변의 다른 세포로부터도 얻는 과정에 대해서 자세히 논하고 있다. 따라서 정답은 보기 A, C.

15. 이 대화에서 논의된 내성 유전자에 대해 추론할 수 있는 것은?

Ⓐ 그것은 모든 박테리아 세포에서 발견된다.

Ⓑ 그것은 항생제에 견뎌낼 수 없다.

Ⓒ 그것은 박테리아 질병 치료를 더욱 어렵게 만든다.

Ⓓ 그것은 박테리아에 대한 신체의 방어 능력에 필수적이다.

추론 문제

어휘 treatment 치료, 취급 (방법)   essential 본질적인

해설 두 학생은 어떤 박테리아는 항생제에 내성이 있으며, 내성 유전자가 항생제를 약화시키고 저지한다는 이야기를 나누고 있다. 이것은 박테리아로 인한 질병 치료가 쉽지 않다는 사실을 암시하는 것이다. 따라서 정답은 보기 C.

16. 대화의 일부를 다시 듣고 질문에 답하라.

🎧 T-15

N *Why does the woman say this?*
F Um, but first of all, though, how many pages do we have left? I told my roommate I'd meet her at the library at seven o'clock.

Ⓐ 남자가 숙제를 했는지 알아보기 위해

Ⓑ 도서관이 문을 열었는지 알아봐 달라고 남자에게 부탁하기 위해

Ⓒ 그녀가 오랫동안 공부를 할 수 없다고 남자에게 알려주기 위해

Ⓓ 남자가 그녀의 룸메이트를 만난 적이 있는지 물어보기 위해

의도 파악 문제

어휘 assignment 과제, 할당

해설 여학생이 이 이야기를 한 것은 룸메이트와의 약속 시간 때문에 오래 머물 수 없다는 사실을 밝힌 것이다. 따라서 정답은 보기 C.

Questions 17-22　　　　　　　　　　　p. 162

N Narrator　P Professor　M Male Student　F Female Student

Script

N Listen to part of a talk in a botany class.

P OK. So we've talked about some different types of root systems of plants, and I've shown you some pretty cool slides, but now I want to talk about the extent of the root system—the overall size of the root system... the depth. I want to tell you about one particular experiment. I think you're going to find this pretty amazing. OK. So there was this scientist... this very meticulous scientist decided that the best place to see a whole root system—to actually see how big the entire system got—the best place would be to grow it... where?

F Um, water?

P In water. So he took rye plants—it was rye plants—and he started growing them in water. Now, you've all heard of growing stuff in water before, right?

M It's done commercially, right? Uh, like to grow vegetables and flowers?

P Right. They grow all kinds of commercial crops in water. So if you're growing things in water, you can add the fertilizer. What do you need to do to that water besides put fertilizer in it? Anyone ever actually tried to grow plants in water? You must bubble water through it. Bubble gas through it. I'm sorry, you must bubble gas through it. So, gas, you have to bubble through. Think about the soil we talked about last week, about growing plants in soil. Think about some of you who have killed your favorite houseplants, 'cause you loved them too much. If you overwater, why do your favorite houseplants die?

F Oh, no oxygen.

P Not enough oxygen for the roots... which do what twenty-four hours a day in all seasons?

F Respiration?

P Respire... respiration... they breathe. So if you just stick rye plants in water, it doesn't make a difference how much fertilizer you add, you also need to bubble gas through the water, so they have access to that oxygen. If they don't have that, they're in big trouble. OK. So this guy—this scientist—grew a rye plant in water so he could see the root system, how big it got—its surface area. I read about this and the book said one thousand kilometers of roots. I kept thinking: this has to be a mistake. It just doesn't make any sense to me that... that... that could be right. But that's what all the books have, and no one's ever corrected it. So let me explain to you about this rye plant. If you take a little seed of many grasses—and remember rye is a grass; if you take a tiny little seed and you germinate it— actually, take one of my least favorite grasses that starts growing about May. What's my least favorite grass that starts

N 식물학 강의의 일부를 들으시오.

P 자, 우리는 다양한 종류의 식물 뿌리 조직에 대해 이야기를 나눠보았고, 근사한 슬라이드도 보았습니다. 하지만 이제 뿌리 조직의 범위, 즉 뿌리 조직의 전체적인 규모… 그 깊이에 대해 알아 봅시다. 나는 여러분에게 한 가지 특이한 실험을 소개하고자 합니다. 이 실험이 대단히 흥미롭다고 생각할 겁니다. 이 실험을 실시한 과학자는… 매우 꼼꼼했던 이 과학자는 뿌리 조직의 전체 모습을 볼 수 있는 가장 좋은 장소, 즉 실제로 그 규모를 파악할 수 있는 장소는 뿌리를 키울 수 있는 가장 좋은 장소라고 생각했는데… 그게 어디일까요?

F 물이요?

P 물속입니다. 그래서 그는 호밀을 택했어요. 호밀을 물속에서 키우기 시작했어요. 여러분 모두 수경재배에 대해 들어본 적이 있을 겁니다. 그렇죠?

M 그건 상업적으로 재배하는 방식이죠? 채소나 꽃 같은 거 말예요?

P 맞습니다. 사람들은 각종 상업 작물을 수경재배하지요. 물속에서 작물을 키울 때는 비료를 첨가할 수도 있습니다. 비료를 넣는 것 외에 어떤 조치가 필요할까요? 실제로 물에서 식물을 키워 본 사람 있습니까? 물을 거품으로 만들어야 합니다. 물속에 가스 거품이요. 미안합니다, 물속에 가스 거품을 만들어줘야 합니다. 가스를 거품으로 분출시켜야 하는 것입니다. 지난주에 우리가 살펴본 토양과, 토양에서 식물을 키우는 것에 대해 나눴던 이야기를 생각해 보세요. 여러분 중에는 아끼는 실내 화초를 지나치게 좋아해서 죽여 버린 사람들도 있었지요. 물을 지나치게 주면 왜 아끼는 화초가 죽을까요?

F 예, 산소 부족 때문입니다.

P 사시사철 하루 24시간 내내 뭔가를 하고 있는… 뿌리에 충분한 산소가 공급되지 못하기 때문입니다. 뿌리는 내내 뭘 하고 있을까요?

F 호흡이요?

P 호흡하죠… 호흡… 뿌리는 숨을 쉽니다. 물속에 호밀을 꽂아 놓으면 첨가하는 비료의 양은 그리 중요하지 않습니다. 그 외에도 물속에 거품을 만들어서 산소를 공급해 줘야 합니다. 산소를 공급 받지 못하면 심각한 문제가 발생합니다. 내가 언급한 그 사람, 그 과학자는 호밀을 물속에 넣고 재배하여 뿌리 조직의 규모가 얼마나 큰지 그 표면적을 알아봤습니다. 나는 이 실험과 관련된 책을 읽었는데, 거기에는 뿌리가 1000km나 된다고 나와 있습니다. 아무리 생각해 봐도 그건 잘못된 것이라고 생각했어요. 도저히 말이 안 되는 얘기였어요. 하지만 모든 책마다 그렇게 나와 있었고, 누구도 그것을 수정한 적이 없었어요. 자, 이 호밀에 대해서 설명해 볼게요. 다양한 종류의 풀의 작은 씨앗을 가지고 - 호밀도

growing about May?

M Crabgrass.

P Crabgrass.

Remember how I showed you in the lab, one little seed starts out producing one little shoot. Then at a week or so later you've got about six shoots, and then, three weeks later you've got about fifteen shoots coming out all directions like this — all those little shoots up there? Well, that's what they did with the rye. And the little seedling started and pretty soon there were several shoots, and then more shoots. In the end, that one single seed produced eighty shoots, with an average of fifty centimeters of height... from one seed. Eighty shoots coming out, average fifty centimeters high. When they looked at the shoot versus the root surface, they found that the shoot surface, with all of its leaves, had a total surface area of about five square meters. Now, here's the biggie, when they looked at the root surface area, you would expect that the root and the shoot would be in balance, right? So they should be pretty close in terms of surface area, right?

M Uh-un.

P What's that? Did somebody say "no?" Well, you're absolutely correct. Instead of five square meters, the root system was found to have more than two hundred square meters of surface area. Where did all of that extra surface area come from? Who did it? Who was responsible for all those extra square meters of surface area? What did roots do to increase their surface area?

F Root hairs.

P Root hairs, that's exactly it. So those root hairs were responsible for an incredible chunk of surface area. They constantly have to be spread out in the water so they can absorb minerals from the fertilizer, and of course they need oxygen access as well.

풀의 일종임을 잊지 마세요. 그 작은 씨앗을 가지고 발아시켜 보세요. 구체적으로, 5월경에 자라기 시작하는데 내가 가장 싫어하는 풀의 씨앗을 가지고 해 보세요. 5월에 자라기 시작하며 내가 가장 싫어하는 풀이 뭔지 아세요?

M 왕바랭이요.

P 왕바랭이.

실험실에서 내가 여러분에게 보여 준 거 기억납니까? 자그마한 씨앗에서 작은 줄기가 나오기 시작했잖아요. 일주일 정도 지나자 줄기가 6개나 되었지요. 그리고 3주 후에는 사방에서 15개의 줄기가 이처럼 솟아났지요. 그럼 저 위에 있는 작은 줄기들은 뭐냐구요? 그건 호밀을 키울 때 생겨난 거죠. 그 작은 식물이 발아하기 시작해 여러 개의 줄기가 나오더니, 곧 더 많은 줄기가 나왔어요. 결국에는 하나의 씨앗에서 평균 높이 50센티미터 정도의 줄기가 80개나 나왔지요 ⋯ 하나의 씨앗에서 말이죠. 평균 50센티미터 높이로 80개의 줄기가 나온 거예요. 그들은 줄기 표면적과 뿌리 표면적을 비교해 보았는데, 모든 잎들을 포함한 줄기의 표면적은 총 5평방 미터였습니다. 그리고 굉장한 사실이 드러났지요. 그들은 뿌리 표면적을 살펴보았는데요, 아마 여러분은 뿌리와 줄기가 균형을 이루고 있을 거라고 생각할 것입니다, 그렇지 않나요? 그러기 위해서는 줄기와 뿌리의 표면적이 상당히 비슷해야 되잖아요, 그렇죠?

M 아니요.

P 뭐라구요? 누가 '아니'라고 했나요? 정말 그렇습니다. 뿌리 조직은 5평방 미터가 아니라 200평방 미터 이상의 표면적을 갖고 있었습니다. 그럼 나머지 면적이 어디에서 생긴 것일까요? 누가 그랬을까요? 누가 표면적을 그렇게 늘려놓았을까요? 뿌리가 어떻게 표면적을 그렇게 증가시켰을까요?

F 뿌리털이요.

P 뿌리털, 바로 그겁니다. 뿌리털 때문에 표면적이 엄청나게 늘어난 겁니다. 뿌리털은 물속에서 계속 퍼져 나가야만 비료에서 미네랄을 흡수할 수 있습니다. 물론 산소도 필요하고요.

어휘

botany 식물학　root system 뿌리체계　extent 범위, 넓이, 크기　overall 전부의, 총체적인　particular 특정한　experiment 실험 meticulous 꼼꼼한, 세심한　entire 전체의, 완전한　rye 호밀　growing stuff in water 수경재배 (= water culture; aquiculture; hydroponics) commercially 상업적으로　crop 작물, 수확물　fertilizer 비료, 화학비료　bubble through 거품으로 분출시키다　overwater 물을 지나치게 주다 respiration 호흡, 호흡작용　surface area 표면적　germinate 발아하다, 생겨나다　crabgrass 왕바랭이　shoot (줄기, 식물의) 새로나온 가지 biggie 중요한 것, 거물　absolutely 절대적으로　root hair 뿌리털　absorb 흡수하다, 열중시키다　mineral 무기물, 미네랄　penetrate 스며들다, 꿰뚫다　wording 표현, 말씨　odor 냄새, 악취　similarity 유사, 비슷함

Reading

Listening

Speaking

Writing

Test 1

Test 2

Test 3

Test 4

17. 이 강의의 주제는 무엇인가?

Ⓐ 뿌리 조직의 규모

Ⓑ 다양한 종류의 뿌리 조직

Ⓒ 호밀에 필요한 영양소들

Ⓓ 두 종류의 식물종 개량하기

내용의 요점을 묻는 문제

어휘 nutrient 영양분　improve 개선하다, 증진하다, (가치, 수요 등이) 증대하다　species (생물) 종

해설 이 강의는 식물의 뿌리 조직과 다른 부분들과 대조되는 점을 논하고 있다. 영양소와 여러 종류의 풀에 대해서도 설명하고 있지만 주로 뿌리의 규모에 초점을 맞추고 있다. 따라서 정답은 보기 A.

18. 교수에 따르면 한 과학자는 왜 호밀을 수경재배했는가?

Ⓐ 뿌리를 햇빛에 노출시키기 위해

Ⓑ 가스로 호밀을 수정시키기 위해

Ⓒ 뿌리 조직 전체를 관찰하기 위해

Ⓓ 미네랄이 뿌리에 흡수되는 과정을 알아보기 위해

세부 정보 찾기 문제

어휘 fertilize 비료를 주다, 비옥하게 하다　penetrate 침투하다

해설 강의의 시작 부분에서 교수는 과학자가 뿌리 전체의 규모를 파악하려고 했다는 사실을 밝히고 있다. 따라서 정답은 보기 C.

19. 교수는 물을 너무 많이 준 실내 화초에 대해 언급하고 있다. 왜 그것을 언급하고 있는가?

Ⓐ 많은 종류의 식물들이 물속에서 자랄 수 있음을 보여 주기 위해

Ⓑ 물속에서 자라는 식물들에 왜 가스 거품이 필요한지 설명하기 위해

Ⓒ 학생들에게 다음 실험의 중요성을 상기시켜 주기 위해

Ⓓ 실내 화초의 뿌리 길이에 대한 의견을 제시하기 위해

구성 파악 문제

해설 수경재배하는 식물은 가스 거품을 통해 산소를 공급 받아야 한다는 사실을 설명하기 위해서다. 정답은 보기 B.

20. 교수에 따르면, 왕바랭이와 호밀의 유사점은 무엇인가?

Ⓐ 둘 다 5월에 자라기 시작한다.

Ⓑ 둘 다 물이 많이 필요한 뿌리 조직을 갖고 있다.

Ⓒ 둘 다 뿌리 표면보다 줄기 표면이 넓다.

Ⓓ 둘 다 하나의 씨앗에서 많은 줄기가 나온다.

세부 정보 찾기 문제

해설 교수가 왕바랭이를 예로 든 것은 학생들이 호밀보다는 더 친숙하기 때문이다. 교수는 호밀이나 왕바랭이 등 다양한 풀 종류가 한 개의 씨앗에서 많은 줄기가 나온다는 사실을 강조하고 있다. 따라서 정답은 보기 D.

21. 강의의 일부를 다시 듣고 질문에 답하라.

🎧 T-17

P　What do you need to do to that water besides put fertilizer in it? Anyone ever actually tried to grow plants in water? You must bubble water through it. Bubble gas through it. I'm sorry, you must bubble gas through it. So, gas, you have to bubble through.

N　*Why did the professor say this?*

P　I'm sorry, you must bubble gas through it.

Ⓐ 그녀는 방금 한 말을 고쳐 말하려는 것이다.

Ⓑ 그녀는 가스 거품을 만들 필요가 없기를 바랐다.

Ⓒ 그녀는 가스 냄새가 불쾌할 수도 있다는 것을 깨달았다.

Ⓓ 그녀는 학생들에게 실험의 한 단계에 대해 말하는 것을 잊었다.

의도 파악 문제

해설 교수는 처음에 "You must bubble water through it."이라고 잘못 말했다. 여기서 it은 water이므로 "You must bubble water through water"라고 말한 셈이 되고, 이 말은 의미가 성립되지 않는다. 그래서 다시 "Bubble gas through it. I'm sorry, you must bubble gas through it."이라고 두 번 반복해서 앞에 진술한 내용을 수정한 것이다. 그러므로 정답은 보기 A.

22. 강의의 일부를 다시 듣고 질문에 답하라.

🎧 T-18

P　I read about this and the book said one thousand kilometers of roots. I kept thinking: this has to be a mistake. It just doesn't make any sense to me that... that... that could be right. But that's what all the books have, and no one's ever corrected it. So let me explain to you about this rye plant.

N　*What does the professor intend to explain?*

Ⓐ 교과서에서 드러난 잘못이 결코 수정되지 않는 이유

Ⓑ 호밀의 뿌리가 1,000km까지 늘어나는 것을 믿지 않는 이유

Ⓒ 호밀의 뿌리 길이가 그렇게 길게 늘어나는 방식

Ⓓ 물에서 자라는 식물이 비료를 이용하는 방식

의도 파악 문제

해설 교수는 책에 나온 내용을 믿을 수 없었지만, 그것이 사실이었다는 점을 지적하면서 그 이유를 설명하고자 한다. 정답은 보기 C.

Questions 23-28 · p. 164

N Narrator · P Professor · M Male Student · F Female Student

Script

N Listen to part of a lecture in a business management class.

P OK. Uh, let's talk about organization and structure in a company. How are companies typically structured?

F Functionally.

P And...?

F By projects.

P Right. By function... and by projects. Twenty years ago companies were organized in function groups, where people with a certain expertise worked together as a unit—the, uh, architects in one unit, the finance people in another unit. Well, nowadays a lot of companies are organized around projects—like a construction company could be building an office building in one city and an apartment house somewhere else, and each project has its own architects and engineers.

Now, the good thing about project organization is that it's easier to change to adapt to the needs of the project—it's a small group, a dedicated team, not the whole company.

Now, with that in mind, here's a question for you: why do we continue to organize ourselves by function, even now, when in fact we admit that projects are the lifeblood of a lot of organizations? Why do some companies maintain a functional organization instead of organizing around projects? Yes?

F Because, um, if you don't have that functional structure within your organization, chances are you'd have a harder time meeting the goals of the projects.

P Why?

F Why?

P Listen, let's say we got four new cars we want to design. Why do we need a functional organization? Why not just organize the company around the four projects—these people make car number one, these other people make car number two...

F Yeah, but who's gonna be responsible for what? You know, the way you tell who's...

P Well... well, we'll appoint a manager: new car number one manager, car number two manager—they're completely responsible. Why should we have a single engineering department that has all four cars passing through it?

F When you design a car, you need the expertise of all the engineers in the company. Each engineer needs to be in touch with the entire engineering department.

P Yeah, but I keep... I keep asking why. I wanna know why. Yes.

M Well, to eliminate redundancy's probably one of the biggest fac-

---

N 경영학 강의의 일부를 들으시오.

P 좋습니다. 어, 회사의 조직과 구조에 대해 논의해 봅시다. 회사는 보통 어떻게 조직되어 있습니까?

F 직무별로요.

P 그리고?

F 프로젝트별로요.

P 그렇습니다. 직무별로, 프로젝트별로 조직되어 있지요. 20년 전에 회사들은 직무 그룹별로 조직되어 있었습니다. 동일한 전문지식을 가진 사람들끼리 한 단위로 구성되어 함께 일했죠. 이를테면 건축가 그룹이 한 단위가 되고 재무 그룹이 또 하나의 단위가 되는 식이었죠. 요즘은 많은 회사들이 프로젝트별로 조직되어 있습니다. 예를 들면 어떤 건설회사가 한 도시에 사무실 건물을 짓고 또 다른 지역에 아파트를 짓는다고 하면, 각 프로젝트마다 건축가들과 엔지니어들을 따로 두고 있습니다.

프로젝트별로 짠 조직의 장점은 프로젝트의 필요에 맞춰 쉽게 변할 수 있다는 것입니다. 이것은 전사적 규모라기보다는 작은 그룹이자 헌신적인 팀이라고 할 수 있지요.

자, 이런 점을 염두에 두었다면, 여러분에게 질문을 하나 하겠습니다. 왜 우리는 계속해서 직무별로 회사를 조직하고 있을까요? 사실 지금도 우리는 프로젝트를 조직의 생명줄과 다름없다고 생각하고 있는데도 말이죠. 왜 상당수의 회사들이 프로젝트가 아닌 직무별로 조직을 유지하고 있을까요? 예, 뭐지요?

F 왜냐하면, 조직이 직무별 구조를 갖추고 있지 않으면, 프로젝트의 목표를 달성하기가 더욱 어려워질 가능성이 있기 때문이에요.

P 왜요?

F 왜냐고요?

P 들어보세요. 우리가 네 종류의 신형 자동차를 제작한다고 합시다. 우리는 왜 직무별 조직이 필요합니까? 네 개의 프로젝트별로 회사를 조직할 수 있잖아요. 한 팀이 첫 번째 자동차를 맡고, 또 하나의 팀이 두 번째 자동차를 맡고…

F 예, 하지만 누가 어떤 책임을 져야 하나요? 그런 식으로는 누가…

P 그래요… 그럼 책임자를 임명하면 되죠. 첫 번째 자동차를 담당하는 책임자, 두 번째 자동차를 담당하는 책임자를 말이죠. 그들이 전적으로 책임을 지는 겁니다. 그런데 왜 우리는 네 종류의 자동차 제작을 총괄하는 기술 부서를 둬야 하는 겁니까?

F 자동차를 설계할 때는 회사 내 모든 기술자들의 전문지식이 필요합니다. 각 기술자는 총괄 기술 부서와 계속 접촉

Reading

Listening

Speaking

Writing

Test 1

Test 2

Test 3

Test 4

tors in an organization. So that, uh... so that there's, there's... standards of... for uniformity and efficiency in the organization.

P OK. And... and that's probably the primary reason for functional organization right there — is that we want some engineering consistency. We want the same kind of technology used in all four cars. If we disperse those four engineers into four parts of the organization and they work by themselves, there's a lot less chance that the technology's gonna be the same from car to car. So instead we maintain the functional organization — that means the engineers work together in one part of the building. And their offices are next to each other because we want them to talk to each other. When an engineer works on a project, they bring the expertise of their whole functional group with them.

But there's a downside of that, though, isn't there? I mean organizing a company into functional groups is not all positive. Where's the allegiance of those engineers? It's to their coordinator, right? It's to that chief engineer. But we really want our one engineer, the engineer that's working on car number one, we want that person's loyalty to be to that project as well as to the head of the engineering group. We... we really want both, don't we? We want to maintain the functional organization, so we can maintain uniformity and technology transfer, and expertise. We want the cutting-edge expertise in every group. But at the same time we also want the engineer to be totally dedicated to the needs of the project. Ideally, we have a ... a hybrid, a combination of both functional and project organization.

But there's a problem with this kind of hybrid structure. When you have both functional and project organization, well, what does that violate in terms of basic management principles?

할 필요가 있지요.

P 예, 하지만 계속 질문할게요. 얘기하세요.

M 중복성을 제거하는 것이 아마 조직에서는 가장 중요한 요소들 중 하나죠. 그래서 조직에서 통일성과 효율성에 관한 기준이 있는 것이죠.

P 그렇습니다. 그것이 아마도 직무별로 조직을 구성하는 가장 큰 이유가 될 것입니다. 즉 기술의 일관성이 필요한 겁니다. 우리는 네 종류의 자동차에 동일한 기술이 이용되기를 원합니다. 만일 네 명의 기술자들을 그 조직의 네 부문으로 분산시키면 그들은 홀로 작업을 할 테고 그 기술은 자동차별로 제각각일 것입니다. 그렇기 때문에 우리는 직무별 조직을 유지하고 있는 것입니다. 이는 기술자들이 건물의 특정한 공간에서 함께 작업한다는 것을 의미하지요. 그리고 그들의 사무실도 가까이 붙여 놓았는데, 이는 그들이 서로 대화를 나누면서 협조하기를 원하기 때문입니다. 한 기술자가 어떤 프로젝트에 참여하고 있다면, 직무별 그룹 전체의 전문지식이 동원됩니다.

하지만 이런 직무별 조직의 단점도 있지 않겠어요? 회사를 직무별로 조직하는 것이 전적으로 바람직하다고는 할 수 없습니다. 그런 기술자들은 어디에 헌신하겠습니까? 그 대상은 책임자가 되겠죠? 수석 엔지니어에게 헌신할 겁니다. 하지만 우리는 기술자 한 사람이, 이를테면 첫 번째 자동차를 제작하는 어떤 기술자가 기술부의 책임자뿐 아니라 프로젝트에도 헌신하기를 원합니다. 우리는 정말 두 가지를 다 원하죠, 그렇지 않겠어요? 우리는 통일성, 기술 이전, 그리고 전문지식을 유지하기 위해 직무별 조직을 원합니다. 모든 그룹이 첨단 지식을 갖고 있기를 원하지요. 하지만 동시에 기술자들 각자가 프로젝트의 요구에 전적으로 헌신하기를 원합니다. 이상적인 것은 직무별 조직과 프로젝트별 조직이 조합된 혼성 조직이죠.

하지만 이런 혼성 조직에도 문제는 있습니다. 직무와 프로젝트의 성격이 혼합된 조직의 경우, 기본적인 경영원칙에 어긋나는 것이 있는데 무엇일까요?

F Unity of command.

P Unity of command. That's exactly right. So this... this is a vicious violation of unity of command, isn't it? It says that this engineer working on a project seems to have two bosses. We... we got the engineering boss, and we got the project manager boss. But the project manager is responsible for the project, and is not the official manager of the engineer who works on the project. And we try to maintain peace in the organizations, and sometimes it's disrupted and we have conflicts, don't we? The project manager for car one wants a car part to fit in a particular way, for a specific situation, a specialized case. Well, the, uh, engineering director says no, we gotta have standardization. We gotta have all the cars done this way. We can't make a special mold for that particular part for that particular car. We're not gonna do that. So we got a conflict.

F 명령 일원화요.

P 명령 일원화, 바로 그겁니다. 그래서 이것은 명령 일원화의 심각한 위반입니다. 어떤 프로젝트에 참여한 기술자는 상사가 두 명이 생기게 됩니다. 기술부의 책임자가 있고 프로젝트의 책임자가 있지요. 하지만 프로젝트의 책임자는 프로젝트를 책임지고 있을 뿐이고, 그 프로젝트에 참여한 기술자의 정식 관리자는 아닙니다. 우리는 조직의 평화를 유지하길 원하지만, 때로는 평화가 깨지고 갈등을 겪게 될 겁니다, 그렇지 않겠어요? 첫 번째 자동차 제작을 담당한 프로젝트 책임자가 특수한 상황이나 전문적인 목적을 위해 자동차 부품 하나를 특별한 방식으로 조립하길 원한다고 합시다. 하지만 기술부 책임자는 이를 거부합니다. 그는 표준화를 고수하려고 합니다. 회사의 모든 차들을 일정한 방식으로 제작해야 하며, 그렇게 특별한 차의 특별한 부품을 위해 특별한 틀을 만들 수는 없습니다. 그렇게 하지 않겠다고 합니다. 그러면 갈등이 생기죠.

어휘

business management 경영학 organization 조직 structure 구조, 조직 typically 보통 functionally 직무별로, 기능별로 expertise 전문지식 architect 건축가, 설계자 finance 재무, 재정 adapt to ~에 조화시키다, 적응시키다 dedicated 헌신적인 lifeblood 생명줄, 원기의 근원 meet the goal 목표를 달성하다 appoint 임명하다, 정하다 engineer 기술자들, 기사 be in touch with ~와 접촉하다 eliminate 제거하다, 삭제하다 redundancy 중복성, 여분 factor 요소, 요인 uniformity 통일성 efficiency 효율성, 능률 primary 주요한, 첫째의 consistency 일관성, 견실성 disperse 분산시키다 downside 단점 allegiance 헌신, 충성 coordinator 책임자, 조정자 technology transfer 기술이전 cutting edge expertise 첨단지식 hybrid 혼성, 잡종 violate 어긋나다, 위반하다 in terms of ~의 관점에서 보면 management principle 경영 원칙 unity of command 명령 일원화 vicious 심각한, 악성의 violation 문제, 방해 disrupt 깨지다, 분열시키다 specific 특수한, 구체적인 standardization 표준화 mold 틀 innovation 혁신

Reading

Listening

Speaking

Writing

Test 1

Test 2

Test 3

Test 4

23. 강의는 주로 무슨 내용을 다루고 있는가?

Ⓐ 자동차 산업의 기술 혁신

Ⓑ 회사의 구조

Ⓒ 기술 부서의 효율성을 개선하는 방안

Ⓓ 조직 내에서 갈등을 해결하는 방안

내용의 요점을 묻는 문제

어휘 resolve 해결하다, 결심하다   conflict 충돌, 갈등

해설 교수는 강의 시작에서 회사의 조직과 구조에 대해 논하겠다고 밝혔다. 그리고 직무별 조직과 프로젝트별 조직, 두 가지 형태의 조직에 대해 설명하고 있다. 따라서 정답은 보기 B.

24. 교수는 왜 여러 도시에서 일감을 맡고 있는 건설회사에 대해 이야기하는가?

Ⓐ 직무별로 구성된 조직의 예를 제시하기 위해

Ⓑ 프로젝트별로 구성된 조직의 예를 제시하기 위해

Ⓒ 직무별로 구성된 조직의 문제점을 설명하기 위해

Ⓓ 회사에서 발생할 수 있는 갈등의 유형을 설명하기 위해

구성 파악 문제

해설 교수는 프로젝트별로 구성된 조직이 일하는 방식을 설명하기 위해 건설회사를 예로 든 것이다. 따라서 정답은 보기 B.

25. '명령 일원화'의 원칙에 어긋나는 사례는 무엇인가?

Ⓐ 두 명 이상이 한 직원을 감독한다.

Ⓑ 회사가 제품들을 표준화하지 않기로 결정한다.

Ⓒ 여러 명의 프로젝트 책임자들이 새로운 제품의 제작에 책임을 진다.

Ⓓ 직원 한 사람이 상사 한 사람의 지시를 따르지 않는다.

세부 정보 찾기 문제

어휘 supervise 감독하다, 관리하다   standardize 표준화하다
instruction 지시, 명령

해설 강의의 마지막 부분에서 교수는 명령 일원화에 심각한 문제가 발생할 수 있음을 한 가지 예를 들어 설명하고 있다. 어떤 프로젝트에 참여한 기술자가 프로젝트 책임자와 회사의 기술 부서 책임자, 두 상사의 관리를 받아야 할 때 갈등이 일어날 수 있다는 것이다. 따라서 정답은 보기 A.

26. 교수에 따르면, 프로젝트와 직무의 성격이 혼합된 조직 구조의 어디에서 갈등이 발생할 수 있는가?

Ⓐ 건축가들과 재무 전문가들

Ⓑ 전문화의 필요성과 표준화의 필요성

Ⓒ 같은 프로젝트에 참여하고 있는 두 명의 기술자들

Ⓓ 여러 도시에서 진행되는 프로젝트의 필요 사항들

세부 정보 찾기 문제

어휘 function 지능, 기능

해설 교수가 예로 들었던 프로젝트 책임자와 기술 부서 책임자와의 갈등은 곧 전문화와 표준화의 갈등이라고 할 수 있다. 따라서 정답은 보기 B.

27. 아래 각 문장이 직무별 조직과 프로젝트별 조직 중 어느 것과 관련 있는지 지적하라. 해당 박스에 체크하라.

	직무별 조직	프로젝트별 조직
A. 비슷한 전문지식을 가진 사람들을 격려하여 서로 긴밀하게 협조하도록 유도한다.	✔	
B. 회사가 빠르게 적응하여 변화하는 요구를 충족시키는 데 유용하다.		✔
C. 프로젝트의 통일성을 갖추는 데 유용하다.	✔	

내용 연결 문제

해설 전문가들을 그룹으로 묶는 것이 직무별 조직이고, 프로젝트에 따라 작은 팀으로 구성하는 것이 프로젝트별 조직이다. 따라서 첫 번째와 세 번째는 직무별 조직에 해당하고, 두 번째는 프로젝트별 조직에 해당한다.

28. 강의의 일부를 다시 듣고 질문에 답하라.

🎧 T-20

P Why should we have a single engineering department that has all four cars passing through it?

F When you design a car, you need the expertise of all the engineers in the company. Each engineer needs to be in touch with the entire engineering department.

P Yeah, but I keep... I keep asking why. I wanna know why.

N *Why does the professor say this?*

P Yeah, but I keep... I keep asking why. I wanna know why.

Ⓐ 그는 이 학생이 기술자들에 대해 이야기하는 이유를 이해하지 못한다.

Ⓑ 그는 기술자들이 그들의 동료들과 어떤 식으로 의사소통을 하는지 알고 싶어 한다.

Ⓒ 이 학생은 그의 질문에 대해 완벽한 대답을 하지 못했다.

Ⓓ 그는 이 학생이 그 주제에 대해 좀 더 조사하기를 원한다.

의도 파악 문제

어휘 communicate 의사를 소통하다, 전달하다   coworker 동료, 협력자   complete 완벽한, 철저한

해설 교수가 질문을 되풀이한 것은 학생의 대답이 만족스럽지 않기 때문이다. 따라서 정답은 보기 C.

SPEAKING

 T-21

Question 1	p. 168

Narrator

Some people who unexpectedly receive a large amount of money spend it on practical things, while others spend it for pleasure only. Which do you think is better and why?

뜻밖에 큰돈을 받으면 어떤 사람은 실용적인 것에 쓰는 반면, 어떤 사람은 단지 즐거움만을 위해 쓰는 사람도 있다. 어느 쪽이 낫다고 생각하며, 그 이유는 무엇인가?

준비 시간 : 15초

답변 시간 : 45초

중요 포인트

이 문제에 답하려면 더 낫다고 생각하는 행동을 택하고 이유를 설명해야 한다. 유효한 답변을 하려면 자신의 의견에 대해 명확한 이유를 제시해야 한다. 점수는 어떤 행동을 선호하느냐에 따라 결정되지 않고, 얼마나 효과적으로 의견을 제시하고 뒷받침할 수 있느냐에 따라 결정된다. 이런 상황에 처한 사람들이 어떻게 행동할지 설명해 개괄적으로 주제에 접근하거나, 아니면 개인적인 관점으로 접근해 자신이 뜻밖에 돈을 받는다면 어떻게 할지 이야기해도 좋다.

실용적인 것에 돈을 쓰는 것과 즐거움에 돈을 쓰는 것 중 어느 쪽을 택하든 구체적인 내용을 제시하고 예를 들어야 한다. 이를테면 실용적인 것에 돈을 쓰기로 선택한다면, 어떤 실용적인 물건이나 경험을 의미하는지 언급하면 된다(예를 들면 가족의 삶을 편리하게 해 주는 새 세탁기나 자동차, 또는 대학 등록금 납부처럼 진로에 도움이 되는 일 등). 만약 즐거움을 위해 돈을 쓰기로 선택한다면, 어떤 것들이 즐거움을 주는지(가장 좋아하는 휴양지로 여행하기, 자선단체에 기부하기, 어머니에게 선물하기 등), 그리고 이유는 무엇인지 구체적으로 진술해야 한다. 또한 다른 선택의 잘못된 점을 설명해 자신의 선택을 옹호해도 좋다.

우수 답변 T-26

If a person receives a large amount of money, I believe it's better for him or her to use it for practical things rather than on pleasure only, because there's been a lot of cases with people who win the lottery and they spent almost all the money for their own pleasure, and once they finish spending, then they don't have any more money to- but the same kind of luxurious lifestyle, and at that point a lot of people have lost their jobs or kind of got... eaten over by all the money and all the greed that's involved, so... I believe we should just spend it on practical things.

채점자 의견

높은 점수를 받은 답변으로 수험자는 실용적인 것에 돈을 쓰겠다는 논지를 전개하기로 하고 이것이 즐거움을 위해 돈을 쓰는 편보다 낫다고 생각하는 이유를 설명한다. 의견을 설명하는 과정에서 수험자는 오류나 어색한 표현이 거의 없이 매우 구체적인 표현을 사용한다. "there's been a lot of cases with people who win the lottery and they spent almost all the money for their own pleasure." ("복권에 당첨된 후 즐거움에 돈을 탕진한 사례들이 많다.") 나아가 수험자는 이것이 "luxurious lifestyle" ("사치스러운 생활 방식")으로 이어진다고 설명하고 이런 생활은 오래 갈 수 없다고 주장한다. 그러나 구체적인 내용이 부족해 완벽한 답변은 아니다. 수험자는 사람들이 어떤 "실용적인 것"에 돈을 써야 한다고 생각하는지 설명하지 않는다. 즉 어떤 곳에 돈을 쓰면 안 되는지는 밝혔지만 어떤 곳에 돈을 쓰면 좋은지는 밝히지 않았다. 마지막으로, 발음은 대체로 또렷하고 쉽게 알아들을 수 있다. 억양과 끊어 말하기는 자연스럽고 적절하며 듣는 사람이 집중하는 데 방해가 되지 않는다. 전반적으로 논지를 적절히 전개한 답변으로 이해하기 쉽다.

중간 수준의 답변 T-27

I think, uh, will spend it for pleasure only is better. Um, my reason, uh, is that, um, first, um... uh, because, uh, now the life is- is so stressful, uh, if you can, if you can buy something or do something to relax is so, uh, important. And, um, second, uh, pleasure is, uh, very important for every people. If, if someone is, uh, always, uh, happy, uh, uh... he or she will have a longer or happier life.

채점자 의견

수험자는 즐거움을 위해 돈을 써야 한다는 의견을 피력했으며, 그 편을 선택한 이유를 포괄적으로 제시한다. 그러나 이유를 구체적으로 설명하지 않는다. 내용이 모호하고 세부 사항이 부족하다. 수험자는 즐거움을 위해 돈을 쓰는 편이 낫다고 말한다. "First, because now the life is so stressful, if you can buy something or do something to relax is so important." ("우선 지금 생활은 스트레스가 많으므로, 무언가를 살 수 있거나 휴식을 취할 수 있다는 것은 아주 중요하다.") 흥미로운 생각이지만, 그 돈으로 무엇을 살지, 그리고 그 행위가 누군가에게 어떤 식으로, 왜 즐거움을 주는지 등 구체적인 정보가 있어야 한다. 기본적인 어휘와 문법은 적절하게 구사하지만 "very"를 써야 할 곳에 "so"를 쓰거나 "life"를 "the life"라고 잘못 말하는 오류를 범한다. 발음은 대체로 명료해 알아듣기 쉽지만 속도가 너무 느리고 단어 하나하나를 따로 발음하는 탓에 억양을 제대로 살리지 못해 유창하지 못하다.

Question 2   p. 168

Narrator

A student has written a letter to the editor of City University's newspaper concerning the campus health center. You have 50 seconds to read the letter. Begin reading now.

어떤 학생이 캠퍼스 보건소와 관련하여 시립대학 학보 편집장에게 투고했다. 편지를 50초 동안 읽으시오. 지금 읽으시오.

Student Health Services Need Improvement

The situation at the health center is unacceptable: you sit in a crowded waiting room for hours waiting to get treatment for minor ailments. Then when it's your turn, you get about three minutes with an overworked doctor. I have two suggestions: first, the health center needs to hire more doctors so that each patient receives quality treatment. And as far as the wait time issue is concerned, the health center is currently open only Monday through Fridays, which means that people who get sick over the weekend wait until the following week to get treatment. So, opening the health center on weekends should solve that problem too.

Sincerely,
Megan Finch

학생 보건 서비스 개선 필요

보건소 상황은 용납할 수 없습니다. 가벼운 질병을 치료 받으려고 붐비는 대기실에서 몇 시간 앉아 기다립니다. 그런 다음 차례가 되면 과로로 지친 의사에게 3분 정도 진료를 받습니다. 두 가지를 제안합니다. 첫째, 모든 환자가 양질의 진료를 받을 수 있도록 보건소에서 의사를 더 고용해야 합니다. 그리고 대기시간 문제에 관한 한 보건소는 현재 월요일부터 금요일까지만 문을 열고 있어서 주말에 아픈 사람은 진료를 받으려면 다음 주까지 기다려야 합니다. 따라서 주말에 보건소를 열면 그 문제도 해결될 것입니다.

메건 핀치

│어휘

health center 보건소, 의료 센터   unacceptable 받아들일 수 없는
treatment 치료   ailment 질병   overworked 혹사당하는
quality 고급의, 양질의   currently 지금, 현재

Narrator Now listen to two students discussing the letter.

W Did you read that letter in the paper?

M Sure. And though she's right about the problems, I don't think what she proposes will do much good.

W Really?

M Yeah, take her first suggestion—I mean, have you seen the health center?

W Of course. Why?

M Well, it's tiny, right? The center suffers from lack of space. So unless they build more treatment rooms or offices or something...

W I see.

M And also, her second suggestion...

W Seems like that'll help things out.

M Well, not necessarily. I mean think about it. A lot of students aren't even here on the weekends.

W That's true.

M They leave town and get away. There's not a lot of people here...

W Yeah, like me... I go home probably at least twice a month.

M Right. And a lot of us leave campus for the weekend even more often than that. So there's just not a lot of demand for treatment then. See what I mean?

해설자 이제 편지에 관해 두 학생이 나누는 대화를 들으시오.

여 신문에 실린 편지 읽었어?

남 그럼. 그녀가 문제들은 제대로 짚었지만, 그녀가 제안한 것들이 그다지 도움이 될 것 같지는 않아.

여 정말?

남 응, 첫 번째 제안을 보면, 내 말은, 보건소에 가봤어?

여 물론이지. 왜?

남 아주 좁지 않아? 보건소는 공간이 부족해 어려움을 겪고 있어. 그러니 치료실이나 진료실 같은 걸 더 짓지 않으면…

여 그렇군.

남 게다가 두 번째 제안도…

여 그게 도움이 될 것 같은데.

남 꼭 그렇진 않아. 생각해 봐. 주말이면 많은 학생들이 여기 없잖아.

여 그렇지.

남 마을을 떠나 멀리 가니까 여기는 사람이 별로 없어…

여 맞아, 나도 그래… 한 달에 적어도 두 번은 집에 가거든.

남 그거야. 우리 중 대다수는 주말을 보내려고 그보다 훨씬 더 자주 캠퍼스를 떠나지. 그래서 그때는 진료 수요가 많지 않아. 내 말이 맞지?

│어휘

tiny 아주 작은   suffer from ~로 고통받다   get away 휴가를 가다, 떠나다   demand 수요

Narrator

The man expresses his opinion about the student's suggestions that are made in the letter. State the man's opinion and explain the reasons he gives for holding that opinion.

남자는 편지에 제시된 학생의 제안에 대해 자신의 의견을 개진한다. 남자의 의견이 무엇이며, 그런 의견을 가지게 된 이유는 무엇인지 설명하시오.

준비 시간 : 30초
답변 시간 : 60초

중요 포인트

남자는 학생의 제안이 보건소 진료 수준이나 대기 시간 개선에 도움이 되지 않는다고 생각한다고 답변하면 된다. 남자가 밝힌 이유로는 보건소에는 추가 인력이 일할 공간이 부족하므로 의사를 더 고용하는 것이 도움이 되지 않는다는 점을 지적해야 한다. 남자는 보건소에 진료실이 더 필요하다는 점을 언급했다고 덧붙여도 좋다. 또한 남자는 주말이면 떠나는 학생들이 많으므로 주말에 보건소를 여는 것이 도움이 되지 않는다고 생각한다는 점 역시 밝혀야 한다.

우수 답변 🎧 T-28

The man states that, eh, the solutions that the students suggest will not help improve the situation, because those solutions don't take into consideration some other issues of the health center. For example, when the man suggests, eh, to hire more doctors, eh... he's not taking into consideration that, eh, there is a lack of space in the health center, so, eh, f- for them to hire more doctors, they also need more treatment rooms. He also mentions that, eh... the suggestion of the- to open weekends is not very viable, because, eh, students are- aren't even on campus on weekends, so there is not a lot of demand of the service on those days, so he doesn't see the need to open the... the health center on those days too. And so the man, eh, refuse- refutes the ideas expose in the newspaper.

채점자 의견

수험자는 편지와 대화에서 제시된 요점들을 효과적으로 조합해 답변했지만 독자 편지의 요점에 관한 더 상세한 내용(예를 들어 보건소의 대기 시간 문제)이 빠졌다. 사소한 오류들이 있지만 어법을 적절히 활용하고 있고 다양한 어휘("take into consideration," "viable")를 사용해 생각을 표현하고 있다. 발음에 모국어의 영향이 두드러지지만 대체로 분명하고 알아듣기 쉽다.

중간 수준의 답변 🎧 T-29

The man's opinion is he think that the students' opinion is not so good, because he think the health center is very tiny, and there are no spaces for more treatment room or office. And he thinks... when at weekends, student go downtown or other place, so almost nobody live in the campus. So he think, uh, the students' opinion on the newspaper is not so useful. And he have his opinion that, um, he think the health center now is just OK, because there's no way to change it.

채점자 의견

수험자는 대화에서 나온 기본적인 정보는 이해하지만 언어 구사력이 부족해 대화에 나온 요점을 효과적으로 전달하거나 대화의 요점과 편지의 요점을 연결하지 못한다. "he think that"처럼 단순한 구절을 반복하거나, 모호한 표현("The man's opinion is he think that a student's opinion is not so good")을 사용해 어휘 및 문법 구사력의 한계가 분명히 드러난다. 또한 문법 오류도 다수 발견된다. 발음은 일부를 제외하면 대체로 분명해서 알아들을 수 있으며 말하는 속도도 무난하다.

Question 3   p. 170

Narrator

Now read the passage about the nature of social interaction. You will have 45 seconds to read the passage. Begin reading now.

사회적 상호작용의 본질에 대한 단락을 읽으시오. 45초 동안 읽으시오. 지금 읽으시오.

Social Loafing

When people work in groups to perform a task, individual group members may feel less motivated to contribute, since no one person is held directly responsible for completing the task. The result is that people may not work as hard, or accomplish as much, as they would if they were working alone and their individual output were being measured. This decrease in personal effort, especially on a simple group task, is known as social loafing. While it is not a deliberate behavior, the consequence of social loafing is less personal efficiency when working in groups than when working on one's own.

사회적 태만

사람들이 과제를 수행하기 위해 팀을 꾸려 일할 때, 어느 누구도 과제 완수에 직접 책임이 없으므로 팀원 개개인은 기여하고자 하는 의욕이 떨어질 수 있다. 그 결과 혼자 일하고 개별로 작업 결과를 평가받을 때만큼 열심히 일하지 않거나 성취 수준이 떨어질 수도 있다. 이처럼 특히 간단한 팀 과제에서 개개인의 노력이 미흡한 경우를 사회적 태만이라고 한다. 고의로 하는 행동은 아니지만, 사회적 태만 탓에 혼자 일할 때보다 집단으로 일할 때 개인의 효율성이 떨어진다.

어휘

social loafing 사회적 태만   perform 수행하다   task 일, 과업   individual 개인의, 각각의   motivated 동기가 부여된   contribute 기여하다, 이바지하다   complete 완료하다   output 생산, 산출   measure 측정하다   decrease 감소   deliberate 고의의, 의도적인   consequence 결과   efficiency 효율성, 능률

Narrator Listen to part of a lecture in a psychology class.

Professor Now, a study was done that illustrated this phenomenon. In the study people were given an ordinary task that everyone has probably done before—they were simply asked to peel potatoes. And to peel as many potatoes as possible in a given amount of time. OK, so some people worked alone—and they were told that the number of potatoes they each peeled would be recorded. Others peeled potatoes together, as part of a group, and they were told that only the total number of potatoes peeled would be recorded. So it would be impossible to tell how many any one person had done.

Then researchers compared the results of the people who worked alone and those that worked together to see if there was any difference. That is, they took the average score of the people working alone and compared it to the average score of the people working together in a group. And they did discover a difference. It turns out that people working as a group peeled significantly fewer potatoes than people who worked alone.

해설자 심리학 강의의 일부를 들으시오.

교수 자, 이런 현상을 분명히 보여 주는 연구가 시행되었습니다. 이 연구에서 사람들은 이전에 누구나 해본 적이 있는 평범한 과제를 받았습니다. 그저 감자 껍질을 벗기라는 요청을 받았죠. 그리고 주어진 시간 내에 가능한 한 감자 껍질을 많이 벗기라는 요청이었죠. 자, 그래서 일부는 혼자 일했는데 그들은 각자 껍질을 벗긴 감자 개수가 기록될 거라고 들었죠. 다른 사람들은 팀을 꾸려 함께 감자 껍질을 벗겼는데, 껍질 벗긴 감자의 총 개수만 기록될 거라고 들었습니다. 따라서 한 사람이 얼마나 많이 했는지는 알 수 없었죠.

그러고 나서 연구원들은 혼자 일한 사람과 함께 일한 사람의 결과를 비교해서 차이가 있는지 알아보았습니다. 즉 혼자 일하는 사람들의 평균 점수를 내서 그것을 팀을 꾸려 함께 일한 사람들의 평균 점수와 비교했죠. 그런데 정말 차이가 있었습니다. 팀을 꾸려 일한 사람들이 혼자 일한 사람들보다 감자 껍질을 훨씬 적게 벗긴 것으로 나타났습니다.

어휘

illustrate 설명하다, 예증하다   phenomenon 현상   ordinary 평범한   peel 껍질을 벗기다   record 기록하다   compare 비교하다   average 평균의   discover 발견하다   significantly 상당히, 크게

중요 포인트

답변으로 사회적 태만의 개념을 설명하고 교수가 든 예시가 사회적 태만과 어떻게 연계되는지 설명해야 한다. 사회적 태만은 사람들이 집단으로 일할 때 생기는 현상을 설명하는 용어다. 집단의 구성원들은 혼자 일할 때만큼 동기부여가 안 될 수도 있고, 혼자 일할 때만큼 일을 많이 못할 수도 있다. 지문에서는 개인이 과제에 대해 책임감을 느끼지 않기 때문에 일어나는 현상이라고 말한다. 교수는 사람들에게 감자 껍질을 벗기도록 한 연구를 예로 들어 사람들의 행동을 설명한다. 혼자 일한 사람도 있고, 단체로 일한 사람도 있었는데 단체로 일한 사람들은 혼자 일한 사람들보다 감자 껍질을 적게 벗겼다. 이 연구는 단체로 일하는 사람들이 혼자 일하는 사람들보다 덜 일한다는 것을 보여 주므로 사회적 태만을 설명하는 좋은 사례다.

우수 답변 🎧 T-30

Social loafing is when people do not feel as motivated to put in their personal effort w- when- because they're working in a group. It means that people who work in a group are- d- do not feel responsible for the res- outcome of the group work, so they put in less effort than they would have if they were to do the activ- same ac- activity while they were on own. For example, when people are asked to peel potatoes, they peel less number of potatoes while they working in a group than they do when they have to peel the potatoes by themselves, and this is because they don't feel responsible for- they're not- they know that they're not going to be held responsible for the number of potatoes that are he- peeled in a group, while they are h- held directly responsible when they peel potatoes, by themselves, so...

채점자 의견

수험자는 문제가 요구하는 과제를 충분하고 명확하게 답변하고 있다. 수험자는 사회적 태만이 무엇이며 왜 일어나는지부터 설명한다("It means that people who work in a group do not feel responsible for the result"). 그런 다음 감자 깎는 사람들의 사례를 설명하고 단체로 일한 사람들이 감자 껍질을 적게 벗긴 이유를 다시 한 번 설명한다

("They know they're not going to be held responsible for the number of potatoes that are peeled in a group"). 즉 수험자는 사례와 지문이 어떻게 연관되는지 효과적으로 설명하고 있다. 발음은 분명하고, 말하는 속도도 적절하다. 이따금 머뭇거리며 몇 가지 사소한 오류가 있지만 생각을 전달하는 데 방해가 되지는 않는다.

중간 수준의 답변 🎧 T-31

Social loafing is, um, loafing is a, um, is a decreasing the, um, individual's efficiency in a- in a work when they're working in- in a group. And then, um, through-through the lecture, there was example of peeling potatoes in certain amount of time, and then some worked alone and some worked group, and then they're not sure how to, um, count how many potatoes they did each when they worked in a group and also they worked alone. And then so they get every score from each and then they discovered that, um... the person who worked alone peeled, um... more potatoes than... who worked in a group. And that's the social loafing. ... They just decrease their, um, individual efficiency when they're working in a group.

채점자 의견

지문과 강의의 중요한 정보를 제공하지만, 둘의 관계를 아주 명확하게 보여 주지는 못한다. 수험자는 정의를 내리는 것부터 시작하는데, 어렵사리 자신의 생각을 어느 정도는 전달할 수 있다("Social loafing is decreasing an individual's efficiency in a work when they're working in a group"). 이후 사례를 설명하지만 필요 없는 정보를 제공하느라 속도가 느려진다("they were not sure how to count how many potatoes they did each when they worked in a group"). 답변 전반에 정확한 말과 어구가 부족하며, 적당한 말을 찾느라 속도가 더디다. 긍정적인 측면을 들자면 수험자는 연구에 관한 중요하고 정확한 정보를 제시하고 있으며, 발음은 대체로 분명하다. 그러나 지문의 자료와 예시를 연결하는 데 어려움을 겪는다. 수험자는 사람들이 단체 내에서 일할 때 효율성이 떨어진다는 점을 이해하고 있지만, 단체에 속한 사람들이 일에 대한 책임감이 적고 의욕이 떨어진다는 매우 중요한 요점을 언급하지 않았다.

Question 4   p. 171

Narrator

Now listen to part of a talk in a psychology class.

이제 심리학 강의 내용의 일부를 들으시오.

Professor OK. Ever thought about the things that happen to you, and what's responsible for them? We psychologists have a term—*locus of control*. Locus of control refers to [*hesitates*] where people think control over their lives comes from: whether it comes from themselves, or from somewhere else. People who think that control is in *themselves* are "internals." And people who think it comes from somewhere else are "externals."

Let's say there're two people going for job interviews. One of them is an "internal"—she has an *internal* locus of control. Since she thinks that control comes from *within* herself, she'll believe that her success and her preparation are really her responsibility. So, she's likely to really work on her interview skills ahead of time. Then, if she gets the job, she'll believe that it's because she's worked so hard, and if she doesn't get it, well... she'll probably be disappointed with herself and try to figure out how she can improve for the next time.

OK, and another job candidate is an "external." He perceives other things—say, his *interviewers*—to have more influence. After all, it's their decision. It depends on what mood they're in, and you know... luck! Now, with his external locus of control, he's not as hard on himself, so he's more likely to take risks. He might interview for a job that he's not completely qualified for. If he gets it, he'll think he's really lucky and, because he believes external forces are in control, he might think it's because the interviewers were having a good day. If he doesn't get it, he'll probably blame the interviewers... or bad luck... rather than look at himself and try to figure out what he could've done better.

교수 좋습니다. 여러분에게 일어나는 일들, 그리고 그런 일들이 왜 일어났는지 생각해 본 적이 있습니까? 우리 심리학자들에게는 '통제 소재'라는 용어가 있습니다. 통제 소재란 [머뭇한다] 자기 자신이든, 아니면 다른 어떤 곳이든, 자신의 삶을 통제하는 것이 비롯된다고 생각하는 위치를 가리킵니다. '자신'이 통제한다고 생각하는 사람은 '내재론자'입니다. 그리고 다른 곳에서 통제한다고 생각하는 사람은 '외재론자'입니다.

두 사람이 취업 면접을 보러 간다고 합시다. 한 사람은 '내재론자'로, '내부'에 통제 소재가 있습니다. 그녀는 통제가 자기 '안'에서 나온다고 생각하므로 성공 여부와 준비는 정말로 자신의 책임이라고 믿을 겁니다. 그러므로 그녀는 면접에 앞서 미리 면접 기술을 정말 열심히 익힐 겁니다. 그리고 취업하게 되면 자신이 매우 열심히 했기 때문이라고 생각할 것이고 취업하지 못한다면, 글쎄… 아마 자신에게 실망하고 다음에는 어떻게 하면 나아질지 생각해 내려고 하겠죠.

자, 그리고 다른 구직자는 '외재론자'입니다. 그는 다른 것, 예를 들어 면접관들이 더 영향력이 많다고 인식하죠. 어쨌든 그들이 결정하니까요. 면접관들 기분이 어떤지에 따라 달라지니까… 운이죠! 이 사람은 통제 소재가 외부에 있으므로 스스로에게 엄격하지 않고, 따라서 무모하게 도전할 확률이 높죠. 그는 전혀 자격이 없는 일자리에 면접을 볼지도 모릅니다. 만약 취업하면 정말 운이 좋다고 생각하겠죠. 왜냐하면 그는 외부의 힘이 통제한다고 믿기 때문에 면접관들이 그날 기분이 좋았기 때문이라고 생각할 수도 있습니다. 취업에 실패하면 스스로를 돌아보고 어떤 것을 더 잘할 수 있었을지 생각하려고 애쓰기보다는 면접관들을 탓하거나 운이 없다고 생각하겠죠.

어휘

psychologist 심리학자   term 용어   refer to 언급하다   internal 내재론자   external 외재론자   preparation 준비   be disappointed with ~에 실망하다   figure out 생각해 내다   candidate 후보   perceive 인지하다   influence 영향력   take risk 위험을 감수하다   qualified 자격이 있는   blame ~을 탓하다

Narrator

Using points and examples from the talk, explain internal and external locus of control.

강의에 나온 논지와 예시를 이용해 내부 및 외부 통제 소재를 설명하시오.

준비 시간 : 20초
답변 시간 : 60초

중요 포인트

통제 소재란 사람들이 자신의 삶에 대한 통제가 비롯된다고 믿는 위치, 즉 내재론(사람 내부)과 외재론(다른 곳)을 가리킨다는 점을 설명해야 한다. 교수가 구직자를 예로 들어 말한 논지를 설명해야 한다. 통제 소재가 내부에 있는 구직자는 성공에 대한 책임이 스스로에게 있다고 본다. 그녀는 취직 여부가 자신이 준비하기 위해 쏟은 노력의 결과라고 생각한다. 통제 소재가 외부에 있는 구직자는 다른 힘들이 통제한다고 인식한다. 그는 취업 여부가 행운이나 면접관들의 기분 같은 다른 요인의 결과라고 생각한다.

Reading   Listening   Speaking   Writing   Test 1   Test 2   Test 3   Test 4

In the example, the interviewee with the, uh, internal locus of control, uh, the interviewee would think that it's her responsibility- his or her responsibility to get the job. Therefore, uhh, she thinks that her readiness, her qualifications, and everything... um, um, everything needed to get the job is- is, uh, within her reach or within her control. She can do things in order to improve herself and ensure that she can get the job. Whereas, uh, the external locus of control believes that the factors that, uh, influence the decision of, um, getting the job comes from his, uh, luck, from the environment, and, like, the mood of the interviewer.

채점자 의견

수험자는 취업 면접자를 예로 들어 논하면서 해당 개념에 대해 자신이 이해한 바를 전달한다. 억양을 매우 효과적으로 사용해 개념을 전달하며 ("it's **her** responsibility to get the job...") 발음은 분명하다. 다양한 어휘와 문법을 정확하게 사용하고 있다. 생각을 정리하느라 가끔 머뭇거리지만 전반적으로 유창하게 말하며 알아듣기 쉽다.

The internal locus of control means one believe that the- she can control her life, and she will response for her life- for her behaviors. And the external control means the opposite. For example, the job, mm, two persons, mm, to make a job interview. The internal locus of control person will work very hard, and, um, thinks the result of the interview will give her confid- the- the- if she get the job, she will feel confidence, uh, if she lost it, she will disappear, and she will improve herself next time. While the external interview- the external person will took the interview just for risk, and he'll think it's- he believe in luck- he believe in luck, and he won't look at himself to improve hersel- himself.

채점자 의견

수험자는 강의에서 나온 개념을 잘 전달할 수 있지만, 어휘 선택과 문법에 문제가 있어 답변을 충분히, 명확하게 전개하지 못한다. 예를 들어, 두 종류의 통제 소재에 대한 정의가 다소 모호하다("internal locus of control means one believe that she can control her life and she will response for her... behaviors, and the external control means the opposite"). 어휘 선택이 부정확해 듣는 사람이 다소 혼란스럽다("if she lost it she would disappear," and "the external person will do the interview just for risk"). 발음도 때때로 알아듣기가 어렵다.

WRITING

Integrated Writing　　　　　　　　　p. 174

Some fuels, known as biofuels, can be extracted from plants that produce natural oils. One kind of biofuel comes from algae, the simplest plant organisms. Some people believe that fuel derived from algae could replace other kinds of fuel as our main source of energy. However, manufacturing fuel from algae creates some unique problems.

To get enough oil from algae, algae would have to be farmed on a large scale; this would require a good deal of land and water. In many parts of the world, however, there are dangerous shortages of farmable land, usable water, and agricultural food products. Since algae farming uses up land and water without producing food, building large-scale algae farming operations could make food shortages worse.

A second problem with using algae as a fuel source is that the equipment required to grow and extract oil from the algae is expensive. The cost of starting an algae farm is high. Companies would have to invest in large facilities to contain the algae and expose them to sunlight, in complicated machines to squeeze oil out of the algae, and in other equipment necessary to make the oil usable as fuel.

Third, farming algae is problematic because algae require a large quantity of carbon dioxide gas to grow. All plants need some carbon dioxide (CO_2), which they generally pull directly from the air. Algae, however, do not thrive without a very high concentration of this gas in their environment. To grow large amounts of algae, farmers would have to pump pure CO_2 into algae-growing tanks. Not all of this CO_2 would be absorbed by the algae; a significant amount would pass into the atmosphere. Since CO_2 is considered a pollutant, this would be harmful to the environment.

바이오 연료라고 알려진, 일부 연료는 천연 오일을 만들어 내는 식물을 통해 추출될 수 있다. 바이오 연료의 한 종류는 가장 단순한 식물 유기체인 해조류에서 나온다. 어떤 사람들은 해조류에서 비롯되는 연료가 우리의 주 에너지 공급원으로서 여러 다른 종류의 연료를 대체할 수 있다고 생각한다. 하지만, 해조류를 통한 연료 제조는 몇몇 독특한 문제를 야기한다.

해조류에서 충분한 오일을 얻으려면, 해조류가 대규모로 양식되어야 할 것이며, 이는 많은 토지와 물을 필요로 할 것이다. 하지만, 전 세계의 많은 지역에서, 경작 가능한 토지와 이용 가능한 물, 그리고 농산 식품이 위태로울 정도로 부족한 수준이다. 해조류 양식이 식량을 생산하지 않고 토지와 물을 소모하기 때문에, 대규모 해조류 양식 사업을 구축하는 것은 식량 부족 문제를 악화시킬 수 있다.

해조류를 연료 공급원으로 이용하는 것과 관련된 두 번째 문제는 해조류를 기르고 오일을 추출하는 데 필요한 장비가 비싸다는 점이다. 해조류 양식장을 시작하는 비용은 높다. 회사들은 해조류를 기르고 햇빛에 노출시키기 위한 대규모 시설물과 해조류에서 오일을 짜낼 복잡한 기계들, 그리고 그 오일을 연료로 사용 가능하게 만들어 주는 데 필요한 기타 장비에 투자해야 할 것이다.

세 번째로, 해조류 양식이 문제가 되는 이유는 해조류를 기르는 데 많은 양의 이산화탄소가 필요하기 때문이다. 모든 식물은 어느 정도의 이산화탄소(CO_2)가 필요한데, 일반적으로 공기 중에서 곧바로 끌어 모은다. 하지만, 해조류는 이 기체의 농도가 매우 높지 않으면 번성하지 못한다. 많은 양의 해조류를 기르려면, 양식자들이 해조류 양식용 탱크에 순수 이산화탄소를 펌프로 주입해야 할 것이다. 이 이산화탄소가 전부 해조류에 의해 흡수되지는 않을 것이며, 상당량은 대기의 일부가 될 것이다. 이산화탄소가 오염 물질로 여겨지기 때문에, 이는 환경에 유해할 것이다.

어휘

biofuel 바이오 연료, 생물 연료　extract 추출하다　algae 해조류　organism 유기체　derived from ~에서 비롯된　replace 대체하다　unique 독특한, 특별한　farm 양식하다, 경작하다　on a large scale 대규모로　shortage 부족　use up 소모하다　operation 사업　invest in ~에 투자하다　facility 시설(물)　complicated 복잡한　squeeze 짜내다　thrive 번성하다　concentration 농도　absorb 흡수하다　significant 상당한　pass into ~의 일부가 되다　atmosphere 대기　pollutant 오염 물질

I think algae-derived biofuel has a bright future despite the concerns you just read about. Let's see how those concerns can be addressed.

Let's talk first about the farmland issue. Your reading says algae farming uses up valuable land and water without giving us food. Actually, this doesn't have to happen with algae farming. Algae can grow pretty much anywhere, even in relatively infertile areas where we cannot grow any other crop. And algae isn't sensitive to the kind of water it grows in: seawater or water that's too dirty to use on food crops works fine. So you can use land and water for growing algae that's useless for growing food; this way nothing at all is wasted.

What you read next is that algae farms have a big start-up cost. But what you may not know is that many kinds of algae can be harvested and re-grown every single week, not just once or twice a year like other plants we use to make fuel—you know, like corn, for example. This means algae can produce something like twenty times more usable fuel each year compared to corn. The income generated by the high volume of fuel production will help algae farmers to make up for the high cost of the equipment very quickly.

Finally, using carbon dioxide gas, or CO_2, should be no cause for concern either. We don't have to generate new CO_2 to feed the algae. Instead, we can use CO_2 that's released by factories as a waste product. You see, CO_2 from factories normally goes straight into the atmosphere and adds to pollution. But if we pump this CO_2 into algae-growing tanks, the algae will absorb some of it, and less of it will end up as pollution. By using CO_2 released by factories, algae farming can actually help lower CO_2 pollution.

해조류에서 비롯되는 바이오 연료는 방금 읽어 본 우려 사항에도 불구하고 미래가 밝다고 생각합니다. 이 우려 사항들이 어떻게 해결될 수 있는지 알아보겠습니다.

양식장 문제와 관련해 먼저 이야기해 보죠. 읽어 본 내용에는 해조류 양식이 우리에게 식량은 제공하지 않으면서 소중한 토지와 물을 소모한다고 나와 있습니다. 실제로, 이는 해조류 양식으로 할 필요가 없습니다. 해조류는 어디서든 꽤 잘 자랄 수 있고, 심지어 우리가 다른 어떤 작물도 재배할 수 없는 비교적 비옥하지 않은 곳에서도 잘 자랍니다. 그리고 해조류는 성장하는 곳에 있는 물의 종류에도 민감하지 않은데, 바닷물이든, 아니면 식용 작물에 사용하기에 너무 더러운 물도 괜찮습니다. 따라서 식량 재배에 유용하지 않은 토지와 물을 해조류를 재배하는 데 이용

할 수 있으며, 이렇게 하면 어떤 것도 전혀 낭비되지 않죠.

다음으로 읽어 본 내용은 해조류 양식장에 초기 비용이 많이 든다는 점입니다. 하지만 여러분이 알지 못하고 있을 수도 있는 부분은 많은 종류의 해조류가 매주 수확되고 다시 재배될 수 있다는 점인데, 우리가 연료를 만드는 데 이용하는 다른 식물들, 그러니까, 예를 들어서, 옥수수처럼 일 년에 겨우 한두 번이 아니라는 거죠. 이는 해조류가 옥수수에 비해 사용 가능한 연료를 매년 스무 배 정도는 더 많이 만들어 낼 수 있다는 뜻입니다. 높은 연료 생산량에 의해 창출되는 수입은 해조류 양식자들이 아주 빠르게 높은 장비 비용을 만회하는 데 도움을 줄 것입니다.

마지막으로, 이산화탄소 기체, 즉 CO_2를 이용하는 것도 우려의 원인이 되지 못할 겁니다. 새로운 CO_2를 만들어 해조류에 공급할 필요가 없습니다. 대신, 공장들이 폐기물로 배출하는 CO_2를 이용하면 됩니다. 말하자면, 공장에서 나오는 CO_2는 보통 대기 중으로 곧장 유입되어 오염을 증가시키죠. 하지만 이 CO_2를 해조류 양식용 탱크에 펌프로 주입하면, 해조류가 그 일부를 흡수하게 되어 결과적으로 더 적은 양이 오염으로 이어집니다. 공장이 배출하는 CO_2를 이용함으로써, 해조류 양식은 실제로 CO_2 오염을 낮추는 데 도움이 될 수 있습니다.

어휘

derived 비롯된　**address** (문제 등을) 해결하다, 처리하다　**relatively** 비교적, 상대적으로　**infertile** 비옥하지 않은, 불모의　**sensitive** 민감한　**harvest** 수확하다　**compared to** ~에 비해　**income** 수입, 수익　**generate** 만들어 내다　**make up for** ~을 만회하다, ~을 보충하다　**release** 배출하다, 방출하다　**atmosphere** 대기　**add to** ~을 증가시키다, ~에 보탬이 되다　**pollution** 오염　**absorb** 흡수하다　**end up as** 결과적으로 ~이 되다　**lower** 낮추다

Question

Summarize the points made in the lecture, being sure to explain how they respond to the specific concerns presented in the reading passage.

강의에서 말하는 요점들이 어떻게 읽기 지문에 제시된 특정 우려 사항에 대해 대응하고 있는지 반드시 설명하면서 요약하시오.

해설

읽기 지문에 제시된 전반적인 요점은 해조류로 만든 바이오 연료가 유망한 청정 에너지 공급원인 것처럼 보일 수 있지만, 그 생산과 관련된 심각한 우려 사항들이 존재한다는 점이다. 그래서 교수는 그러한 우려 사항들을 해결하면서 왜 해조류를 통한 바이오 연료 제조가 좋은 아이디어인지 알려 주고 있다.

고득점 답안은 도입부를 포함해 교수가 말하는 다음 요점들을 다루는 과정에서 어떻게 읽기 지문에 제시된 요점들과 관련되어 있는지 설명해야 한다.

지문의 주요 내용	지문과 대조되는 강의 내용
Farming algae on a large scale means using land and water that needs to be used for growing food.	Algae can grow well in areas too infertile to grow other crops and can use water that is too dirty for other crops; algae can even grow in seawater.
Equipment needed to manufacture fuel from algae is very costly.	Unlike other crops, algae can be harvested every week. The frequent harvesting generates a lot of income, which helps to pay off the start-up costs quickly.
CO$_2$ that algae require for growth is a dangerous pollutant, and some of it might escape into the atmosphere.	Algae farms can use CO$_2$ released by factories as a waste product. Using this source of CO$_2$ can decrease the overall CO$_2$ pollution of the atmosphere.

4점과 5점에 해당하는 답안은 표에 제시된 요점들 및 대조적인 요점들을 이야기하고 연관 지으면서 교수가 언급하는 모든 중요한 뒷받침 세부 정보를 추가해야 한다. 위의 표는 강의의 주된 요점은 포함하고 있지만, 모든 중요한 뒷받침 세부 정보는 포함하지 않을 수 있다.

예제 답안과 채점자 의견

우수 답변

The reading states several disadvantages in the production process of algae based fuel. In the lecture the professer refutes every single point that has been made in the article, therefore expecting a bright future for this specific kind of biofuel.

The first statement made in the passage is that algae farms would have to use up vast amounts as landmass and water and therefore occupy regions that might have been used to decrease the worldwide food scarcity. Contrary to this statement, the professor explains that algae can be grown nearly everywhere, even on land, which is considered infertile for other kind of crops. Furthermore, the needed water might be salty and dirty to still be effecient. In conclusion, no ressources would be wasted by algae farms.

The passage mentions as well the enourmous investment costs that would have to be made in

starting up an algaefuel business. Refuting the article, the professor states that compared to other corps such as corn, farmers are able to harvest algae nearly once a week and are hence able to generate a sales amount up to twenty times bigger than corn would. She believes that the revenues would easily make up the initial investments.

Finally, the reading explains that environmentally harmfull CO$_2$ is needed to feed the plants and the amount that is not absorbed by algaes will be polluting the atmosphere. In the lecture, the professor agrees that CO$_2$ needs to be used but she offers the viable solution to pump it directly from factories to the farmingtanks. The usage of this technique would help to greatly decrease the pollution and help to effectively fight the global warming.

번역

읽기 지문은 해조류 기반 연료의 생산 과정에서 나타나는 여러 단점을 언급하고 있다. 강의에서, 교수는 기사에 제시된 모든 요점을 하나하나 반박하고 있으며, 그에 따라 이 특정 종류의 바이오 연료에 대해 밝은 미래를 예상하고 있다.

지문에 제시된 첫 번째 주장은 해조류 양식장이 엄청나게 많은 땅과 물을 소모함으로써 전 세계의 식량 부족 문제를 감소시키는 데 쓰였을 수도 있는 지역을 차지해야 할 것이라는 점이다. 이 주장과 대조적으로, 교수는 해조류가 거의 어디에서든 재배될 수 있다고 설명하고 있으며, 심지어 다른 종류의 작물에게 비옥하지 않은 것으로 여겨지는 토지에서도 그러하다. 더욱이, 필요한 물은 염분이 있고 더러워도 여전히 효율적일 수 있다. 결론적으로, 어떤 자원도 해조류 양식장에 의해 낭비되지 않을 것이다.

읽기 지문은 해조류 연료 사업을 시작하는 데 있어 이뤄져야 할 엄청난 액수의 투자를 언급하고 있다. 기사 내용을 반박하면서, 교수는 옥수수 같은 다른 작물에 비해, 양식자들이 거의 일주일에 한 번씩 해조류를 수확할 수 있어서 옥수수보다 최대 스무 배는 더 많은 판매액을 창출할 수 있다고 언급하고 있다. 교수는 그 수익이 초기 투자금을 쉽게 만회해 줄 것이라고 생각한다.

마지막으로, 읽기 지문은 환경적으로 유해한 CO$_2$가 그 식물에게 공급하는 데 필요하며, 해조류가 흡수하지 않는 양은 대기를 오염시키게 될 것이라고 설명한다. 강의에서는, 교수가 CO$_2$가 이용되어야 한다는 점에 동의하고 있지만, 공장에서 곧바로 양식장 탱크에 직접 펌프로 주입하는 실행 가능한 해결책을 제안하고 있다. 이러한 기술의 이용은 오염을 크게 감소시키는 데 도움이 될 것이며, 지구 온난화에 효과적으로 맞서는 데 도움이 될 것이다.

채점자 의견

이 답안은 통합형 과제의 고득점 답변에 대한 기준을 충족하고 있다.

▶ 수험자가 강의 및 읽기 지문에 제시된 요점을 잘 선택해 틀을 잡고

연결하고 있다. 글이 전반적으로 잘 정리되어 있으며, 각 중심 단락이 읽기 지문에 제시된 주장들 중 하나를 먼저 간략히 요약한 다음, 그에 대한 교수의 반응을 요약하고 있다.

▶ 교수가 제시하는 모든 중요한 정보가 포함되어 있다.
▶ 어법은 정확하고 효과적으로 사용되었다.

중간 수준의 답변

> Despite the concerns presented in the passage, algae might have a great future in terms of fuel production. These concerns are about farm-land issue , equipments to grow and extract oil,and Carbondioxide need of algae.
>
> It is presented in the passage that fuel derived from algae creates problems due to that algae have to be farmed on larger areas. Since they would cover fertile land, farming may cause food shortages. However, as it is proposed in the listening section that it is quite easy to grow algae in infertile areas. Furthermore, they regrown every single week. For instance; they are 20 times more usable than corn.
>
> In the passage, it is also stated that algae pull a large quantity of Carbondioxide from the air, and not all of them's absorbed by the algae. This forms the other concern for algae extraction to produce oil, whereas as put it in the listening section, less polluted gas can pass into the atmosphere, if the Carbondioxide gas thrown from factories is used for algae. Carbondioxide gas can be pump into algae growing lands,and the amount of Carbondioxide gas pass into the atmosphere can be decreased.
>
> Although manufacturing fuel from algae can create some problems, it is possible to reduce the harmful effects of other pullution causes by using their waste products in algae manufacturing.

채점자 의견

수험자가 읽기 지문에 대한 교수의 반응에 제시된 중요한 요점들은 전달하고 있지만, 글의 일부가 명확하지 않으며, 일부 중요한 정보가 배제되어 있다.

▶ 읽기 지문에 제시된 첫 번째 요점에 대한 교수의 반응 중 오직 일부만 전달함으로써, 더러운 물 또는 바닷물에서 자라는 해조류에 관한 정보를 배제하고 있다.
▶ 교수의 두 번째 요점의 일부 정보를 전달하는 것처럼 보이지만, 그 정보는 모두 명확하지 않으면서 읽기 지문에 제시된 두 번째 요점과 관련되어 있지 않다.
▶ 읽기 지문에 제시된 마지막 요점 및 그에 대한 교수의 반응을 다루고 있지만, 그 범위가 몇몇 곳에서 부정확하다.

Question

Your professor is teaching a class on human resource management. Write a post responding to the professor's question.

In your response, you should do the following.
- Express and support your opinion.
- Make a contribution to the discussion in your own words.

An effective response will contain at least 100 words.

교수가 인적 자원 관리에 관한 수업을 가르치고 있다. 교수의 질문에 답하는 게시물을 작성하시오.
답변을 작성할 때, 다음 사항을 수행해야 한다.
- 자신의 의견을 제시하고 뒷받침할 것.
- 자신만의 글로 논의에 기여할 것.
효과적인 답변은 최소 100자의 단어를 포함한다.

디아즈 박사
이번 주에, 우리는 직업 능력 개발, 즉 직장 내 교육에 대해 이야기하고 있습니다. 일부 직원들은 현재의 직무를 더 잘 하는 데 도움이 될 능력을 개발하는 것을 선호합니다. 다른 이들은 미래의 더 나은 자리를 준비하는 데 도움이 되는 교육에 초점을 맞추는 것을 선호합니다. 어느 종류의 직업 능력 개발 기회가 직원이 이용하는 데 있어 더 중요할까요? 왜 그럴까요?

클레어
현재의 직무와 관련 있는 능력을 확장하는 데 초점을 맞추는 것이 훨씬 더 중요합니다. 즉시 활용할 수 있는 능력을 강화함으로써, 직원들은 상사의 주목을 받게 되어 회사에서 빠르게 승진할 수 있을 것입니다.

폴
회사들은 다양한 교육 프로그램을 제공하며, 직원들은 무엇이든 자신에게 주어지는 기회를 잡아야 합니다, 설사 그것이 현재의 직무와 직접적으로 관련되어 있지 않다 하더라도 말입니다. 언제 더 나은 기회가 나타날지 아무도 모릅니다. 현재의 직무와 관련된 능력에만 초점을 맞춘다고 해서 반드시 더 나은 자리에 대한 최고의 후보자가 되는 것은 아닙니다.

어휘

professional development 직업 능력 개발 training 교육 prefer to do ~하는 것을 선호하다 current 현재의 focus on ~에 초점을 맞추다 take advantage of ~을 이용하다 relevant to ~와 관련된(= related to) strengthen 강화하다 put A to use A를 활용하다 notice 주목하다 be able to do ~할 수 있다 advance 승진하다, 진급하다 a variety of 다양한 present itself 나타나다 not necessarily 반드시 ~하는 것은 아니다 candidate 후보자

Reading

Listening

Speaking

Writing

Test 1

Test 2

Test 3

Test 4

해설

이 온라인 토론 글에서, 교수는 직장 내 교육을 추구하는 직원들이 현재의 일자리를 위해 필요한 능력을 향상시키는 데 초점을 맞춰야 하는지, 아니면 미래에 유용할 수 있는 능력을 터득하는 데 초점을 맞춰야 하는지 묻고 있다. 한 토론 참가자는 현재의 일자리와 관련된 능력을 향상시키는 것이 가장 좋으며, 그렇게 하는 것이 경영진에게 가장 매력적이기도 하다고 주장하는 반면, 다른 참가자는 새로운 취업 기회가 생길 때 새로운 능력을 활용할 수 있을지도 모르기 때문에 다른 분야의 교육 프로그램을 듣는 것이 좋을지도 모른다고 주장한다. 수험자들은 이미 언급된 아이디어들을 파악해 한층 더 자세히 발전시키거나 완전히 새로운 아이디어를 도입할 수 있다. 예를 들어, 일부 수험자들은 심지어 한 사람의 일자리조차 진화하면서 새로운 능력을 필요로 할 가능성이 있다고 주장할 수 있는 반면, 다른 수험자들은 새로운 직장을 찾을 때 가능성을 향상시켜 주는 것이 가능한 가장 다양한 능력을 습득하는 것에 관해 이야기하겠지만, 또 다른 수험자들은 교육을 통해 현재의 일자리에 중요하지만 드물게 쓰이는 능력을 새롭게 하는 것이 얼마나 중요한지 등등을 설명할 수 있다.

예제 답안과 채점자 의견

우수 답변

> I believe it depends on the stage of employment and the year of experience the employee has at the current position. On the one hand, if an employee just joined a new team, it is definitely for the new entrant to focus on training and learning skills that would be helpful for the current position. On the other hand, if an experience employee who is already familiar enough with all current tasks is looking for advancements, it would be helpful to learn new techniques to help them do better in the future. Also, with the development of technology, it is critical to keep learning new technical skills in the fast-changing business world.

번역

저는 고용상의 단계 및 직원이 현재의 일자리에서 얻은 경력의 연차에 따라 다르다고 생각합니다. 한편으로는, 한 직원이 막 새로운 팀에 합류한 경우, 그 신입 사원이 현재의 일자리에 유익할 만한 교육 및 능력 습득에 초점을 맞추는 것이 절대적으로 유리합니다. 다른 한편으로는, 현재의 모든 업무를 이미 충분히 잘 알고 있는 경험 직원이 승진을 바라고 있는 경우, 앞으로 더 잘하도록 도움을 주는 새로운 기술을 배우면 유익할 것입니다. 또한, 기술의 발전으로 인해, 빠르게 변화하는 비즈니스 세계에서 지속적으로 새로운 기술력을 습득하는 것이 아주 중요합니다.

채점자 의견

1. 수험자가 언어 사용에 있어 일관된 능력을 발휘하면서, 온라인 토론에 매우 명확하게 표현된 의견 제시문을 작성했다.
2. 수험자는 직원들이 교육을 위해 활용해야 하는 전략이 회사에 얼마나 오래 머물러 왔는지에 따라 다르다고 명확하게 설명하고 있다.
3. 수험자는 다양한 효과적인 구조 및 정확히 선택한 단어를 활용하고 있지만, 시간이 제한된 상황에서 작성하는 능숙한 수험자에게 예상될 수 있는 단지 몇몇 실수가 존재한다.

중간 수준의 답변

> Its better to get trained in different programmes irrespective of the current skills. World is getting update with technologies . So when companies offer veritie of training programmes all the employees should take oppurtunity to update with new skills. We should always be ready for better and should be bale to always prove best in our current skill along with updated and new skils.
>
> Focusing on current skills and updating will only prove and sustain in current suituation but we will not be able to achieve new skills. For professional development and to get more oppprtunities for all employees compies also should boost employees to get trained irrespective of their personal interest

채점자 의견

1. 수험자는 과제에 대해 부분적으로 성공적인 답변을 제공하고 있다.
2. 대체로 이해 가능하고 대체로 관련되어 있지만, 여러 부분이 불분명하고 어휘 및 문법에 있어 뚜렷한 오류가 존재한다.
3. 주장이 전달되는 방식에 있어, 명료성이 부족한 오류를 보이고 있다.

READING

LOIE FULLER
p. 182

The United States dancer Loie Fuller (1862–1928) found theatrical dance in the late nineteenth century artistically unfulfilling. She considered herself an artist rather than a mere entertainer, and she, in turn, attracted the notice of other artists.

Fuller devised a type of dance that focused on the shifting play of lights and colors on the voluminous skirts or draperies she wore, which she kept in constant motion principally through movements of her arms, sometimes extended with wands concealed under her costumes. She rejected the technical virtuosity of movement in ballet, the most prestigious form of theatrical dance at that time, perhaps because her formal dance training was minimal. Although her early theatrical career had included stints as an actress, she was not primarily interested in storytelling or expressing emotions through dance; the drama of her dancing emanated from her visual effects.

Although she discovered and introduced her art in the United States, she achieved her greatest glory in Paris, where she was engaged by the Folies Bergère in 1892 and soon became "La Loie," the darling of Parisian audiences. Many of her dances represented elements or natural objects—Fire, the Lily, the Butterfly, and so on—and thus accorded well with the fashionable Art Nouveau style, which emphasized nature imagery and fluid, sinuous lines. Her dancing also attracted the attention of French poets and painters of the period, for it appealed to their liking for mystery, their belief in art for art's sake, a nineteenth-century idea that art is valuable in itself rather than because it may have some moral or educational benefit, and their efforts to synthesize form and content.

Fuller had scientific leanings and constantly experimented with electrical lighting (which was then in its infancy), colored gels, slide projections, and other aspects of stage technology. She invented and patented special arrangements of mirrors and concocted chemical dyes for her draperies. Her interest in color and light paralleled the research of several artists of the period, notably the painter Seurat, famed for his Pointillist technique of creating a sense of shapes and light on canvas by applying extremely small dots of color rather than by painting lines. One of Fuller's major inventions was underlighting, in which she stood on a pane of frosted glass illuminated from underneath. This was particularly effective in her *Fire Dance* (1895), performed to the music of Richard Wagner's

로이 풀러

미국 무용가 로이 풀러(1862~1928)는 19세기 말 무용극의 예술성이 불만족스러웠다. 로이 풀러는 자신을 단지 예능인 이라기보다는 예술가로 여겼으며, 이에 따라 다른 예술가들의 주의를 끌었다.

로이 풀러는 자신이 입은 풍성한 치마나 권의(卷衣)에 비추는 조명과 색상의 현란한 변화에 중점을 두는 무용 양식을 창안했으며, 주로 팔 동작을 이용하긴 했지만 때로는 봉을 의상 속에 숨겨 길게 뻗어서 끊임없이 옷자락이 물결치게 했다. 로이 풀러는 당시 무용극의 최고급 표현형식이었던 발레 동작의 기술적 기교를 거부했는데, 정식 무용 교육을 거의 받지 못했기 때문일 것이다. 로이 풀러의 이전 무대 경력에는 배우로서의 기간도 있었지만, 주요 관심사는 춤을 통한 이야기 전개나 감정 표현이 아니었다. 즉 로이 풀러의 춤의 극적 효과는 시각적 효과에서 비롯되었다.

로이 풀러는 미국에서 자신의 예술을 발굴하고 소개했지만, 파리에서 가장 큰 성공을 거두었고, 1892년 그곳에서 폴리 베르제르 뮤직홀에 채용되어 이내 파리 관객들의 총아 '라 로이(La Loie)'가 되었다. 로이 풀러의 많은 춤들이 4대 요소나 자연물—불, 백합, 나비 등—을 표현해서 당시 유행하던 아르누보 스타일과 잘 어울렸는데, 이 스타일은 자연 심상과 유체, 즉 구불구불한 선을 강조했다. 로이 풀러의 무용은 당대 프랑스 시인들과 화가들의 이목도 끌었다. 로이 풀러의 무용이 신비에 대한 그들의 기호, 예술을 위한 예술에 대한 신념, 예술이란 어떤 도덕적이거나 교육적인 이로움이 있어서라기보다는 예술 그 자체로서 가치가 있다는 19세기 사상, 그리고 형식과 의미를 통합하려는 그들의 노력과 일맥상통했기 때문이다.

풀러는 과학적 성향이 있어서 전기 조명(그 당시에는 아직 초창기였다), 컬러필터, 슬라이드 영사, 그리고 무대 기술의 다른 여러 측면을 끊임없이 실험했다. 로이 풀러는 거울을 특수하게 배치하는 방법을 고안하여 특허를 받았고, 권의 염색용 화학 염료를 직접 조제했다. 색상과 빛에 대한 로이 풀러의 관심은 당대의 몇몇 예술가들의 연구에 필적했다. 특히 그 중에서도 선을 그리기보다는 다채로운 색상의 아주 미세한 점을 찍어 캔버스에 형태와 빛의 느낌을 창출하는 점묘화법으로 유명한 화가 쇠라를 꼽을 수 있다. 로이 풀러의 주요 발명품들 중 하나는 하부광이었으며, 풀러는 아래쪽에서 조명을 비추는 서리유리판 위에 올라섰다. 하부광은 리하르트 바그너의 악곡 〈발퀴레의 비행〉을 반주로 하는 〈불의 춤〉(1985)에서 특히 효과적이었다. 이 춤은 화가 앙리 데 툴

Reading
Listening
Speaking
Writing
Test 1
Test 2
Test 3
Test 4

"Ride of the Valkyries." The dance caught the eye of artist Henri de Toulouse-Lautrec, who depicted it in a lithograph.

As her technological expertise grew more sophisticated, so did the other aspects of her dances. **(A)** Although she gave little thought to music in her earliest dances, she later used scores by Gluck, Beethoven, Schubert, Chopin, and Wagner, eventually graduating to Stravinsky, Fauré, Debussy, and Mussorgsky, composers who were then considered progressive. **(B)** She began to address more ambitious themes in her dances such as *The Sea*, in which her dancers invisibly agitated a huge expanse of silk, played upon by colored lights. **(C)** Always open to scientific and technological innovations, she befriended the scientists Marie and Pierre Curie upon their discovery of radium and created a *Radium Dance*, which simulated the phosphorescence of that element. **(D)** She both appeared in films—then in an early stage of development—and made them herself; the hero of her fairy-tale film *Le Lys de la Vie* (1919) was played by Rene Clair, later a leading French film director.

At the Paris Exposition in 1900, she had her own theater, where, in addition to her own dances, she presented pantomimes by the Japanese actress Sada Yacco. She assembled an all-female company at this time and established a school around 1908, but neither.survived her. Although she is remembered today chiefly for her innovations in stage lighting, her activities also touched Isadora Duncan and Ruth St. Denis, two other United States dancers who were experimenting with new types of dance. She sponsored Duncan's first appearance in Europe. Her theater at the Paris Exposition was visited by St. Denis, who found new ideas about stagecraft in Fuller's work and fresh sources for her art in Sada Yacco's plays. In 1924 St. Denis paid tribute to Fuller with the duet *Valse à la Loie*.

루즈-로트렉의 시선을 사로잡았고, 그는 이를 석판화로 묘사했다.

로이 풀러의 기술적 전문 지식이 더욱 정교해지면서 무용의 다른 측면도 발전했다. 초창기 춤에서는 음악에 별로 관심을 두지 않았지만, 나중에는 글룩, 베토벤, 슈베르트, 쇼팽, 바그너의 배경음악을 사용했으며 궁극적으로는 당시 전위적이라는 평을 받던 스트라빈스키, 포레, 드뷔시, 무소르크스키로 범위를 확대했다. 풀러는 〈바다〉 같은 무용 작품에서는 더욱 야심찬 주제를 중점적으로 다루기 시작했으며, 이런 작품에서는 풀러의 무용수들이 모습을 나타내지 않은 채 다채로운 색상의 조명에 맞추어 거대하게 펼쳐진 비단을 흔들었다. 풀러는 항상 과학과 기술의 혁신에 개방적이어서 과학자 부부 피에르 퀴리와 마리 퀴리가 라듐을 발견하자마자 이들의 친구가 되어 〈라듐 댄스〉를 창안했으며, 이 춤은 라듐의 인광성(燐光性)을 흉내냈다. 풀러는 당시 아직 초창기였던 영화에 출연하기도 했고 영화를 직접 제작하기도 했다. 동화를 소재로한 풀러의 영화 〈생명의 백합〉(1919)의 주연을 맡았던 르네 클레어는 훗날 손꼽히는 프랑스 영화감독이 되었다.

1900년 파리 엑스포에서 풀러는 본인 명의의 극장을 세우고 자신의 무용 공연 이외에 일본 여배우 사다 얏코의 팬터마임을 상연했다. 풀러는 이 무렵 여성 무용단을 창단하고 1908년경에는 학교도 설립했지만, 두 곳 모두 풀러가 사망하기 전에 문을 닫았다. 풀러는 오늘날 주로 무대 조명의 혁신으로 기억되지만, 풀러의 활약은 무용의 새 양식을 시도한 미국의 두 무용수 이사도라 던컨과 루스 세인트 데니스에게도 영향을 미쳤다. 풀러는 던컨의 최초 유럽 진출을 후원했다. 파리 엑스포에 있는 풀러의 극장을 방문한 세인트 데니스는 풀러의 작품에서 연출법에 관한 새 아이디어를 얻었고, 사다 얏코의 공연에서는 참신한 소재를 발굴했다. 1924년 세인트 데니스는 2인무 〈라 로이에게 바치는 왈츠〉로 풀러에게 찬사를 바쳤다.

어휘

theatrical dance 무용극, 춤극   unfulfilling 만족스럽지 못한   in turn 이번에는, 차례로   notice 주목, 눈길   devise 고안하다   shifting 이동하는, 바뀌는   voluminous (옷이) 풍성한, 부피가 큰   drapery 권의(卷衣, 천으로 감싸는 식으로 입는 옷)   principally 주로, 대체로   wand 막대기, 지휘봉   conceal 숨기다, 감추다   reject 거절하다, 거부하다   virtuosity 기교   prestigious 유명한, 일류의   stint 일정기간(allotted time)   drama 연출법, 극적효과   emanate ~에서 나오다, 발하다   engage 고용하다   Folies Bergère 폴리 베르제르(파리의 유명한 뮤직홀 겸 극장)   darling 총애(寵兒), 사랑하는 사람   elements 고대 철학 4대 요소(흙, 공기, 불, 물)   accord with ~와 일치하다, 어우러지다   Art Nouveau 아르누보(식물과 꽃을 회화와 건축에 활용하는 예술 양식으로 19세기 말 미국과 유럽에서 유행했다.)   imagery 심상   fluid 흐르는 듯한   sinuous 물결 모양의   liking 취향, 기호   for someone's sake ~을 위하여   in itself 본래, 본질적으로   benefit 이득, 이로움   synthesize 통합하다, 합성하다   leaning 성향, 기호   infancy 초기, 유년기   patent ~의 특허를 얻다   concoct 조제하다, 날조하다   dye 염료   parallel 필적하다   Pointillist 점묘화가, 점묘주의자   underlighting 하부광   pane 판유리   frosted glass 서리유리판   depict 그리다, 묘사하다   lithograph 석판화   expertise 전문지식[기술]   score 배경음악   graduate (범위, 단계 등을) 확대하다, 증진하다   progressive (음악) 전위적인   address ~을 중점적으로 다루다, ~에 본격적으로 착수하다   agitate 흔들다, 선동하다   play upon[on] 연주[연기]하다   be open to ~에 개방적이다   befriend ~와 친구가 되다   simulate ~를 흉내내다   phosphorescence 인광   fairy tale 동화   present 상연하다   pantomime 팬터마임, 무언극   assemble (단체를) 조직하다   company 극단   touch 감동시키다   stagecraft 극작법, 연출법   duet 2인무, 2인극, 2중창   pay tribute to ~에게 경의를 표하다

1. 첫 번째 단락에서 19세기 후반 무용극에 관해 유추할 수 있는 것은?

Ⓐ 무용 분야 밖의 많은 예술가들에게 영향을 미쳤다.
Ⓑ 19세기 초반 무용극과 매우 유사했다.
Ⓒ 순수 예술의 형태라기보다는 예능의 형태에 더 가까웠다.
Ⓓ 미국에서는 비교적 새로운 예술 형태였다.

내용 추론 문제

해설 풀러가 19세기 말 무용극의 예술성에 만족하지 못했고, 자신을 예능인보다 예술가로 여겼다는 설명에서 C를 유추할 수 있다.

2. 두 번째 단락에 따르면, 다음 중 풀러의 무용 양식이 아닌 것은?

Ⓐ 색채를 이용하는 실험
Ⓑ 크고 풍성한 의상
Ⓒ 의상의 끊임없는 움직임
Ⓓ 동작의 기술적 기교

틀린 정보 찾기 문제

해설 풀러는 발레의 기술적 기교를 쓰지 않았다고 했으므로 정답은 D 다.

3. 다음 중 두 번째 단락에 음영으로 표시된 부분의 핵심 정보를 가장 잘 표현한 것은? 정답 외의 보기들은 의미가 상당히 왜곡되거나 본 질적인 정보가 빠져 있다.

Ⓐ 풀러는 춤의 서사나 감정적 가능성보다는 시각적 효과에 더 많은 관심이 있었다.
Ⓑ 풀러는 자신의 작품에서 표현되는 이야기와 감정을 극적으로 표현하기 위해 시각적 효과를 이용했다.
Ⓒ 풀러는 자신의 춤의 극적 효과가 감성적으로 이야기를 풀어내는 방식에서 우러난다고 믿었다.
Ⓓ 시각적 효과에 대한 풀러의 집중적 관심은 여배우로서 일찍이 받은 무대훈련에 기인한다.

문장 재구성 문제

어휘 impact 영향, 효과   narrative 서사   spring from 우러나 다, 솟아나다
해설 풀러는 배우 경력이 있긴 했지만, 보통 배우들처럼 연기나 감정 묘사를 하기보다는 시각적 효과에 더 큰 관심을 두었다고 했으므로 A가 가장 타당하다.

4. 지문의 단어 synthesize와 의미상 가장 가까운 것은?

Ⓐ 향상하다
Ⓑ 정의하다
Ⓒ 단순화하다
Ⓓ 통합하다

어휘 문제

해설 글에서 synthesize는 '통합하다'라는 의미로 쓰였다.

5. 세 번째 단락에 따르면, 풀러의 공연이 파리에서 좋은 평가를 받은 이유는?

Ⓐ 파리 관객들이 미국에서 건너온 예술가들과 예술 운동에 특히 관심이 있었다.
Ⓑ 풀러가 파리에 갔을 때 영향력 있는 시인들이 무용가들로 하여금 풀러의 공연에 관심을 갖도록 노력을 기울였다.
Ⓒ 당시 풀러의 공연은 다른 분야에서 활동하는 프랑스 예술가들에게서 직접적으로 차용된 것이었다.
Ⓓ 풀러의 춤이 파리의 기존 예술적 가치와 조화를 이루었다.

세부 사항 찾기 문제

해설 마지막 문장이 그 이유를 설명하고 있다. 풀러의 춤이 당시 파리 시인들과 화가들의 기호나 믿음, 사상, 시도 등 그들이 예술적으로 가치를 두는 측면들에서 매력이 있었기 때문이다.

6. 네 번째 단락에 따르면, 풀러의 'Fire Dance'가 주목 받은 이유 중 일부라고 할 수 있는 것은?

Ⓐ 유리에 조명을 하기 위해 컬러 패널 사용하기
Ⓑ 불의 이미지를 창출하기 위해 염료와 페인트 사용하기
Ⓒ 아래쪽에서 무용수를 비추는 조명 기법
Ⓓ 쇠라의 점묘화 기법과 유사하게 작은 점들이 찍힌 권의(卷衣)

세부 사항 찾기 문제

해설 Fire Dance와 관련하여 언급된 것은 하부 조명 기법과 바그너의 곡을 배경 음악으로 사용한 것이다.

7. 글쓴이가 풀러의 작품 〈바다〉를 언급한 이유는?

Ⓐ 풀러의 춤 중에서 음악이 중요한 역할을 하지 않았던 춤을 지적하기 위해
Ⓑ 풀러가 가끔 전위적 작곡가들의 음악을 이용한 이유를 설명하기 위해
Ⓒ 풀러가 예술가로서 어떻게 발전해 나갔는지를 하나의 특정한 예를 들어 설명하기 위해
Ⓓ 과학에 대한 풀러의 관심이 공연에 반영된 방식을 설명하기 위해

수사학적 의도 찾기 문제

해설 글쓴이가 무용극 〈바다〉를 언급한 이유는 다섯 번째 단락 첫 문장에서 풀러의 무용이 더욱 발전했다는 설명을 뒷받침할 수 있는 사례이기 때문이다. 즉 여러 음악가들의 곡을 이용한 것에 더불어 더욱 야심찬 주제를 다루기 시작했다고 설명한다. A와 B는 〈바다〉와 직접적인 관련이 없으며, D는 라듐 댄스와 관련이 있으므로 정답이 아니다.

8. 여섯 번째 단락에 따르면, 파리 엑스포의 풀러의 극장에 관해 옳은 것은?

Ⓐ 그곳에서는 풀러의 공연이 아닌 공연도 상연했다.

Ⓑ 그곳에서는 여성 무용수뿐만 아니라 훌륭한 남성 무용수의 특별 공연도 있었다.

Ⓒ 그곳은 풀러를 기리어 이름을 딴 유명한 학교가 되었다.

Ⓓ 그곳은 풀러가 사망한 후에도 극장으로 운영되었다.

세부 사항 찾기 문제

해설 일본 배우 사다 얏코의 팬터마임도 상연했다고 했으므로 A가 정답이다.

9. 지시문: 위에 제시된 지문의 일부를 보시오. 지문에 표시된 **(A)**, **(B)**, **(C)**, **(D)** 중 하나에 다음 문장이 삽입될 수 있다.

For all her originality in dance, her interest expanded beyond it into newly emerging artistic media.

(무용에 뛰어난 창의력이 있었지만, 풀러의 관심은 무용을 넘어 새로이 부상하는 예술 매체로 확대되었다.)

이 문장이 들어갈 가장 적당한 위치는?

As her technological expertise grew more sophisticated, so did the other aspects of her dances. **(A)** Although she gave little thought to music in her earliest dances, she later used scores by Gluck, Beethoven, Schubert, Chopin, and Wagner, eventually graduating to Stravinsky, Fauré, Debussy, and Mussorgsky, composers who were then considered progressive. **(B)** She began to address more ambitious themes in her dances such as *The Sea*, in which her dancers invisibly agitated a huge expanse of silk, played upon by colored lights. **(C)** Always open to scientific and technological innovations, she befriended the scientists Marie and Pierre Curie upon their discovery of radium and created a *Radium Dance*, which simulated the phosphorescence of that element. **(D)** For all her originality in dance, her interest expanded beyond it into newly emerging artistic media. She both appeared in films–then in an early stage of development-and made them herself; the hero of her fairy–tale film *Le Lys de la Vie* (1919) was played by René Clair, later a leading French film director.

Ⓐ   Ⓑ   Ⓒ   Ⓓ

문장 삽입 문제

어휘 originality 독창성

해설 newly emerging artistic media에서 풀러가 무용 이외의 다른 예술 매체에 관심을 가지기 시작했음을 알 수 있다. 따라서 이 문장은 무용에 관한 설명이 끝나고 영화에 관한 이야기로 전환되는 사이, 즉 (D)에 삽입되어야 문맥상 가장 적합하다.

10. 지시문: 지문을 간단히 요약하기 위한 도입 문장이 아래에 제시되어 있다. 아래 보기들 중에서 지문의 가장 중요한 개념을 표현한 문장 3개를 골라 요약을 완성하라. 보기들 중에는 지문에 나오지 않았거나 중요하지 않은 개념이기 때문에 요약문으로 적절치 않은 것들도 있다. 이 문제의 배점은 2점이다.

로이 풀러는 매우 중요한 무용가였던 동시에 혁신적인 무용가였다.

Ⓐ 풀러는 19세기 후반 관객들이 대부분 무용극에 대해 흥미를 잃었다고 생각했다.

Ⓑ 풀러는 시인과 화가들의 작품을 해석하는 무용을 창안함으로써 무용을 부분적으로 변형했다.

Ⓒ 풀러의 작품은 실험적 무용에 관심이 있던 다른 여러 무용가들에게 영향을 미쳤다.

Ⓓ 풀러는 무용극 공연에 많은 기술적 혁신을 도입했다.

Ⓔ 풀러는 현역 기간 내내 지속적 발전을 이룩해 복합적 작품을 더 많이 만들고 예술의 새 영역을 탐구했다.

Ⓕ 1920년대에 이르러, 파리 엑스포의 풀러 극장은 혁신적 무용의 세계적 중심이 되었다.

지문 요약하기 문제

어휘 innovative 혁신적인 transform 변형하다 interpretation (예술 작품의) 해석, (개인적 해석을 바탕으로 하는) 연기, 연주

해설 보기 A는 지문에서 뚜렷이 언급한 적이 없다. 보기 B에 관해서는 세 번째 단락에서 시인과 화가들의 주목을 끌었다는 설명만 있을 뿐 무용과의 직접적 관련을 시사하는 내용이 없다. 보기 F의 경우, 여섯 번째 단락에서 극장을 언급했지만 이후 어떻게 되었는지 알 수 없다.

Icebergs are massive blocks of ice, irregular in shape; they float with only about 12 percent of their mass above the sea surface. They are formed by glaciers—large rivers of ice that begin inland in the snows of Greenland, Antarctica, and Alaska—and move slowly toward the sea. The forward movement, the melting at the base of the glacier where it meets the ocean, and waves and tidal action cause blocks of ice to break off and float out to sea.

Icebergs are ordinarily blue to white, although they sometimes appear dark or opaque because they carry gravel and bits of rock. They may change color with changing light conditions and cloud cover, glowing pink or gold in the morning or evening light, but this color change is generally related to the low angle of the Sun above the horizon. (A) However, travelers to Antarctica have repeatedly reported seeing green icebergs in the Weddell Sea and, more commonly, close to the Amery Ice Shelf in East Antarctica.

(B) One explanation for green icebergs attributes their color to an optical illusion when blue ice is illuminated by a near-horizon red Sun, but green icebergs stand out among white and blue icebergs under a great variety of light conditions. (C) Another suggestion is that the color might be related to ice with high levels of metallic compounds, including copper and iron. (D) Recent expeditions have taken ice samples from green icebergs and ice cores—vertical, cylindrical ice samples reaching down to great depths—from the glacial ice shelves along the Antarctic continent. Analyses of these cores and samples provide a different solution to the problem.

The ice shelf cores, with a total length of 215 meters (705 feet), were long enough to penetrate through glacial ice—which is formed from the compaction of snow and contains air bubbles—and to continue into the clear, bubble-free ice formed from seawater that freezes onto the bottom of the glacial ice. The properties of this clear sea ice were very similar to the ice from the green iceberg. The scientists concluded that green icebergs form when a two-layer block of shelf ice breaks away and capsizes (turns upside down), exposing the bubble-free shelf ice that was formed from seawater.

A green iceberg that stranded just west of the Amery Ice Shelf showed two distinct layers: bubbly blue-white ice and bubble-free green ice separated by a one-meter-long ice layer containing sediments. The green ice portion was textured by seawater erosion. Where cracks were present, the color was light green because of light scattering; where no cracks were present, the color was dark green. No air bubbles were present in the green ice, suggesting that the ice was not formed from the compression of snow but instead from the freezing of seawater. Large concentrations of single-celled organisms with green pigments (coloring substances) occur along

녹색 빙산

빙산은 거대한 얼음 덩어리고, 형태가 일정하지 않다. 빙산은 부피의 12퍼센트만 수면 위로 드러낸 채 떠다닌다. 빙산은 빙하–그린란드, 남극대륙, 알래스카의 내륙 설원에서 발생한 거대한 얼음 강–에 의해 형성되어 바다 쪽으로 서서히 이동한다. 전진운동, 바닷물과 접촉하는 빙산 하부의 용해, 그리고 파도와 조석 작용으로 얼음 덩어리가 갈라져 바다로 떠내려간다.

빙산은 대개 푸르스름한 백색이지만, 가끔 어두워 보이거나 불투명하게 보이기도 하는데, 자갈이과 암석 조각을 함유하기 때문이다. 빙산은 일조 조건이나 운량(雲量)의 변화에 따라 색상이 바뀔 수도 있으며, 아침이나 저녁에 햇빛을 받아 분홍빛이나 금빛을 띠기도 한다. 하지만 이 색상 변화는 대개 낮은 일사각과 연관된 현상이다. 그러나 남극 대륙 여행자들로부터 웨델 해(海)에서, 그리고 더욱 더 흔하게는 남극대륙 동부의 애머리 빙붕 근처에서 녹색 빙산을 목격했다는 보고가 줄을 잇고 있다.

녹색 빙산을 설명하는 한 가지 이론은 청색 얼음이 수평선에 가까운 붉은 태양의 빛을 받아 착시 현상을 일으켜 녹색으로 보인다는 것이다. 그러나 녹색 빙산은 온갖 다양한 일조 조건에서도 백색 빙산과 청색 빙산 사이에서 두드러져 보인다. 다른 가설은 그 색상이 구리와 철 등의 금속성 화합물을 다량으로 함유한 얼음과 관련이 있을 수 있다는 것이다. 최근 탐사에서 녹색 빙산의 얼음 표본과 남극대륙 주변의 빙붕에서 채취한 빙핵—매우 깊은 곳에서 시추한 원통형 얼음 표본—을 채취했다. 이 빙핵과 얼음 표본의 분석 결과는 녹색 빙산의 정체에 관한 색다른 설명을 제시한다.

빙붕핵은 총 길이가 215미터(705피트)이고, 이는 빙하 얼음–눈의 압밀(壓密)에 의해 형성되고 기포를 함유한다–을 관통하기에 충분하고, 해수가 빙하 얼음의 아래쪽에 얼어붙으면서 형성된 맑고 기포가 없는 얼음의 내부로 이어진다. 이 맑은 해수 얼음의 특성은 녹색 빙산의 얼음과 매우 유사하다. 과학자들은 녹색 빙산이 형성되는 경우는 두 개의 층으로 된 빙붕이 갈라져 전복되어(거꾸로 뒤집혀서), 해수로 형성되어 기포가 없는 얼음이 노출될 때라는 결론을 내렸다.

애머리 빙붕의 정서쪽에 얹혀 있는 녹색 빙산은 확연히 구분되는 두 개의 얼음 층을 드러냈다. 즉 기포가 많은 청백색 얼음과 기포가 없는 녹색 얼음이 퇴적물이 함유된 두께 1미터의 얼음층에 의해 나뉘어 있다. 녹색 얼음 부분에는 해수 침식으로 물결 무늬가 있었다. 균열이 있는 부분은 빛의 산란으로 색상이 연녹색이었고, 균열이 없는 부분은 진녹색이다. 녹색 얼음에는 기포가 존재하지 않았고, 이는 눈이 압축되어 형성된 것이 아니라 해수의 결빙으로 형성된 것임을 시사한다. 이 지역 빙붕의 가장자리에는 녹색 색소(색상을 나타내는 물질)가 있는 단세포 생물들이 다량으로 농축되

Reading

Listening

Speaking

Writing

Test 1

Test 2

Test 3

Test 4

the edges of the ice shelves in this region, and the seawater is rich in their decomposing organic material. The green iceberg did not contain large amounts of particles from these organisms, but the ice had accumulated dissolved organic matter from the seawater. It appears that unlike salt, dissolved organic substances are not excluded from the ice in the freezing process. Analysis shows that the dissolved organic material absorbs enough blue wavelengths from solar light to make the ice appear green.

Chemical evidence shows that platelets (minute flat portions) of ice form in the water and then accrete and stick to the bottom of the ice shelf to form a slush (partially melted snow). The slush is compacted by an unknown mechanism, and solid, bubble-free ice is formed from water high in soluble organic substances. When an iceberg separates from the ice shelf and capsizes, the green ice is exposed.

The Amery Ice Shelf appears to be uniquely suited to the production of green icebergs. Once detached from the ice shelf, these bergs drift in the currents and wind systems surrounding Antarctica and can be found scattered among Antarctica's less colorful icebergs.

어 있으며, 바닷물에는 이들이 분해한 유기물질이 풍부하다. 녹색 빙산은 이런 유기체(미생물)를 많이 함유하지는 않지만, 얼음에는 바닷물 속에 용해된 유기물질이 축적되어 있다. 소금과는 달리 용해된 유기 물질은 동결 과정에서 얼음으로부터 방출되지 않는 듯하다. 분석에 의하면, 용해된 유기 물질이 얼음을 녹색으로 보이게 하는 데 충분할 정도의 청색 파장을 태양광에서 흡수한다.

화학적 증거도 물속에서 박판형 결빙(미세한 판형 얼음 결정)이 형성된 다음 뭉쳐져서 커지면서 빙붕의 하부에 들러붙어 슬러시(약간 녹은 눈)가 형성된다는 것을 입증한다. 이 슬러시는 알 수 없는 작용에 의해 압축되고, 단단하고 기포가 없는 얼음은 가용성 유기 물질이 풍부히 함유된 물로 형성된다. 빙산이 빙붕에서 갈라져 전복될 때 녹색 얼음이 노출된다.

애머리 빙붕은 녹색 빙산의 생성에 유일무이하게 적합한 듯하다. 빙산은 일단 빙붕에서 분리되면 남극 대륙 주변의 해류와 풍계(風系)에 의해 표류하다가 남극대륙의 일반 색상의 빙산들 사이에 여기저기 흩어진 채 발견될 수 있다.

어휘

iceberg 빙산 massive 거대한 mass 부피, 큰 덩어리 glacier 빙하 inland 내륙에서 Antarctica 남극 대륙 base 하부, 바닥, 기슭, 기저부 tidal action 조수간만 활동 break off 갈라지다, 파손되다 opaque 불투명한, 어두운 gravel 자갈, 사력층 bits of 약간의, 소량의 light condition 일조 상황[조건] cloud cover 운량(雲量) Weddell Sea 웨들 해(海)(남대서양 남극대륙 만입부의 해협) Amery Ice Shelf 애머리 빙붕 attribute to ~에 원인이 있다 optical illusion 착시 stand out 두드러지다, 눈에 띄다 metallic compound 금속성 화합물 ice core 빙핵(빙하 깊은 곳을 시추해 얻는 원통형 얼음 덩어리) (glacial) ice shelf 빙붕, 대륙붕빙(빙상의 끝 부분이 바다로 밀려 나와 떠 있는 것) penetrate 통과하다, 관통하다 compaction (퇴적물의) 압밀, 압축 air bubble 기포(氣泡) bubble-free 기포가 없는 property 특성 capsize 뒤집히다, 전복하다 strand 좌초하다, 기슭에 올라앉다 sediment 퇴적물, 침전물 portion 일부, 부분 texture 결이 지다, 거칠거칠하다 erosion 침식, 부식 crack 균열, 갈라진 틈새 scattering 산란, 흩뿌려짐 compression 압착, 압축 concentration 농축 single-celled organism 단세포 생물 pigment 색소 rich in ~이 풍부한 decompose 분해하다, 부패시키다 accumulate 축적되다, 퇴적되다 dissolved 용해된, 녹은 exclude 제외하다, 배제하다 wavelength 파장 platelet (ice) 박판형 결빙(추운 바다에서 빙핵의 구실을 하는 얇은 판형 얼음 결정) minute 미세한 accrete 부착하여 커지다 slush 녹기 시작한 눈 soluble 가용성의, 녹는 be suited to ~에 적합하다 detach 분리하다 drift 표류하다, 떠돌다 current 해류 wind system 풍계(계절풍, 무역풍 등 넓은 지역에 걸쳐서 일정하게 부는 바람의 계통)

11. 첫 번째 단락에 따르면, 다음 중 빙산에 대해 사실이 아닌 것은?

Ⓐ 빙산은 형태가 불규칙적이다.

Ⓑ 빙산은 빙하가 바다와 만날 때 형성된다.

Ⓒ 빙산은 대부분의 부피가 수면 위에 드러나 있다.

Ⓓ 파도와 조수가 빙산을 빙하로부터 분리시킨다.

틀린 정보 찾기 문제

해설 전체 부피의 12%만 수면 위로 드러나 있다고 했으므로 C는 사실이 아니다.

12. 두 번째 단락에 따르면, 빙산의 색상이 어두워지거나 불투명하게 되는 원인은 무엇인가?

Ⓐ 많은 운량

Ⓑ 자갈이나 암석 조각

Ⓒ 낮은 일사각

Ⓓ 빙산 표면의 큰 균열

세부 사항 찾기 문제

해설 두 번째 단락 첫 번째 문장에서 자갈과 암석 조각이 섞여 있어서 어둡거나 불투명하게 보인다고 했다.

13. 지문의 단어 penetrate와 의미상 가장 가까운 것은?

Ⓐ 모으다   Ⓑ 꿰뚫다

Ⓒ 녹이다   Ⓓ 견디다

어휘 문제

해설 지문에서 penetrate는 '관통하다' 라는 의미로 쓰였다.

14. 네 번째 단락에 따르면, 빙하는 어떻게 형성되는가?

Ⓐ 눈의 압밀로

Ⓑ 빙붕 하부의 해수 결빙으로

Ⓒ 빙붕에서 갈라져

Ⓓ 두 층으로 된 빙붕이 뒤집혀서

세부 사항 찾기 문제

해설 첫 번째 문장의 glacial ice–which is formed from the compaction of snow에서 눈의 압밀이 빙하 형성의 원인임을 알 수 있다.

15. 네 번째 단락에 따르면, 다음 중 과학자들이 녹색 빙산의 형성 원인을 설명할 수 있도록 빙붕핵이 보여 주는 것은?

Ⓐ 녹색 빙산 하부의 얼음은 해수의 결빙으로 생성되어 기포가 없다.

Ⓑ 기포가 없는 얼음은 빙붕의 상부에서 찾아볼 수 있다.

Ⓒ 빙하 얼음은 해수 얼음보다 더 가볍고 물에 더 잘 뜬다.

Ⓓ 빙붕 하부의 맑은 해수 얼음은 녹색 빙산에서 채취한 얼음과 유사하다.

세부 사항 찾기 문제

해설 두 번째 문장(The properties of this clear sea ice were very similar to the ice from the green iceberg.) 다음에 녹색 빙산의 형성에 관한 과학자들의 결론을 설명하고 있다. 즉 과학자들은 녹색 빙산의 얼음이 해수 얼음과 특성이 비슷하다는 사실에

근거하여 녹색 빙산이 해수로 형성되었다는 결론을 내렸음을 알 수 있다.

16. 글쓴이가 '녹색 얼음 부분은 해수로 인한 침식으로 결이 져 있다.' 라고 언급한 이유는?

Ⓐ 빙산의 균열이 짙은 녹색이 아니라 옅은 녹색으로 보이는 이유를 설명하기 위해

Ⓑ 녹색 얼음이 백색 얼음보다 해수에 부식이 더 잘 된다는 사실을 시사하기 위해

Ⓒ 녹색 얼음이 하부였는데 나중에 뒤집혔다는 견해를 뒷받침하기 위해

Ⓓ 녹색 얼음에서 기포가 제거된 과정을 설명하기 위해

수사학적 의도 찾기 문제

해설 녹색 얼음 부분에 해수로 침식된 흔적이 있다는 말은 원래 바다 속에 잠겨 있었음을 뜻한다. 'the ice was not formed from the compression of snow but instead from the freezing of seawater' 에서 녹색 얼음 부분이 해수의 결빙으로 생성되었음을 알 수 있다. 따라서 녹색 얼음 부분이 해수로 인한 침식으로 결이 져 있었다는 말은 이 부분이 원래는 빙산의 하부였는데 나중에 뒤집혔다는 견해를 뒷받침하기 위한 근거에 해당한다.

17. 지문의 단어 excluded와 의미상 가장 가까운 것은?

Ⓐ 배출되었다

Ⓑ 압착되었다

Ⓒ 손상되었다

Ⓓ 모였다

어휘 문제

어휘 keep out ~을 안에 들이지 않다, 밖에 내놓다

해설 글에서 excluded는 '배출되었다' 라는 의미로 쓰였다.

18. 다음 중 지문에서 뒷받침하는 것은?

Ⓐ 애머리 빙붕은 녹색 빙산만을 생성한다.

Ⓑ 애머리 빙붕이 녹색 빙산을 생성하는 이유는 애머리 빙붕의 얼음이 구리와 철 같은 금속 합성물을 함유하기 때문이다.

Ⓒ 애머리 빙붕이 녹색 빙산을 생성하는 이유는 해수에는 특정 종류의 용해성 유기 물질이 풍부하기 때문이다.

Ⓓ 애머리 빙붕에서 멀리 떨어진 곳에서는 녹색 빙산을 찾아볼 수 없다.

세부 사항 찾기 문제

해설 다섯 번째 단락 마지막 문장에서 용해된 유기 물질이 태양광의 청색 파장을 흡수해서 얼음이 녹색으로 보인다고 했으므로 C가 정답이다. 마지막 단락에서 애머리 빙붕이 빙붕 생성에 유일하게 적합한 듯하다고 했지 녹색 빙산만을 생성한다고 하지는 않았으므로 A는 정답이 아니다. 세 번째 단락에서 언급한 금속 화합물과 녹색 빙산의 색상의 관계는 입증되지 않은 가설에 불과하므로 B 역시 정답이 아니다. 녹색 빙산이 해류에 떠내려가 남극 대륙의 일반 색상의 빙산들 사이에서 발견될 수 있다고 했으므로 D도 옳은 내용이 아니다.

19. 지시문: 위에 제시된 지문의 일부를 보시오. 지문에 표시된 **(A)**, **(B)**, **(C)**, **(D)** 중 하나에 다음 문장이 삽입될 수 있다.

Scientists have differed as to whether icebergs appear green as a result of light conditions or because of something in the ice itself.

(과학자들은 빙산이 녹색으로 보이는 것이 일조 조건의 결과인지 얼음 자체에 함유된 어떤 것 때문인지에 대해 의견을 달리한다.)

이 문장이 들어갈 가장 적당한 위치는?

(A) However, travelers to Antarctica have repeatedly reported seeing green icebergs in the Weddell Sea and, more commonly, close to the Amery Ice Shelf in East Antarctica. **(B)** Scientists have differed as to whether icebergs appear green as a result of light conditions or because of something in the ice itself. One explanation for green icebergs attributes their color to an optical illusion when blue ice is illuminated by a near-horizon red Sun, but green icebergs stand out among white and blue icebergs under a great variety of light conditions. **(C)** Another suggestion is that the color might be related to ice with high levels of metallic compounds, including copper and iron. **(D)** Recent expeditions have taken ice samples from green icebergs and ice cores—vertical, cylindrical ice samples reaching down to great depths—from the glacial ice shelves along the Antarctic continent.

Analyses of these cores and samples provide a different solution to the problem.

Ⓐ   Ⓑ   Ⓒ   Ⓓ

문장 삽입 문제

해설 녹색 빙산의 형성 원인에 대해 과학자들이 의견을 달리한다고 했으므로, 이 문장은 다른 의견의 예시에 해당하는 (B)와 (C)보다 앞서야 한다. 따라서 가장 적합한 곳은 (B)다.

20. 지시문: 지문을 간단히 요약하기 위한 도입 문장이 아래에 제시되어 있다. 아래 보기들 중에서 지문의 가장 중요한 개념을 표현한 문장 3개를 골라 요약을 완성하라. 보기들 중에는 지문에 나오지 않았거나 중요하지 않은 개념이기 때문에 요약문으로 적절치 않은 것들도 있다. 이 문제의 배점은 2점이다.

녹색으로 보이는 빙산들이 있는 이유를 설명하기 위해서, 일조 조건으로부터 금속성 화합물의 존재에 이르기까지 몇 가지 가설들이 제시되었다.

Ⓐ 빙핵은 구리와 철을 비롯한 금속성 화합물이 농축되어 녹색 빙산이 생겼다는 결론을 내리는 데 이용되었다.

Ⓑ 모든 빙붕이 녹색 빙산을 생성할 수 있지만, 애머리 빙붕은 특히 그런 조건을 잘 갖추고 있다.

Ⓒ 녹색 빙산은 두 층으로 이루어진 얼음 덩어리가 빙하에서 갈라져 뒤집혀서 하부가 보이도록 노출되었을 때 형성된다.

Ⓓ 빙핵과 표본은 빙붕과 녹색 빙산에 모두 기포가 있는 빙하 얼음층과 기포가 없는 해수 얼음 층이 있음을 밝혀냈다.

Ⓔ 녹색 빙산은 박판형 결빙과 가용성 유기 녹색 염료를 함유한 해수와 접촉할 때 까지는 백색이었다.

Ⓕ 녹색 빙산의 경우, 해수 얼음에는 해수의 유기물질이 다량 농축되어 있다.

지문 요약하기 문제

어휘 determine (문제 등을) 해결하다, 결론을 내리다   come into contact with ~와 접촉하다

해설 금속성 화합물에 관한 논의는 결론이라기보다는 여러 가설 중 하나에 해당하므로 보기 A는 잘못된 내용이다. 모든 빙붕이 아니라 일부 빙붕이 녹색 빙붕을 생성할 수 있는데, 특히 애머리 빙붕이 적합하므로 보기 B는 옳은 요약이 아니다. 보기 E의 경우 또한, 녹색 빙산은 녹색 유기 염료를 포함하는 해수가 결빙하여 생성되므로 잘못된 요약이고, 보기 C, D는 네 번째 단락, 보기 F는 다섯 번째 단락에서 확인할 수 있다.

LISTENING

 T-34

Questions 1-5   p. 196

N Narrator   P Professor   F Female Student

Script

N Listen to a conversation between a student and a professor.

P Sandy, how's class been going for you this semester?

F Oh, it's great. I really like your business psychology class, but I have one major concern about the last assignment: you know — the one where we have to interview a local business owner, uh, I mean entrepreneur?

P Are you having trouble coming up with interview questions?

F Well, that's just it. I mean I worked on my high school newspaper for years, so I actually have great questions to ask. The thing is... I'm new to the area, and I don't know people off campus... So I was wondering if... well, could you possibly give me the name of someone I could interview... ?

P You don't know anyone who owns a business?

F Well, yeah, back home... my next-door neighbors — they own a shoe store, and they're really successful — but they're not local.

P Well, it wouldn't be fair to the other students if I gave you the name of a contact — but I could help you figure out a way to find someone on your own. Let's see... Do you read the local newspaper?

F Sure, whenever I have the time.

P Well, the business section in the paper often has stories about local business people who've been successful. If you find an article, you could call the person who is profiled.

F You mean, just call them up... out of the blue... and ask them if they'll talk to me?

P Sure, why not?

F Well, aren't people like that awfully busy? Too busy to talk to a random college student.

P Many people enjoy telling the story of how they got started. Remember, this is a business psychology class, and for this assignment, I want you to get some real insight about business owners, their personality, what drives them to become an entrepreneur.

F Like, how they think?

P And what motivates them. Why did they start their business? I'm sure they'd talk to you, especially if you tell them you might start a business someday.

N 교수와 학생 간의 대화를 들으시오.

P 샌디, 이번 학기 수업은 어때요?

F 예, 잘되고 있어요. 교수님의 경영 심리학 강의는 정말 좋아요. 그런데 지난번 과제 때문에 걱정거리가 하나 있어요. 아시겠지만 이 지역의 사업주, 기업인 인터뷰를 하는 과제 말이에요.

P 인터뷰 질문을 준비하는 데 문제 있어요?

F 예, 바로 그 부분이에요. 제가 드리고 싶은 말씀은, 그러니까 고등학교 때 몇 년 동안 학보사에서 일해서 사실 좋은 질문거리는 있어요. 문제가 되는 건, 전 이 지역이 처음이라서 학교 밖의 사람들은 잘 몰라요. 그래서 혹시 인터뷰할 만한 사람을 교수님께서 추천해 주실 수 있으실까요?

P 사업하는 사람을 아무도 모른다고요?

F 예, 고향에 가면 옆집에서 구두 가게를 하는데 장사가 정말 잘 되요. 하지만 그 사람들은 이 지역 사람들이 아니잖아요.

P 음, 샌디에게 만나볼 만한 사람의 이름을 가르쳐 준다면 다른 학생들에게는 불공평하겠지요. 하지만 샌디 스스로 누군가를 찾아낼 수 있는 방법을 생각해 내도록 도와줄 수는 있어요. 어디 보자. 혹시 지역 신문 봐요?

F 물론이에요. 짬 날 때마다요.

P 그러면 신문 경제란에 성공한 지역 사업가들에 대한 기사가 자주 실릴 거예요. 어떤 기사 하나를 찾아서, 거기 신상이 소개된 사람에게 전화를 해 볼 수 있을 거예요.

F 그러니까 그냥 전화를 걸어서 난데없이 인터뷰 해달라고 부탁하라는 말씀이세요?

P 그럼, 당연하지요.

F 저어, 그런 분들은 대단히 바쁘지 않을까요? 너무 바빠서 아무 대학생과 얘기할 수는 없을 텐데요.

P 많은 사람들이 자기가 어떻게 시작했는지 남에게 들려주고 싶어 해요. 잊지 마세요. 이 강의는 경영 심리학 강의고, 난 이 과제를 통해 여러분이 사업가와 그들의 성격, 그리고 무엇에 자극을 받아서 사업가가 되었는지에 관해 진정한 통찰력을 얻기 바래요.

F 이를테면 그들의 사고방식이요?

P 그리고 동기가 무엇인지. 그들은 왜 자영업을 시작했을까요? 틀림없이 샌디에게 얘기해 줄 거예요. 특히 언젠가 샌디도 창업할 거라고 말하면요.

F I'm not sure I'd have the guts to do that. Opening a business seems so risky, so scary.

P Well, you can ask them if they felt that way too. Now you just need to find someone to interview to see if your instincts are correct.

F 제게 그럴 만한 배짱이 있는지 모르겠어요. 창업은 너무 위험하고, 너무 겁나요.

P 그 사람들도 그렇게 느꼈는지 물어볼 수도 있어요. 샌디의 직관이 맞는지 알아 보려면, 인터뷰 대상을 찾기만 하면 되겠네요.

어휘

business psychology 경영 심리학, 비즈니스 심리학   concern 우려, 걱정   assignment 과제, 숙제   entrepreneur 사업가   come up with 생각해내다   off campus 캠퍼스 밖의   next-door neighbor 옆집 사람(이웃)   fair 공평한   figure out (방법, 해결책을) 찾다, 이해하다   on one's own 혼자서, 자력으로   business section (신문) 경제란   article (신문, 잡지) 기사   profile 인물을 소개하다   out of blue 뜻밖에, 난데없이   awfully 대단히, 매우   random 임의의, 닥치는 대로의   insight 통찰력, 식견   personality 성격, 개성   drive someone to do ~하도록 자극하다   motivate 동기를 부여하다   guts 배짱, 용기   risky 위험한, 모험적인   instinct 본능, 직관

---

1. 학생이 교수를 찾아간 이유는 무엇인가?

Ⓐ 인터뷰 질문 작성법에 관해 조언을 구하기 위해
Ⓑ 인터뷰 대상자를 찾는 데 도움을 얻기 위해
Ⓒ 창업에 관해 조언을 구하기 위해
Ⓓ 교수와 인터뷰 약속을 잡기 위해

내용의 목적을 묻는 문제

어휘 ask for advice on ~에 대한 조언을 구하다   schedule 일정을 세우다
해설 학생은 인터뷰 대상자를 선정할 수 없어서 교수에게 적당한 사람을 소개해 달라고 부탁했다.

2. 학생이 자신의 고등학교 학보사를 언급한 이유는?

Ⓐ 인터뷰를 학교 신문에 게재할 계획임을 교수에게 통보하기 위해
Ⓑ 본인에게 과제가 어려운 이유를 설명하기 위해
Ⓒ 학교 신문에 글 쓰기를 즐긴다는 것을 보여 주기 위해
Ⓓ 인터뷰 진행 경험이 있음을 알려 주기 위해서

의도 파악 문제

어휘 print (신문) 게재하다   indicate 보여 주다, 의견을 말하다
해설 학생은 자신이 고등학교 학보사에서 몇 년간 일한 경험이 있어서 좋은 인터뷰 질문이 있다고 말한다. 즉 인터뷰 진행에는 익숙하다는 뜻을 전달하기 위해 학보사를 언급했다.

3. 교수는 학생을 어떻게 도와주는가?

Ⓐ 학생에게 지역 사업주 명단을 준다
Ⓑ 학생이 고향 마을 사업주를 인터뷰하도록 허락한다.
Ⓒ 학생에게 신문 경제란을 읽어 보라고 권한다.
Ⓓ 학생에게 과제를 완료하기 위한 시간을 더 준다.

세부 정보 찾기 문제

해설 교수는 학생에게 신문 경제란을 보면 지역 사업가들의 이야기를 찾을 수 있다고 충고한다.

4. 교수는 학생이 과제에서 무엇을 배우기 원하는가?

Ⓐ 창업의 위험성
Ⓑ 지역 기업에 관한 기사 작성이 중요한 이유
Ⓒ 상세한 사업 계획서 작성법
Ⓓ 사업주들의 전형적 성격 특성

세부 정보 찾기 문제

어휘 traits (성격 등의) 특성, 특색   typical 전형적인
해설 교수는 학생이 사업가를 대상으로 인터뷰를 진행하면서 성격과 창업 동기를 알아 보라고 했으므로 D가 정답이다.

5. 대화의 일부를 다시 듣고 질문에 답하라.

🎧 T-35

P Are you having trouble coming up with interview questions?
S Well, that's just it. I mean I worked on my high school newspaper for years, so I actually have great questions to ask.

N What does the student imply?

Ⓐ 학생이 교수의 반응에 놀랐다.
Ⓑ 교수가 학생의 걱정거리를 제대로 파악하지 못했다.
Ⓒ 교수가 학생의 문제가 무엇인지 알아맞혔다.
Ⓓ 학생이 과제를 마치고 싶어하지 않는다.

의도 파악 문제

어휘 reaction 반응, 태도   identify 확인하다, 식별하다
해설 질문을 생각해내는 데 어려움이 있는지 묻는 교수에게 학생은 학보 기자 생활을 해서 좋은 질문거리는 있다고 했으므로 B가 정답이다.

Questions 6-11

N Narrator P Professor

Script

N Listen to part of a lecture in an anthropology class.

P OK, I, I want to begin today by talking about calendars. I know, some of you are thinking it's not all that fascinating, right? But listen, the next time you look at a calendar, I want you to keep something in mind. There are at least three natural ways of measuring the... the passage of time—by day, by month, and by year. And these are all pretty easy to see, right? I mean a day is based on one rotation of Earth. A month is how long the Moon takes to move around the Earth. And a year is the time it takes for Earth to move around the Sun, right? So they're all based on natural events. But the natural clocks of Earth, the Moon, and the Sun run on different times, and you can't divide any one of these time periods by another one without having some messy fraction left over. I mean one lunar month—that's the time it takes for the Moon to go around Earth—one month is about 29 and a half days... not really a nice round number. And one year is a little more than 365 days. So these are obviously numbers that don't divide into each other very neatly. And this makes it pretty difficult to create some sort of tidy calendar that really works.

Not that different cultures haven't tried. Have any of you ever been to Stonehenge? No... you know, that amazing circle of giant stones in England? Well, if you ever go, and find yourself wondering why this culture way back in prehistoric England would go to so much work to construct this monumental ring of enormous stones,... well, keep in mind that a lot of us think it was designed, at least partially, as a calendar—to mark when the seasons of the year begin, according to the exact day when the Sun comes up from a particular direction. I have colleagues who insist it's a temple, maybe, or a tomb... but they can't deny that it was also used as a calendar... probably to help figure out, for example, when farmers should begin their planting each year.

The Mayans, in Central America, also invented a calendar, but for a different purpose. The Mayans, especially the royalty and priests, wanted to look at long cycles of history—so the calendar they used had to be able to count far into the future as well as far into the past. And not only were the Mayans keeping track of the natural timekeepers we mentioned before—Earth, the Moon, and the Sun—but another natural timekeeper: the planet Venus.

Venus rises in the sky as the morning star every 584 days,

N 문화인류학 강의의 일부를 들으시오.

P 자, 오늘은 달력에 관해 이야기하면서 시작하겠습니다. 여러분 중 일부는 별로 재미없겠다고 생각하고 있겠죠, 그렇죠? 하지만 들어보세요. 여러분이 다음에 달력을 볼 때, 꼭 유념해야 할 사항이 있습니다. 시간의 경과를 측정하는 자연적 방법은 적어도 세 가지가 있습니다. 즉 일, 월, 년입니다. 그리고 이건 모두 너무나 알기 쉬워요. 그렇죠? 하루는 지구의 자전 1회에 근거합니다. 한 달은 달이 지구를 한 번 공전하는 데 걸리는 시간입니다. 그리고 한 해는 지구가 태양을 한 번 공전하는 데 걸리는 시간입니다. 그렇지요? 그러므로 이는 모두 자연 현상에 근거를 두고 있습니다. 하지만 지구, 달, 태양의 자연 시계는 저마다 다른 시간 단위에 따라 작동합니다. 그리고 이 시간들 중 한 단위를 다른 시간 단위로 나누면 항상 까다롭게 남는 부분이 있습니다. 우리가 쓰는 태음월은 달이 지구를 한 번 공전하는 데 걸리는 시간인데, 이 태음월로는 한 달이 약 29일에 반나절이 더 있습니다. 딱 맞아떨어지는 숫자가 결코 아닙니다. 그리고 1년은 365일보다 약간 더 깁니다. 그러므로 이런 시간 단위들은 각기 다른 시간 단위로 나누면 똑 떨어지지 않습니다. 그래서 정말 잘 맞는 만족스러운 달력을 만들기가 어렵습니다.

다른 문화권에서 시도하지 않았던 것은 아닙니다. 여러분들 중 스톤헨지에 가 본 사람 있어요? 없군요… 영국의 그 멋진 환형 거석군 유적 알죠? 만약 언제라도 가보면, 아득한 옛날 선사시대까지 거슬러 올라가는 이 영국 고대문화에서 이처럼 기념비적 환형 거석군을 건축하려고 그토록 수고한 이유가 무엇인지 한번 생각해 보기 바랍니다. 잊지 말아야 할 것은, 우리 중 다수는 적어도 부분적으로나마 이 거석군이 달력으로 쓰기 위해 설계되었다고 생각한다는 사실입니다. 즉 어떤 특정 방향에서 해가 뜨는 정확한 날에 따라, 계절이 언제 시작되는지 표시하기 위한 것입니다. 이 거석군이 사원이나 묘지라고 주장하는 동료들도 있어요. 하지만 이들 역시 이 거석군이 달력으로도 쓰였다는 사실을 부인하지는 못합니다. 어쩌면, 예를 들어, 농부들이 해마다 파종을 시작해야 하는 시기를 파악하는 데 도움이 되었을 것입니다.

중앙 아메리카의 마야인들 역시 달력을 고안했지만 목적은 달랐습니다. 마야인들 중에서도 특히 왕족이나 사제들은 역사의 장기적 주기를 알아보고 싶어했습니다. 그래서 그들이 사용한 달력은 오랜 과거는 물론

and the Venus cycle was incorporated in the Mayan calendar. So the Mayans kept track of long periods of time, and they did it so accurately, in fact, that their calendar is considered about as complicated and sophisticated as any in the world.

Now, the ancient Chinese believed very strongly in astrology—the idea that you can predict future events based on the positions of the stars and planets like, say, Jupiter. Incidentally, the whole Chinese system of astrology was based on the fact that the planet Jupiter goes around the Sun once every 12 years, so one orbit of Jupiter lasts 12 of our Earth years. Apparently, that's why the Chinese calendar has a cycle of 12 years. You know, like, "The Year of the Dragon," "The Year of the Tiger," and so on... all parts of a 12-year astrological cycle, that we get from the orbit of Jupiter.

Calendars based on the orbits of other planets, though, are a lot less common than those based on the cycle of the Moon—the lunar month. I could mention any number of important cultures around the world that have depended on lunar calendars, but there really isn't time.

So let's go right to the calendar that's now used through-out most of the world—a solar calendar—based on the number of days in a year. This calendar's mainly derived from the one the ancient Romans devised a couple thousand years ago. I mean the Romans—with more than a little help from the Greeks—realized that a year actually lasts about 365 and one-quarter days. And so they decided to round off most years to 365 days but make every fourth year into a leap year. I mean, somehow, you have to account for that extra one-fourth of a day each year, so every four years, they made the calendar one day longer. By adding the leap year, the Romans were able to make a calendar that worked so well—that, with a few minor adjustments, this calendar is still widely used today.

먼 미래까지도 전부 계산할 수 있어야 했지요. 마야인들은 앞에서 언급한 자연 시계-지구, 달, 해-뿐만 아니라 다른 자연 시계, 즉 금성도 관측했습니다.

금성은 샛별로서 584일마다 하늘에 떠오르고, 금성의 주기는 마야인들의 달력에 포함되었습니다. 그래서 마야인들은 장기간의 시간을 관측했고, 매우 정확히 관측해서 사실상 마야인의 달력은 세상의 어떤 달력 못지않게 복잡하고 정교한 것으로 간주됩니다.

자, 고대 중국인들은 점성학, 즉 목성과 같은 행성이나 별의 위치에 근거하여 미래의 일을 예상할 수 있다는 사상을 열렬히 신봉했습니다. 덧붙여 말하자면, 중국 점성학 사상의 전체 체계는 목성이 태양을 12년마다 한 번 공전하고, 그래서 목성의 공전은 지구년 기준으로 12년 간 지속된다는 사실에 토대를 두고 있습니다. 분명, 이는 바로 중국 달력이 12년 주기인 이유입니다. 그러니까, '용의 해', '범의 해' 등은 모두 목성의 공전주기에서 알아낸 점성학의 12년 주기의 일부에 해당합니다.

하지만 다른 행성의 공전주기에 근거를 둔 달력은 달의 주기-태음월-에 근거를 둔 달력보다 훨씬 드뭅니다. 음력에 의존했던 세계의 주요 문화권이라면 얼마든지 언급할 수 있지만, 사실상 시간이 부족하네요.

그러면 현재 세계 대부분 지역에서 사용하는 달력-태양력-으로 곧장 넘어가 봅시다. 태양력은 한 해의 날짜 수에 근거합니다. 이 달력은 2천여 년 전 고대 로마인들이 고안한 달력으로부터 대부분 유래했습니다. 로마인들은 그리스인들의 상당한 도움으로 일 년이 사실상 365일과 4분의 1이라는 것을 알아냈습니다. 그래서 대부분의 1년을 365일로 반올림하고 4년마다 한 번씩 윤년을 두기로 했습니다. 아무튼, 매년 남는 4분의 1일을 계산에 넣어야 하므로, 4년마다 하루가 추가된 달력을 만들었습니다. 윤년을 추가해서, 로마인들은 매우 잘 맞는 달력을 만들 수 있었고, 몇 가지 사소한 변경을 거쳐 이 달력은 오늘날까지 널리 사용됩니다.

어휘

anthropology 인류학 keep something in mind 기억해 두다, 유의하다 passage (시간의) 경과 rotation (천체의) 자전 fraction 소량 leave over 남기다 cf. leftover 나머지 lunar month 태음월(太陰月), 음력 달 round number 우수리가 없는 수 neatly 간결히, 깔끔히 tidy 만족스러운, 잘 정돈된 way back 아득한 옛날에, 훨씬 거슬러 올라가 prehistoric 선사시대의, 유사이전의 monumental 기념비적인, 역사적 의미가 있는 colleague 동료 royalty 왕족 priest 사제, 신관 keep track of ~을 기록하다 Venus 금성 incorporate 통합하다 sophisticated 정교한, 세련된 astrology 점성학, 점성술 orbit 공전주기, 궤도 Jupiter 목성 incidentally 덧붙여 말하자면 apparently 분명히 derive from ~에서 유래하다 round off 반올림하다 leap year 윤년 adjustment 조정, 조절

6. 교수가 주로 논의하고 있는 내용은?

ⓐ 초창기 달력의 다양한 오류

ⓑ 사람들이 지구가 태양을 공전한다는 것을 믿게 된 이유

ⓒ 서로 다른 문화권에서 사용된 다양한 달력 유형의 사례

ⓓ 행성과 별의 위치로 미래의 사건을 예측할 수 있다는 믿음

내용의 요점을 묻는 문제

어휘 come to ~하게 되다

해설 강의의 주요 내용은 여러 가지 달력의 예, 특히 여러 문화권에서 서로 다른 방법으로 만들었던 달력의 사례에 관한 설명이다.

7. 교수는 스톤헨지의 용도에 관한 여러 가지 가설을 설명하고 있다. 교수의 의견에 관해 유추할 수 있는 내용은?

ⓐ 교수는 스톤헨지가 달력으로 이용되었다고 확신한다.

ⓑ 교수는 스톤헨지의 주요 용도가 사원이나 묘지였다고 믿는다.

ⓒ 교수는 거석들이 주로 역사적인 사건의 기록으로 이용되었다고 생각한다.

ⓓ 교수는 스톤헨지의 건립 목적이 결코 밝혀지지 않을 수도 있다는 것을 인정한다.

태도 파악 문제

어휘 admit 인정하다

해설 교수 본인을 포함한 대부분 사람들이 스톤헨지가 달력으로 쓰였다고 생각하며, 의견을 달리하는 동료들도 달력의 기능이 있었다는 사실을 부인하지는 못한다고 했다. 따라서 교수는 스톤헨지의 달력 기능을 확신하고 있음을 알 수 있다.

8. 교수에 따르면, 마야 달력의 주된 용도는 무엇인가?

ⓐ 장기적 역사 주기를 기록하기 위해

ⓑ 태음월을 기록하기 위해

ⓒ 왕의 결정이 낳을 결과를 예측하기 위해

ⓓ 사제들이 지구와 금성의 궤도를 비교하게 하기 위해

세부 사항 찾기 문제

어휘 outcome 결과, 성과

해설 교수는 마야의 왕족과 신관들이 역사의 장기적 주기를 살펴보고 싶어 했다고 설명하고 있다.

9. 교수에 따르면, 고대 중국의 점성학 주기의 근거는 무엇인가?

ⓐ 밤낮의 주기

ⓑ 달의 궤도

ⓒ 계절의 주기

ⓓ 목성의 궤도

세부 사항 찾기 문제

해설 목성이 태양 주위를 12년 주기로 공전한다는 사실에 중국 점성학의 전체 체계가 기반을 두고 있다고 설명했다.

10. 로마인들이 어떻게 자신들의 달력을 더욱 정확하게 만들었는가?

ⓐ 한 해에 포함되는 일주일의 횟수를 변경함으로써

ⓑ 4년마다 하루를 추가함으로써

ⓒ 목성의 움직임을 주의 깊게 관찰함으로써

ⓓ 중국 달력의 원리를 채택함으로써

세부 사항 찾기 문제

어휘 adopt (방법 등을) 채택하다

해설 교수는 로마인들이 4년마다 한 번씩 하루가 더 많은 윤년을 추가함으로써 매우 정확한 달력을 만들 수 있었다고 설명했다.

11. 교수는 강의를 어떻게 구성하는가?

ⓐ 달력 제작의 문제점을 언급하고, 이를 해결하기 위한 다양한 시도를 설명함으로써

ⓑ 현대 달력에 관해 먼저 말하고, 이를 이전의 달력과 비교함으로써

ⓒ 선사시대의 달력 하나가 여러 다른 문화권에서 어떻게 변경되었는지 논함으로써

ⓓ 다양한 시간 주기 사용의 장단점을 강조함으로써

구성 파악 문제

어휘 attempt 시도, 노력   adapt 변경하다, 개조하다

해설 강의의 앞 부분은 정확한 달력을 만들기 어려운 이유에 대한 설명이었고, 그 다음은 문화권 별로 각기 다른 방법으로 달력을 만들어 사용한 사례들을 소개하고 있다.

p. 200

N Narrator   E Employee   S Student

Script

N Listen to part of a conversation between a student and a university employee.

E Oh, hello... can I help you?

S Um... yeah... I'm looking for Professor Kirk; is she here? I mean is this her office?

E Yes, you're in the right place — Professor Kirk's office is right behind me — but no... she's not here right now.

S Um, do you know when she'll be back?

E Well, she's teaching all morning. She won't be back until... let me check... hmm, she won't be back until... after lunch. That's when she has her office hours. Perhaps you could come back then?

S Oh, unfortunately no. I have class this afternoon. And I was really hoping to talk to her today. Hey, um, do you know if... she's accepting any more students into her introduction to Biology class?

E You wanna know if you can take the class?

S Yes, if she's letting any more students sign up, I'd like, I'd like to join the class.

E Introduction to Biology is a very popular class, especially when she teaches it. A lot of students take it.

S Yeah, that's why the registrar said it was full. I've got the form the registrar gave me, um, to get her permission to take the class. It's all filled out except for her signature. I'm hoping she'll let me in even though the class is full. You, see, I'm a senior this year, and, uh... this'll be my last semester, so it's my last chance...

E Oh, wow, really. I mean most students fulfill their science requirement the first year.

S Well, I mean, um... to be honest, I kept putting it off. I'm not really a big fan of science classes in general, and with the labs and everything, I've never quite found the time.

E Your advisor didn't say anything?

S Well, to tell you the truth, she's been after me to take a class like this for a while, but I'm double-majoring in art and journalism and so my schedule's been really tight with all the classes I gotta take, so somehow I never...

N 학생과 대학 직원간의 대화 일부를 들으시오.

E 아, 안녕하세요. 도와드릴까요?

S 저, 커크 교수님을 뵈러 왔는데요, 여기 계세요? 여기가 교수님 연구실인가요?

E 예, 제대로 찾아오셨어요. 커크 교수님 연구실은 제 바로 뒤편이에요. 하지만 지금은 안 계세요.

S 혹시 언제 돌아오실지 아세요?

E 글쎄요, 오전 내내 수업이 있어서 안 오실 거예요. 확인해 볼게요. 음, 점심 이후까지는 오시지 않을 거예요. 점심 이후가 교수님 상담시간이에요. 그때 다시 오시겠어요?

S 아, 공교롭게도 안 되겠네요. 오후에 수업이 있어요. 그리고 오늘 교수님께 꼭 말씀드리려 했거든요. 혹시 교수님이 생물학 개론 강의에 학생을 더 받아주실까요?

E 그 수업을 들을 수 있는지 알고 싶으세요?

S 예, 교수님이 더 많은 학생들이 수강 신청하도록 하신다면, 그렇게 할 거예요. 그 강의를 듣고 싶거든요.

E 생물학 개론은 매우 인기 있는 수업이에요. 특히 커크 교수님이 가르치실 때는요. 많은 학생들이 그 수업을 들어요.

S 예, 그래서 학적과 직원이 이미 정원이 다 찼다고 말씀하셨어요. 학적과 직원이 준 수강 신청서를 가져왔는데요, 교수님의 수강 허락을 받으려고요. 다른 건 다 작성했고 교수님 서명만 남았어요. 정원이 다 찼더라도 교수님께서 저를 넣어 주시길 바래요. 보시다시피 전 4학년이고, 이번 학기가 저의 마지막 학기라서 이번이 저의 마지막 기회예요.

E 아, 정말 그렇네요. 그러니까, 대부분의 학생들은 1학년 때 과학 필수과목을 전부 이수해요.

S 솔직히 말해서, 전 계속 미뤄 뒀어요. 일반 과학 강의는 별로 좋아하지 않아요. 그리고 실험과 그밖에 이것저것 있어서 도대체 시간이 나지 않았어요.

E 지도교수님이 아무 말씀 안 하시던가요?

S 사실대로 말하자면, 교수님께서 한동안 저를 따라다니다시피 하시면서 이런 과목을 수강하라 하셨어요. 하지만 전 미술과 언론학을 복수전공하고 있어서 수강해야 할 과목을 모두 듣느라 일정이 정말 빠듯했어요. 그래서 아무튼 전혀 못 들었어요.

E Well, perhaps you could leave the form with me and I'll see if she'll sign it for you.

S You know, I appreciate that, but maybe I should explain the problem to her in person... I didn't want to do it, but I guess I'll have to send her an e-mail.

E Hmm. You know, not all professors check their e-mails regularly—I... I'm not sure if professor Kirk does it or not. Here's an idea... why don't you stick a note explaining your situation under her door and ask her to call you if she needs more information?

S Hey, that's a good idea, and then I can leave the form with you—if you still don't mind.

E 수강 신청서를 맡겨 두고 가시면 교수님께서 서명하실지 제가 알아봐 드릴게요.

S 말씀은 감사하지만, 교수님께 문제를 직접 설명해 드려야 할 텐데요. 내키진 않지만, 교수님께 이메일을 보내야겠어요.

E 아시겠지만, 모든 교수님들이 이메일을 정기적으로 확인하지는 않으세요. 커크 교수님이 그렇게 하시는지 안 하시는지 확실치 않지만요. 좋은 생각이 있어요. 사정을 설명하는 쪽지를 교수님 연구실 문 밑으로 밀어 넣어 두고, 더 알고 싶으시면 전화하시라고 부탁하면 어떨까요?

S 아, 그거 좋은 생각이네요. 그러면 양식을 맡길 수 있겠네요. 아직 괜찮으시다면요.

어휘

office hours 대학교수의 학생상담 시간   introduction 개론, 입문   sign up 등록하다   registrar 학적과 직원   permission 허락, 인가   fill out 기입하다   requirement 필수 과목   advisor 지도교수   be after ~을 따라다니다, 쫓아다니다   double major 복수전공하다   journalism 언론학 tight (일정이) 꽉 찬, 빠듯한   in person 직접   stick 밀어 넣다, 집어넣다

12. 학생이 커크 교수 연구실에 찾아간 이유는?

Ⓐ 졸업하기 위해 특정 과목을 수강해야 하는지 알아보기 위해

Ⓑ 커크 교수의 초대에 응하기 위해

Ⓒ 커크 교수에게 지도교수가 되어달라고 부탁하기 위해

Ⓓ 커크 교수에게 양식에 서명해달라고 부탁하기 위해

내용의 목적을 묻는 문제

어휘 form 양식, 신청서

해설 학생은 정원이 찬 강의를 수강하기 위해 수강 신청서에 커크 교수의 서명을 받고자 한다.

13. 직원이 남학생의 요청에 놀란 이유는?

Ⓐ 학생이 학적과에서 생물학 개론 수강 신청을 하려 하지 않았다.

Ⓑ 학생이 졸업반이 될 때까지 생물학 개론을 수강하지 않았기 때문에

Ⓒ 언론학 전공학생이 생물학 강의를 반드시 수강할 필요는 없다.

Ⓓ 커크 교수가 생물학 개론을 더 이상 가르치지 않는다.

추론 문제

어휘 request 요청, 요구

해설 대부분 학생들이 과학 필수과목을 1학년 때 수강한다는 직원의 말에서 남학생이 4학년이 될 때까지 생물학 개론을 수강하지 않아서 직원이 놀랐음을 알 수 있다.

14. 학생은 자기 지도교수에 관해 뭐라고 말하는가?

Ⓐ 지도교수가 과학 과목 수강을 권장했다.

Ⓑ 지도교수가 언론학 전공을 권장했다.

Ⓒ 지도교수가 남학생의 문제를 인식하지 못한다.

Ⓓ 지도교수가 커크 교수를 매우 존경한다.

세부 사항 찾기 문제

어휘 encourage 권장하다, 장려하다　be aware of ~을 인식하다, 알아차리다　think highly of ~을 존경하다

해설 직원이 지도교수에 관해 묻자 학생은 교수가 따라다니며 과학 과목을 수강하라 했다고 대답했으므로 A가 정답이다.

15. 학생은 커크 교수에게 자신의 문제를 어떻게 알리려 할 것인가?

Ⓐ 전화를 해서

Ⓑ 이메일을 보내서

Ⓒ 쪽지를 남겨서

Ⓓ 상담시간에 찾아가서

세부 사항 찾기 문제

해설 쪽지를 남기라는 직원의 말에 학생이 좋은 생각이라고 대답하는 것으로 미루어 보아 학생은 쪽지를 남길 것으로 짐작할 수 있다.

16. 대화의 일부를 다시 듣고 질문에 답하라.

🎧 T-38

N *Why does the man say this to the woman?*

S You know, I appreciate that, but maybe I should explain the problem to her in person...

학생이 직원에게 이렇게 말하는 이유는 무엇인가?

Ⓐ 문제를 해결해 줘서 고맙다는 말을 하기 위해

Ⓑ 직원의 제의를 정중히 거절하기 위해

Ⓒ 직원의 도움이 필요한 이유를 설명하기 위해

Ⓓ 직원의 바쁜 사정을 이해한다는 것을 알리기 위해

의도 파악 문제

어휘 politely 정중히, 예의 바르게

해설 수강 신청서를 맡겨 두라는 직원의 말에 학생은 감사하지만 교수에게 문제를 설명해야겠다고 하므로 직원의 제의를 거절하고 있음을 알 수 있다.

Reading

Listening

Speaking

Writing

Test 1

Test 2

Test 3

Test 4

Script

N Listen to part of a lecture in an astronomy class.

P I'm sure y'all have been following the news about Mars. A lot of spacecraft have been visiting the planet recently—some have gone into orbit around it, while others have landed on it. And, they've sent back a... an abundance of data that's reshaping our knowledge... our vision of the planet in a lot of ways. Is there anything that you've been particularly struck by in all the news reports?

F Well, they seem to mention water a lot, which kinda surprised me, as I have this picture in my head that Mars is dry... sorta dry and dead.

P You're not the only one. You know, for centuries, most of our knowledge of the planet came from what we saw through telescopes, so, obviously, it was pretty limited—and our views of the planet were formed as much by writers... as they were by serious scientists. When the first science-fiction stories came out, Mars was described as being a lot like Earth except...

M I know: the planet was red and, uh, the people were green. I've seen some of those old movies. What were they thinking? I mean really... they...

P Well, it seems silly to us now, but those ideas were quite imaginative and, occasionally, scary in their time. Anyway, we began to rethink our image of Mars when the first spacecraft flew by the planet in 1965 and sent pictures back to Earth. Those pictures showed a planet that looked a lot more like our Moon than Earth—lots of craters and not much else. It was bitterly cold, it had a very thin atmosphere, and that atmosphere was mostly carbon dioxide. So the view of Mars after this first flyby mission was that dry, dead planet that Lisa mentioned.

But, then there were more visits to the planet in the 1970s—and this time the spacecraft didn't just fly by; they orbited... or landed. This allowed us to receive much more detailed images of the planet, and it turned out to be a pretty interesting place. Mars had... has a lot more than craters—it has giant volcanoes and deep canyons. It also showed signs of dried-up riverbeds and plains that had been formed by massive floods. So we concluded that there must have been water on the planet at one time—billions of years ago. Now, what does it take for water to exist?

M You need to have a warm-enough temperature so that it doesn't freeze.

N 천문학 강의의 일부를 들으시오.

P 화성 관련 뉴스에 다들 귀를 기울여 왔을 것으로 확신합니다. 많은 우주선이 최근 화성을 탐사했습니다. 일부는 화성 궤도에 진입했고, 다른 일부는 화성에 착륙하기도 했습니다. 그리고 우주선은 우리의 지식, 그 행성에 대한 우리의 시각을 여러 면에서 재형성하는 다량의 자료를 전송했습니다. 혹시 그 모든 뉴스 보도 중에서 특히 충격적인 것이라도 있을까요?

F 저어, 뉴스 보도에서는 물을 많이 언급하는 듯해서 좀 놀랐어요. 저는 화성이 메마른 행성, 메마르고 생명이 없는 행성이라고만 생각하거든요.

P 학생만 그런 건 아니에요. 알다시피, 수 세기 동안, 화성에 대한 우리의 지식은 대부분 망원경 관측을 통해서 얻은 것이었고, 그래서 분명 그 지식은 상당히 제한적이었어요. 그리고 화성에 대한 우리의 시각은 전문 과학자들에 의해 형성된 만큼 작가들에 의해서도 형성되었습니다. 공상과학소설이 처음 출간되었을 때, 화성은 우리 지구와 상당히 비슷한 모습으로 묘사되었고, 다만……

M 저도 알아요. 화성은 적색이었고, 어, 화성인들은 녹색이었어요. 그런 옛날 영화를 몇 편 봤는데, 대체 무슨 생각이었던 걸까요? 제 말은, 정말…….

P 자, 이제 그런 생각은 우리에게는 어이없는 소리 같겠지만 당시에는 매우 환상적이었고, 가끔 무섭기도 했어요. 어쨌든, 1965년 최초로 우주탐사선이 화성 주변으로 날아가 지구에 사진을 전송했을 때, 우리는 화성에 대한 이미지를 다르게 생각하기 시작했습니다. 그 사진들은 지구보다는 달과 훨씬 더 비슷한 화성을 보여 주었습니다. 즉 분화구(운석구)만 수두룩하고 다른 건 별로 없었습니다. 화성은 혹독하게 춥고, 대기는 무척 희박하며, 그리고 그 대기는 대부분 탄산가스로 이루어져 있습니다. 그러므로, 이 최초의 화성 근접 탐사 임무 이후 화성에 대한 시각은, 리사가 말한 대로 메마른 죽음의 행성이라는 것이었습니다.

하지만, 그 후 1970년대에 들어 화성 우주선 탐사가 더 많이 이루어졌고, 이번에는 탐사선이 단지 옆을 스쳐 지나가는 것이 아니라 화성 궤도에 진입하거나 착륙했습니다. 이 덕분에 우리는 더욱 자세한 화성 사진을 얻게 되었고, 화성이 상당히 흥미로운 별이라는 사실이 드러났습니다. 화성에는 운석구 말고도 많은 것이 있습니다. 거대한 화산(분화구)과 깊은 계곡이 있습니다. 화성은 말라버린 강바닥과 대규모 홍수로 형성된 평원의 흔적도 보여 주었습니다. 그래서 우리는 한때는, 수십억 년 전에는 화성에 분명 물이 있었다고 결론지었습니다. 자, 물이 존재하려면 무엇이 필요할까요?

P That's one thing—and the other is that you need enough atmospheric pressure, thick-enough air so that the water doesn't instantly vaporize. The Mars we see today doesn't have either of those conditions—it is too cold and the air is too thin—but a long time ago, there may have been a thicker atmosphere that created a greenhouse effect that raised temperatures—and maybe that combination produced water on the surface of the planet. So maybe Mars wasn't just a dead, boring rock; maybe, it was, uh, a fascinating fossil that was once alive and dynamic—worthy of exploration. Now let's jump forward a few decades to the beginning of this century, and a new generation of orbiters and landers that have been sent to Mars. Of course, the scientific instruments now surveying Mars are far more sophisticated than the instruments of the '70s, so we're getting all kinds of new data for analysis. And, not surprisingly, that data is challenging our notions of what Mars is like. Lisa, you mentioned that a lot of the news reports talked about water—do you remember any of the details?

F Well, they were showing these pictures of these long, uh, cuts in the ground, which would be gullies here; I mean on Earth. They say that since, uh, gullies are usually formed by water, it seems like they might be evidence that water still exists on Mars, but I didn't get how that worked.

P I'm not surprised. There're a lot of theories... a lot of speculation... and some argue the formations aren't caused by water at all. But there're some ingenious theories that assume that there's a lot of water right under the planet's surface that somehow is causing the gullies to form. If we could only get a lander there... but the gullies aren't in places where we can send landers yet. Anyway, if there is some kind of water activity, it may change our view of the planet once again... to something that's not dead, not even a fossil, but rather a planet like Earth that undergoes cycles—think of our ice ages—over long periods of time. Maybe Mars could sustain water again at some distant date.

M 얼어붙지 않도록 기온이 충분히 따뜻해야겠지요.

P 그게 한 가지 조건이에요. 다른 조건은 충분한 기압이 있어야 한다는 것인데, 물이 순식간에 증발하지 않도록 충분한 두께의 대기가 있어야 합니다. 오늘날 우리가 보는 화성은 이 조건들을 전혀 갖추고 있지 않습니다. 기온은 너무 낮고 대기는 지나치게 희박하지요. 하지만 아주 오래 전에는, 온실 효과를 발생시켜 기온을 상승시킨 두꺼운 대기가 있었을 겁니다. 그리고 두 조건이 충족되어 화성 표면에 물이 생성되었을 것입니다. 화성은 죽은, 단조로운 암석 덩어리가 아니라, 한때는 생명이 약동하던 화석이었을 수도 있고, 따라서 탐사해볼 만한 가치가 있는 곳이었을 겁니다. 자, 이제 몇 십 년을 건너뛰어 금세기 초, 화성에 궤도 탐사선과 착륙선을 보낸 새로운 세대로 넘어가 보겠습니다. 물론, 현재 화성을 탐사하고 있는 과학 장비들은 1970년대의 장비보다 훨씬 더 정교해서, 우리는 분석에 필요한 온갖 종류의 새 분석용 데이터를 입수하고 있습니다. 그리고, 당연하게도 그 데이터는 화성의 모습에 대한 우리의 관념에 이의를 제기하고 있습니다. 리사, 많은 뉴스 보도에서 물에 관해 얘기했다고 했는데, 세부내용 중 뭐라도 기억나요?

F 뉴스에서 화성 표면에 이처럼 장거리에 걸쳐 발생한 침식 흔적의 사진을 보여 주고 있었는데요, 여기, 여기 지구에서라면 협곡에 해당하겠지요. 뉴스에서는 협곡이 대개 물에 의해 형성되기 때문에, 화성에 아직도 물이 존재한다는 증거가 될 수도 있다고 한 것 같은데요, 어떻게 그럴 수 있는지 이해할 수 없어요.

P 그럴 겁니다. 많은 이론이 있고, 추측도 많습니다. 그리고 어떤 이들은 그 형상이 결코 물에 의해 생성된 것이 아니라고 주장합니다. 하지만 화성의 표면 바로 밑에 협곡을 생성하는 대량의 물이 존재한다고 추정하는 독창적 이론도 있습니다. 만약 우리가 착륙탐사선을 그곳에 보낼 수 있다면, 하지만 협곡은 아직 우리가 착륙탐사선을 보낼 수 있을 만한 곳에 있지 않습니다. 어쨌든, 어떤 형태든 물의 활동이 있다면, 화성에 대한 우리의 견해가 다시 한 번 바뀔 수도 있습니다. 생명이 없는 것도 아니고, 심지어 화석도 아니고 순환을 겪는 지구와 같은 행성—지구의 빙하기를 생각해 보세요—오랜 세월에 걸쳐 순환을 겪는 행성일지도 모르죠. 어쩌면 언젠가 먼 훗날 화성에 다시 물이 고일지도 모릅니다.

어휘

follow (이야기, 뉴스 등에) 귀를 기울이다   spacecraft 우주선   abundance 대량, 풍부   reshape 재형성하다   struck by 강한 인상을 받다   sorta (속어) =sort of 다소, 얼마간   telescope 망원경   silly 어이없는   imaginative 상상력이 풍부한, 창조적인   crater 운석구, 분화구   bitterly 살을 에이는 듯이, 지독하게   sign 흔적, 자취   atmosphere 대기   carbon dioxide 이산화탄소   riverbed 강바닥, 하상(河床)   atmospheric pressure 기압   vaporize 증발하다   combination 조합, 짝맞춤   boring 단조로운   fascinating 매우 흥미로운, 매혹적인   fossil 화석   worthy of ~할 만한 (가치가 있는)   not surprisingly 당연히   notion 개념, 생각   gully (물이 마른) 협곡   speculation 견해, 추론   formation 형태, 형성   ingenious 독창적인   undergo (변화 등을) 겪다   cycle (현상, 계절 등의) 순환, 주기   sustain (생명을) 유지하다, 부양하다

17. 강의는 주로 무엇에 관한 것인가?

Ⓐ 화성이 생명을 유지할 수 없는 이유를 설명하는 다양한 이론

Ⓑ 화성에서 지질학적 변천이 일어난 다양한 원인

Ⓒ 화성의 본질에 대한 견해의 발전

Ⓓ 화성에 관한 정보를 입수하기 어려웠던 이유

내용의 요점을 묻는 문제

어휘 geological change 지질학적 변화, 지형 변이   obtain 입수하다, 획득하다

해설 교수는 강의에서 화성에 대한 인식의 변화를 개괄적으로 설명한다.

18. 교수에 따르면, 1965년에 최초로 우주탐사선이 근접 비행을 한 이후 화성에 대해 어떤 결론을 내렸는가?

Ⓐ 화성에는 흥미로운 지질학적 특성이 거의 없었다.

Ⓑ 화성은 지구와 유사하지만 훨씬 더 춥다.

Ⓒ 화성은 한때 생명을 유지했다.

Ⓓ 화성은 지표 아래에 물이 있었다.

세부 사항 찾기 문제

어휘 feature (두드러진) 특색, 특징, 생김새

해설 교수는 1965년의 근접 탐사로 화성이 달과 비슷하고 운석구가 많다는 것 이외에는 별다른 게 없었다는 것이 밝혀졌다고 설명한다.

19. 수십억 년 전의 화성 상황에 관해 교수가 시사하는 것은? 두 개의 답을 선택하라.

Ⓐ 화성은 현재보다 훨씬 더 메말랐을 것이다.

Ⓑ 대기 압력과 기온이 현재보다 훨씬 더 높았을 수도 있다.

Ⓒ 화성에는 유기체가 서식했으나 이후에 화석이 되었다.

Ⓓ 대홍수가 화성의 지표를 형성하고 있었다.

추론 문제

어휘 inhabit 서식하다, 살다

해설 말라붙은 강바닥과 대홍수로 형성된 평원이 있으므로 수십억 년 전에는 물이 있었을 것이라는 교수의 설명에서 우선 대홍수로 화성의 지표가 형성되었다는 추론이 가능하다. 이후의 추가 설명에 따라 물이 있기 위해서는 대기 압력과 기온이 높았을 것이라는 추론이 가능하다.

20. 최근 수년 이내에 화성에서 발견된 협곡이 중요할 수 있는 이유는?

Ⓐ 협곡은 화성의 현재의 화산 활동을 나타낼지도 모른다.

Ⓑ 협곡은 화성 표면이 더욱 더 건조해지고 있음을 나타낼지도 모른다.

Ⓒ 협곡은 현재 화성에 물이 존재한다는 것을 나타낼지도 모른다.

Ⓓ 협곡에는 한때 화성에 존재했던 유기체의 화석이 매장되어 있지도 모른다.

세부 사항 찾기 문제

어휘 significance 의미, 중요성   increasingly 더욱 더, 점점

해설 협곡은 물이 여전히 존재한다는 증거일 수도 있다는 뉴스 보도를 인용하는 학생의 말과 화성의 표면 아래에 물이 존재해서 협곡 형성을 유발하고 있는지도 모른다는 교수의 부연 설명을 통해 협곡의 의미를 파악할 수 있다.

21. 다음을 듣고 질문에 답하라.

 T-40

N *Why does the professor say this?*
P So maybe Mars wasn't just a dead, boring rock; maybe, it was, uh, a fascinating fossil that was once alive and dynamic — worthy of exploration.

Ⓐ 화성은 더 이상 탐사하기에 흥미롭지 않음을 강조하기 위해

Ⓑ 우주탐사선이 화성에서 가져온 것들을 설명하기 위해

Ⓒ 화석 연구에 관한 자신의 관심사를 말해 주기 위해

Ⓓ 새 증거에 근거하여 화성에 대한 견해가 얼마나 많이 바뀌었는지 보여 주기 위해서

의도 파악 문제

어휘 stress 강조하다   share (생각 등을) 남에게 이야기하다

해설 교수는 1970년대 탐사에 따른 새로운 가설을 설명하고, 이어서 화성은 단지 생명이 없는 암석이 아니라 한때 생명이 있었고 탐사해볼 만한 곳일 수도 있다는 견해의 변화를 시사한다.

22. 강의의 일부를 다시 듣고 질문에 답하라.

🎧 T-41

M I know: the planet was red and, uh, the people were green. I've seen some of those old movies. What were they thinking? I mean really...

N *Why does the student say this?*
M What were they thinking?

Ⓐ 이전에 말한 내용에 대한 명백한 설명을 요청하기 위해

Ⓑ 자신의 의견을 전달하기 위해

Ⓒ 앞서 했던 질문을 바꾸어 말하기 위해

Ⓓ 찬성을 표명하기 위해

의도 파악 문제

어휘 clarification (내용 등을) 명확히 하기   statement 말, 발언   rephrase 고쳐[바꿔] 말하다

해설 학생은 적색 화성과 녹색 화성인에 대해 "대체 무슨 생각이었던 걸까요?"라고 반문한다. 즉 화성에 관한 사실적 정보에 근거하지 않고 영화를 제작했다는 의미다. 따라서 학생은 이런 영화가 전혀 근거 없는 상상의 산물이라는 본인의 의견을 암시하고 있음을 알 수 있다.

🎧 T-42

N Narrator   P Professor

Script

N Listen to part of a lecture in an art history class. The professor has been talking about colossal statues.

P We've been looking at colossal statues—works of exceptionally huge size—and their essentially public role, in commemorating a political or religious figure. We've seen how some of these statues date back thousands of years... like the statues of the pharaohs of ancient Egypt—which you can still visit today—and how others, though surviving only in legend, have fired the imagination of writers and artists right up to our own time, such as the Colossus of Rhodes, that 110-foot statue of the Greek god Helios. Remember, this same word, *colossus*—which means a giant or larger-than-life-size statue—is what today's term *colossal* derives from.

Now, it was one thing to build such statues, at an equally colossal cost, when the funds were being allocated by ancient kings and pharaohs. But if we're going to think about modern-day colossal statues, we need to reexamine more closely their role as social and political symbols, in order to understand why a society today—a society of free, taxpaying citizens—would agree to allocate so much of its resources to erecting them. A good example to start out with would be Mount Rushmore.

Now, many of you have probably seen pictures of Mount Rushmore; perhaps you've actually visited the place. Mount Rushmore, in South Dakota, is a colossal representation of the faces of four U.S. Presidents: George Washington, Thomas Jefferson, Theodore Roosevelt, and Abraham Lincoln, carved directly into a mountain. Imagine: each of those faces in the rock is over 60 feet high! Now, carving their faces took over six and a half years, and cost almost a million dollars. And this was in the 1930s, during the worst economic depression in U.S. history! Does that strike any of you as odd?

Well, I personally think that the Great Depression of the 1930s actually makes this more understandable, not less so. Often it's the case that, precisely at times of hardship—when the very fabric of society seems to be unraveling and confidence is eroding—uh, that people clamor for some public expression of strength and optimism, perhaps as a way of symbolizing its endurance in the face of difficulty.

So with that in mind, let's go back to Mount Rushmore. Actually, the original motivation for a colossal monument in South Dakota had very little to do with all this symbolism... and everything to do with money: you see, it was first conceived of

N 예술사 강의의 일부를 들으시오. 교수는 거대 석상에 대해 이야기하고 있다.

P 우리는 거대 석상, 즉 아주 거대한 작품과 정치나 종교적 인물을 기념한다는 석상 본연의 공적 역할에 대해 알아보고 있었습니다. 이런 석상들 중 일부는 수천 년 전까지 거슬러 올라갑니다. 고대 이집트의 파라오 석상처럼요. 이건 오늘날에도 찾아가 볼 수 있지요. 그리고 다른 것들은 비록 전설로만 남아 있지만, 현재 우리 시대에 이르기까지 작가나 예술가들의 상상력을 뜨겁게 달구었습니다. 33미터나 되는 그리스 신 헬리오스의 조각상이었던 로도스의 거상처럼요. 기억해 두세요. 이와 같은 단어, 'colossus'는 거인이나 실물보다 훨씬 큰 조각상을 의미하고, 이 단어에서 오늘날의 'colossal(거대한)'이라는 말이 유래했습니다.

자, 이런 조각상을 규모에 못지않게 거대한 비용을 들여 짓는다는 것은, 비용을 고대 왕들이나 파라오가 할당하던 시절에는, 별개 사항이었습니다. 하지만 현대 거대 조각상에 관해 생각해 본다면, 사회적·정치적 상징으로서 거대 석상의 역할을 더욱 면밀히 재검토할 필요가 있습니다. 현대 사회, 즉 세금을 납부하는 자유 시민 사회가 거상 건립에 그처럼 막대한 재원을 할당하는 데 동의하는 이유를 파악하려고요. 먼저 검토해 볼 좋은 사례는 러슈모어 산일 겁니다.

자, 여러분 중 많은 분들이 러슈모어 산의 사진을 봤을 겁니다. 어쩌면 실제로 가봤을 수도 있겠지요. 러슈모어 산은 사우스다코타 주에 있으며 미국 대통령 네 명의 거대한 두상이 조각되어 있습니다. 조지 워싱턴, 토머스 제퍼슨, 시어도어 루스벨트, 에이브러햄 링컨의 얼굴이 산에 직접 조각되어 있습니다. 상상해 보세요. 바위에 새겨진 각 얼굴은 높이가 무려 18미터가 넘습니다! 자, 이 얼굴들을 조각하는 데 6년 6개월이 걸렸으며 거의 백만 달러가 들었습니다. 게다가 1930년대, 즉 미국 역사상 최악의 경제 공황기였습니다! 이상하다고 생각하는 사람 없나요?

그런데, 제 개인적인 생각으로는 1930년대 대공황 사태는 사실상 이를 납득하기 어렵게 만드는 것이 아니라 오히려 더 쉽게 합니다. 이런 경우가 종종 있죠. 정확히 고난의 시기, 즉 사회 체제가 낱낱이 와해되고 신념이 무너지는 듯할 때, 국민은 힘과 낙관론의 범국가적인 표출을 소리 높여 요구합니다. 난국에 굴복하지 않고 인내를 상징하는 수단으로서요.

그래서 그 점을 염두에 두고 러슈모어 산을 다시 살펴보겠습니다. 사실상 사우스다코타 주의 거대 기념물을 추진하게 된 본래의 동기는 이 모든 상징성과는 거의 상관이 없었고, 모든 게 다 돈 때문이었습니다. 아시다시피 이 사업은

basically as a tourist attraction, and it was supposed to feature the images of legendary figures of the American West, like the explorers Lewis and Clark. The government of South Dakota thought it would bring lots of money into the state.

It was only later on that the sculptor — the artist who designed and oversaw the project, a man named Gutzon Borglum — decided the project should be a monument honoring four of the most-respected Presidents in U.S. history; much more than a tourist attraction... its very prominence and permanence became perceived as a symbol of the endurance of U.S. ideals and the greatness of the country's early leaders. So, you see, what began as a tourist attraction became something far loftier.

Let's look at another example of this phenomenon.

The Statue of Liberty is another colossal statue — one that I assume a number of you are familiar with. But, umm, I would guess that — like many people today — you don't realize that, when it was designed, over a century ago — by a French sculptor — it was intended to symbolize the long friendship between the people of France and the people of the United States — one which dated back to France's support of the American colonies' war for independence from the British.

But the shift in the statue's meaning started soon after it was built. Back in 1883, Emma Lazarus wrote that famous poem — you know, the one that goes: "Give me your tired, your poor..." and so on and so forth. That poem describes the Statue of Liberty as a beacon of welcome for the entire world. Well, in the early 1900s, it was put on a plaque on the pedestal that the Statue of Liberty stands on.

From that point on, the Statue of Liberty was no longer perceived as just a gift between friendly republics. It now became a tribute to the United States' history of immigration and openness.

This association was strengthened in the imagination of the general public just a few decades after the statue's completion, with the immigration waves of the early twentieth century... especially since the statue happened to be the first sign of America seen by those immigrants sailing into the port of New York. So, as with Mount Rushmore, the original motivation for this colossal statue was forgotten, and the statue is now valued for more important reasons.

원래 관광 명소로서 착상되었고, 탐험가 루이스와 클라크와 같은 미국 서부의 전설적 인물의 이미지를 보여 주기로 되어 있었습니다. 사우스다코타 주정부는 이로 인해 주 수입이 많이 늘어날 것이라 생각했습니다.

나중에서야 조각가, 즉 이 프로젝트를 설계하고 감독한 예술가 거츤 보글럼이라는 사람이 이 프로젝트가 미국 역사상 가장 존경 받는 네 명의 대통령들을 기리는 기념비를 건립하는 일이 되어야 한다는 결단을 내렸습니다. 관광 명소 이상이어야 한다는 것이었습니다. 이 거대 조각상의 탁월함과 영속성은 미국 이상(理想)의 지속성과 초창기 지도자들의 위대함의 상징으로 인식되었습니다. 그래서 아시다시피 한낱 관광 명소로 시작된 일이 훨씬 더 숭고한 사업으로 발돋움했습니다.

이런 현상의 또 다른 사례를 살펴봅시다.

자유의 여신상은 또 하나의 거대 조각상입니다. 여러분 중 많은 분들이 익히 알고 있는 조각상일 겁니다. 하지만 제가 짐작하기로는 오늘날 많은 사람들과 마찬가지로 여러분은 백 년도 더 전에 프랑스 조각가가 이것을 설계했을 당시에는 프랑스 시민들과 미국 시민들의 오랜 친선을 상징하려는 것이 의도였음을 알아차리지 못합니다. 이 친선관계는 영국으로부터 독립하기 위한 미국 식민지 전쟁에 대한 프랑스의 지원까지 거슬러 올라갑니다.

하지만 이 동상의 의미 변화가 건립 직후 시작되었습니다. 1883년, 에마 라자루스는 바로 그 유명한 시를 썼습니다. 알다시피, 이런 구절이 있습니다. "지치고 가난한 자들을 내게 보내다오." 등등입니다. 그 시는 자유의 여신상을 전 세계에 대한 환영의 횃불로 묘사합니다. 1900년대 초 이 구절이 자유의 여신상 받침대의 장식판에 새겨졌습니다.

그 시점부터 줄곧 자유의 여신상은 더 이상 우호국 간의 친선 선물로만 인식되지 않게 되었습니다. 이제는 미국의 이민과 개방정신의 역사를 기리는 기념비가 되었습니다.

이처럼 둘을 연결 짓는 생각은 자유의 여신상이 완공된 지 불과 수십 년 만에 대중의 상상 속에서 강화되었습니다. 20세기 초 이민 물결에 더불어, 특히 자유의 여신상이 뉴욕항으로 배를 타고 들어오는 이민자들에게 가장 먼저 목격되는 미국의 상징이 된 이후 그렇게 되었습니다. 그래서 러슈모어 산의 경우처럼 이 거대 조상은 본래의 동기가 잊혀지고, 이제는 더욱 중요한 이유로 높이 평가 받고 있습니다.

colossal 거대한 colossal statue 거상(巨像)　exceptionally 매우, 대단히　commemorate 기념하다　figure 인물　fire 고무하다, 자극하다
Colossus of Rhodes 로도스의 거상　Helios 헬리오스(태양의 신)　allocate 할당하다　reexamine 재검토하다　resources 재원, 자원
erect 건립하다　Mount Rushmore 러슈모어 산(사우스다코타 주의 산. 워싱턴, 제퍼슨, 링컨, 루즈벨트 대통령의 거대한 두상이 조각되어 있음.)
representation 조각상, 초상　strike (머리에) 떠오르다, 생각나다　odd 이상한, 뜻밖의　hardship 고난, 고초　fabric (사회 등의) 체계, 구조
unravel (체계, 구조 등이) 와해되다, (실타래가) 풀리다　confidence 신념, 확신　erode 부식되다, 침식하다　clamor for ~을 소리 높여 요구하다
endurance 인내력, 참을성　conceive (계획 등을) 착상하다, 생각해내다　tourist attraction 관광 명소　Lewis and Clark 서부개척자 메리웨더 루
이스와 윌리엄 클라크(포틀랜드를 최초로 발견했음.)　oversee 감독하다　prominence 현저함　permanence 영속성　perceive 인지하다　lofty
숭고한, 거룩한　phenomenon 현상, 사건　shift 변화, 변천　so on and so forth ~등등, 기타　beacon 횃불, (교통) 표지　plaque 장식판
pedestal 대좌, 받침돌　tribute 존경을 표시하는 물건, 기념비적 물건　strengthen 강하게 하다, 강화하다　value 높이 평가하다, 소중히 여기다

23. 교수는 주로 무엇을 논하는가?

Ⓐ 자유의 여신상의 설계와 의도

Ⓑ 미국의 거대 조각상 두 개의 건립자들

Ⓒ 거대 조각상의 목적과 상징성

Ⓓ 현대와 과거의 거대 조각상 건립 비용 비교

내용의 요점을 묻는 문제

어휘 versus ~대(對), ~에 대하여

해설 교수는 강의에서 거대 조각상의 건립 이유와 거대 조각상이 상
징하는 의미를 개괄적으로 소개한다.

24. 교수는 오늘날의 거대 조각상들이 사회·정치적 상징으로 높은 평
가를 받는다는 의견을 뒷받침하는 증거로 무엇을 제시하는가?

Ⓐ 거대 조각상은 건립 비용이 매우 많이 든다.

Ⓑ 거대 조각상은 전 세계 강의실에서 연구되고 있다.

Ⓒ 거대 조각상은 수천 년 동안 존속하도록 설계되었다.

Ⓓ 거대 조각상은 훌륭한 시에 고무되었다.

세부 사항 찾기 문제

어휘 inspire 고무하다, 고취하다

해설 교수는 세금을 내는 자유 시민들이 그렇게 많은 돈을 들여 조각
상을 건립하는 데 찬성한 이유를 이해하기 위해 사회·정치적
상징성을 다시 생각해 봐야 한다고 했다. 바꾸어 말하면, 비용이
많이 든다는 사실 자체가 사회·정치적 상징성이 매우 크다는
사실을 뒷받침하는 증거가 될 수 있다.

25. 교수에 따르면, 1930년대 대공황의 한 가지 결과는 무엇이었는가?

Ⓐ 국제 동맹이 약화되었다.

Ⓑ 미국 이민이 증가했다.

Ⓒ 대중이 신념의 상실을 경험했다.

Ⓓ 정부가 예술 기금을 더 이상 지원할 수 없었다.

세부 사항 찾기 문제

어휘 alliance 동맹　fund 기금, 자금

해설 교수는 1930년대 대공황을 설명하면서 이 시기를 국민의 신뢰
가 무너지는 시기라고 했다.

26. 교수에 따르면, 사우스다코타 주가 최초에 거대 조각상을 만들려
고 했던 이유는 무엇이었는가?

Ⓐ 관광 수입을 창출하기 위해　Ⓑ 사회 단합을 상징하기 위해

Ⓒ 대공황을 기념하기 위해　Ⓓ 미국 대통령들을 기리기 위해서

세부 사항 찾기 문제

어휘 originally 원래는, 본래는　generate 창출하다, 일으키다

해설 교수는 거대 조각상이 애초에 관광 명소로 계획되었으며, 주정
부는 이로 인해 수입이 증가할 것으로 기대했다고 설명했다.

27. 교수는 왜 에마 라자루스의 시에 대해 논하는가?

Ⓐ 문학과 조각의 밀접한 관계를 강조하기 위해

Ⓑ 기념비에 관련된 의미가 어떻게 변하는지 설명하기 위해

Ⓒ 프랑스와 미국의 친선의 중요성을 강조하기 위해

Ⓓ 러슈모어 산과 자유의 여신상의 차이를 지적하기 위해

의도 파악 문제

어휘 associate 관련시키다　point out 지적하다

해설 교수는 에마 라자루스의 시에서 자유의 여신상이 이민자들을 위
한 희망의 등불로 묘사된 것을 예로 들어 미국과 프랑스의 친선
이라는 원래 의미가 달라졌다는 사실을 설명한다.

28. 강의의 일부를 다시 듣고 질문에 답하라.

🎧 T-43

P Back in 1883, Emma Lazarus wrote that famous
poem—you know, the one that goes: "Give me
your tired, your poor..." and so on and so forth.
N *What does the professor imply about the poem by
Emma Lazarus?*

Ⓐ 그 시는 교수가 가장 좋아하는 시 중의 하나다.

Ⓑ 그 시를 완독한 사람은 거의 없다.

Ⓒ 교수는 그 시의 전문을 낭송할 필요는 없다.

Ⓓ 라자루스는 그 시를 완성할 수 없었다.

의도 파악 문제

어휘 recite 낭송하다, 낭독하다

해설 교수가 유명한 대목을 말하다가 끊고 등등이라고 얼버무리는 것
으로 보아, 전체 내용을 언급할 필요는 없다는 교수의 의도를 파
악할 수 있다.

SPEAKING

T-44

Question 1   p. 208

Narrator

Some students would prefer to live with roommates. Others would prefer to live alone. Which option would you prefer and why?

어떤 학생들은 룸메이트와 같이 살기를 선호한다. 다른 학생들은 혼자 살기를 선호한다. 어느 쪽을 선호하는지 밝히고 이유를 설명하시오.

준비 시간 : 15초
답변 시간 : 45초

우수 답변   T-49

On the one hand I think to live with a roommate could be a good thing since you always have somebody to talk with when you have problems, or thing like that, and it's a good way to meet people, but on the other hand, you can't really do whatever you want. I mean, if you like parties and if your roommate does not it's not a good thing for you... you are not free to do what you like, and it's not really... interesting... it's... ummm, well, I live by myself and I'm very glad since I can do what I want, I have nobody to tell me what to do, and...

채점자 의견

수험자는 자신의 의견을 명확히 전개하고 있다. 먼저 룸메이트와 함께 사는 것에 대한 장점을 논한 다음 단점에 대해 설명했고 장점보다는 단점을 더 부각했다. 룸메이트가 어떤 문제점이 있을 수 있는지에 대한 예를 든 다음 혼자 사는 것을 더 선호한다 밝히면서 이와 관련한 개인적 경험담을 덧붙였다. 발음은 이해하기 편하고 매우 유창하다. 단어 선택이 몇 가지 부정확했지만 수험자의 의견을 이해하는 데는 지장이 없다.

하위 수준의 답변   T-50

Some students would prefer to live, uh, with a (sic) romantis... uh... whether... uh... I prefer live (pause) in... uh... (sic) illuminism because, uh, they... this, uh, period, they... there is, uh... um... (background chatter)

채점자 의견

답변의 서두에서 수험자는 질문을 소리 내어 읽기만 했을 뿐 실제로 답변을 하지 않고 있다. 발음은 모국어의 영향이 강해서 무슨 말인지 알아들으려면 대단히 신경을 써야 한다. 다음 단어를 생각하느라 여러 번 길게 멈추는 것으로 보아 이 수험자의 단어 구사력은 매우 제한적임을 알 수 있다. 이런 답변이 채점 기준 상 최저점에 해당하는 답변이다.

Narrator

Read the article from the university newspaper about the plan to build new student housing. You will have 50 seconds to read the article. Begin reading now.

새 학생 숙소 건설 계획에 관한 대학신문 기사를 50초 동안 읽으시오. 지금 읽으시오.

University May Build
New Student Apartments Off Campus

The Department of Student Housing is considering whether to build new student housing off campus in a residential area of town. Two of the major factors influencing the decision will be parking and space. Those who support building off campus argue that building new housing on campus would further increase the number of cars on and around campus and consume space that could be better used for future projects that the entire university community could benefit from. Supporters also say that students might even have a richer college experience by being connected to the local community and patronizing stores and other businesses in town.

캠퍼스 외부에 신규 학생 아파트 건립 가능성 있어

학생 숙소 관리부는 캠퍼스 외부 주거 지역에 학생 숙소를 신설하는 계획을 검토하고 있다. 이 결정에 영향을 미치는 두 가지 주요 요소는 주차와 부지다. 캠퍼스 외부 건축을 지지하는 이들은 캠퍼스 내 숙소 신축으로 캠퍼스 내외의 차량 수가 증가하고, 학교 전체에 득이 되는 다른 프로젝트에 더욱 유용하게 사용될 수 있는 부지가 감소한다고 주장한다. 지지자들은 학생들이 지역 사회와 관계를 맺고 마을 상점들과 기타 사업체들을 단골로 이용해 심지어 훨씬 풍부한 대학 생활을 경험할 수 있을 것이라 한다.

어휘

housing 숙소   residential area 주거 지역   consume 소모하다, 소비하다   patronize 단골로 삼다, 거래하다

Narrator

Now listen to two students discussing the article.

이제 기사에 대한 두 학생의 논의를 들으시오.

F   I can't believe these plans. It just doesn't make sense to me.

M   Really? Seemed OK to me, especially the argument about the cars.

F   Yeah, I know. But the thing is, it doesn't matter where students live 'cause they still have to get to class somehow, right? At least if they built new dorms on campus, students would use campus transportation...

M   ... instead of their cars. I see what you're getting at. If they live off campus, they're *still* goging to have to drive and park on campus. Might even create more traffic.

F   Exactly.

M   OK. Still, though... the point about students interacting more with people in the community: that doesn't seem to be a bad thing, does it?

F   But the more time spent off campus, in town, the less time spent on campus. What about all the clubs, shows, discussions, a—all the campus happenings that just kind of... happen? It's important to be on campus to really take advantage of these things. Having a different living experience shouldn't be given up at the expense of not being as much a part of the university community.

여   이런 계획들을 세우다니 믿을 수가 없어. 도대체 이해가 안 돼.

남   정말? 내가 보기엔 괜찮은데. 특히 차량에 관한 주장은 말이야.

여   그래, 나도 알아. 하지만 문제는 학생들이 어디에 사는지는 상관이 없다는 거야. 어떻게든 수업을 받으러 올 테니까. 그렇지? 최소한 캠퍼스 내에 기숙사를 지으면, 학생들이 캠퍼스 교통편을 이용하겠지.

남   자기 차 대신에. 무슨 말인지 알겠어. 학생들이 캠퍼스 밖에 살면, 여전히 운전하고 와서 캠퍼스에 주차해야 해. 오히려 교통량이 더 많아질 거야.

여   맞아.

남   그래. 그렇기는 하지만. 학생들이 지역 주민들과 더 많이 교류한다는 것의 요지는, 그건 그리 나쁜 것 같지 않아, 그렇지?

여   하지만 캠퍼스 밖에서, 즉 시내에서 더 많은 시간을 보내면, 캠퍼스 안에서 보내는 시간이 줄어들겠지. 동아리, 공연, 토론은 어떻게 될까? 캠퍼스에서 일어나는 거의 모든 일들 말이야. 캠퍼스에서 이런 장점들을 실제로 누리려면 캠퍼스 안에 있어야 해. 그만큼 학교 공동체의 일부가 되지 못하는 걸 감수하면서까지 다른 생활을 경험할 필요는 없어.

어휘

make sense 말이 되다, 이해할 수 있다 dorm 기숙사(dormitory)
be getting at ~을 말하려 하다 interact 교류하다 community
공동체 happening 일, 사건 give up 포기하다 at the
expense of ~을 희생하여

Narrator

The woman expresses her opinion of the university's
plan. State her opinion and explain the reasons she
gives for holding that opinion..

여학생은 학교의 계획에 관해 자신의 의견을 피력한다. 여학생의
의견을 진술하고 여학생이 자신의 의견을 뒷받침하기 위해 제시하
는 근거를 설명하시오.

준비 시간 : 30초
답변 시간 : 60초

우수 답변 🎧 T-51

In the woman's opinion, the plans of the university to
build housing—uh, to build new student dorms
outside—off-campus, are not viewed—she, um, is
against that because she thinks that the-the reason that
the university is giving, which is, um... that are too many
cars on campus already and um, there is no space for
more—more dorms and more cars there, uh, doesn't
really work because she says that if people live on
campus they don't even need a car to go to university
but if they live off-campus they will need a car to get
there. That's her one reason, and she also says it's better
for students if they live on campus because that way they
have better possibilities to enjoy all the benefits from their
student life, they can take part in many of student actions
on campus without having to worry how to get there and
how to get away from there again.

채점자 의견

수험자는 상세하고 조리 있게 답변하고 있으며, 신문기사의 주요 논점에
대한 여자의 의견을 정확하고 효율적으로 설명하고 있다. 대화나 지문의
내용 중 중요하지 않은 부분을 언급하느라 시간 낭비를 하는 우를 범하
지 않았다. 말하는 속도는 물 흐르듯 자연스럽고 문장력과 어휘력이 훌
륭하며, 발음 또한 탁월하다.

중간 수준의 답변 🎧 T-52

Uh, she doesn't agree with the plan because she
personally thinks that, um, if the location of, uh, the
students, uh, is on the campus, the-they will not need
cars, uh, so, they will not need parking because they will
use the campus transportation, but, uh, of course if they
are out, they will need cars and it will, um... it will be bad
for the campus and she thinks that, uh, if, um, people are
on the campus they can assist to campus happening and
it's very important because with—that they can be part
of university community, which is more important than,
uh, being out of the campus and, uh, meeting other
people.

채점자 의견

이 수험자는 대화 속 여자의 중요한 논점을 모두 다루고는 있지만 대학
교의 계획이 무엇인지 언급하지 않아 그 여자가 무엇에 반대하고 있는지
확실하게 드러나지 않는다. 단어 선택에서 예를 들면 "attend" 대신에
"assist"를 사용한다든지 하는 사소한 문제가 있기는 하지만 대체로 어
휘와 문법이 괜찮은 수준이다. 말하는 속도는 대개 일정하나, 가끔씩 머
뭇거리는 부분이 있어 집중해서 들어야 한다.

Question 3   p. 210

Narrator

Now read the passage about a topic in psychology. You will have 45 seconds to read the passage. Begin reading now.

심리학 주제에 관한 글을 45초 동안 읽으시오. 지금 읽으시오.

Actor-observer

People account for their own behavior differently from how they account for the behavior of others. When observing the behavior of others, we tend to attribute their actions to their character or their personality rather than to external factors. In contrast, we tend to explain our own behavior in terms of situational factors beyond our own control rather than attributing it to our own character. One explanation for this difference is that people are aware of the situational forces affecting them but not of situational forces affecting other people. Thus, when evaluating someone else's behavior, we focus on the person rather than the situation.

행위자-관찰자

사람들은 타인의 행동을 설명하는 방식과 다른 방식으로 자신의 행동을 설명한다. 타인의 행동을 관찰할 때, 우리는 그들의 행동이 외적 요인보다는 그들의 개성이나 성격 탓이라고 여기는 경향이 있다. 반면, 우리는 우리의 행동을 우리의 성격 탓으로 여기지 않고 우리가 통제할 수 없는 상황적 요인의 관점에서 우리의 행동을 설명하는 경향이 있다. 이런 차이에 대한 설명 중 하나는, 사람들이 자신에게 영향을 미치는 상황적 강제를 인식하지만 타인에게 영향을 미치는 상황적 강제는 인식하지 못한다는 것이다. 그래서 타인의 행동을 평가할 때 우리는 상황보다는 사람에 초점을 맞춘다.

어휘

actor 행위자 observer 관찰자 account for 설명하다 tend to ~하는 경향이 있다, ~하기 쉽다 attribute (원인을) ~의 탓으로 돌리다 in terms of ~의 관점에서 situational force 상황적 강제

Narrator

Now listen to part of a lecture in a psychology class.

심리학 강의의 일부를 들으시오.

P So we encounter this in life all the time, but many of us are unaware that we do this... even psychologists who study it... like me. For example, the other day I was at the store and I was getting in line to buy something. But just before I was actually in line, some guy comes out of nowhere and cuts right in front of me. Well, I was really annoyed and thought, "That was rude!" I assumed he was just a selfish, inconsiderate person when, in fact, I had no idea why he cut in line in front of me or whether he even realized he was doing it. Maybe he didn't think I was actually in line yet... But my immediate reaction was to assume he was a selfish or rude person.

OK, so a few days after that, I was at the store again. Only this time I was in a real hurry—I was late for an important meeting—and I was frustrated that everything was taking so long. And what's worse, all the checkout lines were long, and it seemed like everyone was moving so slowly. But then I saw a slightly shorter line! But some woman with a lot of stuff to buy was walking toward it, so I basically ran to get there first, before her, and, well, I did. Now, I didn't think of myself as a bad or rude person for doing this. I had an important meeting to get to—I was in a hurry, so, you know, I had done nothing wrong.

교수 자, 우리는 살면서 항상 이런 일을 겪지만, 우리들 중 다수가 스스로 그런다는 사실조차 알지 못합니다. 심지어는 이를 연구하는 심리학자들도 모릅니다. 저처럼요. 예를 들어, 일전에 상점에서 뭘 사려고 줄을 서고 있었어요. 그런데 줄을 서기 바로 전에, 어떤 사람이 갑자기 나타나 바로 제 앞에서 새치기를 했습니다. 정말 화가 나서, '정말 무례해!' 라는 생각이 들었습니다. 저는 그 사람을 이기적이고 남을 배려할 줄 모르는 사람이라고 여겼는데, 사실, 그 순간 저는 그 사람이 제 앞에서 새치기한 이유도 몰랐고 자기가 무슨 짓을 하고 있는지 스스로 알고 있는지도 알 수 없었어요. 어쩌면 그 사람은 제가 아직 줄을 서지 않았다고 생각했을지도 모르죠. 하지만 그때 저의 즉각적 반응은 그 사람이 이기적이고 무례한 사람이라고 여긴 것이었습니다.

자, 그러고 나서 며칠 뒤, 전 그 상점에 다시 갔습니다. 이번에는 저는 무척 서두르고 있었습니다. 중요한 회의에 늦었거든요. 그리고 모든 것이 너무 오래 걸려서 쩔쩔매고 있었죠. 설상가상으로 계산대마다 줄이 길게 늘어서 있었고, 모두 아주 느릿느릿 움직이는 듯했어요. 하지만 그때 약간 짧은 줄이 보였어요! 그런데 사려는 물건을 잔뜩 든 여성 한 분이 그쪽으로 걸어가고 있었고,

그래서 전 거기에 먼저 도착하려고 실은 뛰다시피, 그분보다 먼저 그쪽으로 갔고, 그래서 먼저 도착했어요. 이번에는 제가 그렇게 한 데 대해 저 자신을 나쁜 사람이나 무례한 사람으로 여기지 않았습니다. 중요한 회의에 참석해야 해서 서둘렀고, 그래서 아시다시피 잘못한 게 없어요.

어휘

encounter 만나다, 마주치다　　unaware 인식하지 못하는, 모르는　　psychologist 심리학자　　get in the line 줄을 서다　　out of nowhere 갑자기, 불쑥　　inconsiderate 남을 배려할 줄 모르는, 경솔한　　cut in line 새치기하다　　frustrate 좌절시키다　　check-out 계산대(counter)　　basically 요컨대, 실은

Narrator

Explain how the two examples discussed by the professor illustrate differences in the ways people explain behavior.

교수가 논한 두 가지 사례가 사람들이 행동을 해석하는 방식의 차이를 어떻게 보여 주는지 설명하시오.

준비 시간 : 30초
답변 시간 : 60초

우수 답변 🎧 T-53

To begin my statement I have to say that there are two main different kinds of evaluate other people or your own. If you evaluate other people, you look just first on the personality or so-something to connect with the character. If you look at yourself, you see more the surrounding or the situation than you are and not-don't see the full the problems for yourself or what you do by yourself. On to professor is two examples to illustrate this—how people explain behavior. First, he was in line and he—a person jumped before him, he did line jumping and he was very annoyed about this fact because he thought this person was rude or selfish, but just a couple of days later he was (sic) nery attend a important meeting, only meeting and—then—he—did the same and uh—bef—he just explained his behavior due to the fact that he had no time and an important meeting and so—he thought it was no—nothing wrong.

채점자 의견

수험자는 사람들이 자신의 행위를 이해하는 관점과 타인의 행위를 이해하는 관점이 어떻게 다른지를 설명하는 교수의 예시를 명확하게 설명했다. 할당된 시간 안에 주요 논점이 모두 효율적으로 언급되었다. 끊김 없이 일정한 속도를 유지하며 답변했고 발음은 몇 군데 알아듣기 힘든 부분이 있기는 하나 전체적으로 무난하다. 사소한 문법적 실수가 몇 가지 있지만 이해하는 데는 지장이 없으며 전반적으로 괜찮은 수준의 문법을 구사하고 있음을 알 수 있다.

중간 수준의 답변 🎧 T-54

The two examples discussed by the professor, uh—illustrate difference in the ways people, uh, explain behavior because, uh, the first one, uh.... he... he don't—doesn't understand uh—why somebody uh, took his place in the, uh, in the store. He thought, uh, that people was, uh, selfish but, uh, in fact he didn't realize, uh, why, uh, why the people t-took his place. In the second, uh, example, um...he—he was in a hu-hu-hurry and um, he, uh...he, um....he took the place of uh, of uh, somebody else, and uh, this uh, this explain by the fact that uh, when uh, when people explain uh... uh... somebody's behavior, uh, then they base on the... on the character and no—and not on the, on the situation of um... of the... of the other people, the other people.

채점자 의견

수험자는 교수가 언급한 두 가지 예시를 모두 기본적인 선에서 설명했으나, 두 번째 예시와 "사람들은 자기 자신의 행위를 성격적 요인보다는 상황적 요인으로 설명하려 한다"는 지문의 내용을 명확하게 연관 짓지 못했다. 발음은 알아듣기 쉽지만 머뭇거리는 말투가 잦아 잘 이해되지 않는 부분도 있다.

Question 4   p. 211

Narrator

Now listen to part of a lecture in a child development class.

아동발달 강의의 일부를 들으시오.

Professor OK. Young children and art. Research suggests that learning art skills can benefit a young child's development. Umm... two of the ways it can do this is by providing a platform to express complex emotions and by encouraging persistence.

Now, what do I mean when I say "a platform to express complex emotions"? Young children have limited vocabulary. So how would they communicate the feeling of pride, for example? A drawing, though, making a drawing of feeling proud... this is something a young child could do. So a little girl might draw herself jumping up in the air next to her bike. In the drawing, her arms are raised up in the air and she's smiling. Children can communicate their emotions, whether positive or negative, through the drawing—mm—better than they could with words.

And encouraging persistence? Art skills can help children to develop patience and concentration to persist in an activity... the willingness to keep trying to reach a goal. So suppose there's a little boy who wants to mold a lump of clay into the shape of a car. The first attempt doesn't look too much like a car. He's disappointed but wants to try again. The second, third, fourth try still don't look quite right, but there's improvement with every attempt. So, after some time, he gets to the point where he's satisfied with his creation. The newly shaped clay car is an instant reminder of an accomplishment—a success resulting from his persistence. The boy may be able to transfer this lesson toward other situations and activities because, well, he's had the experience of successfully accomplishing a goal through hard work.

교수 어린 아동들과 미술에 관해 살펴보겠습니다. 연구에 의하면, 미술 학습이 어린아이의 발달에 이롭습니다. 그렇게 되는 두 가지 방식은 복잡한 감정을 표현하기 위한 기반을 제공하고, 인내심을 북돋운다는 것이지요.

'복잡한 감정을 표현하기 위한 기반'이란 무엇일까요? 어린이들의 어휘력은 제한적입니다. 예를 들어, 아이들은 자긍심을 어떻게 전달할까요? 그림. 그래도 자긍심을 느끼는 그림 그리기. 이것이 바로 어린아이들이 할 수 있는 것입니다. 어린 여자아이는 자전거 옆에서 공중으로 펄쩍 뛰어오르는 자신의 모습을 그릴 수도 있어요. 그 그림 속에서 아이는 두 팔을 머리 위로 쳐들고 활짝 웃고 있습니다. 아이들은 그림을 그려 감정을 전달할 수 있습니다. 긍정적이든 부정적이든, 그림을 통해서라면 말로 하는 것보다 더욱 잘할 수 있습니다.

그리고 인내심을 북돋운다는 건 무슨 뜻일까요? 미술 솜씨가 있으면 한 가지 활동에 집중하기 위한 인내심과 집중력에 도움이 됩니다. 목적을 달성하려고 기꺼이 계속 시도하는 마음이지요. 자, 진흙 덩어리를 빚어 자동차를 만들려는 어린 남자아이가 있다고 합시다. 첫 번째 시도는 그다지 자동차처럼 보이지 않습니다. 아이는 실망하지만 다시 시도하려 합니다. 두 번째, 세 번째, 네 번째로 시도해도 여전히 제대로 되지 않은 듯하지만 매번 시도할 때마다 발전이 있습니다. 어느 정도 시간이 지나면, 아이는 자신의 작품에 만족하는 순간에 도달합니다. 새로 만든 진흙 자동차는 성취, 즉 인내에 따른 성공을 즉각적으로 상기시키는 것입니다. 아이는 이 교훈을 다른 상황이나 행동으로 전이할 수 있을 것입니다. 열심히 노력해서 목적을 성공적으로 달성한 경험이 있으니까요.

어휘

development 발달, 발전   platform 기반, 토대   persistence 인내, 끈기   limited 한정된 제한된   mold (형체를) 만들다, 형성하다   lump 덩어리   instant 즉각적인   reminder 상기시키는 것(사람)   transfer 전이하다, 옮기다

우수 답변 🎧 T-55

They are two ways in which art can foster a child's development. Uh, one way is um, there's an - a - a platform offered for um, expressing a child's, um, complex emotions, and the other one is, um...yeah, encouraging a child's persistence. Um, a child has very limited vocabulary, um, and that's why cannot express, uh and cannot verbally express, um, its uh, some of co- some complex emotions, like grief and all this, um... So, um, in a drawing, um, a child has the opportunity to actually uh, yeah—show, uh, the way—uh, show what it feels. And also, um, with persistence, um, it's been that a child can keep trying to create something and when it's finally done there's, uh, this success factor and accomplishment.

채점자 의견

수험자는 미술 교육이 아동의 성장에 어떤 영향을 주는지에 대해 설명하기 위해 강의의 요점을 효율적으로 요약했다. 답변은 알아듣기 쉽고 간혹 가다 흐름이 살짝 끊기는 부분이 있긴 하나 전반적으로는 매끄러웠다. 또한 구어 표현에서 사용되는 기본적인 표현과 좀 더 복잡한 문법을 잘 구사했다.

중간 수준의 답변 🎧 T-56

Learning art can be important for children since, uh... (pause) it can be seen as a platform to express, uh... complex emotions, for example, like, pride, since she gave an example of a little boy who wanted to draw a car. His first attempt was bad, but the other one, the third, the fourth, the fifth, were good, so he was satisfied with himself and he achieved thanks to its persistence. (sigh) So art has been good for him, and learning art is also... a good way to learn (sic) art out skills, so it can only be an asset for, uh... for child.

채점자 의견

수험자는 강의를 요약하기는 했지만 내용 상 중요한 실수를 했다. 즉 '미술이 아이들의 정서 발달에 도움이 되는 점 중 하나로 아이들에게 인내심을 가르쳐준다는 점을 꼽을 수 있다'라는 두 번째 논점을 빠뜨렸다. 첫 번째 논점에 대한 요약은 부정확하며, 두 번째 논점의 예시와 첫 번째 논점(미술이 아이들이 감정 표현에 도움이 된다)의 예시를 혼동하고 있다. 발음은 대개 분명하지만, 답변이 논리 정연하게 전개되지 못하여 앞서 했던 말과 다음에 이어지는 말에 어떤 연관성이 있는지 이해하기 쉽지 않다.

WRITING

p. 214

Integrated Writing

Professors are normally found in university classrooms, offices, and libraries doing research and lecturing to their students. More and more, however, they also appear as guests on television news programs, giving expert commentary on the latest events in the world. These television appearances are of great benefit to the professors themselves as well as to their universities and the general public.

Professors benefit from appearing on television because by doing so they acquire reputations as authorities in their academic fields among a much wider audience than they have on campus. If a professor publishes views in an academic journal, only other scholars will learn about and appreciate those views. But when a professor appears on TV, thousands of people outside the narrow academic community become aware of the professor's ideas. So when professors share their ideas with a television audience, the professors' importance as scholars is enhanced.

Universities also benefit from such appearances. The universities receive positive publicity when their professors appear on TV. When people see a knowledgeable faculty member of a university on television, they think more highly of that university. That then leads to an improved reputation for the university. And that improved reputation in turn leads to more donations for the university and more applications from potential students.

Finally, the public gains from professors' appearing on television. Most television viewers normally have no contact with university professors. When professors appear on television, viewers have a chance to learn from experts and to be exposed to views they might otherwise never hear about. Television is generally a medium for commentary that tends to be superficial, not deep or thoughtful. From professors on television, by contrast, viewers get a taste of real expertise and insight.

교수들의 일반적 모습은 대학 강의실, 연구실, 도서관에서 연구를 하거나 학생들에게 강의를 하는 것이다. 하지만 점점 더 텔레비전 뉴스 프로그램에 게스트로 출연하여 최근 세계 정세에 관해 전문가적 논평을 하기도 한다. 교수들의 이러한 텔레비전 출연은 교수들 본인에게는 물론 교수들의 소속 대학이나 일반 대중들에게도 매우 이롭다.

교수들은 텔레비전 출연으로 이득을 본다. 그 덕분에 자신들의 전문 분야에서 권위자라는 명성이 대학 캠퍼스보다 훨씬 더 광범위한 시청자들 사이에 퍼져 나가기 때문이다. 어떤 교수가 학술지에 의견을 게재하면 다른 학자들만 그 의견을 알게 되고 평가한다. 하지만 교수가 TV에 출연하면, 한정된 학계 외부의 수많은 사람들이 그 교수의 의견을 알게 된다. 따라서 교수들이 텔레비전 시청자들에게 자신의 견해를 피력하면, 그 교수는 학자로서 관록이 붙는다.

대학도 교수의 TV출연으로 이득을 얻는다. 소속 교수가 TV에 출연하면 그 대학은 긍정적 평판을 받는다. 사람들은 박식한 대학 교직원을 TV에서 보면 그 대학교를 더욱 높이 평가한다. 그러면 이로 인해 그 대학의 명성도 향상된다. 그리고 향상된 명성으로 이번에는 대학 기부금도 증가하고 잠재 학생들의 지원도 증가한다.

마지막으로, 대중에게도 교수의 TV 출연은 이롭다. 대부분의 TV 시청자들은 대개 대학 교수를 접할 기회가 없다. 교수들이 TV에 출연하면, 시청자들은 전문가로부터 배우고 그렇지 않다면 절대로 들어볼 수 없는 의견을 접하는 기회를 얻는다. 텔레비전은 일반적으로 심오하거나 생각이 깊은 것은 배제하고 피상적 경향이 있는 논평 매체다. 반대로 텔레비전에 출연하는 교수로부터 진정한 전문가적 지식과 통찰력을 경험한다.

어휘

normally 대게, 보통 commentary 논평, 해설 be of benefit to ~에 이롭다 benefit from ~로부터 이득을 얻다 authority 권위자, 대가 view 견해, 의견 appreciate 진가를 알다, 가치를 인정하다 narrow (범위 등이) 제한된, 좁은 academic community 학계 publicity 평판 knowledgeable 박식한 faculty member 교직원 think highly of ~을 높이 평가하다 in turn 이번에는, 다음에는 donation 기부 gain 이득을 얻다 otherwise 그렇지 않다면 superficial 피상적인, 외면상의 get a taste of ~을 경험하다 expertise 전문가적 의견, 전문 지식

Professor

Lately, we've been seeing some professors on television. Though it's sometimes claimed to be a good thing, we should question whether anybody really benefits from it. First of all, it's not good for the professors themselves — not from a professional standpoint. Rightly or wrongly, a professor who appears on TV tends to get the reputation among fellow professors of being someone who is not a serious scholar — someone who chooses to entertain rather than to educate. And for that reason, TV professors may not be invited to important conferences — important meetings to discuss their academic work. They may even have difficulty getting money to do research. So for professors, being a TV celebrity has important disadvantages.

A second point is that being on TV can take a lot of a professor's time — not just the time on TV but also time figuring out what to present and time spent rehearsing, travel time, even time getting made up to look good for the cameras. And all this time comes out of the time the professor can spend doing research, meeting with students, and attending to university business. So you can certainly see there are problems for the university and its students when professors are in the TV studio and not on campus.

So who does benefit? The public? Umm... that's not so clear either. Look, professors do have a lot of knowledge to offer, but TV networks don't want really serious, in-depth academic lectures for after-dinner viewing. What the networks want is the academic title, not the intellectual substance. The material that professors usually present on TV — such as background on current events, or some brief historical introduction to a new movie version of a great literary work — this material is not much different from what viewers would get from a TV reporter who had done a little homework.

최근 우리는 텔레비전에 나오는 교수들을 보고 있습니다. 바람직한 현상이라는 주장도 가끔 있지만, 과연 실제로 누구에게 이득이 있는지 의문을 가져봐야 합니다. 무엇보다도 이는 교수들 본인들에게 좋지 않습니다. 전문가적 입장에서는 좋은 게 아니지요. 옳든 그르든, TV에 출연하는 교수는 동료 교수들로부터 진정한 학자가 아니라는 평판을 받기 쉽습니다. 교육보다는 연예 활동을 택한 사람이라는 겁니다. 그리고 그런

이유로 TV에 출연하는 교수들은 중요한 학술 회의에 초청받지 못할 수도 있습니다. 학술적인 연구를 검토하는 중요한 회의 말이죠. 심지어 연구비를 받는 데도 어려움을 겪을 수 있습니다. 그래서 교수들에게 TV 명사가 되면 심각한 단점이 발생합니다.

두 번째 문제는 TV 출연에 교수의 많은 시간이 소요된다는 것입니다. TV 출연 시간뿐만 아니라 발언 내용을 준비하는 시간, 리허설 시간, 이동 시간, 심지어 카메라에 잘 나오도록 분장하는 시간도 있습니다. 그리고 이 모든 시간은 그 교수가 연구를 하고, 학생들을 만나고, 학사 행정업무를 처리하는 시간에서 나옵니다. 그래서 교수가 캠퍼스에 있지 않고 TV 스튜디오에 있을 때 대학과 학생들에게 문제가 발생한다는 것을 분명히 알 수 있습니다.

그러면 과연 누가 혜택을 받을까요? 일반 대중? 그것도 확실치 않습니다. 자, 교수들은 제공할 지식이 많지만, TV 방송국들은 저녁 식사 후 프로그램에 정말 진지한 심층적 학술 강의를 원치 않습니다. 방송국들이 원하는 것은 학문적 직함이지 지적인 내용은 아닙니다. 교수들이 TV에서 보통 말하는 내용은 현 정세에 관한 배경 정보나 위대한 문학작품을 새롭게 각색한 영화의 역사적 배경을 간략히 소개하는 정도입니다. 이런 내용은 사전 조사를 한 TV 리포터에게서 시청자들이 얻을 수 있는 것과 별반 다르지 않습니다.

어휘

standpoint 관점, 입장 **fellow professor** 동료 교수 **celebrity** 명사, 유명인사 **present** 발표하다, 소개하다 **rehearse** 예행연습[리허설]하다 **make up** 분장하다, 화장하다 **substance** 내용, 요지 **literary work** 문학 작품

Question

Summarize the points made in the lecture, being sure to explain how they respond to the specific concerns presented in the reading passage.

강의에서 말하는 요점들이 어떻게 읽기 지문에 제시된 특정 우려 사항에 대해 대응하고 있는지 반드시 설명하면서 요약하시오.

해설

강의에서 제시된 교수들의 TV 출연이 반드시 바람직하지는 않은 이유를 파악해야 한다. 교수는 교수의 평판, 교수의 시간, 대중 교육에 관해 지문에서 제시한 각각의 장점에 의문을 제기한다. 우수한 답안은 아래와 같은 지문의 요점에 대한 교수의 강의 내용을 포함한다. 4~5점을 받으려면 일반적으로 아래와 같은 요점들을 모두 명확히 설명해야 한다.

지문의 주요 내용	지문과 대조되는 강의 내용
TV appearances improve the professor's reputation.	1. Their reputation suffers, because they are considered entertainers by their peers and not serious scholars.
	2. As a result, they may get fewer invitations to academic conferences or lose research funding.
TV appearances benefit the university and lead to more student applications and more donations.	Professors spend a lot of time preparing for the TV appearances, which takes away from their true academic work, such as teaching and doing research.
TV appearances benefit the public because the public is exposed to more in-depth knowledge about a subject.	Professors generally do not give in-depth academic lectures on TV.

예제 답안과 채점자 의견

우수 답변

The passage introduced three reasons why professors should appear on TV: gaining reputation for the professor, for the college, and to educate the general public. However, the lecture disagrees.

Professors who appear frequently on TV are not generally viewed as a serious scholar. As a result, those professors will receive less invitation to attend academic conferences or less likely to receive research grant. This seriously hinders the professor's opportunity to further grow as a researcher

Professors who frequently appear on TV also has negative effect on students and the university. Appearing on TV takes a lot of time to prepare, including preparation for the material, transportation time, and even time to dress up. This precious time can also be used to teach class, help students, or even do further research. As a result, professors who appear on TV waste a lot of time that they can contribute to teaching and research.

Professors appearing on TV doesn't usually help educating the general public. The TV network is not interested in having the professor explaining the intellectual substances of their researches. Rather, they are interested in having them explain some basic background information or history. This type of information can be easily presented by a serious reporter who has done his work properly.

Because of the above reasons, it is highly questionable whether professors appearing on TV has any advantage. In fact, it could bring negative consequence both to the professors themselves and the universities they teach.

번역
읽기 지문에서는 왜 교수들이 텔레비전에 출연해야 하는지에 대해 3가지 이유를 소개하고 있다. 교수 자신과 학교의 평판을 높일 수 있고, 일반 대중에 대한 교육 효과가 있기 때문이란 것이다. 그러나, 강의자는 이에 동의하지 않는다.

텔레비전에 자주 출연하는 교수들은 일반적으로 진지한 학자로 보이지 않는다. 그 결과, 그런 교수들은 학술회의 참석 초청장을 덜 받게 되거나, 연구 기금을 덜 받게 될 것이다. 이는 교수들이 연구자로서 더욱 성장할 수 있는 기회를 심각히 저해한다.

텔레비전에 자주 출연하는 교수들은 학생과 소속 대학에 부정적인 영향을 준다. 텔레비전 출연은 강의자료 준비를 포함한 많은 준비 시간을 요하며, 이동 시간 및 분장 시간이 든다. 이 귀중한 시간은 강의하거나 학생들을 돕거나 때로는 더 나은 연구를 하는 데 사용될 수도 있는 시간이다. 결과적으로 텔레비전 출연 교수들은 강의나 연구에 기여할 수 있는 많은 시간을 낭비하는 것이다.

텔레비전 출연 교수들은 대개 일반 대중을 교육하는 데 도움이 되지 않는다. 텔레비전 방송국은 교수가 자신의 연구와 관련된 학술적 내용을 설명하는 것에는 관심이 없고, 오히려 기초적인 교양이나 역사에 대하여 설명하도록 만드는데 더 관심이 있다. 그런 유형의 정보는 일을 제대로 해온 진지한 기자라면 얼마든지 설명할 수 있을 것이다.

이와 같은 이유로 교수가 텔레비전에 출연하면서 취할 수 있는 이점이 과연 있는 것인지 대단히 의문스럽다. 사실, 교수 자신에게도, 소속 대학에게도 모두 부정적인 결과를 초래할 수 있다.

채점자 의견
1. 이 답안의 서술은 강의의 세 가지 주요 논점을 잘 전달하고 있으며 논리 정연하다.
2. 첫 문단과 마지막 문단에는 읽기 지문과 강의 사이의 논리적 상관관계가 잘 설명되어 있다. 본론 부문에 해당하는 문단들은 모두 읽기 지문에 있는 논점들을 반박하는 주제 문장으로 시작하여 구체적인 내용이나 예로 이어지면서 강의자의 논점을 전개하고 있다.
3. 하지만 언어 구사력이 완벽한 것은 아니다. "Professors ... has negative effects"처럼 주어와 동사의 수를 일치시키지 않았거나 "preparation for the material", "the universities they teach"같이 전치사 용법에 대한 사소한 실수가 보인다.
4. 그러나, 통합 과제에 대한 채점 기준에 의하면 간혹 사소한 실수가 있더라도 의미나 논리가 부정확하거나 애매하지 않는 이상 5점을 받을 수 있다. 이 답안에서 보이는 실수들은 의미 전달에 지장을 주거나 흐름을 방해하지 않는다.

중간 수준의 답변

The question which is asked is to know if the apparition of a professor on television is a good or a bad think? On this point, the text and the lecture completely disagree.

First, we can think that it is a good thing for the professors themselves. It seems to be something logical because today a lot of people want to be known and the television is perhaps the best thing to be known. But what the lecture say is that such a professor don't have a good reputation. People think they are not very serious when they pass on television. The effect is that they are no more invited to important conferences.

In what concerned the students and the university, the text shows the facts that some of these apparitions can bring some donation to the university, what is very good. But in the other hand according to the lecture, this professor spend a lot of time travelling and during that time, he isn't available for the students or for the researches and the university lose therefore some money.

Finally for the public himself, they could learn some interesting things and it could be a very big chance because a lot of these persons haven't had the chance going in the university. But it is true that such intervention isn't often best as something that a journalist could prepare.

채점자 의견
1. 상당히 정돈된 내용의 답안이다. 간략한 도입부 이후, 읽기 지문의 모든 논점이 간략히 요약되어 있고 각각 상응되는 강의의 논점이 이어지고 있다.
2. 그러나 중간 점수를 받은 이유는 강의 내용 요약에 여러 가지 문제점이 있기 때문이다.
   ▶ 동료 학자들이 아니라 '사람들'이 텔레비전 출연 교수들을 진지하지 않다고 생각한다고 하여 내용이 부정확하고,
   ▶ 텔레비전 방송국은 깊이 있는 강의에는 관심이 없다는 내용이 누락되어 있으며,
   ▶ 대학들이 '일부 기금'을 놓치게 된다는 것과 텔레비전 출연이 교수들이 학교에서 보내는 시간을 빼앗아 간다는 것이 논리적 연관성이 없어 보인다.
3. 가장 중요한 점은 작성자의 영어 구사력이 떨어져 글의 명료함 또한 떨어진다는 것이다. 지문에 표시된 것 같은 단어 선택 오류 때문에 첫 번째 논점에 대한 강의자의 논지가 희미하고 마지막 논점에 대한 답변은 완전히 불명확하다고 할 정도로 의미 전달이 안 되고 있다.
4. 이 답안 작성자는 자신이 쓰고 싶은 것에 대해 많이 알고 있음에도 불구하고 명확한 의미 전달에는 실패했다.

148

Question
Your professor is teaching a class on ecology. Write a post responding to the professor's question.
In your response, you should do the following.
• Express and support your opinion.
• Make a contribution to the discussion in your own words.
An effective response will contain at least 100 words.

교수가 생태학에 관한 수업을 가르치고 있다. 교수의 질문에 답하는 게시물을 작성하시오.
답변을 작성할 때, 다음 사항을 수행해야 한다.
• 자신의 의견을 제시하고 뒷받침할 것.
• 자신만의 글로 논의에 기여할 것.
효과적인 답변은 최소 100자의 단어를 포함한다.

굽타 박사
요즘, 기본적으로 인간 활동에 의해 훼손되지 않은 야생 지역을 의미하는 자연 생태계를 우리가 어떻게 대해야 하는지에 관한 논쟁이 있습니다. 이 자연 생태계는 한때 순전히 개발해야 하는 자원으로 여겨졌지만, 지금은 많은 사람들이 인간의 모든 이용이나 방해로부터 보호받아야 야생 지역이 완전히 자연적으로 계속 조성된다고 생각합니다. 여러분은 어느 정도로 자연 생태계를 보호하고 보존하는 것을 지지하나요? 일부 야생 지역이 인간의 이용으로부터 완전히 보호되어야 할까요?

앤드류
이미 가족들을 먹여 살리기 힘겨워하고 있는 사람들은, 예를 들어, 야생 지역에서의 광업에 대한 금지 조치에 영향받고 있을 가능성이 가장 큰 사람들입니다. 우리는 경제적인 결과 없이 자연 생태계 속의 인간 활동을 금지할 수 없습니다. 저는 인간이 생존을 위해, 그리고 부를 쌓기 위해 천연자원을 이용할 근본적인 권리를 지니고 있다고 생각합니다.

켈리
지구상에 진정한 야생 지역은 거의 남아 있지 않으며, 일단 사라지고 나면, 우리는 절대 되돌릴 수 없습니다. 저는 우리가 남아 있는 자연 생태계를 인간의 방해로부터 보호해야 한다고 생각합니다. 그러한 곳에 있는 동물과 식물에게 유익할 뿐만 아니라, 우리 인간도 그럴 텐데, 우리 자신의 생존이 우리 지구의 건강에 달려 있기 때문입니다.

해설
이 온라인 토론 글에서, 교수는 기본적으로 학생들에게 야생 지역이 보존되어야 하는 정도에 관한 각자의 관점을 이야기하고, 각자의 입장에 대한 근거를 제공하도록 요청하고 있다. 앤드류의 게시물은 경제적인 이유로 인간이 필요에 따라 천연자원을 이용할 권리를 지니고 있다고 생각한다는 내용을 언급하는 반면, 켈리는 인간 생존의 문제로서 야생 지역의 보호를 지지하고 있다. 수험자들은 이 게시물 중 어느 한쪽에 대한 전적인 동의 또는 부분적인 동의를 나타내거나, 완전히 새로운 의견을 제시할 수 있다(아마 지정된 특정 조건 하에 있는 일부 지역은 보호해야 하지만 다른 곳들은 그렇지 않다는 내용일 수 있다). 답변은 수험자의 전반적인 의견이 무엇인지, 그리고 그 의견에 대한 근거를 명확히 밝혀야 한다.

예제 답안과 채점자 의견

우수 답변

All living things are entitled to live on this earth. Humans are the only species that can globally affect other species and make them extinct by altering nature and affecting the lives of other species. I do agree with Kelly that we should try our best to preserve nature as much as possible. Designating areas to be preserved from human living is good. Places like national parks where people are allowed to visit but not allowed to live in, should be an adequate solution. We should still be able to enjoy the nature but not to destroy them. It is also critical to the overall survival of this world.

번역

모든 생명체는 우리 지구에서 살 자격이 있습니다. 인간은 자연을 변화시키고 다른 종의 삶에 영향을 미치는 것으로 전 세계적으로 다른 종에 영향을 미치고 멸종하게 만들 수 있는 유일한 종입니다. 저는 우리가 가능한 한 많이 자연을 보존하기 위해 최선을 다해야 한다는 켈리의 의견에 정말로 동의합니다. 인간의 생활로부터 보존되도록 지역을 지정하는 것이 좋습니다. 사람들이 방문하도록 허용되기는 하지만 거주하도록 허용되지는 않는 국립공원 같은 곳이 적절한 해결책이 될 것입니다. 우리는 여전히 자연을 즐길 수 있어야 하지만, 파괴할 수는 없어야 합니다. 이는 전 세계의 전반적인 생존에 있어서도 중대한 부분입니다.

채점자 의견

1. 토론과 관련되어 있으면서 매우 명확하게 표현된 의견 제시문이며, 언어 사용에 있어 일관된 능력을 보여 주고 있다.
   ▶ 수험자는 "모든 생명체가 우리 지구에서 살 자격이 있다"는 이유로 야생을 보존하자는 입장을 취하고 있다.
   ▶ 수험자는, 켈리의 입장에 동의하면서도, 계속해서 문제에 대한 해결책을 권하고 있다.
2. 거의 존재하지 않는 어휘 또는 문법적 오류와 더불어, 관련성 있으면서 매우 자세히 서술한 설명으로 인해 이 답변은 높은 점수가 보장된다.

중간 수준의 답변

I agree with Andrew there are some peoples who had been already suffered and struggling a lot to feed its families if there are restriction or ban on natural ecosystems then how they survive? They should get or should allowed to use natural ecosystems as its god gift and everyone has right to use it. There will be more possible chance that they get frustated with own lives because they might think they are already not getting good help from government or so and at same time even if this natural source is not available for them then they feel leftover and this effect them very badly and also for the country.

채점자 의견

1. 이 에세이는 토론 주제와 대체로 관련되어 있으면서 이해 가능하지만 언어 사용에 있어 일부 오류가 있다.
2. 수험자는 사람들이 "이미 정부 같은 곳으로부터 좋은 도움을 받고 있지 못하다고 생각할지도 모르기 때문에 자신의 삶에 좌절하게 될 더 많은 가능성이 있을 수 있을 것이고, 동시에 이 천연자원이 그 사람들에게 이용 가능하지 않다 하더라도 남겨져 있는 느낌을 받게 되며, 이는 그 사람들에게 그리고 국가에게도 아주 좋지 않게 영향을 미치게 될" 잠재성과 관련해 세부 정보를 추가하며 앤드루의 의견에 동의한다. 이 답변에는 문장 구조 및 단어 형태에 뚜렷한 어휘 및 문법 관련 오류가 있다
3. 뚜렷한 언어 오류의 존재가 에세이의 명료성에 영향을 미치고 있으며, 이로 인해 이 답변은 높은 점수를 받지 못한다.

READING

ARCHITECTURE
p. 222

Architecture is the art and science of designing structures that organize and enclose space for practical and symbolic purposes. Because architecture grows out of human needs and aspirations, it clearly communicates cultural values. Of all the visual arts, architecture affects our lives most directly for it determines the character of the human environment in major ways.

Architecture is a three-dimensional form. It utilizes space, mass, texture, line, light, and color. To be architecture, a building must achieve a working harmony with a variety of elements. Humans instinctively seek structures that will shelter and enhance their way of life. It is the work of architects to create buildings that are not simply constructions but also offer inspiration and delight. Buildings contribute to human life when they provide shelter, enrich space, complement their site, suit the climate, and are economically feasible. The client who pays for the building and defines its function is an important member of the architectural team. The mediocre design of many contemporary buildings can be traced to both clients and architects.

In order for the structure to achieve the size and strength necessary to meet its purpose, architecture employs methods of support that, because they are based on physical laws, have changed little since people first discovered them—even while building materials have changed dramatically. The world's architectural structures have also been devised in relation to the objective limitations of materials. Structures can be analyzed in terms of how they deal with downward forces created by gravity. They are designed to withstand the forces of *compression* (pushing together), *tension* (pulling apart), *bending*, or a combination of these in different parts of the structure.

Every development in architecture has been the result of major technological changes. Materials and methods of construction are integral parts of the design of architectural structures. In earlier times it was necessary to design structural systems suitable for the materials that were available, such as wood, stone, or brick. Today technology has progressed to the point where it is possible to invent new building materials to suit the type of structure desired. Enormous changes in materials and techniques of construction within the last few generations have made it possible to enclose space with much greater ease and speed and with a

건축

건축은 실용적인 목적과 상징적인 목적으로 공간을 조직하고 에워싸는 구조물을 설계하는 예술이자 과학이다. 건축물은 인간의 필요나 열망에서 생겨나므로 문화적인 가치관을 분명히 드러낸다. 모든 시각 예술 중에서도 건축이 우리 삶에 가장 직접적인 영향을 미치는데, 이는 건축이 주요한 방식으로 인간 환경을 결정하기 때문이다.

건축물은 3차원 형태이며, 공간과 매스, 질감, 선, 빛, 색채를 활용한다. 건축물이 되려면 건물이 다양한 요소들과 효과적으로 조화를 이루어야 한다. 인간은 본능적으로 편히 쉴 수 있고, 삶의 질도 높여주는 건물을 원한다. 그리고 단순한 건축물이 아닌, 영감과 기쁨을 줄 수 있는 건물을 만드는 것이 건축가의 사명이다. 건물이란, 휴식처를 제공하고 공간을 풍요롭게 하고 부지의 약점을 보완하면서, 기후에도 적합하고, 또한 경제적 형편에도 합당해야 비로소 인간 생활에 보탬이 되는 법이다. 건축비를 부담하며 건물의 용도를 결정하는 건축주 역시 건축을 수행하는 전체 팀의 중요한 일원이다. 많은 현대 건축물들의 그저 그런 설계는 건축가와 건축주, 양자 모두에게 책임이 있다고 할 수 있다.

구조물이 본연의 목적 달성에 필요한 규모와 강도를 갖게 하기 위해 지지 기법들이 건축에 활용된다. 이런 기법들은 물리 법칙에 기초하고 있으므로, 건축 자재들은 엄청나게 변해 오는 동안에도 지지 기법들 그 자체는 인류가 처음 발견한 이후로 크게 변한 바가 없다. 세계의 모든 건축 구조물들 역시, 그 건축 자재의 물성적 한계를 고려하여 고안되어 왔다. 구조물은 중력에 따른 하향력을 어떻게 다루는가 하는 측면에서 분석될 수 있다. 구조물은 여러 부분에서 압축력(미는 힘), 인장력(당기는 힘), 휨, 혹은 이러한 힘들의 복합적인 작용을 견딜 수 있도록 설계된다.

건축 분야의 모든 발전은 주요한 과학 기술 변화의 결과였다. 건축 자재 및 구조 기법은 건축물 설계에서 필수불가결한 요소이므로, 고대에는 목재나 석재, 벽돌 등, 구할 수 있는 자재에 맞춰 구조 시스템을 설계해야 했다. 하지만 오늘날의 과학 기술은 원하는 구조 방식에 적합한 신자재 개발이 가능할 정도로 발전했다. 최근 몇 세대 동안 이루어진 건축 자재와 구조 기술은 엄청난 변화로 인해 최소한의 자재로 훨씬 더 간편하고 신속하게 공간을 에워쌀 수 있게 되었다. 이 분야의 발전은 현재 건축되는 건물과 백 년 전에 건축된 비슷한 규모 건물의 무게 차이로 가늠할 수 있다.

Reading
Listening
Speaking
Writing
Test 1
Test 2
Test 3
Test 4

minimum of material. Progress in this area can be measured by the difference in weight between buildings built now and those of comparable size built one hundred years ago.

(A) Modern architectural forms generally have three separate components comparable to elements of the human body: a supporting *skeleton* or frame, an outer *skin* enclosing the interior spaces, and *equipment*, similar to the body's vital organs and systems. **(B)** The equipment includes plumbing, electrical wiring, hot water, and air-conditioning. **(C)** Of course in early architecture—such as igloos and adobe structures—there was no such equipment, and the skeleton and skin were often one. **(D)**

Much of the world's great architecture has been constructed of stone because of its beauty, permanence, and availability. In the past, whole cities grew from the arduous task of cutting and piling stone upon stone. Some of the world's finest stone architecture can be seen in the ruins of the ancient Inca city of Machu Picchu high in the eastern Andes Mountains of Peru. The doorways and windows are made possible by placing over the open spaces thick stone beams that support the weight from above. A structural invention had to be made before the physical limitations of stone could be overcome and new architectural forms could be created. That invention was the arch, a curved structure originally made of separate stone or brick segments. The arch was used by the early cultures of the Mediterranean area chiefly for underground drains, but it was the Romans who first developed and used the arch extensively in aboveground structures. Roman builders perfected the semicircular arch made of separate blocks of stone. As a method of spanning space, the arch can support greater weight than a horizontal beam. It works in compression to divert the weight above it out to the sides, where the weight is borne by the vertical elements on either side of the arch. The arch is among the many important structural breakthroughs that have characterized architecture throughout the centuries.

현대적인 건축 형태는 대체로 인체의 구성 요소와 유사한 세 가지 개별적인 구성 요소들을 갖추고 있다. 즉 몸을 지탱하는 뼈대라고 할 수 있는 골조, 내부 공간을 에워싸고 있는 외피인 외장, 신체 주요 장기 및 순환계와 유사한 설비가 있다. 건축 설비에는 배관 설비, 전기 배선, 온수 공급 설비, 공조 설비가 포함된다. 물론 이글루나 어도비 구조물 등 초창기 건축물들은 이러한 설비들이 없었으며 골조와 외장이 일체인 경우가 많았다.

세계의 위대한 건축물들 중에는 돌로 건축된 것이 많은데, 그 이유는 석재가 아름다울 뿐만 아니라, 내구성도 우수하며, 구하기도 쉬웠기 때문이었다. 과거에는, 석재를 잘라 포개 쌓는 고된 노역 끝에 도시 전체가 생겨났다. 페루 안데스 산맥 동부 고원에 위치한 마추픽추 고대 잉카 도시 유적에서는 세계 최고의 석조 건축물들을 볼 수 있는데, 출입문이나 창문은 빈 공간 위로 위쪽에서 누르는 하중을 지탱하는 두꺼운 석재 인방을 가로질러 설치해 만들 수 있었다. 이러한 석재의 물리적 한계를 극복하고 새로운 건축물 형태가 개발되기 전 하나의 혁신적인 구조물이 고안되어야 했다. 그 고안물은 아치였는데 아치는 원래 돌덩어리들이나 벽돌 조각으로 만들어진 곡선 형태의 구조물이었다. 아치는 초기 지중해 문화권에서 주로 지하 배수로에 쓰였지만, 아치를 최초로 지상 구조물로 개발하고 광범위하게 사용한 이들은 로마인들이었다. 로마 건축가들은 개개의 석재 블록들을 사용하여 반원형 아치를 완성했다. 공간을 가로지르는 방식인 아치는 일반적인 수평 보 구조보다 훨씬 더 무거운 중량을 지탱할 수 있다. 압축 작용으로 상부 하중을 측면으로 분산시켜 아치 양쪽의 수직 부재가 하중을 지탱하게 된다. 아치는 구조물 분야의 비약적인 발전 중 하나로 오랜 세월 동안 건축계를 풍미해 왔다.

어휘

enclose (울타리, 벽 등으로) 둘러[에워]싸다 aspirations 열망, 염원 values 가치관 visual arts (그림, 조각 등의) 시각 예술 determine 결정하다 utilize 활용[이용]하다 mass (미술, 건축) 매스, 부피를 가진 하나의 덩어리 형태 texture 질감 instinctively 본능적으로, 무의식적으로 shelter (비, 바람 등을) 막아주다; 쉴 곳을 제공하다 inspiration 영감, 창조적 자극 delight 기쁨, 즐거움 contribute to ~에 기여하다 enrich 풍요롭게 하다, 질을 높이다 complement 보완하다 site (건물 등의) 부지 suit 어울리다, 잘 맞다 feasible 실현 가능한 define 정의하다, 명확히 하다 mediocre 평범한, 그저 그런 contemporary 현대의, 당대의 be traced to ~로 거슬러 올라가다 employ (기술 등을) 쓰다, 이용하다 method of support 지지 기법 physical laws 물리 법칙 dramatically 극적으로 in relation to ~에 관하여 objective limitation 물질[물성]적 한계 in terms of ~의 측면에서 downward force 하향력 withstand 견디다, 지탱하다 compression 압축 tension 인장 bending 휨 integral (전체를 구성하는 일부로서) 필요 불가결한 suitable for ~에 알맞은 enormous 막대한 with ease 쉽게 comparable 비슷한, 유사한 component (구성) 요소 skeleton 골격, 뼈대 frame (건물의) 골조 skin 가죽, 외피 equipment 설비, 장비 vital organ (신

체) 주요 장기 plumbing 배관 electrical wiring 전기 배선 air-conditioning 공조, 냉난방 igloo 이글루(에스키모의 집) adobe structure (벽돌, 블록 등의) 어도비 구조물 permanence 내구성, 영구성 availability (입수) 가능성 arduous 힘든, 고된 pile 쌓다, 포개다 ruins 폐허, 유적 Machu Picchu (고대 잉카의) 마추픽추 유적 doorway 출입구 beam (건축) 인방, 보 overcome 극복하다 arch 아치, 홍예 separate 별개의, 각각의 segment 단편, 조각 Mediterranean 지중해의 drain 배수관(로) extensively 널리, 광범위하게 aboveground 지상의 perfect 완성하다, 개량하다 semicircular 반원형의 span 가로지르다; (건축) 경간을 잇다 horizontal 수평의 divert 방향을 바꾸다 bear(bore/borne) (무게를) 지탱하다 vertical 수직의 breakthrough (기술 등의) 비약적인 발전 characterize ～의 특징이 되다 throughout ～동안 내내

1. 첫 번째 단락에 따르면, 다음 중 틀린 설명은?

Ⓐ 건축은 시각 예술이다.
Ⓑ 건축은 만든 이의 문화적 가치관을 반영한다.
Ⓒ 건축은 예술적인 측면과 과학적인 측면을 모두 내포하고 있다.
Ⓓ 건축은 삶에 간접적인 영향을 미친다.

틀린 정보 찾기 문제
어휘 reflect 반영하다 indirect 간접적인
해설 마지막 문장에서 건축은 우리 삶에 가장 직접적인 영향을 미친다고 했으므로 보기 D가 옳지 않은 설명이다.

2. 지문의 단어 enhance와 의미상 가장 가까운 것은?

Ⓐ 보호하다
Ⓑ 향상시키다
Ⓒ 조직하다
Ⓓ 조화시키다

어휘 문제
어휘 enhance (가치 등을) 높이다, 향상시키다
       improve 개선하다, 향상시키다
해설 살아가는 방식, 삶의 모습을 더욱 향상시킨다는 의미로 쓰였다.

3. 다음 중 세 번째 단락에 음영으로 표시된 문장이 담고 있는 핵심 정보를 가장 잘 표현한 것은? 정답 외의 보기들은 의미가 상당히 왜곡되거나 필수적인 정보가 빠져 있다.

Ⓐ 물리 법칙은 변함이 없으므로, 오래전에 발견된 자재로 지을 수 있는 건축물은 규모나 강도 측면에서 제약이 있다.
Ⓑ 건물 규모를 키우고 강도를 높이기 위해 건축자재는 바뀌었지만 구조물에 적용되는 물리 법칙들은 변함이 없다.
Ⓒ 건축이 태동되던 당시에 규모와 강도를 키우기 위해 사용한 구조 기법들은 물리 법칙에 기반을 두지 않아 부적합했다.
Ⓓ 건축 자재와 달리, 건축에 쓰이는 지지 기법들은 물리 법칙에 기초를 둔 것들이므로 세월이 흘러도 변하지 않았다.

문장 재구성 문제
어휘 unchanging 변치 않는 inadequate 부적합한
해설 건축 자재는 변했어도 물리 법칙에 근거한 지지 기법은 변하지 않았다는 사실이 핵심적인 내용이므로 보기 D가 정답이다.

4. 지문의 단어 integral과 의미상 가장 가까운 것은?

Ⓐ 필수적인
Ⓑ 가변적인
Ⓒ 실용적인
Ⓓ 독립적인

어휘 문제
어휘 integral (전체를 구성하는 일부로) 필수적인
       essential 필수적인, 극히 중요한
해설 건축물 설계에서 절대 빼놓을 수 없는 '필수적인' 부분이라는 의미로 쓰였다.

5. 네 번째 단락에 따르면, 다음 중 건축에 사용되는 자재에 대한 설명으로 옳은 것은?

Ⓐ 새로운 건축 자재를 찾아내기 힘들기 때문에 지난 몇 세대 동안 건축 기법들은 거의 변하지 않았다.
Ⓑ 이제는 적절한 건축 자재의 입수 가능성이 지으려는 구조물의 유형을 더 이상 제한하지 않는다.
Ⓒ 오늘날 활용할 수 있는 주요 건축 자재는 목재, 석재, 벽돌이다.
Ⓓ 고대의 건축가들에게는 넓은 공간을 에워쌀 수 있는 건축 자재가 부족했다.

세부 사항 찾기 문제
어휘 construction technique 건축 기법
       limit 제한하다 primary 주된, 주요한
해설 세 번째 문장에서 과거에는 자재의 한계 때문에 구조 방식 적용에 제약이 있었다고 했지만, 네 번째 문장에서는 오늘날 기술의 발전으로 원하는 구조 방식에 맞춰 자재를 새로 개발할 수 있다고 했으므로, 보기 B가 올바른 설명이다.

6. 네 번째 단락에서 저자가 현대 건물에 대해 암시하는 것은?

Ⓐ 백 년 전에 지은 건물보다 공간을 훨씬 덜 차지한다.
Ⓑ 몇 세대 전에 지은 건물과 크게 다를 바가 없다.
Ⓒ 백 년 전에 지은 건물보다 규모에 비해 무게가 가볍다.
Ⓓ 건축 공법이 복잡하여 짓는 데 시간이 오래 걸린다.

내용 추론 문제
어휘 imply (생각을) 넌지시 나타내다 occupy (공간 등을) 차지하다, 점유하다 weigh 무게가 나가다
해설 다섯 번째 문장에서, 지난 몇 세대 동안의 자재 및 기술 변혁(발전) 덕분에 자재를 최소화할 수 있게 되었다고 하였으며, 마지막 문장에서는 이러한 발전 덕분에 백 년 전의 건물과 지금의 건물은 중량에서 차이가 난다고 하였으므로, 이를 종합해 보면 건물의 전체 중량이 가벼워졌다는 것을 알 수 있다.

7. 저자가 마추픽추에서 '출입문과 창문들'을 만든 방법을 설명한 이유는?

Ⓐ 마추픽추 석조 건물들의 골조–외피 일체식 구조가 이글루나 어도비 구조물들과 비슷하다는 사실을 보여 주기 위해서

Ⓑ 마추픽추를 건설하기 위해 다양한 종류의 석재들을 잘라 사용했다는 사실을 보여 주기 위해서

Ⓒ 아치가 고안되기 이전의 건축 방법을 사례로 들어 설명하기 위해서

Ⓓ 고대 건축가들이 석재 건물의 공사 시간을 단축시킨 방법을 설명하기 위해서

수사학적 의도 파악 문제

어휘 indicate 나타내다, 보여 주다 combined (단일체가 되도록) 결합한 illustration (설명을 위한) 실례, 예 reduce (크기, 양 등을) 줄이다, 축소하다

해설 마추픽추 석조 건축물들에서 출입문이나 창문 등 개구부를 상부에 석재 인방을 가로지르는 방식으로 만들었다는 설명을 한 이유는 아치 구조가 개발되기 이전 시대에는 자재의 물성적 한계를 어떤 식으로 극복했는지 보여 주기 위해서다.

8. 여섯 번째 단락에 따르면, 다음 중 아치에 대한 설명으로 옳은 것은?

Ⓐ 석조 아치를 가장 처음 사용한 이들은 로마인이다.

Ⓑ 아치의 고안으로 새로운 건축 형태가 개발될 수 있었다.

Ⓒ 아치는 건물의 하중을 아치 중앙부로 배분하는 방식이다.

Ⓓ 로마인들은 이전 시대의 관행에 따라 아치를 활용했다.

세부 사항 찾기 문제

어휘 allow ~ to ~가 …할 수 있도록 하다 distribute 할당하다, 배치하다 follow 뒤를 따르다, 추종하다 practice 실행, 관행

해설 다섯 번째와 여섯 번째 문장에서, 석재의 물성적 한계를 극복하고 새로운 건축 형태가 개발되기 전에 만들어진 구조적 고안물이 아치라고 하였으므로 보기 B가 옳은 설명이다. 아치는 원래 지중해 지역에서 사용했던 구조물이었으며, 하중을 아치 양쪽으로 분산시키는 방식으로, 로마인들이 개량하여 지상 구조물에 사용했다고 설명했으므로, 보기 A, C, D는 모두 옳지 않다.

9. 지시문: 위에 제시된 지문의 일부를 보시오. 지문에 표시된 **(A)**, **(B)**, **(C)**, **(D)** 중 하나에 다음 문장이 삽입될 수 있다.

However, some modern architectural designs, such as those using folded plates of concrete or air-inflated structures, are again unifying skeleton and skin.

(하지만, 콘크리트 절판 구조나 공기 주입식 구조 등을 활용한 현대 건축물들은 골조와 외피를 다시금 일체화시키고 있다.)

이 문장이 들어갈 가장 적당한 위치는?

(A) Modern architectural forms generally have three separate components comparable to elements of the human body: a supporting *skeleton* or frame, an outer *skin* enclosing the interior spaces, and *equipment*, similar to the body's vital organs and systems. **(B)** The equipment includes plumbing, electrical wiring, hot water, and air-conditioning. **(C)** Of course in early architecture—such as igloos and adobe structures—there was no such equipment, and the skeleton and skin were often one. **(D)** However, some modern architectural designs, such as those using folded plates of concrete or air-inflated structures, are again unifying skeleton and skin.

Ⓐ　　　　Ⓑ　　　　Ⓒ　　　　Ⓓ

문장 삽입 문제

어휘 folded plates of concrete 콘크리트 판을 골판 모양 등으로 만들어 하중에 대한 저항을 높인 구조
air-inflated structure 내부에 공기를 불어 넣어 구조체를 형성시키는 멤브레인식 구조

해설 이 문장은 골조와 외피가 분리된 현대 건축의 예외 사례인 동시에, 골조와 외피가 일체였던 초창기 건축과 같은 형식인 사례를 설명하고 있으므로, 이글루와 어도비 구조물 등을 예로 든 문장 뒤에 이어지는 것이 가장 적합하다.

10. 지시문: 이 지문을 간단히 요약하기 위한 도입 문장이 아래에 제시되어 있다. 아래 보기들 중에서 지문의 가장 중요한 개념을 표현한 문장 3개를 골라 요약을 완성하라. 보기들 중에는 지문에 나오지 않았거나 중요하지 않은 개념이기 때문에 요약문으로 적절치 않은 것들도 있다. 이 문제의 배점은 2점이다.

건축은 형태와 공간을 활용하여 문화적 가치관을 표현한다.

Ⓐ 건축가들은 보기에도 아름답고 인간이 쓰기에도 적합한 건물을 지으려고 노력한다.

Ⓑ 일부 현대 건축물들의 그저 그런 설계는 건축주와 건축가, 양쪽 모두에게 책임이 있다.

Ⓒ 건축사 전반에 걸쳐 자재 및 건축 공법의 혁신 덕분에 건축가들은 지금까지 더 큰 표현의 자유를 누릴 수 있었다.

Ⓓ 현대 건물들은 마추픽추 같은 고대 석조 건물들처럼 아름답지 못한 경우가 많다.

Ⓔ 역사상 모든 건물들은 인체와 유사하게 건축되어, 기능을 위한 별도 '내부 장기' 시스템들이 필요했다.

Ⓕ 아치의 발견과 활용이야말로 더욱 효율적인 구조물 양식을 개발해 건축이 발전한 대표적인 사례다.

지문 요약하기 문제

어휘 appealing 매력적인, 마음을 끄는 lack ~이 없다[부족하다] distinct 구별되는, 별개의 typify ~를 대표하다, ~의 표본이 되다

해설 보기 D는 지문에서 언급되지 않은 내용이며, 보기 E는 초창기 건축에는 해당되지 않는 설명이다. 지문의 전체적인 흐름과 대의에 맞는 서술은 보기 A, C, F이며, 보기 B는 중요도가 다소 떨어지는 지엽적인 내용이다.

p. 229

THE LONG-TERM STABILITY OF ECOSYSTEMS

Plant communities assemble themselves flexibly, and their particular structure depends on the specific history of the area. Ecologists use the term "succession" to refer to the changes that happen in plant communities and ecosystems over time. The first community in a succession is called a pioneer community, while the long-lived community at the end of succession is called a climax community. Pioneer and successional plant communities are said to change over periods from 1 to 500 years. These changes—in plant numbers and the mix of species—are cumulative. Climax communities themselves change but over periods of time greater than about 500 years.

An ecologist who studies a pond today may well find it relatively unchanged in a year's time. Individual fish may be replaced, but the number of fish will tend to be the same from one year to the next. We can say that the properties of an ecosystem are more stable than the individual organisms that compose the ecosystem.

At one time, ecologists believed that species diversity made ecosystems stable. They believed that the greater the diversity the more stable the ecosystem. Support for this idea came from the observation that long-lasting climax communities usually have more complex food webs and more species diversity than pioneer communities. Ecologists concluded that the apparent stability of climax ecosystems depended on their complexity. To take an extreme example, farmlands dominated by a single crop are so unstable that one year of bad weather or the invasion of a single pest can destroy the entire crop. In contrast, a complex climax community, such as a temperate forest, will tolerate considerable damage from weather or pests.

The question of ecosystem stability is complicated, however. The first problem is that ecologists do not all agree what "stability" means. Stability can be defined as simply lack of change. In that case, the climax community would be considered the most stable, since, by definition, it changes the least over time. Alternatively, stability can be defined as the speed with which an ecosystem returns to a particular form following a major disturbance, such as a fire. This kind of stability is also called *resilience*. In that case, climax communities would be the most fragile and the *least* stable, since they can require hundreds of years to return to the climax state.

Even the kind of stability defined as simple lack of change is not always associated with maximum diversity. At least in

생태계의 장기 안정성

식물 군락의 형성 양상은 상당히 탄력적인 편으로, 서식지 특유의 이력에 따라 제각기 독특한 구조를 보인다. 생태학자들은 오랜 세월에 걸친 식물 군락들과 생태계의 변천 과정을 가리켜 '천이(遷移)'라는 용어를 쓴다. 천이 과정에서 제일 먼저 등장하는 군락을 '개척자 군락'이라 하며, 천이 과정의 마지막 단계에서 오랜 세월을 이어가는 군락을 '극상 군락'이라고 한다. 개척자 군락을 필두로 하여 그 뒤를 잇는 식물 군락들은 1년에서 500년에 이르는 기간에 걸쳐 변천해 간다고 한다. 이러한 변천—개체수 및 종 구성 측면의—은 점증적으로 이루어진다. 극상 군락들도 변화를 겪긴 하지만, 500년 이상의 오랜 세월에 걸쳐 이루어진다.

오늘날 연못을 연구하는 생태학자라면 1년이라는 시간 동안에는 연못의 생태계가 별로 변하지 않는다는 사실을 잘 알 것이다. 각각의 물고기는 바뀔 수 있지만, 전체 물고기 숫자는 이듬해가 되어도 마찬가지일 가능성이 크다. 그러므로 어떤 한 생태계의 특성은 그 생태계를 구성하는 각각의 유기체들보다 훨씬 안정적이라고 말할 수 있다.

한때 생태학자들은 종의 다양성이 생태계를 안정시킨다고 믿었다. 그들은 종의 다양성이 커질수록 생태계가 더욱 안정된다고 생각했다. 오랜 세월 지속되는 극상 군락은 대개 개척 군락들보다 종의 다양성도 더 크고 더 복잡한 먹이사슬 구조를 보인다는 관찰 결과가 이런 생각을 뒷받침했다. 따라서 생태학자들은 극상 군락이 안정성을 보이는 것은 그 복잡성 덕택이라고 결론지었다. 극단적인 예를 든다면, 가령 농작물 한 가지가 주류를 이루는 농지는 매우 불안정하므로, 한 해 기상이 나쁘거나 해충 한 종류만 설쳐도 작황 전체를 망칠 수 있다. 반면, 온대림 같이 복잡다단한 극상 군락은 어지간한 기후나 해충의 피해에도 끄떡없이 견딜 수 있다.

하지만, 생태계 안정성의 문제는 복잡하다. 첫 번째 문제점은, '안정성'이 무엇을 뜻하는지에 대해, 생태학자들도 의견이 일치하지 않는다는 사실이다. '안정'이란 단순히 변화가 없는 상황이라고 볼 수 있다. 그렇다면, 극상 군락은 세월이 흘러도 변화가 가장 적으므로 가장 안정되었다고 할 수 있다. 그게 아니라면, '안정성'이란 산불 같은 극심한 재해를 겪은 뒤, 생태계가 특정한 형태로 되돌아가는 속도라고 정의할 수도 있다. 이런 종류의 안정성은 '회복력'이라고 표현하기도 한다. 그런 경우라면, 극상 군락들은 가장 취약하며 안정성도 가장 낮다고 해야 할 것이다. 극상의 상태로 다시 회복하기 위해서는 수백 년의 세월이 필요할 수도 있기 때문이다.

단순히 변화가 없다는 의미의 '안정성'도 꼭 다양성의 극대화와 연관이 있다고는 볼 수 없다. 적어도 온대 지역에

temperate zones, maximum diversity is often found in mid-successional stages, not in the climax community. Once a redwood forest matures, for example, the kinds of species and the number of individuals growing on the forest floor are reduced. In general, diversity, by itself, does not ensure stability. Mathematical models of ecosystems likewise suggest that diversity does not guarantee ecosystem stability—just the opposite, in fact. A more complicated system is, in general, more likely than a simple system to break down. (A fifteen-speed racing bicycle is more likely to break down than a child's tricycle.)

(A) Ecologists are especially interested in knowing what factors contribute to the resilience of communities because climax communities all over the world are being severely damaged or destroyed by human activities. (B) The destruction caused by the volcanic explosion of Mount St. Helens, in the northwestern United States, for example, pales in comparison to the destruction caused by humans. (C) We need to know what aspects of a community are most important to the community's resistance to destruction, as well as its recovery. (D)

Many ecologists now think that the relative long-term stability of climax communities comes not from diversity but from the "patchiness" of the environment; an environment that varies from place to place supports more kinds of organisms than an environment that is uniform. A local population that goes extinct is quickly replaced by immigrants from an adjacent community. Even if the new population is of a different species, it can approximately fill the niche vacated by the extinct population and keep the food web intact.

서는, 극상 군락이 아닌 천이 중간 단계에서 다양성이 극대화되는 경우가 종종 발견된다. 예를 들어, 삼나무 숲이 성숙기에 접어들면, 숲 기저부에 서식하는 식물 종과 개체수가 오히려 감소한다. 대체로, 다양성 그 자체만으로는 안정성이 보장되지 않는다. 생태계의 수리 모델에서도 역시 마찬가지로, 다양성이 생태계의 안정성을 보장하지 못한다는 사실을 짐작할 수 있다. 사실상 정반대가 아닐 수 없다. 일반적으로, 복잡한 시스템은 단순한 시스템보다 붕괴되기가 쉽기 때문이다. (아이들의 세발자전거보다 15단 기어 경주용 자전거가 더 고장이 잘 나기 마련이다.)

인간 활동으로 전 세계의 극상 군락들이 심각한 피해를 입거나 파괴되고 있으므로, 생태학자들은 군락 회복력을 높일 수 있는 요인을 알아내는 데 특히 관심이 많다. 예를 들면, 미국 북서부 지역 세인트헬렌스 산의 화산 폭발로 인한 피해도 인간에 의한 피해에 비하면 무색할 지경이다. 어떤 군락 양상이 생태계 파괴에 대한 군락의 회복력뿐만 아니라 파괴에 대한 저항력에 가장 중요한지도 규명할 필요가 있다.

오늘날, 극상 군락이 상대적으로 오랫동안 안정성을 유지하는 것은 다양성 때문이 아니라 '분반성'에 기인한다고 보는 생태학자들도 적지 않다. 즉 여기저기 장소에 따라 달라지는 다변적 환경이 균일한 환경보다 더 많은 생물체들을 부양할 수 있다는 개념이다. 토착 개체군 하나가 멸종되면, 인근 군락에서 넘어온 개체군이 그 자리를 신속하게 메운다. 설령 새로 자리 잡은 개체군의 종이 다를지라도, 원 개체군이 사라진 빈자리를 큰 무리 없이 메울 수 있으므로, 먹이사슬도 온전하게 유지될 수 있다.

Reading

Listening

Speaking

Writing

Test 1

Test 2

Test 3

Test 4

어휘

stability 안정성, 복원성 ecosystem (특정 지역의) 생태계 community (식물의) 군락, (생물의) 군집 assemble 모이다, 모으다 flexibly 유연하게 ecologist 생태학자, 생태[환경] 운동가 succession (생물) 천이(遷移) refer to ~을 가리키다 over time 세월의 흐름에 따라 pioneer community 개척 군락(천이 과정에서 초기 개척 단계의 군락) climax community 극상 군락(천이 과정에서 최종 안정화 단계의 군락) cumulative 누적되는, 점증적인 replace 대체[대신]하다 properties 특성, 속성 stable 안정된, 안정적인 compose 구성하다, ~의 일부를 이루다 species (생물의 기초단위) 종(種) diversity (생물) 다양성 complex 복잡한, 얽히고설킨 food web 먹이사슬 apparent (주로 명사 앞에서) ~으로 보이는, 외견상의 farmland 농(경)지 dominate ~의 가장 큰 특징이 되다, 우위를 차지하다 crop (농)작물, 수확, 작황 invasion 침해, 침범 pest 해충 in contrast 반대로 temperate forest 온대림 tolerate (힘든 환경 등을) 견디다 considerable 어지간한, 상당한 complicated 복잡한, (문제가) 풀기 어려운 define 정의하다 in that case 그런 경우에는, 그렇다면 by definition 정의상, 분명히 alternatively (대안을 소개할 때) 그렇지 않으면 disturbance 소동, 방해, 장애 resilience (생물) 회복력[성] fragile 취약한, 손상되기 쉬운 be associated with ~와 관련되다 redwood 미국삼나무 ensure 보장하다 mathematical model 수리 모형, 수학적 모델 likewise 마찬가지로 just the opposite 정반대(인) break down 망가지다, 허물어지다 volcanic explosion 화산 폭발 pale 무색하다, (색 등이) 옅어지다 in comparison to ~와 비교할 때 aspect 양상, 국면 resistance (생물) 저항력[성] relative 상대적인 patchiness 분반성, 패치화 from place to place 이곳저곳, 여기저기 uniform 획일적인, 균일한 local population (생물) 토착 개체군 go extinct 멸종되다 immigrant (생태) 귀화식물, 외래종 adjacent 인접한, 이웃의 approximately 대체로, 거의 niche 틈새; (생태) 생태적 지위 vacate 떠나다, 비우다 intact 온전한, 그대로인

11. 지문의 단어 particular와 의미상 가장 가까운 것은?

Ⓐ 자연스러운
Ⓑ 최종적인
Ⓒ 독특한
Ⓓ 복잡한

어휘 문제

어휘 particular 특정한, 독특한 specific 특유의, 독특한

해설 여기서는 다른 것과 구별되는 '특유의', '독특한' 이라는 의미로 쓰였다.

12. 두 번째 단락에 따르면, 다음 중 연못 관찰 연구를 통해 알 수 있는 생태계의 원리는?

Ⓐ 생태계의 특성은 생태계를 구성하는 개체들보다 더 느리게 변한다.
Ⓑ 한 생태계의 안정도는 개체들이 대체되면 변하기가 쉽다.
Ⓒ 각각의 유기체들은 이듬해로 넘어가도 안정적이다.
Ⓓ 한 유기체 개체수의 변동은 생태계의 특성에 영향을 미치지 않는다.

세부 사항 찾기 문제

어휘 principle 원리, 법칙 individual (생물) 개체

해설 생태계 자체의 속성이 그 생태계 내의 개체들보다 안정적이라는 표현은 변화가 없거나 혹은 변화가 더 느리게 진행된다는 의미로 A가 바른 설명이다. 보기 B와 C는 두 번째 문장의 내용과 맞지 않으며, 보기 D는 지문에서 명확히 언급되지 않은 내용이다.

13. 네 번째 단락에 따르면, 생태계 안정성의 문제가 복잡한 이유는?

Ⓐ 생태계가 변화하는 이유가 항상 분명한 것은 아니기 때문에
Ⓑ 생태학자들이 '안정성'과 '회복력'을 혼동하기 때문에
Ⓒ '안정성'의 정확한 의미에 대해서 생태학자들 사이에 논란이 있기 때문에
Ⓓ 생태학 관련 문제에는 여러 가지 답이 있을 수 있기 때문에

세부 사항 찾기 문제

어휘 clear 명백한, 확실한 confuse A with B A를 B와 혼동하다 debate 논쟁하다, 토론하다

해설 두 번째 문장에서 '안정성'의 의미에 대해 생태학자들의 의견이 일치되지 않는다고 언급되었으므로 정확한 설명은 보기 C다.

14. 네 번째 단락에 따르면, 다음 중 극상 군락에 대한 설명으로 옳은 것은?

Ⓐ 개척 군락보다 회복력이 뛰어나다.
Ⓑ 가장 안정적인 동시에 가장 불안정한 군락으로 볼 수 있다.
Ⓒ 큰 재해를 입은 후에 신속히 회복하므로 안정적이라고 할 수 있다.
Ⓓ 세월이 흘러도 가장 변화가 적기 때문에 가장 회복력이 뛰어난 군락이라고 할 수 있다.

세부 사항 찾기 문제

어휘 resilient (충격 등에 대해) 회복력 있는

해설 네 번째 문장과 마지막 문장에서 극상 군락의 극단적인 두 가지 측면을 확인할 수 있다. 변화가 없다는 측면에서는 가장 안정적이지만, 회복력이 떨어진다는 측면에서는 가장 불안정한 군락이라고 할 수 있으므로 보기 B가 옳은 설명이다.

15. 다음 중 다섯 번째 단락의 삼나무 숲에 관한 내용에서 추론할 수 있는 것은?

Ⓐ 성숙기에 접어들면 안정성이 떨어진다.
Ⓑ 극상 단계에 이르면 많은 종들을 부양한다.
Ⓒ 온대 지역에서 볼 수 있다.
Ⓓ 천이 중간 단계에서는 다양성이 줄어든다.

내용 추론 문제

어휘 mature 완전히 발달한, 성숙한 temperate zone 온대 지방

해설 두 번째 문장에서 온대 지역에서 극도의 다양성이 발현되는 경우가 종종 있다고 언급한 뒤, 이어서 그 예로 삼나무 숲의 상황을 제시했으므로 삼나무 숲은 온대 지방에서 볼 수 있는 군락임을 알 수 있다.

16. 다섯 번째 단락에 음영으로 표시된 문장을 저자가 덧붙인 이유는?

Ⓐ 시스템의 안정성에 대한 일반적인 원리를 일상적인 예를 통해 설명하기 위해서
Ⓑ 생태계의 안정성을 이해하면 다른 상황의 안정성도 이해하기 쉽다는 것을 보여 주기 위해서
Ⓒ 비교 설명을 통해, 대체로 다양성은 안정성 증대의 요인이 된다는 주장을 뒷받침하기 위해
Ⓓ 생태계의 수리 모델과 대조되는 예를 제시하기 위해

수사학적 의도 파악 문제

어휘 illustrate 예를 들어 보여 주다 apply (규칙을) 적용하다, (원리를) 응용하다 comparison 비교, 비유 claim 주장

해설 여섯 번째 문장에서, 복잡한 시스템은 간단한 시스템보다 고장이 나기 쉽다는 설명을 통해 안정성의 일반적인 원리를 언급하고, 그에 대한 일상적인 예를 든 것이므로 보기 A가 옳은 이유이다.

17. 다음 중 지문에 음영으로 표시된 문장이 담고 있는 핵심 정보를 가장 잘 표현한 것은? 정답 외의 보기들은 의미가 상당히 왜곡되거나 필수적인 정보가 빠져 있다.

Ⓐ 현재 생태학자들은 어떤 한 환경이 안정된 양상을 보이는 것은 분반성보다는 다양성 덕분이라고 여긴다.
Ⓑ 장소에 따라 변하는 분반적 환경은 종 다양성이 높지 않은 경우가 많다.
Ⓒ 균일한 환경은 분반적인 환경보다 부양할 수 있는 유기체 형태들이 적기 때문에 극상 군락을 형성할 수 없다.
Ⓓ 분반적 환경은 다양한 유기체를 부양할 수 있으므로 안정성을 높이는 요인으로 간주된다.

문장 재구성 문제

어휘 patchy 고르지 못한, 뒤죽박죽인 support (필요한 것을 제공하여) 살게[존재하게] 하다, 부양하다

해설 다양한 유기체가 살 수 있는 환경이 되는 분반적 환경이야말로 장기간 안정 상태를 유지하는 극상 군락의 발현 요인으로 본다는 내용이므로, 보기 D가 가장 적절한 요약이다. 보기 A는 표시된 부분의 내용과 상반되는 설명이므로 옳지 않으며, 분반적 환경으로 다양성이 유발된다는 보기 B의 설명도 타당하지 않다. 보기 C의 경우, 균일적 환경은 언급되지 않은 요소이므로, 이 역시 옳지 못한 설명이다.

Reading

Listening

Speaking

Writing

Test 1

Test 2

Test 3

Test 4

18. 지문의 단어 adjacent와 의미상 가장 가까운 것은?

Ⓐ 외래의

Ⓑ 안정적인

Ⓒ 유동적인

Ⓓ 이웃하는

어휘 문제

어휘 adjacent (지역 등이) 인접한, 가까운 fluid (상황 등이) 유동적인, 가변적인 neighboring 이웃하는, 인근의, 인접한

해설 '바로 가까이에 있는', '인접하는' 등의 의미로 쓰인다.

19. 지시문: 위에 제시된 지문의 일부를 보시오. 지문에 표시된 **(A)**, **(B)**, **(C)**, **(D)** 중 하나에 다음 문장이 삽입될 수 있다.

In fact, damage to the environment by humans is often much more severe than by natural events and processes.

(실제로, 인간이 환경에 입히는 피해는 천재지변이나 자연적인 변화 과정보다 훨씬 더 심각한 결과를 초래할 때가 많다.)

이 문장이 들어갈 가장 적당한 위치는?

(A) Ecologists are especially interested in knowing what factors contribute to the resilience of communities because climax communities all over the world are being severely damaged or destroyed by human activities. **(B)** In fact, damage to the environment by humans is often much more severe than by natural events and processes. The destruction caused by the volcanic explosion of Mount St. Helens, in the northwestern United States, for example, pales in comparison to the destruction caused by humans. **(C)** We need to know what aspects of a community are most important to the community's resistance to destruction, as well as its recovery. **(D)**

Ⓐ   Ⓑ   Ⓒ   Ⓓ

문장 삽입 문제

어휘 event (중요한) 사건, 사변

process (자연스러운 변화가 일어나는) 과정

해설 세인트헬렌스 화산 폭발과 인간으로 인한 피해를 비교하는 두 번째 문장은 인간이 천재지변보다 더 큰 피해를 야기할 때가 많다는 주장에 대한 부연 설명이므로, (B)가 가장 적합한 위치다.

20. 지시문: 이 지문을 간단히 요약하기 위한 도입 문장이 아래에 제시되어 있다. 아래 보기들 중에서 지문의 가장 중요한 개념을 표현한 문장 3개를 골라 요약을 완성하라. 보기들 중에는 지문에 나오지 않았거나 중요하지 않은 개념이기 때문에 요약문으로 적절치 않은 것들도 있다. 이 문제의 배점은 2점이다.

천이의 과정과 극상 군락의 안정성은 세월의 흐름에 따라 변할 수 있다.

Ⓐ 개척 군락부터 극상 군락에 이르는 생태계 변화는 인간이 한 세대에 관찰할 수 있는 현상이다.

Ⓑ 생태학자들은 극상 군락이 가장 안정된 형태의 생태계라는 사실에 동의한다.

Ⓒ 종 다양성의 수준이 높다고 해서 반드시 생태계가 안정되는 것은 아니다.

Ⓓ '안정'이라는 용어 정의에 대한 의견이 일치하지 않아, 안정성이 가장 높은 생태계가 무엇인지 규정하기가 쉽지 않다.

Ⓔ 특정 식물 군락의 회복도는 장기 안정성에 기여한다.

Ⓕ 극상 군락은 회복력 덕분에 인간에 의한 파괴를 견뎌낼 수 있다.

지문 요약하기 문제

어휘 one human generation 한 세대(보통 부모가 자식에게 대를 물릴 때까지의 기간, 약 30년) result in (결과적으로) ~를 야기하다 disagreement 의견 불일치[차이] contribute to ~에 기여하다, ~에 도움이 되다 resistant ~에 잘 견디는, 저항력이 있는

해설 보기 C, D, E가 지문의 전반적인 내용과 부합되는 요약 설명이다. 보기 A의 경우, 첫 번째 단락에서 개척 군락과 그 뒤를 잇는 천이 단계 군락들의 변천이 길게는 500년에 걸쳐 이루어질 수도 있다고 했으므로, 결코 한 세대에 가능한 일이 아니다. 보기 B의 경우, 네 번째 단락과 다섯 번째 단락에서 극상 군락이 가장 안정성이 높은 경우가 아닌 예도 소개되었으므로, 종합적인 요약문으로는 합당하지 않다. 또한 극상 군락이 회복력 측면에서 가장 취약하며(네 번째 단락), 인류로 인해 극상 군락들이 극심한 피해를 입는다고 했으므로(여섯 번째 단락), 보기 F도 틀린 설명이다.

LISTENING

Questions 1-5   p. 236

N Narrator   S Supervisor   F Female Student

Script

N Listen to a conversation between a student and a supervisor in the university buildings department.

S When all of this is over, Lynne, I'll be glad to write you a letter of recommendation.

F Can I ask you again in a couple of years? That's probably when I'll start looking...

S Why don't I write something while it's still fresh in my mind, and you can save it for later.

F OK. Thanks. So, which building will I be showing?

S Buildings. Even though you'll be assigned to just one, each guide for the Green Buildings Tour will have to learn about two buildings. If a guide cancels unexpectedly, you'd first show your group around your building then around the other.

F How do I learn about the buildings?

S I'll walk you through them and give you written materials. Uh, as you know from the list I e-mailed, visitors will tour all ten sustainable buildings on campus. Eight are older buildings that were retrofitted with a variety of sustainable features, like insulated windows and tanks to harvest rainwater. The other two are new construction. Both were designed to save energy costs. The engineering library was completed last year... and Lightstone Dormitory shortly after. Its first residents just moved in.

F Lightstone! Wasn't that constructed with materials salvaged from demolished city buildings?

S Yeah. And it's totally off the electrical grid—no utility bills! Electricity is generated by solar energy, and with energy from deep under the ground; this geothermal energy provides radiant heat. In fact, the heat-pump technology we use was invented right here at the university. The pump transports and amplifies geothermal heat through a network of pipes beneath the floorboards.

F I learned about radiant heat when I did a project in my architecture class. I could tell visitors how the floor heats objects in the rooms, which then heats the space.

N 학생과 대학 건물 관리팀 책임자의 대화를 들으시오.

S 린, 이 모든 게 끝나면, 기꺼이 추천서를 써 줄게요.

F 제가 2년 후에 다시 여쭤 봐도 될까요? 그땐 아마 제가 찾기 시작할…

S 내 머리 속에 아직 생생할 때 뭔가 써 놓으면 어떨까요? 그럼 나중을 위해 갖고 있을 수 있으니까요.

F 네. 감사합니다. 그럼, 제가 어느 건물들을 소개하게 되는 건가요?

S 건물들이죠. 단지 하나만 배정받게 된다 하더라도, 친환경 건물 투어의 각 가이드는 두 곳의 건물에 관해 배워야 할 겁니다. 한 가이드가 예기치 못하게 취소하는 경우, 배정된 건물 곳곳을 담당 그룹에게 먼저 소개한 다음, 나머지 한 곳의 건물 곳곳을 소개하게 될 겁니다.

F 그 건물들에 관해서 어떻게 배우죠?

S 내가 차근차근 설명한 다음, 문서 자료를 제공해 줄 겁니다. 어, 이메일로 보내 준 목록을 보면 알겠지만, 방문객들이 캠퍼스에 있는 열 곳의 지속 가능한 건물을 모두 둘러 볼 거예요. 여덟 곳은 절연 처리가 된 창문 및 빗물 수집을 위한 탱크 같은, 다양한 지속 가능한 특징들로 보강된 더 오래된 건물입니다. 나머지 두 곳은 새로 지은 것이고요. 이 두 곳은 모두 에너지 비용을 절약하도록 설계되었습니다. 공학 도서관은 작년에 완공되었고… 라이트스톤 기숙사도 그 직후예요. 첫 기숙생들이 막 입주했습니다.

F 라이트스톤이요! 그곳은 철거된 도시 건물들에서 가져온 자재로 지어지지 않았나요?

S 네. 그리고 전력망에서 완전히 벗어나 있기 때문에, 공과금이 들지 않아요! 전기는 태양열 에너지로, 그리고 지하 깊은 곳에서 나오는 에너지로 생산되죠. 이 지열 에너지가 방사열을 제공합니다. 실제로, 우리가 이용하는 열 펌프 기술이 바로 이곳 우리 대학에서 발명되었어요. 그 펌프가 바닥재 아래에 있는 파이프망을 통해 지열을 이동시키고 증폭시키죠.

F 제가 건축학 수업 시간에 프로젝트를 하나 하면서 방사열에 관해 배웠어요. 제가 방문객들에게 그 바닥이 어떻게 방 안에 있는 물건들을, 그리고 그 후에는 공간을 따뜻하게 만드는지 이야기해 드릴 수 있어요.

Reading

Listening

Speaking

Writing

Test 1

Test 2

Test 3

Test 4

S Right... unlike conventional heating systems, where warm air rises to the ceiling, radiant heat stays lower in the room. So the rooms feel warm even though the thermostat is set at a relatively low temperature. That's the reason we're having this event in winter... so people can "feel" how radiant heat works.

F Could you assign me to Lightstone Hall, then?

S Sure, Lightstone Hall it is.

F Y'know, maybe I could get a bunch of details from the engineer who invented that heat-pump technology.

S I guess. But remember, each group will walk all over campus, through ten buildings... and last year, hundreds of people attended these tours.

F Oh... right... so they can't take too long.

S Right. So which building would you like to cover if someone cancels?

F How 'bout the fitness center, even though it's not on the list. The treadmills use zero electricity. The user's foot action recharges a battery. And the battery powers a display panel that shows information about your workout.

S Yes, the treadmills... but there's nothing special about the building itself.

S 그렇군요… 온기가 천장으로 올라가는 전통적인 난방 시스템과 달리, 방사열은 방 안의 더 낮은 곳에 머무릅니다. 그래서 온도 조절 장치가 비교적 낮은 온도로 설정되어 있다 하더라도 방이 따뜻하게 느껴지죠. 이게 바로 우리가 이 행사를 겨울에 하는 이유입니다… 그래야 사람들이 어떻게 방사열이 작용하는지 '느낄' 수 있죠.

F 그럼, 저에게 라이트스톤 홀을 배정해 주실 수 있으세요?

S 그럼요, 라이트스톤 홀이 맞군요.

F 있잖아요, 제가 그 열 펌프 기술을 발명한 엔지니어를 통해 세부 정보를 한 가득 얻을 수 있을 거예요.

S 그럴 것 같아요. 하지만 기억해야 하는 건, 각 그룹이 캠퍼스 전역에서, 열 곳의 건물을 거쳐 걸어 다닐 거예요… 그리고 작년에는, 수백 명의 사람들이 이 투어에 참석했어요.

F 아… 알겠습니다… 그럼 너무 오래 걸리면 안 되겠네요.

S 그렇죠. 그럼 누군가 취소하는 경우에 어느 건물을 담당하고 싶은가요?

F 피트니스 센터는 어떤가요? 목록에 있지는 않지만요. 러닝머신이 전기를 전혀 사용하지 않거든요. 이용자의 발 움직임으로 배터리를 충전해요. 그리고 그 배터리는 운동과 관련된 정보를 보여 주는 디스플레이 패널에 전력을 공급하고요.

S 네, 러닝머신이라… 하지만 그 건물 자체와 관련해서는 특별한 게 없어요.

어휘

assign 배정하다, 할당하다   cancel 취소하다   unexpectedly 예기치 못하게   walk A through B A에게 B를 차근차근 설명하다   material 자료, 자재, 재료   sustainable (환경 파괴 없이) 지속 가능한   retrofit 보강하다   a variety of 다양한   feature 기능   insulated 절연 처리된   harvest 모으다, 거둬들이다   salvage 구하다, 이용하다   demolish 철거하다   electrical grid 전력망   utility bills 공과금   generate 만들어 내다   geothermal energy 지열 에너지   radiant heat 방사열, 복사열   invent 발명하다   transport 이동시키다   amplify 증폭시키다   conventional 전통적인, 관습적인   thermostat 온도 조절 장치   relatively 비교적, 상대적으로   a bunch of 한 가득한, 다수의   details 세부 정보   cover 담당하다, 다루다   treadmill 러닝머신   recharge 충전하다   power 전력을 공급하다   workout 운동

1. 학생이 왜 남자를 만나러 갔는가?

Ⓐ 수업 프로젝트에 필요한 정보를 얻기 위해

Ⓑ 다가오는 행사에 대한 참여를 논의하기 위해

Ⓒ 일자리에 필요한 추천서를 요청하기 위해

Ⓓ 새 건축 프로젝트에 대한 의견을 제공하기 위해

내용의 목적을 묻는 문제

어휘 participation 참여, 참가   upcoming 다가오는   input 의견
(의 제공)

해설 여자는 친환경 건물 투어의 가이드로서 알아 두어야 하는 정보
와 관련해 남자와 이야기하고 있으므로 B가 정답이다.

2. 화자들이 라이트스톤 기숙사에 관해 무슨 말을 하는가?
2개의 답안을 고르시오.

Ⓐ 비전통적인 전력 공급원을 이용한다.

Ⓑ 공학 도서관 옆에 위치해 있다.

Ⓒ 빗물을 수집하는 설비가 갖춰져 있다.

Ⓓ 재활용 자재로 지어졌다.

세부 정보 찾기 문제

어휘 unconventional 비전통적인   equipped 갖춰진   recycled
materials 재활용 자재

해설 남자가 라이트스톤 기숙사에서 에너지가 만들어지는 독특한 과
정을 설명하고 있으며, 철거된 건물들에서 나온 자재로 지어졌
는지 여자가 묻는 것에 대해 그렇다고 대답하고 있으므로 A와
D가 정답이다.

3. 남자의 말에 따르면, 친환경 건물 투어가 왜 겨울에 진행되는가?

Ⓐ 더 많은 투어 가이드가 겨울에 시간이 난다.

Ⓑ 방문객들에게 방사열의 효과를 경험할 수 있게 해 준다.

Ⓒ 새 건축 프로젝트가 일반적으로 추운 겨울이 시작되기 전에 완료
된다.

Ⓓ 대학교에서 겨울 기간 중에 친환경 디자인에 관한 강의를 제공한
다.

세부 정보 찾기 문제

어휘 available 시간이 나는, 이용 가능한   allow A to do A에게
~할 수 있게 해 주다   set in 시작되다   green 친환경의

해설 방문객들이 투어를 통해 어떻게 방사열이 작용하는지 확인할 수
있도록 겨울에 행사를 진행한다고 언급하고 있으므로 B가 정답
이다.

4. 남자가 피트니스 센터와 관련해 암시하는 것은 무엇인가?

Ⓐ 그곳의 러닝머신이 전기를 사용하지 않는다는 사실을 알지 못했
다.

Ⓑ 오직 몇몇 러닝머신만 그곳에서 전기를 사용하지 않는다.

Ⓒ 피트니스 센터가 있는 건물은 지속 가능한 특징이 부족하다.

Ⓓ 피트니스 센터가 이전 투어에 포함되어 있었다.

추론 문제

어휘 aware 알고 있는   house 제공하다, 수용하다

해설 여자가 투어 장소의 하나로 피트니스 센터를 제안하자, 남자는
그 건물 자체와 관련해서는 특별한 게 없다는 말로 피트니스 센
터가 있는 건물에 어떤 지속 가능한 특징도 있지 않다는 뜻을
나타내고 있으므로 C가 정답이다.

5. 대화의 일부를 다시 듣고 질문에 답하라.

F Y'know, maybe I could get a bunch of details from
the engineer who invented that heat-pump
technology.

S I guess. But remember, each group will walk all
over campus, through ten buildings... and last
year, hundreds of people attended these tours.

N *Why does the man say this:*

S I guess. But remember, each group will walk all
over campus, through ten buildings... and last year,
hundreds of people attended these tours.

Ⓐ 여자에게 더 많은 투어 가이드가 건물 개방 행사에 필요하다는
사실을 상기시키기 위해

Ⓑ 일부 정보가 오직 엔지니어들에게만 흥미로울지도 모른다는 뜻을
나타내기 위해

Ⓒ 여자가 가이드 시 시간 내 설명할 수 있는 것보다 더 많은 정보
를 수집하지 못하게 하기 위해

Ⓓ 많은 방문객들이 이미 열 펌프 기술에 익숙하다는 뜻을 나타내기
위해

의도 파악 문제

어휘 remind 상기시키다   discourage A from -ing A가 ~하지
못하게 하다   share 공유하다   be familiar with ~에 익숙하
다

해설 여자가 엔지니어를 통해 세부 정보를 많이 얻을 수 있다고 말하
자, 남자가 캠퍼스 투어에 포함된 건물의 숫자와 많은 투어 참가
자를 언급하고 있다. 이는 투어 진행 중에 그 모든 정보를 제공
할 시간이 충분하지 않을 것이라는 뜻이며, 결국 여자에게 너무
많은 정보를 수집하지 못하게 하려는 것이므로 C가 정답이다.

Script

N Listen to part of a lecture in an environmental science class.

P Now, we've been talking about the loss of animal habitat from housing developments, um, growing cities... small habitat losses. But today I want to begin talking about what happens when habitat is reduced across a large area. There are, of course, animal species that require large areas of habitat... and, um, some migrate over very long distances. So what's the impact of habitat loss on those animals? Animals that need large areas of habitat?

Well, I'll use the hummingbirds as an example. Now, you know a hummingbird is amazingly small. But even though it's really tiny, it migrates over very long distances... travels up and down the Western Hemisphere... the Americas... back and forth between where it breeds in the summer and the warmer climates where it spends the winter. So we would say that this whole area over which it migrates is its habitat, because on this long-distance journey, it needs to come down to feed and sleep every so often, right?

Well, the hummingbird beats its wings — get this — about 3,000 times per minute. So you think, wow, it must need a lot of energy, a lot of food, right? Well, it does — it drinks a lot of nectar from flowers and feeds on some insects — but it's energy-efficient, too. You can't say it isn't. I mean as it flies all the way across the Gulf of Mexico, it uses up almost none of its body fat. But that doesn't mean it doesn't need to eat! So hummingbirds have to rely on plants in their natural habitat. And it goes without saying, but... well, the opposite is true as well. Plants depend on hummingbirds too. There are some flowers that can only be pollinated by the hummingbird. Without it stopping to feed and spreading pollen from flower to flower, these plants would cease to exist!

But the problem, well... as natural habitat along these migration routes is developed by humans for housing or agriculture, or, um, cleared for raising cattle, for instance... there's less food available for migrating hummingbirds. Their nesting sites are affected, too... the same... by the same sorts of human activities. And all of these activities pose a real threat to the hummingbird population.

So, to help them survive, we need to preserve their habitats... And one of the concrete ways people have been doing this is by cleaning up polluted habitat areas... and then replanting flowers, uh, replanting native flowers that hummingbirds feed on. Promoting ecological tourism is another way to help save their habitat. As the number of

N 환경학 강의의 한 부분을 들으시오.

P 자, 지금까지 주택 개발로 동물 서식지들이 줄어들고 있다는 이야기를 했는데, 음… 도시가 커지면… 조그만 자연 서식지들은 사라지고 말죠. 하지만 오늘은, 자연 서식지가 넓은 지역에 걸쳐 감소되면, 과연 어떤 일이 벌어지는지부터 살펴보기로 하겠습니다. 물론, 넓은 서식지가 필요한 동물 종들이 있죠… 그리고, 음, 일부는 아주 먼 거리를 이동하죠. 그렇다면, 서식지 감소가 녀석들에게 어떤 영향을 미칠까요? 넓은 서식지가 필요한 동물들에게는요?

음, 벌새를 예로 들어 보겠습니다. 자, 벌새가 굉장히 조그만 새라는 건 잘 알고 있겠죠. 하지만 몸집은 정말 조그맣지만, 아주 먼 거리를 이동해 다니죠… 서반구와… 아메리카 대륙들을 오르내리며… 여름철 번식하는 곳과 겨울을 보내는 따뜻한 기후 지역 사이를 오가죠. 그러니까 벌새가 오가는 지역 전체가 벌새의 서식지라고 할 수 있습니다. 이처럼 먼 거리를 이동하게 되면, 먹이를 구하고 잠을 자기 위해 가끔 아래로 내려와야 할 테니까요. 그렇죠?

음, 벌새는 날갯짓을, 그렇죠, 1분에 약 3천 번이나 합니다. 그렇다면 이런 생각이 들겠죠. 와, 에너지도 많이 필요하고, 먹이도 많이 먹겠네… 그렇죠? 음, 그렇긴 하죠. 꽃에서 많은 꿀을 섭취하고 곤충들도 잡아먹죠. 하지만 에너지 효율도 좋습니다. 아니라곤 결코 말할 수 없죠. 벌새는 멕시코만 전역을 줄곧 날아다니면서도 체지방은 거의 소모하지 않는다는 말입니다. 하지만 그렇다고 해서 안 먹어도 된다는 뜻은 아니죠! 그러니까, 벌새는 자연 서식지 내에 있는 식물들에 의지할 수밖에 없죠. 두말할 필요도 없는 일이지만… 그 반대 역시 마찬가지입니다. 식물들도 벌새에 의존하니까요. 벌새에만 꽃가루받이를 의존하는 꽃들도 있습니다. 벌새가 잠시 멈춰 먹이를 먹으며 꽃들 간에 꽃가루를 옮겨주지 않는다면, 이런 식물들은 살아남을 수 없겠죠!

하지만 문제는, 음… 이러한 이동 경로상의 자연 서식지가 인간들의 주거지나 농지로 개발되거나, 혹은, 이를테면 소떼 사육을 위해 개간되면서… 벌새들이 이동 중에 구할 수 있는 먹이가 줄어드는 겁니다. 똑같은… 똑같은 식의 인간 활동들에 의해 벌새들의 보금자리들도 피해를 입고 있어요… 그래서 이러한 모든 활동이 벌새들에게는 진짜 위협이 되고 있습니다.

그러므로, 벌새들이 살아남을 수 있도록 돕기 위해서는, 우리가 그들의 서식지를 보존해야 하죠… 그리고 사람들이 실천하고 있는 구체적인 방법들 중 하나가 오염된 자연 서식지를 정화하는 일이예요… 그리고 그런 다음 벌새들이 먹이로 삼는 재래종 꽃들을 다시 심는 거죠. 생태 관광을 장려하는 것은 벌새 서식지를 보존하는 데 도움이 되는 또 한 가지 방법입니다. 관광객들, 그러니까 벌새를 보기 위해 벌새

visitors—ecotourists who come to hummingbird habitats to watch the birds—the more the number of visitors grows, the more local businesses profit. So ecological tourism can bring financial rewards. All the more reason to value these beautiful little creatures and their habitat, right?

But to understand more about how to protect and support hummingbirds the best we can, we've gotta learn more about their breeding... nesting... sites and, uh, migration routes—and also about the natural habitats we find there. That should help us determine how to prevent further decline in the population.

A good research method... a good way to learn more... is by, um, running a banding study. Banding the birds allows us to track them over their lifetime. It's a practice that's been used by researchers for years. In fact, most of what we know about hummingbirds comes from banding studies... where we, uh, capture a hummingbird and make sure all the information about it—like... its weight and, um, age and length—are all recorded... put into international... an international information database. And, then we place an extremely lightweight band around one of its legs... well, what looks like a leg—although, technically it's considered part of the bird's foot. Anyway, these bands are perfectly safe. And some hummingbirds have worn them for years with no evidence of any problems. The band is labeled with a tracking number... oh, and there's a phone number on the band for people to call, for free, to report a banded bird they've found or recaptured.

So when a banded bird is recaptured and reported, we learn about its migration route, its growth... and how long it's been alive... its life span. One recaptured bird had been banded almost 12 years earlier! She's one of the oldest hummingbirds on record.

Another interesting thing we've learned is... that some hummingbirds, uh, they no longer use a certain route; they travel by a different route to reach their destination. And findings like these have been of interest to biologists and environmental scientists in a number of countries, who are trying to understand the complexities of how changes in a habitat... affect the species in it—species like the hummingbirds.

서식지를 찾는 생태 관광객의 수가 늘어날수록, 지역 경제도 더욱 윤택해집니다. 그러므로, 생태 관광은 경제적으로도 득이 됩니다. 그러니까 더욱 더 이 아름답고 작은 새들과 녀석들의 서식지를 소중히 해야겠죠, 그렇죠?

하지만 최선을 다해 벌새들을 보호하고 지원하는 길을 더 잘 알기 위해서는, 벌새들의 번식지와… 보금자리… 그리고 이동 경로들, 그리고 그 경로들에서 발견하는 자연 서식지들에 대해서도 좀 더 잘 알아야 합니다. 그래야 벌새의 수가 더 이상 줄어드는 것을 막을 방법을 결정하는 데 도움이 될 겁니다.

좋은 연구 방법… 더 많은 것을 알 수 있는 방법은… 음, 바로 (조류) 표지법이죠. 새들에게 인식표를 달고 놓아 주면, 새들의 일생을 추적 관찰할 수 있으니까요. 이건 학자들이 오랫동안 사용해 온 방법이기도 합니다. 실제로, 우리가 벌새에 대해 알고 있는 사실들은 대부분 표지법 연구를 통해 얻은 것들이죠… 그러니까 벌새를 포획하여, 몸무게라든가, 나이, 몸 길이 등… 모든 정보를 확인해 전부 기록한 다음… 국제 정보 데이터베이스에 입력합니다. 그런 다음, 아주 가벼운 인식표찰을 그 벌새의 한쪽 다리에 다는 거죠… 음, 다리처럼 보이긴 해도 엄밀히 말하면 발의 일부라고 해야겠죠. 어쨌든, 이런 인식표찰은 절대 안전합니다. 여러 해 동안 아무런 문제 없이 인식표를 차고 다니는 벌새들도 있으니까요. 이 인식표에는 일련 번호가 있고… 아, 그리고 인식표를 찬 새를 발견하거나 재포획했을 경우 연락할 수 있는 무료 전화번호도 기재되어 있죠.

그러므로 인식표를 찬 새가 재포획되어 보고되면, 그 새가 이동한 경로와 성장 정도… 그리고 얼마나 오래 살았는지… 즉 수명도 알게 되죠. 12년 전에 인식표를 단 새 한 마리가 재포획된 경우도 있었죠! 녀석은 지금껏 가장 오래 산 벌새 중 하나로 기록되고 있습니다.

또 한 가지 흥미로운 사실이 확인되었는데… 어떤 벌새들은 특정 경로를 더 이상 이용하지 않는다는 겁니다. 즉 다른 경로를 통해 목적지로 간다는 거죠. 이런 발견들에 여러 나라의 생물학자들과 환경학자들이 관심을 보이고 있습니다. 이들은 서식지 환경의 변화가… 그 안에서 살아가는 종, 즉 벌새 같은 종에게 미치는 영향의 복합적 특성들을 규명하고자 노력하고 있습니다.

어휘

habitat (동식물의) 서식지 migrate 이동하다 hummingbird 벌새 tiny 아주 작은 Western Hemisphere 서반구 breed 새끼를 낳다, 번식하다 feed 먹이를 먹다 every so often 가끔, 때때로 beat 날갯짓하다 get this 얘기 좀 들어봐 nectar (꽃의) 꿀 energy-efficient 에너지 효율적인 body fat 체지방 it goes without saying 말할 나위도 없다 pollinate 수분하다 spread (여러 장소로) 퍼트리다 pollen 꽃가루 cease 그치다, 멎다 migration route 이동 경로 clear 개척[개간]하다 nesting site 보금자리 threat 위협, 위험 concrete 구체적인 replant (식물을) 옮겨 심다, 다시 심다 ecological tourism 생태 관광 ecotourist 생태 관광객 reward 보상, 대가 all the more (그만큼) 더, 더욱 더 value 소중하게 여기다 decline 감소 banding 조류 표지법(bird-banding) track 추적하다, 지켜보다 technically 엄밀히 말하면 evidence 흔적 recapture 다시 붙잡다, 재포획하다 life span 수명 destination 목적지, 도착지

Reading

Listening

Speaking

Writing

Test 1

Test 2

Test 3

Test 4

6. 교수가 주로 다루고 있는 내용은?

Ⓐ 벌새의 이동 형태에서 나타난 큰 변화

Ⓑ 벌새의 도시 환경 적응

Ⓒ 벌새 서식지 감소에 대한 우려

Ⓓ 생태 관광이 벌새 무리에게 미치는 영향

내용의 요점을 묻는 문제

어휘 adaptation 적응   concern 우려, 걱정

해설 자연 서식지의 감소라는 큰 주제 하에, 갖가지 생물 종들에게 미칠 영향을 우려하면서 특히 벌새를 주된 사례로 들어 토론하고 있으므로 보기 C가 강의의 주요 내용이라고 할 수 있다.

7. 교수가 벌새의 감소 원인으로 암시하는 것은?

Ⓐ 생태 관광 산업의 발전

Ⓑ 경작지 및 목축지의 증대

Ⓒ 조류 표지법 연구의 감소

Ⓓ 철새 이동 거리의 감소

추론 문제

어휘 imply (생각을) 넌지시 나타내다, 암시하다
   raise (작물을) 재배하다; (가축을) 사육하다

해설 농경지나 목축지 개발 등으로 자연 서식지가 파괴되면서 벌새들이 이동 중에 구할 수 있는 먹이도 줄어들고, 보금자리까지도 영향을 받고 있다고 했으므로, 보기 B가 가장 합당한 원인이다.

8. 교수는 벌새들의 생존을 위해 사람들이 어떤 일을 했다고 말하는가?

Ⓐ 벌새들이 먹이 먹는 장소들을 마련했다.

Ⓑ 야생 동물 서식지를 오염시키는 사람들을 처벌하는 새로운 법안을 지지했다.

Ⓒ 오염되었던 지역에 재래종 꽃들을 다시 심었다.

Ⓓ 다양한 벌새 종들을 식별하는 법을 배웠다.

세부 정보 찾기 문제

어휘 feeding station 먹이 먹는 장소   wildlife 야생 동물
   identify 알아보다, 식별하다

해설 사람들이 벌새를 보호하고 지원하기 위해 오염되었던 자연 서식지들을 정화하고 토종꽃들을 다시 심었다고 언급했다.

9. 이동하는 벌새들에 대한 정보를 수집하는 방법으로 교수가 언급하는 것은?

Ⓐ 전자 추적 장비로 무선 신호를 수신하는 방법

Ⓑ 인식표를 찬 새를 재포획한 사람들로부터 연락을 받는 방법

Ⓒ 매년 같은 지역으로 돌아오는 새들의 숫자를 세어 보는 방법

Ⓓ 나이 든 새들과 젊은 새들의 이동 경로를 비교하는 방법

세부 정보 찾기 문제

어휘 radio signal 무선 신호
   contact (전화, 편지 등으로) 연락하다

해설 교수가 언급한 조류 표지법은 새를 포획하여 정보를 수집한 뒤 인식표를 달아 놓아주었다가, 그 새가 누군가에게 다시 잡혔을 때 인식표에 기재된 무료 전화번호로 연락을 받아 이전 자료와 비교하여 그 새에 대한 각종 정보를 얻는 방법이다.

10. 교수의 설명에서, 학자들이 벌새의 이동을 연구하면서 알게 된 사실이라고 짐작되는 것은?

Ⓐ 일부 나라에서는 최근의 서식지 파괴로 벌새들이 완전히 자취를 감추었다.

Ⓑ 벌새 서식지에 재래종 꽃들을 다시 심는 프로그램은 성공을 거두지 못하고 있다.

Ⓒ 이동 형태가 바뀐 벌새 무리들도 있다.

Ⓓ 벌새에게 수분 활동을 의존하는 식물 종 일부는 멸종되었다.

내용 연결 문제

어휘 totally 완전히   due to ~ 때문에   extinct 멸종된

해설 교수가 마지막 단락에서 '특정 경로를 이용하지 않고, 다른 경로로 목적지까지 가는 벌새들도 있다'라고 언급한 부분에서, 벌새들의 이동 형태가 바뀐 경우도 있음을 짐작할 수 있다.

11. 강의의 일부를 다시 듣고 질문에 답하라.

🎧 T-60

P So hummingbirds have to rely on plants in their natural habitat. And it goes without saying, but... well, the opposite is true as well. Plants depend on hummingbirds too.

N *What does the professor imply when she says this?*

P And it goes without saying...

Ⓐ 교수가 제시한 의견에 동의하지 않는 이들도 있다.

Ⓑ 자세한 내용들을 다 설명할 생각은 없다.

Ⓒ 다음에 언급할 내용은 방금 말한 내용과 모순될 수도 있다.

Ⓓ 다음에 말할 내용은 학생들도 분명히 알고 있을 내용이다.

의도 파악 문제

어휘 present 제시하다, 발표하다   contradict 모순되다
   obvious 분명한, 확실한

해설 'It goes without saying'은 관용어구로 '두말할 나위도 없이'라는 뜻이다. 너무나 당연한 사실이라는 점을 강조하기 위해 쓰인 표현이다.

Script

N Listen to part of a lecture in a film history class.

P Okay, we've been discussing film in the 1920s and '30s, and, ah, how back then, film categories as we know them today had not yet been established. We, ah, said that, by today's standards, many of the films of the '20s and '30s would be considered "hybrids"; that is, a mixture of styles that wouldn't exactly fit into any of today's categories. And in that context, today we're going to talk about a, a filmmaker who began making very unique films in the late 1920s. He was French, and his name was Jean Painlevé.

Jean Painlevé was born in 1902. He made his first film in 1928. Now, in a way, Painlevé's films conform to norms of the '20s and '30s; that is, they don't fit very neatly into the categories we use to classify films today. That said, even by the standards of the '20s and '30s, Painlevé's films were a unique hybrid of styles. He had a special way of fusing—or, or some people might say confusing—science and fiction; his films begin with facts, but then they become more and more fictional—they gradually add more and more fictional elements. In fact, Painlevé was known for saying that "science is fiction."

Painlevé was a, a pioneer in underwater filmmaking, and a lot of his short films focus on the aquatic animal world. He liked to show small underwater creatures displaying what seemed like familiar human characteristics—what we think of as unique to humans. He might take a, a clip of a mollusk going up and down in the water and set it to music—you know, to make it look as if the mollusk were dancing to the music like a human being. That sort of thing. But then he'd suddenly change the image or narration to remind us how different the animals are, how unlike humans. He confused his audience in the way he portrayed the animals he filmed, mixing up our notions of the categories "human" and "animal." The films make us a little uncomfortable at times because we're uncertain about what we're seeing. It gives his films an uncanny feature... the familiar made unfamiliar, the normal made suspicious. He liked twists; he liked the unusual. In fact, one of his favorite sea animals was the sea horse because with sea horses, it's the male that gets pregnant, it's the male that carries the babies. And he thought that was great. His first and most celebrated underwater film is about the sea horse.

Susan? You have a question?

N 영화사 강의의 일부를 들으시오.

P 자, 지금까지 1920년대와 1930년대의 영화들을 둘러보면서, 아, 그 당시에는, 오늘날 우리가 알고 있는 영화의 장르들이 미처 확립되지 못했다는 이야기를 했습니다. 오늘날의 기준으로 본다면, 20년대와 30년대 영화들은 대부분 '혼합 장르'였다고 할 수 있겠죠. 즉 오늘날의 장르 분류로는 어디에도 정확히 들어맞지 않는 양식들의 혼합인 셈이죠. 그러면 오늘은, 이런 맥락에서, 1920년대 말에 아주 독특한 영화를 만들기 시작했던 감독에 대해 이야기하도록 하겠습니다. 프랑스인, 장 팽르베라는 인물입니다.

장 팽르베는 1902년에 태어났습니다. 그리고 처음으로 영화를 만든 것은 1928년이었죠. 자, 어떤 면으로는, 팽르베의 영화도 20년대와 30년대의 전형을 따르고 있습니다. 즉 오늘날 우리가 구분하는 영화 장르들 중 그 어디에도 깔끔하게 들어맞지 않죠. 그렇긴 하지만, 심지어 20년대와 30년대의 기준에서도, 팽르베의 영화는 독특한 혼성 스타일이었습니다. 그는 사이언스와 픽션을 한데 융합시키는—아니, 융합이 아니라 혼돈이라고 말하는 이들도 있겠지만—그런 특별한 기법을 썼습니다. 그의 영화들은 사실에서 출발하긴 하지만, 허구적인 성격이 점점 더 강해져서—허구적인 요소들이 차츰 차츰 늘어나죠. 사실, 팽르베는 "사이언스는 곧 픽션이다"라는 말로 유명한 인물이기도 하죠.

팽르베는 수중 영화 제작의 선구자로, 수중 동물 세계에 초점을 맞춘 단편 영화들을 많이 만들었습니다. 익숙한 인간의 특성—우리가 인간 고유의 특성이라고 생각하는 것들—과 흡사한 모습을 보여 주는 조그만 수중 생물을 즐겨 보여 주곤 했죠. 이를테면, 연체 동물 한 마리가 물 속에서 오르락내리락하는 장면을 찍고 거기에 음악을 넣는 거죠. 마치 연체 동물이 사람처럼 음악에 맞춰 춤을 추는 것처럼 보이게 만드는, 그런 식의 연출을 했습니다. 하지만 그러고는 영상이나 내레이션을 돌변시켜, 동물들이 인간과 얼마나 다른지를 상기시켜 주곤 했죠. 그는 자신의 영화에 등장하는 동물들을 표현할 때, 우리가 생각하는 '인간'과 '동물'의 범주에 대한 개념을 뒤섞어 버리는 방식을 써서 관객들을 혼란에 빠뜨렸습니다. 그의 영화는 무얼 보고 있는지 알 수 없어 좀 거북할 때도 있습니다. 그 때문에 그의 영화들에는 기묘한 특징이 있죠… 익숙한 것을 낯설게 만들고, 통상적인 것도 수상쩍게 만듭니다. 그는 배배 꼬기를 좋아했고, 특이한 것들을 즐겼습니다. 실제로, 그가 가장 좋아했던 수중 동물 하나가 바로 해마였죠. 해마의 경우, 새끼를 배는 쪽이 수컷이니까요. 그래서 그는 그 점이 멋지다고 생각했죠. 그의 첫 작품이자 가장 많은 찬사를 받았던 수중 영화도 해마를 주제로 한 작품이었죠.

수잔? 질문 있나요?

F 하지만 수중 영화가 그렇게 특이했던 건 아니잖아요, 그

Reading

Listening

Speaking

Writing

Test 1

Test 2

Test 3

Test 4

F But underwater filmmaking wasn't that unusual, was it? I mean weren't there other people making movies underwater?

P Well, actually it was pretty rare at that time. I mean we're talking the early 1930s here.

F But what about Jacques Cousteau? Wasn't he, like, an innovator, you know, with underwater photography, too?

P Ah, Jacques Cousteau. Well, Painlevé and Cousteau did both film underwater, and they were both innovators, so you're right in that sense, but that's pretty much where the similarities end. First of all, Painlevé was about 20 years ahead of Cousteau... Um, and Cousteau's adventures were high-tech, with lots of fancy equipment, whereas Painlevé kind of patched equipment together as he needed it... Uh, Cousteau usually filmed large animals, usually in the open sea, whereas Painlevé generally filmed smaller animals, and, and he liked to film in shallow water... Uh, what else? Well, the main difference was that Cousteau simply investigated and presented the facts; he, he didn't mix in fiction. He was a strict documentarist; he set the standard, really, for the nature documentary. Painlevé, on the other hand, as we said before, mixed in elements of fiction, and his films are much more artistic, incorporating music as an important element.

John, you have a question?

M Well, maybe I shouldn't be asking this... Uh, but if Painlevé's films are so special, so good, why haven't we ever heard of them? I mean everyone's heard of Jacques Cousteau...

P Well, that's a fair question. Uh, the short answer is that Painlevé's style just never caught on with the general public. I mean it probably goes back, at least in part, to what we mentioned earlier, that, that people didn't know what to make of his films, that they were confused by them. Whereas Cousteau's documentaries were very straightforward, uh, met people's expectations more than Painlevé's films did. But your true film-history buffs know about him, and Painlevé's still highly respected in many circles.

렇지 않나요? 다른 사람들도 수중 영화를 만들지 않았나요?

P 음, 실제로 당시에는 무척 드물었죠. 우리가 지금 논하고 있는 건 1930년대 초반이니까요.

F 하지만 자크 쿠스토도 있잖아요? 그 사람도, 음, 수중 사진 촬영의 혁신자라고 할 수 있지 않나요?

P 아, 자크 쿠스토 말이군요. 음, 팽르베와 쿠스토, 두 사람 다 수중 영화를 만든 혁신적 인물이었으니까, 그런 면에서는 옳은 말이죠. 하지만 두 사람의 유사점은 그게 전부입니다. 무엇보다도, 팽르베는 쿠스토보다 약 20년 앞섰고… 음, 그리고 쿠스토의 수중 탐험은 근사한 장비들을 잔뜩 갖춘 하이테크 작업인 반면, 팽르베는 필요에 따라 장비들을 이리저리 끼워 맞추는 식으로 했죠… 음, 쿠스토는 대개 외해에 나가 몸집이 큰 동물들을 촬영했지만, 반면 팽르베는 대체로 작은 동물들을 촬영했고, 또한 얕은 바다에서 촬영하기를 좋아했죠… 어, 그 외에 또 뭐가 있을까요? 음, 가장 큰 차이라고 한다면, 쿠스토는 탐사해서 밝혀낸 사실을 제시하기만 했다는 거죠. 그는 허구를 추가하지 않았습니다. 쿠스토는 엄격한 다큐멘터리 작가였죠. 이에 반해, 팽르베는 앞에서 말했듯이, 허구적인 요소들을 추가했으며, 또한 음악을 중요한 요소로 포함시켰으므로, 예술성은 훨씬 더 높았다고 할 수 있죠.

존, 질문 있나요?

M 음, 이런 질문은 하면 안 될지도 모르지만… 어, 그런데 팽르베의 영화들이 그토록 특별하고 훌륭하다면, 왜 저희가 한 번도 들어 보질 못했을까요? 그러니까, 자크 쿠스토는 모르는 사람이 없는데…

P 아, 적절한 질문입니다. 음, 간단히 답하자면, 팽르베의 작품 스타일이 일반 대중에게 인기가 없었기 때문이죠. 그러니까 아마도, 우리가 앞에서 언급했던 사실이 적어도 부분적으로는 그 원인이 되겠죠. 즉 사람들은 그의 영화들을 이해하지 못했고, 혼란스러워했으니까요. 반면, 쿠스토의 다큐멘터리 영화들은 아주 단순하고, 음, 팽르베의 영화들보다 더 사람들의 기대에 부응했습니다. 하지만 진정한 영화사광이라면 팽르베를 알고 있으며, 또한 팽르베를 여전히 높게 평가하는 사람들도 많습니다.

어휘

film categories 영화 장르　**establish** 확립하다, 정착시키다　**hybrid** 혼성체, 혼합물　**fit into** ～에 꼭 들어맞다　**in that context** 그런 맥락에서　**filmmaker** 영화 제작자, 영화감독　**Jean Painlevé** 장 팽르베(1902-1989; 프랑스의 영화 제작자)　**conform** 일치하다　**classify** 분류[구분]하다　**fuse** 융합하다　**confusing** 혼란스러운, 헷갈리는　**underwater** 수중의　**focus on** ～에 주력하다, ～에 초점을 맞추다　**aquatic animal** 수생[수중] 동물　**human characteristics** 인간의 특성[특질]　**clip** (영화) 클립(일부만 따로 떼어 보여 주는 부분)　**mollusk** 연체 동물　**portray** 묘사[표현]하다　**mix up** ～을 뒤섞다　**uncanny** 기괴한, 비정상적인　**suspicious** 의심스러운, 수상쩍은　**twist** 꼰 것, 뒤틀기　**sea horse** 해마　**carry a baby** 임신하다, 새끼를 배다　**rare** 드문, 보기 힘든　**Jacques Cousteau** 자크 쿠스토(1910-1997; 프랑스의 탐험가, 생태학자, 영화 제작자)　**innovator** 혁신자　**fancy** 복잡한, 멋진, 일류의　**patch together** 이어 맞추다　**open sea** 외해, 대해　**shallow water** 얕은 물, 천해　**mix in** ～와 합치다, ～를 더하다　**strict** 엄격한, 순전한　**documentarist**(= documentarian) 다큐멘터리 작가　**incorporate** 포함하다, 통합하다　**fair question** 적절한 질문　**catch on with** ～의 인기를 얻다　**make of** ～을 생각하다[해석하다]　**straightforward** 직접적인, 간단한　**buff** ～광, 애호가

12. 강의의 주요 목적은 무엇인가?

Ⓐ 어느 초기 영화 제작자의 스타일을 논의하는 것

Ⓑ 1930년대의 여러 가지 영화 제작 방식들을 설명하는 것

Ⓒ 다큐멘터리 영화의 탄생에 대해 논의하는 것

Ⓓ 팽르베가 오늘날의 SF 영화들에 미친 영향을 설명하는 것

내용의 목적을 묻는 문제

어휘 emergence 나타남, 출현   influence on ~에 대한 영향

해설 1920년대 후반부터 사이언스와 픽션을 혼합하는 독특한 영화를 만들기 시작했던 팽르베 감독에 대한 설명이 강의의 골자를 이루고 있다. 사이언스와 픽션을 결합한다는 측면에서는 오늘날의 SF 영화와 유사하지만, 전반적인 내용은 팽르베 감독의 영화 제작 스타일과 기법에 대한 자세한 설명이므로 보기 D보다는 보기 A가 더 적합한 강의 목적이다.

13. 팽르베의 영화가 1920년대와 1930년대의 전형적인 영화라고 할 수 있는 이유는?

Ⓐ 음향이 없어서

Ⓑ 수중에서 촬영해서

Ⓒ 이해하기가 쉬워서

Ⓓ 장르를 분류하기 어려워서

내용 연결 문제

어휘 typical of 전형적인, 대표적인   categorize 분류하다

해설 팽르베의 영화가 1920년대와 1930년대의 전형을 따르고 있으며, 그 당시의 영화는 오늘날의 어떤 영화 장르에도 정확히 들어맞지 않는 '혼합 장르'라고 했으므로, 장르 분류가 어렵다는 점이 이유가 된다.

14. 교수의 설명에 따르면, 팽르베의 영화는 어떤 식으로 관객들을 혼란스럽게 했는가?

Ⓐ 자연 서식지에서 벗어난 동물들을 보여 준다.

Ⓑ 동물들을 인간과 동물의 특성들을 모두 지닌 존재로 묘사한다.

Ⓒ 내레이션이 전문적이고 이해하기 어렵다.

Ⓓ 1920년대와 1930년대의 관객들은 수중에서 촬영된 영화에 익숙하지 않았다.

세부 정보 찾기 문제

어휘 out of ~에서 떨어져서[벗어나서]

scientific 과학적인, 전문적인 지식을 담은

해설 팽르베 감독은 영화 속에서 동물들을 표현할 때, 일반적인 '인간'과 '동물'의 개념을 뒤섞어 버리는 방식을 써서 관객들을 혼란스럽게 만들었다고 설명했다.

15. 교수가 해마를 언급한 이유는?

Ⓐ 1930년대에 해마를 촬영하기 어려웠다는 것을 설명하기 위해서

Ⓑ 쿠스토가 해마에 관한 다큐멘터리를 만들었다는 점을 지적하기 위해서

Ⓒ 팽르베가 특이한 동물들에 매료된 사례를 보여 주기 위해서

Ⓓ 팽르베의 수중 영화들이 성공을 거두지 못한 이유를 설명하기 위해서

구성 파악 문제

어휘 illustrate 사례를 들어 설명하다

fascination 매료됨, 마음이 홀린 상태

해설 교수가 해마를 언급한 이유는 팽르베가 특이한 것을 유난히 좋아했다는 실례를 보여 주기 위한 것이다. 수컷이 새끼를 배는 아주 특이한 동물인 해마를 사례로 들어 팽르베 감독의 그런 성향을 보여 주려는 것이다.

16. 교수가 자크 쿠스토와 장 팽르베의 영화 스타일을 비교한 이유는?

Ⓐ 팽르베가 쿠스토에게 어떤 영향을 끼쳤는지를 설명하기 위해서

Ⓑ 팽르베의 영화 스타일이 독특하다는 것을 강조하기 위해서

Ⓒ 쿠스토의 다큐멘터리 영화들이 지닌 예술적인 가치를 강조하기 위해서

Ⓓ 팽르베의 영화 제작 장비들이 더 우수했다는 사실을 입증하기 위해서

내용 연결 문제

어휘 emphasize (중요성을) 강조하다   superiority (~에 대한) 우월(성), 우위   demonstrate 증거를 들어 입증하다[보여 주다]

해설 제작 시기나 촬영 장비, 표현 방식 등 두 사람의 차이를 자세히 비교 설명한 것은 팽르베의 영화에 대해 의혹을 제기한 여학생의 질문에 대한 대답이자, 팽르베의 스타일이 독특했다는 사실을 더욱 강조하기 위해서였다.

17. 다음을 듣고 질문에 답하라.

🎧 T-62

N *What does the student imply when he says this?*
M *Well, maybe I shouldn't be asking this... Uh, but if Painlevé's films are so special, so good, why haven't we ever heard of them? I mean everyone's heard of Jacques Cousteau...*

Ⓐ 장 팽르베 감독의 영화를 좋아하지 않는다.

Ⓑ 교수가 자크 쿠스토의 영화에 대해 더 많은 시간을 할애하여 논의해야 한다고 생각한다.

Ⓒ 훌륭한 영화 제작자는 대개 유명할 것이라고 생각한다.

Ⓓ 장 팽르베의 영화가 부당하게 무시당해 왔다고 생각한다.

의도 파악 문제

어휘 unfairly 부당하게   overlook 간과하다, 무시하다

해설 팽르베의 영화가 그토록 대단하다면 어째서 자크 쿠스토만큼 유명하지 않느냐는 남학생의 반문 속에는 영화가 훌륭하다면 당연히 유명하기 마련이라는 생각이 깔려 있다.

Questions 18-22 p. 242

N Narrator　M Male Student　P Professor

Script

N Listen to a conversation between a student and a professor.

M Hi, Professor Archer. You know how in class last week you said that you were looking for students who were interested in volunteering for your archaeology project?

P Of course. Are you volunteering?

M Yes, I am. It sounds really interesting. But, ummm, do I need to have any experience with these kinds of projects?

P No, not really. I assume that most students taking the introductory-level class will have little or no experience with archaeological research, but that's OK.

M Oh, good—that's a relief. Actually, that's why I'm volunteering for the project—to get experience. What kind of work is it?

P Well, as you know, we're studying the history of the campus this semester. This used to be an agricultural area, and we already know that where the main lecture hall now stands there once were a farmhouse and barn that were erected in the late 1700s. We're excavating near the lecture hall to see what types of artifacts we find—you know, things people used in the past that got buried when the campus was constructed. We've already begun to find some very interesting items like, um, old bottles, buttons, pieces of clay pottery...

M Buttons and clay pottery? Did the old owners leave in such a hurry that they left their clothes and dishes behind?

P That's just one of the questions we hope to answer with this project.

M Wow—and it's all right here on campus...

P That's right, no traveling involved. I wouldn't expect volunteers to travel to a site, especially in the middle of the semester. We expect to find many more things, but we do need more people to help.

M So... how many student volunteers are you looking for?

P I'm hoping to get five or six. I've asked for volunteers in all the classes I teach, but no one's responded. You're the first person to express interest.

M Uh... sounds like it could be a lot of work. Is there... umm... is there any way I can use the experience to get some extra credit in class? I mean can I write a paper about it?

N 학생과 교수의 대화를 들으시오.

M 아처 교수님, 안녕하세요. 지난주 강의 시간에 교수님의 고고학 프로젝트에 지원하고 싶은 학생을 찾는 중이라고 하셨죠?

P 그랬죠. 지원할 생각이 있나요?

M 예, 그렇습니다. 정말 흥미로워 보여서요. 그런데, 저어, 이런 류의 프로젝트에 참가해 본 경험이 있어야만 합니까?

P 아니요, 그렇진 않죠. 입문 강좌 수강생들은 고고학 조사 활동에 대해서 경험이 거의 없거나 전무한 경우가 대부분이죠. 하지만 그래도 상관없어요.

M 아, 잘됐네요. 그럼 다행이네요. 사실, 그래서 프로젝트에 지원하려고 합니다. 경험을 쌓으려고 말이죠. 어떤 일을 하게 되죠?

P 음, 학생도 알다시피, 이번 학기에는 우리 대학 캠퍼스의 역사를 연구하고 있죠. 이곳은 원래 농경지였고, 현재 본관 강의동 자리는 1700년대에 세운 농가와 헛간이 있던 곳이라는 건 이미 알고 있죠. 그래서 어떤 종류의 유물들을 찾을 수 있는지 확인하기 위해 강의동 부근을 발굴하고 있어요. 그러니까, 대학 캠퍼스 건립 당시 묻힌 옛 주민들의 물건들을 찾는 거죠. 벌써 아주 흥미로운 물건들이 나오기 시작했는데, 그러니까, 음, 오래된 병들이나 단추, 토기 파편 등…

M 단추와 토기요? 옛 주민들이 옷과 그릇까지 놔두고 갈 정도로 서둘러 떠났나요?

P 이 프로젝트를 통해 우리가 풀고자 하는 의문점들 중 하나가 바로 그 점이죠.

M 와, 여기 캠퍼스에 모든 게 다 있군요…

P 그래요, 이동이 필요 없죠. 지원 학생들이 먼 곳에 있는 현장을 다닐 거라고는 생각하지 않아요. 특히 학기 중에는 더욱 그렇죠. 유물들이 훨씬 더 많이 나올 것 같지만, 도와줄 사람들이 더 많이 필요해요.

M 그러시다면… 지원자를 몇 명이나 받을 생각이신가요?

P 대여섯 명 정도를 바라고 있어요. 내가 맡은 모든 수업에서 자원봉사를 요청했지만, 찾아온 학생은 아무도 없었죠. 관심을 보인 건 학생이 처음이에요.

M 어… 할 일이 많을 수도 있겠군요. 그러니까… 저어… 이번 경험을 활용해서 가산점을 받을 수 있는 길이 혹시 없을까요? 그러니까, 프로젝트에 대한 보고서를 제출한다든지 해서 말이죠.

P I think it'll depend on what type of work you do in the excavation, but I imagine we can arrange something. Well, actually, I've been considering offering extra credit for class because I've been having a tough time getting volunteers... Extra credit is always a good incentive for students.

M And... how often would you want the volunteers to work?

P We're asking for three or four hours per week, depending on your schedule. A senior researcher—I think you know John Franklin, my assistant—is on-site every day.

M Sure, I know John. By the way, will there be some sort of training?

P Yes, uh, I wanna wait till Friday to see how many students volunteer. And then I'll schedule a training class next week at a time that's convenient for everyone.

M OK, I'll wait to hear from you. Thanks a lot for accepting me!

P 그건 발굴 조사에서 학생이 어떤 일을 하느냐에 따라 다르겠지만, 어떤 안을 마련할 수 있겠죠. 음, 사실은 지원자를 구하기가 힘들어서 가산점을 줄 것을 고려하고 있었어요… 가산점은 학생들에게 언제나 훌륭한 자극제니까요.

M 그리고… 지원자들이 얼마나 자주 작업에 참여하길 바라시나요?

P 학생 일정에 따라 일주일에 서너 시간 정도는 해줬으면 해요. 내 조교인 존 프랭클린은 학생도 알고 있겠죠, 존이 수석 연구원으로 매일 현장에 있어요.

M 물론입니다. 알고 있죠. 그런데, 교육 같은 것을 받아야 하나요?

P 그래요, 음, 금요일까지 지원하는 학생이 얼마나 있을지 기다려 볼 생각이에요. 그런 다음, 다음 주에 모두가 편한 때로 교육 일정을 잡을 거예요.

M 알겠습니다. 연락 주시길 기다리겠습니다. 받아주셔서 정말 감사합니다!

어휘

archaeology[archeology] 고고학   assume 추측하다, 간주하다   introductory-level 입문 단계   relief 안도, 안심   farmhouse 농가, 농장 안의 본채   barn 헛간[창고], 가축 우리   erect 건립하다, 세우다   excavate 파다, 발굴하다   artifact 공예품, 인공 유물   get buried 묻히다, 매몰되다   button (옷의) 단추   clay pottery 토기, 오지그릇   in a hurry 서둘러, 급히   respond 반응을 보이다   extra credit 추가 점수, 가산점   arrange 마련하다, 주선하다   have a tough time 힘이 들다, 혼이 나다   incentive 유인책, 자극제   senior researcher 수석[선임] 연구원   assistant (대학의) 조교   on-site 현장에서

18. 학생이 교수를 찾아간 이유는?

Ⓐ 과제에 대해 물어 보려고

Ⓑ 학기 중에 진행되는 프로젝트에 대해 알아 보려고

Ⓒ 여름 방학 아르바이트에 대한 정보를 얻으려고

Ⓓ 성적을 올릴 수 있는 방법을 의논하려고

내용의 목적을 묻는 문제

어휘 assignment (학생의) 숙제, 연구 과제 mid-semester 학기 중간(의) summer job 여름방학 아르바이트

해설 대화 첫머리에서 학생이 교수가 진행하는 고고학 프로젝트에 흥미를 느껴 찾아왔다는 뜻을 밝혔으며, 학기 중에 학생들이 먼 곳까지 현장 조사를 나갈 것으로 기대하지 않는다는 교수의 말에서 이 고고학 프로젝트는 학기 중에 진행되는 것임을 알 수 있다.

19. 강의동 자리는 원래 무엇이 있던 곳인가?

Ⓐ 농가

Ⓑ 도자기 공장

Ⓒ 옷 가게

Ⓓ 병 제조 공장

세부 정보 찾기 문제

어휘 manufacture (기계를 이용해 대량으로) 제조하다, 생산하다

해설 현재 강의동이 있는 자리에는 1700년대 말에 세운 농가와 헛간이 있었다고 교수가 설명했다.

20. 이 프로젝트에 참여하는 것의 장점으로 언급된 것은?

Ⓐ 교외 현장 이동 경비를 지원받는다.

Ⓑ 강의 시간에 일찍 나가는 것이 허용된다.

Ⓒ 다니기 편한 곳에 현장이 있다.

Ⓓ 졸업 필수 요건을 충족한다.

세부 정보 찾기 문제

어휘 off-campus 대학 캠퍼스 밖의, 교외의
graduation requirements 졸업 자격[요건]

해설 프로젝트 현장이 학교 구내임이 여러 차례 언급되었으며, 쉽게 다닐 수 있다는 것이 이 프로젝트의 장점이라는 점을 교수와 학생 모두 인정하고 있다.

21. 지원자를 늘리기 위해 교수가 고려하고 있는 방법은?

Ⓐ 가산점을 부여하는 것

Ⓑ 참여 학생들에게 시간당 보수를 주는 것

Ⓒ 수강생이 아닌 학생들에게도 자원봉사를 요청하는 것

Ⓓ 작업 시간을 선택할 수 있게 해 주는 것

세부 정보 찾기 문제

어휘 class credit 이수 학점
flexible work schedules 근무시간 자유 선택제

해설 프로젝트에 지원하면 가산점을 받을 수 있느냐는 학생의 질문에 대한 대답으로, 교수는 지원자를 늘리기 위해 가산점 제공을 실제로 고려하고 있다고 말했다.

22. 학생이 교수에게 얻어야 할 정보는?

Ⓐ 수석 연구원의 이름

Ⓑ 다음 강의 전에 읽어야 할 책

Ⓒ 프로젝트 관련 교육을 받게 될 시점

Ⓓ 프로젝트 현장 위치

내용 연결 문제

어휘 session (특정한 활동을 위한) 시간[기간]

해설 교수는 다음 주 중에 교육 일정을 잡을 계획이라고만 했고 학생은 연락을 기다리겠다고 대답했으므로, 아직 정확한 시기가 결정되지 않은 상황이다. 따라서 정확한 날짜와 시간을 알려 주어야 한다.

Questions 23-28　　　　　　　　　　　　p. 244

N Narrator　P Professor

Script

N Listen to part of a lecture in an art history class.

P We've talked a lot in this course about still lifes. And I guess if there's one thing you thought it was safe to assume about still lifes, it'd probably be that they're depictions of things that are... still, right? A bowl of fruit, a vase of flowers, a stack of books. But today we're gonna look at some modern-day artists who are innovating with still lifes. In fact, some of them are even taking the still—out—of still lifes!

　Now, still lifes are scarce in the contemporary art scene, but some artists are looking for ways to make them new for a contemporary audience. For example, historically we think of still lifes as paintings. But more and more, artists are employing nonpaint media like photography, digital art, even animation.

　Now animation doesn't sound like a likely medium for a still life, but one pair of contemporary artists is using it. What they've done is make an exact replica of a painting by the still life painter Ambrosius Bosschaert the Elder.

　Bosschaert was a seventeenth-century Dutch painter known for his still lifes of rare, exotic flowers. Here, take a look at this piece.

　At the time this was originally painted, there was a national obsession in the Netherlands with flowers—especially tulips, which had only recently begun to be imported from Turkey and were still considered exotic. But Bosschaert mainly specialized in painting lots of rare and expensive flowers together in a single, dazzling bouquet. It was irrelevant to him whether these flowers could be assembled together in real life—often they couldn't, because they bloomed at different times of the year. But, who cares, right? The imaginary bouquets made a great picture.

　OK, so a pair of contemporary artists—Rob and Nick Carter—recently decided to reproduce this particular painting.

N 예술사 강의의 일부를 들으시오.

P 이 강의 중에 정물화와 관련해 많은 이야기를 해 왔습니다. 그리고 여러분이 정물화와 관련해 추정하기 안전하다고 생각한 한 가지가 있다면, 그건 아마 정지되어 있는… 사물에 대한 묘사라는 점일 거라고 생각합니다, 그렇죠? 그릇에 담은 과일, 화병이 꽂힌 꽃, 쌓여 있는 책이 그렇습니다. 하지만 오늘은, 정물화로 혁신을 일으키고 있는 몇몇 현대 미술가들을 살펴볼 예정입니다. 실제로, 이 미술가들 중 일부는 심지어 정지 상태에서 벗어난 정물화 작업을 하고 있습니다!

　자, 정물화가 현대 미술계에서 드물기는 하지만, 일부 미술가들은 현대의 관람객들을 위해 정물화를 새롭게 만들기 위한 방법을 찾고 있죠. 예를 들어, 역사적으로 우리는 정물화를 그림으로 생각하고 있습니다. 하지만 점점 더 많은 미술가들이 사진과 디지털 아트, 그리고 심지어 애니메이션 같은 물감이 아닌 수단을 활용하고 있습니다.

　자, 애니메이션이 정물화를 위한 수단일 가능성이 있을 것 같지 않지만, 부부가 된 현대 미술가들이 이를 이용하고 있습니다. 이들이 해 온 것은 정물화 미술가 암브로시우스 보스샤르트 1세의 그림을 정확한 복제품으로 만드는 것입니다. 보스샤르트는 희귀하고 이국적인 꽃들을 담은 정물화로 알려진 17세기 네덜란드 미술가였습니다. 여기, 이 작품을 한번 보세요. 이 작품이 처음 그려졌을 당시, 네덜란드에서는 꽃, 특히 튤립에 대한 전국적인 강박 관념이 존재했고, 튤립은 그 당시가 되어서야 터키에서 수입되기 시작했기 때문에 여전히 이국적인 것으로 여겨졌습니다. 하지만 보스샤르트는 단 하나의 눈부신 꽃다발에 함께 담긴 많은 희귀하고 비싼 꽃들을 그리는 것을 주로 전문으로 했습니다. 이 꽃들이 현실에서 함께 모여 있을 수 있는지는 그에게 상관없었는데, 흔히 그럴 수 없었고, 그 이유는 이 꽃들이 일 년 중 서로 다른 시기에 꽃을 피웠기 때문이었죠. 하지만 누가 신경이나 쓸까요? 이 상상의 꽃다발은 훌륭한 그림이 되었습니다. 자, 그래서 부부 현대 미술가인 롭 카터와 닉 카터는 최근 이 특정 그림을 복제하기로 결정했습니다.

The Carters worked with a crew of animators to make a three-hour digitalized film that brings the painting to life. When you see their piece in an art gallery, you actually watch it on a computer screen that's been placed in a wooden frame like a painting would be. And if you watch closely, you'll realize that ever so slowly, elements of the composition change. Clouds pass by. Caterpillars eat the leaves of the flowers. The light changes from dawn to daylight, to evening to nighttime. During the dark of night, the video loops and starts back over.

It's interesting; we know that a viewer at an art gallery will look at an artwork for an average of about six seconds. One of the things the artists said about creating this piece was that they really wanted people to... slow down and look. And it seems to have worked. When you're at a gallery with one of these animated paintings, you'll see people watching it for a long time. They want to catch something changing in the picture. Kids, even, will watch for a long time.

A moving still life may seem nontraditional, but the artists have created quite a lot of continuity with the original painting. Bosschaert—because of the flowers he wanted in his compositions—employed hundreds of people in his studio to observe and draw flowers at all different times of year. They drew them at different times of day, from different angles... And then Bosschaert would work from their sketches to produce his paintings. He was meticulous about realism. Same with the Carters. They took lots of video of real flowers—in different lighting, opening and closing—and then they employed 25 animators to watch these videos and digitally paint each flower in a way that's true to life. Their animated video took several years to produce, but it really preserves Bosschaert's emphasis on realism.

Now, of course, there are some... issues introduced into the work because it's animated. I mentioned caterpillars eating the leaves, but . . . like I said, the video loops. So... what do you do about these chewed-up leaves? The artists had to be kind of clever about it. At the end of the video, during the nighttime period, the wind begins to blow. The leaves turn horizontal in the wind, so you're looking at them from the side and can't see the holes. When the wind stops and the leaves return to their original positions, the caterpillars' holes have been refilled.

카터 부부는 애니메이션 작가 한 팀과 협업해 세 시간 길이의 디지털화된 영화를 만들면서 그 그림에 생명을 불어 넣었습니다. 미술관에서 이들의 작품을 볼 때, 실제로 그림 같은 느낌의 나무 액자에 담긴 컴퓨터 스크린을 통해 관람합니다. 그리고 자세히 지켜보면, 굉장히 느리게, 그 작품의 요소들이 변한다는 사실을 알게 될 겁니다. 구름이 지나갑니다. 애벌레들은 꽃에서 잎을 먹습니다. 빛은 새벽에서 한낮으로, 그리고 저녁에서 밤 시간으로 바뀝니다. 어두운 밤 시간에, 이 영상이 반복되면서 다시 시작됩니다.

흥미롭게도, 우리는 미술관의 관람객이 평균 약 6초 동안 미술 작품을 보게 된다는 사실을 알고 있습니다. 이 미술가들이 이 작품을 만든 것과 관련해 한 말들 중 한 가지는 이들이 정말로 사람들에게… 느긋함을 갖고 보기를 원했다는 점이었습니다. 그리고 효과가 있었던 것으로 보입니다. 이 애니메이션 그림들 중 하나가 있는 미술관에 가면, 사람들이 오랫동안 지켜 보는 것을 보게 됩니다. 사람들은 그 그림 속에서 변화하는 뭔가를 포착해 내고 싶어 합니다. 심지어 아이들조차 오랫동안 지켜봅니다.

움직이는 정물화가 비전통적인 것처럼 보일 수 있지만, 이 미술가들은 원작 그림에 대해 상당히 많은 연속성을 만들어 냈습니다. 보스샤르트는, 자신의 작품에 담기를 원했던 꽃들 때문에, 일 년 중 모든 다른 시기에 꽃들을 관찰하고 그리기 위해 자신의 작업실에 수백 명의 사람들을 고용했습니다. 이들은 하루 중 서로 다른 시간에, 서로 다른 각도로 그렸죠… 그리고 그 후에 보스샤르트는 그 스케치를 통해 작업하면서 그림을 만들어 냈습니다. 그는 사실주의에 대해 세심했습니다. 카터 부부도 마찬가지입니다. 실제 꽃들이 다른 조명에 비친 모습, 피고 지는 모습을 영상으로 많이 촬영했으며, 그 후에 이 영상들을 보고 디지털로 각각의 꽃을 사실적인 방식으로 그리기 위해 25명의 애니메이션 작가를 고용했습니다. 이들의 애니메이션 영상은 제작하는 데 몇 년이나 소요됐지만, 보스샤르트가 강조한 사실주의를 정말로 유지하고 있습니다.

자, 물론, 애니메이션으로 만들어진 것이기 때문에 이 작품에 포함된 몇 가지… 문제들이 존재합니다. 잎을 먹는 애벌레들을 언급했는데… 말했듯이, 이 영상은 반복됩니다. 그래서… 이 씹어 먹은 잎들에 대해 어떻게 할까요? 이 미술가들은 이 부분과 관련해 좀 기발해야 했습니다. 영상 마지막 부분인, 밤 시간에, 바람이 불기 시작합니다. 이 잎들은 바람이 불 때 수평 상태가 되기 때문에, 측면에서 잎들을 보게 되어 구멍들을 확인할 수 없습니다. 바람이 멈추고 잎들이 원래의 위치로 돌아가면, 애벌레들이 만든 구멍들이 다시 채워진 상태가 되죠.

Now, all of this might offend purists who would argue that the Carters have ruined Bosschaert's work by animating it. But for me the artists' thorough, careful treatment of Bosschaert's painting ultimately draws attention to the mastery of the original.

자, 이 모든 게 카터 부부가 애니메이션으로 만들면서 보스샤르트의 작품을 망쳐 놓았다고 주장할 순수주의자들에겐 불쾌할지도 모릅니다. 하지만 내가 볼 때, 보스샤르트의 그림에 대한 이 미술가들의 철저하고 신중한 처리로 인해 궁극적으로 원작이 얼마나 뛰어난 수준인지에 관심이 집중됩니다.

어휘

still life 정물화   assume 추정하다   depiction 묘사   innovate 혁신을 일으키다   contemporary 현대의, 동시대의   employ 활용하다   medium 수단, 매체   replica 복제물   exotic 이국적인   obsession 강박 관념   specialize in ~을 전문으로 하다   dazzling 눈부신   irrelevant 상관없는   assemble 모으다   bloom 꽃을 피우다   reproduce 복제하다   element 요소   composition (그림, 음악 등의) 작품   caterpillar 애벌레   loop 반복되다   catch 포착하다   nontraditional 비전통적인   continuity 연속성   observe 관찰하다   meticulous 세심한   preserve 유지하다, 보존하다   emphasis 강조   introduced into ~에 들어가 있는   chew up 씹어 먹다   horizontal 수평의   refill 다시 채우다   offend 불쾌하게 하다   ruin 망치다   thorough 철저한   treatment 처리, 다룸   ultimately 궁극적으로   draw attention to ~에 관심이 집중되다   mastery 통달, 숙달

23. 강의는 주로 무엇에 관한 것인가?

Ⓐ 한 네덜란드 화가가 정물화를 그리는 방법

Ⓑ 정물화가 현대 미술에 드문 이유에 관한 이론

Ⓒ 한 오래된 그림의 새로운 발견

Ⓓ 한 가지 전통 미술 양식에 대한 새로운 접근 방식

내용의 요점을 묻는 문제

어휘 method 방법　discovery 발견　approach 접근하다　traditional 전통적인

해설 전통 미술 양식에 속한 정물화가 현대의 관람객들을 위해 새롭게 변모하게 된 한 가지 방식을 주로 이야기하고 있으므로 D가 정답이다.

24. 교수의 말에 따르면, 보스샤르트의 그림에 있는 일부 꽃다발이 왜 현실에서는 존재할 수 없었을 것인가?

Ⓐ 그 꽃들이 전 세계 여러 지역에 폭넓게 분리되어 자란다.

Ⓑ 그 꽃들 중 일부가 너무 독성이 강해서 꺾을 수 없다.

Ⓒ 그 꽃들이 일 년 중 여러 다른 시기에 핀다.

Ⓓ 그렇게 이국적인 꽃다발의 가격은 엄두도 못 낼 정도였을 것이다.

세부 정보 찾기 문제

어휘 separated 분리된　region 지역　toxic 독성이 있는　pick (꽃을) 꺾다　bloom 꽃을 피우다　prohibitive 엄두도 못 낼 정도인

해설 보스샤르트의 그림에 있는 꽃들이 일 년 중 서로 다른 시기에 꽃을 피웠기 때문에 실제 꽃다발로 존재할 수 없었을 것임을 이야기하고 있으므로 C가 정답이다.

25. 교수가 왜 사람들이 한 미술 작품을 보는 평균 시간 길이를 언급하는가?

Ⓐ 작품을 만드는 데 있어 카터 부부의 목표들 중 하나를 소개하기 위해

Ⓑ 카터 부부의 작품이 지닌 기술적 문제를 설명하기 위해

Ⓒ 정물화에 대한 개념이 시간에 따라 어떻게 변화되었는지 설명하기 위해

Ⓓ 아이들이 카터 부부의 작품을 좋아하는 여러 이유를 소개하기 위해

구성 파악 문제

어휘 piece (그림, 글 등의) 작품

해설 관람객이 평균 약 6초 동안 미술 작품을 보게 된다는 사실과 함께 카터 부부가 정말로 사람들에게 원했던 것을 언급하면서 그 효과가 있었던 것으로 보인다고 이야기하고 있다. 이는 작품을 보는 시간이 카터 부부가 사람들을 위해 작품을 만든 목표와 관련되어 있다는 것을 의미하므로 A가 정답이다.

26. 교수는 왜 카터 부부가 실제 꽃에 대한 영상 기록을 만들었다는 점을 언급하는가?

Ⓐ 두 사람의 예술적 기교와 보스샤르트의 것 사이에 존재하는 유사성을 강조하기 위해

Ⓑ 기술이 예술적 능력에 대한 대체물로 쓰일 수 없다는 점을 강조하기 위해

Ⓒ 카터 부부의 작품이 정물화로 여겨지지 말아야 한다고 주장하기 위해

Ⓓ 기술이 어떻게 예술적 과정을 향상시키는 데 쓰일 수 있는지 알려 주기 위해

구성 파악 문제

어휘 emphasize 강조하다　similarity 유사성　substitute 대체(물)　be considered A A로 여겨지다　improve 향상시키다

해설 보스샤르트가 그림을 사실적으로 만들기 위해 활용한 방법 및 다른 미술가들과의 협업한 사실을 언급한 다음, 마찬가지로 카터 부부도 사실적인 작품을 위해 실제 꽃 영상을 많이 촬영한 점과 다른 애니메이션 작가들과 협업한 사실을 이야기하고 있다. 이는 보스샤르트와 카터 부부 사이의 유사성을 말하는 것이므로 A가 정답이다.

27. 교수의 말에 따르면, 왜 애니메이션 영상에서 돌풍이 불었는가?

Ⓐ 영상을 더 현실적으로 보이게 만들기 위해

Ⓑ 관람객이 반드시 영상의 마지막까지 관심을 잃지 않도록 하기 위해

Ⓒ 영상의 마지막에서 처음으로 더 매끄러운 전환을 가능하게 하기 위해

Ⓓ 자연의 파괴적인 힘을 상징하기 위해

세부 정보 찾기 문제

어휘 ensure that 반드시 ~하도록 하다　smooth 매끄러운　transition 전환　symbolize 상징하다

해설 영상이 반복되는 특성상, 다시 처음으로 돌아갈 때 애벌레들이 이미 먹은 부분을 원래의 상태로 돌려 놓기 위한 방법으로 바람을 이용한다고 설명하고 있으므로 C가 정답이다.

28. 카터 부부가 보스샤르트의 작품을 다루는 방식에 대한 교수의 의견은 어떠한가?

Ⓐ 화가로서 보스샤르트의 명예를 훼손하고 있다.

Ⓑ 원작 그림의 수준을 강조하고 있다.

Ⓒ 정물화에 대한 익숙함 부족 문제를 보여 준다.

Ⓓ 정물화를 애니메이션화하려는 다른 시도들보다 우수하다.

태도 파악 문제

어휘 reputation 명예, 명성　demonstrate 보여 주다　familiarity 익숙함　superior to ~보다 더 우수한　attempt 시도

해설 카터 부부가 철저하고 신중하게 보스샤르트의 그림을 다룬 것이 원작의 탁월한 수준에 관심을 집중시켰다고 언급하고 있다. 이는 원작의 수준을 강조하는 방식이 되었으므로 B가 정답이다.

Reading

Listening

Speaking

Writing

Test 1

Test 2

Test 3

Test 4

SPEAKING

T-65

| Question 1 | p. 248 |

Narrator

Some students prefer to work on class assignments by themselves. Others believe it is better to work in a group. Which do you prefer? Explain why.

과제를 혼자서 해결하기를 좋아하는 학생들도 있지만, 여럿이 모여 하는 쪽을 더 좋아하는 학생들도 있다. 어느 쪽을 선호하는가? 그 이유도 같이 설명하시오.

준비 시간 : 15초
답변 시간 : 45초

중요 포인트

수업 과제를 여럿이 모여서 함께 하기를 좋아하는지, 아니면 혼자 해결하는 편인지, 본인의 성향을 밝히고 이어서 그 이유도 설명해야 한다. "I prefer to work in groups because it is more interesting plus many people help and also you can learn from other people... (친구들과 모여서 하는 것을 더 좋아하는 편인데, 왜냐하면 그쪽이 더 재미가 있고, 사람들이 많으면 도움도 되는 데다가, 다른 친구들한테서 배우는 것들도 있으니까…)"처럼 여러 가지 이유들을 단순히 나열하는 것은 별로 바람직하지 않다. 그보다는 한두 가지 이유를 제대로 설명하는 편이 더 낫다. 예를 들어, 모여서 하는 쪽을 더 좋아한다면, 이런 식으로 답변할 수도 있다: "I prefer working in groups because usually in group work, different people know different things about the topic, and because of that, you get a deeper understanding of the assignment. For example, there was a student from Venezuela in a group assignment I had, and we were supposed to describe how crude oil prices are set. She helped us understand problems in oil production in a much deeper way because her parents worked in oil production..." ("친구들과 모여서 하는 쪽을 더 좋아하는데, 왜냐하면, 대개 공동 작업의 경우에는 사람들마다 제각기 주제에 대해 다른 지식을 갖고 있으므로, 과제를 좀 더 깊이 있게 파악할 수 있죠. 한 예를 들면, 베네수엘라에서 온 학생과 같이 공동 과제를 수행한 적이 있는데, 원유 가격이 어떻게 결정되는지를 설명해야 하는 과제였죠. 마침 그 친구 부모님이 석유 생산 회사에 근무하시는 분들이라, 석유 생산에 관련된 문제들을 이해하는 데 그 친구가 도움이 됐죠…")

우수 답변 T-70

If I work on a class assignment, I prefer to work on myself better to work in a group, uh, simply because I like to do things the way I see them. Uh, for example, sometimes I've got very particular opinions on—on a topic, and I really want to express them. If I'm work in a group I have to adjust to other people's opinions. Um, and I can monitor my t- my time on my own. I'm quite good at that and like to have a very structured approach to things and finish things at certain times. If I always have to rely on other people in a group, things might not be finished in time. I want them to be finished so I prefer to work on my own.

채점자 의견

상당히 우수한 수준의 답변이다. 혼자서 하는 쪽을 더 좋아하는 근거 – 자신의 의견을 확실하게 피력할 수 있고, 시간 관리에도 더 유리하다 – 두 가지를 든 다음, 왜 그러한지를 명확히 설명했다. 답변도 유창하며, 억양이나 강세도 적절하여('I see them'에서 'I'를 강하게 발음한 경우 등) 의미가 분명하게 전달되고 있다. 또한 'structured approach'처럼 상당히 수준 높은 표현과 문장들을 무리 없이 구사하고 있다.

하위 수준의 답변 T-71

Um, both of this assignments have their (pause) good things. So first of all, in the group, you have different ideas and everybody knows something else from the topic, and, you can... um... um... yes. (pause) Um, another point is that you have more time for other things and you don't have to do everything by your own. But, alone, it's better, you are independent, and you can... um...

채점자 의견

발음은 그런대로 분명한 편이지만, 'advantages'나 'benefits' 등으로 표현해야 할 곳에서 그냥 'good things'라고 얼버무리고 넘어가는 등, 적절한 어휘를 찾지 못해 의미를 제대로 전달하지 못한 부분들이 많다. 또한 과제를 공동으로 할 경우와 혼자서 하는 경우의 장점들을 모두 설명하느라 시간을 너무 소비한 탓에, 혼자서 하는 쪽이 낫다는 본인의 의견을 제대로 설명하지 못하고 그저 독립성이 더 보장된다는 간단한 설명으로만 그쳤다. 전체적으로 산만하고 미흡한 부분이 많은 답변이며, 문장 구사력도 아주 기초적인 수준을 넘지 못하고 있다.

Question 2
p. 248

Narrator

The university's Dining Services Department has announced a change. Read an announcement about this change. You will have 45 seconds to read the announcement. Begin reading now.

대학 구내식당이 변경 사항을 공지하고 있다. 이 변경 공고문을 45초 동안 읽으시오. 지금 읽으시오.

Hot Breakfasts Eliminated

Beginning next month, Dining Services will no longer serve hot breakfast foods at university dining halls. Instead, students will be offered a wide assortment of cold breakfast items in the morning. These cold breakfast foods, such as breads, fruit, and yogurt, are healthier than many of the hot breakfast items that we will stop serving, so health-conscious students should welcome this change. Students will benefit in another way as well, because limiting the breakfast selection to cold food items will save money and allow us to keep our meal plans affordable.

아침 시간 주문 조리 메뉴 철시

다음 달부터, 대학 구내식당에서는 아침 메뉴로 따뜻한 요리를 더 이상 제공하지 않을 예정입니다. 대신, 학생들에게 다양한 종류의 차가운 메뉴들을 제공할 것입니다. 빵, 과일, 요구르트 같은 차가운 아침 메뉴들은 철시 예정인 여러 뜨거운 아침 메뉴들보다 건강에 더 좋으므로 건강에 신경 쓰는 학생들은 이번 메뉴 변경을 환영할 것입니다. 또한 아침 식사 메뉴를 차가운 음식들로 국한하면 비용이 절약되고 식대 또한 계속 저렴하게 유지될 수 있으므로, 학생들에게 또 다른 혜택이 될 것입니다.

어휘

eliminate 없애다, 배제하다   hot food (주문을 받고 조리해서 나오는) 따뜻한 음식   dining hall 식당   wide assortment of 다양하게 갖춰 놓은   cold food (미리 만들어 두어 별도의 조리가 필요 없는) 상온 음식   health-conscious 건강에 신경 쓰는   benefit 혜택을 받다   selection 선택 가능한 것들(의 집합)   affordable (가격, 비용 등이) 감당할 수 있는

Narrator

Now listen to two students discussing the announcement.

이 공고문에 대해 두 학생이 나누는 대화를 들으시오.

W Do you believe any of this? It's ridiculous.

M What do you mean? It is important to eat healthy foods...

W Sure it is, but they're saying yogurt's better for you than an omelet... or than hot cereal? I mean whether something's hot or cold, that shouldn't be the issue. Except maybe on a really cold morning, but in that case, which is going to be better for you—a bowl of cold cereal or a nice warm omelet? It's obvious; there's no question.

M I'm not going to argue with you there.

W And this whole thing about saving money...

M What about it?

W Well, they're actually going to make things worse for us, not better. 'Cause if they start cutting back and we can't get what we want right here, on campus, well, we're going to be going off campus and pay off-campus prices, and you know what? That will be expensive. Even if it's only two or three mornings a week, it can add up.

여 이게 하나라도 말이 되는 소리야? 정말 터무니없어.

남 무슨 말이야? 건강한 음식을 먹는 건 중요해…

여 그야 그렇지. 하지만 요구르트가 오믈렛이나… 죽보다 건강에 더 좋다는 소리잖아! 내 말은 뜨겁든, 차갑든, 그건 문제가 아니야. 아주 추운 아침만 아니라면 말이야. 하지만 그런 날이라면, 차가운 시리얼, 그리고 따끈따끈하고 맛있는 오믈렛, 둘 중에 어떤 게 더 좋겠니? 분명하잖아, 두말하면 잔소리지.

남 그 문제라면 나도 할 말이 없네.

여 그리고 비용이 절약된다는 이 말은…

남 그게 뭐 어때서?

여 실은 우리에게 좋은 게 아니라 더 나빠지는 꼴이거든. 메뉴가 줄어들면, 우리가 먹고 싶은 음식을 여기 캠퍼스 내에서 구하지 못하는 경우가 생길 테고, 그러면, 결국 캠퍼스 바깥까지 나가서 일반 가격으로 사 먹겠지. 너도 알지? 아무래도 비쌀 거잖아. 일주일에 두세 번만 그렇게 해도 지출이 늘게 돼.

어휘

ridiculous 말도 안 되는, 터무니없는   hot cereal (곡물) 죽   issue (논의의) 주제, 쟁점   there's no question 의심의 여지가 없다   cut back (규모 등을) 줄이다, 축소하다   off-campus price (구내 할인가격이 아닌) 일반 시중 가격   add up (조금씩) 늘어나다

Narrator

The woman expresses her opinion of the change that has been announced. State her opinion and explain her reasons for holding that opinion.

여학생이 변경 공지에 대한 의견을 피력하고 있다. 그녀의 의견이 무엇인지, 그리고 그렇게 생각하는 근거로 언급한 내용들을 설명하시오.

준비 시간 : 30초
답변 시간 : 60초

중요 포인트

구내식당이 아침에는 더 이상 따뜻한 메뉴를 내지 않겠다는 것은 잘못이라고 여학생이 주장하고 있다. 그리고 건강 문제라면 음식의 온도는 문제가 아니라고 했다(따뜻한 음식이 더 나은 추운 날이 아니라면). 또한 학생들이 먹고 싶은 음식을 구내식당에서 먹지 못하게 되면, 학교 밖까지 나가 더 비싼 값을 치르고 먹을 수밖에 없으므로 아침 식사 비용이 절약되기는커녕 오히려 늘어날 것이라고 주장했다.

우수 답변 🎧 T-72

The woman has the opinion that, uh, the whole new food change is pretty ridiculous because she thinks it's no issue if the food is hot or cold in concern of what is healthy or not, because she says on a cold day it's much better to eat something, uh, warm like a soup or an omelet, instead of yogurt or bread or olives and fruit because when it's cold, you could get sick. And um, she also thinks that there is no chance of saving money in this new program, in this new dining service change, because she will go off-campus and other students too will go off-campus to get food that they like, and that will become more expensive than if they would just stay on the campus and eat the food they would get there. So she's — she has the opinion that the dining change is pretty ridiculous because she would like warm food.

채점자 의견

공고문과 대화에서 언급된 중요 사항들을 하나도 빠짐없이, 매우 분명하고 자세하게 설명한 답변이다. 발음도 매우 분명하고, 말하는 속도나 억양도 적절하다. 다양한 어휘와 관용어구들을 구사하여, 본인의 생각을 명확히 표현하고 있다.

중간 수준의 답변 🎧 T-73

First of all, she thinks that if food is healthy or not doesn't depend on if it's cold or warm. Then... she says the difficulty is if the university stops serving hot food in the morning, and... it is like... and the offer is their last offer for choosing breakfast, and if you — if it's a cold morning and you come to university and wanna eat something hot, you wanna e- you wanna warm up, and there's nothing wa — no warm food to eat, it's... that is horrible, so when... might (sigh) be not able to get used to it. And the last thing re — she refers to is about the money, that it's very expensive then to go out, to eat off campus and buy hot food.

채점자 의견

공고문 내용이 불만스러운 여학생의 입장을 상당히 잘 설명하긴 했으나, 결코 매끄럽지는 못한 답변이다. 적합한 어휘나 표현을 생각하느라 말이 끊기는 때가 많고, 어휘 지식의 부족으로 생각을 명확하게 표현하지 못하는 경우도 보인다. (예: 'the offer is their last offer for choosing'이라는 표현은 무슨 뜻인지 의미가 분명치 않다.) 발음은 대체로 알아듣기 쉬운 편이지만, 주의 깊게 듣지 않으면 알아듣기 힘든 경우도 가끔 있다.

Question 3   p. 250

Narrator

Read the passage from a sociology textbook. You have 50 seconds to read the passage. Begin reading now.

사회학 교재의 한 부분을 50초 동안 읽으시오. 지금 읽으시오.

Cognitive Dissonance

Individuals sometimes experience a contradiction between their actions and their beliefs — between what they are doing and what they believe they should be doing. These contradictions can cause a kind of mental discomfort known as *cognitive dissonance*. People experiencing cognitive dissonance often do not want to change the way they are acting, so they resolve the contradictory situation in another way: they change their interpretation of the situation in a way that minimizes the contradiction between what they are doing and what they believe they should be doing.

인지 부조화

사람들은 가끔 자신의 생각과 행동 사이의 모순을 경험한다. 즉 자신이 하고 있는 행동과, 어떻게 행동해야 한다고 믿는 바가 서로 어긋나는 현상이다. 이러한 모순은 '인지 부조화'라고 하는 일종의 정신적 불안을 유발한다. 인지 부조화를 겪는 사람들은 행동 방식을 바꾸려고 하지 않고, 대신 다른 방법으로 모순된 상황을 해결하곤 한다. 즉 실제 행동과 해야 한다고 믿는 행동 간의 모순을 최소화하는 방식으로 그 상황에 대한 해석을 바꾸는 것이다.

어휘

sociology 사회학   cognitive dissonance 인지 부조화(자신의 행동과 신념이 서로 모순될 경우 행동보다는 관점을 바꿔 불편함을 덜려고 한다는 이론)   contradiction 모순   cause 유발하다   mental discomfort 정신적 불안   resolve (문제 등을) 해결[해소]하다   interpretation 이해, 해석[판단]   in a way that ~하는 식으로   minimize 최소화하다, 축소하다

Narrator

Now listen to part of a lecture about this topic in a sociology class.

이 주제를 다루는 사회학 강의 내용의 일부를 들으시오.

Professor This is a true story — from my own life. In my first year in high school, I was addicted to video games. I played them all the time, and I wasn't studying enough — I was failing chemistry; that was my hardest class. So this was a conflict for me because I wanted a good job when I grew up, and I believed — I knew — that if you want a good career, you gotta do well in school. But... I just couldn't give up video games.

I was completely torn. And my solution was to... to change my perspective. See, the only class I was doing really badly in was chemistry. In the others I was, I was okay. So I asked myself if I wanted to be a chemist when I grew up, and the fact is I didn't. I was pretty sure I wanted to be a sociologist. So... I told myself my chemistry class didn't matter because sociologists don't really need to know chemistry. In other words, I changed my understanding of what it meant to do well in school. I reinterpreted my situation: I used to think that doing well in school meant doing well in all my classes, but now I decided that succeeding in school meant only doing well in the classes that related directly to my future career.

I eliminated the conflict, at least in my mind.

교수 이건 제가 실제 겪었던 경험담입니다. 고등학교 1학년 때, 저는 비디오 게임에 푹 빠져 있었죠. 항상 게임을 했고, 공부는 제대로 하지 않았습니다. 저는 화학 과목에서 낙제를 하게 될 지경에 처했죠. 제겐 가장 어려운 과목이었으니까요. 그래서 전 갈등했죠. 커서 훌륭한 직장에 취직하고 싶었고, 그리고 사회에서 성공하려면 학업 성적이 좋아야 한다고 생각했으니까요. 하지만… 비디오 게임은 도저히 끊을 수가 없었죠.

정말 갈피를 잡을 수가 없었습니다. 그래서 제 해결책은… 관점을 바꾸는 것이었죠. 자, 정말로 성적이 안 좋은 건 화학 과목뿐이잖아. 다른 과목은, 그래, 그런대로 괜찮잖아. 그래서 저는 커서 화학자가 되고 싶은지 자문해 봤습니다. 사실 아니었죠. 반드시 사회학자가 되고 싶었으니까요. 그래서… 스스로에게 말했죠, 사회학자에겐 화학 지식이 꼭 필요한 게 아니니까, 결국 화학 과목은 크게 중요하지 않다고 말이죠. 달리 말하면, 학업 성적이 좋아야 한다는 데 대한 해석을 바꾼 거죠. 상황을 재해석한 것입니다. 즉, 예전에는 공부를 잘한다는 것이 모든 과목의 성적이 우수하다는 의미라고 생각했지만, 이젠, 장래의 직업과 직접 상관이 있는 과목만 잘하면 된다는 의미라고 판단한 겁니다.

적어도 마음속의 갈등은 해소된 셈이었죠.

be addicted to ~에 빠지다, 중독되다 **fail** 시험에 떨어지다, 낙제하다 **conflict** 갈등 **career** 직장, 사회 생활 **give up** 포기하다, (나쁜 습관 등을) 버리다 **be torn** 갈피를 잡지 못하다, 어쩔 줄 모르다 **perspective** 관점, 시각 **matter** 중요하다, 문제되다 **in other words** 다시 말해서, 바꿔 말하면 **reinterpret** 재해석하다, 다른 식으로 보다 **situation** 상황, 처지

Narrator

Using the example discussed by the professor, explain what cognitive dissonance is and how people often deal with it.

교수가 말한 사례를 활용하여, 인지 부조화가 무엇이며, 사람들은 그 문제를 대개 어떤 식으로 해결하는지 설명하시오.

준비 시간 : 30초
답변 시간 : 60초

중요 포인트

인지 부조화는 생각과 행동이 서로 일치하지 않는 현상이다. 사람들은 이러한 인지 부조화를 해결하기 위해, 상황을 바라보는 관점을 바꾸는 쪽을 택하곤 한다. 그 예로, 교수는 고교 시절에 화학 과목에 낙제하게 된다는 걸 알면서도 비디오 게임을 끊지 못했다. 그래서, 자신의 꿈은 사회학자가 되는 것이니까, 화학 성적은 굳이 좋을 필요가 없다는 식으로 생각을 바꾸어 자기 행동을 합리화했다.

우수 답변 🎧 T-74

Cognitive dissonance (clears throat) is a conflict between your actions and your beliefs. The co-consequence of this conflict you, uh, don't change, uh, your actions, but you just change your interpretation of your situation. For example, the lecturer of socio-sociology was addicted to video games in his first, uh, university year, um, and he was bad at chemistry. And sh- he just couldn't give up playing video games so he, uh, said to himself, well, why do I need chemistry? I am going to be a sociologist. I am quite bad at chemistry, but it doesn't matter! I just change the perspective and reinterpret the situation and so everything is okay, and my future is safe.

채점자 의견

인지 부조화의 개념은 물론, 교수의 경험담처럼 사람들이 인지 부조화를 해소하는 방식을 정확하고 효과적으로 설명한 답변이다. 답변도 매끄러울 뿐 아니라, 억양이나 강세도 적절하여 강조하고자 하는 의미를 정확히 전달하고 있다. 예를 들면, 'actions'와 'interpretation'에 강세를 두어 강조하는 식으로, 사람들이 인지 부조화 현상을 어떻게 해결하는지 (행동을 바꾸기보다 상황을 보는 관점을 바꾸는 방식)를 명확히 밝히고 있다. 또한 고급 수준의 어휘를 정확하고 능숙하게 구사하고 있다.

중간 수준의 답변 🎧 T-75

Cognitive dissonance is when there's a contradiction between actions that people do and their belief. Um, so for example, if, um, someone is addicted to video games, but he can't stop it, although he's writing really bad marks at school, and he just can't stop it, then he begins to make up his own opinion, for example that he says that, um, his bad marks in chemistry are not that, um, bad for him because he doesn't' want to do anything with chemistry later in life, and so it doesn't really matter what his marks are like... and (sigh)...

채점자 의견

문제에서 요구한 내용을 그런대로 적절히 설명한 편이지만, 내용이 정확하지 못한 부분도 있다. 한 예로, 교수의 경험담을 설명하는 대목에서, 상황을 달리 해석(interpretation)했다고 표현하는 대신에, '독자적인 생각을 꾸며내기(make up his own opinion)' 시작했다고 표현한 부분을 들 수 있다. 발음은 비교적 분명하지만 중간에 말이 끊기거나 머뭇거리는 곳들이 많은 편이다.

| Question 4 | p. 251 |

Narrator

Now listen to part of a lecture in a psychology class. The professor is discussing advertising strategies.

이제 심리학 강의의 일부를 들으시오. 교수는 광고 전략에 대해 강의하고 있다.

Professor In advertising, various strategies are used to persuade people to buy products. In order to sell more products, advertisers will often try to make us believe that a product will meet our needs or desires perfectly... even if it's not true. The strategies they use can be subtle, uh, "friendly" forms of persuasion that are sometimes hard to recognize.

In a lot of ads, repetition is a key strategy. Research shows that repeated exposure to a message, even something meaningless or untrue, is enough to make people accept it or see it in a positive light. You've all seen the car commercials on TV... like... uh, the one that refers to its "roomy" cars... over and over again. You know which one I mean... this guy is driving around and he keeps stopping to pick up different people—he picks up 3 or 4 people. And each time, the narrator says, "Plenty of room for friends, plenty of room for family, plenty of room for everybody." The same message is repeated several times in the course of the commercial. Now, the car, uh, the car actually looks kind of small... it's not a very big car at all, but you get the sense that it's pretty spacious. You'd think that the viewer would reach the logical conclusion that the slogan, uh, misrepresents the product. Instead, what usually happens is that when the statement "plenty of room" is repeated often enough, people are actually convinced it's true.

Um, another strategy they use is to get a celebrity to advertise a product. It turns out that we're more likely to accept an advertising claim made by somebody famous—a person we admire and find appealing. We tend to think they're trustworthy. So... um, you might have a car commercial that features a well-known race car driver. Now, it may not be a very fast car—uh, it could even be an inexpensive vehicle with a low performance rating. But if a popular race car driver is shown driving it, and saying, "I like my cars fast!" then people will believe the car is impressive for its speed.

교수 광고에는, 사람들의 구매를 유도하기 위한 다양한 전략들이 동원되죠. 상품을 더 많이 팔기 위해, 광고업자들은 흔히 이 상품이 우리의 필요나 열망에 딱 맞는 상품이라고 소비자들이 곧이듣게끔 하려고 애쓰죠… 그게 사실이 아니더라도 말이죠. 이들이 쓰는 수법들은 교묘한, 그러니까, 정말 알아채기 힘들 정도로 '친근한' 설득의 형태가 될 수도 있습니다.

수많은 광고에서 '반복'이 핵심 전략입니다. 연구 결과에 따르면, 사람들이 어떤 메시지를 반복하여 계속 접하게 되면, 설령 별 뜻이 없거나 사실이 아닌 말이라도, 수긍하거나 긍정적으로 받아들이게 된다고 합니다. 여러분들 모두 자동차 TV 광고를 본 적이 있죠… 그러니까… 음, "실내 공간이 넓다"고 선전하죠… 거듭 반복해서 말이죠. 어떤 광고를 말하는지 알겠죠… 출연자가 차를 몰고 여기저기 돌아다니며 계속 차를 멈추고 사람들을 태웁니다. 서너 명을 태우죠. 그리고 그렇게 사람을 태울 때마다, "친구들을 태우기에 넉넉한 실내 공간, 가족을 태우기에 넉넉한 실내 공간, 누구에게나 넉넉한 실내 공간"이라는 소개말이 흐르죠. 광고 도중에 동일한 메시지가 몇 차례 반복됩니다. 자, 그런데 이 차는, 음, 사실상 좀 작아 보입니다… 아주 큰 차는 결코 아닙니다, 하지만 그래도 실내 공간은 꽤 넓다는 느낌을 받게 되죠. 시청자가 저런 선전문구는 상품의 진실을 왜곡한다는 생각을 당연히 할 것 같지만, 대개의 경우는, "실내 공간이 넓다"는 말을 충분히 반복하면, 사람들은 그 말이 사실이라고 믿게 됩니다.

음, 또 한 가지 전략은 유명인을 내세워 상품을 광고하는 것이죠. 사람들은 자신이 동경하거나 매력적이라고 느끼는 유명 인사가 하는 홍보성 발언을 잘 받아들이는 경향이 있다고 합니다. 믿을 수 있는 사람이라고 생각하기 쉬우니까요. 그래서… 음, 유명한 카 레이서가 등장하는 자동차 광고를 본 적이 있을 거예요. 자, 이 차는 속력이 아주 빠른 차가 아닐 수도 있고, 음, 심지어는 성능이 별로 뛰어나지 않은 저렴한 차일 수도 있습니다. 하지만 유명한 카 레이서가 그 차를 몰면서, "난 빠른 차가 좋아!"라고 말하는 걸 보면, 사람들은 그 차가 속도 하나는 끝내주는 차라고 믿게 되겠죠.

| 어휘 |

advertising 광고(의) strategy 전략, 수법 persuade 설득하다 desire 욕구 subtle 교묘한, 영리한 friendly 친근한 recognize 알아보다, 눈치채다 repeated exposure 계속적인 노출, 반복적인 체험 meaningless 중요하지 않은, 아무 의미가 없는 accept 받아들이다, 인정하다 in a positive light 긍정적인 시각에서 commercial (TV, 라디오의) 광고 refer to ~를 가리키다 roomy 넓은, 널찍한 pick up ~를 (차에) 태우다 in the course of ~ 동안 get the sense 인식을 갖다, 느낌을 받다 spacious (방, 건물 등이) 넓은 viewer 보는 사람, 시청자 logical conclusion 논리적 결론, 당연한 결과 slogan 슬로건, 선전문구 misrepresent 잘못 전하다, 오도하다 convince 설득하다 celebrity 유명 인사 turn out ~인 것으로 드러나다 be likely to ~할 것 같다, ~하기 쉽다 claim 주장, 단언 appealing 매력적인, 마음을 끄는 trustworthy 신뢰할 수 있

는, 믿을 수 있는 feature 출연시키다 inexpensive 비싸지 않은, 저렴한 performance rating 성능 등급[평가] impressive 인상적인, 대단한

Narrator

Using the examples from the talk, explain how persuasive strategies are used in advertising.

강의에서 언급된 사례들을 활용하여, 광고에서 어떤 판촉 전략이 사용되는지 설명하시오.

준비 시간 : 20초
답변 시간 : 60초

중요 포인트

광고업자들은 각종 판촉 전략들을 활용하여 소비자들의 구매를 유도한다. 그런 전략들 중 한 가지는, 메시지를 반복적으로 되풀이하는 방법(내용이 사실이 아닐 수도 있다)인데, 그 예로, 소형차 광고에서 내부 공간이 넓다는 말을 반복해서 강조하는 경우를 들 수 있다. 또 다른 전략 하나는 유명인을 출연시켜 사람들의 신뢰를 얻는 방법이다. 그 예로는, 유명한 카 레이서를 자동차 광고에 출연시키는 경우를 꼽을 수 있다(설령 사실이 아닐지라도, 빠른 차라는 인식을 사람들에게 심어줄 수 있다).

우수 답변 🎧 T-76

The psychology professor presents... two techniques, um, employed in, um, advertising strategy, um meant to subtle — to send subtle messages to the watching customer, and she underlines these, uh, strategies, um, and the techniques employed in them, um, through examples from car advertising. Um, s—technique one that she's referring to is, um, repetition of, um, a certain feature of a car, which might us, cause to — cause to believe that this car actually has this feature, even though, um, we do not obviously, uh, recognize it when seeing the car. Um, and her example cites. The second technique is to use a celebrity, which, um... we might feel, uf — appealing or trustworthy about, um, which, um, can also transmit a feature of a car to use that we would not, um, perceive ourselves.

채점자 의견

강의의 핵심적인 내용과 근거들을 빠짐없이 설명한 답변이다. 비록 'subtle'의 발음이 약간 부정확하지만, 전체적인 내용을 이해하는 데는 전혀 지장이 없으며, 전반적으로 매우 명확하고 매끄러운 답변이다. 말할 내용을 머릿속으로 떠올리느라 답변 속도가 잠시 느려지는 부분들도 있지만, 내용 전달에는 전혀 무리가 없다. 또한 상당히 고급 수준의 어휘와 문장들을 능숙하게 구사하고 있다.

중간 수준의 답변 🎧 T-77

Persuading strategies are used in advertising to improve the reputation. Uh, for example, if one method is repeat it all the time, uh, fi — for example, uh, lots of your friends have space in it, the listener is conwee — convenienced with it. Uh, another strategy is that firm persons, um, are realized that in their advertising because... uh, we trust the famous persons and we know their faces, and so we believe what they are saying. That's all.

채점자 의견

강의에서 언급한 광고 전략 두 가지를 모두 설명하기는 했지만, 표현이 다소 모호하여 뜻이 분명하지 않은 부분들도 있다. 예를 들면, 첫 번째 광고 전략을 소개할 때는 자동차 광고라는 말을 하지 않은 탓에, 'lots of your friends have space in it(친구들 여러 명이 탈 자리가 넉넉하다)'라는 메시지를 반복한다고 하는 말의 의미가 불분명했다. 발음은 알아듣기 쉬운 편이지만, 말이 중간에 끊길 때가 많고 어휘나 문장 구사 능력도 그리 뛰어난 편은 아니다.

WRITING

Integrated Writing   p. 254

Rembrandt is the most famous of the seventeenth-century Dutch painters. However, there are doubts whether some paintings attributed to Rembrandt were actually painted by him. One such painting is known as *Portrait of an Elderly Woman in a White Bonnet*. The painting was attributed to Rembrandt because of its style, and indeed the representation of the woman's face is very much like that of portraits known to be by Rembrandt. But there are problems with the painting that suggest it could not be a work by Rembrandt.

First, there is something inconsistent about the way the woman in the portrait is dressed. She is wearing a white linen cap of a kind that only servants would wear — yet the coat she is wearing has a luxurious fur collar that no servant could afford. Rembrandt, who was known for his attention to the details of his subjects' clothing, would not have been guilty of such an inconsistency.

Second, Rembrandt was a master of painting light and shadow, but in this painting these elements do not fit together. The face appears to be illuminated by light reflected onto it from below. But below the face is the dark fur collar, which would absorb light rather than reflect it. So the face should appear partially in shadow — which is not how it appears. Rembrandt would never have made such an error.

Finally, examination of the back of the painting reveals that it was painted on a panel made of several pieces of wood glued together. Although Rembrandt often painted on wood panels, no painting known to be by Rembrandt uses a panel glued together in this way from several pieces of wood.

For these reasons the painting was removed from the official catalog of Rembrandt's paintings in the 1930s.

렘브란트는 17세기 네덜란드 화가들 중 가장 유명한 인물이다. 하지만, 렘브란트의 작품이라고 생각되는 그림들 가운데 일부는 실제로 그가 그린 것이 아니라는 의혹을 받는 작품들이 있다. 그런 그림들 중 하나가 바로 〈하얀 보닛을 쓴 늙은 여인의 초상〉이라는 작품이다. 이 그림을 렘브란트의 작품으로 여겼던 것은 화풍 때문이었다. 그리고 사실, 여인의 얼굴을 묘사한 기법이 렘브란트의 작품으로 알려진 다른 초상화들과 대단히 흡사하다. 하지만 이 그림이 렘브란트의 작품이 아닐 수도 있음을 시사하는 의문점들이 있다.

첫째, 초상화 속 여인의 차림새에 모순점이 있다. 머리에는 하인들이나 쓰는 흰색 리넨 모자를 쓰고 있는데, 입고 있는 외투에는 하인이라면 엄두도 내지 못할 호화스러운 모피 칼라가 달려 있다. 인물의 의복을 세밀하게 묘사하기로 유명했던 렘브란트가 이렇게 앞뒤 안 맞는 실수를 범했을 리는 만무하다.

둘째, 렘브란트는 빛과 음영 표현의 대가였는데, 이 그림에서는 이런 요소들이 서로 어우러지지 않는다. 여인의 얼굴은 아래쪽으로부터 반사되는 빛을 받아 환히 빛난다. 하지만 얼굴 아래의 짙은 색 모피 칼라는 빛을 받는다기보다는 오히려 빛을 흡수하게 되어 있다. 그렇다면 얼굴에도 일부 그림자가 져야 하는데, 실제 모습은 그렇지 않다. 렘브란트라면 이런 실수를 결코 하지 않았을 것이다.

마지막으로, 그림의 뒷면을 조사한 결과, 이 그림은 목판 여러 장을 붙여서 만든 패널 위에 그려졌다는 사실이 밝혀졌다. 렘브란트가 자주 목재 패널 위에 그림을 그리긴 했지만, 그의 그림으로 알려진 것들 중에서 이런 식으로 여러 장의 목판을 붙여 만든 패널을 쓴 작품은 하나도 없다.

이러한 이유로, 이 작품은 1930년대에 렘브란트의 공식 작품 목록에서 삭제되었다.

어휘

Rembrandt 렘브란트(1606–1669; 바로크 시대의 네덜란드 화가) Dutch 네덜란드(인)의 doubt 의혹, 의심 attribute (글, 그림 등을) ~의 것[책임]이라고 보다 portrait (특히 어깨 윗부분까지 그린) 초상화 elderly 나이가 든, 초로의 bonnet 보닛, 턱 밑에서 끈을 매는 형식으로 아이나 여자들이 많이 쓰는 모자의 일종 representation 묘사, 표현 inconsistent 모순되는 linen 리넨, 아마포 luxurious 호화로운, 사치스러운 fur collar 모피 깃 afford (금전적) 여유[형편]가 되다 attention 관심, 처리[손질] be guilty of (좋지 못한 행동을) 범하다 fit together 서로 잘 맞다, 어울리다 illuminate (빛, 불을) 비추다, 밝히다 reflect (빛 등을) 반사하다 absorb (열, 빛 등을) 흡수하다 reveal 드러내다 glue together 접합하다, 맞붙이다 remove 없애다, 삭제하다 official catalog 공식 목록

Narrator

Now listen to part of a lecture on the topic you just read about.

Professor

Everything you just read about *Portrait of an Elderly Woman in a White Bonnet* is true, and yet, after a thorough reexamination of the painting, a panel of experts has recently concluded that it's indeed a work by Rembrandt. And here's why.

First, the fur collar. X-rays and analysis of the pigments in the paint have shown that the fur collar wasn't part of the original painting. The fur collar was painted over the top of the original painting about a hundred years after the painting was made. Why? Someone probably wanted to increase the value of the painting by making it look like a formal portrait of an aristocratic lady.

Second, the supposed error with light and shadow. Once the paint of the added fur collar was removed, the original painting could be seen. In the original painting the woman is wearing a simple collar of light-colored cloth. The light-colored cloth of this collar reflects light that illuminates part of the woman's face. That's why the face is not in partial shadow. So in the original painting, light and shadow are very realistic and just what we would expect from Rembrandt.

Finally, the wood panel. It turns out that when the fur collar was added, the wood panel was also enlarged with extra wood pieces glued to the sides and the top to make the painting more grand—and more valuable. So the original painting is actually painted on a single piece of wood—as would be expected from a Rembrandt painting. And in fact, researchers have found that the piece of wood in the original form of *Portrait of an Elderly Woman in a White Bonnet* is from the very same tree as the wood panel used for another painting by Rembrandt, his *Self-Portrait with a Hat*.

해설자 방금 읽은 내용에 대해 논하는 강의의 일부를 들으시오.

교수 〈하얀 보닛을 쓴 늙은 여인의 초상〉에 대해 여러분이 방금 읽은 내용은 모두 사실입니다. 그렇지만, 작품을 다시 면밀히 조사한 전문가들은 이 작품이 렘브란트의 작품이 맞다고 최근에 결론 내렸습니다. 이유는 이렇습니다.

우선, 모피 칼라 문제입니다. 엑스선 검사와 물감 안료 분석 결과, 모피 칼라는 원작에 없었던 부분임이 밝혀졌습니다. 작품이 완성되고 백여 년이 흐른 뒤 원작 위에 덧그렸다는 겁니다. 왜 그랬을까요? 누군가가 그것을 귀부인 공식 초상화처럼 보이게 만들어 작품의 가치를 높이고 싶었던 거겠죠.

두 번째로, 빛과 음영이 안 맞는다는 문제입니다. 덧그린 모피 칼라를 지워 보니 원작의 모습이 드러났습니다. 원작에서 여인은 밝은색 천으로 된 소박한 칼라를 하고 있었습니다. 이 칼라의 밝은색 천이 빛을 반사해 여인의 얼굴 한쪽 면을 환하게 밝히고 있죠. 그래서 여인의 얼굴에 부분적으로 그림자가 드리워지지 않은 겁니다. 그러므로, 원작은 빛과 음영 묘사가 매우 사실적이며, 우리가 렘브란트의 작품에서 기대하는 그대로입니다.

마지막으로, 목재 패널 문제입니다. 모피 칼라를 덧그릴 당시, 원작의 위쪽과 양옆에 목판을 추가로 붙여 크기를 키웠다는 사실이 밝혀졌습니다. 작품을 더 웅장하고 값어치 있게 보이게 하려는 목적이었겠죠. 그러므로, 원작은 사실상 목판 한 장에 그린 작품이었습니다. 렘브란트 작품에서 기대할 수 있는 그대로 말이죠. 그리고 실제로, 연구자들은 〈하얀 보닛을 쓴 늙은 여인의 초상〉 원작 목판과 〈모자를 쓴 자화상〉이라는 렘브란트 작품의 목재 패널이 같은 나무로 만들어졌다는 사실을 발견했습니다.

어휘

thorough 철저한 **reexamination** 재검토 **a panel of** ~위원회, (전문가) 집단 **indeed** 정말로, 확실히 **pigment** 안료, 물감 재료 **formal** 제대로 된, 의례를 갖춘 **aristocratic** 귀족적인, 귀족의 **light-colored** 밝은색의, 색이 옅은 **realistic** 실제 같은, 실물 같은 **enlarge** 확대하다, 크기를 키우다 **grand** 웅대한, 당당한 **self-portrait** 자화상

Question

Summarize the points made in the lecture, being sure to explain how they respond to the specific concerns presented in the reading passage.

강의에서 말하는 요점들이 어떻게 읽기 지문에 제시된 특정 우려 사항에 대해 대응하고 있는지 반드시 설명하면서 요약하시오.

해설

지문에서 제기한 의문점들을 강의에서 어떻게 풀어나갔는지 분명히 파악해야 한다. 지문에서는 〈하얀 보닛을 쓴 늙은 여인의 초상〉은 렘브란트의 작품이 아니라는 근거들을 제시했지만, 강의에서는 이 그림이 렘브란트의 작품이 맞다는 것을 입증하는 새로운 증거들을 소개하였다.

이 문제에서 높은 점수를 받으려면, 지문의 의문점들에 대해 교수가 설명한 다음과 같은 핵심 사항들을 빠짐없이 언급하는 답안을 작성해야 한다. 4~5점을 받으려면 표에 제시된 주요 논점들이 모두 분명하게 언급되어야 한다.

Reading

Listening

Speaking

Writing

Test 1

Test 2

Test 3

Test 4

지문의 주요 내용	지문과 대조되는 강의 내용
The fur collar in the painting does not match clothing typical of a servant woman, a detail that Rembrandt would not have overlooked.	The fur collar was added later in an attempt to increase the painting's value.
The light and shadow appear incorrectly in the painting, but Rembrandt was a master of painting light and shadow.	The light and shadow appeared incorrectly because of the fur collar that was added later. Once the fur collar was removed, revealing the original white collar, the light and shadow appeared correctly.
The portrait was painted on multiple wood panels, which was not typical of Rembrandt's works.	The original was painted on a single wood panel. Additional wood panels were added to the painting later in an attempt to increase its value.

예제 답안과 채점자 의견

우수 답변

Both texts deal with the question wheather or not the painting "Portrait of an Elderly Woman in a White Bonnet" was painted by the most famous Dutch painter Rembrandt. The text clearly states, that many facts prove that it wasn't painted by Rembrandt himself, but just attributed to him because of its style. In the lecture however the professor gives proof why it is in fact a work of the famous Dutch painter.

The first contradicting fact are the clothes of the woman in the portrait. She is wearing a white linen cap which gives her the appearance of a simple servant, whereas the luxurious fur collar she also wears doesn't fit. In the lecture is said, that after a thorough research people found out that the fur collar was added to the painting about 100 years later in order to increase the value of the workpiece, because now it illustrated an aristocratic lady instead of a servant.

Another problem with the painting was the display of light and shadow. Rembandt was known as a master of painting light and shadow, yet contradictionally the elements in the work don't fit

together. But this problem could also be explained by now. By removing the additional fur collar one could see that the lady is wearing a simple light colored cloth, which reflects light into her face.

The third aspect which let people wonder about the origins of the painting was the fact, that the panel was made of several pieces of wood glued together instead of just one panel which was usual for works of Rembrandt. But the additional panels were also added later to enlarge the paiting. by doing this the painting seemed to be more valuable.

Another interesting fact is, that the main panel is made from the same tree like another painting of Rembrandt, 'Selfportrait with a hat'.

In the end it is clear that this painting is indeed a work of the Dutch painter and it should be reintegrated in the catalog of Rembrandt's paintings.

번역

지문과 강의 모두 〈하얀 보닛을 쓴 늙은 여인의 초상〉이라는 그림이 과연 네덜란드의 가장 유명한 화가 렘브란트가 그린 작품인지에 대한 의문을 다루고 있다. 지문에서는 렘브란트 본인이 그린 작품이 아니라는 것이 여러 가지 사실로 입증되고 있지만, 단지 그림의 화풍 때문에 렘브란트의 작품으로 생각되었을 따름이었다고 단언한다. 하지만 강의에서는 이 그림이 실제로 그 유명한 네덜란드 화가의 작품이라는 증거를 제시하고 있다.

첫 번째 모순되는 사실은 초상화 속 여인의 차림새다. 여인은 소박한 하인 같은 차림새인 하얀 리넨 모자를 쓰고 있으면서도 그에 어울리지 않는 화려한 모피 칼라를 걸치고 있다. 강의에서는, 철저한 조사 결과 그 모피 칼라는 작품의 가치를 높이려고 100년쯤 후에 덧그렸다는 사실이 밝혀졌으며, 그렇게 하면 하인의 초상화가 아니라 귀부인의 초상화처럼 보였기 때문이라고 설명했다.

그림의 또 한 가지 문제점은 빛과 음영 표현이었다. 렘브란트는 빛과 음영을 그림으로 표현해 내는 대가로 유명했는데, 그에 걸맞지 않게, 이 작품의 빛과 음영들은 서로 어울리지 않는다. 하지만 이 문제 역시 이제는 설명이 가능하다. 덧그린 모피 칼라를 제거하면, 초상화 속 여인이 밝은색의 천을 걸치고 있으며, 여기서 반사되는 빛이 얼굴을 밝히고 있는 모습을 볼 수 있다.

이 그림의 출처에 대해 사람들이 의문을 가지게 되는 세 번째 측면은 그림의 패널이 렘브란트의 작품에서 일반적으로 볼 수 있는 것처럼 한 장으로 된 것이 아니라 목판 몇 장을 붙여서 만든 것이라는 사실이다. 하지만 덧댄 패널들 역시 작품의 크기를 키우기 위해 나중에 덧댄 것들이다. 그렇게 하여 작품의 가치가 더욱 높아졌던 것 같다.

또 한 가지 흥미로운 사실은, 중심 패널이 렘브란트의 다른 작품인 〈모자를 쓴 자화상〉과 같은 나무로 만들어졌다는 것이다.

결국 분명한 점은, 이 그림은 정말로 그 네덜란드 화가의 작품이므로 렘브란트의 작품 목록에 다시 등재되어야 한다는 것이다.

1. 이 답변이 높은 점수를 받은 이유는 지문과 강의의 대조되는 요점들을 훌륭히 설명했을 뿐만 아니라, 핵심 사항들은 물론 세부적인 내용들까지도 모두 빠짐없이 기술했기 때문이다.

2. 글의 서두와 결론 부분에서 주제를 명확하게 다루고, 핵심 사항들을 단락 별로 구분하여 기술하는 형식을 취한 전체 글의 구성 또한 적절했다. 예를 들면, 두 번째 단락에서는 모피 칼라는 작품의 가치를 높이려는 의도로 후대에 덧그렸다는 사실을 정확히 밝혔고, 세 번째 단락에서는 두 번째 단락처럼 구체적으로 밝혀지는 않았어도, 어쨌든 빛과 음영이 안 맞는 문제를 대략적으로 소개한 다음, 그 이유를 밝혔다.

3. "Another problem," "By removing the additional fur collar," "In the end" 등 앞뒤 내용을 이어주는 어구나 표현들도 적절히 사용했으며, "In the lecture is said(문법 오류: In the lecture it is said)," "after a thorough research(관사 오류: after thorough research)," "contradictionally(어휘/표현 오류: yet contradictorily, 혹은 there are contradictory elements in the work.)" 등 사소한 실수 몇 개 외에는 문장이나 표현들도 거의 정확하게 구사했다.

중간 수준의 답변

There are doubts whether Rembramdt painted Portrait of an Elderly Woman in a White Bonnet. The reading says that the painting wasn't paint by Rembrandt because of the leck of consistency observed. On the other hand the lecture says that Rembrandt is the real painter. The opinion expressed in the lecture is based on a third examination of the painting when the experts decided that Rembrandt is the real painter because of the examination of the fur colar, the light and shadow that were realistic and finally the elements of the wood panel.

Examining the fur colar from the painting, the experts noticed that the actual colar was painted over the top of the original painting over 100 years later. The reason of doing this was to increase the value of the painting.

Further on the light and color were very realistic, says the lecture. This opinion is formulated in opossition to the one from the reading that says that in this painting this elements do not fit together.

Finally the last reason why the lecture affirms that the painting belongs to Rebmrandt is based on the examination of the wood panel. Even though the wood panel was enlarged it was used the same tree that Rembrandt used in Self Portrait with a Hat.

In conclusion it seems that the argument given by the lecture overpower the reading part.

1. 첫 번째 단락에서 지문과 강의의 주장이 서로 상반된다는 사실을 명확히 밝히긴 했지만, 양측 주장의 근거가 되는 핵심적인 사항 세 가지를 완벽하게 설명하지 못한 탓으로 중간 점수를 받은 답안이다.

2. 두 번째 단락에서, 모피 칼라는 작품의 가치를 높이려고 100년 뒤에 덧그린 부분이라는 강의 내용은 소개했지만, 모피 칼라는 여인의 다른 차림새와 서로 어울리지 않는다는 지문 내용을 전혀 언급하지 않았다. 따라서 지문과 강의의 내용을 잘 모르는 사람은 이 부분을 이해하기 힘들 수도 있다.

3. 그에 반해, 세 번째 단락에서는 빛과 색 표현이 매우 사실적이라는 강의의 주장과, 그런 요소들이 서로 맞지 않는다는 지문의 주장이 대조적이라고만 언급했을 뿐, 구체적인 설명은 누락되어 있다. 또한 네 번째 단락은 표현 자체가 분명치 않다.

4. 렘브란트의 다른 작품에 쓰인 패널과 똑같은 목재가 쓰였다는 연구 결과로 진품임을 입증할 수 있다고 했는데, 원래의 목판과 덧댄 목판 중 어느 쪽을 말하는지 분명치 않으며, 게다가 목판의 크기를 키운 이유도 언급하지 않았다.

5. 전반적으로 보면 중요한 세 가지 사항들을 모두 기술했다고 할 수 있으나, 내용면으로는 모호하거나 부족한 부분들이 꽤 있는 답안이다. 표현은 대체적으로 깔끔한 편이지만, "the painting wasn't paint by Rembrandt," "this elements do not fit together" 등 가벼운 실수들이 이따금 보인다.

Writing for an Academic Discussion

p. 256

Question

Your professor is teaching a class on sociology. Write a post responding to the professor's question.

In your response, you should do the following.
- Express and support your opinion.
- Make a contribution to the discussion in your own words.

An effective response will contain at least 100 words.

교수가 사회학에 관한 수업을 가르치고 있다. 교수의 질문에 답하는 게시물을 작성하시오.

답변을 작성할 때, 다음 사항을 수행해야 한다.
- 자신의 의견을 제시하고 뒷받침할 것.
- 자신만의 글로 논의에 기여할 것.

효과적인 답변은 최소 100자의 단어를 포함한다.

디아즈 박사

이번 주에, 우리는 식품 쇼핑의 경향을 공부할 예정입니다. 그 중 한 가지가 밀키트 웹사이트입니다. 이런 사이트에서 고객이 먼저 한 가지 이상의 식사를 선택하면, 회사가 조리 설명서와 함께 선택된 식사를 준비하는 데 딱 충분한 식료품 재료를 집으로 배송해 줍니다. 고객은 그 후 집에서 식사를 준비합니다. 여러분이 이것이 긍정적인 경향이라고 생각하나요? 그런 이유, 또는 그렇지 않은 이유를 설명하세요.

앤드류

어떤 요리 능력도 지니고 있지 않은 경우에 특히 긍정적입니다. 제가 그런 종류의 서비스를 이용해 본 적이 있는데, 제가 요리를 잘 하는 사람이 아닌데도 불구하고, 식사가 꽤 맛이 좋게 만들어졌습니다. 요리하는 법을 배우게 될 것 같아요! 아마 식료품점에서 가장 좋은 재료를 선택하는 방법조차 알지 못할지도 모르는, 더 젊은 사람들에게 특히 유용할 겁니다.

클레어

편리할지는 모르겠지만, 분명 긍정적인 경향은 아닙니다. 매주, 도시 전역에 걸쳐, 그 모든 집으로 단지 몇 번의 식사를 위해 그 모든 트럭이 포장된 식료품을 배송하는 것이 환경에 미치는 영향을 생각해 보세요! 우리는 정말로 환경적 영향보다 편리함의 편에 서는 것을 멈춰야 합니다.

해설

이 온라인 토론 글에서, 교수는 밀키트 배송이 긍정적인 경향인지에 관해 학생들의 의견을 요청하면서, 각자의 관점을 설명하도록 요구하고 있다. 첫 번째 학생인 앤드류는 긍정적으로 생각하고 있는데, 젊은 사람들이 요리하는 법을 배우는 데 도움이 될 수 있기 때문이며, 이는 실제로 그에게도 도움이 되었다. 클레어는 편리하다는 데 동의하긴 하지만, 다수의 가정으로 배송되는 포장재의 환경적 영향과 관련해 걱정하고 있으므로, 부정적인 경향이라고 생각한다. 수험자는 완전히 새로운 아이디어를 제시하거나, 클레어 또는 앤드류의 의견을 다루거나 더 자세히 설명함으로써, 또는 혼합한 의견을 제공함으로써, 이 주제와 관련해 자신만의 의견을 제공해야 한다. 예를 들어, 전체적으로, 긍정적인 경향이라고 말하면서 이유를 설명한 다음, 몇몇 비교적 부정적이면서 크게 중요하지

예제 답안과 채점자 의견

우수 답변

Meal-kit websites have started an interesting trend—on the one hand, they try to ensure a healthy home-cooked meal and on the other hand there is a concern of additional truck traffic on the roadways hurting the environment. The important part is to stike the right balance, which is always hard to achieve. The advantages of this trend, however, might outweigh the negatives. It enables families that are busy to relax and enjoy a home-cooked meal—it can also bring families together since cooking together at home can be fun. One needs to understand that the alternative would be for individuals to potentially still get in their vehicles and drive to the grocery stores and purchase ingredients themselves, or to order delivery or pick-up food, or eat out. All of these actions also result in additional vehicle trips that affect the environment. Ultimately, it is important for individuals to ensure the right balance but overall, meal-kit websites seem to present a positive trend.

번역

밀키트 웹 사이트들이 흥미로운 경향을 시작했으며, 한편으로는, 이 사이트들이 집에서 조리하는 건강한 식사를 보장하기 위해 노력하고 있지만, 다른 한편으로는, 환경에 해를 끼치는 도로상의 추가적인 트럭 교통량에 대한 우려도 존재합니다. 중요한 부분은 올바른 균형을 유지하는 것이지만, 이는 언제나 이루기 어려운 일입니다. 하지만, 이러한 경향의 장점이 부정적인 측면보다 더 많을지도 모릅니다. 바쁜 가정에서 느긋하게 집에서 조리한 식사를 즐기게 해 줄 수 있으며, 가족을 화합시킬 수도 있는데, 집에서 함께 요리하는 것이 즐거울 수 있기 때문입니다. 알아 두어야 하는 점은, 그 대안이 사람들이 잠재적으로 여전히 차량을 타고 운전해 식료품점으로 가서 직접 재료를 구입하거나, 배달 또는 포장 음식을 주문하는 것, 아니면 외식하는 것일 수 있습니다. 이 모든 행위도 환경에 영향을 미치는 추가적인 차량 이동이라는 결과를 낳습니다. 궁극적으로, 사람들이 반드시 올바른 균형을 이루는 것이 중요하지만, 전반적으로, 밀키트 웹 사이트들이 긍정적인 경향을 제시하는 것으로 보입니다.

채점자 의견

1. 수준 높은 이 답변은 토론 게시판에 매우 성공적이면서, 관련성 있고 명확하게 표현된 의견 제시문을 더해 주고 있다.
2. 이 답변은 앤드류와 클레어에 의해 표현되는 상반된 관점("집에서 조리하는 건강한 식사를 보장하기 위해 노력하고 있지만"과 "도로상의 추가적인 트럭 교통량")을 언급한 다음, 계속해서 밀키트 경향의 장

점이 단점보다 더 많다고 말한 뒤로, 이러한 관점을 뒷받침하는 상세 설명이 이어진다.

3. 이 답변은 다양한 문법 구조 및 정확하고 효과적인 단어 선택을 활용하고 있으며, 어휘 또는 문법 어느 쪽도 오류가 거의 없다.

중간 수준의 답변

I would support Andrew.

Getting the grocery for each week will reduce the amount of people going to grocery shopping, it saves the time of each individual also. It helps in not buying extra grocery items. Its in favor of customers. It may not impact enviromental impacts as too many people driving to get the grocery will reducing to one truck delivering all the grocery. The other reason why i suppor tthis it helps each invidual to cook and since they also give the recipe it would be favaourable for customer, in one shot they get the recipe , grocery and try out home food, which would be more healtier and cheaper comparing to ordering restaurant food.

채점자 의견

1. 이 중간 수준의 답변은 분명 토론에 기여하기는 하지만, 전적으로 성공적이지는 못한데, 언어 오류의 빈번함이 그 주된 이유이다.

2. 수험자는 밀키트가 긍정적인 경향이라는 앤드류의 의견에 동의하면서 몇 가지 이유를 간략히 설명하고 있다. 이 답변은 그 후 이어서 식료품 매장으로 운전해서 가는 것보다 환경에 훨씬 더 많은 영향을 미치는 밀키트 배송에 반대한다고 주장한 다음(클레어의 관점과 반대), 밀키트 배송이 긍정적인 경향인 것에 대한 추가적인 이유를 제공하고 있다.

3. 대부분의 아이디어들이 "이는 환경적 영향에 영향을 미치지 않을 수 있는데"와 "모든 식료품을 배송하는 하나의 트럭으로 줄어들 것이기", 그리고 "이것을 지지하는 또 다른 이유는 … 도움이 된다는 점이며"와 같이, 언어 사용상의 오류로 인해 약간 모호하다.

4. "이는 고객들에게 유리합니다."라는 문장의 의미도 불분명하다.

Notes

Reading

Listening

Speaking

Writing

Test 1

Test 2

Test 3

Test 4

READING

INDUSTRIALIZATION IN THE NETHERLANDS AND SCANDINAVIA

p. 262

While some European countries, such as England and Germany, began to industrialize in the eighteenth century, the Netherlands and the Scandinavian countries of Denmark, Norway, and Sweden developed later. **(A)** All four of these countries lagged considerably behind in the early nineteenth century. **(B)** However, they industrialized rapidly in the second half of the century, especially in the last two or three decades. **(C)** In view of their later start and their lack of coal—undoubtedly the main reason they were not among the early industrializers—it is important to understand the sources of their success. **(D)**

All had small populations. At the beginning of the nineteenth century, Denmark and Norway had fewer than 1 million people, while Sweden and the Netherlands had fewer than 2.5 million inhabitants. All exhibited moderate growth rates in the course of the century (Denmark the highest and Sweden the lowest), but all more than doubled in population by 1900. Density varied greatly. The Netherlands had one of the highest population densities in Europe, whereas Norway and Sweden had the lowest. Denmark was in between but closer to the Netherlands.

Considering human capital as a characteristic of the population, however, all four countries were advantaged by the large percentages of their populations who could read and write. In both 1850 and 1914, the Scandinavian countries had the highest literacy rates in Europe, or in the world, and the Netherlands was well above the European average. This fact was of enormous value in helping the national economies find their niches in the evolving currents of the international economy.

Location was an important factor for all four countries. All had immediate access to the sea, and this had important implications for a significant international resource, fish, as well as for cheap transport, merchant marines, and the shipbuilding industry. Each took advantage of these opportunities in its own way. The people of the Netherlands, with a long tradition of fisheries and mercantile shipping, had difficulty in developing good harbors suitable for steamships; eventually they did so at Rotterdam and Amsterdam, with exceptional results for transit trade with Germany and central Europe and for the processing of overseas foodstuffs and raw materials (sugar, tobacco, chocolate, grain, and eventually oil). Denmark also had an admirable commercial history, particularly

네덜란드와 스칸디나비아의 산업화

영국, 독일 등 일부 유럽 국가들이 18세기에 산업화를 시작한 반면, 네덜란드와 덴마크, 노르웨이, 스웨덴 같은 스칸디나비아 국가들은 이후에 발전하였다. 19세기 초에는 이들 4개국 모두 상당히 뒤처져 있었다. 그러나 이들 국가는 19세기 후반기, 특히 마지막 20, 30년 동안 급속하게 산업화되었다. 이 국가들이 후발 주자라는 점, 그리고 석탄이 부족했다는 점—분명 일찍 산업화된 국가에 속하지 못한 주된 이유—을 고려할 때, 성공의 원천을 이해하는 것이 중요하다.

모두 인구가 적었다. 19세기 초, 덴마크와 노르웨이의 인구는 100만 명 미만이었고, 스웨덴과 네덜란드 거주민은 250만 명 미만이었다. 모두 19세기 동안 완만한 성장률을 보였으나(덴마크가 가장 높았고 스웨덴이 가장 낮음) 1900년에는 모두 인구가 두 배 이상 증가했다. 인구밀도는 천차만별이었다. 네덜란드는 유럽에서 인구밀도가 가장 높은 축에 속한 반면 노르웨이와 스웨덴은 가장 낮았다. 덴마크는 그 사이에 있었지만 네덜란드에 더 가까웠다.

그러나 인적 자본을 인구의 한 가지 특징으로 본다면, 4개국 모두 읽고 쓸 수 있는 인구의 비율이 높아서 유리했다. 1850년과 1914년에 스칸디나비아 국가들은 유럽, 아니 세계에서 문자해독률이 가장 높았으며 네덜란드는 유럽 평균을 훨씬 웃돌았다. 이 사실은 발전하는 국제 경제의 흐름에서 국가 경제에 적합한 틈새 시장을 찾도록 돕는 데 엄청난 가치가 있었다.

입지는 4개국 모두에게 중요한 요소였다. 모두 바다에 바로 접근할 수 있었는데 이는 저렴한 수송, 상선, 조선업뿐만 아니라 중요한 국제 자원, 어류에도 중대한 의미를 지니고 있었다. 각국은 이런 기회를 나름대로 이용했다. 오랜 어업과 상업 해상운송의 전통을 가진 네덜란드인은 증기선에 적합한 좋은 항구를 개발하는 데 어려움을 겪었는데 마침내 로테르담과 암스테르담에서 좋은 항구를 개발했고 독일, 중부 유럽과의 통과무역, 해외 식품과 원자재(설탕, 담배, 초콜릿, 곡물, 그리고 최종적으로는 석유) 가공에서 특출한 결과를 얻었다. 또한 덴마크는 탄복할 만한 상업의 역사를 지니고 있었는데 특히 사운드해협(덴마크와 스웨덴을 가르는 해협)을 통한 운송이 그랬다. 1857년, 다른 상업 국가들로부터 6300만 크로노를 지불 받는 대가로 덴마크는 1497년 이후 사운드해협 이용료로 징수했던 사운드해협 통행세를 폐지했다. 자유무역을 향한 다른 정책 변화와 더불어 이 조치로 사운드해협과 코펜하겐 항구를 통과하는 운행량이 상당히 증

Reading

Listening

Speaking

Writing

Test 1

Test 2

Test 3

Test 4

with respect to traffic through the Sound (the strait separating Denmark and Sweden). In 1857, in return for a payment of 63 million kronor from other commercial nations, Denmark abolished the Sound toll dues, the fees it had collected since 1497 for the use of the Sound. This, along with other policy shifts toward free trade, resulted in a significant increase in traffic through the Sound and in the port of Copenhagen.

The political institutions of the four countries posed no significant barriers to industrialization or economic growth. The nineteenth century passed relatively peacefully for these countries, with progressive democratization taking place in all of them. They were reasonably well governed, without notable corruption or grandiose state projects, although in all of them the government gave some aid to railways, and in Sweden the state built the main lines. As small countries dependent on foreign markets, they had few or low barriers to foreign trade in the main, though a protectionist movement developed in Sweden. In Denmark and Sweden agricultural reforms took place gradually from the late eighteenth century through the first half of the nineteenth, resulting in a new class of peasant landowners with a definite market orientation.

The key factor in the success of these countries (along with high literacy, which contributed to it) was their ability to adapt to the international division of labor determined by the early industrializers and to stake out areas of specialization in international markets for which they were especially well suited. This meant a great dependence on international commerce, which had notorious fluctuations; however, it also meant high returns to those aspects of production that were fortunate enough to be well placed in times of prosperity. In Sweden exports accounted for 18 percent of the national income in 1870, and in 1913, 22 percent of a much larger national income. In the early twentieth century, Denmark exported 63 percent of its agricultural production: butter, pork products, and eggs. It exported 80 percent of its butter, almost all to Great Britain, where it accounted for 40 percent of British butter imports.

가했다.

4개국의 정치 제도는 산업화나 경제성장에 큰 걸림돌이 되지 않았다. 이들 국가는 19세기를 비교적 평화롭게 보냈고 모든 국가들에서 점진적인 민주화가 이루어졌다. 4개국 모두 정부가 철도에 일정 부분 지원을 했고 스웨덴에서는 국가가 주요 노선을 건설했지만 두드러진 부정부패나 거창한 국책사업 없이 상당히 잘 통치되었다. 이들 국가는 해외시장에 의존하는 작은 나라로서, 스웨덴에서 보호무역주의 운동이 전개되긴 했지만 대체로 대외무역에 장벽이 거의 없거나 낮았다. 18세기 말부터 19세기 전반까지 덴마크와 스웨덴에서 농업개혁이 점진적으로 이루어졌고, 그 결과 시장 지향이 확실한 새로운 농민 지주계층이 생겨났다.

이들 국가의 성공에 기여한 핵심 요소는 (높은 문자해독률과 함께) 초기 산업국가들에 의해 결정된 국제 노동분업에 적응하는 능력과 국제시장에서 특히 잘 맞는 전문 영역을 자신의 것으로 만들 수 있는 능력이었다. 이는 변동성이 크기로 악명 높은 국제 무역에 대한 의존도가 높다는 것을 의미했다. 하지만 한편으로는 운 좋게 번영의 시대에 잘 편승한 생산의 어떤 측면에서 높은 수익을 얻을 수 있었다는 의미이기도 했다. 1870년 스웨덴에서는 수출이 국민소득의 18%를 차지했고, 1913년에는 국민소득이 크게 늘었는데 수출이 국민소득의 22%를 차지했다. 20세기 초 덴마크는 버터, 돼지고기 제품, 달걀 등 농업 생산품의 63%를 수출했다. 덴마크는 버터의 80%를 거의 전부 영국으로 수출했는데, 이는 영국 버터 수입의 40%를 차지했다.

어휘

industrialization 산업화 lag 뒤처지다 considerably 상당히 decade 10년 in view of ~을 고려하여 coal 석탄 undoubtedly 확실히 population 인구 inhabitant 거주민 exhibit 보이다 moderate 온건한, 완만한 growth rate 성장률, 증가율 density (인구) 밀도 vary 다르다 whereas ~인 반면 human capital 인적 자본 characteristic 특징 literacy rate 문자해독률 niche 틈새, 적합한 분야 evolve 발달하다, 진화하다 immediate 당장, 즉각적인 access 접근, 이용 가능함 implication 의미, 영향 significant 중대한 resource 자원 transport 운송, 수송 merchant marine 상선 take advantage of ~을 이용하다 opportunity 기회 mercantile 상업의 harbor 항구

suitable for ~에 적합한   steamship 증기선   exceptional 특출한, 예외적인   transit trade 통과무역   processing 가공   raw material 원자재   admirable 탄복할 만한   commercial 상업의   strait 해협   in return for ~의 대가로   abolish 폐지하다   toll due 통행세   policy 정책   port 항만, 항구   institution 제도   pose 야기하다   barrier 장벽, 걸림돌   progressive 점진적인, 진행하는   democratization 민주화   reasonably 합리적으로, 상당히   govern 통치하다   notable 두드러진   corruption 부정부패   grandiose 거창한   state project 국책사업   dependent on ~에 의존하는   protectionist 보호무역주의의   agricultural 농업의   reform 개혁   peasant 농민   landowner 지주   definite 확실한   market orientation 시장 지향(생산의 입지 선택이 시장인자에 영향을 받거나 결정되는 상태)   contribute to ~에 기여하다   adapt to ~에 적응하다   division of labor 노동분업   determine 결정하다   stake out 자기 소유임을 분명히 하다   specialization 특화   commerce 상업, 무역   fluctuation 변동성   return 수익   fortunate 운이 좋은   prosperity 번영   export 수출   account for 차지하다   income 소득, 수입   import 수입

1. 다음 영국과 독일에 관한 개념들 중 첫 번째 단락에서 뒷받침하고 있는 것은?

Ⓐ 19세기 초에 완전히 산업화되었다.

Ⓑ 석탄 저장량이 풍부했다.

Ⓒ 19세기 초에 네덜란드와 스칸디나비아에게 경제적으로 추월당했다.

Ⓓ 네덜란드와 스칸디나비아와 같은 이유로 성공했다.

내용 추론 문제

어휘 possess 보유하다   plentiful 풍부한   supplies 보급품, 물자   overtake 추월하다

해설 첫 번째 문장에서 영국과 독일은 일찍 산업화되었다고 했으며 네 번째 문장에서 네덜란드와 스칸디나비아 국가들이 산업화가 늦은 이유는 석탄 부족 때문이라고 했다. 이 두 문장을 통해 석탄이 초기 근대화에 중요했다는 사실을 추론할 수 있으며 따라서 영국과 독일은 석탄이 있었다고 유추할 수 있으므로 정답은 보기 B이다. 영국과 독일이 18세기에 산업화를 시작했다고 했으나 19세기 초에 산업화 과정이 완성되었다는 언급은 없으므로 A는 정답이 될 수 없다. 네덜란드와 스칸디나비아 등 4개국은 모두 19세기 초에 상당히 뒤처진 상태라고 했으므로 보기 C는 지문과 상반된다. 영국과 독일은 석탄을 보유했고 네덜란드와 스칸디나비아 국가는 석탄이 부족했다고 했다. 따라서 산업화에 성공한 이유가 동일하다고 할 수 없으므로 보기 D도 정답이 아니다.

2. 두 번째 단락과 세 번째 단락에 따르면, 다음 중 네덜란드와 스칸디나비아의 성공적인 경제 발전에 크게 기여한 것은?

Ⓐ 인구 규모가 비교적 작았음

Ⓑ 인구가 빨리 성장했음

Ⓒ 투자에 쓸 수 있는 자본이 많았음

Ⓓ 교육 받은 시민의 비율이 높았음

세부 정보 찾기 문제

어휘 relatively 비교적   amount 양   available 이용 가능한

해설 세 번째 단락 첫 번째 문장에서 네덜란드와 스칸디나비아 국가들이 읽고 쓸 수 있는 인구의 비율이 높아서 유리했다고 했으므로 보기 D가 정답이다.

3. 지문의 단어 abolished와 의미상 가장 가까운 것은?

Ⓐ 끝냈다   Ⓑ 높였다

Ⓒ 되돌려 줬다   Ⓓ 낮췄다

어휘 문제

어휘 lower 낮추다

해설 abolish는 법률이나 제도, 관습 등을 '폐지하다'는 의미이다.

4. 네 번째 단락에 따르면, 다음 중 산업화를 시작할 당시 위치 때문에 네덜란드와 스칸디나비아 국가들이 모두 갖고 있었던 장점이 아닌 것은?

Ⓐ 저렴한 물품 수송 비용

Ⓑ 어류에 접근하기 쉬움

Ⓒ 조선업

Ⓓ 해상 군사 통제

틀린 정보 찾기 문제

어휘 military 군사의

해설 네덜란드와 스칸디나비아 국가가 위치 때문에 무역과 상업에서 유리했다고 했고 그 예로 저렴한 운송, 어장 접근, 조선업 등을 들고 있다. 군사 행동에 관한 내용은 언급되지 않았으므로 보기 D가 정답이다.

5. 저자가 "스웨덴에서 보호무역주의 운동이 전개되었다"는 정보를 넣은 이유는?

Ⓐ 4개국의 정치 제도가 산업화나 경제성장에 큰 걸림돌이 되지 않았다는 주장을 뒷받침하기 위해

Ⓑ 무역장벽이 적거나 낮은 일반적인 경향에 대한 예외를 밝히기 위해

Ⓒ 스웨덴이 다른 스칸디나비아 국가들과 네덜란드보다 산업화가 더 뎠던 이유를 설명하기 위해

Ⓓ 농업 개혁이 무역 장벽이 없는 나라보다 무역 장벽이 적거나 낮은 나라에서 더 빨리 일어난다는 증거를 대기 위해

수사학적 의도 파악 문제

어휘 identify 식별하다, 밝히다   exception 예외   evidence 증거

해설 네 번째 문장에서 네덜란드와 스칸디나비아 국가들은 대체로 무역을 장려하는 정책을 썼다고 했다. 그러나 보호무역주의 운동의 부상은 무역에는 불리한 움직임이므로 보기 B가 정답이다.

Reading

Listening

Speaking

Writing

Test 1

Test 2

Test 3

Test 4

6. 다섯 번째 단락에 따르면, 다음 중 네덜란드와 스칸디나비아의 산업화에 긍정적으로 기여한 요인이 아닌 것은?

Ⓐ 해외무역의 장애물이 없음
Ⓑ 국가에서 수행한 대형 프로젝트
Ⓒ 비교적 부정부패가 없는 정부
Ⓓ 사회적, 정치적 분란이 비교적 없음

틀린 정보 찾기 문제

어휘 obstacle 장애물   uncorrupt 부패하지 않은   disruption 분란, 분열

해설 세 번째 문장에서 네덜란드와 스칸디나비아 국가 정부는 거창한 국책사업을 추진하지 않았다고 했으므로 보기 B가 정답이다. 이들 국가는 무역 장벽이 거의 없거나 낮았다고 했으므로 보기 A는 지문과 일치하며 뚜렷한 부정부패가 없었다고 했으므로 보기 C도 지문과 일치한다. 또 19세기는 비교적 평화롭게 지나갔다고 했으므로 보기 D 역시 지문과 일치한다.

7. 다음 중 지문에서 음영으로 표시된 문장이 담고 있는 핵심 정보를 가장 잘 표현한 것은? 정답 외의 보기들은 의미가 상당히 왜곡되거나 필수적인 정보가 빠져 있다.

Ⓐ 초기 산업국가들은 국제 경제의 대부분을 지배했고, 이들 국가들은 주변부를 따라 새로운 전문 분야를 개척하게 되었다.
Ⓑ 높은 문자해독률 덕분에 이들 국가는 확립된 국제 시장 내에서 전문 영역을 차지할 수 있었다.
Ⓒ 높은 문자해독률 덕분에 이들 국가는 국제 시장을 장악하고 그들의 강점에 맞게 국제 분업을 조정할 수 있었다.
Ⓓ 초기 산업국가들에 의해 확립된 국제 노동분업이 이들 국가에게 잘 맞았는데, 이는 성공의 핵심 요소였다.

문장 재구성 문제

어휘 claim 차지하다   established 확립된   enable 가능하게 만들다

해설 보기 B가 강조된 문장의 핵심을 잘 짚어냈다. 전문 분야를 개척한 것은 뒤늦게 산업화된 네덜란드와 스칸디나비아 국가이므로 보기 A는 틀린 내용이다. 국제 시장을 통제하고 노동분업을 결정한 것은 네덜란드와 스칸디나비아 국가들이 아니므로 보기 C 역시 틀렸다. 보기 D는 이들 국가가 특화된 분야를 개발해서 성공했다는 핵심 정보가 빠져 있다.

8. 여섯 번째 단락에 따르면, 국제 시장에 크게 의존할 때 생기는 중요한 문제는?

Ⓐ 국제 시장은 안정성이 결여되었다.
Ⓑ 국제 시장은 농업 생산품에 적합하지 않았다.
Ⓒ 국제 시장은 초기 산업국가들에 크게 휘둘렸다.
Ⓓ 국제 시장은 지역 산업의 느린 성장으로 이어졌다.

세부 정보 찾기 문제

어휘 stability 안정성

해설 국제 시장은 변동성으로 악명 높다고 했으므로 보기 A가 정답이다. 덴마크는 버터의 80퍼센트를 수출했다고 했으므로 보기 B는 지문과 상반되는 내용이다. 초기 산업국가들이 국제 시장을 좌지우지한 것이 '중요한 문제'라는 언급은 없으므로 보기 C는 정답이 될 수 없다. 국제 시장에 크게 의존해 성장이 느려졌다는 내

용도 없으므로 보기 D 역시 정답이 될 수 없다.

9. **지시문:** 위에 제시된 지문의 일부를 보시오. 지문에 표시된 **(A)**, **(B)**, **(C)**, **(D)** 중 하나에 다음 문장이 삽입될 수 있다.

During this period, Sweden had the highest rate of growth of output per capita of any country in Europe, and Denmark was second.
(이 기간 동안 스웨덴은 유럽 어느 나라보다 1인당 생산량 증가율이 가장 높았고 덴마크는 두 번째였다.)

이 문장이 들어갈 가장 적당한 위치는?

While some European countries, such as England and Germany, began to industrialize in the eighteenth century, the Netherlands and the Scandinavian countries of Denmark, Norway, and Sweden developed later. **(A)** All four of these countries lagged considerably behind in the early nineteenth century. **(B)** However, they industrialized rapidly in the second half of the century, especially in the last two or three decades. **(C)** During this period, Sweden had the highest rate of growth of output per capita of any country in Europe, and Denmark was second. In view of their later start and their lack of coal—undoubtedly the main reason they were not among the early industrializers—it is important to understand the sources of their success. **(D)**

All had small populations.

Ⓐ   Ⓑ   Ⓒ   Ⓓ

문장 삽입 문제

어휘 output 생산량   per capita 1인당

해설 '이 기간 동안'이 '마지막 20, 30년'을 가리키며, 네덜란드와 스칸디나비아 국가들이 19세기 후반기에 급속히 산업화되었다는 문장 뒤에 스웨덴과 덴마크의 구체적인 성장을 언급하는 것이 자연스러우므로 (C) 위치가 적합하다. 첫 번째 문장에서 네덜란드와 스칸디나비아 국가는 18세기 이후에 발전했다고 했으므로 삽입 문장이 (A)에 오면 이 기간 동안이 18세기를 가리키게 되므로 맞지 않다. 두 번째 문장에서 네덜란드와 스칸디나비아 국가는 19세기 초반에 상당히 뒤처졌다고 했으므로 삽입문과 상반되는 내용이므로 (B) 역시 적합하지 않다. (D) 앞 문장은 네덜란드와 스칸디나비아 국가의 성공 원인이라는 새로운 주제를 말하고 있는데 삽입 문장에는 관련 정보가 없으므로 (D) 역시 적합하지 않다.

10. **지시문:** 이 지문을 간단히 요약하기 위한 도입 문장이 아래에 제시되어 있다. 아래 보기들 중에서 지문의 가장 중요한 개념을 표현한 문장 3개를 골라 요약을 완성하라. 보기들 중에는 지문에 나오지 않았거나 중요하지 않은 개념이기 때문에 요약문으로 적절치 않은 것들도 있다. 이 문제의 배점은 2점이다.

답으로 선택한 보기를 지정된 공간에 쓰시오. 선택한 보기의 번호를 쓰거나 문장을 옮겨 쓰시오.

네덜란드와 스칸디나비아는 상대적으로 늦게 산업화를 시작했지만, 매우 성공적으로 산업화를 이루었다.

A 비록 이들 국가 모두 규모도 작고 교육 받지 못한 인구로 시작했지만, 산업화는 상당한 인구 증가와 높은 문자해독률로 이어졌다.

B 이들 국가는 바다에 쉽게 접근할 수 있었던 덕분에 상업 해운, 어업, 조선업에서 이점을 누렸다.

C 이들 국가 모두 증기선을 위한 좋은 항구를 보유하고 있었으므로 통과무역 경쟁에서 중요한 우위를 점하고 시작했다.

D 이들 국가는 자국 정부가 비교적 안정적이고 정직하며 전반적으로 교역을 차단하기보다는 장려하는 정책을 펼쳤다는 사실에 도움을 받았다.

E 이들 국가는 주로 높은 문자해독률 덕분에 특화된 틈새 시장을 메웠기 때문에 성공했다.

F 이들 국가는 결코 국제 무역에 완전히 의존하지 않았기 때문에, 변동성으로 악명 높은 국제 시장에서 살아남을 수 있었다.

지문 요약하기 문제

어휘 competition 경쟁　stable 안정적인　encourage 장려하다　primarily 주로　survive 살아남다

해설 높은 문자해독률 덕분에 산업화에 유리했다고 했고 산업화가 높은 문자해독률로 이어진 것은 아니므로 A는 사실과 다르다. 네 번째 단락에서 바다에 가까운 위치 덕분에 어업, 무역, 조선업이 발전했다고 했으므로 B는 지문과 일치한다. 네덜란드는 처음에는 증기선을 위한 좋은 항구가 없었다고 했으므로 C는 사실과 다르다. 다섯 번째 단락에서 평화롭고 부정부패가 적은 정부, 무역에 우호적인 정책이 산업화에 도움이 되었다고 했으므로 D는 지문의 핵심 내용이다. 여섯 번째 단락에서 높은 문자해독률 덕분에 기존 국제 시장에서 특화된 분야를 만들 수 있다고 했으므로 E 역시 지문과 일치한다. 지문에서 시장 변동성에서 살아남은 이유는 언급하지 않았으므로 F는 핵심 내용이 될 수 없다.

Reading

Listening

Speaking

Writing

Test 1

Test 2

Test 3

THE MYSTERY OF YAWNING

p. 269

According to conventional theory, yawning takes place when people are bored or sleepy and serves the function of increasing alertness by reversing, through deeper breathing, the drop in blood oxygen levels that are caused by the shallow breathing that accompanies lack of sleep or boredom. Unfortunately, the few scientific investigations of yawning have failed to find any connection between how often someone yawns and how much sleep they have had or how tired they are. About the closest any research has come to supporting the tiredness theory is to confirm that adults yawn more often on weekdays than at weekends, and that school children yawn more frequently in their first year at primary school than they do in kindergarten.

Another flaw of the tiredness theory is that yawning does not raise alertness or physiological activity, as the theory would predict. When researchers measured the heart rate, muscle tension, and skin conductance of people before, during, and after yawning, they did detect some changes in skin conductance following yawning, indicating a slight increase in physiological activity. However, similar changes occurred when the subjects were asked simply to open their mouths or to breathe deeply. Yawning did nothing special to their state of physiological activity. Experiments have also cast serious doubt on the belief that yawning is triggered by a drop in blood oxygen or a rise in blood carbon dioxide. **(A)** Volunteers were told to think about yawning while they breathed either normal air, pure oxygen, or an air mixture with an above-normal level of carbon dioxide. **(B)** If the theory was correct, breathing air with extra carbon dioxide should have triggered yawning, while breathing pure oxygen should have suppressed yawning. **(C)** In fact, neither condition made any difference to the frequency of yawning, which remained constant at about 24 yawns per hour. **(D)** Another experiment demonstrated that physical exercise, which was sufficiently vigorous to double the rate of breathing, had no effect on the frequency of yawning. Again, the implication is that yawning has little or nothing to do with oxygen.

A completely different theory holds that yawning assists in the physical development of the lungs early in life, but has no remaining biological function in adults. It has been suggested that yawning and hiccupping might serve to clear out the fetus's airways. The lungs of a fetus secrete a liquid that then mixes with its mother's amniotic fluid. Babies with congenital blockages that prevent this fluid from escaping from their lungs are sometimes born with deformed lungs. It might be that yawning helps to clear

하품의 신비

통설에 따르면, 하품은 사람들이 지루하거나 졸릴 때 발생하며 수면 부족이나 지루함에 따르는 얕은 호흡으로 혈중 산소 수치가 떨어지는데, 하품을 하면 더 깊은 호흡을 통해 이 수치를 뒤집어 경각심을 높이는 기능을 한다. 안타깝게도 얼마 안 되는 하품에 대한 과학적 연구가 이루어졌지만 잠을 얼마나 잤는지 혹은 얼마나 피곤한지와 얼마나 자주 하품을 하는지 사이에 어떤 연관성도 발견하지 못했다. 피곤이론을 뒷받침하는 가장 가까운 연구는 어른들이 주말보다 평일에 더 자주 하품하고, 초등학생들이 유치원 때보다 초등학생 첫해에 더 자주 하품한다는 것을 확인한 것이다.

피곤이론의 또 다른 결함은 이 이론이 예견하는 대로 하품이 경각심이나 생리 활동을 높이지 않는다는 점이다. 연구자들이 하품을 하기 전과 중간, 이후 사람의 심박수, 근육의 긴장, 피부 전도도를 측정했는데 하품 이후 약간의 피부전도 변화가 감지되어 생리 활동이 약간 증가했음이 드러났다. 그러나 피실험자들에게 단순히 입을 벌리거나 깊이 숨쉬라고 했을 때도 비슷한 변화가 일어났다. 하품은 그들의 생리 활동 상태에 특별한 영향을 끼치지 않았다. 또한 실험 결과는 하품이 혈중 산소의 저하나 혈중 이산화탄소의 증가에 의해 유발된다는 믿음에 심각한 의문을 던지고 있다. 지원자들은 보통의 공기, 순수한 산소, 또는 정상치가 넘는 이산화탄소가 혼합된 공기를 마시는 동안 하품에 대해 생각하라는 지시를 받았다. 피곤이론이 옳다면 추가 이산화탄소가 있는 공기를 호흡하면 하품이 촉발되어야 했고, 순수 산소를 호흡하면 하품이 억제되어야 했다. 실제로 어떤 조건에서도 하품 빈도는 아무런 차이 없이 시간당 24회 정도로 일정하게 유지되었다. 또 다른 실험 결과 호흡의 비율이 두 배가 될 정도로 충분히 격렬한 신체 운동은 하품 빈도에 아무런 영향을 미치지 않았다. 이 역시 하품이 산소와 거의 관계가 없거나 전혀 관계가 없다는 것을 의미한다.

완전히 다른 이론은 하품이 생명의 초기 단계에서 폐의 신체적 발달을 돕지만, 성인에게는 생물학적 기능이 남아 있지 않다고 주장한다. 하품과 딸꾹질이 태아의 기도를 깨끗하게 하는 역할을 할 수도 있다는 주장이 제기되었다. 태아의 폐는 액체를 분비하는데 이 액체는 엄마의 양수와 섞인다. 선천적으로 막혀 있어 이 액체가 폐에서 빠져나가지 못하는 아기들은 때때로 기형적인 폐를 가지고 태어난다. 하품을 하면 주기적으로 폐 안의 압력이 낮아져 폐를 깨끗하게 만드는 데 도움이 될 수도 있다. 이 이론에 따르면, 성인에게 하품은 생물학적 기능이 없는 발육 단계의 화석일 뿐이다. 그러나 생명의 모든 것이 다윈의 진화론으로 설명될 수 없다는 것을 받아들인다 해도, 성인에게 하품이 갖는 역할에 대한 문제를 회피하는 이런 이론에 여전히 회의적인 데는 적

out the lungs by periodically lowering the pressure in them. According to this theory, yawning in adults is just a developmental fossil with no biological function. But, while accepting that not everything in life can be explained by Darwinian evolution, there are sound reasons for being skeptical of theories like this one, which avoid the issue of what yawning does for adults. Yawning is distracting, consumes energy, and takes time. It is almost certainly doing something significant in adults as well as in fetuses. What could it be?

The empirical evidence, such as it is, suggests an altogether different function for yawning—namely, that yawning prepares us for a change in activity level. Support for this theory came from a study of yawning behavior in everyday life. Volunteers wore wrist-mounted devices that automatically recorded their physical activity for up to two weeks; the volunteers also recorded their yawns by pressing a button on the device each time they yawned. The data showed that yawning tended to occur about 15 minutes before a period of increased behavioral activity. Yawning bore no relationship to sleep patterns, however. This accords with anecdotal evidence that people often yawn in situations where they are neither tired nor bored, but are preparing for impending mental and physical activity. Such yawning is often referred to as "incongruous" because it seems out of place, at least in the tiredness view: soldiers yawning before combat, musicians yawning before performing, and athletes yawning before competing. Their yawning seems to have nothing to do with sleepiness or boredom—quite the reverse—but it does precede a change in activity level.

절한 이유가 있다. 하품은 정신을 산만하게 하고 에너지를 소모하며 시간이 걸린다. 하품은 태아뿐만 아니라 어른에게도 분명히 중요한 어떤 역할을 하고 있다. 그게 무엇일까?

미약하나마 경험적 증거에 따르면, 하품은 완전히 다른 기능, 즉 활동 수준의 변화에 대비하도록 한다. 이 이론을 뒷받침하는 근거는 일상생활 속 하품 행동에 대한 연구에서 나왔다. 지원자들은 최대 2주 동안 자동으로 신체 활동을 기록하는 손목 장치를 착용했다. 지원자들은 또한 하품할 때마다 장치의 버튼을 눌러 기록했다. 이 자료에 따르면, 증가된 행동 활동기 약 15분 전에 하품이 나오는 경향이 있었다. 하지만 하품은 수면 패턴과 아무런 관계가 없었다. 이는 사람들이 피곤하지도, 지루하지도 않지만 임박한 정신적, 신체적 활동을 준비하고 있을 때 하품을 한다는 일화적 증거와 일치한다. 이런 하품은 적어도 피곤이론 관점에서는 적절하지 않아 보이므로 흔히 "어색하다"고 부른다. 병사들은 전투 전에 하품하며, 음악가는 공연하기 전에 하품하며, 운동선수들은 겨루기 전에 하품한다. 이들의 하품은 졸림이나 지루함과는 무관해 보이며, 반대로, 활동 수준의 변화에 앞서 일어난다.

어휘

yawning 하품 conventional 종래의, 판에 박힌 alertness 경각심, 빈틈없음 reverse 뒤집다 shallow 얕은 accompany 따르다, 동행하다 boredom 지루함 investigation 연구, 조사 frequently 자주 flaw 결함, 흠 physiological 생리적인 predict 예측하다 measure 측정하다 heart rate 심박수 conductance 전도도 detect 감지하다 indicate 표시하다 slight 약간의 increase 증가 subject 피실험자 experiment 실험 cast 던지다 trigger 촉발하다 carbon dioxide 이산화탄소 suppress 억제하다 frequency 빈도 constant 일관된, 지속적인 demonstrate 보여 주다 physical 신체의 sufficiently 충분히 vigorous 격렬한 have effect on ~에 영향을 미치다 implication 의미 have nothing to do with ~와 아무 관계가 없다 completely 완전히 lung 폐 biological 생물학적인 hiccup 딸꾹질하다 fetus 태아 airway 기도 secrete 분비하다; 분비물 liquid 액체 amniotic fluid 양수 congenital 선천적인 blockage 봉쇄, 막힘 prevent A from -ing A가 ~하는 것을 막다 deformed 기형의 periodically 주기적으로 developmental 발육의, 발달 상의 fossil 화석 evolution 진화 skeptical 회의적인 avoid 피하다 distracting 정신을 산만하게 하는 consume 소비하다 significant 중대한 empirical evidence 경험적 증거 behavior 행동, 행위 wrist-mounted 손목에 차는 device 장치 anecdotal evidence 일화적 증거(개인의 직접 경험에 대한 보고나 타인의 경험에 대한 보고를 통해 모인 증거) impending 임박한 refer to ~라고 부르다 incongruous 어색한, 어울리지 않는 out of place 적절하지 않은 combat 전투 perform 공연하다 compete 겨루다, (시합에) 참가하다 precede 앞서다, 선행하다

Reading

Listening

Speaking

Writing

Test 1

Test 2

Test 3

Test 4

11. 다음 중 지문에서 음영으로 표시된 문장이 담고 있는 핵심 정보를 가장 잘 표현한 것은? 정답 외의 보기들은 의미가 상당히 왜곡되거나 필수적인 정보가 빠져 있다.

Ⓐ 지루하거나 졸릴 때 호흡이 얕아 혈중 산소 수치가 떨어지는 경우가 많다는 것이 통설이다.

Ⓑ 하품을 하면 혈중 산소 수치가 높아져 결국 경각심이 높아지므로 지루하거나 졸릴 때 하품을 한다는 것이 통설이다.

Ⓒ 통설에 따르면, 하품은 기민하거나 깊게 숨쉴 때보다 지루하거나 졸릴 때 일어날 가능성이 더 높다.

Ⓓ 통설에 따르면, 하품은 지루함이나 수면 부족에 의해 발생하며 더 깊은 호흡을 통해 피할 수 있다.

문장 재구성 문제

어휘 due to ~ 때문에   in turn 결국, 결과적으로   be likely to ~할 것 같다

해설 강조된 문장의 핵심 정보를 모두 담고 있는 보기 B가 정답이다. 통설이 말하는 하품하는 이유에 대한 핵심 정보가 빠져 있으므로 보기 A는 정답이 될 수 없다. 통설에서 말하는 하품을 하는 이유와 하품이 경각심을 높이는 이유에 관한 핵심 정보가 없으므로 보기 C 역시 정답이 될 수 없다. 하품을 피하는 방법에 관한 정보는 강조된 내용에 없으므로 보기 D 역시 적절하지 않다.

12. 첫 번째 단락에서 저자는 하품의 피곤이론에 대한 증거에 대해 무엇을 지적하는가?

Ⓐ 하품과 피로를 연결하는 과학적 증거는 없다.

Ⓑ 그 증거는 여러 연령층을 포함하므로 포괄적이다.

Ⓒ 그 증거는 오랜 기간에 걸쳐 수집되었으므로 신뢰할 수 있다.

Ⓓ 어린이와 어른의 하품 패턴은 달라야 하므로 그 증거는 의심스럽다.

세부 정보 찾기 문제

어휘 wide-ranging 포괄적인, 광범위한   reliable 신뢰할 만한

해설 두 번째 문장에서 하품과 피로를 연결하는 어떤 증거도 찾지 못했다고 했으므로 보기 A가 정답이다. 보기 B, C, D는 모두 본문에 어긋나거나 본문에 없는 내용이므로 정답이 될 수 없다.

13. 지문의 단어 flaw와 의미상 가장 가까운 것은?

Ⓐ 결함   Ⓑ 측면

Ⓒ 혼란   Ⓓ 비밀

어휘 문제

어휘 fault 결함   confusion 혼란

해설 flaw는 '결점'이라는 의미이다.

14. 두 번째 단락에서 저자가 피실험자들이 단순히 입을 벌리거나 깊게 숨을 쉴 때 일어나는 생리적 변화와 사람들이 하품할 때 일어나는 생리적 변화를 비교하는 이유는?

Ⓐ 피곤이론을 뒷받침하는 논거를 제시하기 위해

Ⓑ 심박수, 근육의 긴장 및 피부 전도도를 측정한 테스트의 신뢰성에 의문을 제기하기 위해

Ⓒ 하품이 경각심을 높이거나 생리 활동을 증가시키는 특별한 방법이라는 가설을 반박하기 위해

Ⓓ 입을 벌리거나 깊게 호흡하는 것이 혈중 산소 수치에 영향을 미칠 수 있다는 견해를 뒷받침하기 위해

수사학적 의도 파악 문제

어휘 compare 비교하다   present 제시하다   argument 논거   reliability 신뢰성   hypothesis 가설

해설 두 번째 단락에서 입을 벌리는 행위, 깊이 숨쉬는 행위, 하품 이 세 가지 행동을 비교하면서 하품과 마찬가지로 입을 벌리는 행위와 깊이 숨쉬는 행위에도 동일한 생리 변화가 있었다고 했다. 즉 이는 하품이 피곤해서 경각심을 높이려는 행위라는 피곤이론을 반박하고 있으므로 보기 C가 정답이다.

15. 다음 하품에 관한 질문 중 두 번째 단락에서 대답이 나오지 않은 것은?

Ⓐ 하품이 경각심이나 생리 활동을 증가시키는가?

Ⓑ 하품에 대해 생각하면 하품에 대해 생각하지 않는 것보다 하품을 더 많이 하게 되는가?

Ⓒ 공기 중 이산화탄소와 산소의 양이 하품을 하는 비율에 영향을 미치는가?

Ⓓ 호흡 비율이 사람들이 하품하는 비율에 영향을 미치는가?

틀린 정보 찾기 문제

어휘 affect 영향을 미치다

해설 지문에서 하품에 대해 생각하면서 여러 종류의 공기를 마시게 하는 실험이 언급되지만 이는 여러 공기들이 하품에 미치는 영향을 측정한 실험으로, 단순히 하품에 대해 생각하는 것이 하품에 미치는 영향을 측정한 실험이 아니었다. 따라서 정답은 보기 B이다. 하품 이후 약간의 피부전도도 변화가 감지되었다는 내용은 보기 A에 대한 대답이며, 이산화탄소와 산소 양은 하품의 비율에 영향을 미치지 않는다는 내용은 보기 C에 대한 대답이며, 호흡의 비율이 두 배가 되어도 하품 빈도에는 아무런 영향을 미치지 않았다는 내용은 보기 D에 대한 대답이다.

16. 세 번째 단락에 제시된 하품의 발달이론에 따르면, 하품의 역할은 무엇인가?

Ⓐ 딸꾹질을 유발해 폐의 발달을 돕는다.

Ⓑ 폐가 다른 발달하는 장기에 가하는 압력의 양을 조절한다.

Ⓒ 양수가 폐로 들어가는 것을 방지한다.

Ⓓ 폐에서 잠재적으로 해로운 액체를 제거한다.

세부 정보 찾기 문제

어휘 organ (인체의) 장기   potentially 잠재적으로

해설 세 번째, 네 번째 문장에서 태아의 폐 속에 있는 액체가 분비되지 못하면 폐가 기형이 될 수도 있다고 했다. 그리고 발달이론은 태아의 하품과 딸꾹질이 이런 액체가 폐에서 나가도록 돕는다고 주장하므로 보기 D가 정답이다. 하품이 딸꾹질을 유발하는 것은 아니므로 보기 A는 맞지 않는다. 폐에서 액체가 빠지면 폐의 압력이 낮아지지만 폐가 다른 장기를 누른다는 내용은 없으므로 보기 B 역시 틀린 내용이다. 폐에서 액체가 나오지 못하고 막히면 기형이 된다고 했지만 양수가 폐로 들어가지 못하도록 방지한다는 내용은 없으므로 보기 C 역시 정답이 될 수 없다.

17. 지문의 단어 empirical과 의미상 가장 가까운 것은?

Ⓐ 신뢰할 만한 　　　Ⓑ 상식에 근거한
Ⓒ 적절한 　　　　　Ⓓ 관찰에 근거한

어휘 문제

어휘 common sense 상식　relevant 적절한, 관련이 있는
해설 empirical은 '경험적인'이라는 의미이다.

18. 다음 중 네 번째 단락에서 논의된 하품 행동 연구가 뒷받침하는 결론은?

Ⓐ 하품은 신체 활동의 증가에 대한 기대와 관련이 있다.
Ⓑ 하품은 하품을 기록하도록 요구 받을 때 더 자주 발생한다.
Ⓒ 사람들은 피곤하거나 지루해지기 15분 전에 하품을 하는 경향이 있다.
Ⓓ 정신적 또는 신체적 스트레스는 하품을 유발하는 경향이 있다.

내용 추론 문제

어휘 be associated with ～와 관련이 있다　expectation 기대, 예상
해설 네 번째 문장에서 활동 약 15분 전에 하품이 나오는 경향이 있다고 했으므로 보기 A가 정답이다. 장치의 버튼을 눌러 하품을 기록한 것과 하품 횟수에 대한 연관성은 본문에 없으므로 보기 B는 정답이 될 수 없다. 또한 활동하기 약 15분 전에 하품하며, 피곤하거나 지루해지기 전에 하품하는 것이 아니므로 보기 C 역시 맞지 않다. 본문에 정신적, 신체적 스트레스에 대한 내용은 없으므로 보기 D도 정답이 될 수 없다.

19. 지시문: 위에 제시된 지문의 일부를 보시오. 지문에 표시된 **(A)**, **(B)**, **(C)**, **(D)** 중 하나에 다음 문장이 삽입될 수 있다.

This, however, was not the case.

(그러나 그렇지 않았다.)

이 문장이 들어갈 가장 적당한 위치는?

Another flaw of the tiredness theory is that yawning does not raise alertness or physiological activity, as the theory would predict. When researchers measured the heart rate, muscle tension and skin conductance of people before, during and after yawning, they did detect some changes in skin conductance following yawning, indicating a slight increase in physiological activity. However, similar changes occurred when the subjects were asked simply to open their mouths or to breathe deeply. Yawning did nothing special to their state of physiological activity. Experiments have also cast serious doubt on the belief that yawning is triggered by a drop in blood oxygen or a rise in blood carbon dioxide. **(A)** Volunteers were told to think about yawning while they breathed either normal air, pure oxygen, or an air mixture with an above-normal level of carbon dioxide. **(B)** If the theory was correct, breathing air with extra carbon dioxide should have triggered yawning, while breathing pure oxygen should have suppressed yawning. **(C)** This, however, was not the case. In fact, neither condition made any difference to the frequency

of yawning, which remained constant at about 24 yawns per hour. **(D)** Another experiment demonstrated that physical exercise, which was sufficiently vigorous to double the rate of breathing, had no effect on the frequency of yawning. Again, the implication is that yawning has little or nothing to do with oxygen.

Ⓐ　　　Ⓑ　　　Ⓒ　　　Ⓓ

문장 삽입 문제

해설 삽입 문장은 어떤 것이 사실이 아니었다는 것이므로 연구 결과 실제로 일어나지 않은 일 뒤에 와야 한다. 따라서 이산화탄소가 많은 공기를 호흡하면 하품이 촉발되고 순수 산소를 호흡하면 하품이 억제되어야 한다는 가설이 실제와 어긋나므로 이 문장 뒤, 즉 (C) 위치에 들어가는 것이 가장 알맞다.

20. 지시문: 이 지문을 간단히 요약하기 위한 도입 문장이 아래에 제시되어 있다. 아래 보기들 중에서 지문의 가장 중요한 개념을 표현한 문장 3개를 골라 요약을 완성하라. 보기들 중에는 지문에 나오지 않았거나 중요하지 않은 개념이기 때문에 요약문으로 적절치 않은 것들도 있다. 이 문제의 배점은 2점이다.

답으로 선택한 보기를 지정된 공간에 쓰시오. 선택한 보기의 번호를 쓰거나 문장을 옮겨 쓰시오.

하품의 피곤이론은 하품이 왜 발생하는지 설명하지 못하는 듯하다.

Ⓐ 이전의 과학 연구들이 피곤이론을 강하게 지지했지만, 새로운 증거는 이러한 발견들에 의문을 던져 왔다.
Ⓑ 증거에 따르면, 하품은 혈중 산소의 양과 거의 전적으로 무관하며 수면 행동과도 관련이 없다.
Ⓒ 일부는 출생 전 하품이 폐의 발육에 기여한다는 의견을 제시했지만, 성인에게도 하품이 용도가 있는 듯하다.
Ⓓ 태아의 폐에 있는 액체는 하품이 일어나는 것을 방지하는데, 이는 하품 발달이론의 오류를 입증한다.
Ⓔ 일화적 증거와 함께 새로운 연구들은 장기간 활동이 없는 동안 하품 빈도가 증가한다는 것을 보여 주었다.
Ⓕ 하품이 활동 수준의 변화를 위해 몸과 마음을 준비시킨다는 증거가 있다.

지문 요약하기 문제

어휘 unrelated 무관한　disprove 오류를 입증하다　extended 늘어난, 장기간에 걸친
해설 첫 번째, 두 번째 단락에서 수면과 하품 사이에는 연관성이 없으며 산소와도 거의 관계가 없거나 전혀 관계가 없다고 했다. 이는 피곤이론을 반박하는 핵심 견해이므로 B는 요약에 포함되어야 한다. 세 번째 단락에서 또 하나의 이론인 발달이론을 제시하고 발달이론의 결함을 설명하고 있으므로 C 역시 핵심 내용이다. 네 번째 단락에서 하품이 활동 수준의 변화에 앞서 발생한다는 경험 증거를 제시하고 있으므로 F 역시 핵심 내용이다. 피곤이론과 하품 사이에 연관성을 발견한 연구는 거의 없다고 했으므로 A는 본문과 일치하지 않는다. 지문 세 번째 단락에서 하품이 태아의 폐에서 액체를 내보낸다고 했으며, 액체가 하품을 방지한다는 내용은 없으므로 D 역시 본문과 일치하지 않는다. 네 번째 단락에서 하품은 활동이 있기 전에 발생한다고 설명하는데, 장기간 무활동이 하품 증가로 이어진다는 내용은 없으므로 E 역시 본문에 없는 내용이다.

LISTENING

Questions 1-5   p. 276

N *Narrator*   M *Male Student*   A *Administrator*

Script

N Listen to a conversation between a student and an A in the university employment office.

M Hi, I hope you can help me. I just transferred from Northeastern State University, near Chicago...

A Well, welcome to Central University. But Chicago's such a great city, why did you leave?

M Everyone asks that... it's my hometown, and it was sure convenient to go to a school nearby. But Northeastern is still fairly small, and it doesn't have the program I'm interested in... I want to major in international studies and the only program in the state is here.

A We do have a great program. How did you get interested in international studies?

M My family hosted a few foreign-exchange students while I was growing up... then I took part in an international summer program after I graduated from high school. I found I really like meeting people from all over, getting to know them...

A Oh, OK. And that led you to our program. Right now, though, I assume you're looking for a job.

M Yeah, a part-time job on campus... I thought I'd save money, being away from the big city... but it doesn't seem to be working that way. Anyway, I'm not having much luck.

A I'm not surprised. Most of our campus jobs are taken in the first week or two of the semester. What work experience have you had?

M Well, I worked in the university library last year. But I already checked at the library here... they said their remaining positions were for work-study students getting financial aid. I've never run into that before.

A Well, I guess each school has its own policies. We really don't have much right now. You might be better off waiting until next semester... if you really want something... How are your computer skills?

M About average, I'd say. I helped teach some of the basic computer classes Northeastern offers for new users, if that helps any.

N 학생과 대학 고용처 관리자 간의 대화를 들으시오.

M 안녕하세요, 도와주셨으면 합니다. 저는 시카고 인근 노스이스턴 주립대학교에서 막 편입했어요…

A 센트럴대학교에 오신 걸 환영합니다. 시카고는 아주 큰 도시인데 왜 떠나셨죠?

M 모두들 묻더군요… 시카고는 제 고향이고, 학교도 근처에 있어서 다니기에 분명 편했어요. 하지만 노스이스턴은 아직 꽤 작고 제가 관심 있는 프로그램이 없어요… 저는 국제지역학을 전공하고 싶은데 여기에 주에서 유일한 프로그램이 있어요.

A 우린 훌륭한 프로그램이 있죠. 어떻게 해서 국제지역학에 관심을 갖게 되었나요?

M 제가 자랄 때 우리 가족이 외국 교환학생 몇 명을 초대했어요… 그리고 저는 고등학교 졸업 후에 국제 여름 프로그램에 참가했고요. 제가 각지에서 온 사람들을 만나고, 알게 되는 것을 정말 좋아한다는 걸 알게 되었어요.

A 그렇군요. 그래서 우리 프로그램을 찾은 거네요. 하지만 지금 당장은 일자리를 찾고 있을 테죠.

M 맞습니다, 교내 시간제 일이요… 대도시에서 떨어져 살면 돈을 모을 거라고 생각했는데, 안 되는 것 같아요. 어쨌든, 운이 별로 없네요.

A 놀랍지 않아요. 교내 일자리는 대부분 학기 첫 주나 둘째 주에 없어져요. 어떤 일을 해보셨어요?

M 음, 지난해에 대학 도서관에서 일했습니다. 하지만 여기 도서관에 이미 확인해 봤는데, 남은 자리는 재정 지원을 받는 근로학생 자리라고 했어요. 이런 일은 처음이에요.

A 어, 학교마다 나름의 정책이 있는 것 같아요. 지금은 정말 일자리가 별로 없어요. 다음 학기까지 기다리는 게 나을지도 모르겠네요… 만약 정말 원한다면… 컴퓨터 실력은 어때요?

M 평균 정도예요. 노스이스턴이 새로운 사용자들에게 제공하는 컴퓨터 기초 수업이 있었는데, 그 수업 중 일부를 가르칠 때 도와줬어요. 그게 도움이 될지 모르겠지만요.

A OK... Uh, the technology support department needs people to work at its helpdesk. It's basically a customer-service job... answering questions, helping people solve their computer problems... give you a chance to develop your people skills.

M Something every diplomat needs. But, is there some problem? I mean, why's the job still open?

A Well, they have extended hours... from 6 A.M. to 2 A.M. every day, so they need a large staff. But right now they only need people early mornings, late nights, and weekends. You'd probably end up with a bit of everything rather than a regular spot. On the bright side, you'd probably be able to get some studying done between calls. At least it'd be a start and then you can try for better hours next semester.

M Hmm, I see where the hours might be a problem. But... I guess I can't afford to be too picky if I want a job. Still, maybe we can work something out.

A 좋아요… 어, 기술지원부에서 업무지원센터에서 일할 사람이 필요해요. 기본적으로 고객 서비스 일이에요… 질문에 대답하고, 컴퓨터 문제를 해결하도록 도와주는 거죠. 사람을 상대하는 기술을 발전시킬 기회가 되죠.

M 외교관이라면 누구에게나 필요한 기술이죠. 하지만 무슨 문제라도 있나요? 그러니까 왜 아직도 그 일자리가 남아 있는 거죠?

A 어, 매일 아침 6시부터 새벽 2시까지 시간을 연장해서 직원이 많이 필요해요. 하지만 지금 당장은 이른 아침, 늦은 밤, 그리고 주말에 일할 사람만 있으면 되요. 아마 고정으로 일하기보다는 이것저것 골고루 하게 될 거예요. 긍정적인 면이라면 전화를 받는 사이 사이에 공부를 좀 할 수도 있을 거예요. 이건 일단 시작으로 삼고 다음 학기에는 더 좋은 시간대를 노려 보세요.

M 흠, 시간이 문제가 될 만하네요. 하지만… 일자리를 원하면 너무 까다롭게 굴 처지는 아닌 것 같네요. 그래도 어찌어찌 해결할 수 있겠죠.

어휘

transfer 전학[전근]하다, 옮기다   convenient 편리한   be interested in ~에 관심이 있다   international studies 국제지역학   host (주인으로 손님을) 초대하다, 접대하다   exchange student 교환학생   take part in ~에 참가하다   assume 짐작하다   semester 학기   experience 경험, 경력   remaining 남아 있는   financial 재정의   aid 도움, 지원   run into (주로 안 좋은 상황과) 만나다, 부딪히다   policy 정책   support 지원   customer-service 고객 서비스   diplomat 외교관   extend (시간, 분량 등을) 늘리다   a bit of everything 이것저것 골고루   afford to ~할 여유가 있다   picky 까다로운   work out 해결하다

198

1. 학생이 대학 고용처를 찾은 이유는 무엇인가?

Ⓐ 대학 도서관 일자리에 지원하기 위해

Ⓑ 교환학생 초대에 관한 정보를 얻기 위해

Ⓒ 교내에 남은 일자리가 있는지 알아 보기 위해

Ⓓ 컴퓨터실 시간을 알아 보기 위해

내용의 목적을 묻는 문제

어휘 apply for ~에 지원하다   available 이용할 수 있는, 얻을 수 있는

해설 편입 이유에 관한 대화가 오간 후 관리자가 일자리를 찾으러 온 것인지 묻자 학생이 교내 시간제 일을 찾는다고 했으므로 보기 C가 정답이다.

2. 학생이 센트럴대학교로 편입한 이유는 무엇인가?

Ⓐ 학업 프로그램을 이용하기 위해

Ⓑ 교환학생 프로그램에 참여하기 위해

Ⓒ 전에 다니던 대학보다 더 작은 대학을 다니기 위해

Ⓓ 센트럴대학교의 국제적 명성에서 득을 보기 위해

세부 정보 찾기 문제

어휘 take advantage of ~을 이용하다   participate in ~에 참여하다   benefit from ~에서 이익을 얻다   reputation 명성

해설 대화 초반부에서 시카고에서 다니던 대학에는 국제지역학 프로그램이 없어 센트럴대학교로 편입했다고 했으므로 보기 A가 정답이다. 학생은 국제 여름 프로그램에 참가했고 교환학생 프로그램에 참여한 것이 아니므로 보기 B는 본문과 일치하지 않는다. 센트럴대학교가 국제적인 명성이 있다는 내용은 없으므로 보기 D 역시 정답이 될 수 없다.

3. 학생이 외국 교환학생 초대를 언급한 이유는 무엇인가?

Ⓐ 특정 학문 분야에 대한 관심을 설명하기 위해

Ⓑ 학기 중 뒤늦게 일자리를 찾는 이유를 설명하기 위해

Ⓒ 이듬해에 교환학생이 되고 싶은 이유를 설명하기 위해

Ⓓ 컴퓨터 기술을 어떻게 배웠는지 설명하기 위해

구성 파악 문제

어휘 particular 특정한   field 분야

해설 학생이 외국 교환학생 초대에 대해 언급한 것은 국제지역학에 관심을 갖게 된 경위를 묻는 관리자의 질문에 대답한 것이므로 보기 A가 정답이다.

4. 기술지원 업무지원센터 일자리에 지원하는 학생들에 관해 추론할 수 있는 것은?

Ⓐ 컴퓨터 강좌에 등록해야 한다.

Ⓑ 주말에만 일할 수 있을 것이다.

Ⓒ 일하는 날마다 기꺼이 많은 시간을 일하려고 한다.

Ⓓ 시간이 불규칙해도 기꺼이 일하려고 한다.

추론 문제

어휘 enroll 등록하다   irregular 불규칙한

해설 관리자가 이른 아침, 늦은 밤, 그리고 주말에 일할 사람이 필요하며 고정으로 일하기보다는 이것저것 골고루 하게 될 것이라고 했다. 따라서 업무지원센터에서는 시간이 불규칙해도 일할 사람이 필요하다고 추론할 수 있으므로 보기 D가 정답이다.

5. 대화의 일부를 다시 듣고 질문에 답하라.

🎧 T-79

> **A** We really don't have much right now. You might be better off waiting until next semester... if you really want something
>
> **N** *Why does the woman say this?*
> **A** if you really want something

Ⓐ 당장 일을 시작하지 않도록 학생을 설득하기 위해

Ⓑ 교정 밖에서 일자리를 구하라고 제안하기 위해

Ⓒ 학생이 지금 비어 있는 일자리가 내키지 않을 수도 있다는 것을 암시하기 위해

Ⓓ 학생에게 근로학생 프로그램에 지원하라고 권장하기 위해

의도 파악 문제

어휘 dissuade ~하지 않도록 설득하다   encourage 권장하다

해설 고용처 관리자는 일자리가 별로 없다고 하면서 다음 학기까지 기다리는 게 나을지도 모른다고 했다. 따라서 지금 남아 있는 일자리는 별로 내키지 않을 수도 있음을 암시하므로 보기 C가 정답이다.

Reading

Listening

Speaking

Writing

Test 1

Test 2

Test 3

Test 4

Script

N Listen to part of a lecture in an art history class.

P Today, we'll continue our examination of ancient Roman sculpture. We've already looked at portrait sculpture—which are busts created to commemorate people who had died—and we've looked at relief sculpture, or sculpting on walls. And today we look at yet another category of sculpture—copies. Roman sculptors often made copies of famous Greek sculptures.

F Why did they do that?

P Well, no one knows for sure. You see, in the late fourth century B.C., the Romans began a campaign to expand the Roman Empire... and in 300 years they had conquered most of the Mediterranean area and parts of Europe. You know the saying, "To the victor belong the spoils?" Well, the Roman army returned to Rome with many works of Greek art. It's probably fair to say that the Romans were impressed by Greek art and culture—and they began making copies of the Greek statues. Now, the dominant view in traditional art history is that Roman artists lacked creativity and skill, especially compared to the Greek artists who came before them. Essentially, the traditional view—a view that's been prevalent for over 250 years—is that the Romans copied Greek sculptures because they couldn't create sculpture of their own.

But, finally, some contemporary art historians have challenged this view. One is Elaine Gazda.

Gazda says that there might be other reasons that Romans made copies. She wasn't convinced that it was because of a lack of creativity. Can anyone think of another possible reason?

M Well... maybe they just admired the sculptures, you know, they liked the way they looked.

P Yes! That's one of Gazda's points. Another is that while nowadays reproduction is easy, it was not so easy in Roman times. Copying statues required a lot of skill, time, and effort. So, Gazda hypothesizes that copying didn't indicate a lack of artistic imagination—or skill—on the part of Roman artists, but rather, the Romans made copies because they admired Greek sculpture. Classical Greek statues represented an idealization of the human body and were considered quite beautiful at the time.

Gazda also believes that it's been a mistake to dismiss the Roman copies as, well, copies for copies' sake, and not to

N 예술사 수업의 강의 일부를 들으시오.

P 오늘은 고대 로마 조각을 계속 고찰해 보겠습니다. 죽은 자들을 기리기 위해 만들어진 흉상인 인물 조각에 대해 이미 살펴봤죠. 그리고 벽에 조각하는 돋을새김 조각을 살펴보았습니다. 그러면 오늘은 또 다른 범주의 조각품, 즉 모사품을 살펴보겠습니다. 로마의 조각가들은 종종 유명한 그리스 조각품들을 베꼈습니다.

F 왜 그랬죠?

P 음, 확실한 건 아무도 모릅니다. BC 4세기 후반 로마인들은 로마제국을 확장하기 위한 운동을 벌였죠… 그리고 300년 후 그들은 지중해 지역 대부분과 유럽 일부를 정복했습니다. "전리품은 승자 차지"라는 속담, 알죠? 로마군은 많은 그리스 예술작품을 가지고 로마로 돌아왔습니다. 로마인들이 그리스 예술과 문화에 감명 받았다는 게 맞을 겁니다. 그리고 그들은 그리스 조각상들을 모방하기 시작했습니다. 현재, 전통 미술사의 지배적인 관점은 로마 예술가들이 특히 그들보다 이전에 있었던 그리스 예술가들에 비해 창의력과 기술이 부족했다는 것입니다. 본질적으로 전통적인 견해, 즉 250년 이상 동안 지배적이었던 관점은 로마인들이 자신들만의 조각품을 만들 수 없었기 때문에 그리스 조각품을 모방했다는 것입니다.

그러나 마침내 몇몇 현대 미술사학자들이 이 견해에 이의를 제기했죠. 그중 한 사람이 일레인 가즈다입니다.

가즈다는 로마인들이 모사품을 만든 데는 다른 이유가 있었다고 말합니다. 그녀는 창의력 부족 때문이라고 믿지 않았습니다. 가능성 있는 다른 이유 생각나는 사람?

M 음… 그들은 그저 조각품에 감탄했을 수도 있어요, 그러니까 조각품의 모습이 마음에 들었던 거죠.

P 맞습니다! 그 점도 가즈다가 지적한 사항 중 하나예요. 또 하나는 요즘은 복제가 쉽지만, 로마 시대에는 그렇게 쉽지 않았다는 거죠. 조각상을 복제하려면 많은 기술과 시간, 노력이 필요했습니다. 그래서 가즈다는 복제가 로마 예술가들의 예술적 상상력, 혹은 기술 부족을 나타내는 것이 아니라, 오히려 로마인들이 그리스 조각품에 경탄했기 때문에 복제했다는 가설을 내세우죠. 고전적인 그리스 조각상은 인체를 이상적으로 나타냈고 당시에는 상당히 아름답다고 여겼습니다.

가즈다는 또한 로마 복제품을 복제를 위한 복제라고 무시하고 그 조각에 깃든 로마의 기능과 의미를 고려하지 않는 것은 실수라고 믿습니다.

F 로마의 기능이라니 무슨 뜻인가요? 그냥 장식품 아니었나요?

P 글쎄요, 꼭 그렇지만은 않아요. 로마제국 전성기인 아우구스투스 황제가 다스리던 시절 인물 조각상을 제국 전역으로 보냈습니다… 인물 조각상은 황제와 황실에 대한 구체적

Reading

Listening

Speaking

Writing

Test 1

Test 2

Test 3

Test 4

consider the Roman function and meaning of the statues.

F What do you mean... the Roman function? Weren't they just for decoration?

P Well, not necessarily. Under the emperor Augustus, at the height of the Roman Empire, portrait statues were sent throughout the empire... they were supposed to communicate specific ideas about the emperor and the imperial family, and to help inhabitants of the conquered areas become familiar with the Roman way of life. You know, Roman coins were also distributed throughout the empire. Anybody care to guess what was on them?

M The emperor's face?

P That's right. The coins were easy to distribute, and they allowed people to see the emperor, or at least his likeness, and served as an additional reminder to let them know, well, who was in charge. And the images helped people become familiar with the emperor—statues of him in different roles were sent all over the empire. Now, actually some Roman sculptures were original, but others were exact copies of Greek statues. And some Roman sculptures were combinations of some sort; some combined more than one Greek statue, and others combined a Greek god or an athlete with a Roman's head. At the time of Julius Caesar, it wasn't uncommon to create statues that had the body of a god and the head of an emperor.

And the Romans were clever... what they did was, they made plaster casts from molds of the sculptures. Then, they shipped these plaster casts to workshops all over the empire, where they were replicated in marble or bronze. And on some statues the heads were removable—they could put an emperor's head on different bodies showing him doing different things. And then later, when the time came, they could even use the head of the next emperor on the same body!

인 개념을 전달하고 정복지 주민들이 로마의 생활방식에 익숙해지도록 돕는 역할을 했습니다. 알다시피, 로마 동전도 제국 전역에 배포되었죠. 동전에 뭐가 있었는지 맞혀볼 사람?

M 황제의 얼굴이요?

P 맞습니다. 동전은 배포하기 쉬웠고 사용자는 동전을 통해 황제의 얼굴, 아니 적어도 초상을 볼 수 있었습니다. 따라서 동전은 사람들이 누가 통치하고 있는지 알게 해 주는 물건이었죠. 그 이미지는 사람들이 황제에게 친숙해지도록 도왔습니다. 황제의 조각상은 다른 역할로 제국 전역으로 전달되었죠. 사실, 몇몇 로마 조각상들은 독창적이었습니다. 하지만 다른 조각상들은 그리스 조각상들을 그대로 베낀 모사품이었습니다. 그리고 일부 로마 조각품들은 일종의 조합이었습니다. 어떤 조각상들은 그리스 조각상 하나 이상을 조합했고 또 어떤 조각상들은 그리스 신이나 운동선수에 로마인의 머리를 조합했죠. 줄리어스 시저 시대에, 신의 몸에 황제의 머리를 가진 동상을 만드는 일은 드물지 않았습니다.

그리고 로마인들은 영리했습니다… 그들이 한 일은, 그들은 조각상 주형으로 석고 틀을 만들었습니다. 그들은 이 석고 틀을 제국 전역의 작업장으로 보냈고 여기서 대리석이나 청동으로 복제했죠. 그리고 일부 조각상은 머리를 분리할 수 있었죠—그들은 황제의 다른 행동을 보여 주는 다른 몸에 황제의 머리를 놓을 수 있었습니다. 그리고 나중에 때가 되면 같은 몸에 다음 황제의 머리까지 쓸 수 있었답니다!

어휘

continue 계속하다　sculpture 조각(품)　portrait 인물 묘사, 초상화　bust 흉상　commemorate (중요한 사건이나 인물을) 기념하다, 기리다　relief sculpture 돋을새김 조각　sculptor 조각가　expand 확장[확대]하다　conquer 정복하다　Mediterranean 지중해의　victor 승자　spoil 전리품, 약탈품　fair 정당한　impressed 깊은 인상을 받은, 감명 받은　statue 조각상, 동상　dominant 지배적인　compared to ~에 비해　prevalent 널리 퍼진　contemporary 현대의, 동시대의　convinced 확신하는　admire 경탄하다, 동경하다　reproduction 복제(품)　hypothesize 가설을 세우다　indicate 나타내다　represent 나타내다　idealization 이상화　dismiss 무시하다　function 기능　not necessarily 반드시 ~은 아닌　emperor 황제　be supposed to ~하기로 되어 있다　specific 구체적인　imperial 황제의, 제국의　inhabitant 주민　familiar with ~에 익숙한　distribute 배포하다, 퍼트리다　likeness 초상　reminder 상기시키는 것　in charge ~을 책임 지는　combine 조합[결합]하다　athlete 운동선수　uncommon 드문　plaster 석고　cast 틀, 주형　mold 틀　replicate 모사하다, 복제하다　bronze 청동　removable 분리할 수 있는, 뗄 수 있는

6. 이 강의의 주제는 무엇인가?

Ⓐ 고대 로마 시대에 유행한 조각의 유형에 대한 다양한 견해

Ⓑ 로마인에게 뛰어난 예술적 역량이 있었다는 증거

Ⓒ 그리스 조각과 로마 조각의 차이점

Ⓓ 고대 로마 시대의 예술과 정치의 관계

내용의 요점을 묻는 문제

어휘 popular 유행하는, 인기 있는   outstanding 뛰어난
politics 정치

해설 교수는 로마 조각가들이 그리스 조각을 모방했다고 한 뒤 과거 대대수 미술사학자들의 견해를 제시한다. 이어서 현대 미술사학자의 다른 견해를 소개하고 있으므로 보기 A가 정답이다.

7. 종래의 미술사학자들에 따르면, 로마인들이 그리스 조각을 모방한 이유는 무엇인가?

Ⓐ 로마 대중은 독창적인 예술 작품에는 관심이 없었다.

Ⓑ 로마 정부는 다른 형태의 예술은 지원하지 않았다.

Ⓒ 로마 예술가들은 독창적인 조각품을 창조할 만한 역량이 충분하지 않았다.

Ⓓ 로마인들은 자신들이 동경하는 예술을 모방하고 싶어했다.

세부 정보 찾기 문제

어휘 imitate 모방하다, 흉내 내다

해설 교수에 따르면 전통 미술사의 지배적인 관점은 로마 예술가들이 그리스 예술가들에 비해 창의력과 기술이 부족했기 때문에 그리스 조각품을 모방했다는 견해이다. 따라서 보기 C가 정답이다. 보기 A, B는 본문에 없는 내용이며 보기 D는 현대 학자인 일레인 가즈다의 견해이다.

8. 로마인이 그리스 조각상을 모방한 것에 대한 가즈다의 견해는 무엇인가?

Ⓐ 모사품은 로마 사회가 그리스 사회와 비슷하다는 생각을 드러냈다.

Ⓑ 모사품은 로마제국의 시민에게 그리스 역사를 소개했다.

Ⓒ 모사품은 원본 조각상보다 열등했다.

Ⓓ 모사품에는 예술적 기능과 정치적 기능이 모두 있었다.

내용 연결 문제

어휘 similar 유사한   inferior 열등한

해설 가즈다는 모사품 제작에는 예술적 역량이 필요했다고 지적하는 한편 로마인들이 정복지 주민의 충성심을 고취하기 위해 황제의 조각상을 제국 곳곳에 퍼트렸다고 했다. 따라서 조각상에는 예술적 기능과 정치적 목적이 모두 있었으므로 정답은 보기 D이다.

9. 교수가 로마 동전을 언급한 이유는 무엇인가?

Ⓐ 조각상과 동전에 찍힌 황제 초상의 유사성을 보여 주기 위해

Ⓑ 황제의 형상을 제국 전역에 퍼트리는 로마의 정책을 설명하기 위해

Ⓒ 로마제국의 시민들이 꽤 부유해졌다는 것을 암시하기 위해

Ⓓ 로마인이 동전에도 그리스 예술을 모방했다는 것을 암시하기 위해

구성 파악 문제

어휘 illustrate 설명하다, 예시를 들다   wealthy 부유한

해설 로마 황제들의 조각상을 제국 곳곳에 퍼트릴 필요가 있었다고 언급한 뒤 황제의 얼굴이 찍힌 동전은 작고 가벼워 배포하기 쉬웠다고 했다. 따라서 보기 B가 정답이다. 조각상과 동전에 찍힌 황제 초상의 유사성을 보여 주는 것이 교수의 목적은 아니므로 보기 A는 정답이 될 수 없다.

10. 교수에 따르면 로마인들이 때때로 조각상에서 황제의 머리를 분리한 이유는 무엇인가?
정답 2개를 고르시오.

Ⓐ 머리 때문에 조각상을 운반하기 너무 무거웠다.

Ⓑ 다른 조각상의 몸에 머리를 놓았다.

Ⓒ 황제가 권좌에서 물러났다.

Ⓓ 황제가 조각상의 수준에 만족하지 않았다.

세부 정보 찾기 문제

어휘 satisfied 만족한

해설 교수에 따르면 첫째, 다양한 조각상에 부착하기 위해 머리를 분리했고, 둘째, 다른 황제가 권좌에 올랐을 때 머리만 교체했다고 했다. 따라서 보기 B, C가 정답이다.

11. 강의의 일부를 다시 듣고 질문에 답하시오.

🎧 T-81

P Essentially, the traditional view—a view that's been prevalent for over 250 years—is that the Romans copied Greek sculptures because they couldn't create sculpture of their own. But, finally, some contemporary art historians have challenged this view.

N *What does the professor imply when he says this?*

P But, finally, some contemporary art historians have challenged this view.

Ⓐ 미술사학자들은 자주 견해를 바꾼다.

Ⓑ 현대의 견해는 이해하기 쉽지 않다.

Ⓒ 로마인들이 그리스 조각상을 모방한 이유를 판단하기는 어렵지 않다.

Ⓓ 종래의 미술사학자들의 견해가 틀릴 수도 있다.

의도 파악 문제

어휘 frequently 자주   incorrect 틀린

해설 교수가 지배적이었던 견해를 소개한 뒤 마침내 현대 미술사가들이 전통적인 견해에 의문을 제기하고 있다고 했으므로 보기 D가 정답이다.

N Narrator　　P Professor　　M Male Student

Script

N Listen to a conversation between a student and his sociology professor.

P Well, I'm glad you redid your outline. Um, I've made a few comments, but nothing you have to act on. It's in good enough shape for you to start writing your paper.

M Thanks. At first I was afraid all that prep work would be a waste of time.

P Well, especially with a challenging topic like yours—factors leading to the emergence of sociology as an academic discipline. There's just so much history to consider, you could get lost without a solid outline. Uh, so, did you have a question?

M Yeah, it's about.... You mentioned needing volunteers for a research study?

P Yep. It's not my study, it's my colleague's in the marketing department. She needs people to watch various new TV programs that haven't been broadcast yet. Then indicate on a survey whether they liked it, why, if they'd watch another episode.... It'd be kinda fun, plus participants get a $50 gift certificate.

M Oh, well, I like the sound of that! But—so they're trying to predict if these shows are gonna succeed or fail, right? Based on students' opinions? Why would they care what we think?

P Hey, don't sell yourself short—people your age are a very attractive market for advertisers who promote their products on television. The study's sponsored by a TV network. If enough students don't like a show, the network may actually reconsider putting it on the air.

M OK, well, how do I sign up?

P You just add your name and phone number to this list and check a time slot. Although it looks like the only times left are next Monday morning and Thursday evening.

M Oh, well.... I have marketing and economics Monday mornings, and Thursday.

P Oh, you're taking a marketing class? Who's teaching it?

M It's, uh, Professor Larkin, intro to marketing. He hasn't mentioned the study, though.

P Oh. Well... the marketing department's pretty big. I happen to be friends with the woman who's doing the TV study. OK, well, we don't want you missing class... how's Thursday?

N 학생과 사회학 교수간의 대화를 들으시오.

P 음, 네가 개요를 고쳐서 기쁘구나. 내가 몇 가지 의견을 내긴 했지만 네가 그대로 따를 필요는 없어. 리포트 작성을 시작할 수 있을 만큼 상태가 괜찮아.

M 감사합니다. 처음에는 이런 준비 작업이 모두 시간 낭비가 될까 걱정했어요.

P 음, 특히 너처럼 녹록하지 않은 주제라면—사회학이 분과학문으로 부상하게 된 요인들 말이야. 고려해야 할 역사가 너무 많아서, 탄탄한 개요가 없으면 길을 잃을 수도 있지. 어, 그럼, 질문 있니?

M 예, 그게…. 연구를 위해 지원자가 필요하다고 하셨죠?

P 내 연구는 아니고 마케팅과에 있는 동료의 연구야. 아직 방송되지 않은 다양한 신규 TV 프로그램을 시청할 사람들이 필요하다고 해. 그리고 나서 마음에 드는지, 이유는 무엇인지, 다른 에피소드도 시청할 의향이 있는지 설문지에 표시하는 건데 재미있을 거야. 게다가 참가자는 50달러짜리 상품권도 받아.

M 오, 괜찮을 것 같아요! 하지만—그러니까 이 쇼들이 성공할지 실패할지 예측하려고 하는 거죠? 학생들의 의견을 토대로? 왜 우리 생각에 신경 쓰죠?

P 저런, 자신을 과소평가하지 마. 네 나이대 사람들은 TV에서 제품을 홍보하는 광고주들에게 매우 매력적인 시장이야. 그 연구는 TV 방송국의 후원을 받아. 만약 충분한 학생들이 쇼를 좋아하지 않는다면, 방송국은 정말 방송을 재고할 수도 있어.

M 그렇군요, 어떻게 신청하죠?

P 이 목록에 이름과 전화번호를 추가하고 시간대를 확인하기만 하면 돼. 남은 시간은 다음 주 월요일 아침과 목요일 저녁뿐인 것 같지만.

M 아, 이런…. 월요일 아침과 목요일에는 마케팅, 경제학 수업이 있어요.

P 마케팅 수업을 듣고 있니? 누가 가르치지?

M 라킨 교수님의 마케팅 입문이에요. 그런데 교수님은 그 연구에 대해 말씀이 없으셨어요.

P 아, 그래… 마케팅과는 꽤 크지. 나는 TV 연구를 하고 있는 여성분과 마침 친구 사이거든. 그래, 수업을 빠지면 안 되지…. 목요일은 어때?

M Oh, I work from five till nine that night.

P Hmm. No flexibility with your schedule? Where do you work?

M At Fox's Diner. I'm a server.

P Oh, I love Fox's. I eat there every week. Maybe you could switch shifts with someone.

M I'm still in training, and the only night my trainer works is Thursday.

P Look, I know the owners there really well. Why don't you let me give them a call and explain the situation?

M OK. It'd be cool to be part of a real research study. And the gift certificate wouldn't hurt, either!

M 그날 밤에는 다섯 시부터 아홉 시까지 일해요.

P 흠. 일정을 바꿀 여지는 없어? 어디서 일하는데?

M 폭스 다이너예요. 저는 웨이터예요.

P 폭스 정말 좋아. 매주 거기서 먹거든. 다른 사람과 교대 근무 시간을 바꿀 수 있지 않을까.

M 전 아직 교육 기간이라 제 교육 담당이 목요일 밤에만 일해요.

P 이봐, 나 거기 주인들을 정말 잘 알아. 내가 그들에게 전화해서 상황을 설명하면 어때?

M 좋아요. 실제 연구에 참여하면 멋질 거예요. 그리고 상품권도 나쁠 건 없죠!

어휘

redo 고치다　act on ~에 따라 행동하다　prep work 준비 작업　emergence 부상, 출현　sociology 사회학　academic discipline 분과학문　solid 탄탄한　volunteer 지원자　various 다양한　indicate 나타내다　survey 설문조사(서)　participant 참가자　gift certificate 상품권　predict 예측하다　sell oneself short 자신을 과소평가하다　attractive 매력적인　advertiser 광고주　promote 홍보하다　sign up 신청하다　time slot 시간대　economics 경제학　mention 언급하다　flexibility 융통성　shift 교대 근무 (시간), 교대조　situation 상황

12. 대화의 주제는 무엇인가?

Ⓐ 남자의 연구 리포트 주제

Ⓑ 진행 중인 사회학 연구 프로젝트

Ⓒ 효과적인 사회학 연구 수행 방법

Ⓓ 남자가 참가할 수도 있는 연구 프로젝트

내용의 요점을 묻는 문제

어휘 effective 효과적인 conduct 수행하다 participation 참가

해설 대화 초반부에 과제물 작성에 관한 이야기 뒤에 교수가 질문이 있는지 묻자 학생이 지원하고 싶어하는 연구 프로젝트에 관한 이야기가 쭉 이어지므로 보기 D가 정답이다.

13. 남자의 개요에 관해 교수가 암시하는 것은?

Ⓐ 그가 리포트의 논점을 제한해야 한다는 것이 드러났다.

Ⓑ 그가 리포트를 작성하기에 충분한 정보가 없다.

Ⓒ 그가 복잡한 주제에 대해 명료하게 쓸 수 있도록 도움을 준다.

Ⓓ 사회학과 마케팅 사이의 연관성을 과장한다.

추론 문제

어휘 limit 제한하다 overstate 과장하다 connection 연관성

해설 교수는 학생의 리포트 주제가 탄탄한 개요가 없으면 길을 잃을 수도 있다고 언급했다. 앞서 교수는 학생이 개요를 고쳐서 리포트 작성을 시작할 수 있을 만큼 상태가 괜찮다고 했으므로 개요가 어려운 주제를 다루는 데 도움이 된다는 것을 추론할 수 있으므로 보기 C가 정답이다.

14. 교수의 동료가 수행하고 있는 연구의 주요 목표는 무엇인가?

Ⓐ 어떤 TV 쇼가 특정 연령대의 사람에게 인기가 있을지 알아 보는 것

Ⓑ 대학생들이 좋아하는 식품에 관한 정보를 수집하는 것

Ⓒ 새로운 텔레비전 쇼에 대한 아이디어를 짜내는 것

Ⓓ 사람들의 텔레비전 시청 선호도와 관련된 사회학적 요인을 판단하는 것

세부 정보 찾기 문제

어휘 generate 만들어 내다 related to ~와 관련된 preference 선호

해설 교수는 마케팅과에서 아직 방송되지 않은 신규 TV 프로그램에 대한 의견을 구하는데 학생 나이대 사람들이 쇼를 좋아하는지 여부에 따라 방송국이 방송 여부를 결정할 수도 있다고 했으므로 보기 A가 정답이다.

15. 교수가 폭스 다이너 주인들에 관해 암시하는 것은?

Ⓐ 아마도 그녀의 부탁을 들어줄 것이다.

Ⓑ 남자의 요청을 받아들이지 않을 것이다.

Ⓒ 조사 연구에 참여하는 것을 좋아할 것이다.

Ⓓ 텔레비전에 자주 광고한다.

추론 문제

어휘 do a favor 부탁을 들어 주다 be unlikely to ~할 것 같지 않다 advertise 광고하다

해설 학생이 근무시간을 바꾸기 어렵다고 말하자 교수는 식당 주인들을 잘 알고 있다면서 전화해서 설명해 보겠다고 했다. 따라서 식당 주인들이 교수를 도와줄 수 있음을 암시하므로 정답은 보기 A이다.

16. 대화의 일부를 다시 듣고 질문에 답하시오.

🎧 T-83

> P Oh, you're taking a marketing class? Who's teaching it?
>
> M It's, uh, Professor Larkin, intro to marketing. He hasn't mentioned the study, though.
>
> P Oh. Well... the marketing department's pretty big. I happen to be friends with the woman who's doing the TV study.
>
> N *What does the professor mean when she says this?*
>
> P Oh. Well... the marketing department's pretty big.

Ⓐ 학생은 아마도 사회학에 관심이 있는 마케팅 교수를 찾을 수 있을 것이다.

Ⓑ 학생의 마케팅 교수는 텔레비전 연구에 대해 모를 수도 있다.

Ⓒ 텔레비전 연구에 참여할 학생이 더 이상 필요하지 않다.

Ⓓ 마케팅과에서 몇 가지 조사 연구로 학생이 필요하다.

의도 파악 문제

어휘 have an interest in ~에 관심이 있다

해설 학생이 라킨 교수는 조사 연구에 대해 아무런 언급이 없었다고 하자 교수가 마케팅과는 꽤 크다고 대답했으므로 보기 B가 정답이다.

N Narrator   P Professor

Script

N   Listen to part of a lecture in a European history class.

P   In order to really study the social history of the Middle Ages, you have to understand the role of spices. Now, this might sound a little surprising, even a little strange, but what seem like little things now were, back then, actually rather big things. So, first let's define what a spice is. Technically speaking, a spice is part of an aromatic plant that is not a leaf, or herb. Spices can come from tree bark, like, ah, cinnamon, plant roots like ginger, flower buds like cloves. And in the Middle Ages, Europeans were familiar with lots of different spices, the most important being pepper, cloves, ginger, cinnamon, mace, and nutmeg. These spices literally dominated the way Europeans lived for centuries—how they traded and, uh, even how they used their imaginations. So why this medieval fascination with spices? We can boil it down to three general ideas, briefly. One was cost and rarity, ah, two was exotic taste and fragrance, and third, mysterious origins and a kind of mythical status.

Now, for cost and rarity: Spices aren't native to Europe, and they had to be imported. Spices only grew in the East Indies, and of course transportation costs were astronomical. So spices were incredibly valuable, even from the very beginning. Here's an example, um, in 408 A.D., the Gothic general who'd captured Rome demanded payment. He wanted 5,000 pounds of gold, among other things, but he also wanted 3,000 pounds of pepper. Maybe that'll give you an idea of exactly where pepper stood at the time. By the Middle Ages, spices were regarded as so important and expensive, they were used in diplomacy—as gifts by heads of state and ambassadors.

Now, for the taste, the diet then was relatively bland compared to today's. There wasn't much variety. Uh, especially the aristocracy, who tended to eat a lot of meat, um, they were always looking for new ways to prepare it—new sauces, new tastes, and this is where spices came in. Now this is a good point to mention one of the biggest myths about spices: It's commonly said that medieval Europeans wanted spices to cover up the taste of spoiled meat, but this isn't really true. Anyone who had to worry about spoiled meat couldn't afford spices in the first place. If you could afford spices, you could definitely afford fresh meat. We also have evidence that various medieval markets employed a kind of police, to make sure that people didn't sell spoiled food. And if you were

N   유럽사 수업의 강의 일부를 들으시오.

P   중세 사회사를 제대로 연구하려면 향신료의 역할을 이해해야 합니다. 자, 좀 놀라운 얘기일 수도 있고, 심지어 좀 이상하게 들릴 수도 있겠지만, 지금 별것 아니어 보이는 것이 당시에는 사실 좀 대단했습니다. 자, 먼저 향신료가 무엇인지 정의해 봅시다. 엄밀히 말해 향신료는 잎이나 허브가 아닌 향료 식물의 일부입니다. 계피처럼 향신료가 나무껍질에서 나올 수도 있고, 생강처럼 식물의 뿌리에서 나올 수도 있죠. 정향처럼 꽃봉오리에서 나오기도 하고요. 그리고 중세 유럽인들은 다양한 수많은 향료에 익숙했는데 후추, 정향, 생강, 계피, 육두구 가루, 육두구 등이 가장 중요한 향신료였죠. 이 향신료들은 수세기 동안 말 그대로 유럽인들의 생활 방식을 지배했습니다. 그들의 무역 방식, 심지어 그들의 상상력을 활용하는 방식까지도 말이죠. 그런데 왜 중세는 향신료에 매료되었을까요? 간단히 세 가지 개념으로 요약할 수 있습니다. 하나는 가격과 희귀성, 어, 두 번째는 이국적인 맛과 향기였고, 세 번째는 신비한 기원과 일종의 신화적 위상입니다.

자, 가격과 희소성을 보죠. 향신료는 유럽이 원산지가 아니어서 수입해야 했죠. 향신료는 동인도에서만 자랐고 물론 운송비가 천문학적이었죠. 따라서 향신료는 처음부터 믿을 수 없을 정도로 귀했습니다. 예를 들어, 음, 서기 408년에, 로마를 점령한 고트 족 장군이 지급물을 요구했습니다. 그는 무엇보다 5000파운드의 금을 원했는데 후추 3000파운드도 원했죠. 아마 이것으로 당시 후추의 위상이 정확히 어땠는지 알 수 있을 겁니다. 중세에 향신료는 매우 중요하고 비싼 물품으로 인식되었고, 국가 원수나 사절의 선물로 외교에 활용되었죠.

이제, 맛으로 가서, 당시 식단은 오늘날에 비해 상대적으로 밍밍했죠. 그다지 다양하지 않았습니다. 어, 특히 고기를 많이 먹는 경향이 있는 귀족들은, 음, 항상 고기를 요리할 새로운 방법을 찾고 있었습니다. 새로운 소스, 새로운 맛, 그리고 여기서 향신료가 들어오죠. 이쯤에서 향신료에 관한 최대의 그릇된 통념 중 하나를 언급하는 게 좋겠어요. 흔히 중세 유럽인들이 상한 고기의 맛을 덮기 위해 향신료를 원했다고 하지만, 이건 사실이 아닙니다. 상한 고기를 걱정해야 하는 사람은 애당초 향신료를 살 여유가 없었죠. 향신료를 살 여유가 있다면 신선한 고기를 살 여유가 분명 있었을 테니까요. 사람들이 상한 음식을 팔지 못하도록 다양한 중세 시장에서 일종의 경찰을 고용했다는 증거도 있습니다. 상한 음식을 팔다가 걸리면 다양한 벌금에, 공개적 처벌 받는 굴욕을 당했습니다. 그래서, 실상은 이랬습니다. 겨울에 먹을

Reading

Listening

Speaking

Writing

Test 1

Test 2

Test 3

Test 4

caught doing it, you were subject to various fines, humiliating public punishments. So, what actually was true was this: In order to have meat for the winter, people would preserve it in salt—not a spice. Spices, actually, aren't very effective as preservatives. And, uh, throughout winter they would eat salted meat, but the taste of the stuff could grow really boring and, and depressing after a while. So the cooks started looking for new ways to improve the taste, and spices were the answer.

Which brings us to mysterious origins and mythical status. Now the ancient Romans had a thriving spice trade, and they sent their ships to the east and back. But when Rome collapsed in the fifth century and the Middle Ages began, um, direct trade stopped, and, uh, so did that kind of hands-on knowledge of travel and geography. Spices now came by way of the trade routes, with lots of intermediaries between the producer and the consumer. So these spices took on an air of mystery. Their origins were shrouded in exotic travels; they had the allure of the unknown, of wild places. Myths grew up of fantasy lands, magical faraway places made entirely of food and spices. Add to that, spices themselves had always been considered special, or magical—not just for eating—and this was already true in the ancient world where legends about spices were abundant. Spices inspired the medieval imagination, they were used as medicines to ward off diseases, and mixed into perfumes, incense. They were used in religious rituals for thousands of years. They took on a life of their own, and they inspired the medieval imagination, spurred on the age of discovery in the fifteenth and sixteenth centuries. When famous explorers like Columbus and Da Gama and Magellan left Europe in their ships, they weren't looking for a new world; they were looking for spices. And we know what important historical repercussions some of those voyages had.

고기를 보관하기 위해서 고기를 향신료가 아니라 소금에 절였습니다. 사실 향신료는 그다지 방부 효과는 뛰어나지 않습니다. 그리고, 어, 겨울 내내 소금에 절인 고기를 먹곤 했지만, 한참 지나면 맛이 식상하고 떨어졌죠. 그래서 요리사들은 맛을 끌어올릴 새로운 방식을 찾았는데 향신료가 해답이었습니다.

이것으로 신비한 기원과 신화적인 위상에 이르게 되었군요. 고대 로마에서 향신료 무역이 번창했고, 배를 동쪽으로 보내 다시 돌아오게 했죠. 그러나 5세기에 로마가 붕괴되고 중세 시대가 시작되자, 음, 직접 교역이 중단되었고, 어, 여행과 지리학에 대한 실제적인 지식도 멈추었습니다. 향신료는 이제 무역로를 거쳐 들어왔고, 생산자와 소비자 사이에 중개 상인들도 많았죠. 이리하여 이 향신료들은 신비한 분위기를 풍겼습니다. 향신료의 기원은 이국적인 여행이라는 베일에 싸여 있었고 미지의, 야생의 장소라는 매력을 갖게 되었죠. 환상의 땅, 전적으로 음식과 향신료로 만들어진 마법 같은 머나먼 곳들이라는 그릇된 통념이 생겨났습니다. 게다가 향신료 자체는 단지 먹기 위한 것이 아니라 언제나 특별한 것, 신비한 것으로 인식되었고 향신료에 관한 전설이 풍성했던 고대 세계에서는 이미 그랬죠. 향신료는 중세의 상상력에 영감을 불어넣었죠. 향신료는 질병을 물리치기 위한 약으로 사용되었고 향수와 향에도 섞어 넣었습니다. 향신료는 수천 년 동안 종교 의식에도 사용되었죠. 향신료는 향신료만의 생명을 이어나갔고, 15세기와 16세기 발견의 시대에 박차를 가하면서 중세 상상력에 영감을 불어넣었습니다. 콜럼버스와 다 가마, 마젤란 같은 유명한 탐험가들이 배로 유럽을 떠날 때 그들은 신세계를 찾아 나선 것이 아니었습니다. 그들은 향신료를 찾고 있었습니다. 우리는 그러한 항해들 중 일부가 역사에 어떤 영향을 미쳤는지 알고 있습니다.

어휘

spice 향신료   define 정의하다   bark 나무껍질   clove 정향   familiar with ~에 친숙한   mace 육두구 가루   nutmeg 육두구   literally 말 그대로   dominate 지배하다   medieval 중세의   fascination 매료, 매혹   boil down 요약하다   briefly 간단히   rarity 희소성   exotic 이국적인   fragrance 향   mythical 신화적인   status 지위   import 수입하다   transportation 운송, 수송   astronomical 천문학적인   incredibly 믿을 수 없이   valuable 귀한   Gothic 고트 족의   capture 점령하다   demand 요구하다   expensive 비싼   diplomacy 외교   ambassador 사절, 대사   relatively 비교적   bland 밍밍한, 자극이 적은   compared to ~에 비해   aristocracy 귀족   myth 그릇된 통념   commonly 흔히, 일반적으로   spoiled 상한   afford 여유가 있다   definitely 분명히   evidence 증거   employ 고용하다   be subject to 받다, 대상이다   fine 벌금   humiliating 굴욕적인   punishment 처벌   preserve 보존하다   effective 효과적인   preservative 방부제   depressing 우울하게 만드는   improve 개선하다   thriving 번창하는   collapse 붕괴하다   hands-on 실제적인   geography 지리   intermediary 중개자   consumer 소비자   shroud 덮이다, 싸이다   allure 매혹   abundant 풍부한   inspire 영감을 불어넣다   ward off 물리치다   disease 질병   incense 향   ritual 의식   spur 박차를 가하다   explorer 탐험가   repercussion 영향   voyage 항해

17. 강의의 주요 목적은 무엇인가?

Ⓐ 중세 요리에서 향신료의 용도 탐구하기

Ⓑ 중세 사회에서 향신료의 중요성 설명하기

Ⓒ 중세 유럽에서 향신료 무역이 발달한 경위 설명하기

Ⓓ 중세 시대 향신료 역할의 변화 살펴보기

내용의 목적을 묻는 문제

어휘 significance 중요성   describe 설명하다   evolve 발달하다, 진화하다

해설 강의 첫머리에서 교수가 중세를 제대로 연구하려면 향신료의 역할을 이해해야 한다고 했고 이후 강의 전반에 걸쳐 중세에서 향신료가 중요했던 이유를 설명하고 있으므로 보기 B가 정답이다.

18. 강의 내용에 근거하여 중세 유럽의 향신료에 관해 기술한 다음 각 문장이 사실인지 여부를 표시하라.

아래 '예' 혹은 '아니오'에 표시하라.

	예	아니오
A. 수입해야 했다.	✓	
B. 많은 사람들에게는 너무 비쌌다.	✓	
C. 겨울 동안 고기를 보존하는 데 사용되었다.		✓
D. 사람들은 약효 속성이 있다고 믿었다.	✓	
E. 공설 시장에서는 판매가 엄격히 규제되었다.		✓

내용 연결 문제

어휘 unaffordable 너무 비싼   medicinal 약효가 있는   property 속성, 성질   regulate 규제하다

해설 향신료는 유럽이 원산지가 아니라고 했으므로 A는 본문과 일치한다. 또한 향신료가 너무 비싸 다수가 이용할 수 없었다고 했고 중세에서 향신료는 치료용으로도 사용되었다고 했으므로 B, D 역시 사실이다.

19. 중세 유럽인들이 상한 고기의 맛을 덮기 위해 향신료를 쓰지 않은 이유를 설명하는 두 가지 요인은 무엇인가?

정답 2개를 고르시오.

Ⓐ 신선한 고기가 향신료보다 쌌다.

Ⓑ 향신료는 주로 향과 향수에 사용되었다.

Ⓒ 상한 음식을 파는 것이 금지되었다.

Ⓓ 대다수 향신료보다 소금이 더 쌌다.

세부 정보 찾기 문제

어휘 mainly 주로   prohibit 금지하다

해설 향신료로 상한 고기의 냄새를 감추었다는 주장에 비싼 향신료를 살 수 있으면 신선한 고기를 살 수 있었다고 반박했으므로 보기 A가 정답이다. 또한 경찰을 도입해 상한 음식을 팔지 못하게 했다고 했으므로 보기 C도 정답이다.

20. 교수가 로마제국의 붕괴를 언급한 이유는 무엇인가?

Ⓐ 향신료 무역이 더 직접적으로 이루어졌음을 보여 주기 위해

Ⓑ 후추 가격이 갑자기 오른 이유를 설명하기 위해

Ⓒ 유럽에서 수 세기 동안 향신료를 구할 수 없었음을 보여 주기 위해

Ⓓ 향신료의 기원이 더욱 신비에 싸인 이유를 설명하기 위해

구성 파악 문제

어휘 available 구할 수 있는, 이용할 수 있는

해설 로마제국의 붕괴로 로마와 아시아 간의 직접 교역이 중단되자 로마인들에게 향신료는 더욱 이국적이고 신비로운 대상이 되었다고 했으므로 보기 D가 정답이다.

21. 발견의 시대 유럽 탐험가들에 관해 교수가 언급한 것은 무엇인가?

Ⓐ 그들의 발견으로 특정 향신료의 가격이 올랐다.

Ⓑ 그들은 향신료 수요에 부응하고 있었다.

Ⓒ 탐험 도중 향신료를 발견하리라 기대하지 않았다.

Ⓓ 그들의 주된 목표는 미지의 땅을 발견하는 것이었다.

세부 정보 찾기 문제

어휘 increase 오르다, 증가하다   demand 수요   exploration 탐험

해설 강의 말미에 교수는 향신료가 더욱 특별하게 인식되면서 콜럼버스 같은 유명한 탐험가들이 신세계가 아닌 향신료를 찾아 나섰다고 했다. 따라서 보기 B가 정답이다.

22. 강의의 일부를 다시 듣고 질문에 답하시오.

🎧 T-85

> P Here's an example, um, in 408 A.D., the Gothic general who'd captured Rome demanded payment. He wanted 5,000 pounds of gold, among other things, but he also wanted 3,000 pounds of pepper. Maybe that'll give you an idea of exactly where pepper stood at the time.
>
> N *Why does the professor say this?*
>
> P Maybe that'll give you an idea of exactly where pepper stood at the time.

Ⓐ 후추가 지불 수단으로 널리 사용되었음을 보여 주기 위해

Ⓑ 당시 후추가 발견되었던 곳을 보여 주기 위해

Ⓒ 당시 후추가 귀했음을 강조하기 위해

Ⓓ 후추가 금에 버금갈 만큼 풍부했음을 암시하기 위해

의도 파악 문제

어휘 emphasize 강조하다   nearly 거의   plentiful 풍부한

해설 교수는 로마를 정복한 장군이 금과 후추를 요구했다는 일화를 통해 금에 맞먹는 후추의 위상을 지적한다. 따라서 당시 후추의 가치를 강조하기 위한 말이므로 보기 C가 정답이다.

Questions 23-28
p. 284

N Narrator P Professor M Male Student

Script

N Listen to part of a lecture in a biology class.

P Well, it's finally looking like spring is arriving—the last of the winter snow will be melting away in a few days. So before we close today, I thought I'd mention, uh, a biological event that's part of the transition from winter to spring... something you can go outside and watch, if you have some patience. There's a small creature that lives in this area—you've probably seen it: it's the North American wood frog.

Now the wood frog's not that easy to spot, since it stays pretty close to the ground, under leaves and things, and it blends in really well with its background, as you can see. But they're worth the effort, because they do something very unusual—something you might not have even thought possible.

OK, North American wood frogs live over a very broad territory, or range—they're found all over the northeastern United States, and all through Canada and Alaska—even inside the Arctic Circle. No other frog is able to live that far north. But wherever they live, once the weather starts to turn cold, and the temperatures start to drop below freezing—as soon as the frog even touches an ice crystal or a bit of frozen ground... well, it begins to freeze. Yes, Jimmy? You look a bit taken aback.

M Wait. You mean, it's still alive, but it freezes? Solid?

P Well, almost. Ice forms in all the spaces outside cells, but never within a cell.

M But... then, how does its heart beat?

P It doesn't.

M But—how can it do....

P How can it do such a thing? Well, that first touch of ice apparently triggers a biological response inside the frog, that first of all starts drawing water away from the center of its body. So the middle part of the frog, its internal organs—its heart, lungs, liver—these start getting drier and drier, while the water that's being pulled away is forming a puddle around the organs, just underneath the skin. And then that puddle of water starts to freeze.

OK, up to now the frog's heart is still beating, right? Slower and slower, but.... And in those last few hours before it freezes, it distributes glucose—a blood sugar—throughout its body, its circulatory system. Sort of acts like an antifreeze....

M A solution of antifreeze, like you put in your car in the winter?

N 생물학 수업의 강의 일부를 들으시오.

P 드디어 봄이 오는 것 같네요—며칠 있으면 마지막 남은 겨울 눈도 다 녹아 없어질 겁니다. 그래서 오늘 마치기 전에, 어, 겨울에서 봄으로 넘어가는 생물학적 사건에 대해 얘기해 보려고 합니다… 참을성만 있다면 밖으로 나가서 볼 수 있습니다. 이 지역에 사는 작은 생물이 있습니다—아마 여러분도 봤을 겁니다: 북아메리카에 사는 나무숲산개구리입니다.

나무숲산개구리는 나뭇잎 같은 물체 아래 땅 가까이에 살고 보다시피 배경과 잘 섞이기 때문에 녀석을 보기가 그렇게 쉽지 않죠. 하지만 녀석들은 아주 특별한 행동을 하기 때문에 공들일 만한 가치가 있어요. 아마 가능하다고 생각조차 못한 일일 겁니다.

자, 북아메리카 나무숲산개구리는 매우 넓은 영역, 즉 범위에 걸쳐 살고 있어서—미국 북동부 전역, 그리고 캐나다, 알래스카 전역, 심지어 북극권에서도 발견됩니다. 다른 개구리들은 그렇게 멀리 북쪽에서 살 수 없습니다. 그런데 녀석들이 어디에 살건 날씨가 추워지기 시작하고 기온이 영하로 떨어지기 시작하면—녀석이 얼음 결정체나 얼어붙은 땅을 건드리자마자… 녀석은 얼어붙기 시작합니다. 그래, 지미? 좀 놀란 것 같구나.

M 잠깐만요. 그러니까 아직 살아 있는데 얼어붙는 건가요? 단단하게요?

P 거의 그래요. 세포 밖에 있는 모든 공간에 얼음이 형성되죠, 하지만 세포 안은 절대 얼어붙지 않아요.

M 하지만… 그럼 심장은 어떻게 뛰죠?

P 안 뜁니다.

M 하지만—어떻게 그럴 수 있죠…

P 어떻게 그런 일이 가능하냐고? 음, 처음 얼음을 건드리면 개구리 내부에서 생물학적 반응이 촉발됩니다. 우선 몸 중심에서 물을 끌어내기 시작합니다. 그러면 개구리의 중심부, 내부 장기인 심장, 폐, 간이 점점 마르죠. 빠져 나온 물이 장기 주변, 피부 바로 밑에 웅덩이를 형성하죠. 그러면 물 웅덩이가 얼기 시작합니다.

자, 지금까지 개구리의 심장은 여전히 뛰고 있습니다, 그렇죠? 점점 느리게, 하지만… 그리고 얼기 전 몇 시간 동안 녀석은 포도당—혈당—을 온몸과 순환기관에 분배합니다. 부동액과 비슷한 역할이죠…

M 겨울에 차에 넣는 부동액처럼요?

P 글쎄, 본인이 답을 알고 있을 듯한데요. 개구리 안에서 여러분의 포도당이 세포 안의 물이 얼기 어렵게 만듭니다. 그래서 세포들은 겨우 겨울을 날 수 있을 정도로 살짝 수분이

P Well, you tell me. In frogs, the extra glucose makes it harder for the water inside the cells to freeze, so the cells stay just slightly wet—enough so that they can survive the winter. Then after that, the heart stops beating altogether. So, is that the same?

M I don't really know, but uh... how long does it stay that way?

P Well, it could be days or even months—all winter, in fact. But, um, see, the heart really doesn't need to do any pumping now, because the blood is frozen too.

M I just... I guess I just don't see how it isn't—y'know, clinically dead.

P Well, that's the amazing thing. And how it revives is pretty amazing too. After months without a heartbeat, springtime comes around again, the Earth starts to warm up, and suddenly one day—ping! A pulse—followed by another one, then another, until—maybe ten, twelve hours later, the animal is fully recovered.

M And—does the, uh, thawing process have some kind of trigger as well?

P Well, we're not sure, actually. The peculiar thing is, even though the sun is warming the frog up on the outside, its insides thaw out first—the heart and brain and everything. But somehow, it all just happens that way every spring.

M And after they thaw? Does it affect them? Like their life span?

P Well, hmm... we really don't know a lot about how long a wood frog normally lives—probably just a few years. But there's no evidence that the freezing process affects its longevity. It does have some other impacts, though. In studies we've found that, when it comes to reproduction, freezing diminishes the mating performance of males: after they've been frozen, and thawed of course, they don't seem quite as vocal, they move slower—and they seem to have a harder time recognizing a potential mate. So if a male frog could manage not to go through this freezing cycle, he'd probably have more success at mating.

남은 상태죠. 그런 다음 심장이 완전히 박동을 멈춥니다. 그래서 똑같나요?

M 잘 모르겠어요, 그런데… 언제까지 그 상태로 있죠?

P 글쎄, 며칠, 심지어 몇 달이 될 수도 있죠. 사실 겨울 내내 그 상태입니다. 그런데, 어, 혈액도 얼어 있기 때문에 심장은 이제 펌프처럼 혈액을 내보낼 필요가 없습니다.

M 전 그냥… 그러니까 이게 어떻게 임상학적으로 사망이 아닌지 모르겠어요.

P 어, 그게 놀라운 점이죠. 녀석이 되살아나는 것 역시 놀랍고요. 몇 달 동안 심장 박동이 없다가 다시 봄이 와서 지구가 따뜻해지기 시작하면 어느 날 갑자기 핑! 하나, 하나 박동이 시작되고 10시간, 12시간쯤 후에 이 동물은 완전히 회복됩니다.

M 녹는 과정에도 어떤 기폭제가 있나요?

P 글쎄, 사실 확실하지 않습니다. 특이한 것은, 태양이 바깥에서 개구리를 데우고 있는데, 개구리 내부, 즉 심장과 뇌, 그리고 모든 것이 먼저 녹는다는 것입니다. 하지만 어찌된 일인지, 해마다 봄이면 이 모든 일이 일어납니다.

M 그리고 녀석들이 녹은 다음에는요? 그게 녀석들에게 영향을 끼치나요? 수명 같은 것?

P 글쎄요, 음… 나무숲산개구리가 보통 얼마나 사는지 별로 아는 게 없어요. 아마 고작 몇 년 정도일 겁니다. 하지만 냉동 과정이 수명에 영향을 미친다는 증거는 없습니다. 하지만 다른 영향은 끼칩니다. 연구에서 발견한 바에 따르면 번식에서 냉동이 수컷의 짝짓기 성과를 떨어뜨립니다. 수컷들은 얼었다가 녹은 후에, 소리를 잘 내지 않는 것 같고, 더 느리게 움직입니다—따라서 수컷은 짝이 될 만한 개체를 알아보는 데 어려움을 겪는 것 같습니다. 따라서 만약 수컷 개구리가 어찌어찌 이 냉동 주기를 거치지 않을 수 있다면 아마 녀석은 짝짓기에 더 성공할 겁니다.

어휘

melt away 녹아 없어지다 transition 이행 patience 인내심 wood frog 나무숲산개구리 blend 섞이다 territory 영역 temperature 기온, 온도 taken aback 깜짝 놀란 solid 단단한 apparently 겉보기에 trigger 촉발하다 lung 폐 liver 간 organ 장기 puddle 웅덩이 distribute 분배하다 glucose 포도당 circulatory system 순환기관 antifreeze 부동액 clinically 임상학적으로 revive 소생하다 thaw 녹다 peculiar 특이한, 기이한 life span 수명 evidence 증거 longevity 수명, 장수 impact 영향 reproduction 번식 diminish 줄이다 mating 짝짓기 performance 성과 vocal 시끄러운 recognize 인식하다 potential 잠재적인

23. 강의의 주요 목적은 무엇인가?

Ⓐ 북아메리카 나무숲산개구리에게 일어나는 신체 변화의 생물학적 이점에 대해 설명하기

Ⓑ 북아메리카 나무숲산개구리의 서식지가 확대된 이유 설명하기

Ⓒ 북아메리카 나무숲산개구리의 순환기관의 기능에 대해 설명하기

Ⓓ 북아메리카 나무숲산개구리에게 영향을 미치는 특이한 현상을 학생들에게 소개하기

내용의 목적을 묻는 문제

어휘 habitat 서식지　expand 확대되다　phenomenon 현상

해설 교수는 북아메리카 나무숲산개구리의 특이한 생물학적 현상을 상세히 설명하고 있으므로 정답은 보기 D이다. 동결 현상에 따른 짝짓기 확률 감소 등 부정적 영향은 언급되었으나 장점은 언급된 바 없으므로 보기 A는 정답이 될 수 없다. 순환기관도 언급되었지만 동결 과정을 설명하기 위한 세부 정보이므로 보기 C 역시 정답이 될 수 없다.

24. 교수가 봄이 온 것을 처음 언급한 이유는 무엇인가?

Ⓐ 학생들에게 녹고 있는 나무숲산개구리를 찾아보도록 권장하기 위해

Ⓑ 개구리가 짝짓기하는 시기를 지적하기 위해

Ⓒ 그 반이 곧 나무숲산개구리로 실험하는 이유를 설명하기 위해

Ⓓ 녹는 과정의 속도를 강조하기 위해

구성 파악 문제

어휘 experiment 실험　emphasize 강조하다

해설 봄은 북아메리카 나무숲산개구리가 녹기 시작하는 계절이기 때문에 언급했으며 보기가 어렵지만 아주 특별한 행동을 하기 때문에 공들일 만한 가치가 있다고 했으므로 정답은 보기 A이다.

25. 나무숲산개구리가 얼기 시작할 때 일어나는 일은 무엇인가?

Ⓐ 피가 몸 중앙으로 몰린다.

Ⓑ 피가 당 생산을 멈춘다.

Ⓒ 내부 장기에서 물이 빠져나간다.

Ⓓ 피부 바로 밑에 있는 물이 증발하기 시작한다.

세부 정보 찾기 문제

어휘 concentrate 집중시키다　evaporate 증발하다, 사라지다

해설 나무숲산개구리가 얼음을 건드리면 몸 중심에서 물이 빠져나가 장기가 점점 마른다고 했으므로 정답은 보기 C이다.

26. 나무숲산개구리의 녹는 과정에 대해 교수가 지적한 두 가지 요점은 무엇인가?
정답 2개를 고르시오.

Ⓐ 녹는 과정이 완전히 규명되지는 않았다.

Ⓑ 녹는 과정이 어는 과정보다 더 오래 걸린다.

Ⓒ 개구리의 외피가 녹기 전에 내부 장기가 녹는다.

Ⓓ 개구리의 심장이 포도당을 몸에 보낼 때 녹는다.

내용 연결 문제

어휘 internal 내부의

해설 녹는 과정을 촉발하는 것이 무엇인지 묻는 학생의 질문에 교수가 알 수 없다고 했고, 태양이 밖에서 데우지만 내부가 먼저 녹는다고 했으므로 보기 A, C가 본문의 내용과 일치한다.

27. 녹은 나무숲산개구리에게 동결이 미치는 영향은 무엇인가?

Ⓐ 번식 성공률을 높인다.

Ⓑ 수명을 줄인다.

Ⓒ 더 시끄럽고 활동적으로 만든다.

Ⓓ 짝이 될 만한 개체를 식별하는 능력을 떨어뜨린다.

세부 정보 찾기 문제

어휘 reproductive 번식의

해설 강의 말미에 교수는 어느 과정이 개구리의 수명에는 영향을 미치지 않지만 번식에 부정적 영향을 미친다고 설명한다. 특히 짝을 식별하는 데 문제가 있다고 했으므로 보기 D가 정답이다. 보기 A는 본문 내용과 상반된다.

28. 강의의 일부를 다시 듣고 질문에 답하라.

🎧 T-87

> M A solution of antifreeze, like you put in your car in the winter?
> P Well, you tell me. In frogs, the extra glucose makes it harder for the water inside the cells to freeze, so the cells stay just slightly wet — enough so that they can survive the winter. Then after that, the heart stops beating altogether. So, is that the same?
> N *What does the professor imply when she says this?*
> P Well, you tell me.

Ⓐ 학생이 질문을 분명히 말하길 원한다.

Ⓑ 학생이 스스로 결론을 도출하길 원한다.

Ⓒ 학생이 자동차 부동액의 작동 원리를 이해하지 못한다고 생각한다.

Ⓓ 학생이 논점을 오해했다고 생각한다.

의도 파악 문제

어휘 clarify 분명하게 말하다　draw a conclusion 결론을 도출하다

해설 학생이 포도당 분비가 자동차 부동액과 비슷한 원리인지 묻자 교수는 직접 대답하는 대신 포도당이 어는 효과를 감소시키는 과정을 설명한다. 그러고 나서 학생에게 스스로 생각해 보도록 되묻고 있으므로 보기 B가 정답이다.

SPEAKING

 T-88

Question 1
p. 288

Narrator

Do you agree or disagree with the following statement?

It is important to learn about other cultures.

Use details and examples to explain your opinion.

다음 논제에 대한 찬성 또는 반대 의견을 서술하시오.
다른 문화에 대해 배우는 것은 중요하다.
세부 사항과 사례를 들어 의견을 설명하시오.

준비 시간 : 15초
답변 시간 : 45초

중요 포인트

수험자는 대답할 때 우선 자신이 논제를 믿는지 여부를 진술해야 한다. 어느 쪽이든 선택할 수 있으며 어떤 선택을 하느냐는 평가의 대상이 아니다. 얼마나 완벽하고 명확하게 자신의 생각을 설명하고 의견을 뒷받침하는지가 평가 기준이다. 논제에 동의한다면, 중요한 영역(해외 사업, 여행 및 관광 등)을 기술한 다음, 세부 사항과 구체적인 예를 제시하여 설명할 수 있다. 논제에 동의하지 않는다면, 역시 적어도 하나의 이유와 구체적인 내용과 예를 제시해 자신의 의견을 뒷받침해야 한다.

우수 답변   T-93

I think it is, uh, important to learn about other cultures. First of all, it, uh, gives you the opportunity to understand your culture better. Uh, then uh… it, uh, helps you to understand, uh, other people from other cultures better because if you know the background of their behavior, then, uh, it is easier to understand it and not judge it. And, uh, in addition to that, if you know other cultures, then, uh, you do not offend people because, uh, you know how-how to behave in certain situations and you know better how to react on, uh, uh, when… on others' people behavior.

채점자 의견

대체로 매우 명료하고 이해하기 쉽다. 수험자는 효과적으로 멈추어 구절을 분리하고 있고 구절 내에서 중요한 단어를 강조하기 때문에 듣는 사람이 메시지를 쉽게 이해할 수 있다. ("First of all, it uh **gives** you the **opportunity** to **understand** your culture **better**.") 비록 가끔 사소한 어법 오류를 범하지만, 정확한 구절과 문장을 만들어 내는 능력을 갖추고 있다. 자신의 의견에 대한 일반적 근거("it helps you understand other people…")와 타인의 문화를 이해하면 그들에게 상처 주지 않는다 등 구체적인 사례와 세부 내용을 모두 제시해 자신의 의견을 뒷받침하고 있다.

중간 수준의 답변   T-94

Yeah, uh, actually I think, uh, it's so important and it's really significantly will affect my, uh, personal, uh, life knowing about a new culture and other cultures. It's firstly will make me more open-minded and more tolerant toward others. Then I'm gonna really expand my verizon of thoughts and philosopher… philosophical, uh, ideas because I'm gonna inter… interact with other backgrounds and that's really give me the chance to acquire good values from other nations.

채점자 의견

대체로 명확하고 이해하기 쉽다. 그러나 때때로 어법과 어휘의 한계 때문에 쉽게 이해할 수 없는 부분도 있다. 예를 들어, 다소 정교하게 의견을 피력하려고 하지만 단어 선택, 단어 형태, 그리고 특히 수일치 오류 때문에 의미가 명확하지 않다. 예를 들어 다음과 같은 문장이다. "I'm gonna really expand my verizon of thoughts and philosopher philosophical, uh, ideas because I'm gonna inter… interact with other back grounds and that's really give me the chance to acquire good values from other nations." 이 문장은 "Interacting with other cultures could help me to expand my horizons/open me up to new experiences and ideas."("다른 문화와 교류하면 시야를 넓히고 새로운 경험과 사고에 나를 개방하는 데 도움이 될 수 있다.")로 표현하면 좀 더 효과적이고 간단하다.

Question 2
p. 288

Narrator

City University's choir is changing its performance schedule next year. Read an article about it in the student newspaper. You will have 50 seconds to read the article. Begin reading now.

시립대학교 합창단이 내년 공연 일정을 바꾸고 있다. 학보에 실린 관련 기사를 50초 동안 읽으시오. 지금 읽으시오.

University Choir to Enter Off-Campus Singing Competitions

Currently, the university choir gives singing concerts only on campus. Next year, however, the choir will add competitive events at other locations to its schedule. The choir's new director feels that entering singing competitions will make the quality of the choir's performance even better than it is now. "Competitions will motivate students in the choir to pursue a higher standard of excellence in singing," he said. In addition, it is hoped that getting the choir off campus and out in the public will strengthen the reputation of the university's music program. This in turn will help the program grow.

대학 합창단 교외 노래 경연대회 참가

현재, 대학 합창단은 캠퍼스에서만 노래 콘서트를 열고 있다. 하지만 내년에는 다른 장소에서 열리는 경연 행사를 일정에 추가할 예정이다. 합창단의 신임 단장은 노래 경연대회에 참가하면 합창단의 공연 수준이 지금보다 훨씬 나아질 것이라고 생각한다. "경연대회는 합창단 학생들이 노래에서 더 높은 수준의 탁월함을 추구하도록 동기를 부여할 것입니다."라고 그는 말했다. 또한 합창단을 캠퍼스에서 벗어나 대중 앞에 나오게 하면 대학 음악 프로그램의 명성이 높아지리라 기대한다. 이는 결국 프로그램이 성장하는 데 도움을 줄 것이다.

어휘

choir 합창단 competition 경연대회 currently 현재
competitive 경쟁하는 performance 공연 motivate 동기를 부여하다 pursue 추구하다 strengthen 강화하다 reputation 명성

Narrator

Now listen to two students discussing the article.

이제 기사에 관해 두 학생이 나누는 대화를 들으시오.

F Jim, you're in the choir, right? Whaddaya think about what they're doing next year... this article?

M I really like it.

F Yeah?

M Yeah. The new director's right that it will motivate us.

F How's that?

M Well, some of the other schools are really good... so we'll really have to work hard to go up against them.

F Yeah...

M I mean, right now we don't rehearse more than once a week, but if we know we'd be competing with other schools, we'd probably rehearse more often and improve our singing a lot.

F That's true. The more you practice, the better you get. So, um... What about what the article said about how this will help the program?

M I hope it works! Right now, our program is pretty small, but we have some really talented people. And it would be great to attract even more people.

F So how will this plan help?

M Well, if we go to these off campus events and other people hear us and think we're really good, we might be able to get some new students interested in coming to this university... to be a part of our music program and perform in our choir concerts.

F You're right. I hadn't really thought about that.

여 짐, 너 합창단원이지? 내년에 하는 일… 이 기사 어떻게 생각해?

남 아주 마음에 들어.

여 그래?

남 응. 우리한테 동기부여가 될 거라는데, 이건 신임 단장 말이 옳아.

여 어째서?

남 일부 다른 학교들은 정말 잘하거든… 그래서 경쟁해서 올라가려면 우리도 정말 열심히 해야 해.

여 그렇구나…

남 그러니까 지금은 우리가 일주일에 한 번밖에 연습을 안 해. 그런데 다른 학교랑 경쟁하는 걸 알면 아마 더 자주 연습할 거고 노래 실력도 많이 늘 거야.

Reading Listening Speaking Writing Test 1 Test 2 Test 3 **Test 4**

여	그건 그래. 연습을 많이 하면 나아지지. 그래서, 음… 이게 프로그램에 도움이 된다는 기사 내용은 어떻게 생각해?
남	그러길 바래! 지금 우리 프로그램은 아주 소규모지만 정말 재능 있는 사람들이 몇 명 있어. 더 많은 사람이 오게 되면 좋을 거야.
여	그래서 이 계획이 어떻게 도움이 될까?
남	이런 교외 행사에 나가면 다른 사람도 우리 노래를 듣고 우리가 정말 잘한다고 생각하겠지. 그러면 이 학교에 오는 데 관심 갖는 신입생들을 더 많이 끌어올 수 있을 거야. 우리 음악 프로그램의 일원이 되어서 합창단 콘서트에서 공연하려고 말이지.
여	맞아. 정말 그건 생각 못했어.

어휘

rehearse (예행) 연습하다 improve 개선하다 attract 끌어들이다, 유치하다

Narrator

The man expresses his opinion about the change described in the article. Briefly summarize the change. Then state his opinion about the change and explain the reasons he gives for holding that opinion.

남자는 기사에 서술된 변화에 대해 의견을 피력한다. 어떤 변화인지 간략하게 요약하시오. 그런 다음 변화에 대한 남자의 의견은 무엇이며, 그런 의견을 갖게 된 이유는 무엇인지 설명하시오.

준비 시간 : 30초
답변 시간 : 60초

중요 포인트

수험자는 읽기와 듣기에서 나온 정보를 모두 다루어야 한다. 기사에서 언급된 변화, 즉 대학 합창단이 앞으로는 (지금처럼 캠퍼스 안에서만 노래를 부르는 것이 아니라) 캠퍼스 밖에서 열리는 대회에 참가한다고 간단히 설명하는 것으로 시작할 수 있다. 그 다음 남자가 변화에 동의한다는 점을 설명해야 한다. 첫째, 남자는 대회에서 공연하려면 합창단이 더 자주 연습해야 하므로 합창단의 실력이 향상될 것이라는 단장의 의견에 동의한다. 그리고 음악 프로그램이 성장하는 데 도움이 될 것이라는 단장의 생각에도 남자는 동의한다는 점을 설명해야 한다. 남자는 합창단이 대회에 참가해 사람들이 합창단의 노래를 듣는다면, 이 대학에 다니는 것 (그리고 합창단에 들어가는 것)에 관심을 갖게 될 것이라고 말한다.

우수 답변 🎧 T-95

The choir, choir's about to change the… mm-uh, their-their schedule… Um, because they want to take now some off-campus competition because the director think that students will be more motivated, um, then because they are get into competition with other choirs. Furthermore, he thinks, em, that the guys then are more and, um… eh, will do a better performance than before and probably the program will grow. The student, he actually agrees, um, with all these… with all these, um…or he, he thinks that the changes are very good and he agrees with the opinion of the, um, director, eh, who thinks that they will, uh, perform better and they will be more motivated because he thinks when they are in com-… eh, when they are in-in competition with other very good choirs, they will practice more-more often… maybe have more than one rehearsal a-a week and he thinks that other students will be attracted when they hear them in off-campus competitions join the studen… university.

채점자 의견

수험자의 답변은 정보가 충분하고 명료하다. 생각을 가다듬는 동안 이따금 멈추고 시작하지만, 전체적으로 상당히 유창하고 알아듣기 쉬우며 어휘는 정확하고 다양하다. "furthermore" 같은 전환어는 듣는 사람의 이해를 돕는다. "the director think" 같은 사소한 문법 오류가 있지만 이해하는 데는 문제가 없다. 필요 이상으로 자세히 읽기 지문을 요약했는데, 변경 계획에 동의하는 이유를 설명할 때 해당 정보를 통합했으면 훨씬 효율적인 대답이 되었을 것이다. 그러나 수험자의 대답에는 핵심 정보가 모두 들어 있다.

중간 수준의 답변 🎧 T-96

The man we just heard is mainly… he's pretty happy with the change undertook by… ac-… by-by the director. He states that they currently, eh, practice very little because they don't really have very regu-regular or, um… re-… um… rehearsal times. By practicing more in preparation for competitions, they will improve their singing quality at the same time that they, eh…that they can level up their singing—their singing proficiency with the compe-… with the-the current competition in other universities. That way will, eh… and that way, they will also establish a cycle where future improvements will enqu… encourage the students to rehearsal more and practice more.

채점자 의견

수험자는 높은 수준의 어휘("pretty happy with the change undertook", "level up their singing proficiency")를 사용하지만, 이해하기 어려운 부분도 있다. 일부 발음 오류와 느린 속도 때문에 이해하려면 노력이 필요하다. 내용 또한 때때로 명확하지 않다. 단장의 계획이 합창단을 위한 것이라는 점이 충분히 설명되지 않았고, 합창단이 학교 밖에서 경쟁하는 것이 새로운 학생을 대학에 유치하는 방안이 되는 이유가 빠져 있다. 조금 더 유창하게 말하고 속도를 개선하면 60초 안에 주요 개념을 더 효율적으로 전달할 수 있을 것이다.

214

Question 3   p. 290

Narrator

Read a passage about relict behaviors from a biology textbook. You will have 50 seconds to read the passage. Begin reading now.

생물학 교재에 나오는 잔존 행동에 대한 지문을 50초 동안 읽으시오. 지금 읽으시오.

Relict Behaviors

In general, animals act in ways that help them to survive within their specific habitats. However, sometimes an animal species may display a behavior that no longer serves a clear purpose. The original purpose for the behavior may have disappeared long ago, even thousands of years before. These behaviors, known as relict behaviors, were useful to the animal when the species' habitat was different; but now, because of changed conditions, the behavior no longer serves its original purpose. Left over from an earlier time, the behavior remains as a relict, or remnant, long after the environmental circumstance that influenced its evolution has vanished.

잔존 행동

일반적으로 동물은 특정 서식지 안에서 살아남는 데 도움이 되는 방식으로 행동한다. 그러나 때때로 동물 종은 더 이상 뚜렷한 목적에 기여하지 않는 행동을 보이기도 한다. 그 행동의 원래 목적은 오래전, 심지어 수천 년 전에 사라졌을 수도 있다. 잔존 행동이라고 하는 이러한 행동은 그 종의 서식지가 달랐을 때는 그 동물에게 유용했다. 하지만 지금은 상황이 바뀌었기 때문에 그 행동은 더 이상 원래의 목적에 기여하지 못한다. 이전 시대에서 잔존한 이런 행동은 진화에 영향을 준 환경 상황이 사라진 후에도 오랫동안 잔존물, 즉 유물로 남아 있다.

어휘

relict 잔존하는; 잔존물   behavior 행동   specific 특정한 habitat 서식지   purpose 목적   disappear 사라지다   remnant 유물, 남은 것   environmental 환경의   circumstance 상황 influence 영향을 미치다   evolution 진화   vanish 사라지다

Narrator

Now listen to part of a lecture in a biology class.

이제 생물학 수업의 강의 일부를 들으시오.

Professor OK, so a good example of this—found right here in North America—is something an animal called the American pronghorn does. Pronghorns, as you may know, are a kinda deer-like animal... they live out on the open, grassy plains... somewhat in the middle of North America....

And they are super fast. Pronghorns are, in fact, noted for being the fastest animal in the Western Hemisphere. Once a pronghorn starts running—zoom!—none of its present-day predators, like the... bobcat... or coyote, can even hope to catch up with it... it's off in a flash!

OK, so why then do pronghorns run so fast? That's the question.

Well, it turns out that quite a long time ago... I'm talking tens of thousands of years... things on the grassy plains used to be very different for the pronghorns.

Because back then lions used to live on the plains... chasing and preying upon the pronghorns. And lions, of course, are a very swift-moving mammal... much faster than the bobcat or coyote, or other predators that you find on the plains today....

But, now, however, lions are all extinct in North America. They're no longer a predator of the pronghorn. Tens of thousands of years ago, though, the lions were there, chasing the pronghorns. So, back then, the pronghorn's speed was critical to its survival.

교수 자, 이것의 좋은 예가 바로 여기 북아메리카에서 발견되는 가지뿔영양이라는 동물이 하는 행동입니다. 가지뿔영양은 알다시피 사슴과 비슷한 동물로… 북아메리카 중부, 탁 트인 초원에 삽니다.

녀석들은 엄청나게 빠릅니다. 가지뿔영양은 사실 서반구에서 가장 빠른 동물로 유명합니다. 가지뿔영양이 달리기 시작하면—붕!—붉은스라소니, 코요테 같은 오늘날의 포식자들은 따라잡을 희망조차 없습니다… 녀석은 눈 깜짝할 새 사라집니다!

그렇다면 가지뿔영양은 왜 그렇게 빨리 달리는 걸까요? 이게 의문입니다.

아주 오래전… 그러니까 수만 년 전 초원은 가지뿔영양에게 무척 다른 곳이었습니다.

당시에는 초원에 사자가 살고 있어 가지뿔영양을 쫓고 사냥해서 잡아먹었습니다. 물론 사자는 아주 재빨리 움직이는 포유류로 오늘날 초원에서 볼 수 있는 붉은스라소니나 코요테, 혹은 다른 포식자들보다 훨씬 빠릅니다.

하지만 지금 북아메리카에서 사자는 모두 멸종했습니다. 이제는 가지뿔영양의 포식자가 아니죠. 하지만 수만 년 전 사자는 거기에서 가지뿔영양을 쫓았습니다. 따라서 당시에 가지뿔영양의 속도는 생존에 대단히 중요했습니다.

어휘

pronghorn 가지뿔영양 grassy 풀이 많은 plain 평원 be noted for ~으로 유명하다 hemisphere 반구 predator 포식자 bobcat 붉은스라소니 catch up with ~을 따라잡다 chase 쫓다 prey upon ~을 잡아먹다 extinct 멸종한 critical 대단히 중요한

Narrator

Using the example of the pronghorn and lion, explain the concept of a relict behavior.

가지뿔영양과 사자의 사례를 활용해 잔존 행동의 개념을 설명하시오.

준비 시간 : 30초
답변 시간 : 60초

중요 포인트

우선 잔존 행동이 무엇인지 간략히 설명해야 한다. 잔존 행동이란 과거에는 목적을 위해 필요했지만 더 이상 목적에 기여하지 않는 동물의 행동이다. 그런 다음 가지뿔영양의 사례를 들어 이 개념과 연결해 논의해야 한다. 가지뿔영양은 매우 빨리 달릴 수 있는데, 과거에는 이 행동이 빠른 포식자인 사자를 피하기 위한 행동이었다. 그런데 지금은 서식지인 북아메리카에서 사자가 멸종했고, 현재 포식자인 붉은스라소니와 코요테는 사자만큼 빠르지 않기 때문에 가지뿔영양은 빨리 달릴 필요가 없다. 이처럼 읽기 지문과 강의 양쪽의 정보를 포괄해 가지뿔영양의 달리기가 잔존 행동임을 설명해야 한다.

우수 답변 🎧 T-97

A relic behavior is a behavior or a quality that, um, a creature still shows, although the reasons for having developed that behavior or quality has long disappeared, um, the-... For example, in the evolution, animals needed to-to flee, uh, from their predators—like the pronghorns had to flee from lions who were preying upon them. Um, thus they needed to be very fast and would have to run, um, very fast. But nowadays the lions are extinct in North America and, um, the current enemies of the pronghorns—the bobcats and the coyotes—are much slower than the lions used to be. Um, and the pronghorns actually don't need to run that fast anymore but they still have the ability to do so and still show that behavior.

채점자 의견

수험자의 대답은 전반적으로 분명하며 속도는 적절해서 알아듣기 쉽다. 마지막 문장에서 "need"를 강조하는 등 억양과 어휘 강세로 의미를 강조하고 있다. 다양한 어법 구조를 효과적으로 사용하고 있으며("...the reasons for having developed that behavior or quality has long disappeared", "...the pronghorns had to flee from lions who were preying upon them") 어휘 선택도 효과적이고 정확하다. 잔존 행동의 정의로 시작해 사례가 이 개념과 어떻게 연결되는지 생각을 효과적으로 전개하고 있다. 마지막 문장에서 잔존 행동이라는 용어를 다시 한 번 사용했으면 더 명확했겠지만, 잔존 행동의 개념과 사례를 잘 연결해 설명하고 있다.

중간 수준의 답변 🎧 T-98

The concept of a relic behavior, um, based on the example that was given, uh, shows that, uh-uh, this can be genetic-... uh, genetically inherit like with the example of the pronghorn that, uh, tens of thousands of years ago were...they used to be chased by lions. Um, uh, this, uh, this proves that was inherited to nowadays when...even now, uh, even if now lions are extinct in the North America—uh, pronghorn, uh, still are the fastest, um, animals, um, on the-the North, eh, hemisphere and uh-uh, they have this-it... which then was critical for their survival... now, it-it's just something that just, they have it. It's not survival for them, but it just have.

채점자 의견

수험자의 답변은 일부 정확한 내용이 있고 잔존 행동의 개념과 사례를 연결하려고 시도했지만 제대로 생각을 전개하지 못해 대체로 명확하지 못하고 불완전하다. 답변 초반에 잔존 행동에 대해 언급하지만 "can be genetically inherit"라는 말만 하고 분명하게 설명하지 못한다. 이후 핵심 세부 사항을 제시했지만 전체적으로 불분명하며 내용 사이에 공백이 있어 이해하기가 어렵다. 예를 들어 가지뿔영양의 속도가 가장 중요한 내용인데 답변 중반 이후에야 언급된다. 또한 "This proves that was inherited..."에서 대명사가 가리키는 것이 명확하지 않아 혼란스럽다. 가지뿔영양의 속도가 잔존 행동이라는 점을 구체적으로 설명했다면 더 명확한 답변이 되었을 것이다. 더 큰 문제는 어법과 어휘 사용이 정확하지 않고 제한되어 생각이 분명하게 전개되지 못한다는 점이다.

Question 4　　　　　　　　　p. 291

Narrator

Listen to part of a lecture in a business class.

경영학 수업의 강의 일부를 들으시오.

Professor People who are likely to buy a company's product are called target customers. And these target customers influence a company's marketing strategy. In order to develop a marketing strategy, a company will look at certain characteristics of the target customers to decide when and where to advertise... so that they'll reach the target customers most effectively. I'd like to talk to you today about two characteristics of target customers that can influence marketing strategy, specifically age and geographic location of the target customers.

Say a company makes toy cars. Who are its target customers? Kids, right? So, if the company wants to make sure its television advertising reaches its target customers, it'd want to advertise during times when kids are actually watching television, like during children's television shows. That way it can make sure that kids see the advertisements. And that way the company'd get people in that age group to go buy toy cars, or to ask their parents to buy 'em at least.

Now, another important characteristic to consider is geographic location... places where the company's target customers live. Think about a company that makes boats. Its target customers are people who own homes near oceans or lakes, places where they can use boats. After all, people who don't live near water don't have much use for boats. So, by placing advertisements on signs along the road or on television in cities and towns that are near oceans or lakes, the company'd be more likely to reach the target customers for its boats... and sell more of 'em as a result.

교수 어떤 회사 제품을 살 가능성이 있는 사람을 목표 고객이라고 부릅니다. 그리고 이 목표 고객이 회사의 마케팅 전략에 영향을 미치죠. 마케팅 전략을 짜려면 회사는 목표 고객의 어떤 특징들을 살펴서 언제, 어디에 광고할지 결정합니다… 그래야 가장 효과적으로 목표 고객에 다가갈 수 있죠. 오늘 여러분에게 마케팅 전략에 영향을 미칠 수 있는 목

표 고객의 두 가지 특징, 특히 목표 고객의 나이와 지리적 장소에 대해 이야기하려고 합니다.

장난감 차를 만드는 회사라고 합시다. 목표 고객이 누구일까요? 어린이, 그렇죠? 그렇다면 텔레비전 광고가 목표 고객에게 다가가도록 회사가 확실히 하고 싶다면 어린이 텔레비전 프로그램처럼 어린이들이 실제로 텔레비전을 시청하는 시간대에 광고를 하고 싶을 겁니다. 이렇게 해야 어린이들이 광고를 보도록 할 수 있으니까요. 또 이렇게 해야 회사는 그 나이대 사람들이 가서 장난감 차를 사도록 만들거나 적어도 부모에게 사 달라고 부탁하게 만들 수 있겠죠.

또 고려해야 하는 중요한 특징은 지리적 위치로 회사의 목표 고객이 사는 장소입니다. 배를 만드는 회사를 생각해 봅시다. 목표 고객은 배를 활용할 수 있는 곳, 즉 바다나 호수 근처에 집을 소유하고 있는 사람들이겠죠. 어쨌거나 물 근처에 살지 않는 사람은 배를 이용할 일이 많지 않으니까요. 따라서 바다나 호수 인근에 있는 도시나 마을의 텔레비전에 광고를 하거나 도로를 따라 광고판을 내건다면 회사는 배 목표 고객에게 다가갈 확률이 높고 결과적으로 배를 더 많이 팔 확률이 높습니다.

어휘

target customer 목표 고객　　influence 영향을 미치다
characteristic 특징　　decide 정하다　　advertise 광고하다
effectively 효과적으로　　geographic 지리적인　　at least 적어도

Narrator

Using points and examples from the lecture, explain how the characteristics of target customers influence marketing strategy for products.

강의에 나오는 논지와 예들을 이용해 목표 고객의 특징들이 제품 마케팅 전략에 어떻게 영향을 미치는지 설명하시오.

준비 시간 : 20초
답변 시간 : 60초

중요 포인트

목표 고객의 개념을 설명하되 교수가 논하고 있는 목표 고객의 특징에 집중해야 한다. 교수는 나이와 지리적 장소를 마케팅 전략에 영향을 미치는 특징으로 지적했다. 나이에 관해서는 어린이가 목표 고객이라면 어린이들이 텔레비전을 시청하는 시간대에 광고를 해야 한다. 지리적 장소에 관해서는 배를 만드는 회사라면 물 근처에 사는 사람들이 목표 고객이므로 물 근처 도시에서 광고해야 한다. 강의에 나온 이 두 가지 정보와 구체적인 사례가 답변에 포함되어야 한다.

우수 답변 🎧 T-99

Target customers influence marketing strategy because it answers the question where and when should the company advertise. For example, uh, two major points of, um, target customer is age and geographical location. So knowing the age, for example, of target customer which is a child, you should know where the

Reading　Listening　Speaking　Writing　Test 1　Test 2　Test 3　Test 4 ad-ad-advertise between, um, the s-… or the things the children watch, and this will be the proper time to advertise your toy cars, for example. Knowing the geographical location is also important because, uh, for example—if you're selling a boat, it's important that you sell a boat to people that actually need it and how you reach it is, um, you try to find where people who need it live. So people who need it mainly live near the rivers or near the water… that's so they could have use of that. In this way, it's important to know target customers.

채점자 의견

첫 번째 문장이 조금 불명확하긴 하지만 대체로 명확하고 완결된 답변이다. 수험자는 강의의 중요한 논지들을 모두 다루었으며 for example, so, also, in this way 등 연결어를 적절히 활용해 전개가 매끄러웠다. 발음이 전체적으로 좋으며 어린이와 텔레비전을 논하는 부분에서 사소한 몇 가지 문제가 있지만 이해하기에 큰 어려움은 없다. 멈추는 부분도 주로 정보를 떠올리기 위한 목적이므로 이해하기에 지장은 없다. 또한 다양한 문장 구조를 효과적으로 사용했다("and this will be the proper time to advertise your toy cars, for example"). "how you reach it is…" 등 애매한 부분이 있지만 요점을 파악하는 데 방해가 되지는 않는다. 전반적으로 강의를 잘 요약했다.

중간 수준의 답변 🎧 T-100

Actually, it's, uh… it's, eh… it's the… it's influence the strategies of companies directly because they are the target of the company. So, eh, companies usually seek to, uh, put their promotions and advertisement, eh, as much as it might be exposed for the targeted, uh, customer. So if they are, eh, aiming to buy for kids, they-they put their advertisement in areas which could… kids mostly happen to, uh, expose to it. And similar and, uh-uh, example of, eh, people who are interested in, eh, buying boat, or eh… So they are usually advertise it in the coast—and it's, eh… and the coasts.

채점자 의견

수험자의 답변은 강의의 요점을 대부분 전달하고 있지만 정확성과 완결성이 부족해 고득점을 받지 못했다. 답변 속도와 발음은 대체로 괜찮아서 전체 의미에 방해가 되지는 않지만 계속 끊기는 부분이 있어 알아듣기가 어렵다. 처음에 "it" 대신 "target customer"라고 했으면 의미가 더 분명했을 것이다. 정확하지 않은 어법과 어휘("so companies usually seek to put their promotions and advertisement as much as it might be exposed for the targeted customer", "they are aiming to buy for kids,") 때문에 설명이 모호해졌다. 전반적으로 더 상세한 정보가 포함되었어야 하며 완결성 있는 답변이 되려면 어휘나 어법이 더 발전해야 한다.

WRITING

Integrated Writing   p. 294

In the 1950s *Torreya taxifolia*, a type of evergreen tree once very common in the state of Florida, started to die out. No one is sure exactly what caused the decline, but chances are good that if nothing is done, *Torreya* will soon become extinct. Experts are considering three ways to address the decline of *Torreya*.

The first option is to reestablish *Torreya* in the same location in which it thrived for thousands of years. *Torreya* used to be found in abundance in the northern part of Florida, which has a specific microclimate. A microclimate exists when weather conditions inside a relatively small area differ from the region of which that area is a part. Northern Florida's microclimate is very favorable to *Torreya*'s growth. This microclimate is wetter and cooler than the surrounding region's relatively dry, warm climate. Scientists have been working to plant *Torreya* seeds in the coolest, dampest areas of the microclimate.

The second option is to move *Torreya* to an entirely different location, far from its Florida microclimate. Torreya seeds and saplings have been successfully planted and grown in forests further north, where the temperature is significantly cooler. Some scientists believe that *Torreya* probably thrived in areas much further north in the distant past, so by relocating it now, in a process known as assisted migration, humans would simply be helping *Torreya* return to an environment that is more suited to its survival.

The third option is to preserve *Torreya* in research centers. Seeds and saplings can be moved from the wild and preserved in a closely monitored environment where it will be easier for scientists both to protect the species and to conduct research on *Torreya*. This research can then be used to ensure the continued survival of the species.

1950년대 플로리다 주에서 한때 매우 흔했던 상록수의 일종인 토레이야 탁시폴리아가 죽어 없어지기 시작했다. 쇠퇴 원인이 무엇인지 누구도 정확히 모르지만, 아무 조치도 취하지 않으면 토레이야가 곧 멸종할 가능성이 높다. 전문가들은 토레이야의 쇠퇴를 해결하기 위해 세 가지 방법을 고려하고 있다.

첫 번째 선택은 토레이야가 수천 년 동안 번성했던 바로 그 장소에 재건하는 것이다. 토레이야는 특정한 미기후를 가진 플로리다 주 북부 지역에서 많이 발견되곤 했다. 미기후는 상대적으로 좁은 지역 내부의 기상 조건이 해당 장소가 속한 지역과 다를 때 생긴다. 플로리다 주 북부의 미기후는 토레이야의 성장에 매우 유리하다. 이 미기후는 비교적 건조하고 따뜻한 주변 지역의 기후보다 더 습하고 선선하다. 과학자들은 이 미기후에서 가장 시원하고 습한 지역에 토레이야 씨를 심는 작업을 해 왔다.

두 번째 선택은 토레이야를 플로리다 주의 미기후와는 거리가 먼 완전히 다른 곳으로 옮기는 것이다. 토레이야 씨앗과 묘목은 기온이 현저히 낮은 북쪽 숲에 성공적으로 식목되고 자랐다. 일부 과학자들은 토레이야가 아마도 아주 옛날에는 훨씬 먼 북쪽 지역에서 번성했으리라 믿는다. 따라서 지금 토레이야를 옮긴다면 원조 이주라는 과정에서 단지 토레이야가 생존에 더 적합한 환경으로 되돌아가도록 인간이 돕게 된다.

세 번째 선택은 토레이야를 연구소에 보존하는 것이다. 야생에서 씨앗과 묘목을 옮겨 와 과학자들이 그 종을 보호하고 토레이야를 연구하기 더 쉬운 곳, 면밀히 관찰할 수 있는 환경에서 보존하는 것이다. 그렇다면 이 연구를 종의 지속적인 생존을 보장하는 데 활용할 수 있다.

어휘

common 흔한   decline 쇠퇴   extinct 멸종한   expert 전문가   address 해결하다   reestablish 재건하다, 복구하다   thrive 번성하다   in abundance 풍부하게   microclimate 미기후   relatively 비교적   favorable 유리한, 호의적인   surrounding 주변의   damp 습한   entirely 완전히   sapling 묘목   temperature 기온, 온도   significantly 현저히   relocate 옮기다   migration 이주   suited 적합한   preserve 보존하다   environment 환경   species 종

Professor

You've just read about three ways to save *Torreya taxifolia*. Unfortunately, none of these three options provides a satisfactory solution.

About the first solution, reestablishing *Torreya* in the same location. That's unlikely to be successful because of what's happening to the coolest, dampest areas within *Torreya's* microclimate. These areas are being strongly affected by changes in the climate of the larger region. This could be because global warming has contributed to an increase in overall temperatures in the region or because wetlands throughout Florida have been drained. Either way, many areas across the region are becoming drier. So it's unlikely that *Torreya* would have the conditions it needs to survive anywhere within its original Florida microclimate.

Now, about the second solution, relocating *Torreya* far from where it currently grows. Well, let's look at what happened when humans helped another tree, the black locust tree, move north to a new environment.

When they did this, the black locust tree spread so quickly that it killed off many plants and trees in the new environment—and some of these plants and trees were themselves already in danger of becoming extinct. So assisted migration can have unpredicted outcomes for the new environment.

Third, research centers are probably not a solution either. That's because the population of *Torreya* trees that can be kept in the centers will probably not be able to resist diseases. For a population of trees to survive a disease, it needs to be relatively large and it needs to be genetically diverse. Tree populations in the wild usually satisfy those criteria. But research centers would simply not have enough capacity to keep a large and diverse population of *Torreya* trees, so trees in such centers will not be capable of surviving diseases in the long term.

교수 여러분은 방금 토레이야 탁시폴리아를 구하는 세 가지 방법에 대해 읽었습니다. 안타깝게도 이 세 가지 선택 모두 만족할 만한 해법은 되지 못합니다.

첫 번째 해법은 같은 장소에 토레이야를 재건한다는 것입니다. 토레이야의 미기후 안에서 가장 시원하고 습한 지역에서 일어나고 있는 일 때문에 이 방법은 성공 가능성이 낮습니다. 이 지역은 더 넓은 지역의 기후 변화에 크게 영향 받고 있습니다. 지구온난화가 이 지역의 전반적인 기온 상승에 기여했거나 플로리다 전역의 습지가 고갈되었기 때문에

그럴 수 있습니다. 어느 쪽이든, 이 지역의 많은 영역들이 점점 더 건조해지고 있습니다. 따라서 원래의 플로리다 미기후 안에서는 어느 곳이든 토레이야가 살아남기에 필요한 조건을 갖추지 못할 것 같습니다.

자, 토레이야를 현재 자라는 곳에서 멀리 옮긴다는 것이 두 번째 해결책입니다. 자, 인간이 또 다른 나무인 아까시나무가 새로운 환경인 북쪽으로 옮기도록 도왔을 때 어떤 일이 일어났는지 살펴봅시다.

이렇게 하자 아까시나무는 너무 빨리 퍼져 새로운 환경에 있는 많은 초목을 죽여 없앴습니다. 그리고 이들 초목 중 일부는 이미 멸종 위기에 처해 있는 상태였습니다. 따라서 원조 이주는 새로운 환경에 예기치 못한 결과를 가져올 수 있습니다.

셋째, 어쩌면 연구소도 해결책이 아닙니다. 연구소에 보존할 수 있는 토레이야 나무 개체군이 아마도 질병에 저항할 수 없을 것이기 때문입니다. 나무 개체군이 질병에서 살아남으려면 비교적 개체군이 크고 유전적으로 다양해야 합니다. 야생의 나무 개체군은 보통 그러한 기준을 충족합니다. 그러나 연구소는 크고 다양한 토레이야 나무 개체군을 수용할 수 없습니다. 따라서 연구소에 있는 나무들은 장기적으로 보아 질병에서 살아남을 수 없을 겁니다.

어휘

unfortunately 안타깝게도 provide 제공하다 satisfactory 만족스러운 reestablish 재건하다 unlikely ~할 것 같지 않은, 가망이 없는 damp 습한 affect 영향을 미치다 contribute 기여하다 overall 전반적인 temperature 기온, 온도 drain 배수하다, 물을 빼내다 relocate 옮기다 currently 현재 spread 퍼지다 extinct 멸종한 unpredicted 예기치 못한 outcome 결과 population 개체군 resist 저항하다 disease 질병 relatively 비교적 genetically 유전적으로 diverse 다양한 criteria 기준 capacity 수용 능력 be capable of ~할 수 있다 in the long term 장기적으로 보아

Question

Summarize the points made in the lecture, being sure to explain how they respond to the specific concerns presented in the reading passage.

강의에서 말하는 요점들이 어떻게 읽기 지문에 제시된 특정 우려 사항에 대해 대응하고 있는지 반드시 설명하면서 요약하시오.

해설

토레이야 나무를 구하기 위한 다양한 방법들이 왜 효과가 없는지 강의에서 제시한 이유를 이해해야 한다. 교수는 읽기 지문에서 제안된 해결책, 즉 토레이야를 원래 자라던 지역에 심기, 새로운 지역에 심기, 연구소에 보존하는 것, 모두에 의문을 던진다. 고득점을 받으려면 다음처럼 읽기 지문에서 제시한 요점과 이에 대해 설명하는 교수의 설명이 포함되어야 한다.

Reading

Listening

Speaking

Writing

Test 1

Test 2

Test 3

Test 4

지문의 주요 내용	지문과 대조되는 강의 내용
Torreya trees could be planted in areas where they used to grow because those areas have a favorable cool and wet microclimate.	Unfortunately, global warming and human activities have made the locations where *Torreya* used to grow warmer and drier.
Torreya trees could be introduced in other areas whose environmental conditions are suitable for *Torreya* growth.	Introducing a tree in a new area can endanger other plants that already grow there. This has happened previously when the black locust tree was introduced in a new area.
If *Torreya* trees are grown in research centers, they can be both preserved and studied there.	Since research centers are small, the population of *Torreya* trees grown there would not be large and diverse enough to resist diseases.

Research centres cannot provide a large space for the population to be reestablished.

번역

토레이야 탁시폴리아는 플로리다 지역에서 한때 흔했던 상록수다. 1950년대부터 멸종 위기에 처해 있고 과학자들은 이 나무를 구하기 위해 다양한 방법을 고려하고 있다.

플로리다에 토레이야를 다시 심으려는 계획은 강의 교수에 의해 배제되었다. 왜냐하면 지구 온난화로 나무가 자라고 번성하기에는 그 지역의 기후가 악화되었기 때문이다. 플로리다 지역의 습지 또한 말라버려서 이러한 기후 변화가 나무의 성장을 감퇴시켰고 같은 지역에 다시 정착하기가 매우 어렵다.

두 번째 선택은 그 지역의 토착종에게 매우 위험할 수 있다. 교수는 아까시나무라는 또 다른 예를 들며 설명한다. 아까시나무가 새로운 환경으로 이식되자 너무 광범위하게 성장해 많은 수의 지역 초목을 죽이는 바람에 이 초목들이 멸종위기에 처했다. 따라서 다른 종들을 제거해 한 종을 키우는 것은 현명하지 못하다. 그래서 실험은 위험하다.

세 번째 해결책 역시 적절하지 않다. 왜냐하면 개체군이 성공하려면 질병에 저항할 수 있도록 비교적 크고 유전적으로 다양해야 하기 때문이다. 연구소는 개체군이 다시 정착하기 위한 넓은 공간을 제공할 수 없다.

채점자 의견

1. 이 에세이에는 강의와 읽기 지문의 중요한 정보가 대부분 담겨 있다. 첫 번째 문단에 멸종 위기에 있는 나무를 구한다는 주제를 소개한 뒤 각 해법의 결함을 논의했다.
2. 교수가 말한 결함을 중점적으로 언급했지만 읽기 지문의 해법도 분명하게 언급하고 있다.
3. 대체로 조리 있게 구성되어 있다. 세 번째 문단 마지막 문장이 미완성이지만 에세이의 수준에는 영향을 미치지 않는다. 사소한 실수가 있고 일부 개념이 제대로 표현되지 않았지만 고득점 에세이에도 작은 실수는 용납된다.

예제 답안과 채점자 의견

우수 답변

Torreya taxifolia is an evergreen tree that was once common in Florida region. From 1950's it is in danger of becoming extinct and scientists are considering different ways to save it.

Plans to reestablish Torreya in Florida has been ruled out by the professor in the lecture because global warming has resulted in a worse climate in that area for the tree to grow and flourish. Wetlands in Florida area have also dried up so these changes in the climate has caused the decreased growth of the tree and it is very hard to reestablish in the same area.

The second option could be very dangerous for the native species of that area. The professor explains by citing another example of black locust tree. When it was taken to a new environment, it grew to such an extent that it killed a large number of local plants and trees and hence they became endangered. So, it's not wise to grow one species by eliminating others. So it is at risk to experi

The third solution is again not appropriate because for a population to be successfull it should be relatively large and genetically diverse so that it is able to resist diseases.

중간 수준의 답변

Giving that Torreya started to die out in its naturel location, three solutions were be proposed, but none of them worked.

The first solution is to reestablish the tree in Florida, its naturel home, because historicaly this kind of tree lives thanks to the microclimat of this state. But the plan fall because of the changing of the climat in this area. Benefits of the microclimat, which is specific climat of an area, do not exist yet. So Torreya loose its natural environnement.

The second solution is to establish the tree in a completely different climat, meanning in the north. But as the professor explains, this solution fall in the past with the black locust tree. This historical exemple explains how it is difficult to change the ecosystem, because it is very dangerous to provoc a migration.

Eventuelly, the last solution is to preserve *Torreya* in reserch centres. One more time this proposition is not good, because all experiences of capted population show that every preserve population lost its capacity to resist to deseas and external atacs. Then even if humans try to recreat a reel diversity, it is not possible, because the recreat area can not be enought to be large and diverse as the nature is.

채점자 의견

1. 중간 정도 점수를 받은 에세이로 읽기 지문과 교수의 주장을 대부분 이해하고 있다.
2. 어법에서 중요한 실수가 잦아서 전달하려는 생각과 의미가 모호해졌고 중요한 정보가 빠져 있다. 또한 교수는 생태계를 바꾸는 것이 어렵다는 주장을 하지 않았다.
   ▶ "were be", "fail"을 "fall"로 썼고 시제 오류 등 어법의 실수가 있다.
   ▶ "Benefits of the microclimate... do not exist yet"에서 yet 대신 anymore를 써야 한다.
3. 독자가 실수한 표현들을 제대로 해석한다면 세 번째 주장의 중요한 부분은 명확하다. 그러나 다양성이 없고 커질 수 없는 것은 "area"가 아니라 연구소에서 재배되는 나무의 개체군이다.

Writing for an Academic Discussion | p. 296

Question

Your professor is teaching a class on psychology. Write a post responding to the professor's question.

In your response, you should do the following.
- Express and support your opinion.
- Make a contribution to the discussion in your own words.

An effective response will contain at least 100 words.

교수가 심리학에 관한 수업을 가르치고 있다. 교수의 질문에 답하는 게시물을 작성하시오.

답변을 작성할 때, 다음 사항을 수행해야 한다.
- 자신의 의견을 제시하고 뒷받침할 것.
- 자신만의 글로 논의에 기여할 것.

효과적인 답변은 최소 100자의 단어를 포함한다.

디아즈 박사

이번 주에, 우리는 인간의 행복에 관한 연구를 계속 살펴 보고 있습니다. 한 전문가가 모순되어 보일 수 있는 두 가지 조언을 하는데, "자신을 더 행복하게 만들려면, 다른 사람들을 행복하게 만드는 데 초점을 맞추세요. 다른 사람들을 행복하게 만드는 최고의 방법들 중 하나는 자기 자신의 행복에 더욱 초점을 맞추는 것입니다."라는 말입니다. 자기 자신의 행복을 증진하기 위해, 여러분은 이 두 가지 모두에 초점을 맞추는 것과 한 가지에만 초점을 맞추는 것 중에서 어느 쪽이 더 효과적이라고 생각하나요? 그 이유는 무엇인가요?

앤드류

저는 이 두 아이디어가 모두 사실이라고 생각합니다. 제가 보기엔 분명 다른 사람들을 돕는 즐거움이 존재합니다. 동시에, 어떤 사람이 자신을 행복하게 만드는 데 초점을 맞추지 못한다면, 그 사람은 절대로 사회에 큰 기여를 할 수 없을 텐데, 그 이유는 그렇게 하는 데 필요한 에너지와 열정이 부족할 것이기 때문입니다.

클레어

저는 다른 사람들을 행복하게 만드는 데에만 초점을 맞추는 것이 더 낫다고 주장할 것 같아요. 제가 볼 때, 자기 자신의 행복에 더 초점을 맞추는 것에 관한 그 조언이 이기심으로 향하는 단계이자, 자기 자신의 이익을 주변에 있는 모든 사람의 이익과 분리되어 있으면서 어쩌면 심지어 상충하는 것으로 보게 되는 단계인데, 이건 제가 누구든 불행을 줄이려 노력하는 사람에게 권할 것 같지 않습니다.

해설

질문과 토론 내용을 수험자가 명확히 이해해야 한다. 그 구성이 수험자에게 매력적이면서 관련되어 있기 때문에, 그 사안의 양 측면 모두에 대해 명확하고 충분한 의견 및 의견 제시문을 이끌어내야 한다. 교수의 중심 질문은 자기 자신의 행복뿐만 아니라 다른 이들을 행복하게 만드는 것 두 가지 모두에 초점을 맞추는 것이 더 좋은가, 아니면 그저 둘 중 하나에만 초점을 맞춰야 하는가 하는 점이다. 앤드류는 그 초점이 두 가지 모두에 맞춰져야 한다고 주장하는 반면, 클레어는 오직 다른 이들을 행복하게 만드는 데에만 초점을 맞추는 것이 더 좋다고 생각한다.

수험자는 다수의 방식으로 이 토론에 기여할 수 있다. 두 가지 모두가 중요하다는 앤드류의 아이디어를 더 자세히 설명할 수도 있고, 다른 이들을 행복하게 만드는 데에만 초점을 맞춰야 한다는 클레어의 주장에 동의할 수도 있으며, 아니면 예를 들어, 사람들은 오직 자신을 행복하게 만드는 것에 대해서만 걱정해야 한다는(아마 심지어 다른 이들을 행복하게 만드는 것과 상충하지 않을 것이라고 덧붙이면서) 완전히 다른 관점을 취할 수도 있다. 관점과 상관없이, 수험자는 각자의 의견에 대한 명확한 설명을 제공해야 한다.

예제 답안과 채점자 의견

우수 답변

I agree with Andrew's point that we need to focus on making ourselves happy. Happy persons are more able to help people around them. But I think Claire is right too, when she suggests that selfishness may be a risk in looking too close for your own happiness. In avoiding this danger, a good strategie could be helping others not in the way we would like to be helped, but in the way they would like to be helped. Then your happiness would not only be the condition for the happiness of people around you, but also something you owe to them (and in the measure your happiness helps them).

번역

저는 우리가 자기 자신을 행복하게 만드는 데 초점을 맞춰야 한다는 앤드류의 주장에 동의합니다. 행복한 사람은 주변에 있는 사람들을 돕는 것을 더 잘 할 수 있습니다. 하지만 클레어가 이기심이 너무 철저하게 자기 자신의 행복을 찾는 데 있어 위험 요소가 될 수 있다는 뜻을 나타낼 때, 그 말도 옳다고 생각합니다. 이러한 위험 요소를 피하는 데 있어, 한 가지 좋은 전략은 우리가 도움 받고자 하는 방식이 아니라, 다른 사람들이 도움 받고자 하는 방식으로 그 사람들을 돕는 것일 수 있습니다. 그러면 자신의 행복이 주변에 있는 사람들의 행복을 위한 조건이 될 뿐만 아니라, 그 사람들 덕택인 것이 되기도 할 것입니다(자신의 행복이 다른 사람에게 도움이 된다는 기준 하에서).

채점자 의견

1. 토론 주제와 관련지어 명확하게 의견을 제시하고 있다.
2. 수험자는 두 의견 제시자의 주장에 모두 동의하는 것으로 중간 입장을 취하고 있다. 그 후 계속해서 사람들을 돕는 가장 좋은 방법이 "우리가 도움 받고자 하는 방식이 아니라, 다른 사람들이 도움 받고자 하는 방식으로 그 사람들을 돕는 것"이라고 언급함으로써 두 사람의 의견 제시문을 토론에 덧붙이고 있다
3. 수험자는 한 사람의 행복이 어떻게 "주변에 있는 사람들의 행복을 위한 조건이 될 뿐만 아니라, 그 사람들 덕택인 것이 되기도 할 것인지" 언급함으로써 두 사람의 답변에 대해 끝을 맺고 있다.

중간 수준의 답변

I disagree, Claire. Why do you think that focusing on your own happines is selfish? From my point of view, there nothing more important than own happines and doing your best to increase your happines is must. Also, it very hard to make someone happy while you completely not satisfied with own life. I agree with Andrew regarding this. I can tell from own experience that people start to like me more and enjoy spend time with me once I got happier myself. I able to help people with confidence when I got more confident myself.

채점자 의견

1. 중간 점수를 받은 에세이로 토론의 주제와 관련지었지만 낮은 수준의 언어 표현과 문법적 오류가 빈번하다.
2. 수험자는 클레어의 의견에 동의하지 않으며, "자기 자신의 행에 초점을 맞추는 것이 왜 이기적이라고 생각하는 건가요?"라는 말로 그 입장에 의문을 갖고 있는데, 이 답변은 단어 선택 및 문장 구조에 있어 뚜렷한 어휘 및 문법 오류의 형태로 나타나는 언어 능력 문제를 포함하고 있다.
3. "자기 자신의 삶에 전적으로 만족하지 못하면서 누군가를 행복하게 만드는 건 아주 어려운 일"과 "제 자신이 더 자신감을 가졌을 때 자신감 있게 사람들을 도울 수 있습니다"라는 표현에서 언어 능력 및 문법 표현의 오류를 드러내고 있다.

Reading

Listening

Speaking

Writing

Test 1

Test 2

Test 3

Test 4

Notes